Antique Trader®

Bottles

IDENTIFICATION & PRICE GUIDE

6th Edition

Michael Polak

© 2008 Michael Polak

krause publications
An Imprint of F+W Media, Inc.
700 East State Street • Iola, WI 54990-0001
715-445-2214 • 888-457-2873
www.krausebooks.com

Please call or write for a free catalog of publications.
The toll-free number to place any order or to request a free catalog is (800) 258-0929, or use our regular business number (715) 445-2214.

Library of Congress Control Number: 2008928411
ISBN-13: 978-0-89689-733-5
ISBN-10: 0-89689-733-8

Designed by Marilyn McGrane
Edited by Dan Brownell

Front cover photos courtesy of Jeff Wichman and American Bottle Auctions.
Back cover images courtesy of Jim Hagenbuch and Glass Works Auctions.

More Great Books in the Antique Trader® Series:

Antiques & Collectibles Annual Price Guide

Book Collector's Price Guide

Collectible Cookbooks Price Guide

Collectible Paperback Price Guide

Furniture Price Guide

Guide to Fakes & Reproductions

Indian Arrowheads Price Guide

Jewelry Price Guide

Kitchen Collectibles Price Guide

Limoges Price Guide

Lunch Boxes

Perfume Bottles Price Guide

Pottery and Porcelain Ceramics Price Guide

Radio & Television Price Guide

Royal Doulton Price Guide

Salt and Pepper Shaker Price Guide

Stoneware and Blue & White Pottery Price Guide

Teapots Price Guide

Tools Price Guide

Vintage Clothing Price Guide

Vintage Magazines Price Guide

Dedication

The 6th edition is dedicated to all those collectors making the dirt fly in the dumps and outhouses, buying, selling, and trading at antique and bottle shows, and scouring the flea markets and garage sales in search of that special bottle. Never stop!

Keep having fun with the hobby of bottle collecting.

Mike Polak

Photo Credits

Rodney Baer

Frank Bartlett

Charles and Julie Blake

Collector Books/Schroeder
 Publishing (Avon photos)

Jim Hagenbuch (Antique
 Bottle & Glass Collector
 Magazine, Glass Works
 Auctions)

Bud Hastin (Avon Collector's
 Encyclopedia)

Norman C. Heckler (Norman
 C. Heckler and Company
 Auctions)

David Graci

International Association
 of Jim Beam Bottle and
 Specialties Club

Samia Koudsi

Gary and Vickie Lewis

Bob Moore

Randall Monsen

Steve Ritter (Steve Ritter
 Auctions)

Bob Snyder

David Spaid

Rick Sweeney

Jennifer Tai

John Tutton

Jeff Wichmann (American
 Bottle Auctions)

Willy Young

Acknowledgments

Rodney Baer: Thank you for your contribution of photographs of perfume bottles and your overall support of the project.

Charles and Julie Blake: Thank you for your contribution of the great photographs and background information and pricing on cobalt blue medicine bottles.

Collector Books/Schroeder Publishing: Thank you for the contribution of beautiful Avon photographs.

Penny Dolnick: Thank you for writing the great introduction article for the perfume and cologne chapter, along with pricing input and background information.

Jim Hagenbuch (Antique Bottle & Glass Collector & Glass Works Auctions): Thank you for the great assortment of photographs, pricing input, and overall support of the project.

Bud Hastin (*Avon Collector's Encyclopedia*): Thanks for the great photographs and your help with the Avon collectibles pricing.

Norm Heckler (Heckler Auctions): Thank you for your contribution of photographs and your support of the project.

Fred Holabird: Thanks for your great friendship and your continued help with understanding Nevada bottles.

David Graci: Thanks for your contribution of photographs and background information on soda and beer bottle closures.

Bob Kay: Thanks for your pricing input on miniature bottles and your support of the project.

Gary and Vickie Lewis: Thanks for your contribution of photographs of ACL soda bottles and your overall support of the project.

Randall Monsen: Thank you for your contribution of photographs of perfume bottles and your overall support of the project.

Jacque Pace Polak: A special thank you to my wife for your continued patience and invaluable moral support.

Steve Ritter (Steve Ritter Auctioneering): Thanks for your help in obtaining the ACL soda bottle photographs and your help with the pricing input.

Jan Rutland (Director, National Bottle Museum): Thanks for all your help, support, and overall contribution towards the writing of the chapter on the National Bottle Museum.

David Spaid: Thanks for your help with understanding the world of miniature bottles and your support of the project.

Rick Sweeney: Thanks for your help and understanding with the pricing input for applied color label soda bottles.

John Tutton: Thank you for your contribution of photographs of milk bottles and your overall support of the project.

Violin Bottle Collectors Association and Members: Thanks for all of your help with the contribution of photographs and an overall understanding of violin bottles. A special thank you to Bob Linden, Frank Bartlett, Samia Koudsi, and Bob Moore for their time and effort in providing photographs, pricing data, and resource information.

Jeff Wichmann (American Bottle Auctions): Thanks for your great assortment of Western bottle photographs, for the cover photos, and overall support of the project.

Contents

Introduction

Welcome again to the fun hobby of antique bottle collecting with the 6th edition of *Antique Trader Bottles: Identification and Price Guide*. Once again, a special **thank you** to all of my readers for your support in making the 5th edition a huge success. With the publication of each edition, the positive and valuable input and helpful comments from bottle collectors, clubs, and dealers across the United States, Europe, and Asia-Pacific continues to be overwhelming. I have enjoyed writing and updating the 6th edition as much as the first five editions, incorporating all of the positive feedback, and living up to the nickname "The Bottle Bible," given the book by collectors, clubs, and dealers.

In order to continue making this book the most informative reference and pricing guide available, I have provided beginner and veteran collectors with a broader range of detailed pricing information and reference data. The 6th edition introduces two new chapters on the fastest growing segments of bottle collecting: "Ginger Bottles" and "Portable Soda Pop Dispensers." In addition, I have added a chapter that will highlight a different museum, auction, or show in each new edition. The 6th edition will feature the National Bottle Museum in Ballston Spa, N.Y.

This edition also includes extensive updates and revisions to chapters covering the history and origin of glass and bottles, how to start a collection, bottle facts, bottle sources, bottle handling, and one of my favorite topics—digging for bottles. In addition to a number of valuable illustrations, this edition features 600 stunning color photographs. The 6th edition also provides complete pricing updates and revisions for both old bottles (pre-1900) and new bottles (post-1900). To help you better understand the details of how to price and evaluate a bottle, the chapter titled "Determining Bottle Values" has also been updated and expanded along with the reference and research sections on trademarks, bottle clubs, glossary, and bibliography.

Interest in bottle collecting continues to grow, with new bottle clubs forming throughout the United States and Europe. More collectors are spending their free time digging through old dumps and foraging through old ghost towns digging out old outhouses (that's right), exploring abandoned mineshafts, and searching their favorite bottle or antique shows, swap meets, flea markets, and garage sales. In addition, the Internet has greatly expanded, offering collectors numerous opportunities and resources to buy and sell bottles with many new auction Web sites, without even leaving the house. Many bottle clubs now have Web sites providing even more information for the collector. These new technologies and resources have helped bottle collecting to continue to grow and gain interest.

Most collectors, however, still look beyond the type and value of a bottle to its origin and history. I find that researching the history of a bottle is almost as interesting as finding the bottle itself. I enjoy both pursuits for their close ties to the rich history of the settling of the United States and the early methods of merchandising.

My goal has always been to enhance bottle collecting for both beginning and expert collectors, to help them experience the excitement of antique bottle collecting, especially the thrill of making a special find. I hope the 6th edition continues to bring you an increased understanding and enjoyment of the hobby.

If you would like to provide information or input regarding the 6th edition, or just talk bottles, I can be contacted at my e-mail address: bottleking@earthlink.net or through my Web site: www.bottlebible.com.

Good bottle hunting and have fun with the hobby of bottle collecting.

How to Use This Book

The 6th edition continues to be formatted to assist all collectors, from the novice to the seasoned veteran. The table of contents clearly indicates those chapters, such as "The Beginning Collector," that the veteran collector may want to skip. However, other introductory chapters, including "History and Origin," "Bottle Facts," "Bottle Sources," "Bottle Handling," and the three new chapters: "Ginger Beers," "Portable Soda Pop Dispensers," and "Bottle Museum," highlighting the National Bottle Museum in Ballston Spa, N.Y., will contribute valuable information and resource materials to even the expert's store of knowledge about bottles and collecting.

The pricing information has been divided into two sections. The first section begins on page 103 and covers older collectibles, those manufactured almost exclusively before 1900, categorized by physical type and the bottle's original contents. Where applicable, trade names are listed alphabetically within these sections.

In some categories, such as flasks, trade names were not embossed on the bottles, so pieces are listed by other embossing or identification that appears on the bottle. Descriptive terms used to identify these pieces are explained in the introductory sections and are also listed in the glossary at the end of the book.

The second pricing section, which begins on page 367, is a guide to pieces produced after the turn of the century, broken down by manufacturer or type, such as Avon bottles, Jim Beam bottles, applied color label (ACL) soda bottles, and miniature bottles.

Since it is difficult to list prices for every bottle, I've produced a detailed cross-section of bottles in various price ranges with the dollar amount for each listing indicating the value of that particular piece. Similar but not identical bottles could be more or less valuable than those specifically mentioned. This listing will provide a good starting point for pricing pieces you are considering as additions to your collection.

The reference and research chapters, which include "Trademark Identification" (page 468), "Bottle Clubs" (page 485), "Auction Companies" (page 521), "Museum and Research Resources" (page 526), "Glossary" (page 529), and "Bibliography" (page 539), will provide additional help to all collectors.

Bottle Collecting News

What's happening with bottle collecting? Everything! Antique bottle collecting continues to gain popularity and has brought a greater awareness to a wide range of antique collectors.

In October 2007, 2,400 bottles of Jack Daniels whiskey, some 100 years old, were seized during warehouse raids in Nashville and Lynchburg, Tennesee, by Tennessee Alcoholic Beverage Commission authorities. The authorities suspected the whiskey was being sold by someone without a license. The estimated value of the whiskey is $1,000,000, due in large part to the value of the antique bottles. One 1914 bottle with an unbroken seal is estimated to be worth $10,000. In January 2008, a suspect was indicted, with another hearing scheduled for September 2008. Until a judgment is determined, the whiskey is being stored in a Nashville vault, getting better with age.

Can you handle 184-proof whiskey? The Bruichladdich distillery off Scotland's west coast, founded in 1881, is reviving a 17th-century recipe "purely for fun," said managing director Mark Reynier. The recipe, known in Gaelic as usquebaugh-baul, translates as "perilous water of life." But you'll have to wait a while if you're brave enough to try a drink. The whiskey will be aged in an oak barrel for ten years before it's ready for release.

While I'm on the subject of old whiskey, George Washington's still is back in business again after a 200-year hiatus. On March 30, 2007, George

Washington's Mount Vernon estate officially opened a $2.1 million reconstruction of Washington's original distillery on the exact site where it was located in 1799. Mount Vernon officials said the distillery is the only one in the nation, and possibly the world, that authentically demonstrates 18th century distilling techniques. The whiskey will be made only on special occasions and will be available for purchase at the estate. But be ready for a kick when you take a drink. Washington did not age his whiskey as distillers do today, so Mount Vernon director James Rees compares it to "white lightning."

If a 200-year still isn't old enough for you, how about digging out a 400-year-old well at historic Jamestown, Virginia? In July 2006, a team of 12 archeologists found an intact ceramic bottle called a Bartmann jug, or a "bearded man," made in Germany and dating back to 1590. The English landed in Jamestown in 1607, which was the first permanent British settlement in America. It was also the site of the first attempt to manufacture glass in America, which was a failure.

Coca-Cola is at it again with another new drink called "Coca-Cola Blak." In simple terms, it's Coke with coffee. Coke spokesman Scott Williamson said, "People are looking for different things to drink at different times of the day, so it's incumbent on us to innovate." The new drink is actually a flurry of a group of new products being introduced to the consumer: a new chocolate coffee drink in partnership with Godiva, Coke Zero (reformulated Diet Coke), Coke C2 (a middle-ground between diet and regular Coke), Diet Coke with Splenda, and a number of varieties flavored with lemon and lime.

Can your budget handle $17,000 for a target ball? That's what one sold for on July 5, 2006, during an auction held by American Bottle Auctions in San Francisco, California. The item, a rare Bogardus glass target ball, was part of the Alex Kerr (Kerr Glass Company) collection. This specific auction included 10 balls that ended up going for a total of $45,000, a new world record. What are target balls? They are approximately 3-inch round spheres of various designs and colors manufactured in the mid 1870s. They were made to be tossed in the air by a mechanical thrower so marksmen could test their aim. In the same auction, an 1870 thrower sold for $3,520.

So you think that $17,000 is big? On November 17, 2006, David Rago Auctions achieved a world-record price of $216,000 for a 1939 Lalique perfume bottle known as Tresor de la Mer (Treasure from the Sea). The oyster-shell-form box and pearl-form bottle were designed specifically for a 1939 Lalique exhibit at Saks Fifth Avenue in New York. Overall, the auction netted a total of $1.2 million for the entire collection of Lalique and other perfume bottles.

Recently, an 1885 Chinese cemetery was discovered in Los Angeles by the Metropolitan Transportation Authority while building an extension of the Gold Line commuter rail. Historians believe the site may be a potter's field that was obscured by development after the 1920s. Many medicine and opium bottles were found during excavation.

More digging was taking place in Ventura, California, in July 2007. Archaeologists excavating a housing site in what used to be the center of Ventura located a 130-year-old outhouse. Among the many treasures, the crew found a pistol dating to the 1800s, a Bowie knife, and

several whiskey flasks. Here's the fun part of the story. They aren't sure whether it was the women's outhouse or the men's.

Bottle collecting has hit the Travel Channel. On February 6th and 10th, 2007, the Travel Channel aired a half-hour segment of the series *Cash & Treasures* devoted to bottle collecting. The focus of the segment was the 2006 Saratoga, N.Y., Bottle Show, the Saratoga National Bottle Museum, and a bottle dig conducted by museum trustees Fran Hughes and Roy Topka with his son Mike. There was also film shot in other out-of-state locations. The "digging" portion of the show gave the audience an opportunity to share the excitement of finding the treasures along with conveying the importance of respect for artifacts and the property of others. As you can see, the discoveries and news events include all aspects of antique bottle collecting and increases the interest and fun in the hobby.

Elmer Long's Bottle Tree Ranch

Elmer Long is an artist and the owner of the Bottle Tree Ranch, located on historic Route 66 in Oro Grande, California, between Victorville and Barstow. Long integrates sculpture and local artifacts with his bottle trees to show the role these items have played in our society. Note the central role of bottles in the ranch. Perhaps that is a reflection of just how important bottles have been in our culture, as they have reliably stored perishables for centuries before refrigeration was available. One wonders if our ancestors could have successfully settled this country without bottles to store the food and drink essential to their survival.

The plaque at the entrance of the Bottle Tree Ranch. Long founded the ranch in 2000 and dedicated it to those "who have lived and died on the mother road."

Elmer Long stands next to one of his "bottle tree" creations.

Another bottle tree, topped by a MobilGas sign. Gas back then, just as it is now, was the lifeblood of our mobile society.

The bottle trees here are surrounded by artifacts reminiscent of California and Route 66. Note the large Coca-Cola sign, elk horns, and Route 66 and speed limit signs. These items and all the bottles certainly are iconic and capture life along Route 66 during its heyday.

A bottle tree "cactus," and a motor oil sign next to it. It seems appropriate that the bottles and motor oil sign are adjacent, as both motor oil and our favorite beverages have been such an important part of our heritage.

A bottle tree topped by miners' picks. No doubt the '49ers brought bottles with them to quench their thirst after a long day of digging for gold.

Bottles: History and Origin

Glass bottles are not as new as some people believe. In fact, the glass bottle has been around for about 3,000 years. During the 2nd century B.C., Roman glass was free-blown with metal blowpipes and shaped with tongs that were used to change the shape of the bottle or vessel. The finished item was then decorated with enameling and engraving. The Romans even get credit for originating what we think of today as the basic "store bottle" and early merchandising techniques.

In the late 1st century B.C., the Romans began making glass vials that local doctors and pharmacists used to dispense pills, healing powders, and miscellaneous potions. The vials were 3 to 4 inches long and very narrow. The majority of early bottles made after Roman times were sealed with a cork or a glass stopper, whereas the Romans used a small stone rolled in tar as their stopper. The finished vials contained

Roman bottles, jars, and glass objects, 1st-3rd century A.D., found in the baths and necropolises of Cimiez Nice, France.

many impurities such as sand particles and bubbles because of the crude manufacturing process. The thickness of the glass and the crude finish, however, made Roman glass very resilient compared to the glass of later times, which accounts for the survival and good preservation of some Roman bottles, which have been dated as old as 2,500 years.

The first attempt to manufacture glass in America is thought to have taken place at the Jamestown settlement in Virginia around 1608. It is interesting to note that the majority of glass produced at the Jamestown settlement was earmarked for shipment back to England (due to its lack of resources) and not for the new settlements. As it turned out, the Jamestown glasshouse enterprise ended up a failure almost before it got started. The poor quality of glass produced and the small quantity simply couldn't support England's needs.

The first successful American glasshouse was opened in 1739 in New Jersey by Caspar Wistar, a brass button manufacturer who emigrated from Germany to Philadelphia, Pennsylvania, in 1717. During a trip in Salem County, New Jersey, Wistar noticed the abundance of white sand and the proximity of clay, wood, and water transportation. He soon bought 2,000 acres of the heavily wooded land and made arrangements for experienced glass workers to come from Europe, and the factory was completed in the fall of 1739. Since English law prohibited the colonists from manufacturing anything in competition with England, Wistar kept a low profile. In fact, most of what was written during the factory's operation implied that it was less than successful. Caspar Wistar died in 1752 a very wealthy man and left the factory to his son Richard.

Henry Stiegel started the next major glasshouse operation in the Manheim, Pennsylvania, area between 1763 and 1774, and eventually established several more. The Pitkin Glass Works was opened in East Hartford, Connecticut, around 1783 and was the first American glasshouse to provide figured flask and also the most successful of its time until it closed around 1830 due to the high cost of wood for fuel.

To understand the successes and far more numerous failures of early glasshouses, it is essential that the reader get an overview of the challenges that glass workers faced in acquiring raw materials and constructing the glasshouse. The glass factory of the nineteenth century was usually built near an abundant source of sand and wood or coal, and near numerous roads, rivers, and other waterways for transportation of raw materials and finished products to the major Eastern markets of Boston, New York, and Philadelphia. Finding a suitable location was usually not a problem but once production was underway resources quickly diminished. The next major challenge was constructing the glasshouse building, which was usually a large wooden structure that housed a primitive furnace and was about nine feet in diameter and shaped like a beehive.

A major financial drain on the glass companies (and one of the causes of so many of the businesses failing) was the expense of the large melting pots, which held the molten glass inside the furnace. Each pot, which cost about a hundred dollars and took eight months to make, was formed by hand from a long coil of clay and was the only substance known that would not melt when the glass was heated to 2,700 degrees F. The pot's lifespan was only about eight weeks, as exposure to high temperature over a long time caused the clay itself to turn into glass. The cost of regularly replacing melting pots proved to be the downfall of many early glass factories.

Throughout the 19th century, glasshouses continued to open and close because of changes in demand and technological improvements. Between 1840 and 1890, an enormous demand for glass containers developed to satisfy the whiskey, beer, medicine, and food packing industries. Largely because of the steady demand, glass manufacturing in the United States finally grew into a stable industry. This demand was due in large part to the settling of the western United States and the great gold and silver strikes between 1850 and 1900.

While the eastern glasshouses had been in production since 1739, the West didn't begin its entry into glass manufacturing until 1858, when Baker & Cutting started the first glasshouse in San Francisco, California. Until then, the West had to depend on glass bottles from the eastern glasshouses. The glass manufactured by Baker & Cutting, however, was considered to be poor quality, and production was eventually discontinued. In 1862, Carlton Newman and Patrick Brennan founded Pacific Glass Works in San Francisco, California. In 1876, San Francisco Glass Works bought Pacific Glass Works and renamed the company San Francisco and Pacific Glass Works (SFPGW). Today, these early bottles manufactured in San Francisco are the most desired by Western collectors.

Unlike other industries of the time that saw major changes in manufacturing processes, the process for producing the glass bottles remained the same. It was a process that gave each bottle a special character, producing unique shapes, imperfections, irregularities, and various colors until 1900.

At the turn of the century, Michael J. Owens invented the first fully automated bottle-making machine. Although many fine bottles were manufactured between 1900 and 1930, Owens' invention ended an era of unique bottle design that no machine process could ever duplicate.

Bottle-Making Through History

In order for a bottle collector, especially a new bottle collector, to better understand the history and origin of antique bottles, it is important to take a look at the development of the manufacturing process.

Free-Blown Bottles: B.C.-1860 (Figure 1)

Around the 1st century B.C., the blowpipe, a long hollow metal rod, was invented. After dipping the tip into the molten glass, the glass blower blew into the pipe to form the molten glass into a bottle or other container.

◆ PONTIL MARKS: 1618-1866

Once the bottle was blown, it had to be removed from the blowpipe. To do this, a three-foot-long metal pontil rod was dipped into the tank of molten glass to gather a small glob on the end to act as a "glue." The rod with the "glue" was applied to the bottom of the bottle to attach and hold it. The neck of the bottle was then touched with a tool dipped in cold water to break it from the blowpipe. With the blowpipe removed, the glassblower could do any finishing work on the neck and lip of the bottle. When the neck and lip were complete, the pontil rod was no longer needed to hold the bottle, and it too could be removed. The pontil rod was tapped to break it from the bottle, leaving a circular scar on the bottom of the bottle called a pontil mark.

FIGURE 1 • FREE-BLOWN BOTTLES: B.C.-1860

1 The blowpipe was inserted into the pot of hot "metal" (liquid glass) and twisted to gather the requisite amount onto the end of the pipe.

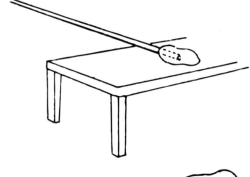

2 The blowpipe was then rolled slowly on a metal table to allow the red-hot glass to cool slightly on the outside and to sag.

3 The blower then blew into the pipe to form an internal central bubble.

4 The glass was further expanded and sometimes turned in a wooden block that had been dipped in cold water to prevent charring, or possibly rolled again on the metal table.

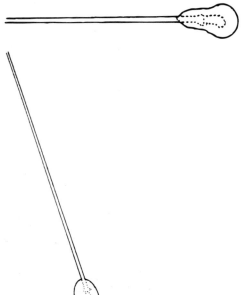

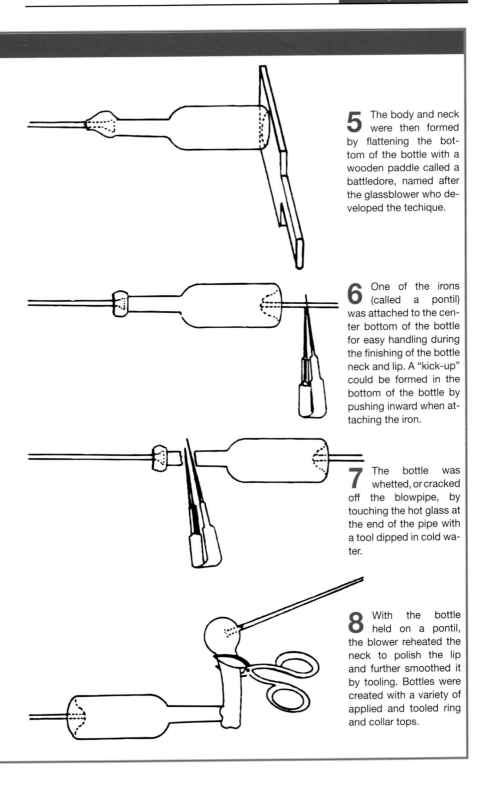

5 The body and neck were then formed by flattening the bottom of the bottle with a wooden paddle called a battledore, named after the glassblower who developed the techique.

6 One of the irons (called a pontil) was attached to the center bottom of the bottle for easy handling during the finishing of the bottle neck and lip. A "kick-up" could be formed in the bottom of the bottle by pushing inward when attaching the iron.

7 The bottle was whetted, or cracked off the blowpipe, by touching the hot glass at the end of the pipe with a tool dipped in cold water.

8 With the bottle held on a pontil, the blower reheated the neck to polish the lip and further smoothed it by tooling. Bottles were created with a variety of applied and tooled ring and collar tops.

ᑌᕱ SNAP CASES: 1860-1903 (FIGURE 2)

Between 1850 and 1860, the snap case was developed to replace the pontil rod. This was the first major invention for bottle making since the blowpipe was created. The snap case was a five-foot metal rod with claws to grasp the bottle. A snap locked the claw into place to hold the bottle securely while the neck was being finished. Each snap case was made to fit bottles of a certain size and shape. Bottles made with a snap case have no pontil marks, which left the bases free for lettering or design. The claw device, however, sometimes left small grip marks on the side of the bottle. The snap-case was used for small-mouth bottle production until the invention of the automatic bottle machine in 1903.

FIGURE 2

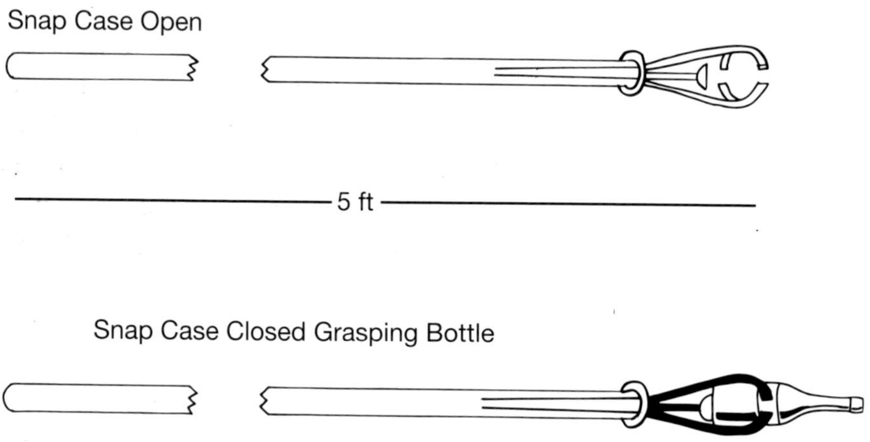

Snap Case Open

————— 5 ft —————

Snap Case Closed Grasping Bottle

🦎 MOLDED BOTTLES: B.C.-1900

The use of molds in bottle making, which really took hold in the early 1800s, actually dates back to the 1st century with the Romans. As detailed in the free-blown process, the glassblower shaped the bottle or vessel by blowing and turning it in the air. When using a mold, the worker would blow a few puffs while lowering the red-hot mass of molten glass into the hollow mold. The worker would continue blowing air into the tube until the glass pushed against the sides of the mold to acquire the finished shape. Most of these bottle molds were made of clay or wood, and formed only the base and body of the container. The neck had to be free-blown and attached later.

Molds were usually made in two or more sections to facilitate removal of the hardened bottle. Since it was impossible to create perfectly fitting molds, the seams showed on the surface of the finished article, leaving evidence of the molding process. Mold were categorized as either "open," in which only the body of the bottle was forced, with the neck and lip being added afterward, or "closed," in which the neck and lip were part of the original mold (Figure 3). The average life for a wooden mold was between 100 and 1,000 castings, depending of the thickness of the glass blown into them. The most common mold used after 1860 was the cast-iron mold, which proved the best and most economical way to manufacture inexpensive bottles.

By 1900, a number of improvements, such as tightly locking mold components, allowed for vent holes to be drilled into the mold to allow air within to escape while being replaced with hot glass. These vent holes were bored in the shoulders and bases of the mold. Then, the hot glass penetrated partway into the holes, leaving a mark on the glass about the size of a pinhead. These marks are very noticeable on the shoulders of quart whiskey bottles of the 1900s. Often, the vent mark was incorporated into the design on the bottles. Later two general types of molds came into use:

(1) The Three-Piece Mold, used between 1809 and 1880, which consisted of two kinds: the three-piece dip mold and the full-height mold.

(2) The Turn Mold or Paste Mold, used between 1880 and 1900. The introduction of the three-piece mold helped the bottle industry become stronger in the 19th century by increasing production to keep up with demand.

FIGURE 3

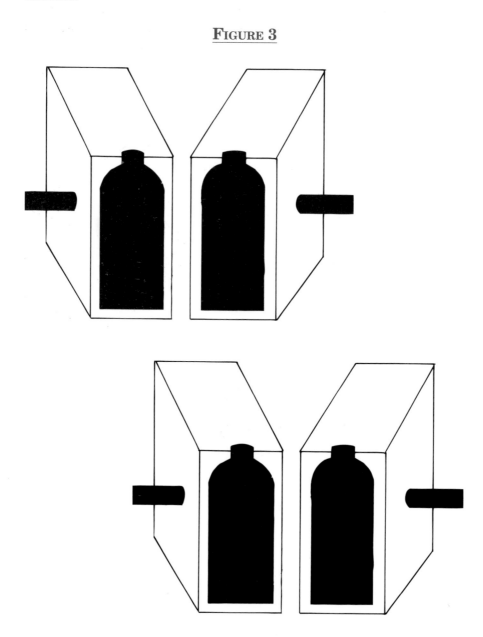

☙ THREE-PIECE MOLDS (FIGURE 4)

◆ THREE-PIECE DIP MOLD

The bottom section of the bottle mold was one piece, while the top, from the shoulder up, was two separate pieces. The mold seams circled the bottle at the shoulder and on each side of the neck.

FIGURE 4

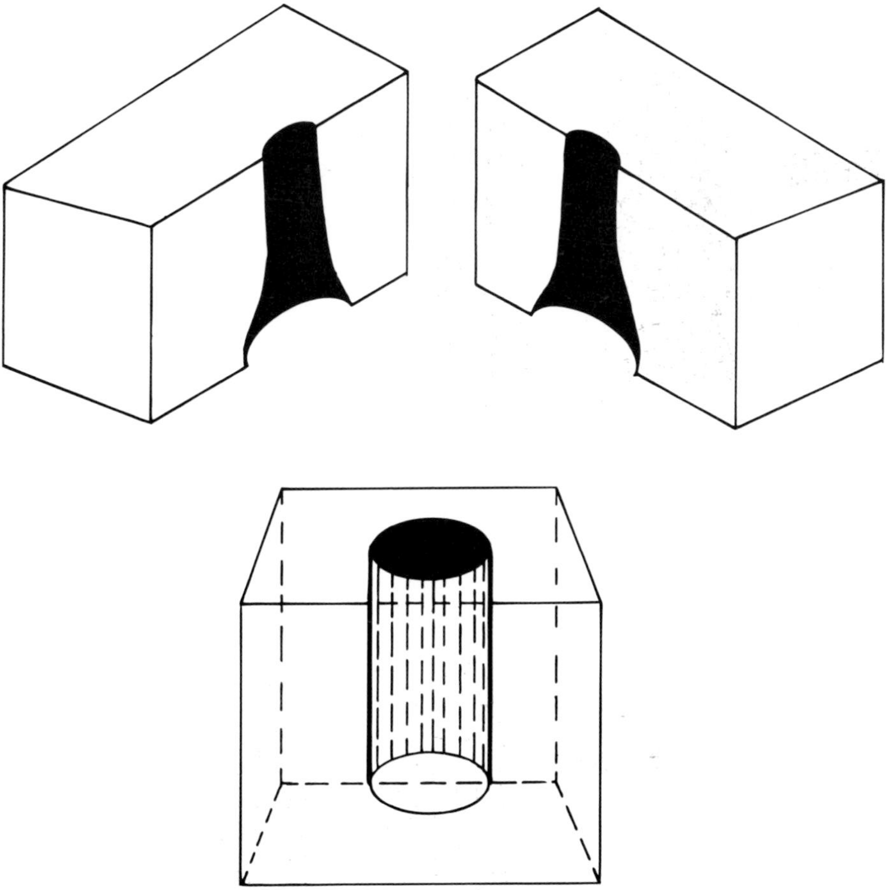

◆ FULL-HEIGHT MOLD

The entire bottle was formed in the mold, forming vertical seams on both sides that ran from the bottom of the bottle to below the lip.

Full height metal mold: front view.

Full height metal mold: side view.

⁀ Turn Mold or Paste Mold

Wooden molds were kept wet to prevent the hot glass from igniting or charring the wood. Turning the bottle in the wet mold erased all seams and mold marks and gave the glass a high luster. After metal molds replaced wooden molds, manufacturers used a paste inside the mold that allowed the bottle to slide easily during the turning process, which explains the origin of the terms "turn mold" and "paste mold."

⁀ Mason Jars: 1858

In 1858, John L. Mason invented the wide-mouth jar that became famous as a food preservative container. The new screw-top jar was formed in the same mold as the body. The jar was then broken from the blowpipe and sent to the annealing oven to temper the glass, making it more resistant to breakage. Then the jagged edges of the rims were ground down. Earlier jars can be distinguished from later ones by the rough and sharp edges produced by the grinding process.

⁀ Press and Blow Process: 1892

In 1892, a semi-automatic process called "press and blow" was invented to manufacture wide-mouth containers such as fruit jars and

Press and blow milk mold used by Thatcher milk bottles, Lockport Glass Co., Lockport, NY, circa 1927.

milk bottles. First, molten glass was pressed into the mold to form the mouth and lip. Then a metal plunger was inserted through the mouth and air pressure was applied to form the body.

FIGURE 1

THE ORIGINAL OWENS PROCESS

The basic invention of the Owens Bottle Machine is fixed on this crude vacuum device. The story fully describes the method of operation.

The Original Owens Process
The basic invention of the Owens Bottle Machine is fixed on this crude vacuum device.

THE AUTOMATIC BOTTLE MAKING MACHINE: 1903

Michael J. Owens, recognized as the inventor of the first automatic bottle-making machine, started as a glassblower in 1874 at the young age of 15. Owens proved to be a capable inventor and, in 1888, while working in Toledo, Ohio, for the American Lamp Chimney Company, he invented a semi-automatic machine for tumblers and lantern chimneys. Utilizing his engineering talent and his background and experience in glassmaking, he developed his first bottle-making machine in 1899 (Figure 1). After experimenting with three machines, he perfected the process with his fourth machine in 1903 (Figures 2, 3, and 4). Owens continued to make improvements and introduced Machine No.5 (Figure 5) in 1904. This final improvement allowed the continuous movement of the machine, which eliminated the intermittent stopping of the rotation of both machine and glass tank and increased the quantity and quality of bottles. A major advantage with these new machines was that the neck and top of the bottle no longer required hand finishing.

At first, Owens machine made only heavy bottles because they were in the greatest demand, but in 1909, improvements to the machine made it possible to produce small prescription bottles. Between 1909 and 1917, numerous other automatic bottle-making machines were invented, and soon all bottles were formed automatically throughout the world. In 1904, Owens' first machine produced 13,000 bottles a day, but by 1917 machine No. 5 was producing approximately 60,000 bottles a day. In 1917, the "gob feeder" was developed, which produced a measured amount of molten glass from which a bottle could be blown. In this process, a gob of glass is drawn from the tank and cut off by shears. Early in 1910, the Owens Bottle Company installed an automatic conveyor system in their factories to eliminate "carry in" boys who previously gathered bottles from the machine and carried them to the annealer oven.

FIGURE 2

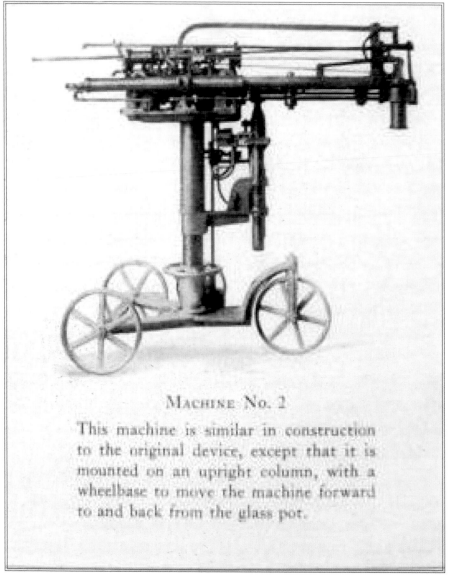

MACHINE No. 2

This machine is similar in construction to the original device, except that it is mounted on an upright column, with a wheelbase to move the machine forward to and back from the glass pot.

Machine No. 2
This machine is similar in construction to the original device, except that it is mounted on an upright column, with a wheelbase to move the machine forward to and back from the glass pot.

FIGURE 3

MACHINE NO. 3

This was the first rotating machine, and was very novel in construction. It was for the requirements of this machine that the revolving glass tank was developed.

Machine No. 3

This was the first rotating machine, and was novel in construction. It was for the requirements of this machine that the revolving glass tank was developed.

FIGURE 4

MACHINE No. 4

This machine was the outgrowth of the great encouragement Mr. Owens received from the operation of No. 3, and at the time it was built was considered a marvelous specimen of engineering skill.

Machine No. 4
This machine was the outgrowth of the great encouragement Mr. Owens received from the the operation of No. 3, and at the time it was built was considered a marvelous specimen of engineering skill.

FIGURE 5

Machine No. 5

This machine shows a great improvement over No. 4. It formed the foundation for the general type in use at the present day.

掔 SCREW-TOPPED BOTTLES

One last note about bottle making concerns the process of producing screw-topped bottles. Early glass blowers produced bottles with inside and outside screw caps long before the bottle making machines mechanized the process. But because early methods of production were so complex, screw-topped bottles produced before the 1800s were considered specialty bottles and expensive to replace. Today they are considered rare and collectable. In fact, the conventional screw-top bottle did not become common until after 1924, when the glass industry standardized the threads.

The Beginning Collector

N ow that you have learned some basics about the history, origin, and process of producing a bottle, it's time to provide information about how to approach the hobby of bottle collecting, as well as suggestions on books and reference guides, startup costs, old vs. new bottles, and information on bottle clubs and dealers.

So what approach should you take towards getting started, and what might influence that approach? The first thing to understand about antique bottle collecting is that there aren't set rules. Everyone's finances, spare time, storage space, and preferences are different, so you will need to tailor your collecting to your own individual circumstances. As a collector, you will need to think about whether to specialize in a specific type of bottle or to be a general or "maverick" collector who acquires everything that becomes available.

Most bottle collectors that I have known over the years, including me, took the maverick approach as new collectors. We grabbed everything in sight, ending up with bottles of every type, shape, and color. Now, after 31 years of collecting, my recommendation to newcomers is to just do a small amount of maverick collecting and focus on a specific or specialized bottle or group of bottles. Taking the more general approach in the early years has given me more breadth of knowledge about bottles and glass, but specializing has the following distinct advantages over the maverick approach:

- It helps focus a collection, which will provide more time for organization, study, and research.
- It allows a collector to become an authority on bottles in a specific field.
- Trading becomes easier with other specialists who may have duplicate or unwanted bottles.
- By becoming more of an authority within a specialty, the collector can negotiate a better deal by spotting bottles that are underpriced.

I need to mention, however, that specialized collectors may be tempted by bottles that don't quite fit into their collections. So, they cheat a little and give into that maverick urge. This occasional cheating sometimes results in a smaller side collection, or in some cases, turns the collector away from a specialty and back to being a maverick. But, that's OK. Remember, there are no set rules, with the exception of having a lot of fun.

Now, what does it cost to start a collection and how can you determine the value of a bottle? Aside from digging excursions, which involves travel and daily expenses, collectors can start a collection by spending just a few dollars or maybe just a few cents per bottle. Digging, which is discussed in detail in the chapter "Digging for Bottles" is in my opinion, the ultimate way of adding to your collection and is how I started my addiction to the hobby.

Knowing what and where the best deals are obviously takes time and experience. But, the beginner can do well with just a few pointers. Let's start with buying bottles, instead of digging for bottles, since this is a quicker approach with more sources available for the new bottle collector.

Over the years, I've developed a "quick look" method of buying bottles by grouping candidates into one of three categories:

Low-End or Common Bottles

Bottles in this category show noticeable wear, and labels are usually missing or not very visible. In most cases, the label is completely gone and there is no embossing or identifying markings. The bottle is dirty (although it can usually be cleaned), and has some scrapes, but is free of chips. These bottles are usually clear.

Average Grade / Common Bottles

Bottles of this type show some wear, and a label may be visible but usually is faded. They are generally clear in color or aqua and free of scrapes or chips. Some may have minimal embossing, but not likely.

⚝ HIGH-END AND UNIQUE BOTTLES

These bottles can be empty, partially full, or completely full, with the original stopper and label or embossing. They can be clear but usually are green, teal blue, yellow, or yellow green. The bottle will have no chips, scrapes, and very little wear. If it has been stored in a box, the bottle is most likely in good or excellent condition. Also, the box must be in very good condition.

Price ranges will be discussed only briefly here since pricing and values are covered in more detail in the "Determining Bottle Values" chapter. Usually the low-end category can be found for $1 to $5, the average grade will range from $5 to $20, and the high-end will range from $20 to $100. Anything above $100 should be examined closely by someone who has been collecting for a while and is knowledgeable.

I try not to spend more than $2 per bottle for low-end or $5 to $7 for average grade. It's easier to stick to this guideline when you've done your homework, but sometimes you just get lucky. As an example, during a number of bottle and antique shows, I have found tables where the seller had "grab bags" full of bottles for $2 a bag. I never pass up this opportunity due to the low price and the lure of hidden treasure. After one show, when I examined my purchase, I discovered nine bottles, some purple, all pre-1900, in great shape, with embossing for a total cost of 22 cents per bottle. Now what could be better than that? Well, what was better was that I found a Tonopah, Nevada, medicine bottle valued at $100.

In the high-end category, deals are usually made after some good old horse trading and bartering. But, hey, that's part of the fun. Always let the seller know that you are a new collector with a limited budget. It really helps. I have never run across a bottle seller who wouldn't work with a new collector to try to give the best deal for a limited budget.

A collector should also be aware of the characteristics of old bottles versus new bottles and what makes a bottle antique. New collectors often assume that any old bottle is an antique, and if a bottle isn't old it isn't collectible. In the antique world, an antique is defined as an article more than 100 years old. But quite a number of bottles listed in this book are less than 100 years old yet are just as valuable—perhaps more so—than those that are officially antiques. As discussed earlier, the history, origin, background, use, and rarity of the bottle can be more important to a bottle collector than its age.

The number and variety of old and antique bottles is greater than the new collectible items in today's market. On the other hand, the Jim Beams, Ezra Brooks, Avons, recent Coke bottles, figurals, and miniature soda and liquor bottles manufactured more recently are very desirable and collectible and are in fact made for that purpose. If you decide you want to collect new bottles, the best time to buy is when the first issue comes out on the market. When the first issues are gone, the collector market is the only available source, which limits availability and will drive the price up considerably.

An example of a company that has produced a great deal of collector items is the Coca-Cola Company. When Coca-Cola reissued the 8-ounce junior size Coke bottle in the Los Angeles area to garner attention in a marketplace full of cans, the word spread fast among collectors. The 8-ounce bottle had the same contour as the 6-1/2 ounce bottle that was a Coke standard from the 1920s into the 1950s and has also been issued as a special Christmas issue every year since 1992. The 6-1/2 ounce bottle is available in a few parts of the United States, most noteably in Atlanta, Georgia, where Coca-Cola is headquartered. When these 8-ounce bottles were issued, the "heavy duty collectors" paid in advance and picked up entire case lots from the bottling operations before they hit the retail market. The most recent example occurred in December 2007, when Coca-Cola issued a replica of the 1899 Coca-Cola bottles in a six-pack. They sold as a novelty for $3.99 and disappeared as soon as they hit the shelves. Some of the dealers are now selling these six-packs for $20-$25 each.

For the beginner collector, and even the old-timer, books, references guides, magazines, and other similar literature are readily available at libraries and bookstores. The bibliography at the back of this book lists various types of literature to get you started. Also, joining a bottle club can be of great value, as this will provide numerous new sources of information, as well as an occasional digging expedition. Various bottle clubs are also listed in a separate chapter of this book.

I want to finish with a final note on reproductions and repaired bottles. Always check a bottle, jar, or piece of pottery carefully to make sure that there have been no repairs or special treatments. It's best to hold the item up to the light or take it outside with the dealer to look for cracks, nicks, or dings. Be sure to check for scratches that may have occurred during cleaning. There are also a number of bottles and jars that have reproduction closures. The proper closure can make a difference in the value of the bottle, so it's important to make sure the closure fits securely, and that the metal lid is stamped with the correct patent dates or lettering. If you need help, don't hesitate to ask an experienced collector. In order to better understand the hobby, new bottle collectors should learn about identification, grading, labeling, and glass imperfections and peculiarities, which are explained in more detail in the following chapters.

Now, get out to the antique and bottle shows, flea markets, swap meets, garage sales, and antique shops. Pick up those bottles, handle that glass, ask plenty of questions, and soon you will be surprised by how much you have learned, not to mention how much fun you'll have.

Bottle Facts

As mentioned in the introduction, the first question from a novice is, "How do you know how old a bottle is" or "How can you tell it is really an antique bottle?" Two of the most common methods for determining the age are by the mold seams and the color variations. Also, details on the lip, or top of the bottle, will provide some further identification.

ఆ Mold Seams (Figure 1)

Prior to 1900, bottles were manufactured using either a blowpipe (free-blown) until 1860 or with a mold until 1900. In this process, the mouth or lip of the bottle was formed last and applied to the bottle after completion (applied lip). An applied lip can be identified by observing the mold seam, which runs from the base up to the neck and near the end of the lip. On a machine-made bottle, the lip is formed first and the mold seam runs over the lip. Therefore, the closer to the top of the bottle the seam extends, the more recent the bottle.

On the earliest bottles manufactured before 1860, the mold seams will end low on the neck or at the shoulder. On bottles made between 1860 and 1880, the mold seam stops right below the mouth and makes it easy to detect that the lip was separately formed. Around 1880, the closed mold began to be used. With the closed mold, the neck and lip were mechanically shaped. Then the bottle was severed from the blowpipe and the ridge on the lip evened off by hand sanding or filing. The closed mold seam usually ends within one-quarter inch from the top of the bottle. After 1900, the seam extends all the way to the top.

IDENTIFYING BOTTLE AGE BY MOLD SEAMS

FIGURE 1

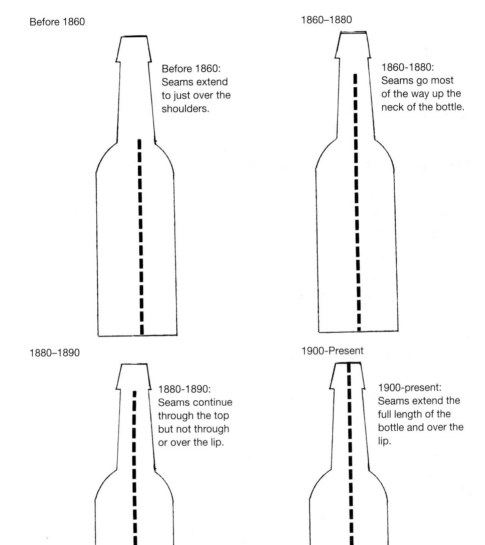

Before 1860

Before 1860: Seams extend to just over the shoulders.

1860–1880

1860-1880: Seams go most of the way up the neck of the bottle.

1880–1890

1880-1890: Seams continue through the top but not through or over the lip.

1900-Present

1900-present: Seams extend the full length of the bottle and over the lip.

↷ Lips and Tops (Figures 2a, 2b, 3 and 4)

Since the lip, or top, was an integral part the bottle-making process, it is important to understand that process. One of the best ways to identify bottles manufactured prior to 1840 is by the presence of a "sheared lip." This type of lip was formed by cutting or snipping the glass free of the blowpipe with a pair of shears, a process that leaves the lip with a stovepipe look. Since hot glass can be stretched, some of these stovepipes have a very distinctive appearance.

Around 1840, bottle manufacturers began to apply a glass ring around the sheared lip, forming a "laid-on-ring" lip. Between 1840 and 1880, numerous variations of lips or tops were produced using a variety of tools. After 1880, manufacturers started to pool their processing information, resulting in a more evenly finished and uniform top. As a general rule, the more uneven and crude the lip or top, the older the bottle.

Neck-Finishing Tools

Figure 2a

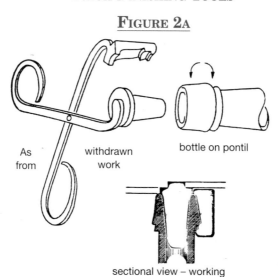

As from   withdrawn work   bottle on pontil

sectional view – working

A. The line drawings were developed from a description that appeared in the seventh edition (1842) of the *Encyclopedia Britannica*, vol. X, p. 579: "The finisher then warms the bottle at the furnace, and taking out a small quantity of metal on what is termed a ring iron, he turns it once round the mouth forming the ring seen at the mouth of bottles. He then employs the shears to give shape to the neck. One of the blades of the shears has a piece of brass in the center, tapered like a common cork, which forms the inside of the mouth, to the other blade is attached a piece of brass, used to form the ring." This did not appear in the sixth edition (1823), though it is probable the method of forming collars was practiced in some glasshouses at that time.

FIGURE 2B

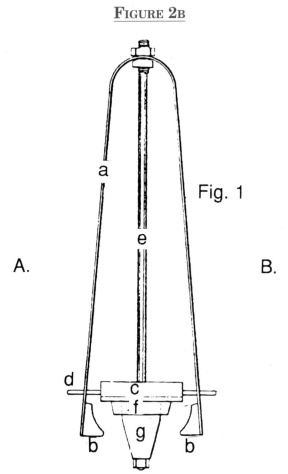

Fig. 1

A.   B.

B. The exact period in which neck finishing tools evolved having metal springs with two jaws instead of one, to form collars, is undetermined. It doubtless was some time before Amosa Stone of Philadelphia patented his "improved tool," which was of simpler construction, as were many later ones. Like Stone's, the interior of the jaws [was] made in such shape as to give the outside of the nozzle of the bottle or neck of the vessel formed the desired shape as it [was] rotated between the jaws in a plastic state..." U.S. Patent Office. From specifications for (A. Stone) patent No. 15,738, September 23, 1856.

☞ Tooled Bottle Lips / Tops Identification

Figure 3

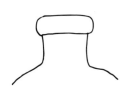

1 Tooled, rounded, rolled-over collar

2 Tooled, flanged, with flat top and squared edges

3 Tooled, rounded above 3/4-inch flat band

4 Tooled, flat ring below thickened plain lip

5 Tooled, narrow beveled fillet below thickened plain lip

6 Tooled, broad sloping collar above beveled ring

7 Tooled, plain broad sloping collar

8 Tooled, broad sloping collar with beveled edges at top and bottom

9 Tooled, broad flat collar sloping to heavy rounded ring

10 Tooled, broad flat vertical collar with uneven lower edge

11 Tooled, double rounded collar, upper deeper than lower; neck slightly pinched at base of collar

12 Tooled, broad round collar with lower level

Bottle Lips / Other Tops Identification

Figure 4

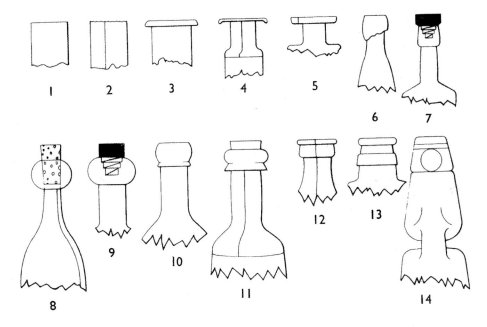

1. Free-blown
2. Sheared
3. Rolled
4. Flared
5. Laid-on ring
6. Applied top
7. Internal threads
8. Blob-top (cork use)
9. Blob-top (internal thread)
10. Improved applied lip on a two-piece mold bottle
11. Improved applied lip on a three-piece mold bottle
12. 20th Century lip
13. Collar below lip
14. Hiram Codd lip

☙ CLOSURES / STOPPERS

As mentioned in the "Bottles: History and Origin" chapter, the Romans used small stones rolled in tar as stoppers. The following centuries saw little advance in the methods of closure. During most of the 15th and 16th centuries, the closure consisted of a sized cloth tied down with heavy thread or string. Beneath the cover was a stopper made of wax or bombase (cotton wadding). Cotton wool was also dipped in wax to be used as a stopper, along with coverings of parchment, paper, or leather. Corks and glass stoppers were still used in great numbers, with the cork sometimes being tied or wired down for effervescent liquids. When the closed mold came into existence, however, the shape of the lip was more accurately controlled, which made it possible to invent and manufacture many different capping devices.

Glass stoppers, 1850-1900.

Example of glass stopper with cork as insulator for poison bottles, 1890-1910.

S.A. Whitney, who owned Whitney Glass Works in Glasborough, N.J, introduced an early closure device when he received Patent No. 31,046 on January 1, 1861, for an internal screw stopper (Figure 5). A unique closure was developed on July 23, 1872, when a British inventor, Hiram Codd, invented a bottle made with a groove inside the neck and was granted Patent No. 129,652 (Figure 6). A glass marble was inserted and then a ring of cork or rubber was fitted into the groove to confine the marble within the neck. The gas released by an effervescing liquid forced the marble to the top of the neck, sealing the bottle. A second patent, No. 138,230, issued April 29, 1873, contained the interior lug, which was a ball-holding element (Figure 7). It is interesting to note that many young boys broke the bottle to get the marble.

More interesting is that the Codd stopper closure isn't dead. The Sangaria Corporation, a Japanese company that distributes carbonated soft drinks in the United States, has re-issued and duplicated this same stopper design with the glass marble. In fact, a warning note on the back of the bottle reads, "Do not try to remove the marble from the bottle to avoid injury."

S.A. WHITNEY BOTTLE STOPPER

FIGURE 5

No. 31046   Patented Jan. 1, 1861

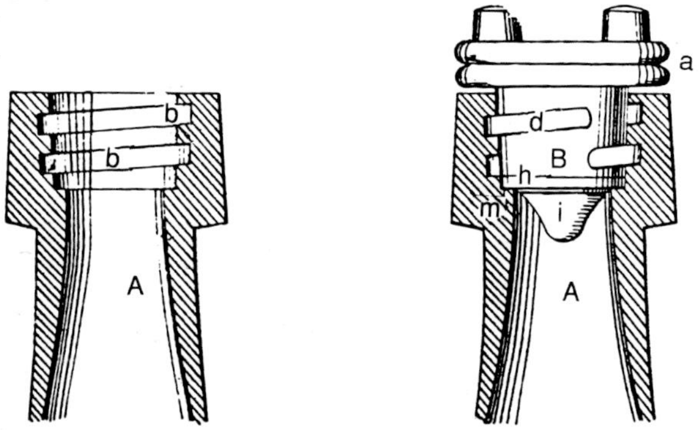

From Samuel A. Whitney's specification for his "Bottle Stopper," Patent No. 31,046, Jan. 1, 1861. The drawing on the left shows grooves in the neck of the bottle. In the drawing on the right, in which "h" is a cork washer, the stopper is in place. "The stopper is formed by pressing or casting the molten...glass in molds of the desired shape...Although...applicable to a variety of bottles and jars, it is especially well adapted to and has been more especiallly designed for use in connection with mineral-water bottles, and such as contain effervescing wines, malt liquors, &c., the corks in this class of bottles, if not lost, being generally so mutilated as to be unfit for second use when the bottles are refilled." (U.S. Patent Office.)

The Hutchinson stopper was awarded Patent No. 213,992 on April 8, 1879, and was a popular closure until the early 1900s (Figure 8). The stopper incorporated a heavy wire loop to control a rubber gasket that remained inside the neck of the bottle. After filling the bottle, the gasket was pulled up against the shoulders and was kept in place by the carbonation. Since it was simple to use, the Hutchinson stopper was easily adaptable to a number of other bottle types.

The lightning stopper (Figure 9), used from 1880 to the early 1900s, was the best closure for beer bottles before the invention of the crown cap. The lightning stopper featured a porcelain or rubber plug anchored to the outside of the bottle by means of a permanently attached wire. The wire formed a bar that controlled the opening and closing of the bottle. Since the lightning stopper cost more than the Hutchinson stopper, it wasn't used for soft drinks.

In 1892, William Painter invented the crown cap, which revolutionized the soft drink and beer bottling industry (Figure 10). By 1915 all major bottlers had switched to the crown-type cap. It was reported that Painter's "crown cork" system had taken him three years of constant work to perfect and cost $100,000, a considerable amount of money in 1892. It wasn't until 1960, with the introduction of the screw cap for beer and soda pop bottles, that the crown-type cap began to disappear.

Finally, in 1902, threads were manufactured on the outside of the lip to enable a

FIGURE 6

Hiram Codd interior ball stopper, Patent #129,652, July 23, 1872.

FIGURE 7

Hiram Codd interior ball stopper, Patent #138,230, April 29, 1873.

FIGURE 8

Charles G. Hutchinson stopper, Patent #213,992, April 8, (year uncertain).

FIGURE 9

Lightning stopper, used from
1880 to early 1900s.

FIGURE 10

William Painter crown cap,
Patent #468,226, Feb. 2, 1890.

FIGURE 11

Dumfries Ale (English)
depicting inside threads.

FIGURE 12

Dumfries Ale (English),
full bottle depicting inside
threads.

threaded cap to be screwed onto the mouth of the bottle. This was not a new idea. Early glassblowers produced bottles with inside and outside screw caps long before bottle-making machines came along. Early methods of production were so complex, however, that screw-topped bottles produced before the 1800s were considered specialty bottles. They were expensive to replace and today are considered rare and quite collectible. In fact, the conventional screw-top bottle did not become common until after 1924 when the glass industry standardized the threads.

In 1875 some glass manufacturers introduced an inside screw-neck whiskey bottle that used a rubber stopper (Figures 11 and 12). This invention wasn't very popular because the alcohol interacted with the rubber, discoloring the rubber and making the whiskey bitter. The following table lists some of the brands of embossed whiskeys that featured the inside threaded neck and the approximate dates of circulation:

WHISKEY COMPANY	DATE OF CIRCULATION	WHISKEY COMPANY	DATE OF CIRCULATION
Adolph Harris	1907-1912	O'Hearns	1907-1916
Chevalier Castle	1907-1910	Posner	1905-1915
Crown (squatty)	1905-1912	Roth (aqua)	1903-1911
Crown (pint)	1896-1899	Roth (amber sq.)	1898-1909
Donnelly Rye	1910-1917	Roth (amber fluted	
El Monte	1910-1918	shoulder)	1903-1911
H.L. Nye	1900-1905	Roth (amber qt.)	1903-1911
Hall Luhrs	1880-1918	Rusconi-Fisher	1902-1915
Hanley	1905-1911	Taussig (clear)	1915-1918
J.C. Donnelly	1907-1915	Weeks/Potter	1860-1875
McDonald/Cohn	1903-1912	Whitney	1860-1875
Mini Taylor/Williams	1881-1900	Wilmerding/Loewe	1907-1917
Old Gilt Edge	1907-1912		

⌘ GLASS COLOR

The next most common method for determining the age of a bottle is by examining the color of the glass. The basic ingredients for glass production (sand, soda, and lime) have remained the same for 3,000 years. These ingredients, when mixed together, are collectively called the batch. When the batch is heated to a molten state, it is referred to as the metal. In its soft or plastic stage, the metal can be molded into objects, which when cooled, become the solid material we know as glass.

Producing colored and perfectly clear glass were both major challenges for glass manufactures for centuries. In the 13th and 14th centuries, the Venetians produced clear glass by using crushed quartz in place of sand. In 1668, the English tried to improve on this process by using ground flint to produce clear glass, and by 1675 an Englishman named George perfected lead glass. Today, this lead glass is referred to as "flint glass." Before 1840, intentionally colored or colorless glass was reserved for fancy figured flasks and vessels.

In naturally colored glass, the color was considered unimportant until 1880, when food preservation packers began to demand clear glass for food products. Since most glass produced previously was green, glass manufacturers began using manganese to bleach out the green tinge produced by the iron content to satisfy the increased demand for clear glass. Only then did clear bottles become common.

Iron slag was used up to 1860 and produced a dark olive green or olive amber glass that has become known as "black glass" and was used for wine and beverage bottles that needed protection from light. Natural glass colors are brown, amber, olive green, and aqua.

The true colors of blue, green, and purple were produced by the metallic oxides added to the glass batch. Cobalt was added for blue glass; sulfur for yellow and green; manganese and nickel for purple; nickel for brown; copper or gold for red; and tin or zinc for milk-colored glass (for apothecary vials, druggist bottles, and pocket bottles). The Hocking

Glass Company discovered a process for making a brilliant red-colored glass described as copper-ruby. The color was achieved by adding copper oxide to a glass batch as it was cooling and then immediately reheating the batch before use. Since these bright colors were expensive to produce, they are very rare and sought after by most collectors.

Many bottle collectors consider purple glass the most appealing and, therefore, it is prized above other glass. As discussed earlier, the iron contained in sand caused glass to take on a color between green and blue. Glass manufacturers used manganese, which counteracted the aqua to produce clear glass. Glass with manganese content was most common in bottle production between 1880 and 1914. When exposed to the ultraviolet rays of the sun, the manganese in the glass oxidizes, or combines with oxygen, and turns the glass purple. The longer the glass is exposed to the ultraviolet rays from the sun, the deeper the purple color. Purple glass is also known as "desert glass" or "sun-colored" glass because the color is activated as a result of exposure to UV rays in intense sunlight.

Because Germany was the main source of manganese, the supply ceased with the outbreak of World War I. By 1916 the glassmaking industry began to use selenium as a neutralizing agent. Glass that was produced between 1914 and 1930 is glass that is most likely to change to an amber or straw color.

The following chart shows how color is achieved by adding various oxides to the batch:

COLOR	OXIDES ADDED TO THE BATCH
Aqua	Iron oxide in sand
Black	Iron oxide, manganese, cobalt, iron
Clear	Selenium
Yellow	Nickel
Red	Gold, copper, or selenium
Blue	Cobalt oxide
Blue-Green	Iron in silicate-based glass
Amber	Manganese oxide, sulfur, carbon oxide
Dark Brown	Sulphide of copper and sulphide of sodium
Amethyst (Purple)	Sulphide of nickel
Rose Tinted	Selenium added directly into the batch
Orange Red	Selenium mixed first with cadmium sulphide
Dark Reddish-Brown	Sodium sulphide
Reddish Yellow	Sulphide of sodium and molybdenite
Yellow Green	Uranium oxide
Green	Iron oxide
Milk Glass	Tin or zinc oxide
Olive Green	Iron oxide and black oxide of manganese
Purple	Manganese
Orange	Oxide of iron and manganese

❧ IMPERFECTIONS

Imperfections and blemishes also provide clues to how old a bottle is and often add to the charm and value of an individual piece. Blemishes usually show up as bubbles or "seeds" in the glass. In the process of making glass, air bubbles form and rise to the surface where they pop. As the "fining out" (elimination process) became more advanced around 1920), these bubbles or seeds were eliminated.

Another peculiarity of the antique bottle is the uneven thickness of the glass. Often one side of the base has a one-inch thick side that slants off to paper thinness on the opposite edge. This imperfection was eliminated with the introduction of the Owens bottle-making machine in 1903.

In addition, the various marks of stress and strain, sunken sides, twisted necks, and whittle marks (usually at the neck where the wood mold made impressions in the glass) also give clues that a bottle was produced before 1900.

❧ Labeling and Embossing

While embossing and labeling were common practices in the rest of the world for a number of centuries, American bottle manufacturers did not adopt the inscription process until 1869. These inscriptions included information about the contents, manufacturer, distributor, and slogans or other messages advertising the product. Raised lettering on various bottles was produced with a plate mold, sometimes called a "slug plate" fitted inside the casting mold. This plate created a sunken area that makes them a special value to collectors. Irregularities such as a misspelled name add to the value of a bottle, as will any name embossed with hand etching or other method of crude grinding. These bottles are very old and valuable.

Inscription and embossing customs came to an end with the production of machine-made bottles in 1903 and with the introduction of paper labels. In 1933, with the repeal of prohibition, the distilling of whiskey and other spirits was resumed under strict government regulations. One of the major regulations was that the following statement was required to be embossed on all bottles containing alcohol: "Federal Law Forbids Sale or Re-Use of this Bottle." This regulation was in effect until 1964 and is an excellent method of dating spirit bottles from 1933 to 1964.

Determining Bottle Values

C ollectors and dealers typically use the following factors to determine a bottle's value: rarity, age, condition, and color.

✤ SUPPLY AND DEMAND

As with any product, when demand increases and supply decreases, the price goes up.

✤ CONDITION

Mint: An empty or full bottle (preferably full) with a label or embossing. Bottle must be clean and have good color, with no chips, scrapes, or wear. If the bottle comes in a box, the box must be in perfect condition too. There should be absolutely no damage. Tumbled bottles are not considered Mint.

Extra Fine/Near Mint: An empty or full bottle with slight wear on the label or embossing. Slight wear or damage is defined as tiny nicks, light scratches, small open bubbles, and light stains. Bottle must be clean with clear color, and no chips or scrapes. There is usually no box, or the box is not in very good condition.

Very Good/Excellent: Bottle has some light or minor wear and label is usually missing or not very visible. Most likely there is no embossing and no box.

Good: Bottle shows additional wear and label is completely absent. Color is usually faded and bottle is dirty. Usually some scrapes and minor chips. Most likely there is no box.

Fair or Average: Bottle shows considerable wear, label is missing, and embossing is damaged.

Poor/Damaged: Bottle has large cracks and large pieces chipped away.

✑ RARITY

It is important to know that while rarity is a strong factor in establishing a high price for a bottle, there is no guarantee that a bottle will always retain its "rare" status. There have been occurrences in which only 1 to 5 bottles of a particular bottle were known to be in existence until an estate went to auction and 3 more examples surfaced.

Unique: A bottle is considered to be unique if only one is known to exist. These bottles are also the most valuable and expensive.

Extremely Rare: Only 5 to 10 known specimens.

Very Rare: Only 10 to 20 known specimens.

Rare: Only 20 to 40 known specimens.

Very Scarce: No more than 50 known specimens.

Scarce: No more than 100 known specimens.

Common: Common bottles, such as clear 1880 to 1900 medicine bottles, are abundant, easy to acquire, usually very inexpensive, and great bottles for the beginning collector.

✑ HISTORIC AND GEOGRAPHIC APPEAL

These bottles are valuable because of the significance of where they were made. For example, bottles made in territories have special value because they were produced in areas that had not yet received statehood. Another good example is that of Western whiskey collectors, who focus especially on bottles from San Francisco and in general northern California, while collectors in the East focus on historical flasks because these flasks portray figures and events that are especially relevant to East coast states.

✑ EMBOSSING LABELING AND DESIGN

Bottles without embossing are common and have little dollar value to many collectors. Exceptions are hand-blown bottles made before 1840, which usually don't have embossing.

Embossing describes the name of the contents, manufacturer, state, city, dates, trademarks, and other valuable information. Embossed images and trademarks can also enhance and increase the value of the bottle.

Labeling found intact with all the specific information about the bottle also enhances and increases the value of the bottle.

ᠻ AGE

While age can play an important role in the value of a bottle, there's not always a direct correlation. As stated in "The Beginning Collector" chapter, the history, rarity, and use of a bottle can be more important than age to a collector.

ᠻ COLOR

To collectors, rare colors are the major factor in determining the value of bottles within a specific bottle category.

Low Price: clear, aqua, amber

Average Price: milk glass, green, black, basic olive green

High Price: teal blue, cobalt blue, purple (amethyst), yellow, yellow green, puce

ᠻ UNIQUE FEATURES

The following characteristics can also significantly affect value: pontil marks, whittle marks, glass imperfections (thickness and bubbles), slug plates, and crudely applied lips and tops.

Even with the above guidelines, it's important to consult more detailed references, especially concerning rare and valuable bottles. See the bibliography and the Web site listing at the back of this book. Remember, never miss a chance to ask other collectors and dealers for advice and assistance.

Bottle Sources

Antique and collectible bottles can be found in a variety of places and sometimes where you least expect them. Excluding digging, the following sources are good potential hiding places for much sought-after bottles.

☙ THE INTERNET

In the 30 years that I've been collecting, I have never seen anything impact the hobby of bottle collecting as much as the Internet. Go to the Internet, type in the words "Antique Bottle Collecting," and you'll be amazed at the amount of instant data at your fingertips. Numerous Web sites throughout the United States, Canada, Europe, and Asia, provide information about clubs, dealers, antique publications, and auction companies. These sites have opened up the entire world and are convenient and in-expensive resources for collectors and dealers.

☙ FLEA MARKETS, SWAP MEETS, THRIFT STORES, GARAGE SALES, SALVAGE COMPANIES, AND SECONDHAND STORES

For beginning collectors, these sources will likely be the most fun (next to digging) and yield the most bottles at the best prices. The majority of bottles found at these sources will fall into the common or common-but-above-average category.

Flea markets, Swap Meets, and Thrift Stores: Target areas where household goods are being sold. It's a good bet they will have bottles.

Garage Sales: Focus on the older areas of town, since the items will be older, more collectible, and more likely to fall into a rare or scarce category.

Salvage Stores or Salvage Yards: These are great places to search for bottles, since these businesses buy from companies that tear down old houses, apartments, and businesses. A New York salvage company discovered an untouched illegal prohibition-era distillery complete with bottles, unused labels, and equipment. What a find!

❧ Local Bottle Clubs and Collectors

By joining a local bottle club or working with other collectors, you will find more ways to add your collection, gather information, and do more digging. Members usually have quantities of unwanted or duplicate bottles, which they will sell very reasonably, trade, or sometimes even give away, especially to an enthusiastic new collector.

❧ Bottle Shows

Bottle shows not only expose collectors to bottles of every type, shape, color, and variety, but also provide them the opportunity to talk with experts in specialized fields. In addition, publications dealing with all aspects of bottle collecting are usually available for sale or even free. Bottle shows can be rewarding learning experiences not only for beginning collectors but also for veteran collectors. They take place almost every weekend all across the country, and they always offer something new to learn and share and, of course, bottles to buy or trade.

Make sure you look under the tables at these shows because many great bargains in the form of duplicates and unwanted items may be lurking where you least expect it. Quite often, diggers find so many bottles that they don't even bother to clean them. Instead, they offer them as is for a very low price. Hey, for a low price, I'll clean bottles!

❧ Auction and Estate Sales

Auction houses have become a good source of bottles and glassware over the last few years. When evaluating auction houses, look for an auction company that specializes in antiques and estate buyouts. To promote itself and provide buyers with a better idea of what will be presented for sale, an auction house usually publishes a catalog that provides bottle descriptions, conditions, and photographs. I recommend, however, that you first visit an auction as a spectator to learn how the process works before you decide to participate. When buying, be sure of the color and condition of the bottle, and terms of the sale. These guidelines also apply to all Internet auctions. Use caution and follow these general rules:

◆ BUYING AT AUCTIONS

- ☞ Purchase the catalog and review all the items in the auction. At live auctions, a preview is usually held to inspect the items by the customers.
- ☞ After reviewing the catalog and making your choice, phone or mail your bid. A 10 to 20 percent buyer's premium is usually added to the sale price.
- ☞ Callbacks allow bidders to increase the previous high bid on certain items after the close of the auction.
- ☞ The winning bidder receives an invoice in the mail. After the bidder's check clears, the bottles are shipped.
- ☞ Most auction houses have a return policy, as well as a refund policy, for items that differ from the description in the catalog.

The "Auction Companies" chapter lists a number of quality auction houses that specialize in bottles, pottery, and related glass items.

◆ SELLING AT AUCTIONS

- ☞ Check and evaluate the auction source before consigning any merchandise. Make sure that the auction venue is legitimate and has not had any problems with payments or product.
- ☞ Package the item with plenty of bubble wrap, insure your bottle, and mail the package by certified mail, signed receipt requested.
- ☞ Allow 30 days to receive payment and be aware that most firms charge a 15 percent commission on the sales price.

ᴄ❧ ESTATE SALES

An estate sale is a great source for bottles if the home is in a very old neighborhood or section of the city that has historical significance. These sales are a lot of fun, especially when the people running the sale let you look over and handle the items to be able to make careful selections. Prices are usually good and are always negotiable.

ᴄ❧ KNIFE AND GUN SHOWS

Bottles at a knife and gun shows? Yes! Quite a few gun and knife enthusiasts are also great fans of the West and keep an eye open for related artifacts. Every knife and gun show I've attended has had at least 10 dealers with bottles on their tables (or under the tables) for sale. And the prices were about right, since they were more interested in selling their knives and guns than the bottles. Plus, these dealers will often provide information on where they made their finds, which you can put to good use later.

ᴄ❧ RETAIL ANTIQUE DEALERS

This group includes dealers who sell bottles at or near full market prices. Buying from dealers has advantages and disadvantages. They usually have a large selection and will provide helpful information and details about the bottles. And it's a safe bet that the bottles for sale are authentic. On the other hand, it s can be very expensive to build a collection this way. But these shops are a good place to browse and learn.

ᴄ❧ GENERAL ANTIQUE AND SPECIALTY SHOPS

The difference between general and retail antique shops is that general shops usually have lower prices and a more limited selection than retail shops. This is partly because merchants in general shops are not as well informed about bottles and may overlook critical characteristics. If a collector is well informed, general antique dealers can provide the opportunity to acquire underpriced quality merchandise.

Digging For Bottles

There are many ways to begin your search for collectible bottles, but few searches are as satisfying and fun as digging up bottles yourself. While the goal is to find a bottle, the adventure of the hunt is as exciting as the actual find. From a beginner's viewpoint, digging is a relatively inexpensive way to start your collection. The efforts of individual and bottle club digging expeditions have turned up numerous important historical finds. These digs revealed valuable information about the early decades of our country and the history of bottle and glass manufacturing in the United States. The following discussion of how to plan a digging expedition covers the essentials: locating the digging sites, equipment and tools, general rules and helpful hints, as well as a section on privy/outhouse digging for the real adventurer.

LOCATING THE DIGGING SITE

Prior to any dig, you will need to learn as much as possible about the area you plan to explore. Do not overlook valuable resources in your own community. You will likely be able to collect important information from your local library, local and state historical societies, various types of maps, and city directories (useful for information about people who once lived on a particular piece of property). The National Office of Cartography in Washington D.C. and the National Archives are excellent resources as well.

In my experience, old maps are the best guides for locating digging areas with good potential. These maps show what the town looked like in an earlier era and provide clues to where stores, saloons, hotels, red light districts, and the town dump were located. All are ripe for exploring. The two types of maps that will prove most useful are the plat maps and Sanborn Fire Insurance maps.

A plat map, which will show every home and business in the city or area you wish to dig, can be compared to current maps that identify the older structures or determine where they once stood. The Sanborn Insurance maps are the most detailed, accurate, and helpful of all for choosing a digging site. These maps, which have also been published under other names, provide detailed information on each lot illustrating the location of houses, factories, cisterns, wells, privies, streets, and property lines. These maps were produced for nearly every city and town between 1867 to1920 and are dated so that it's possible to determine the age of the sites you're considering. Another new tool in the hunt for surveying remote digging sites is Google Earth. It allows you to view the entire site from space. Hey, we've got the Internet, let's use it.

Figure 1 depicts an 1890 Sanborn Perris map section of East Los Angeles. This map section was used to locate an outhouse in East Los Angeles dated between 1885 and 1905. A dig on that site turned up more than 50 bottles. Knowing the approximate age of the digging site also helps to determine the age and types of bottles or artifacts you find there.

Local chambers of commerce, law enforcement agencies, and residents who have lived in the community for a number of years can be very helpful in your search for information. Other great resource for publications about the area's history are local antique and gift shops, which often carry old books, maps, and other literature about the town, county, and surrounding communities.

Since most early settlers handled garbage themselves, buried bottles can be unearthed almost anywhere, but a little knowledge of past customs can narrow the search to a location that's likely to hold some treasures. Usually, the garbage was hauled and dumped within one mile of the town limits. Often, settlers or storeowners would dig a hole about 25 yards out from the back of their home or business for garbage and refuse. Many hotels and saloons had a basement or underground storage area where empty bottles were kept.

Ravines, ditches, and washes are also prime digging spots because heavy rains or melting snow often washed debris down from other areas. Bottles can quite often be found beside houses and under porches. Residents would store or throw their bottles under their porches when porches were common building features in the late 19th and 20th centuries. Explore wagon trails, old railroad tracks, sewers, and abandoned roads where houses or cabins once stood. Old battlegrounds and military encampments are excellent places to dig, when legal. Cisterns and wells are other good sources of bottles and period artifacts.

The first love of this bottle hound, and high on the list of most collectors, is an expedition to a ghost town. It's fun and a lesson in history. The best places to search in ghost towns are near saloons, trade stores, train stations, the red light district, and the town dump (prior to 1900). The Tonopah, Nevada, town dump was the start of my digging experiences and is still a favorite spot.

FIGURE 1

Sanborn Perris map section of East Lost Angeles 1885-1905.

❧ PRIVY / OUTHOUSE DIGGING

"You've dug bottles out of an old outhouse? You've got to be kidding!" Telling your family and friends about this unique experience will usually kick the conversation into high gear. I'm quite serious when I say that one of the best places to find old bottles—old bottles that can be very rare and in great condition—is in an old outhouse. Prior to 1870, most bottles were not hauled out to the dump. Why would anybody bother when they could simply toss old bottles down the outhouse hole in the back of a house or business? In fact, very few pontil age (pre-Civil War) bottles are ever found in dumps. At that time people either dug a pit in their backyard for trash, or used the outhouse. These outhouses, or privies, have been known to yield all kinds of other artifacts such as guns, coins, knives, crockery, dishes, marbles, pipes, and other household items.

To develop a better sense of where privies can be found, it is important to have an understanding of their construction and uses. The privies of the 19th century (which produce the best results) were deep holes constructed with wood, brick, or sides called "liners." You'll find privies in a variety of shapes: square, round, rectangular, and oval. The chart below summarizes the different types of privies, their locations, and depth.

TYPES OF PRIVIES

CONSTRUCTION	SHAPE	LOCATION	DEPTH
BRICK	Oval, round, rectangular, square	Big towns and cities, behind brick buildings	Not less than six feet deep
Stone	Round, square, rectangular	Limestone often used in areas where stone is common	Rectangular, less than 10 feet deep; round, often 20 feet or more
Wood	Square or rectangular	Farms, small towns	May be one privy on plot not more than 10 to 15 feet deep; often very shallow
Barrel	Round	Cities and towns	8 to 12 feet deep

In general, privies in cities are fairly deep and usually provide more bottles and artifacts. Privies in rural areas are shallower and do not contain as many bottles. Outhouses on farms are very difficult to locate and digs often produce few results.

How long was an outhouse used? The lifespan of a privy is anywhere from 10 to 20 years. It was possible to extend its useful life by cleaning it out or relining it with new wood, brick, or stone. In fact, nearly all older privies show some evidence of cleaning.

At some point, old privies were filled and abandoned. The materials used to fill them included ashes, bricks, plaster, sand, rocks, building materials, and soil, which had been dug out when a new or additional privy was added to the house. Often, bottles or other artifacts were thrown in with the fill. The depth of the privy determined the amount of the fill required. In any case, the result was a privy containing layers of various materials, with the bottom layer being the "use" layer or "trash" layer as shown in Figure 2.

It is possible to locate these old outhouses due to the characteristic differences in density and composition of the undisturbed earth. Because of the manner of construction, it is fairly easy to locate them by probing the area with a metal rod or "probe."

OLDER PRIVIES

FIGURE 2

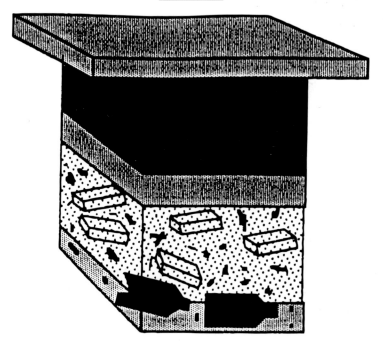

Your own community is a great place to begin the hunt for a privy. A good starting point is to find an old house. Those dating from 1880 to 1920 usually had a least one privy in the backyard. Try to locate a small lot with few buildings or obstructions to get in the way of your dig. First look for depressions in the ground, since materials used to fill privies have a tendency to settle. A subtle depression may indicate where a septic tank, well, or privy was once located. In addition, like most household dumps, outhouses were usually located 15 to 30 yards behind a residence or business. Another good indicator of an old privy site is an unexpected grouping of vegetation such as bushes or trees, which flourishes above the rich fertilized ground. Privies were sometimes located near old trees for shade and privacy.

The most common privy locations were (1) directly outside the back door, (2) along a property line, (3) in one of the back corners or the rear middle of the lot, and (4) the middle of the yard. Figure 3 depicts patterns of typical outhouse locations.

TYPICAL PRIVY CONFIGURATIONS

FIGURE 3

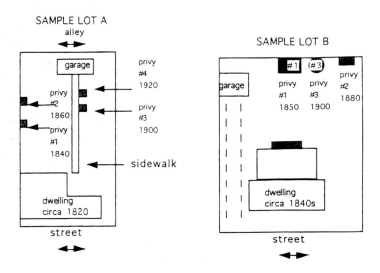

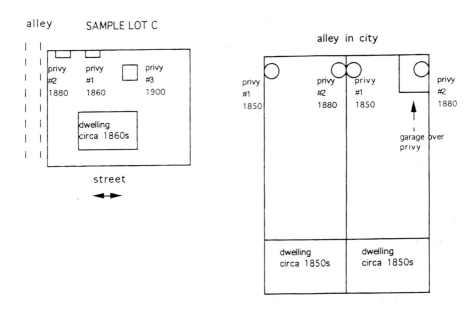

Now that you've located that privy (with luck it's full of great bottles), it's time to open up the hole. The approximate dimensions of the hole can usually be determined with your probe. If you know, or even suspect, that the hole is deeper than you are tall, it is extremely important to open the entire hole to avoid a cave-in. Never try to dig half a hole in hopes of getting to the trash layer quicker. Remember that the fill is looser than the surrounding ground and could come down on you. Also, always dig to the bottom and check the corners carefully. Privies were occasionally cleaned out, but very often bottles and artifacts were missed in the corners or on the sides. If you are not sure whether you've hit the bottom, check with the probe. It's easier to determine if you can feel the fill below what you may think is the bottom. In brick and stone-lined holes, if the wall keeps going down, you are not on the bottom.

Quite often it is difficult to date a privy without the use of detailed and accurate maps. But it is possible to determine the age of the privy by the type and age of items found in the hole. The chart on the following page lists some types of bottles you might find in a dig and shows how their age relates to the age of the privy.

Material	1920+	1900-1919	1880-1900	1860-1880	1840-1860	Pre-1840
Crown Tops	Yes	Yes	No	No	No	No
Screw Tops	Yes	Yes	No	No	No	No
Aqua Glass	Yes	Some	Yes	Yes	Yes	Yes
Clear Glass	All	Most	Some	Some	Some	Some
Ground Lip Fruit Jar	No	Rare	Yes	Yes	Rare	No
Hinge Mold	No	No	No	Yes	Yes	No
Pontiled	No	No	No	Yes	Yes	Yes
Free-Blown	No	No	No	No	No	Yes
Historical Flasks	No	No	No	Yes	Yes	Yes
Stoneware (Crockery)	No	No	Yes	Yes	Yes	Yes

While finding a prized bottle is great, digging and refilling the hole can be hard work and very tiring. To help make this chore easier, put down a tarp on the ground surrounding the hole as you dig, and shovel the dirt on the tarp. Then, shovel the dirt off the tarp and fill five-gallon plastic buckets. The first benefit of this method is the time and energy you'll save filling the hole. The second benefit, and maybe the biggest, is that you'll leave no mess. This becomes important for building a relationship with the property owner. The less mess, the more likely you'll get permission to dig again.

Also, the dig will be safer and easier if you use a walk board. Place an 8-foot long 2 x 8 plank over the hole. The digger, who is standing on the board pulling up buckets of dirt (let's all take turns), can do so without hitting the sides. This also reduces the risk of the bucketman falling in or caving in a portion of the hole. Setting up a tripod with a pulley over the hole will help save time and prevent strain on the back.

The short few paragraphs presented here are really just an outline of privy/outhouse digging. There are two books that discuss the art of privy/outhouse digging in detail, and I recommend everyone obtain them for their library: *The Secrets of Privy Digging* by John Odell and *Privy Digging 101* by Mark Churchill. See the bibliography for complete publishing information on these fine works. Now, let's have some "outhouse" fun.

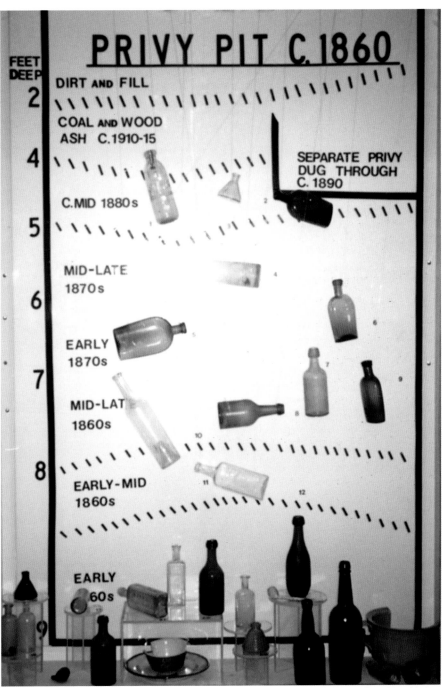

Privy pit display, circa 1860 (actual dug pit), National Bottle Museum, Ballston, Spa, New York.

⁀ THE PROBE

Regardless of whether you're digging in outhouses, old town dumps, or beneath a structure, a probe is an essential tool. The probe, shown in Figure 4, is a simple device, usually five to six feet long (a taller person may find that a longer probe works better) with a handle made of hollow or solid pipe, tapered to a point at the end so it's easier to penetrate the ground. Welding a ball bearing on the end of the rod will help in collecting soil samples. As discussed earlier, examining the soil samples is critical to finding privies. To make probing easier, add weight to the handle by filing the pipe with lead or welding a solid steel bar directly under the handle. The additional weight will reduce the effort needed to sink the probe.

While probing, press down slowly and try to feel for differences in the consistency of the soil. Unless you are probing into sand, you should reach a point where it becomes difficult to push, which means you have hit a natural bottom. If you find you can probe deeper in an adjacent spot, you may have found an outhouse. When this happens, pull out the probe and plunge it in again, this time at an angle to see if you feel a brick or wood liner. After some practice, you'll be able to determine what type of material you are hitting. Glass, brick, crockery, and rocks all have their own distinctive sound and feel. While you can purchase probes in a number of places, you might want to have one custom made to conform to your body height and weight for more comfortable use.

Bottle Probe

Figure 4

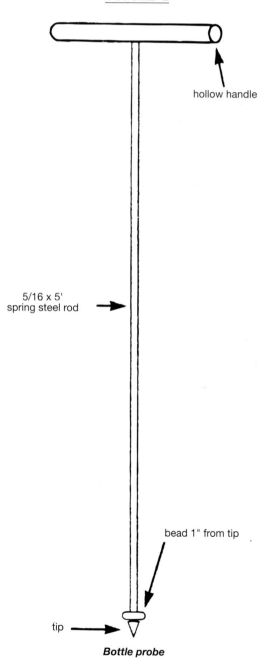

hollow handle

5/16 x 5'
spring steel rod

bead 1" from tip

tip

Bottle probe

ON A PRIVY DIG WITH RICK WEINER AND PAUL SEIDEL

Rick Weiner starting a dig in an 1850s privy near Easton, Pennsylvania, in September 2006. This privy yielded so many cobalt blue bottles that it earned the nickname "Cobalt Hole."

An impressive selection of cleaned cobalt blue bottles.

A closeup of one of the cobalt blue bottles recovered from the dig.

A tub full of bottles before cleaning, including some non-cobalt blue bottles. All, however, are typical of what our ancestors used more than 100 years ago. What a change, considering that we now depend largely on plastic bottles and aluminum cans. We rarely use glass bottles anymore.

Example of a stone-lined privy dug by Rick Weiner and Paul Seidel.

Example of a wood-lined privy dug by Rick Weiner and Paul Seidel.

Rick Weiner holding a cobalt blue bottle found at the dig at the Bowery House near Easton, Pennsylvania, in January 2008.

🦎 DIGGING EQUIPMENT AND TOOLS

When I first started digging, I took only a shovel and my luck. I learned I was doing things the hard way, and the result was a few broken bottles. Since then, I've refined my list of tools and equipment. The following list includes those items I have found useful and recommended by veteran diggers.

🦎 GENERAL DIGGING EQUIPMENT

- Probe
- Long handled shovel
- Short handled shovel
- Long handled potato rake
- Small hand rake
- Old table knives
- Old spoons
- Hard and soft bristle brushes
- Gloves/boots/eye protection/durable clothes
- Insect repellent, snake bite kit, first aid kit
- Extra water and hat
- Dirt sifter (for coins or other items, a 2' x 2' wooden frame with chicken wire).
- Hunting knife
- Boxes for packing and storing bottles

🦎 PRIVY / OUTHOUSE DIGGING EQUIPMENT

- Long handled shovel*
- Five-foot probe*
- Slam probe
- Pick*
- Root cutters*
- Short handled garden scratcher*
- Rope, 1" x 15'+ with clip
- Tripod with pulley
- Walk board*
- Short-handled shovel
- Ten-foot probes*
- Posthole digger
- Pry bar
- Ax
- Five-gallon buckets
- Heavy tarps
- Hardhat and gloves

*Indicates essential item

✺ GENERAL RULES AND HELPFUL HINTS

Although I said there were no rules to bottle collecting, when digging there are two major rules you always need to follow.

◆ RULE NO. 1:

Always be responsible and respectful and ask for permission to dig. As a safety precaution, do not leave any holes open overnight. Do not damage shrubs, trees, or flowers unless the owner approves. When the digging is complete, always leave the site looking better than when you started. I can't stress this enough. That means filling in all holes and raking over the area. Take out your trash as well as trash left by previous prospectors or others. Always offer to give the owner some of the bottles. They may not want any, but they will appreciate the gesture. If you adhere to these few rules, the community or owner will thank you, and future bottle diggers will be welcomed. The following is a summary of the "Bottle Digger's Code of Ethics" (compliments of the San Diego Bottle Club).

• Respect property rights and all warning signs.

• To respect both public and private property, always obtain valid permission to search, probe, or dig on the property.

• Do not park illegally and do park so that other vehicles can get out.

• Upon entering public or private property, do not damage or destroy any property improvements on the site.

• After digging on a site, try to leave all land and vegetation as it was by taking the necessary time to properly fill all holes and re-root plants when possible.

• Remove or bury existing litter and all unwanted items from your search area, leaving it cleaner than you found it.

• As a representative of all bottle collectors and diggers, be thoughtful, considerate, and courteous at all times.

◆ RULE NO. 2:

Do not, under any circumstances, do any digging alone. Ignoring this rule is extremely dangerous. When digging an outhouse, my recommendation is to go with no fewer than three people, and be sure to tell someone exactly where you're going and how long you expect to be gone.

There were two tragic instances, one in 2002 and one in 2003, of what can happen if this rule isn't followed. On September 23, 2002, in Honolulu, Hawaii, a 55-year old bottle collector was digging for bottles in a trench at the Waipahu Sugar Mill, which is a prized area because of the numerous plantations that were in the area. Without warning, the trench collapsed and he was buried under six feet of dirt and suffocated. The other tragedy happened in March 2003 in Ramona, California, when an avid bottle collector and digger, digging in a ravine soaked by several days of heavy rain, was crushed by concrete, stone, dirt, and a large boulder when the unstable ground collapsed.

To highlight the dangers of digging, here's a recent example of a tragedy in which a fatality occurred in a group of experienced bottle diggers even though they were following the rules. In June 2005, the group was digging in downtown Los Angeles, California, at an old brewing company site when without warning, a 5 foot berm collapsed, pouring tons of earth and gravel over one of the club members. Firefighters tried desperately for 45 minutes to dig out the individual but loose dirt continued to fall back on the digger. They couldn't get him out in time and he was slowly crushed to death. This is a tragic and terrible story, but it's a reminder that safety is the most important issue. Follow all rules and don't dig alone!

When you start digging, don't be discouraged if you don't find any bottles. If you unearth other objects such as coins, broken dishes, or bottle tops, continue to dig deeper and in a wider circle. If you still don't find any bottles, move to another spot. Always work from the edge to the center of the hole. Don't give up! Even the best have come home with empty bags and boxes but never without the memory of a good time. When you do find a bottle, stop digging and remove the surrounding dirt a little at a time with a small tool, brush, or spoon. Handle the bottle very carefully, since old bottles are very fragile.

Now, that you know how to dig, what are you waiting for? Grab those tools, get those maps, and get started making the discoveries of a lifetime.

Bottle Handling

W hile selling bottles and listening to buyers at various shows, I am inevitably asked questions about cleaning, handling, and storing old bottles. Some collectors believe that cleaning a bottle diminishes its collectible value and desirability.

Leaving a bottle in its natural state, as it was found, can be special. Others prefer to remove as much dirt and residue as possible. The choice rests with the owner. The following information will provide some help with how to clean, store, and take care of those special finds.

ᘯ Bottle Cleaning

Never attempt to clean a find in the field. In the excitement of the moment, it's easy to break the bottle or otherwise damage the embossing. With the exception of soda and ale bottles, glass bottles manufactured prior to 1875 usually have very thin walls. But even bottles with thicker walls should be handled very carefully. Improper handling or cleaning may result in additional damage, as these bottles are fragile.

First, remove as much loose dirt, sand, or other particles as possible with a small hand brush or a soft bristled toothbrush, followed by a quick warm water rinse. Then, using a warm water solution and bleach (stir the mixture first), soak the bottles for a number of days (depending upon the amount of caked on dirt). This should remove most of the excess grime. Adding a little vinegar to warm water will give an extra sparkle to the glass.

Other experienced collectors use cleaning mixtures such as straight ammonia, kerosene, lime-a-away, Mr. Clean, and chlorine Borax bleach. Do not use mixtures that are not recommended for cleaning glass, never mix cleaners, and do not clean with acids of any type. Mixing cleaners has been known to release toxic gases and poisonous vapors and fumes. A fellow bottle collector from Arizona has his own cleaning technique. He buys a special polish for rock polishing and mixes it with warm water to form a compound. He then lightly rubs the bottle, continuing to use cool water on the surface. I have seen a number of his bottles, and the finish results are fantastic.

After soaking, the bottles may then be cleaned with a bottle brush, steel wool, an old toothbrush, any semi-stiff brush, Q-tips, or used dental picks.

At this point, you may want to soak the bottles again in lukewarm water to remove any traces of cleaning materials. Either let the bottles air dry or dry them with a soft towel. If the bottle has a paper label, the work will become more painstaking since soaking is not a cleaning option. I've used a Q-tip to clean and dry the residue around the paper label.

Don't clean your bottles in a dishwasher. While the hot water and detergent may produce a very clean bottle, older bottles were not designed to withstand the extreme heat of a dishwasher. As a result, the heat, combined with the shaking could crack or even shatter the fragile old bottles. Bottles with any type of a painted label may also be subjected to severe damage.

Another option is finding a professional who will clean your rare bottles with special tumbling, or cleaning machines. These machines work on the same principle as a rock tumbler, with two horizontal parallel bars acting as a "cradle" for the cleaning canisters. The machine cleaning process uses two types of oxides, one for polishing and one for cutting. The polishing oxides include aluminum, cerium, and tin, which remove stains and give the glass a crystal clean and polished appearance, but do not damage the embossing. The cutting oxides, such as silicon carbide, remove the etching and scratching. Many individuals clean bottles professionally, or you can purchase the machines to use yourself. If you do decide to go to a professional, request to look at examples of his work and try to find someone who's been recommended by another collector.

⚡ DISPLAY

Now that you have clean, beautiful bottles, display them to their best advantage. My advice is to arrange your bottles in a cabinet rather than on wall shelving or randomly around the house. While the last two options are more decorative, they also leave the bottles more susceptible to damage. When choosing a cabinet, look for one with glass sides, which will provide more light and better viewing. As an added touch, a light fixture will set off your collection beautifully.

If you still want a wall shelving arrangement, make sure the shelf is approximately 12 inches wide with a front lip for added protection. The lip can be made from quarter-round molding. After the bottle is placed in its spot, draw an outline around the base of the bottle and then drill four 1/4" holes just outside that outline for pegs. These pegs will provide further stability for the bottle. If you have picked up any other goodies from your digging—like coins, tokens, railroad spikes, or gambling chips—scatter them around the bottles for a little Western flavor.

PROTECTION

Because of earthquake activity, like that in California, bottle collectors across the country have taken added steps to protect their valuable pieces. Since most of us have our collections in some type of display cabinet, it's important to know how to best secure it.

First, fasten the cabinet to the wall with brackets and bolts. If you are working with drywall and it's not possible to secure the cabinet to a stud, use butterfly bolts to provide a tight hold. Always secure the cabinet at both the top and bottom for extra protection.

Next, lock or latch the cabinet doors. This will prevent the doors from flying open. If your cabinet has glass shelves, be sure to not overload them. In an earthquake, the glass shelving can break under the stress of excess weight.

Finally, it's important to secure the bottles to the shelves. A number of materials can be used, such as microcrystalline wax, beeswax, silicone adhesive, double-sided foam tape, or adhesive-backed Velcro spots or strips. These materials are available at local home improvement centers and hardware stores. One of the newest and most commonly used adhesives is called Quake Hold. This substance, available in wax, putty, and gel, is similar to the wax product now used extensively by numerous museums to secure their artwork, sculptures, and various glass pieces and is readily available to the general public at many home improvement stores and antique shops.

⚘ STORAGE

For those bottles you've chosen not to display, the best method for storing them is to place them in empty liquor boxes with cardboard dividers (which prevent bottles from bumping into each other). As added protection, you might want to wrap the individual bottles in paper prior to packing them in the boxes.

⚘ RECORD KEEPING

Last but not least, it's a good idea to keep records of your collection. Use index cards detailing where the bottle was found or purchased, including the dealer's name and price you paid. Also, assign a catalog number to each bottle, record it on the card, and then make an index. Many collectors keep records using a photocopier. If the bottle has embossing or a label, put the bottle on the machine and make a photocopy of it. Another method is to make a pencil sketch by applying white paper to the bottle and rubbing over the embossing with a number 2 pencil. Then, type all the pertinent information on the back of the image and put it in a binder. When it comes to trading and selling, excellent record keeping will prove to be invaluable.

The National Bottle Museum, Ballston Spa, New York: A Legacy for Bottle Collectors

🦎 THE MISSION

The museum's mission is to preserve the history of our nation's first major industry: bottle making. Millions of glass bottles per year were manufactured by hand for the mineral waters of Saratoga County alone, enabling the area to participate in world commerce during the early 1800s. A glassworks set in the wilderness above the nearby town of Greenfield employed hundreds of workers and glassblowers from the 1840s to the 1860s. In that era, all bottles were manufactured exclusively with hand tools and lung power.

Sign hanging above the front entrance of the National Bottle Museum in Ballston Spa, N.Y. The museum has more than 2,000 bottles on display and a research library. It also offers flameworking classes and other hands-on learning activities. *(Photo Courtesy of Museum Director Jan Rutland)*

View of the left side of bottle museum just inside the entrance. The oak ladders roll along the shelves, so visitors can get an up-close look at all bottles. With so many on display, enthusiasts could spend days studying their favorite bottles.

The worldwide mineral water industry was just one of many industries creating a tremendous demand for glass bottles. America was the world's largest producer of fine essence oils. The West was being settled, creating a demand for millions of whiskey flasks and spirit bottles to help men cope with loneliness and hardship. Every pharmacy, every producer of patent medicines, every brewery, dairy farm and manufacturer required handmade glass bottles. Machine-made bottles were not manufactured until after Michael Owens patented his inventions in 1903.

Well planned museum exhibits allow visitors to view a variety of beautiful and colorful glass bottles produced by strong men who toiled in intense heat for twelve hours a day, six days a week. In those days, the demand for glass containers was staggering. It was an era when vast commercial empires rose and fell. In many cases, only the glass bottles remain as witness to the drama.

One entire wall of the museum's first floor is covered with approximately 2,000 bottles of many colors, shapes, and forms. This is consid-

Exhibit explaining various bottle dating methods. In the center is a blowpipe, at left towards the bottom is a two-piece hinged wooden mold, and at bottom right the bases of two bottles are raised to display their pontils.

ered "open storage," and all of these bottles are accessioned into the collection to be held in trust for the public. When creating interpretive exhibits, borrowed bottles and related objects are often combined with those from the collection. In some cases, all exhibit objects may be borrowed. The museum has access to collections all over the United States, and borrowing objects from members makes frequent changes and more spectacular exhibits possible. The museum also has a research library available during museum hours.

The museum sponsors a 160-table antique bottle show and sale every June. A special area set aside from the sales floor is reserved for the beautiful educational exhibits. This popular event draws visitors and antique bottle dealers from coast to coast in the U.S. and Canada, as well as area residents. The general public is welcome and encouraged to enjoy this once-a-year event.

⌐ THE MUSEUM'S BEGINNING

According to director Jan Rutland, the museum, located in Ballston Spa, N.Y., near the world famous town of Saratoga Springs, got its start in 1978 when a group of collectors was given a historic Victorian home to create a museum. Exhibits were created from objects that were either loaned or donated. Monthly meetings were held to exchange bottle collecting information. Covered dish suppers and show-and-tell sessions among local collectors became increasingly popular, and educational programs open to the public created a great deal of interest. In the beginning, the museum was an informal organization of friends who enjoyed socializing and exchanging information, but in 1996 the museum received an official New York State charter. (In New York, chartered museums are incorporated under the umbrella of the state university system and file annual reports to the education department.) Chartering is the basis for a 501 C (3) status with the IRS, which allows donors to take deductions on their taxes. The museum currently operates using universally accepted museum practices as defined by the American Association of Museums.

The museum's first home was the Verbeck House, a Queen Ann Victorian mansion. With a New York State Preservation Grant, the mu-

A two-piece hinged violin bottle mold. Violin bottles have been classified in great detail, allowing collectors to precisely identify their styles, manufacturers, years of production, markings, sizes, and even the molds from which they came.

seum restored the exterior paint, slate and copper roof, and brick chimneys of the historic home. In 1994 the museum purchased a three-story brick commercial building in the heart of historic Ballston Spa.

❧ THE MUSEUM NOW

The present museum is located directly across the street from where the renowned Sans Souci Hotel stood in the 1800s. Built in 1803, it was the largest resort hotel in the country, accommodating 250 guests. The Sans Souci mineral water spring still flows freely in Wiswall Park on Front St. just around the corner from the museum. Originally built in 1901 as Tracey's Hardware, the current museum building sits on the site of an older building that burned to the ground. The museum occupies two of the three floors, each containing 2,000 square feet of space. The first floor features fourteen-and-a-half foot ceilings and huge show windows facing Route 50. Rolling oak ladders allow access to floor-to-ceiling shelves displaying parts of the museum's collection.

Demijohn display, 1850 to 1890. Demijohns were designed to transport and store large quantities of liquids such as wine, liquor, and olive oil, and also held seeds. They were often given a wicker cover. The wicker cover on the bottle at left not only added convenient handles to the bottle, but also helped protect it from damage.

Various size holes can be seen in the floor, where ropes and chains were pulled from the basement and measured out for waiting customers of the hardware store.

ꝯ Successes and Challenges

With the assistance of the village of Ballston Spa, the museum has been attempting to obtain a grant to turn the third floor of the building into a dormitory and dining room for students who attend classes at the Museum Glassworks, a teaching facility close to the museum and owned and operated by the museum. The glassworks is equipped with a 200 lb. capacity glass furnace and torches with which to teach flame-working. Unfortunately, the glass furnace was turned off because the rising cost of travel and accommodations along with the rising price of power has made lessons unaffordable for many. The museum's goal, however, is to provide room and board at a reasonable cost for students who wish to take one- or two-week-long classes, making them more affordable.

Poison bottle display, 1860-1920. As the sign indicates, Aunt Hannah's Liquid Death Drops, like other poisons, were intended to send bugs and other vermin to an early grave. Of course, there was always the danger of accidental ingestion. To help prevent this, poison bottles were molded with textured surfaces to warn of their deadly contents.

"While most non-profits the size of the National Bottle Museum are subsidized," Rutland commented, "this museum operates independently, raising all of its own operating funds through memberships, donations, and special events such as its annual bottle show in June. Proceeds from the glassworks also help to pay operating expenses, which include securing, insuring, and cataloguing every item, requiring many man-hours by its trained staff."

When the museum opened the glassworks to the public, members of the Northeast Region of the American Scientific Glassblowers Society provided demonstrations of flameworking techniques. According to Rutland, "So many people showed up that they blocked the street to traffic. The building was filled to capacity. Musicians arrived to entertain the crowd, but found that they could not get in. A sustained crowd of over one hundred was thrilled by hot glass demonstrations by world-renowned scientific glassblowers."

In the beginning, the studio was equipped with the assistance of a Safe Places Grant administered by the Saratoga County Youth Bureau, designed to provide young people with a safe and accessible place to learn and play after school under the supervision of positive role

Display of various pieces of vaseline glass, also known as uranium glass. Note the greenish yellow glow created by the presence of uranium salts. Genuine vaseline glass fluoresces bright green under ultraviolet light (black light) because it is slightly radioactive, and for that reason little was produced after World War II. Small pieces are now being produced, however, so not all fluorescing glass is old.

models. Free flameworking lessons for kids between 13 and 18 years of age were tremendously popular. Some of the teenagers who began with the program have gone on to open their own art glass studios, some have continued their training at major universities, and some are teaching.

Rutland said that "although the grant ended, student interest did not." To help cover expenses, the museum charged the young students $5 for two hours of instruction, including materials. In order to subsidize the teen program, classes were offered to adults at $12.50 per hour. In addition, the museum received a generous inheritance from a local schoolteacher who stated in her will that she wished the money to be used to further develop the Museum Glassworks. With these funds, the museum purchased the glass furnace, a "glory hole," a large annealer, hand tools, and blowpipes. In addition, Princeton University donated a large glass lathe and a glass grinder to the studio.

Rutland was awarded an associate membership in the American Scientific Glassblowers Society, and the Northeast Region of that organization held an annual seminar in Saratoga Springs and used the museum's glassworks for classes for the junior members. During the seminar, glassblowers from all over the world created art glass objects that were auctioned for the benefit of the museum. The museum offered glassblowing classes and a program allowing interested members of the public to spend an hour or two making paperweights at the furnace. The glassblowing classes drew students of all ages from Boston, Philadelphia, Chicago, and Canada.

"Unfortunately, as the price of power increased, so did the cost of travel and accommodations. Finally, the program became too expensive to sustain, and the furnace was shut down," Rutland explained. At present, the museum offers flameworking lessons on Tuesday evenings and Saturdays. On occasion, it offers two-day flameworking classes with world-renowned guest artists.

✎ THE FUTURE

Originally, the Glassworks was created and designed to help pay operating expenses of the museum. Potentially, it could be used to demonstrate bottle making or to create objects made to order. The museum is still hoping to attract area schools and colleges who will design programs for credit, using its equipment and facility, rather than purchasing over $150,000 worth of their own.

But regardless of the financial challenges, the museum's mission has never changed. In the 1970s, two of the museum's original founders, Ralph and Eleanor Work, created its constitution and bylaws, which are still adhered to today. A few minor revisions were necessary to better conform with education law, but the same documents continue to serve the museum well. Rutland's long-term plan is to "continue to develop the museum as an educational institution, relying on the existing constitution and bylaws as a guide, and ultimately to gain accreditation by the American Association of Museums, as grant money is far more accessible with accreditation." Some museum support organizations are urging passage of legislation that would provide operating funds for museums to develop curriculum-based programs for public schools. This wouldn't change the museum's direction or interfere with the services it already provides to members and the collecting community in general, as education is the museum's primary mission.

Gary Moeller, Museum Collection Manager. Moeller and other staff have a big job of securing, insuring, and cataloguing every item in the museum.

The museum's greatest challenge is to find ways to sustain its operations. It needs funds to hire additional staff, including a museum educator and a director with experience in museum management. Rutland has worked full time (and more) for the museum for over 20 years and her husband has worked part time at the Museum Glassworks for at least ten, yet neither has ever taken a salary. They are looking for people to help continue their work and secure the future of the museum. They would like to be ready with prepared school programs should legislation be passed to provide ongoing funds for this service.

In the meantime, a new initiative has been created to attract new people to the museum. Two bare brick walls on the museum's second floor are available for artists to exhibit their work. Gallery openings and changing art exhibits bring many people to the museum for the first time, and the museum receives a percentage of the price of any artwork sold. The museum offers memberships starting at $10 per year. Members receive a newsletter with informative articles and news of museum activities. Currently, members reside in all but two states in

Author Mike Polak and Museum Director Jan Rutland. Polak is a great fan of the museum and is enthusiastic about the opportunity bottle collectors have to use the facility to increase their knowledge. One of Rutland's main jobs is to secure the museum's permanent financial future to ensure that it will always be there for future collectors to enjoy.

the U.S. The museum is also partially funded by donations from bottle clubs around the country. The Village of Ballston Spa, the Ballston Spa Rotary Club, and local banks also provide annual donations in support of the museum.

A WELCOME TO ALL VISITORS

The museum extends a warm welcome to all who would like to visit and learn more about bottle collecting. Whether you are a new collector or a veteran, there is always much to learn about this fascinating hobby, and where better to learn than at the National Bottle Museum? So be sure to stop in if you are in the area! To receive information about visiting or becoming a member, call the museum at (518) 885-7589, visit www.nationalbottlemuseum.org, or e-mail nbm@crisny.org.

Old Bottles: Pre-1900

The bottles in this section have been categorized by physical type and/or by the original contents of the bottle. For most categories, the trade names can be found in alphabetical order if they exist. Note that in the case of certain early bottles, such as flasks, a trade name does not appear on the bottle. These bottles have been listed by subject according to the embossing, label, or other identification on the bottle.

Since it is impossible to list every bottle available, I've provided a representative selection of bottles in various price ranges and categories, rather than listing only the rarest or most collectible pieces.

The pricing shown reflects the value of the particular bottle listed. Similar bottles could have higher or lower values than the bottles specifically listed in this book, but the listings following provide collectors an excellent starting point for determining a reasonable price range.

Ale and Gin Bottles

Since ale and gin bottles are almost identical in style, it can be difficult to determine what the bottle originally contained unless information is provided on the bottle itself. Ale bottles should not be confused with beer bottles, a common mistake due to the similarities in shape.

Ale was a more popular beverage at a time when available wines were not as palatable. Ale quickly became a favorite alternative and even the very best ale was not expensive to make or buy. The bottles used by Colonial ale makers were made of pottery and imported from England. When searching for these bottles, keep in mind that the oldest ones had a matte or unglazed surface. Unlike ale, gin doesn't have an ancient origin, but it certainly does have a unique one.

In the 17th century, a Dutch physician named Francesco De La Bor prepared gin as a medical compound to for the treatment of kidney disease. While its effectiveness to purify the blood was questionable, gin drinking became very popular. It became so popular, in fact, that many chemists went into the gin brewing business full time to meet the growing demaand. During the 19th century, gin consumption in America increased at a steady rate.

The design of the gin bottle, which has a squat body, facilitated the case packing and prevented shifting and possible damage in shipping. The first case bottles were octagonal with short necks and were manufactured with straight sides that allowed four to twelve bottles to fit tightly into a wooden packing case. Designs that were introduced later featured longer necks.

Bottles with tapered collars are dated to the 19th century. The case bottle sizes vary in size from half-pints to multiple gallons. The early bottles were crudely made and have distinct pontil scars.

A.M. Bininger & Co., Old Dock Gin, brillant green, 8", American 1860-1870, $150-250.

Anderson & Co / Home Brewed Ale / Albany, N.Y., yellow with olive tone, 7-1/4", American 1865-1875, $500-700.

Black glass ale , deep olive green, 8-1/8", European 1780-1800, $200-300.

A.M. Bininger & Co / No 375 Broadway N.Y.
Medium pink amethyst, 9-3/4", smooth base, applied mouth, American 1865-1875 .... **$1,400-1,800**

Anderson & Co / Home Brewed Ale / Albany, N.Y.
Yellow with olive tone, 7-1/4", smooth base, applied blob mouth, rare, American 1865-1875...... **$500-700**

Black Glass Ale
Deep olive green with amber tone, 8-1/8", pontil-scarred base, sheared mouth with applied string lip, blown in a dip mold, English 1780-1800 .... **$200-300**

Black Glass Ale
Deep olive amber, 8-3/4", pontil-scarred base, applied mouth, blown in a dip mold, English 1790-1820
.... **$100-200**

Black Glass Ale
Deep olive amber, 9", pontil-scarred base, applied mouth, blown in a dip mold, English 1790-1820
.... **$100-200**

Black Glass Ale – Rev John Browder's Bottle – He Died in the Year 1815 (hand painted lettering)
Medium olive amber, 9", pontil-scarred base, applied mouth, blown in a dip mold, English 1790-1815
.... **$200-300**

Black glass ale, Rev. John Browder's Bottle – He Died in the Year 1815, medium olive amber, 9", English 1790-1815, $200-300.

Black glass ale, emerald green, 10", English 1790-1800, $375-450.

Large case gin, 18", yellow olive green, Dutch 1740-1760, $1,500-2,000.

Black Glass Ale
Emerald green, 10", pontil-scarred base, sheared mouth with applied string lip, English 1790-1800 ....**$375-450**

Case Gin – Double Sealed – Seal on Shoulder (J. Pfaff / 16 Exchange / Street / Boston) Second Seal at Side of Shoulder (Schiedam / Schnapps)
Olive amber, 9-3/4", smooth base, applied mouth, American 1865-1880 ....**$700-$900**

Case Gin – Large Dip Mold
Medium yellowish olive green, 10", open pontil, sheared mouth with applied lip, Dutch 1770-1810 ....**$100-$150**

Case Gin Bottle
Medium yellow olive, 10-3/8", open pontil, outward rolled lip, Dutch 1770-1800 ....**$150-$200**

Case Gin – Large Dip Mold
Medium olive green, 11-1/8", open pontil, applied mouth, Dutch 1770-1800 ....**$140-180**

Case Gin
Dark olive yellow, 12-1/2", straight sided form, applied flared lip, smooth base, English 1800-1825 .... **$300-$600**

Case Gin – Large Dip Mold
Medium yellowish olive green, 13", pontil-scarred base, sheared mouth with applied lip, Dutch 1770-1810 .... **$200-$300**

Case Gin – Large Dip Mold
Deep yellow olive, 15", square tapering form, tubular pontil scar, tooled mushroom mouth, Netherlands 1780-1820.. **$800-1600**

Case Gin – Large Dip Mold
Yellowish olive green, 18" h., 6-1/4" base diameter, pontil-scarred base, sheared and tooled lip with applied string ring, blown in a dip mold, rare size, Dutch 1740-1760.............................**$1,500-$2,000**

Case Gin – Freeblown
Yellow olive, 19-1/4", square tapered form, tooled sloping collared mouth with ring, tubular pontil scar, extremely rare size, Netherlands 1780-1820 ....**$1,000-2,000**

Case Gin – Freeblown
Yellow olive, 19-3/4", square tapered form, tooled flared mouth, tubular pontil scar, extremely rare size, Netherlands 1780-1820 ....**$1,250-$2,500**

Cream/ale, A. Templeton / Louisville,
deep red amber quart, American
1870-1880, $250-300.

Dr. Cronk Gibbons & Co / Superior
Ale / Buffalo / N.Y., blue green, 6-3/4",
American 1840-1860, $400-600.

Charles – London – Cordial Gin
  Medium blue green, 8", smooth base, applied sloping
  collar mouth, American 1860-1870 .... **$180-220**

Charles – London – Cordial Gin
  Deep olive amber, 8-1/4", smooth base, applied
  tapered mouth, American 1860-1875 .... **$125-175**

Charles – London – Cordial Gin
  Medium blue green, 8-1/4", smooth base, applied
  tapered mouth American 1860-1875 .... **$125-175**

**Child's London / Cordial Gin – Schnapps – Post &
Thompson / Sole Agents**
  Dark olive green, 9-5/8", smooth base, applied tapered
  mouth, American 1860-1870 .... **$350-450**

**Cream / Ale – A. Templeton / Louisville (around
mug base) L & W**
  Deep reddish amber, quart, smooth base, applied
  sloping double collar, American 1870-1880 **$250-350**

**Dr. Cronk Gibbons & Co / Superior Ale / Buffalo /
N.Y.**
  Deep blue green, 6-3/4", iron pontil, applied blob
  mouth, American 1840-1860 .... **$400-600**

Royal Imperial Gin, London, sapphire
blue, 9 7/8", American 1860-1870,
$1,000-1,200.

London / Jockey – Club House / Gin,
light blue green, 9-3/8", American
1855-1865, $500-700.

M. Keane – XXX Ale, deep cobalt
blue, 9-1/8", American 1865-1875,
$600-800.

Half-Sized Octagonal Ale
Deep olive amber, 7-1/2", 8-sided, pontil-scarred base, sheared and tooled mouth
with applied string lip, Dutch 1770-1800 ....**$600-800**

J.W. Boot – Black Glass Sealed Ale Bottle – Dip Mold Blown
Deep yellow olive, 7-5/8", cylindrical with applied seal, pontil scar, applied sloping
collared mouth with ring, American 1800-1820 .... **$1,000-2,000**

Large Square Storage Gin – Golden Floral Decoration on one side
Medium blue green, 11-3/8", open pontil, sheared and tooled flared-out mouth,
blown in dip mold, original pewter neck band and screw-on cap, extremely rare,
German 1700-1730 ....**$1,500-2,000**

London / Jockey – Club House / Gin (motif of jockey on running horse)
Light blue green, 9-3/8", smooth base, applied sloping collar mouth, American
1855-1865..**$500-700**

London – Royal – Imperial Gin
Medium cobalt blue, 9-7/8", smooth base, applied mouth, American 1865-1875
....**$600-900**

Old Holland Gin – Greene & Gladding – 62 Cortlandt St / New York, medium blue green 9-1/4", $150-200.

M. Keane – XXX Ale
Deep cobalt blue, 9-1/8", smooth base, applied "top hat" mouth, rare, American 1865-1850 ....**$600-800**

Old Holland Gin – Greene & Gladding – 62 Cortlandt St. / New York
Medium blue green, 9-1/4", smooth base, applied sloping mouth, American 1865-1875 ....**$150-200**

Perrine's – Apple – Ginger – Phila / Perrine's (motif of an apple) Ginger
Medium amber to yellow amber in upper third of bottle, 9-3/4", smooth base, tooled lip, original embossed metal closure, American 1880-1890 ....**$275-400**

Swan Brewery Co. XXX Ale
Medium olive green, 7", smooth base, applied top, American 1870-1890 .. **$500-800**

T. Perkins – Sealed Ale Bottle
Yellow olive, 11-7/8", cylindrical with applied seal, pontil scar, applied sloping collared mouth with string rim, American 1820-1840 ....**$750-1,500**

Udolpho Wolfe's – Schiedam – Holland Gin
Orange amber, 9-5/8", smooth base, applied tapered mouth, American 1860-1870, rare **$150-200**

Barber Bottles

Starting in the mid-1860s and continuing to 1920, barbers in America used colorful decorated bottles filled with various tonics and colognes. The end of these unique and colorful pieces came when the Pure Food and Drug Act of 1906 restricted the use of alcohol-based ingredients in unlabeled or refillable containers.

Very early examples have rough pontil scars and numerous types of ornamentation such as fancy pressed designs, paintings, and labels under glass. The bottles were usually fitted with a cork, metal, or porcelain-type closure. Since the value of barber bottles is very dependent upon the painted or enameled lettering or decoration, it is important to note that any type of wear such as faded decoration or color, faded lettering, or chipping will lower their value.

Barber bottle, fiery opalescent turquoise blue, stars and stripes, 7", American 1885-1925, $250-350.

Labeled barber bottle, Bay Water, aqua, 9-5/8", American 1840-1860, $80-130.

Advertising Barber Bottle – Uno Tonique For The Hair Refressing and Pleasing Made by Fred Dolle, Chicago ILL.

Opalescent milk glass, light mint green background, 9-3/8", pontil-scarred base, rolled lip, extremely rare, American 1885-1925 ....**$400-500**

August Kern / Barber Supply / St. Louis – Bay Rum (floral decoration)

Milk glass, 9-1/8", smooth base, tooled mouth, American 1885-1925 .....**$250-300**

Bay Water – Early Labeled Barber Bottle

Aqua, 9-5/8", open pontil, applied mouth, American 1840-1860...............**$80-150**

Barber Bottle – Art Nouveau Style Cameo Decoration – Vegederma

Deep purple amethyst, white enamel, 8", pontil-scarred base, tooled mouth, American 1885-1925 ....**$375-450**

Barber Bottle – Buerger Bros. Supply Co. – Since 1885 Denver Colorado – Not For Sale, Used in Barber Show at Pueblo about 1885

Deep turquoise blue with cut glass fluted sides, neck ring and mouth, 10", polished pontil, applied mouth, American 1883-1885..**$200-300**

Barber bottle, Art Nouveau, dark amethyst, 8-1/2", American 1885-1925, $180-275.

Barber bottle, Art Nouveau, amethyst, 7-3/4", American 1885-1925, $200-350.

Barber bottle, Art Nouveau, medium frosted yellow topaz, 8-1/4", American 1885-1925, $200-275.

Barber bottle, Mary Gregory, turquoise blue, 7-3/4", American 1885-1925, $200-300.

Barber bottle, yellow green, sheared lip, 7-7/8", American 1885-1925, $140-180.

Barber bottle, toilet water, fiery opalescent milk glass, 8-3/4", American 1885-1925, $250-350.

Barber Bottle – Cameo Mary Gregory
Clear glass with light amber flashing, 8-1/2", coinspot pattern, pinkish white enamel, smooth base, tooled lip, rare color and pattern, American 1885-1925 ....**$175-350**

Barber Bottle – (cherubs reading a song book decoration)
Opaque milk glass, multicolored enamel decoration, 8-1/8", pontil-scarred base, sheared and tooled lip, American 1885-1925 ....**$150-200**

Barber Bottle – (cherub with dove and cage decoration)
Milk glass, 7-3/4", ground pontil, rolled lip, American 1885-1925 ....**$150-200**

Barber Bottle – Crème De Rose Broyer Baume Italiene, France Italian Parfum C, Paris Messian (Label)
Deep yellowish green, vertical rib-pattern with orange, white, and gold enamel floral decoration, 6-7/8", pontil-scarred base, tooled lip, American 1885-1925 .**$150-200**

Barber Bottle – Hair Oil – E. Berninghaus Cincinnati O Trade Mark Climax
Opalescent milk glass, 8-3/4", pontil-scarred base, applied lip, American 1885-1925 ....**$250-300**

Barber Bottle – Herringbone Pattern – Corset Waist Form
Opalescent cranberry with white, 7-1/4", smooth base, tooled mouth, very rare, American 1885-1925 ....**$400-700**

Barber Bottle – (Mary Gregory boy with butterfly net decoration)
Medium yellowish green, 8", pontil-scarred base, rolled lip, scarce color, American 1885-1925 ....**$250-350**

Barber bottle, Lus-Tra / Tonic / Sweeps / Dandruff / Ludwig Bros / Milwaukee, bisque pottery whisk broom, 7-1/4", American 1890-1925, $375-475.

Barber bottle, Bay Rum, amethyst, 7-1/2", American 1885-1925, $170-250.

Barber bottle, Bay Rum, deep fiery opalescent milk glass, 8-7/8", American 1885-1925, $200-275.

Barber Bottle – (Mary Gregory girl playing tennis decoration)
Cobalt blue with white, 8", pontil-scarred base, rolled lip, American 1885-1925 ....**$200-300**

Barber Bottle – Palm Tree
Frosted clear glass, green and while enamel decoration, 8", smooth base, tooled mouth, extremely rare (only two known examples), American 1885-1925.**$500-800**

Barber Bottle – Shampoo
Opalescent blue gray milk glass, multicolored enamel decoration of ski lodge, pontil-scarred base, rolled lip, American 1885-1925 ....**$250-350**

Barber Bottle – (floral decoration)
Deep cobalt blue, 7-5/8", rib-pattern with white and gold enamel, pontil-scarred base, tooled mouth, American 1885-1925 ....**$70-90**

Barber Bottle – (fox hunt decoration)
Milk glass with multicolored enamel, 7-1/2", pontil-scarred base, tooled mouth, American 1885-1925 ....**$140-180**

Barber Bottle – Bay Rum (Grist Mill decoration)
Deep purple amethyst, 7-3/4", rib-pattern with white enamel, pontil-scarred base, rolled lip, American 1885-1925 ....**$300-450**

Barber Bottle – Stag Decoration
Cobalt blue, 8", rib-pattern with multicolored enamel, pontil-scarred base, tooled lip, American 1885-1925 ....**$250-350**

Barber bottle, Hair Tonic, amethyst, 7-3/4", American 1885-1925, $150-200.

Barber bottle, Hair Tonic, cobalt blue, 10-3/8", American 1885-1925, $375-475.

Barber bottle, fiery opalescent cranberry red, 8-5/8", American 1885-1925, $150-250.

Barber Bottle – Hair Tonic (windmill decoration)
  Deep purple amethyst, rib-pattern with white enamel, pontil-scarred base, rolled lip, American 1885-1925 .... **$300-400**

Barber Bottle – Hobnail Pattern
  Yellow amber, 6-7/8", polished pontil, rolled lip, American 1885-1925 .... **$100-150**

Barber Bottle – Hobnail Pattern
  Turquoise blue, 6-7/8", polished pontil, rolled lip, American 1885-1925 .... **$120-140**

Barber Bottle
  Fiery opalescent cranberry red glass with pink overlay and coin spot pattern, melon rib sides, 8-1/2", smooth base, rolled lip, American 1885-1925 .... **$150-250**

Barber Bottle
  Medium emerald green with white enamel decoration, 7-3/8", pontil-scarred base, tooled mouth, American 1885-1925 .... **$150-200**

Barber Bottle
  Turquoise blue, rib-pattern with white and gold floral decoration, bulbous form, 8", pontil-scarred base, tooled mouth, American 1885-1925 .... **$170-200**

Barber bottle, fiery opalescent vaseline, 10-3/4", American 1885-1925, $250-350.

Label under glass barber bottle, opaque milk glass, cologne, 9-1/4", American 1885-1925, $375-475.

Barber bottle, cobalt blue, 8-1/2", American 1900-1925, $140-200.

Personalized barber bottle, J. Kaufmann / Tonic, 10-1/4", American 1885-1925, $600-800.

Barber Bottle
Clear glass with ruby red flashing, rib-pattern with yellow and silver floral decoration, 7-7/8", pontil-scarred base, rolled lip, American 1885-1925 ....**$250-300**

Barber Bottle
Purple amethyst, 7-1/2", rib-pattern with yellow enamel fleur-de-lis decoration, pontil-scarred base, tooled mouth, rare and unusual decoration, American 1885-1925 ....**$350-450**

Barber Bottle
Deep purple amethyst, 7-1/8", vertical rib-pattern, white and gold fleur-de-lis and diamond enameled decoration, pontil-scarred base, tooled mouth, American 1885-1925 ....**$120-180**

Brillantine Barber Bottle
Cobalt blue rib pattern with orange, yellow, and white enamel decoration, 4-3/8", sheared and ground lip, original metal screw cap on metal dispenser, American 1885-1925 ....**$140-180**

Cremex / Shampooing / Vase / Registered Design
Cobalt blue, 7-3/4", smooth base, tooled lip, bent neck with finger grooves on back to prevent from slipping, American 1885-1925 ....**$180-250**

Personalized Barber Bottle – Adam S. Eberhard – Tonic (multicolored with rose decoration)
Opaque milk glass, 9-1/2", smooth base (W.T. & CO.), ground lip, American 1885-1925 ....**$200-300**

Personalized Barber Bottle – H. Hildebrand – Bay Rum (multicolored floral decoration)
Milk glass, 8-3/4", smooth base, tooled mouth, American 1885-1925 .....**$300-400**

Personalized Barber Bottle – J. Kaufmann – Tonic (two deer running across a field near the woods with mountains in the background)
Milk glass, 10-1/4", smooth base, ground lip with original screw cap, American 1885-1925..**$600-800**

Personalized Barber Bottle – C.V. Wolf – (lighthouse and ship decoration)
Milk glass, 9-5/8", smooth base (W.T. & CO), ground lip with original pewter screw cap, American 1885-1925 ....**$375-475**

Personalized Barber Bottle – Thos. L. Kirk (running horse decoration)
Milk glass, 9-1/2", smooth base, ground lip, original pewter screw cap, American 1885-1925..**$400-600**

Personalized Barber Bottle – Wm. F. Stolte – Tonic (sailing boat surround by flowers)
Opaque milk glass, 9-1/2", smooth base (W.T. & CO.), ground lip, American 1885-1925 ....**$450-550**

Personalized Barber Bottle – W.T. Hillborn – Bay Rum (dancer decoration)
Milk glass, 9-5/8", smooth base (W.T. & CO), ground lip with original pewter screw cap, American 1885-1925 ....**$375-475**

T. Noonan & CO / Barbers / Supplies / Boston, Mass
Deep cobalt blue, 8", smooth base, tooled mouth, American 1885-1925.....**$70-90**

Beer Bottles

Attempting to find an American beer bottle made before the mid-19th century is a difficult task. Until then, most bottles used for beer and spirits were imported. The majority of these imported bottles were black glass pontiled bottles made in three-piece molds and rarely embossed. There are four types of early beer bottles:

1. The porter, which is the most common: 1820 to 1920
2. The ale: 1845 to 1850
3. Early lager: 1847 to 1850 - Rare
4. Late lager: 1850 to 1860

In spite of the large amounts of beer consumed in America before 1860, beer bottles were very rare and all have pontiled bases. Most beer manufactured during this time was distributed and dispensed from wooden barrels, or kegs, and sold to local taverns and private bottlers. Collectors often ask why various breweries did not bottle the beer they manufactured. During the Civil War, the federal government placed a special tax on all brewed beverages that was levied by the barrel. This taxing system prevented the brewery from making the beer and bottling it in the same building. Selling the beer to taverns and private bottlers was much simpler than erecting another building just for bottling. This entire process changed after 1890 when the federal government revised the law to allow breweries to bottle the beer straight from the beer lines.

Along with the brewing processes, the federal government also revised guidelines for bottle cleanliness. The chart below show the age and rarity of beer bottles.

YEAR	RARE	SCARCE	SEMI-COMMON	COMMON
1860-1870	X			
1870-1880		X		
1880-1890			X	
1890-1930				X

Embossed bottles marked "ale" or "porter" were manufactured between 1850 and 1860. In the late 1860s, the breweries began to emboss their bottles with names and promotional messages. This practice continued into the 20th century. It is interesting to note that Pennsylvania breweries made most of the beer bottles from the second half of the 19th century. By 1890, beer was readily available in bottles in most of the country.

The first bottles used for beer in the United States were made of pottery, not glass. Glass did not become widely used until after the Civil War (1865). A wholesaler for Adolphus Busch named C. Conrad sold the original Budweiser beer from 1877 to 1890. The Budweiser name was a trademark of C. Conrad, but in 1891, it was sold to the Anheuser-Busch Brewing Association.

Before the 1870s, beer bottles were sealed with cork stoppers. Late in the 19th century, the lightning stopper was invented. It proved a convenient way of sealing and resealing blob top bottles. In 1891 corks were replaced with the crown cork closure invented by William Painter. The closure made use of a thin slice of cork within a tight-fitting metal cap. Once these were removed, they couldn't be used again.

Until the 1930s, beer came in green glass bottles. After Prohibition, brown glass came into use, since it was thought to filter out the damaging rays of the sun and preserve freshness.

Albion – Burnell & Co. – S.F. – Brewery
Medium green, half-pint, smooth base, crown top, American 1920-1930.**$550-650**

A.G. Boehm / 78-82 Essex St. / Lawrence / Mass / Registered – This Bottle / Not To Be Sold
Orange amber, 9-3/8", smooth base, tooled blob mouth, American 1885-1900
....**$70-100**

A. G. Van Nostrano / Charlestown / Mass. / Bunker Hill Lager (inside banner) / Bunker Hill / Breweries / Established 1821 / Registered August Stoehr / Milwaukee / Lager / Manchester, N.H. – This Bottle / Not To / Be Sold
Medium amber, 9-5/8", smooth base, tooled mouth, original lightning-style closure, American 1885-1900 ....**$70-100**

August Reinig / 2107 / Germantown / Ave / Philada. – This Bottle / Not To / Be Sold
Yellow with olive tone, 9-1/2", smooth base (1A), tooled blob mouth, American 1885-1900..**$70-100**

August Stoehr / Milwaukee / Lager / Manchester, N.H. – This Bottle / Not To / Be Sold
Medium yellow olive, 9", smooth base (No. 2), tooled mouth, original lightning closure, American1885-1900 ....**$70-90**

B & CO / (monogram inside diamond) A. Bierweiler & CO / Boston / Mass. / Registered
Medium golden yellow amber, mug-base, 9-1/4", smooth base, tooled mouth, American 1885-1900 ....**$70-100**

Bay View – Brewing Co – Seattle Wash.
Medium green, 9", quart, smooth base, tooled top, American 1890-1905
....**$175-225**

Beer Steam Bottling Co. – (monogram WG & Son in diamond) – Wm Goeppert & Son – San Francisco
Medium amber, quart, smooth base, applied top, rare, American 1882-1884
....**$700-800**

Buffalo Brewing Co. – (monogram BBC) – S.F. Agency
Medium green, pint, 7-1/2", smooth base, applied top, American 1885-1900
....**$250-300**

Buffalo BR'G CO. – Sacramento – This Bottle Not To Be Sold
Medium amber, quart, smooth base, applied top, American 1885-1900 ......**$85-95**

C. Conrad & Cos. – Original Budweiser U.S. – Patent No. 6376
Aqua, 9", quart, smooth base, applied top, American 1890-1905............**$100-150**

C.D. Postel – (monogram wheat stalks T.M.) – S. F. Cal.
Deep amber, quart, smooth base, applied top, American 1884................**$500-600**

C.D. Postel – (monogram wheat stalks T.M.) – S. F. Cal.
Medium amber, quart, smooth base, applied top, American 1884......**$2,500-3,000**

C.D. Postel – (monogram wheat stalks T.M.) – S. F. Cal.
Dark amber, quart, smooth base, applied top, American 1884..........**$1,300-1,500**

Ogdens Porter, blue aqua, 7", American 1840-1860, $150-200.

J.B. Edwards – Columbia Pa. – Brown Stout, emerald green, 6-1/4", American 1840-1860, $375-475.

Chas D. Kaier / KDK (monogram) Mahanoy City / PA – This Bottle / Not To / Be Sold

Medium green, 9-3/8", smooth base (Putnam 26), applied blob type mouth, American 1880-1890 ....**$250-350**

Chas Joly / No. 9 / So Seventh St / Philadelphia – This Bottle / Not To / Be Sold

Medium olive green, 9-1/2", smooth base, tooled mouth, American 1885-1900 ....**$70-100**

Chicago Lager Beer – Chicago Brewing – S.F.

Medium amber, quart, smooth base, applied top, American 1887-1990 ......**$35-40**

Colombia Weiss Beer Brewery – St. Louis Mo. – This Bottle Is Never Sold

Medium amber, 8-7/8", smooth base, tooled top, American 1885-1900 ......**$50-75**

Coors

Light amethyst, pint, smooth base, tooled top, American 1910-1920.........**$75-110**

Consumers – (monogram CBCo.) Bottle Co.

Deep amber, half-pint, smooth base, tooled top, American 1885-1900........**$75-85**

Consumer's – (monogram CBCo.) Bottling Co. – S.F. CAL.

Medium amber, quart, smooth base, tooled top, American 1885-1900....**$300-400**

O.G. M. Gaines – Columbia Pa. – Brown Stout, blue green, 6 3/8", $350-450.

Dr. Cronk's / Compound / Sarsaparilla Beer, blue aqua, 8-5/8", American 1840-1860, $400-600.

E. Wagner / Trade W (inside cross) Mark / Manchester / N.H. – The Property / Of / E. Wagner / Not Sold

Light to medium yellow with olive tone, 9-1/8", smooth base, tooled mouth, original lightning style closure, American 1885-1900 .... **$80-120**

E. Wagner / Trade W (inside cross) Mark / Manchester / N.H. – The Property / Of / E. Wagner / Not Sold

Light to medium yellow with olive tone, 9-3/8", smooth base, tooled mouth, original lightning style closure, American 1885-1900 .... **$80-120**

F.J. Kastner / FJK (diamond monogram inside) Newark N.J. – This Bottle / Not To / Be Sold

Medium golden yellow with amber tone, 9-3/8", applied mouth, American 1885-1900 .... **$80-120**

F. Jacob Jockers / 803-805 / Dickinson St / Phila, PA. / Registered – Contents 12-1/2 Oz

Light to medium cobalt blue, 9", smooth base, tooled mouth, few tall blob beers were made in cobalt blue, American 1885-1900 .... **$100-150**

F.O. Brandt – Healdsburg CAL.

Medium amber, quart, smooth base, tooled top, scarce, American 1885-1900 .... **$100-125**

Geo. Braun Bottler – (monogram GB) – 2210 Pine St. S.F.

Dark amber, half-pint, smooth base, tooled top, American 1885-1900 .... **$75-85**

Golden Gate Bottling Works – Chas. Roschmann – San Francisco (reverse side – Trade – photo of bear – Mark

Medium amber, half-pint, smooth base, tooled top, American 1885-1900 .... **$150-200**

H. Clausen & Son / Brewing Co / 888-890 – 2nd Ave / New York / Phoenix Bottling – This Bottle / Not To / Be Sold

Medium olive green, 9-1/8", smooth base, tooled mouth, American 1885-1900 .... **$80-120**

H. Koehler & Co / Fidelio / Beer / New York

Deep amber, 8-5/8", smooth base, tooled mouth, American 1885-1900 .... **$70-100**

Hoosac Bottling Works / JLG (monogram) Hoosick Falls. N.Y. – This Bottle / Not To / Be Sold

Medium amber, 9-1/8", smooth base, tooled mouth, American 1885-1900 .... **$80-120**

Honolulu Brewing Co. – Honolulu – H.T.
Light green, quart, smooth base, tooled top, American 1890-1905 .... **$75-85**

J.B. Cueno – San Francisco
Medium amber, pint, smooth base, tooled top, American 1885-1900 .... **$150-200**

J. Gahn / Trade (motif of mug) Mark / Boston / Mass – Milwaukee / Lager Beer
Medium yellow amber, 9-3/8", smooth base, tooled mouth, American 1885-1900 .... **$50-70**

J. Proll Bottling Works – Bottling – U.S. Lager – S.F. CAL
Medium amber, pint, smooth base, tooled mouth, rare, American 1885-1905 .... **$375-425**

John Wieland's – Export Beer – SF
Medium amber, 5-3/4" (sample size), smooth base, tooled top, American 1895-1905 .... **$250-325**

John Wieland's – Export Beer – S.F.
Deep amber, pint, smooth base, tooled top, American 1895-1905.. **$100-125**

Lynch Bros / Plymouth, PA – This Bottle / Not To / Be Sold
Medium citron green, 9-1/4", smooth base, tooled mouth, original lightning-style closure, rare colored blob top beer, American 1885-1900............. **$80-120**

Mirasoul – Bros – S.F.
Medium amber, pint, smooth base, tooled top, American 1885-1905 .... **$35-45**

National Bottling Works (Trade Mark – eagle) San Francisco, CA – Not To Be Sold
Amber, 9", smooth base, tooled mouth, American 1895-1901.. **$175-250**

National Brewing Co. – San Francisco
Medium amber, quart, smooth base, tooled top, American 1885-1900 .... **$45-55**

Pacific Bottling Co. (monogram J) – S.F.
Light amber, quart, smooth base, tooled top, American 1885-1900 rare **$135-145**

Philadelphia Bottling Co. – (monogram eagle In nest) – Lager Beer – Lang Bros' Props' – 1318 S. F. Scott St.
Medium amber, quart, smooth base, applied top, American 1886-1889 .... **$1,000-1,200**

E.A. Olendorf / Sarsaparilla Lager (in slug plate) This Bottle / Is Never Sold, medium orange amber, 9-1/4", American 1885-1895, $250-300.

E.N. Lewis / Sarsaparilla / Beer, deep blue aqua, 6-3/4", American 1865-1880, $200-300.

Phillips Bros. / Champion / Bottling Works / Trade (motif of two boxers) Mark / Registered / Baltimore MD. U.S.A. / This Bottle Is Registered / Not To / Be Sold
Amber, 9-1/8", smooth base, tooled mouth, American 1885-1900............**$70-100**
Registered / The W.H. Cawley Co. / Somerville / Dover / Flemington / NJ / This Bottle / Not To Be Sold
Light green, 9", smooth base (C), tooled mouth, lightning-style closure, American 1885-1800...**$70-100**
Registered / Wagner and Matthes / Lawrence, Mass. / Registered
Deep amber, 9-1/4", smooth base, tooled mouth, American 1885-1900....**$70-100**
Richmond – Bottling Works
Light amber, half-pint, smooth base, tooled top, American 1885-1900.........**$75-85**
Richmond – Bottling Works
Clear, half-pint, smooth base, tooled top, American 1885-1905 ....**$80-90**
Robert Portner / Brewing Co / Trade / Tivoli / Mark / Alexandria, VA – This Bottle / Not To / Be Sold
Deep olive green, 9-3/8", smooth base, applied blob mouth, American 1885-1900
....**$70-100**
Santa Clara – County – Bottling Co. – San Jose
Dark amber, quart, smooth base, tooled top, American 1885-1900 ....**$40-50**
Santa Fe Bottling Co. – C.V. & CO. – S.F.
Medium amber, pint, smooth base, tooled top, American 1885-1900 rare ...**$40-35**
Schlitz Milwaukee Lager Howe & Streeter – Manchester, N.H.
Brilliant yellow, 9", smooth base, tooled top, American 1885-1900 ....**$150-200**
Schroeder's / B.W.B. Co / St. Louis, MO.
Yellow green, 9-1/8", smooth base, tooled mouth, original porcelain stopper and wire lightning-style closure, American 1885-1900.......................................**$40-70**
Schroeder's / B.W.B. Co / St. Louis, MO.
Yellow green, 10", smooth base, tooled mouth, original porcelain stopper and wire lightning-style closure, American 1885-1900..**$40-70**
S.F. Stock Brewing – S.F.S.B. – San Francisco, CAL.
Medium amber, pint, smooth base, tooled top, American 1885-1900 ......**$400-500**
Sunset Bottling – (monogram SBCo.) – San Francisco, CAL.
Amber, pint, smooth base, tooled top, American 1880-1900 ....**$65-75**
Tacoma Bottling Co. – S.F. CAL.
Dark amber, half-pint, smooth base, tooled top, American 1885-1905........**$35-45**
Tettner & Thoma Weiss Beer – Brewery – St. Louis
Medium amber, pint, smooth base, tooled top, American 1885-1890 ....**$50-75**
Union Brewing and Malting Co. – S.F. CAL.
Medium amber, pint, smooth base, applied top, American 1885-1900.........**$30-45**

Bitters

Bitters have long been a favorite of bottle collectors. Because of their uniqueness, they were saved in great numbers, giving the collector of today great opportunities to build a special and varied collection.

Bitters, which originated in England, were originally a type of medicine made from bitter tasting roots or herbs, giving the concoction its name. During the 18th century, bitters were added to water, ale, or spirits with the intent to cure all types of ailments. Because of the pretense that those mixtures had some medicinal value, bitters became popular in America since Colonists could import them from England without paying the liquor tax. While most bitters had low alcohol content, some brands were as much as 120 proof, higher than most hard liquor available at the time. As physicians became convinced that bitters did have some healing value, the drink became socially acceptable, promoting use among people who normally weren't liquor drinkers.

The best known among the physicians who made their own bitters for patients was Dr. Jacob Hostetter. After his retirement in 1853, he gave permission to his son David to manufacture it commercially. Hostetter Bitters was known for its colorful, dramatic, and extreme advertising. While Hostetters said it wouldn't cure everything, the list of ailments it claimed to alleviate with regular use covered most everything: indigestion, diarrhea, dysentery, chills and fever, liver ailments, and pains and weakness that came with old age (at that time, a euphemism for impotence). Despite these claims, in 1888 David Hostetter died from kidney failure that should have been cured by his own bitters formula.

One of the most sought after bitters is the Drakes Plantation Bitters that first appeared in 1860 and received a patent in 1862.

The Drakes Bitters is shaped like a log cabin and can be found in a four-log and a six-log variant with colors in various shades of amber, yellow, citron, puce, green, and black. Another interesting characteristic of the Drake bitters is the miscellaneous dots and marks, including the "X" on the base of the bottles, that are thought to be identification marks of the various glass houses that manufactured the bottles.

Most of the bitters bottles—over 1,000 types—were manufactured between 1860 and 1905. The more unique shapes called "figurals" were in the likeness of cannons, drums, pigs, fish, and ears of corn. Others were round, square, rectangular, barrel-shaped, gin-bottle shaped, twelve-sided, and flask-shaped. The embossed varieties are also the oldest and most valuable.

The most common color was amber (pale golden yellow to dark amber brown), then aqua (light blue), followed by green or clear glass. The rarest and most collectible colors are dark blue, amethyst, milk glass, and puce (a purplish brown).

1834 / John Roots Bitters – 1834 / Buffalo, N.Y. – medium blue green, 10-1/4", American 1860-1870, $2,500-3,000.

Botanic (motif of sphinx) Bitters – Herzberg & Bros. – New York, yellow amber, 9-7/8", American 1875-1880, $400-600.

Old Sachem / Bitters / And / Wigwam Tonic, orange amber, 9-1/4", American 1860-1870, $300-400.

Baker's / Orange Grove – Bitters
Medium to deep strawberry puce, 9-5/8", roped corners, smooth base, applied tapered collar mouth, American 1865-1875 ....**$1,000-1,500**

Bell's / Cocktail / Bitters / Jas. M. Bell & Co / New York
Medium copper puce, 10-1/2", lady's leg form, smooth base, applied mouth, American 1865-1880 ....**$500-700**

Bissell's / Tonic Bitters / Patented. Jany, 21. 1868 – O.P. Bissel / Peoria III
Bright yellow amber, 9", smooth base (L & W), applied sloping mouth collar, American 1868-1875......................................**$200-275**

Bourbon Whiskey / Bitters
Medium copper puce, 9-1/4", barrel form, smooth base, applied mouth, American 1865-1875......................................**$375-475**

Brophy's Bitters (in a crescent moon and star) Trade Mark / Nokomis / Illinois
Aqua, 7-3/8", smooth base, tooled lip, American 1880-1890...................**$175-250**

Burdock / Blood Bitters – Foster Milburn & Co – Buffalo, N.Y.
Aqua, 4-1/8", smooth base, tooled lip, rare sample, American 1890-1900 bitters **$80-120**

C. Gautiers / Native / Wine Bitters
Yellow olive green, 9-7/8", flowerpot-form bottle, smooth base (Washington, D.C. Patented 1867) applied mouth, rare, American 1867-1875 ....**$1,000-1,500**

C. Sandhegers / Famous / Stomach Bitters / Cincinnati / Ohio (inside an etched wine glass) Trade Mark
Clear, 10-1/8", smooth base, tooled lip, American 1890-1900 ....**$275-375**

C.C. Seely's / Strengthening / Stomach Bitters / Pittsburgh, PA
Medium amber, 9-3/8", rectangular form with indented chamfered corner panels on three sides, red iron pontil, applied mouth, extremely rare, American 1845-1860 ....**$10,000-15,000**

Hall's / Bitters – E.E. Hall, New Haven / Established 1842 – yellow with amber tone, American 1860-1870, $400-600.

Dr. B. F. Sherman's/ Compound / Prickley Ash / Bitters, yellow olive, 9-1/4", American 1870-1880, $500-700.

Colton's Stomach Bitter – Back Bar Bottle
Black olive amber, 11-3/4", smooth base, applied ring mouth, American 1870-1880 .... **$275-375**

Cooley's / Anti- / Dispeptic / Or / Jaundice / Bitters
Blue aqua, 6-1/4", oval form with chamfered corner indented front panel and 8-paneled roof, open pontil, applied tapered collar mouth, American 1840-1860 .... **$1,000-1,500**

Curtis & Perkins / Wild Cherry / Bitters
Aqua, 6-3/4", open pontil, applied mouth, American 1840-1860... **$75-120**

XXX / Dandelion / Bitters
Clear, 6-7/8", smooth base, tooled lip, American 1890-1900 .... **$75-100**

Dr. A.W. Coleman's – Anti Dyspeptic / And / Tonic Bitters
Deep olive green, 9-1/2", smooth base, applied sloping collar mouth, American 1855-1865 ...... **$1,000-1,500**

Dr. Blake's – Aromatic / Bitters – New York
Aqua, 7", open pontil, applied mouth, American 1840-1860 .... **$150-200**

Dr. Corbett's – Renovating – Shaker Bitters
Aqua, 9-1/2", open pontil, applied double collar mouth, American 1840-1860 .... **$1,400-1,800**

Dr. De Andries – Sarsaparilla / Bitters – E.M. Rusha / New Orleans
Yellow amber, 9-3/4", smooth base, applied sloping collar mouth, American 1855-1865 .... **$800-1,200**

Dr. Flint's – Quaker Bitters – Providence, R.I. – Paper Label reads: Dr. H. S. Flint & Co. – Celebrated – Quaker – Root and Herb – Choice – Bitters – "Try This and Thou Shalt Be Benefitted"
Aqua, 9-1/2", smooth base, applied mouth, American 1872-1880... **$250-350**

Dr. Geo. Pierce's – Indian / Restorative / Bitters – Lowell, Mass
Blue aqua, 7-5/8", open pontil, applied mouth, American 1840-1860 .... **$150-250**

Dr. J. Boveedods – Imperial / / Wine Bitters – New York
Aqua, 10-1/8", smooth base, applied double collar mouth, American 1855-1865 .... **$300-400**

Dr. J. Henry Salisbury / Hinsdale, N.Y. / 1869 – Mountain Herb and / Root Bitters / I.S.P. – I.N.
Deep amber, 9-3/4", smooth base, applied mouth, rare, American 1869-1875 .... **$375-475**

Dr. Jacob's Bitters – S.A. Spencer – New Haven, CT

Bluish aqua, 10", open pontil, applied mouth, American 1840-1860 .... **$200-275**

Dr. Loew's Celebrated / Stomach Bitters & / Nerve Tonic – The / Loew & Sons Co / Cleveland, O

Medium yellow lime green, 9-1/2", fluted neck and shoulder, smooth base, tooled lip, American 1890-1900 .... **$275-375**

Dr. Loew's Celebrated / Stomach Bitters & / Nerve Tonic – The / Loew & Sons Co / Cleveland, O

Medium yellow lime green, 3-7/8", fluted neck and shoulder, smooth base, tooled lip, sample size, American 1890-1900 .... **$375-475**

Dr. XX / Lovegood's – Family – Bitters

Deep amber, 9-3/8", cabin form, smooth base, applied tapered collar mouth, American 1865-1875 .... **$1,000-1,500**

Dr. M. Pearl & Co – Peruvian Bark / Bitters – New Orleans, LA

Medium apple green, 10-1/8", smooth base, applied mouth, extremely rare, American 1870-1880 .... **$1,000-1,500**

Dr. Mampe's / Oshkosh, Wis

Aqua, 7-1/4", smooth base, tooled lip, American 1890-1900 .... **$75-100**

Dr. Marcus – Universal / Bitters – Philada

Bluish aqua, 8-1/8", open pontil, applied mouth, extremely rare, American 1840-1860 .... **$550-750**

Dr. Renz's / Herb Bitters

Deep yellow amber, 10", smooth base, applied mouth, American 1855-1870 .... **$500-700**

Dr. Renz's / Herb Bitters

Medium to deep amber, 10-1/8", smooth base, applied mouth, American 1855-1870 .... **$375-475**

Dr. S.B. Hartman & Co. – Mishler's Herb Bitters – Table Spoon Graduation

Medium yellow copper topaz, 9", smooth base (Stoeckels Grad Pat. Feb. 11, 66) applied collar mouth, American 1865-1875 .... **$350-450**

Dr. Shepards / Compound / Wahoo Bitters / Grand Rapids, Mich

Ice blue, 7-1/2", smooth base, applied mouth, American 1865-1875 .... **$200-275**

Label under glass bitters bottle, Lutz's / German / Stomach / Bitters / Reading, PA /Registered, amber 7-3/4", American 1885-1900, $1,200-1,600.

Celebrated Nectar / Stomach Bitters / And Nerve Tonic – The / Nectar Bitter Co ./ Toledo, O, bright yellow green, 9-3/8", American 1890-1900, $275-475.

Dr. J.C. Chelsey's / Golden Bitters / Manufd At The / Durham Med Int, blue aqua, 9", American 1865-1875, $275-375.

Dr. Varena's – Japan Bitters–medium yellow amber, 8-7/8", American 1885-1895, $250-350.

Victor / Roberg's – Prussian / Bitters, yellow amber, case gin form, 9-7/8", American, 1865-1875, $800-1,200.

Dr. Skinner's / Celebrated / 25 Cent Bitters / So Reading, Mass

Aqua, 8-1/2", rectangular with wide beveled corner panels, pontil-scarred base, applied double collar mouth, American 1840-1860 .... **$175-375**

Dr. Skinner's / Celebrated / 25 Cent Bitters / So Reading, Mass – Label reads: Dr. W.M. Skinner's Celebrated Bitters, For Sale at the Doctor's Laboratory, South Reading, Mass

Aqua, 8-3/4", rectangular with wide beveled corner panels, pontil-scarred base, applied double collar mouth, American 1840-1860 .... **$250-350**

Dr. Walkinshaw's – Curative Bitters – Batavia, N.Y.

Amber, 10", smooth base, applied mouth, American 1865-1875 ....**$400-600**

Dr. Washington's / American / Life Bitters

Medium amber, 9-1/4", smooth base, tooled lip, extremely rare, American 1880-1890 ....**$200-300**

Dr. Wheeler's / Tonic / Sherry Wine Bitters – Established / 1849 (inside a shield) – Boston

Bluish aqua, 9-1/2", roped corners, smooth base, applied mouth, American 1865-1875 ....**$4,000-6,000**

Dr. Whitney's / Bitters – Orlean, N.Y. / U.S.A.

Amber, 7-1/4", semi-oval form, smooth base, tooled lip, extremely rare form, American 1885-1895 ....**$200-300**

Dr. Wise's / Olive Bitters / Cincinnati / O

Clear, 9-3/4", smooth base, tooled lip, American 1890-1910 rare **$300-400**

Dr. Zabriskie's – Bitters – Jersey city / N.J.

Clear moonstone glass, 6", pontil-scarred base, tool flared-out lip, extremely rare, American 1845-1860 ....**$400-600**

Drs. Lowerre & Lyon's / Restorative Bitters
  Bluish aqua, 8-3/4", open pontil, applied mouth
  extremely rare, American 1840-1860 .... **$400-600**

Doctor / Fischs Bitters – W. H. Ware / Patented 1866
  Yellow amber, 11-5/8", fish form, smooth base, applied
  mouth, American 1866-1875 .... **$400-500**

E. Dexter Loveridge / Wahoo Bitters / (bird with arrow) E. Dexter Loveridge / Wahoo Bitters – DWD – 1863 – XXX – PATD
  Medium amber, 10-1/8", smooth base, applied ring
  lip, American 1860-1870............................ **$700-800**

EDW. Brehr – Thuringer – Aromatic / Stomach / Bitters
  Deep yellow olive green, 8-3/4", open pontil, applied
  mouth, American 1845-1860 .... **$700-900**

Established / 1845 / Schroeder's / Bitters / Louisville / And Cincinnati – Embossed on Metal Neck: Schroeder's Cocktail Bitters Co
  Amber, 5-1/4", lady's leg, smooth base, tooled lip rare
  sample size, American 1890-1900 .... **$500-800**

Established / 1845 / Schroeder's / Bitters / Louisville / Henry H. Shufeldt & Co / Peoria, Ill / Sole Owners
  Amber, 11-5/8", lady's leg, smooth base, tooled lip
  rare, American 1890-1900 .... **$800-1200**

Fritz Reuter Bitters (reverse of bottle same)
  Milk glass, 9-7/8", tapered gin form, smooth base,
  applied mouth, American 1880-1895 .... **$250-350**

Geo. Benz / & / Sons / Appetine / Bitters / St. Paul, Minn
  Deep amber, 8-1/8", smooth base (Pat. / Nov 23 /
  1897), tooled lip, American 1897-1900 ...... **$150-200**

Germania (motif of a seated lady) Bitters – label reads: Germania Brand Magen Stomach Bitters, Luhenthal Bros. & Co., Cleveland, Ohio
  Milk glass, 9-5/8", tapered gin form, smooth base,
  applied mouth, rarest of tapered milk glass bitters
  bottles, only three or four known examples, American
  1880-1895... **$1,500-2,000**

Hart's / Star Bitters / (Letters O-B-L-P-C and the date "1868" inside a star) Philadelphia / PA
  Clear glass, 9-1/8", fish form, smooth base, tooled lip,
  American 1880-1890 .... **$400-600**

Dr. Taylor's – Female / Bitters – blue aqua, 6-1/8", American 1840-1860, $400-700.

Germania (motif of a seated lady) / Bitters, label reads: Germania Brand Magen Stomach Bitters, Luhenthal Bros. & Co., Cleveland, Ohio, milk glass, tapered gin form, 9-5/8", American 1880-1895, $1,500-2,000.

Label under glass bitters bottle – Herb's / Pure / Wild Cherry / Bark / Bitters Wertz & Field / Reading, PA, amber 8", American 1885-1900, $1,500-2,000.

Herkules Bitter / GA Monogram / 4 Fl. Oz., bright green, 4-1/8", rare sample size, American 1885-1900, $600-900.

Hartwig Kantorowicz / Posen / Ham / Burg / Ger / Many

Milk glass, 3-7/8", case gin form, smooth base, applied mouth, rare sample bitters, American 1890-1900 .... **$150-200**

Hartwig Kantorowicz / Posen / Ham / Burg / Ger / Many

Milk glass, 5-3/8", case gin form, smooth base, applied mouth, American 1890-1900 .... **$200-250**

Hartwig Kantorowicz / Posen / Ham / Burg / Ger / Many

Milk glass, 9-1/8", case gin form, smooth base, applied mouth, American 1890-1900 .... **$200-250**

Harvey's – Prairie – Bitters – Patented

Medium amber to yellow amber, 9-3/4", smooth base, applied sloping collar mouth, whiskey barrel corners and a corncob domed top, one of the top five or six most desirable bitters bottles, American 1860-1870 .... **$15,000-30,000**

Herb's / Pure / Wild (Tree) Cherry / Bark / Bitters / Wertz & Field / Reading, Pa (Label under glass)

Amber, 8", smooth base (H.M. Co.), tooled lip, American 1885-1900 .... **$1,500-2,000**

Herkules Bitter (GA monogram) 4 FL. OZ

Bright medium green, 4-1/8", smooth base, tooled liprare sample bitters bottle, three or four known examples, American 1885-1900 .... **$600-900**

Hertrich's Gesundheits Bitter / Hans / Hertrich / Hof / Erfinder U. Allien / Destillateur – Gesetzlich Geschutzt

Olive green, 12", smooth base, applied double collar mouth, German 1880-1890 .... **$375-475**

Honi Soit Qui Mal Y Pense (in banner) Royal Pepsin / Stomach Bitters / L & A Scharff / Sole Agents / St. Louis, U.S. & Canada

Amber, 7-1/2", smooth base, tooled mouth, American 1890-1900 .... **$150-250**

Hops / & / Malt / Bitters (on all four roof and shoulder panels) Hops & Malt / Trade (sheaf of grain) Mark / Bitters

Medium amber, 9-1/2", semi-cabin form, smooth base, applied sloping color mouth, American 1875-1885 .... **$400-600**

J. W. Colton's Nervine / Strengthening Bitters, golden yellow amber, 8-3/8", American 1885-1895, $150-200.

Warner's / Safe / Tonic Bitters (motif of safe) Trade Mark / Rochester. N.Y., yellow amber, 7-1/2", American 1880-1895, $500-700.

B. Page Jr & Co. – Boerhaves / Holland Bitters – Pittsburgh, PA, yellow amber, 7-7/8", American 1850-1860, $180-275.

Isaac D. Lutz / Reading, PA – Label under glass reads: Lutz's / German / Stomach / Bitters / Reading, Pa. / Registered

Amber, 7-3/4", smooth base, tooled lip, American 1885-1900 ....**$1,200-1,600**

Keystone Bitters

Orange amber, 9-3/4", barrel form, smooth base, applied tapered collar mouth, American 1865-1875 ....**$700-900**

Khoosh – Bitters

Yellow olive, 8-1/4", smooth base, applied double collar mouth, English 1880-1900 ....**$120-140**

King Solomon's Bitters – Seattle Wash – Label reads: King Solomon Stomach Bitters

Amber, 8-3/8", smooth base, tooled mouth, American 1890-1900..........**$250-350**

Koehler & Hinrichs / Red Star / Stomach Bitters / St. Paul, Minn.

Yellow amber, 11-1/2", fluted panels around shoulder and about base, smooth base, tooled lip, American 1900-1905 ....**$350-350**

Laughlin / Smith & Co. – Old Home / Bitters – Wheeling, W. VA

Deep yellow amber, 10", semi-cabin form, smooth base, applied mouth, American 1865-1875..**$1,200-1,800**

Lediard's – Celebrated – Stomach Bitters

Teal blue, 10-1/8", smooth base, applied sloping double collar mouth, American 1860-1875..**$1,800-2,000**

H.F. Eilert / Cleveland, Ohio (on both side panels) – Eilert's / Waldhäuser / Brand / Magen / Stomach / Bitters / Prepared with Choice Herbs and Roots Distributed by / H.E. Eilert / 2539-2453 Lorain Ave. / Cleveland, O, clear glass, 10-1/4", American 1885-1900, $275-350.

N.W. Med. Co. / Bitters, medium amber, 7-3/8", American, 1880-1895, $200-300.

Litthauer Stomach Bitters / Invented 1864 By / Josef Loewenthal, Berlin
Milk glass, 9-1/2", case gin form, smooth base, applied mouth, American 1875-1890 .... **$200-275**

Lohengrin / Bitters / Adolf Marcus / Von Buton / Germany, Front Label reads: Lohengrin, Celebrated Stomach Bitters, Smaller Label Under Embossing Reads: Adolf Marcut, Tucker Hardy Co., Sole Distributors, Chicago
Milk glass, 9-3/8", tapered gin form, 9-3/8", smooth base, applied mouth, rare, American 1880-1895 .... **$800-1,200**

Malabac Bitters – M. Cziner Chemist
Yellow amber, 11-3/4", lady's leg, smooth base (This Bottle Not To Be Sold), applied double collar mouth, blown in three-piece mold, rare, American 1870-1880 .... **$400-600**

Mills Bitters / A.M. Gilman / Sole Proprietor
Medium yellow amber, 11-1/4", lady's leg, smooth base, applied ring lip, American 1870-1890 .... **$4,000-6,000**

Morning (Star) Bitters / Inceptum 5869 – Patented / 5869
Medium amber, 7-3/8", oval form, smooth base, tooled mouth, American 1865-1875 .... **$200-300**

Moulton's Olorosa Bitters / Trade (motif of pineapple) Mark
Blue aqua, 11-1/4", fluted neck, shoulder and side at base panels, smooth base, applied mouth, American 1865-1880 .... **$300-400**

National / Bitters
Medium amber, 12-1/4", ear-of-corn form, smooth base, applied mouth, American 1865-1875 **$400-500**

N.W. Med. Co. / Bitters
Medium amber, 7-3/8", oval form, smooth base, tooled mouth extremely rare, American 1880-1895 .... **$200-300**

Old Dr. Solomon's – Great Indian Bitters, label reads: Old Doctor Jas. M. Solomon's Great Indian Wine Bitters
Aqua, 8-3/4", smooth base, applied mouth, American 1870-1880 .... **$250-350**

Old Dominion, Vegetable Bitter (Capitol Building) E.W. Mills, Fredericksburg, Va (label only)
Clear glass, 6", flask, smooth base, tooled lip, American 1890-1910 .... **$120-160**

Label only bitters bottle – Old Dominion / Vegetable Bitters / E.W.Mills / Fredericksburg, Va, clear glass, 6", American 1890-1910, $150-175.

Peruvian Tonic – Bitters, label reads: Peruvian Tonic Bitters, For the Cure of Dyspepsia, Headache / General Debility / W.G. Phillips & Co, Wholesale Druggists, Portland, Me, amber, 9-1/2", American 1875-1885, $400-700.

Parhan's – German Bitters / For The Cure Of / Dyspepsia – Liver Complaint – Prepared By / Dr. C. Parham / Philada

Aqua, 6-3/8", open pontil, applied ring mouth, extremely rare bitters/cure combination, American 1840 -1860 ....**$1,500-2,000**

Pat'd 1884 / Dr. Petzold's / Genuine / German / Bitters / Incpt 1862

Amber, 10-1/4", semi-cabin form, smooth base, tooled mouth, American 1885-1895 ....**$200-275**

Pat'd 1884 / Dr. Petzold's / Genuine / German / Bitters / Incpt 1862

Yellow amber, 8", semi-cabin form, smooth base, tooled mouth, American 1885-1895 ....**$400-500**

Pepsin / Calisaya Bitters – Dr. Russel Med. Co.

Deep green, 4-5/8", smooth base, tooled lip, American 1895-1905 ....**$150-200**

Pepsin / Calisaya Bitters – Dr. Russel Med. Co.

Light green, 8-1/8", smooth base, tooled lip, American 1895-1905..........**$150-200**

Peruvian / Bitters – W & K

Yellow amber, 9-1/4", smooth base, applied mouth, American 1875-1885. **$120-150**

Philadelphia / Hop / Bitters (African man holding a bottle)

Deep blue aqua, 9-3/8", semi-cabin form, smooth base, applied mouth, Australian 1880-1890..**$275-375**

R.B. Samuels – Century Stomach Bitters – Back Bar Bottle

Dark olive green, 12-1/4", inscribed pewter label in a fancy recessed panel, smooth base, applied ring mouth, American 1870-1880......................................**$275-375**

Royal Pepsin / Stomach Bitters / L & A Scharff / Sole Agents / St. Louis, U.S. & Canada (rampart lion and unicorn on either side of shield)

Reddish amber, 9", smooth base, tooled double collar mouth, American 1885-1900 ....**$100-150**

Russ' / Stomach / Bitters / New York, medium yellow amber, 10-1/8", American 1860-1865, $6,000-8,000.

Sanborn's / Kidney / And / Liver / Vegetable / Laxative / Bitters, amber, 10", American 1890-1900, $80-120.

Russ / Stomach / Bitters / New York
Medium yellow amber, 10-1/8", lady's leg, iron pontil, applied ring mouth, American 1860-1865 .**$6,000-8,000**

Sanborn's / Kidney / and / Liver / Vegetable / Laxative / Bitters
Amber, 10", smooth base, tooled lip, American 1890-1900 .... **$80-120**

Sazerac Aromatic Bitters (monogram PHD & CO)
Milk glass, lady's leg, 11-3/4", smooth base, applied mouth, American 1865-1875 .... **$350-450**

Schroeder's / Bitters / Louisville, KY
Medium amber, 9", lady's leg, smooth base (S.B. & G. CO), tooled lip, blown in four-piece mold, American 1885-1895 .... **$400-600**

Sharp's – Mountain Herb – Bitters
Medium amber, 98-3/4" smooth base, applied sloping collar mouth, scarce bitter, American 1870-1880 .... **$250-350**

Simon's Centennial Bitters – Trade Mark
Blue aqua, 10-1/8", bust of George Washington, smooth base, applied double collar mouth, American 1876, manufactured to capitalize on the 1876 Centennial **$700-900**

St / Drake's / 1860 / Plantation / X / Bitters – Patented / 1862
Medium olive yellow, 9-7/8", 6-log cabin, smooth base, applied tapered mouth, American 1862-1870 .... **$1,000-1,500**

Smyrna / Stomach / Bitters – Prolongs Life / Dayton, Ohio
Medium amber, 9", smooth base, tooled lip, rare, American 1880-1895 .... **$400-700**

The Great Tonic / Caldwells / Herb Bitters
Yellow amber, 12-1/4", triangular form, iron pontil, applied mouth, American 1865-1875 .... **$300-400**

The Great Tonic / Caldwells / Herb Bitters
Yellow amber, 12-1/2", triangular form, smooth base, applied mouth, American 1865-1875 .... **$275-375**

The Royal – Bitters – Geo. A. Clement / Niagara, Ont
Deep blue aqua, 8-3/8", oval with strap sides form, smooth base, applied double collar mouth, very rare, Canadian 1875-1885 .... **$400-600**

Thos A. Hurleys – Stomach / Bitters – Louisville, KY
Yellow amber, 10-1/2", smooth base, applied mouth, extremely rare, American 1865-1875 .... **$375-475**

St / Drakes / 1860 / Plantation / X / Bitters – Patented / 1862, yellow green (citron), 9-3/4", American 1862-1875, $1,500-2,500.

West India/Stomach Bitters – St. Louis Mo, medium amber, 8-3/4", American 1870-1880, $100-150.

W.L./Richardson-Bitters – South/ Reading-Mass, aqua, 7", American 1840-1860, $140-180.

Travelers – Walking Man With Cane – Bitters – 1834 / 1870
Yellow amber, 10-1/2", smooth base, applied tapered collar mouth, American 1865-1875 ...... **$3,500-5,000**

Yerba Buena – Bitters, S.F. Cal. label reads: Dr. Warren's Yerba Buena Bitters, The Greatest Medical Discovery of the Age, H. Williams & Co. Proprietors, San Francisco, Ca
Yellow amber, 8-1/4", strap sided, smooth base, applied mouth, American 1880-1890 .... **$275-375**

W.C. Bitters / Brobst & Rentschler / Reading, PA.
Yellow amber, 10-3/4", barrel form, smooth base, tooled lip, American 1885-1895 .... **$600-800**

W.L. / Richardson's – Bitters – South / Reading – Mass
Blue aqua, 7", open pontil, applied mouth, American 1840-1860 .... **$275-375**

Weis / Bros. / Knickerbocker / Stomach / Bitters (all on applied shoulder seal)
Orange amber, 12-1/8", lady's leg, smooth base, tooled mouth, American 1885-1895 ..... **$2,000-3,000**

Zingari / Bitters – F. Rahter
Medium amber, 12-1/4", lady's leg, smooth base, applied ring mouth, American 1865-1875 .. **$350-450**

Weis / Bros. / Knickerbocker / Stomach / Bitters (on applied shoulder seal) orange amber 12-1/8", American 1885-1895, $2,000-3,000.

Blown Bottles

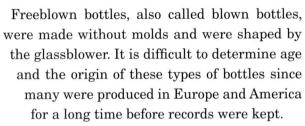

Freeblown bottles, also called blown bottles, were made without molds and were shaped by the glassblower. It is difficult to determine age and the origin of these types of bottles since many were produced in Europe and America for a long time before records were kept.

Another type of blown bottle, the blown three-mold, was formed from a three-piece mold. These bottles were manufactured between 1820 and 1840 in Europe and the United States, and, it is quite difficult to distinguish bottles from different sides of the Atlantic. Since blown three-mold and pressed three-mold are similar, it is important to know how to differentiate between the two types. With blown glass, the mold impression can be felt on the inside, while pressed glass impressions can only be felt on the outside. Most blown three-mold bottles were made in amethyst (purple), sapphire blue, and a variety of greens.

Blown globular bottle, dark olive amber (black), 7-7/8", American 1810-1820, $300-400.

Rib pattern molded flask, medium olive green, 6-3/8", American 1810-1820, $500-700.

Black Glass Demijohn – Blown in Dip Mold
Deep amber, 10-7/8", pontil-scarred base, applied sloping collar mouth, American 1790-1810...**$200-275**

Blown Globular Bottle
Dark olive amber, 7-7/8", pontil-scarred base, outward rolled lip, American 1810-1820, Zanesville Ohio Glass Works **$300-400**

Blown Globular Bottle
Amber, 8-1/8", pontil-scarred base, outward rolled lip, American 1810-1820, Zanesville Ohio Glass Works **$300-400**

Blown Nailsea Handled Jug
Deep apple green with overall white splotch pattern, 9-1/2", pontil-scarred base, applied sloping double collar mouth and handle, English 1800-1825, blown at either Nailsea Glass Works, Bristol, England, or Alloa Glass Works, Scotland...**$800-1,400**

Blown Shaft and Globe "B.I.G.I." Sealed Wine Bottle (Begi Winery founded 1880 in Orvieto, Italy)
Light to medium green, 9", smooth base, tooled mouth, Italian 1880 ....**$150-300**

Blown Three-Mold Bar Bottle
Bright yellow green, pint, barrel form, pontil-scarred base, applied sloping collared mouth, American 1820-1840 ....**$2,000-4,000**

Blown Three-Mold Decanter
Brilliant yellow olive, 7-1/2", barrel form, pontil-scarred base, applied sloping collared mouth, American 1820-1840 ....**$500-1,000**

Blown Three-Mold Decanter
Yellow olive, quart, pontil-scarred base, tooled flared mouth, American 1820-1840, Mount Vernon Glassworks, Mount Vernon, New York.............................**$800-1,600**

Pattern-molded chestnut flask, light olive, 7", American 1815-1835, $200-250.

Pattern-molded chestnut flask, deep olive, 5-1/8", American 1780-1830, $250-300.

Black glass sealed wine bottle, distressed swan being chased by a rampart lion (on applied seal) olive green, blown in a three-part mold, 11-5/8", English 1830-1850, $200-300.

Blown Three-Mold Decanter
Yellow olive green, 7", pontil-scarred base, tool flared-out lip, American 1815-1835, Mount Vernon Glassworks, New York **$2,500-3,500**

Blown Three-Mold Decanter
Medium olive green, 8", pontil-scarred base, applied double collar medicine type mouth, rare, American 1815-1835, Keene Glassworks, New Hampshire **$5,000-7,000**

Blown Three-Mold Decanter
Medium olive green, 10-1/8", pontil-scarred base, applied double collar medicine type mouth, American 1815-1835, Keene Glassworks, New Hampshire **$4,500-6,500**

Blown Three-Mold Decanter
Clear, 11-1/2", pontil-scarred base, tooled flared-out lip, original ground stopper, American 1815-1835 .... **$275-375**

Blown Three-Mold Flask
Clear, 5-5/8", flattened flask form, pontil-scarred base, inward tooled mouth, rare in blown three-mold glass, American 1820-1840, Boston & Sandwich Glass Works, Sandwich, Mass....................... **$1,000-2,000**

Blown Three-Mold Toilet Water Bottle
Deep cobalt blue, 5-3/4", 30-rib pattern swirled to left, pontil-scarred base, flared-out tooled lip, original stopper, American 1815-1845.................... **$350-450**

Blown three-mold toilet water bottle, dark cobalt blue, 5-3/8", American 1815-1835, $200-250.

Freeblown chestnut flask, deep red amber, 5", American
1800-1815, $200-300.

Vertical rib flask, medium green pint, American 1815-
1825, $600-800.

Blown Three-Mold Toilet Water Bottle
Deep lavender blue, 6-1/8", heavy swirls of color,
pontil-scarred base, flared lip, American 1815-1835
.... **$200-300**

Blown Three-Mold Syrup Decanter
Clear glass with daisy pattern, 8-1/8", smooth base,
sheared lip with applied hinged pewter lid, applied
handle, American 1815-1835 .... **$350-450**

**Demijohn Storage Bottle – Blown in Two-Part
Mold**
Dark blue green, 17-1/4", pontil-scarred base, applied
mouth, American 1850-1870 .... **$275-375**

Freeblown Chestnut Flask
Deep reddish amber, 5", pontil-scarred base, sheared
and tooled lip, American 1800-1815 .... **$200-300**

Freeblown Chestnut Flask
Blue aqua, 6-7/8", pontil-scarred base, sheared and
tooled lip, American 1800-1810 .... **$150-200**

Blown three-mold toilet water bottle,
medium cobalt blue, 5-3/4", American 1815-1835, $300-400.

Freeblown creamer, cobalt blue, 3-3/4", American 1800-1830, $375-450.

Pattern molded club bottle, yellow amber with olive tone, 8-5/8", American 1815-1835, $3,500-4,500.

Freeblown Flattened Chestnut Flask
Medium blue green, 5", pontil-scarred base, sheared lip, applied pewter mouth with screw-on cap, blown using the German half-post method, German 1760-1790 .... **$600-900**

Freeblown Flattened Chestnut Flask
Olive yellow, 8", paddle flattened sides, open pontil, applied mouth, American 1780-1810 .... **$300-400**

Freeblown Flattened Chestnut Bottle
Olive amber, 9-3/8", open pontil, applied mouth, American 1800-1820 .... **$275-375**

Freeblown Chestnut Bottle – "Camphor" Neck Label
Light yellow olive, 5-1/4', pontil-scarred base, outward rolled mouth, American 1783-1830 .... **$500-1,000**

Freeblown Chestnut Bottle
Yellow olive, 6-5/8", pontil-scarred base, applied mouth, American 1783-1830 .... **$200-400**

Freeblown Chestnut Flask
Light to medium green olive, 8", open pontil applied mouth, American 1780-1810 .... **$300-400**

Pattern molded club bottle, medium cobalt blue, 8-1/4", American 1815-1835, $3,500-4,500.

Freeblown globular bottle, yellow amber, 8-1/2", American 1780-1810, $150-250.

Freeblown globular bottle, straw yellow, 7-5/8", American 1790-1815, $375-475.

Freeblown Chestnut Bottle
Forest green, 8-1/8", tubular pontil scar, heavy applied mouth, American 1780-1820 .... **$500-1,000**

Freeblown Demijohn
Medium puce amber, 12", squatty bulbous form, smooth base, sheared mouth with string rim, German 1800-1830... **$300-600**

Freeblown Demijohn
Cornflower blue, 12-1/2", cylindrical, crude rough pontil scar, heavy applied collared mouth, American 1840-1860... **$500-1,000**

Freeblown Handled Jug
Puce amber, 8", cylindrical with bulbous mid-section, pontil-scarred base, applied sloping collar, American 1840-1860... **$500-1,000**

Freeblown Globular Bottle
Blue green, 9-1/8", squatty form, pontil scar base, flared sheared mouth, American 1820-1840....... **$800-1,600**

Freeblown Globular Bottle
Light to medium blue green, 9-3/4", pontil-scarred base, outward rolled lip, American 1780-1810 ....**$350-500**

Freeblown Globular Bottle
Light blue green, 11-1/4", open pontil, thick outward rolled lip, American 1780-1810 .... **$350-450**

Freeblown globular bottle, medium olive green, 5-1/4, European 1760-1780, $400-550.

Freeblown globular bottle, amber, 4-1/8", American 1790-1820, $300-400.

Spirits flask, clear glass, 5-3/8", German 1780-1820, blown in German half-post method, $200-300.

Spirits flask, medium amethyst, 9", German 1750-1770, $400-700.

Freeblown Half-Size Dutch Squat Wine Bottle

Medium yellow olive, 5-5/8", squat form with long tapering neck, sheared mouth with string rim, Netherlands 1730-1760 ....**$1,000-2,000**

Freeblown Full Size Dutch Wine Bottle – Painted Ship Scene on Bottle

Yellow olive, 10-1/2", pontil-scarred base, sheared mouth with wide string rim, Netherlands 1740-1780 ....**$1,500-3,000**

Freeblown Jar

Yellow olive, 8-1/2", large pontil scar, tooled slightly flared mouth, American 1820-1840 ....**$300-600**

Freeblown Miniature Flattened Globular Bottle

Yellow olive amber, 3-7/8", open pontil, tooled mouth with applied string lip, Dutch 1730-1760..**$700-800**

Freeblown Miniature Globular Bottle

Light olive yellow, 3-3/8", pontil-scarred base, applied tool mouth, New England 1783-1830..**$1,000-2,000**

Freeblown Miniature Globular Bottle

Light yellow green, 2-5/8", pontil-scarred base, tooled flared mouth, American 1783-1830, rare color..**$1,000-2,000**

Freeblown Small Pocket Bottle

Brilliant amethyst, 4", flattened bulbous form, pontil-scarred base, sheared mouth, extremely rare, American 1763-1775, Steigel's American Flint Glass, Manheim, Pennsylvania **$500-1,000**

Freeblown Pocket Flask

Red amber, 4-7/8", pontil-scarred base, sheared mouth, American 1783-1830 ....**$200-600**

Freeblown Oversized Tear Drop Flask

Medium emerald green, 9-3/4", pontil-scarred base, thick outward rolled lip, European 1770-1810..**$300-450**

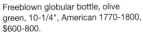

Freeblown globular bottle, olive green, 10-1/4", American 1770-1800, $600-800.

Pitkin flask, medium olive yellow, 4-7/8", American 1775-1800, $700-1,000.

Pitkin flask, brilliant aqua, 4-7/8", American 1775-1800, $350-400.

Freeblown "Thomas Cains" Decanters (matching pair)
Clear glass, 7-7/8", pontil-scarred base, tooled flared-out mouth, applied neck band and chain type bands around body of decanter, American 1815-1835, South Boston Flint Glassworks **$1,200-1,600**

Freeblown Utility Bottle
Olive green, 7-1/4", open pontil, tool flared-out lip, European 1780-1810.**$250-350**

Blown Half-Pint Decanter with Stopper
Sapphire blue, 6-1/2", pontil-scarred base, tooled rim American 1820-1840, Sandwich Glass Works, Sandwich, Massachusetts..................................**$500-800**

Large Bulbous Freeblown Jar
Yellow olive, 8-3/4", pontil-scarred base, tooled wide neck and mouth with sheared mouth with string rim, American 1780-1830......................................**$1,500-3,000**

Large Freeblown Globular Bottle
Light to medium yellow olive, 10-1/4", pontil-scarred base, crude outward rolled collared mouth, American 1780-1830 ....**$800-1,600**

Large Blown Three-Mold Flask
Clear, 9-3/4", tear drop form, pontil-scarred base, tooled collared mouth, extremely rare, American 1820-1840 ....**$1,000-2,000**

Pitkin Flask – Blown in German Half-Post method
Medium yellow olive, 4-7/8'", 32-rib pattern swirled to left, open pontil-scarred base, sheared and tooled lip, rare smaller size, American 1775-1800, Pitkin Glass Works, East Manchester, Connecticut..**$700-1,000**

Pitkin Flask – Blown in German Half-Post method

Medium yellow olive, 5-3/8", 36-rib pattern swirled to right, pontil-scarred base, sheared and tooled lip, American 1780-1810, Pitkin Glass Works, East Manchester, Connecticut **$600-800**

Pitkin flask, medium yellow olive, 5-3/8", American 1780-1810, $600-800.

Pitkin flask, blue green, 6-3/8", American 1815-1825, $500-700.

Pitkin flask, clear glass, 4-5/8", European 1780-1820, $300-400.

Cobalt Blue Medicine Bottles

One of the most sought after colors by bottle collectors is brilliant cobalt blue. As discussed in the "Bottle Facts" chapter, colors natural to bottle glass production are brown, amber, olive green, and aqua. The true blue, green, and purple colors were produced by metallic oxides added to the glass batch. The blue was specifically produced by adding cobalt oxide to the basic glass batch. Since blue and other bright colors were expensive to produce and were usually manufactured for specialty items, bottles with these colors are very rare and highly desired. Since cobalt blue bottles stood out among all other colors, many chemist, druggist, and pharmacist bottles were made with cobalt along with elaborate monograms, pictures, and unique designs.

This chapter presents a cross-section of many cobalt blue medicine bottles manufactured prior to 1920 across the United States. For a complete and detailed collection of these brilliant bottles, I recommend adding the following book to your reference file: *Cobalt Medicine Bottles* by Charles E. Blake (e-mail dig632@aol.com).

Ayer's – Hair Vigor, deep cobalt blue, 6-1/2", American 1890-1910, $120-140.

C.Heimstreet & Co. / Troy, N.Y., medium cobalt blue, 5-1/8", American 1840-1860, $275-375.

Hubbell, light cobalt blue, 5-5/8", American 1840-1860, $800-1,200.

Ackerman & Stewart – Druggist – Palatka, FLA
Medium cobalt blue, 5", smooth base, tooled top, American 1885-1900 .... **$100-150**

Allan's / Anti-Fat – Botanic Medicine Co. – Buffalo, N.Y.
Medium cobalt blue, 7-5/8", smooth base, applied mouth, American 1875-1885 .... **$200-300**

Apothecary Jar with black wording on jar reading: Pulv. Lapis. P
Dark cobalt blue glaze, 6-5/8", smooth base, wide mouth English 1860-1880 .... **$400-600**

C. Heimstreet & Co / Troy, N.Y.
Deep cobalt blue, 7", 8-sided, smooth base, applied double collar mouth American 1855-1865 . **$275-375**

C. Heimstreet & Co / Troy, N.Y.
Deep cobalt blue, 7-1/8", 8-sided, smooth base, applied double collar mouth American 1865-1875
.... **$120-160**

Dickey Chemist – SF – Pioneer 1850
Medium cobalt blue, 6", smooth base, tooled top American 1880-1910 .... **$50-100**

For External Use Only – Prescription – Reese Chem Co. – External Use Four Time Daily – Reese Chem Co. – Cleveland OH
Medium cobalt blue, 5", smooth base, ABM top American 1900-1910 .... **$50-60**

Gargling Oil / Lockport. N.Y., deep cobalt blue, 5-7/8", American, 1910-1915, $160-220.

Gooch's – Extract Of / Sarsaparilla / Cincinnati, O, light cobalt blue, 9-1/2", American 1875-1890, $140-180.

I.C. Morrison's / Sarsaparilla – 188 Greenwich St. – New York, deep cobalt blue, 9-1/2", American 1840-1860, $4,000-6,000.

Gargling Oil / Lockport. N.Y.
Deep cobalt blue, 5-7/8", smooth base, ABM mouth American 1910-1915 .. **$160-200**

Heimstreet & Co Troy NY
Dark cobalt blue, 7", 8-sided, smooth base, applied top American 1885-1900 ....**$100-200**

J & C. Maguire / Chemists & Druggist / St. Louis. Mo
Medium cobalt blue, 8", iron pontil, applied double collar mouth American 1845-1860 ....**$1,200-1,600**

Jerome's Hair Color – Restorer
Medium cobalt blue, 6-1/2", smooth base, flared lip American 1855-1865 ....**$800-1,500**

Johnson & Johnson – New York – Label reads: Linton Moist Gauze Poison
Medium cobalt blue, 6", smooth base, ground top with glass lid and metal band American 1900-1910 ....**$300-400**

Kickapoo / Sage / Hair Tonic
Deep cobalt blue, 4-1/2", smooth base, tooled mouth American 1885-1895 .... **$200-300**

I.C. Morrison's / Sarsaparilla – 188 Greenwich St. – New York
Rich cobalt blue, 9-1/2", iron pontil, applied mouth American 1840-1860 ....**$4,000-6,000**

Maximo M. Diaz / Druggist / Ybor City, FLA
Cobalt blue, 5-1/8", smooth base (WT. & CO / U.S.A.), tooled lip American 1890-1910 ....**$100-150**

Geo. W. Laird & Co. /,Oleo-Chyle, medium cobalt blue, 9-7/8", American 1885-1895, $250-350.

Pure / Cod Liver / Oil – Reed / Carnick / & / Adrus-Chemists – New York, deep cobalt blue, 10-1/8", American 1885-1895, $200-300.

Mortons Citrate Of Magnesia – Milwaukee, medium cobalt blue, 7-3/8", American 1885-1895, $350-450.

Nelson's Extract Of Roses And Rosemary Wakelee & CO – Sole Agent
Deep cobalt blue, 7-1/4", smooth base, tooled top England 1880-1900 ..**$100-150**
N.Y. Medical – University (embossed measure) – Label reads: Compound Fluid Extract of Cancer – Plant, Directions for Taking, etc, and Prepared by the New York Medical University, Nos 6 & 8 University Place, New York City
Deep cobalt blue, 7-3/8", smooth base, tooled lip American 1885-1900 ....**$300-400**
Prof. J.R. Tilton – The Great / Hair / Producer – The / Crown of / Science – S.F. CAL
Medium cobalt blue, 7", smooth base, applied mouth American 1870-1880 ....**$375-500**
Pure / Cod Liver / Oil – Reed / Carnick / & / Andrus – Chemists – New York
Deep cobalt blue, 10-1/8", smooth base, tooled mouth American 1885-1895 ....**$200-300**
Sanford's Extract / Of / Hamamelis Witch Hazel (on indented panel)
Cobalt blue, 11-1/4 ", smooth base, applied square collared mouth American 1860-1880 ....**$500-1,000**
Sanford's Extract / Of / Hamamelis / Or Witch Hazel (on indented panel)
Cobalt blue, 10-3/8", smooth base, tooled mouth American 1880-1895 ..**$275-375**
Sanford's – Radical Cure
Cobalt blue, 7-1/2", smooth base (Potter Drug & Chem Corporation / Boston / Mass USA), applied mouth American 1870-1880 ....**$100-150**

Boswell & Warner's Colorific, deep cobalt blue, 5-5/8", American 1880-1890, $150-200.

Swift's / Syphilitic Specific, deep cobalt blue, 9-1/8", American 1870-1880, $800-1,200.

Upper / Blue Lick / Water – Stanton & Pierce / Proprietors / Maysville, KY, medium cobalt blue, 10", American 1865-1875, $700-900.

Sassafras (motif of eye above eye cup) Eye Lotion / Sassafras / Eye Lotion Co / Mauch Chunk, PA

Cobalt blue, 5-3/4", smooth base (W.T. Co / U.S.A.), tooled mouth, very rare bottle, American 1890-1910 ....**$150-200**

Skookum Root – Hair Grower

Cobalt blue, 6-5/8", smooth base, tooled lip, American 1885-1900 ....**$75-125**

Stearns

Medium cobalt blue, 7-1/8", cylinder form, smooth base, applied double collar mouth, American 1865-1875 ....**$140-180**

Swifts Syphlitic Specific

Medium cobalt blue, 8", smooth base, applied top, applied square collars, American 1865-1880..**$400-500**

T.K. Hibbert / Pittsburgh

Medium cobalt blue, 6-1/8", open pontil, applied collar mouth, extremely rare, American 1840-1860 ....**$600-800**

The Owl Drug Co.

Dark cobalt blue, 6", smooth base, applied top, American 1885-1900 .....**$100-200**

The Owl Drug Co.

Deep cobalt blue, 8", smooth base, applied top, American 1885-1900 ....**$150-250**

Upper / Blue Lick / Water – Stanton & Pierce / Proprietors / Maysville, KY

Medium cobalt blue, 10" oval form, smooth base (McC & CO / Pitts Pa), applied mouth, American 1865-1875 ....**$700-900**

U.S.A. / Hosp. Dept., medium cobalt blue, 9-1/8", American 1863-1870, $1,800-2,500.

Edwin J. Kuhns – Druggist & Chemist – Lansdale, PA., cobalt blue, 6-1/4", American 1890-1910, $275-375.

Wynkoop's / Katharismic Honduras / Sarsaparilla – New York, deep cobalt blue, 10-1/4", American 1840-1860, $3,500-4,500.

Unembossed Ammonia Bottle
Medium cobalt blue, quart, smooth base, applied top, American 1885-1900 ....**$100-200**

U.S.A. / Hosp. Dept
Medium cobalt blue, 3-1/4", smooth base, tooled lip, American 1865-1875 ....**$250-300**

U.S.A. Hosp. Dept
Medium cobalt blue, 4", smooth base, flared lip, American 1865-1875 ....**$400-500**

W.A. Batchelor's / Moldavia Cream / Manufactured Only At 16 Bond Street / New York
Deep cobalt blue, 2-1/8", smooth base, ground lip, rare cream jar, American 1860-1875 ....**$375-500**

Wakelee's Cameline
Dark cobalt blue, 5", smooth base, applied top, American 1885-1895 .....**$300-400**

Wakelee's Cameline
Medium cobalt blue, 6-1/4", smooth base, applied top, American 1885-1895 ....**$400-500**

W.E. Hagan & Co – Troy N.Y.
Dark cobalt blue, 7", smooth base, applied top, American 1885-1900 .....**$200-300**

Weiss Pharmacy – Philada PA
Medium cobalt blue, 5", smooth base, tooled top, American 1885-1910 .**$200-300**

Wynkoop's / Katharismic Honduras / Sarsaparilla – New York
Deep cobalt blue, 10-1/4", open pontil, applied sloping collar mouth, American 1840-1860 ....**$3,500-4,000**

Cosmetic and Hair Restorer Bottles

This category includes bottles that originally contained products to improve personal appearance, such as treatment for skin, teeth, and the scalp (hair and restoring agents). The more popular of these are the hair treatment bottles.

Hair bottles are popular as collector items due to their distinctive colors such as amethyst and various shades of blues. The main producer of American-made perfume bottles in the 18th century was Casper Wistar, whose clients included Martha Washington. Another major manufacturer of the 18th century was Henry William Stiegel. While most of Wistar's bottles were plain, Stiegel's were decorative and are more appealing to collectors.

In the 1840s, Solon Palmer started to manufacture and sell perfumes. By 1879, his products were being sold in drugstores around the country. Today, Palmer bottles are sought after for their brilliant emerald green color.

R.P. Hall's Improved Preparation for The Hair, medium cobalt blue, 7-1/2", American 1870-1880, $150-200.

Ballards / No 1 / Hair Dye / New York
Aqua, 3-3/4", open pontil, rolled lip, American 1840-1860 .... **$80-120**

Bears (in arch) Oil
Blue aqua, 2-7/8", open pontil, inward rolled lip, American 1840-1860 .... **$150-250**
Bears Oil was one of the earliest hair preparation dating to early 1820s.

Bears / Oil (horizontally)
Blue aqua, 2-3/4", open pontil, inward rolled lip, American 1840-1860 .... **$150-250**

Bears / Oil (vertically)
Blue aqua, 2-3/4", open pontil, inward rolled lip, American 1840-1860 .... **$150-250**

Bush's / Argentine / Hair Dye – Almond / No 1 / Water – Lowell – Mass
Aqua, 3-1/2", open pontil, rolled lip, American 1840-1860 .... **$100-150**

Bush / Argen / Tine – No. 2 Hair Dye
Aqua, 4-1/2", open pontil, rolled lip, American 1840-1860 .... **$100-150**

C. Brinckerhoffs – Health Restorative – Price $1.00 – New York
Medium to deep yellow olive green, 7-3/8", pontil-scarred base, applied mouth, American 1840-1860 .... **$1,500-2,000**

"C. A. P. Mason / Alpine / Hair Balm / Providence, R.I."
Deep olive green, 6-3/4", smooth base, rectangular with indented panels and beveled corners, applied double collared mouth, rare, American 1860-1870 .... **$1,500-3,000**

C. Sines – Genuine – Philada, PA – Sines – Electric / Hair / Oil
Blue aqua, 5-1/4", open pontil, inward rolled lip, American 1840-1860 .... **$200-300**

Chews – Hair Dye – No 1
Aqua, 3-1/2", open pontil, rolled lip, very rare, American 1840-1860 .... **$100-150**

Cook's / Hair / invigorator / Lewiston, ME (partial label)
Aquamarine, 6", rectangular, pontil-scarred base, double collar mouth, American 1840-1860 **$200-400**

D. Mitchell's – Tonic For – The Hair – Rochester, N.Y.
Clear, 6-3/8", open pontil, applied double collar mouth, American 1840-1860 .... **$150-250**

Demonet / & Meyers – Hair Dye – N.Y. – NO 1
Aqua, 4-1/8", open pontil, inward rolled lip, very rare, American 1840-1860 .... **$100-150**

Dr. Comstock's – Hair Dye
Aqua, 5", open pontil, applied mouth, very rare, American 1840-1860 .... **$140-180**

Dr. D. Jayne / Hair Tonic – Philada
Aqua, 4-1/2", open pontil, rolled lip, American 1840-1860 .... **$75-125**

Dr. D. Jayne – Liquid / Hair Dye – Phila. – No 1
Aqua, 3", open pontil, flared-out lip, American 1840-1860 .... **$75-125**

F. B. Strouse / New York – Label reads: Superior Pomade, Felix Strouse, New York
Clear glass, 2-3/4", barrel form, smooth base, sheared and ground lip, American 1860-1870 .... **$80-120**

Figural Hair Bottle – Label reads: "Bowens / Genuine / Crude Oil / Hair Grower / Liquid Velvet" and produced by "The Genuine / Crude Oil Company / 37 5th
Clear glass, 6-3/8", oil derrick form, smooth base, tooled rounded top, American 1870-1890 .... **$250-500**

Fountain Of Youth / Hair Restorer / Trenton
Olive green, 7-1/8", rectangular form, smooth base, tooled mouth, American 1885-1895 .... **$400-500**

Franklin's Eagle – Hair Restorer / Columbus, OH
Medium amber, 8-1/4", smooth base, (W.T. & Co. U.S.A.), tooled lip, scarce, American 1885-1895 .... **$200-250**

George's Hair Dye – No 1
Aqua, 3-3/8", open pontil, inward rolled lip, American 1840-1860 .... **$100-150**

Hover's – Hair Dye – Philada
Aqua, 2-3/4", 6-sided, open pontil, rolled lip, American 1840-1860 .... **$100-150**

Hurd's / Hair / Restorer
Blue aqua, 7-3/4", iron pontil, applied mouth, American 1840-1860 .... **$150-200**

Circassian Hair Restorative – Cincinnati, 7-3/8", American 1870-1880, $150-200.

Buckingham Whisker
Dye, medium amber, 5",
American 1890-1910,
$50-100.

I. Morant – No 1 – J. Hambleton / Phila
Blue aqua, 3-1/4", open pontil, applied mouth, American 1840-1860 ......**$120-160**

J. Cristadoro's – Hair Preservative & / Beautifier, N.Y.
Aqua, 3", open pontil, rolled lip, American 1840-1860| **$70-100**

J. Cristadoro – Liquid – Hair Dye – No 2
Aqua, 6-3/4", open pontil, applied mouth, American 1840-1860 ....**$70-100**

Jerome's – Hair Color – Restorer
Medium cobalt blue, 6-1/2", smooth base, flared lip, American 1855-1860
....**$800-1,500**

Jerome's – Hair Color – Restorer
Medium yellow olive, 6-5/8", open pontil, flared lip, American 1855-1960... **$400-700**

Kalopean – Hair Dye – No 1
Cornflower blue, 3-1/2", open pontil, thin flared-out lip, very rare, American 1840-
1860 ....**$100-150**

L. Miller's / Hair / invigorator / N.Y.
Aqua, 5 -7/8", oval form, open pontil, applied mouth, American 1840-1860 . **$140-180**

**Label Under Glass Barber Bottle – Label reads: Hyki Tonic / The World's /
Greatest / Dandruff / Remedy / Prepared by / The Hyki Co. / Cleveland, Ohio
– Dandruff Indicates Approaching Baldness**
Clear glass, 8-1/4", smooth base, tooled lip, American 1890-1915 ....**$300-400**

**Label Under Glass Barber Bottle – Label reads: Pompeian / Hair / Massage
/ Formerly Hyki / Removes / Dandruff / Pompeian Mfg. Co. Cleveland, Don't
Wait Until Too Late**
Clear glass, 8-1/4", smooth base, tooled lip, American 1890-1915 ....**$250-350**

Laird's – Bloom Of Youth / Or / Liquid Pearl / For The / Complexion & Skin – Broadway N.Y.
Fiery opalescent milk glass, 4-7/8", smooth base, tooled mouth, extremely rare, American 1870-1880 .... **$400-600**

Lyon's – Indian – Hair Dye – No. 1
Aqua, 3-1/4", open pontil, rolled lip, rare, American 1840-1860 .... **$200-275**

Log Cabin – Scalpine – Rochester, N.Y. – Label reads: Warner's / Log / Cabin / Hair Tonic / Roots & Herbs Preparations / For / The Head and The Hair
Amber, 9", smooth base (Pat. Sept 6th / 1887), tooled mouth, American 1887-1895 .... **$1,500-2,500**

Lombard & / Cundall / Springfield Mass – Excelsior – Hair Tonic
Aqua, 6-1/2", open pontil, applied double collar mouth, American 1840-1860 .... **$150-200**

Loomis's Cream Liniment
Emerald green, 5", pontiled base, flared lip and tooled mouth, rare, American 1850-1860 .... **$2,500-3,500**

Louden / & Co's – Liquid – Hair Dye – No 2
Aqua, 3", open pontil, rolled lip, American 1840-1860 .... **$100-150**

M. Zimmer – Hair Dye – No. 2
Blue aqua, 3-5/8", open pontil, inward rolled lip, American 1840-1860 .... **$100-150**

Madame Girard's "Hygienic" Hair Restorer
Bright green, 7", smooth base, tooled top, English 1860-1880 .... **$350-500**

Mills Capillus / For The Hair – Shedden & Nelrgaard / Agents, N.Y.
Aqua, 6", open pontil, applied mouth, American 1840-1860 .... **$180-220**

Noxzema / Medicated / Shave / Contents 2 LBS / Distributed By / Noxzema Chemical Co.
Cobalt blue, jar, smooth base, ABM smooth lip, original tin lid, American 1905-1925 .... **$10-20**

Oldridges / Balm / Of Columbia – For Restoring / Hair / Philadelphia
Aqua, 5-1/8", open pontil, flared-out mouth, American 1840-1860 .... **$140-180**

Packard's – Regenerator / And / Reproducer – Of The Hair
Aqua, 7", open pontil, applied mouth, extremely rare, American 1840-1860 .... **$350-450**

Oldridge's Balm of Columbia – For Restoring Hair – Philadelphia, aqua, 5-1/8", American 1840-1860, $150-250.

Professor Woods / Hair
Restorative – Depot
St. Louis, Mo – And
New York, teal, 9-1/8",
American 1840-1860,
$375-475.

Pierce's – Rosetta / Hair Tonic – Boston Mass

Blue aqua, 6", open pontil, applied double collar mouth, American 1840-1860
....**$250-350**

Prof. J.R. Tilton – The Great / Hair / Producer – The / Crown Of / Science – S.F. CAL

Medium cobalt blue, 7", smooth base, applied mouth, American 1870-1880
....**$400-500**

R.G. Gardner – Liquid – Hair Dye

Aqua, 3-1/2", open pontil, thin flared-out lip, American 1840-1860 ....**$100-150**

Riker's / American / Hair Restorer

Orange amber, 6-3/4", smooth base, tooled mouth, American 1875-1885...**$120-140**

Riker's / American / Hair Restorer

Yellow amber, 7", oval form, smooth base, applied mouth, American 1875-1885...**$150-250**

Shaker – Hair Restorer

Yellow amber, 7-7/8", smooth base, tooled double collar mouth, American 1880-1890 ....**$350-450**

Storrs – Chemical / Hair invigorator – Philada

Blue aqua, 6", open pontil, applied mouth, American 1840-1860.............**$100-150**

W.A. Batchelor's / Moldavia Cream / Manufactured Only At 16 Bond Street / New York, deep cobalt blue, 2-1/8", American 1860-1875, $375-500.

"The / Royal / Ispahan / Hair Dye" Jar
Cobalt blue, 2-3/8", octagonal form, smooth base, ground mouth with metal lid, extremely rare, American 1860-1888, Boston and Sandwich Glass Works **$750-1,500**

This Bottle / For Wildroot Hair / Preparations Only / Wildroot Inc. / Buffalo, N.Y. – Label reads: Wildroot Original Formula for the Hair Removes Loose Dandruff – Grooms the Hair – Improves Appearance, Wildroot Company, Inc. Buffalo, N.Y. Contents 10 Fl. Ozs.
Clear glass, black and white pyro label, 8-3/8", smooth base, ABM lip, original glass stopper with dauber, American 1920-1935 ....**$120-160**

W.A. Batchelor's / Moldavia Cream / Manufactured Only at 16 Bond Street / New York
Deep cobalt blue, 2-7/8" jar, smooth base, sheared and ground lip, American 1860-1880 ....**$75-100**

White's / Hair / Restorative
Aqua, 6-3/8" open pontil, oval form, applied sloping collar mouth, extremely rare, American 1840-1860 ....**$200-275**

Wilson's – Hair Colorer
Aqua, 5", open pontil, rolled lip, American 1840-1860..............................**$150-200**

Crocks and Stoneware

Although crocks are made of pottery rather than glass, many bottle collectors also have crock collections, since they have been found wherever bottles are buried. Crock containers were manufactured in America as early as 1641, and were used extensively in the sale of retail products during the 19th and early 20th centuries. Miniature stoneware jugs were often used for advertising, as were some stoneware canning jars. Storeowners favored crocks since they kept beverages cooler and extended the shelf life of certain products. Crocks appeal to collectors because of their interesting shapes, painted and stenciled decorations, lustrous finishes, and folk art value. In addition, molded stoneware shouldn't be considered mass produced, since a great deal of detailed design and handwork had to be done on each crock.

In the late 1800s, the discovery of disease-causing bacteria prompted

many medicine makers to seize a profitable if not unethical opportunity. An undocumented number of fraudulent cures were peddled to gullible and unsuspecting customers. The most infamous of these so-called cures were produced and sold in pottery containers by William Radam. He was given a patent for his "Microbe Killer" in 1886 and stayed in business until 1907, when the Pure Food and Drug Act ended his scheme. His "cure" was nothing more than watered down wine (wine comprised only 1 percent of the total contents.)

With the invention of the automatic bottle machine in 1903, glass bottles became cheaper to make and hence more common. This contributed to the steady decline of production and use of pottery crocks and containers.

Miniature pottery whiskey jug, cream body, with dark brown glaze, 4", American 1885-1910, $150-250.

Miniature bisque pottery whiskey jug, Mark Twain Hotel – Hannibal, Mo. , dark brown glaze, 2-3/4", American 1905-1935, $100-150.

Advertising Stoneware Jug – Firm of Matthews M'F'Rs of Carbonated Beverage, Sirups & C 333 East 26th Street N.Y.

Gray pottery with cobalt slip over lettering, 9", handled, smooth base, American 1880-1900 .... **$175-250**

One Quart Ovoid Cream Pot

Medium gray, 6-1/2", brushed flower design, smooth base American 1870, Shenfelder Factory **$700-1,000**

One-Half Gallon Advertising Jug – Storrs & Curtis / Syracuse / N.Y.

Dark brown, 7", smooth base, American 1880 .... **$200-400**

One-Half Gallon Canning Jar

Dark gray, 8", accent stripes at base and rim, 4-teardrop brushed blue design in the center, smooth base, American 1860 .... **$100-125**

Large-size stoneware Bellarmine jug, brown salt-glazed pottery, 14-1/2", Germany 17th century, $1,500-2,500.

Compliments of – Hicheimer & Co. – Willows – Cal, tan mini-jug, 3", American 1880-1895, $400-500.

Compliments of – C. L. Beebe – Mondamin, Iowa, two-tone cream and brown mini-jug, 3", American 1880-1895.

One-Half Gallon Canning Jar

Dark gray, 8-1/2", brushed blue accents stripes at top and bottom, accented with 10 graduated teardrops in middle, smooth base, American 1860............**$150-220**

One Gallon Advertising Stoneware Jug – Quintard & Thompson / Ship Chandlers & Grocers / No. 28 South St. N. York

Dark brown, 9" beehive-shape form, smooth base, American 1870 ....**$80-130**

One Gallon Cake Crock – Moore, Nichols & Co. – Williamsport

Gray, 5-1/2", dotted flower decoration, blue accents at handles, smooth base, American 1878..**$200-400**

One Gallon Ovoid Jug – P. Pugler & Co. – Buffalo, NY

Light cream, 11", brushed flower and stem decoration, smooth base, American 1850 ....**$1,500-1,700**

One Gallon Preserve Jar with Stoneware Lid – Cowden & Wilcox

Gray, 9-1/2", man in the mood design in blue, American 1870..........**$6,000-8,000**

One Gallon Preserve Jar – Hamilton & Jones – Greensboro PA

Dark gray, 9-1/2", name in blue stencil on front, smooth base, American 1870 ....**$70-80**

Stoneware jar, Collins
& Wright Pittsburgh /
Patented Oct. 27, 1868 /
Re-Issued Sept 14 1869,
brown mottled glaze jar,
7-1/4", American 1869-
1875, $400-600.

One Gallon Saltglaze Stoneware Jug

Brownish, 10-1/2", bullet-head form, handled, stamped "J.B. Caire & Co./Pokeepsie, N.Y." on shoulder above a cobalt skip flower and number 1, smooth base, American 1865-1880 ....**$200-300**

One Gallon Stoneware Jug – J. & E. Norton Bennington, VT

Cream, 10-1/2", one-of-a-kind decoration of a large plump strawberry, smooth base very rare, possibly a special order, American 1855 ....**$500-1,000**

One Gallon Stoneware Pitcher

Gray, 10-1/2", thick blue vine and flower design at the midsection and neck, smooth base, American 1850 ....**$1,200-1,400**

One and One-Half Gallon Ovoid Crock – Liberty Forev Warne & Letts – 1807 S. Amboy – N. Jersey

Cream, 10", blue filled scallop design above the name, blue accents under the ears, accented with impressed dental molding around the rim, smooth base, American 1807 ....**$20,000-24,000**

One and One-Half Gallon Jar – F.B. Norton Sons – Worcester Mass

Cream, 10-1/2", dove design, smooth base, American 1886 ....**$700-1,000**

One and One-Half Gallon Preserve Jar

Medium brown, 12", cylinder shape, four flower drapes around the shoulder, smooth base, American 1850 ....**$60-120**

Two-gallon Red Wing stoneware crock, gray, 9-1/2",
American 1890-1915, $120-160.

Three-gallon saltglaze stoneware crock – E.L. Farrar / Iper-
ville, Q., tan, 10-1/4", Canadian 1860-1880, $250-300.

Two Gallon Cake Crock
Gray, 6", blue drape design repeated in the front and back, blue accents at the applied ears, smooth base, American 1850 ....**$150-250**

Two Gallon Cream Pot – G. Haidle & Co. – Union Pottery – Flemington, N.J.
Cream, 9-1/2", swan on a lake with "Old Scotch" in blue, American 1870 .. **$800-1,000**

Two Gallon Ovoid Crock
Cream, 13", blue accented lollipop flower outline at shoulder, smooth base, American 1830 ....**$150-175**

Two Gallon Ovoid Jug – Paul Cushman
Dark cream, 14", maker's mark in large letters impressed at shoulder, smooth base, American 1807..**$1,000-1,400**

Two Gallon Saltglaze Stoneware Crock – F.H. Cowden Harrisburg 2
Gray pottery with cobalt spitting flower decoration, 11-1/4", close handles, smooth base, American 1881-1888..**$200-300**

Two Gallon Saltglaze Stoneware Crock – F.H. Cowden Harrisburg 2
Gray pottery with cobalt stenciled decoration, 11-3/4", close handles, smooth base, American 1881-1888 ....**$120-150**

Two Gallon Stoneware Jug – C. Crolius Manufacturer – Wells, New York
Cream, 13", brushed blue accents at the handle, smooth base, American 1830 ....**$1,300-1,500**

Two Gallon Stoneware Jug – Brewer & Halm Havana
Cream, 13-1/2", dotted tulip and leaf decoration, back is splattered with cobalt blue, smooth base, American 1852 ....**$350-450**

Two Gallon Stoneware Jug – Somerset Pottery Works
Cream, 14-1/2", blue double flower and vase decoration, smooth base, American 1870 ....**$200-250**

Three Gallon Saltglaze Stoneware Crock – E. L. Farrar / Iperville, Q
Cobalt blue slip flower on front, 10-1/4", smooth base, Canadian 1860-1880 **$250-300**

Three Gallon Blue and White Stoneware Cooler – The Robinson Clay Products Co., Akron, Ohio

Raised decoration of a man pondering at a well with a cabin, tree trunk, as, and tree in background, on the other side a cornucopia of flowers, 12-1/4", smooth base, American 1890-1910...................... **$200-250**

Three Gallon Blue and White Stoneware "Ice Water" Cooler

Raised decoration of flower and leafs with flowers on the back side, 16", original metal faucet, American 1890-1910.. **$375-475**

Three Gallon Stoneware Crock

Dark gray pottery with cobalt flower decoration on both sides, 12-7/8", close handles, smooth base, American 1825-1845.. **$200-275**

Four Gallon Advertising Crock – Philbrick & Spaulding / 23 Washington St / Haverhill

Cream, 11-1/2", impressed name is framed with a double feather design, smooth base, American 1870 .... **$90-130**

Four Gallon Crock – Tyler & Co – Troy NY

Cream, 11-1/2", design of a shore bird with snowflakes, smooth base, American 1860 .... **$3,000-4,000**

Four Gallon Ovoid Crock – Thomas D. Chollar – Cortland

Gray pottery, 13-1/2", brushed cobalt blue flower design, smooth base, American 1845 .... **$150-300**

Four Gallon Water Cooler – Cortland

Cream, 17-1/2", double handled, four bud potted flower fills the front, blue accents at the handle and drain hole, smooth base, American 1870 .... **$1,500-3,000**

Five Gallon Advertising Jug – 1/2 Gallon / M. Farrell & Co. / 95 Haverhill St.

Cream, 9-1/2", patriotic hand incised eagle design with a banner (1872) in its mouth, smooth base, rare, American 1872..................................... **$1,700-1,900**

Five Gallon Ovoid Crock

Cream, 16", design of cobalt blue birds in a flower tree on front and Germanic-style tulips on back, double handled, smooth base, American 1840 .... **$40,000-43,000**

Five Gallon Handled Advertising Jug – E. A. Buck & Co / Blackstone St / Boston, Mass

Cream, 17-1/2", fancy chicken in light blue pecking at corn, smooth base, American 1880 .... **$700-1,000**

Three-gallon stoneware "Ice Water" cooler, blue and white, 16", American 1890-1910, $375-475.

McKenna Whiskey – The Best Made in KY – Distilled by H. McKenna – Fairfield, KY, 3-3/4", American 1885-1910, $90-120.

Saltglaze stoneware, one-gallon jug, J.B. Caire & Co. / Pokeepsie, N.Y., tan brown, 10-1/2", American 1865-1880, $200-300.

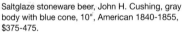

Saltglaze stoneware beer, John H. Cushing, gray body with blue cone, 10", American 1840-1855, $375-475.

Five Gallon Saltglaze Stoneware Jug – 5 Poland Mineral Spring Water, Hiram Ricker & Sons, Proprietors, South Poland, ME, None Genuine Unless Sealed with the Trademark

Dark gray pottery with cobalt glaze over wording, 18-1/4", handled with a hand-tooled internal pour spout, smooth base, very rare   American 1880-1895 ....**$400-700**

Six Gallon Crock – Adam Caire – Pokeepsie, N.Y.

Gray, 13-1/2", bird on a dotted stump design, large crow's foot and glazed spider in front the of left ear, smooth base, American 1880 ....**$300-400**

Sixteen Gallon Crock – Thompson Williams Co., Morgantown, W. VA

Gray pottery with cobalt stencil and decoration, 24", closed ear handles, smooth base, very rare, American 1880-1895 ....**$1,500-2,500**

Saltglaze Advertising Crock – H. J. Heinz Co.

Cream, 5-1/2", impressed and blue accented logo on front, tooled blue accent bands on top and bottom, smooth base, American 1880-1890 ....**$350-450**

Saltglaze Stoneware Crock – Thomas D. Chollar, Cortland

Gray pottery with cobalt fern decoration, 9", closed handles, smooth base, American 1832-1842...**$140-180**

Saltglaze stoneware beer, Watte / Root / Beer, gray with cobalt slip over mouth, 9-3/8", American 1850-1870, $100-150.

Saltglaze stoneware bitters jug, Clendenin's / Golden Tonic / Bitters 21 Congress St. / Boston, cream, 15-1/4", American 1880-1890, $500-700.

Saltglaze stoneware beer, Wells Red – Top – Root – Beer / Springfield. Mass. 1845, cream with brown glazed shoulder, 9-3/4", American 1850-1870, $100-150.

Saltglaze Stoneware Crock – Goodwin & Webster
Cream pottery, 12-5/8", sailing ship on front, close handles, smooth base, American 1820-1840 .... **$2,500-3,000**

Saltglaze Stoneware Jug
Cobalt blue wash with impressed swan, 11", smooth base, American 1880-1890........................ **$200-300**

Saltglaze Stoneware Handled Jug – Goodale / Stedman / Hartford
Gray pottery, 14", incised leaf and upper body of a bald naked man, light cobalt blue across name, ringed neck, American 1822-1825.................. **$1,500-2,000**

Saltglaze stoneware jug, brown, 11", American 1880-1900, $200-300.

Stoneware Crock – G.A.R. Buckingham Post No 12, Nov 21, 1883
Medium brown glaze, 2-3/4", lid, smooth base, American 1863-1870 .....**$275-375**

Stoneware "Bullet Head" Jug
Dark brown with incised swirled lines decoration around shoulder, 18-5/8", smooth base, handled, American 1820-1840 ....**$300-400**

Stoneware Fruit Jar – Los Angeles (motif of olive on branch) Olive Growers Ass'n – Los Angeles, CAL
Two-tone with medium brown on top, cream on bottom half, quart size, wire bail, top reads "THE WEIR PAT MAR. 1, 1892," smooth base, American 1892 ......**$300-400**

Stoneware Poison Jug – "It Kills Bed Bugs / Roaches / National Mining & Milling Co., Baltimore, Md"
Cream with blue lettering, 6-3/4", cylindrical handled jug, smooth base rare, American 1880-1890...**$1,000-2,000**

Stoneware crock, G.A.R. Buckingham Post No. 12, Nov. 21, 1883, medium brown glaze, 2-3/4", American 1863-1870, $275-375.

Stoneware figural female pig, two-tone brown glaze, 2-7/8" h. x 7-1/4" l., American 1875-1890, $140-180.

Figural Bottles

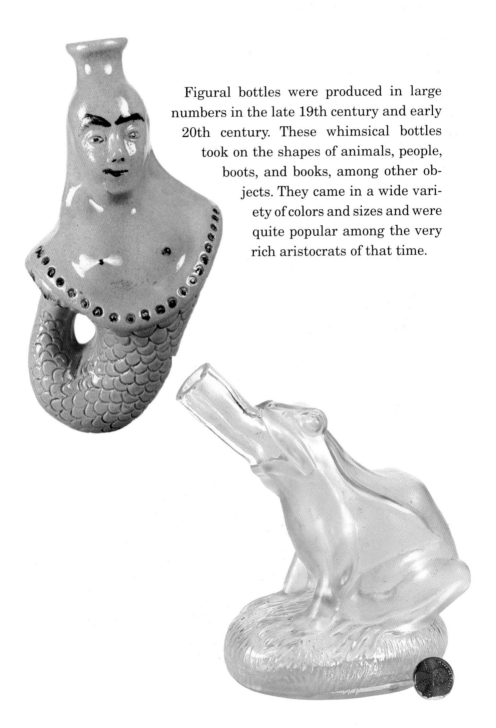

Figural bottles were produced in large numbers in the late 19th century and early 20th century. These whimsical bottles took on the shapes of animals, people, boots, and books, among other objects. They came in a wide variety of colors and sizes and were quite popular among the very rich aristocrats of that time.

Figural bear pomade jar, 3-3/4", American 1850-1870, $350-450.

Figural bottle, mermaid, yellow ware glaze, 7", English 1870-1890, $150-250.

Figural bottle, shore bird, milk glass, 12-1/2", American 1880-1900, $700-900.

Alligator

Milk glass, 10", pontil-scarred base, sheared and tooled mouth, French 1880-1910 ....**$275-375**

Applied Face Sitting Bear

Black olive amber, 10-1/4", smooth base, sheared and tooled lip, applied nose and mouth, American 1880-1895 ....**$400-600**

Bather on Rocks

Clear glass, 11-3/4", pontil-scarred base (depose), tooled mouth, glass stopper, French 1880-1915.......**$100-150**

Bear – Original label on bottom of Bear's paws reads: "Bears Oil"

Clear glass, 2" h., 4" l., smooth base (C.F. Knapp / Philada), tooled lip, American 1890-1910 ....**$200-300**

Bear – Original label on bottom of bear's paws reads: "Bears Oil"

Deep blue green, 2" h., 4" l., smooth base (C.F. Knapp / Philada), rough sheared unfinished lip, extremely rare, American 1890-1910 ....**$400-600**

Bearded Man Holding Bag and Broom

Clear glass, 7-1/2", smooth base, sheared lip, American 1890-1915...**$150-200**

Binoculars (Lot of two)

Clear glass, 2-3/4" and 3-5/8", taller example is embossed (PAT. / APLD / FOR) on both front lenses, rough sheared and ground lips, both have original brass fixtures, American 1890-1910 ....**$300-400**

Figural bottle, Columbus column, milk glass, 18-1/4", originally contained whiskey sold by James Sims and Company of Philadelphia, American 1893-1895, $400-600.

Columbus monument, 18", American 1893-1900, $300-450 (Patented by Julius Librowicz on January 19, 1993, orginally contained rye whiskey).

Figural Bunker Hill monument, 12", American 1860-1880, $200-300.

Bird Cage

Light teal blue, original gold paint, smooth base (PAT. / APL'D / FOR), glass lid, American 1920-1935 .... **$100-150**

Bust of the "Czarine"

Satin finish opaque milk glass, 10-1/2", pontil-scarred base (L), sheared and tooled lip, original blown ground glass head, French 1896, made to commemorate the 1896 visit of the Russian Czar and Czarine to Paris, France....................................... **$500-800**

Bust of the "Czar"

Satin finish opaque milk glass, 10-1/2", pontil-scarred base (L), sheared and tooled lip, original blown ground glass head, French 1896, made to commemorate the 1896 visit of Russian Czar and Czarine to Paris, France....................................... **$500-800**

Bust of Washington – "WASHINGTON – PAT APRIL 11, 1876"

Clear glass, 4-1/4", rough sheared and ground base, missing lid, American 1876 .... **$250-350**

Chick Hatching from Egg – "Easter"

Milk glass, original gold paint, 3-1/8", smooth base, American 1890-1910 .... **$100-150**

Child Hatching from Egg

Milk glass, 2-3/8", smooth base, ground lip, American 1890-1910.. **$80-120**

Child in Rocking Chair

Milk glass, 5-1/8", smooth base, sheared and ground lip, rare in milk glass, American 1880-1910 **$400-600**

Child on Tricycle

Clear glass, 4", smooth base, tooled lip, American 1890-1910.. **$90-125**

Figural Liberty Bell, "Proclaim Liberty Throughout All The Land – 1776 Exposition 1876, Patd Nov 17, 1874 by S.C. Upham Phila, 6", American, $250-300.

Figural of boy and girl climbing a tree, 11-3/4", French 1890-1915, $120-150.

Figural bottle, clown in moon, clear glass 10", French 1890-1915, $170-250.

Figural ear of corn, 9-3/4", American 1870-1880, $150-200.

Child in Long Dress

Clear glass, 7-1/2", smooth base, tooled lip, American 1890-1910.. **$90-125**

Clock – "Here Is To You / Merry Christmas / Happy / New Century / And / Many Of Them (clock face and the letters "BIC")

Opaque milk glass, 4-1/2", original gold paint, smooth base, ground lip, screw metal cap, scarce flask with original screw-on closure, American 1900.. **$400-600**

Clown in Moon – AU CLAIR DE LA LUNE – MON AM PIERROF (embossed on back side of the moon)

Clear glass, 10", pontil-scarred base, tooled lip, French 1890-1915.. **$170-250**

Cluster of Grapes

Cobalt blue, 5-1/2" l., sheared and ground lip, brass chain for hanging, European 1880-1910 .... **$150-200**

Coachman Bottle

Opaque milk glass, 10-3/8", smooth base, sheared and ground lip, rare, American 1880-1910.... **$1,200-1,600**

Dice Bottle

Opaque milk glass, 3-1/2", black dice numbers, top panel (Pat. MCH. 24 1891), smooth base, tooled lip, American 1890-1910 .... **$170-250**

Dressing Case – "Patent / T&C (monogram) / Dressing Case"

Clear glass, 5-3/8", smooth base, tooled mouth, rare, American 1890-1915 .... **$150-200**

Duck on Nest Candy Container

Clear glass with remains of original yellow, red, and blue paint, 2-3/4", original metal screw-on lid, rare, American 1915-1930 .... **$300-400**

Freeblown Mouse Bottle – Label on mouse's back reads: "Rose Geranium" and another label reads: "Love"

Opaque milk glass, 2-3/4" l., applied curved tail, ears, and red glass eyes, tooled mouth, American 1890-1910 .... **$200-275**

Klondyke Nugget Flask

Milk glass, 5-7/8", smooth base, ground lip, "Klondyke" on original metal screw-on cap, American 1900-1915 .... **$120-140**

Lion Bottle

Clear glass, 3-1/4", 4" l., smooth base, ground lip, American 1890-1910 .... **$120-140**

Figural bottle, frog, clear glass 5-1/2", German 1890-1915, $120-160.

Figural cottage bottle, 3-1/4", European 1920-1930, $60-90.

Figural bottle, cluster of asparagus, clear glass 12-1/2", European 1890-1915, $120-160.

Man in Night Cap Holding a Mug
Rockingham-type glaze, 8-3/4", smooth base (Manufacturer / Wadtincote), English 1860-1880 .... **$100-180**

Man Riding a Three-Wheel Bicycle
Man's torso made of clear glass, bicycle made of intricate twisted wire, cap is brass, 4-3/8", smooth base, sheared and ground lip, extremely rare, American 1890-1910 .... **$450-600**

Men Riding Tricycle (Lot of 2)
Clear glass, 4-1/4", pontil-scarred bases (HP), tooled lips, one has original multicolored paint, other has an original ground glass stopper, European 1890-1910 .... **$200-300**

Monk in Robe Bottle
Opaque milk glass, 9-1/4", smooth base, tooled mouth, European 1890-1910 .... **$200-300**

Octopus on Silver Dollar Flask
Milk glass flask with 95% original gold paint on the coin and red paint on the octopus, 4-1/2", smooth base, ground lip, original screw-on cap, American 1901 .... **$1,000-1,500**

Oriental Man Sitting Cross Legged on a Throne
Clear glass, 4-5/8", pontil-scarred base, tooled flared-out lip, very rare, French 1890-1910 .... **$275-375**

Figural four bust bottle, 10-1/4", European 1880-1900, $250-350.

Figural bottle, sitting monkey, milk glass 4-1/2", American 1885-1900, $250-350.

Oriental Man
Clear glass, 7-3/4", pontil-scarred base, tooled flared-out lips, both have the letter "PD" on the side at base, French 1890-1910 .... **$100-175**

Oriental Woman
Clear glass, 7-3/4", pontil-scarred base, tooled flared-out lips, both have the letter "PD" on the side at base, French 1890-1910 .... **$100-175**

Pickle Bottle
Teal blue, 4-1/2" l, smooth base, sheared and ground lip, American 1890-1910 .... **$80-140**

Portly Child with Hands in Pockets
Clear glass, 6-7/8", smooth base, tooled mouth, American 1890-1915 .... **$100-150**

Puss-in-Boot Candy Container
Milk glass, 3", missing closure, smooth base, American 1915-1930 .... **$80-120**

Sitting Monkey with Hat
Milk glass, 4-1/2", smooth base (T), tooled lip, rare, American 1885-1900 .... **$250-350**

Sitting Oriental Man Atomizer Bottle
Opaque milk glass body with "Oriental" embossed on front at base, 5-3/4", brass removable head, smooth base, sheared and ground lip, American 1890-1910 .... **$150-200**

Sitting Rabbit Bottle
Opaque milk glass, 7-1/8", smooth base, sheared and ground lip, European 1910 .... **$700-1,000**

Poodle Sitting Up on a Pedestal Bottle
Fiery opalescent milk glass, 7-1/8", pontil-scarred base, tooled lip, QT 425 embossed on side of pedestal, French 1850-1870 .... **$600-900**

Standing Indian Bottle (lot of two)
Clear glass, 5-1/4" and 8-1/8", pontil-scarred bases, tooled lips, French 1890-1910 .... **$200-350**

Figural cigar, From Isaac W. Keim – Dealer in Wines & Liquors – Reading, 5-1/4" l., American 1890-1900, $80-120.

Figural bottle, violin, amber 14-1/2", American 1870-1880, $250-350.

Figural Joan of Arc Praying at Stake, Jeanne D Arc, 14", French 1885-1910, $200-300.

Figural woman with basket, 10-1/8", American 1890-1915, $120-160.

Standing Man / Soldier Bottle

Cobalt blue, 7-1/4", pontil-scarred base, tooled flared-out lip, rare in cobalt blue, American 1890-1900 ....**$1,800-2,750**

Standing Woman Bottle (Lot of 2)

Clear, 7" and 7-3/4", pontil-scarred bases, tooled flared-out lips, French 1890-1910 ....**$200-300**

Uncle Sam Hat

Milk glass with original red and blue paint, 2-1/2", smooth base, tooled rim, original tin insert and cardboard closure that reads: "Republican Nominees, Wm. H. Taft, President" and "James S. Sherman, Vice President," American 1908.......**$600-800**

Violin Bottle

Fiery opalescent milk glass, 10-1/8", smooth base, ground lip, extremely rare, American 1890-1910 ....**$700-950**

Woman in Long Dress with Apron Bottle

Opaque milk glass, 11-1/8", smooth base, ground lip, rare, European 1890-1910 ....**$400-600**

Woman in a Robe Bottle

Opaque milk glass, 6-7/8", smooth base, tooled lip, American 1890-1910...**$275-375**

Yellow Kid Bottle – "Say / Ain't I Hot Stuff" (on back)

Opaque milk glass with frosted clear glass head, 6-1/2", 50% original yellow and black paint, smooth base, ground lip, extremely rare, American 1895-1905 ....**$1,500-2,500**

The Yellow Kid was created for Truth magazine in 1894 by Richard F. Outcault, who later worked for William Randolph Hearst.

Fire Grenades

Fire grenades are a highly prized item among bottle collectors and represent one of the first modern improvements in firefighting. A fire grenade is a water-filled bottle about the size of a baseball. Its use was simple. It was designed to be thrown into a fire, where it would break and—hopefully—extinguish the flames. The fire grenades worked best when the fire was noticed immediately.

The first American patent on a fire grenade was issued in 1863 to Alanson Crane of Fortress Monroe, Virginia. The best known manufacturer of these specialized bottles, the Halden Fire Extinguisher Co., Chicago, Illinois, was awarded a patent in August of 1871.

The grenades were manufactured in large numbers by companies with names as unique as the bottles themselves: Dash-Out, Diamond, Harkness Fire Destroyer, Hazelton's High Pressure Chemical Firekeg, Magic Fire, and Y-Burn. The fire grenade became obsolete with the invention of the fire extinguisher in 1905. Many of these grenades can still be found with the original closures, contents, and labels.

Babcock – Hand Grenade – Non – Freezing, medium cobalt blue, 7-1/2", American 1880-1895, $1,000-1,500.

Babcock – Hand Grenade – Non – Freezing, light amber, 7-1/2", American 1880-1895, $1,000-1,500.

Grenade / L'Urbaine, medium orange amber, 6-3/8", French 1880-1900, $400-600.

Acme – Fire / Ext'r – Pat'd / June 29th / 1869

Yellow amber, 6", smooth base, sheared and ground lip, very rare, American 1880-1895 .... **$1,500-2,500**

American / Fire / Extinguisher / Co. / Hand Grenade

Clear glass, 6-1/8", smooth base, tooled lip, original light blue contents, rare, American 1870-1895 .... **$600-900**

Babcock / Hand Grenade / Non-Freezing / Manufactured By American LA France Fire Engine Co. / Elmira N.Y.

Light aqua, 7-1/2", smooth base, sheared and tooled lip, extremely rare, American 1880-1895 .... **$600-800**

Barnum's / Hand Fire / Ext. – Diamond – Pat'd / June 26th / 1869 – Diamond

Blue aqua, 6", smooth base (diamond), tooled lip, original contents, American 1885-1900 .... **$700-1,000**

Barnum's / Hand Fire / Ext. – Diamond – Pat'd / June 26th / 1869 – Diamond

Yellow amber, 6-1/8", smooth base (diamond), tooled lip, original contents, rare, American 1870-1895 .... **$800-1,200**

C. & NW. RY (Chicago & Northwest Railroad)

Clear glass, 17-3/4", tube-style grenade, smooth rounded base, rough and sheared ground lip, American 1885-1900 .... **$140-180**

California Fire Extinguisher (walking bear in panel)

Medium amber, 6-5/8", horizontal rib pattern with label panel on reverse, smooth base, applied mouth, American 1885-1900, only fire grenade made in California **$3,500-5,500**

Diamond – Fire / Ext'r – PAT'D / June 29th / 1869 – Diamond

Yellow amber, 6", smooth base, tooled lip, American 1870-1895 .... **$1,500-2,500**

Du Progres – Grenades – Extinctives – Grenades

Medium yellow amber, 5-1/8", pontil-scarred base (TC 2367), tooled lip, rare, German 1880-1900 .... **$375-475**

Fire Grenade and Rack – Grenade / Unic / Extinctrice, medium amber, rib-pattern, 5-5/8", French 1885-1900, $400-500.

Grenade/Francaise, bright lime green, 6-5/8", French 1889-1900, $800-1,200.

Fire Grenade – Label only reads: Patented Aug. 8th 1871 / Liquid / Patented Sept. 19th 1876 / and / February 5th 1878 / Improved 1881

Deep cobalt blue, 6-1/8", smooth base, sheared and ground lip, American 1870-1895 ....**$375-475**

Fire Grenade – PAT NOV / 28, 1884

Yellow amber, 6-1/4", smooth base, sheared and ground lip, original neck seal and contents, Canadian 1884-1895...**$250-300**

Fire Grenade – PSN (monogram)

Amber, 7", smooth base, rough sheared lip, American 1870-1895 ....**$250-350**

Flagg's / Fire / Extinguisher – Pat'd Aug. 4th 1868

Yellow amber, 5-7/8", smooth base, rough sheared lip, American 1870-1895 ....**$600-800**

Flagg's / Fire / Extinguisher – Pat'd Aug. 4th 1868

Yellow amber, 6-1/2", smooth base, sheared and ground lip, rare specimen of the two Flagg variants with the horizontal Pat'd Aug 4th 1868 embossing, American 1870-1895..**$600-800**

Francaise / Grenade

Bright lime green, 6-5/8", rib pattern and below center band, smooth base (GF/14) sheared and ground lip, original contents, extremely rare, French 1889-1900 ....**$800-1,200**

Grenade / L.B., medium turquoise blue, 5-1/8", French 1880-1900, $800-1,200.

Hand / Letter "H" inside a shield / Grenade, deep cobalt blue, 6-1/4", English 1880-1900, $800-1,200.

Grenade / L.B.
Medium turquoise blue, 5-1/8", vertical rib pattern, smooth base, sheared and ground lip, original contents, French 1880-1900 ....**$800-1,200**

Grenade / Unic / Extingtrice (embossed on four indented circular panels)
Orange amber, 5-1/2", vertical rib pattern, smooth base, sheared and ground lip, French 1880-1900 ....**$350-450**

Hand / (letter "H" inside a shield) Grenade
Deep cobalt blue, 6-1/4", raised hobnails around entire grenade, smooth base (RD No 421256) sheared and ground lip, extremely rare due to hobnails, English 1880-1900 ....**$800-1,200**

Harden's Improved – Grenade Fire – Extinguisher PAT – Oct 7th 1884
Cobalt blue, 2-1/2", smooth base (2) rough sheared and ground lip, American 1885-1900 ....**$120-160**

Harden's Hand / Extinguisher / Grenada / Patented
Medium cobalt blue, 4-7/8", footed smooth base, rough sheared and ground lip, original contents, scarce in this color and size, American 1885-1900 ....**$140-180**

Harden's Hand / Fire / Extinguisher / Grenada – Patented
Turquoise blue, 5-1/8", footed smooth base, rough sheared and ground lip, original contents, American 1885-1900...**$120-140**

Harden's Improved / Hand Grenade / PAT'D OCT / NO. 1 / 1884 / Fire Extinguisher (on two of three sections)
Three-section grenade: two sections are clear glass, the third section is amber, 3-7/8", smooth bases, referred to as a cluster grenade and is considered the most rare of all fire grenades, American 1885-1900 ....**$700-900**

New York / Hayward Hand Grenade – Fire Extinguisher – American 1880-1900, $300-400.

Hayward Hand Grenade Fire Extinguisher – No 407 Broadway New York, deep grape amethyst, 6", American 1875-1895, $800-1,400.

Harden's Improved – Grenade Fire-Extinguisher PAT OCT 7th 1884 (embossed on both sections) Label reads: Throw This Genade so as to Break it / and Deliver its Contents into the Fire / Harden's / Nest / Grenade / Fire / Extinguisher / Manufactured / At / 247 / So. Canal St. / Chicago, Ill

Two clear glass sections held together by copper wire, 4-7/8", "No. 3" on one base and "97" orange and black label on other, both sections have rough and sheared lips, grenade is rarely seen with original wire and label, American 1885-1900 .... **$375-450**

Harden's Hand / Fire / Extinguisher / Grenada – Patented / No 1 / Aug 8, 1871 / Aug 14, 1883

Turquoise blue, 6-1/4", footed base (2), rough sheared and ground lip, American 1885-1900...**$80-150**

Harden's Hand / Fire / Extinguisher / Grenada – Patented / No 1 / Aug 8, 1871 / Aug 14, 1883

Turquoise blue, 6-1/4", footed base, rough sheared and ground lip, original contents, 97% – Label reads: "How To Use," American 1885-1900..........................**$80-150**

Harden's Hand / Fire / Extinguisher – Patented (original contents and top of mouth label reads: Semper Paratos (grenade) Trade Mark

Turquoise blue, 6-1/4", footed base, rough sheared and ground lip, American 1885-1900 ....**$80-120**

Hayward Hand Grenade Fire Extinguisher – New York, medium cobalt blue, 5-7/8", American 1880-1895, $250-350.

Imperial Fire Extinguisher Co. – Fire Grenade – Providence, R.I., cobalt blue, 6-1/4", American 1875-1900, $400-600.

Hayward's / Hand / Fire / Grenade – Patented / Aug / 8 / 1871 – S.F. Hayward / 407 / Broadway / N.Y. (in diamond panel) – Original red lettering on black background label reads: In case of fire throw or break the grenade so that the contents will be scattered over the flames

Yellow amber, 6", smooth base (3), tooled lip, original contents, American 1877-1895 ....**$300-400**

Hazelton's / High Pressure / Chemical / Fire Keg

Yellow amber, keg form, 11", smooth base, tooled lip, original contents, metal neck band and handle, American 1885-1900 ....**$250-300**

Hazelton's / High Pressure / Chemical / Fire Keg – Label on base reads: In Case of Fire Break Keg Upon the Flames, Frank R. Hazelton, Concord, N.H. Patent Applied For

Orange amber, 11-1/8", barrel form, smooth base, tooled mouth, American 1885-1900 ....**$250-375**

Healy's Hand Fire – Extinguisher

Olive yellow, 10-3/4", smooth base, tooled lip, American 1880-1895 ....**$800-1,000**

Imperial / Hand D.R.P. Granate (inside a belt) / Fire / Feverloscher

Medium yellow green, 6-1/2", smooth base, sheared and ground lip, European 1885-1900 ....**$180-175**

Sinclair's Hand Grenade, deep cobalt blue, 7-1/2", English 1880-1900, $175-275.

Pat Nov / 28 1884, yellow amber, 6-1/8", Canadian 1884-1900, $500-700.

Little Giant / Fire Extinguisher – Label reads: The Automatic Fire Extinguisher, Buffalo, N.Y. Directions – Place this extinguisher where fire is most likely to occur. The fuse will ignite and break it.
Aqua pint, 6-1/2", smooth base, tooled mouth, American 1885-1900...**$700-1,000**

P.R.R. (Pennsylvania Railroad Fire Grenade)
Clear glass, 7-1/8", horizontal rib pattern, original contents, rare, American 1880-1895 ....**$800-1,200**

Pronto Fire Extinguisher – The Allen Corporation, New York, Stops Fire Quick (label only)
Amber, 11", ABM lip, American early 20th Century.......................................**$50-75**

Pyrofite Fluid Fire Extinguisher, Pull Cork Dash Contents on Fire, by C.J. Cross M'F'G'Co. New York (label only)
Aqua, 11", smooth base (Pyrofite on side of base), tooled lip, American 1900-1920 ....**$75-100**

Pyrofite Fluid Fire Extinguisher, Pull Cork Dash Contents on Fire, by C.J. Cross M'F'G'Co. New York (label only)
Clear, 11", smooth base (Pyrofite on side of base), ABM lip, American 1900-1920 ....**$75-100**

Pyrofite Fluid Fire Extinguisher, Pull Cork Dash Contents on Fire, by C.J. Cross M'F'G'Co. New York (label only)
Amber, 11", smooth base (EXO 5 on side of base), ABM lip, American 1900-1920 ....**$75-100**

Fire Grenades (set of two), medium green,
5-5/8", French 1885-1900, $700-900.

Securite – Extincteur – Grenade
Yellow copper amber, 5-5/8", twisted rib pattern above and below center band, smooth base, sheared and ground lip, very rare, fewer than five known examples, French 1880-1900 ....**$400-600**

Sinclair & Co, Hand Grenade, 19 Elson St. London (label only)
Deep cobalt blue, 7-1/4", smooth base (tool), sheared and ground lip, original monogram impressed neck seal and contents, English 1880-1900..........**$375-475**

(Star inside an embossed star) / Harden Hand Grenade – Fire Extinguisher
Deep yellow green, 6-1/4", smooth base, sheared and ground lip, original neck plug and contents, very rare in this color, American 1880-1895 ....**$800-1,200**

(Star inside an embossed star) / Harden Star Hand Grenade – Fire Extinguisher
Clear glass with some aqua, 6-3/4", smooth base (10490), rough sheared and ground lip, original contents, English 1885-1900......................................**$250-350**

(Star inside an embossed Star) / Harden Hand Grenade – Fire Extinguisher
Turquoise blue, 6-3/4", smooth base, rough sheared and ground lip, American 1885-1900..**$140-250**

(Star inside an embossed star) / Harden Hand Grenade – Fire Extinguisher
Clear glass, quart, 8-1/4", smooth base (May 27, 84), sheared and tooled lip, American 1885-1900 ....**$600-900**

(Star inside an embossed star) / Harden Grenade / S.P. Rinkler
Deep cobalt blue, 17-3/4", tubular grenade, smooth base (RD / NO.60064), tooled lip, original contents and metal pull ring, English 1885-1900..................**$800-1,200**

The Imperial Grenade -
Fire - Extinguisher (with
original metal carrier)
(English), 1880-1900,
6-5/8", $600-800.

The / Harden / Star (inside a star) / Tubular / Grenade

Clear glass, 17-3/4", tubular grenade, smooth round bottom, sheared and tooled lip, original contents and cast iron wall mounts, American 1885-1900 .... **$350-450**

The Imperial Grenade (inside a belt) / Fire / Extinguisher

Medium yellow green, 6-1/2", smooth base, rough sheared lip, part original contents and red neck foil, English 1885-1900 .... **$250-300**

The Kalamazoo / Automatic And / Hand Fire Extinguisher

Cobalt blue, 11-1/8", smooth base, tooled lip, American 1880-1895 .... **$300-400**

The Royal Grenade / Fire / Extinguisher – Patent Applied For / June 1884

Medium cobalt blue, 5-1/4", four circular raised panels and overall raised hobnail pattern, smooth base, sheared and ground lip, extremely rare, Canadian 1884-1895 .... **$2,500-3,500**

Unembossed Fire Grenade

Yellow amber, 6-1/8", smooth base, rough sheared lip, original contents, rare, Canadian 1885-1895 .... **$375-450**

Vertical Rib Pattern Fire Grenade

Deep olive green, 6-3/4", vertical rib pattern around entire grenade, smooth base has grooves for a metal rack, outward rolled lip, rare, American 1885-1890 .... **$350-450**

W. D. Allen – Manufacturing – Company – Chicago – Illinois (crescent moon)

Cobalt blue, 8-1/8", melon sided, smooth base, ground lip, rare, American 1880-1895 .... **$1,500-2,500**

Whiz Fire Extinguisher – The R.M. Hollingshead Co, Camden, N.J. (label only)

Amber, 11", ABM lips, American early 20th Century **$50-75**

Flasks

Flasks have become a most popular and prized item among collectors due to the variety of decorative, historical, and pictorial depictions on many pieces. The outstanding colors have a major effect on the value of these pieces, more so than most other collectible bottles.

American flasks were first manufactured by the Pitkin Glasshouse in Connecticut around 1815, and quickly spread to other glasshouses around the country. Early flasks were freeblown and represent some of the better craftsmanship with more intricate designs. By 1850, approximately 400 designs had been used. Black graphite pontil marks were left on the bottles because the pontils were coated with powdered iron, allowing the flask's bottom to break away without damaging the glass. The flasks made between 1850 and 1870, however, had no such markings because of the widespread use of the newly invented snapcase.

Since flasks were intended to be refilled with whiskey or other spirits, more time and effort was expended in manufacturing than most other types of bottles. Flasks soon became a popular item for use with all types of causes and promotions. Mottos frequently were embossed on flasks and included

a number of patriotic sayings and slogans. George Washington's face commonly appeared on flasks, as did Andrew Jackson's and John Quincy Adams's, the candidates for the presidential elections of 1824 and 1828. Events of the time were also portrayed on flasks.

One of the more controversial flasks was the Masonic flasks, which bore the order's emblem on one side and the American eagle on the other side. At first, the design drew strong opposition from the public, but the controversy soon passed, and Masonic flasks are now a specialty items for collectors.

Another highly collectible flask was the Pitkin-type flasks named for the Pitkin Glassworks, where it was exclusively manufactured. While Pitkin-type flask and ink bottles are common, Pitkin bottles, jugs, and jars are very rare. German Pitkin flasks are heavier and straight-ribbed, while the American patterns are swirled and broken-ribbed with unusual colors such as dark blue.

Because flasks were widely used for promoting various political and special interest agendas, they represent a major historical record of the people and events of those times.

Label under glass, A Merry Christmas / And / Happy New Year, Good Luck, clear glass, 6-1/8", American $150-200.

Label under glass, A Merry Christmas / Happy New Year, clear glass, 6", American $500-700.

A Merry Christmas – And Happy New Year (label under glass with Santa Claus)

Clear, 6", smooth base, screw top with cap, ground lip American 1905-1915 .... **$1,000-1,300**

A Merry Christmas – Cooking Good Stuff – Happy New Year (label under glass)

Clear, 6", smooth base, screw top with pewter cap, ground lip American 1905-1915 .... **$550-650**

A. Livingston – Wholesale and Retail – Carson City, Nev

Clear, pint, smooth base, tooled top, rare, American 1885-1905 .... **$1,000-1,300**

A.M. Smith's – A.D. 1892 249 Hen. Av. – Minneapolis Minn. – California Wine Depot

Clear, 4-1/2", pumpkinseed form, smooth base, tooled top, American 1880-1895 .... **$100-160**

H.C. Heidtmann – Becker's – Reno, Nev

Clear, half-pint, coffin flask form, smooth base, tooled top, American 1900-1918 .... **$650-850**

Baltimore / Anchor / Glass Works – Bird Above Flames / Resurgam

Yellow amber, pint, smooth base, applied double collar mouth, scarce color, American 1865-1870, Baltimore Glass Works, Baltimore, Maryland **$500-800**

A. Livingston – Wholesale & Retail – Carson City, Nev, clear, pint, American 1865-1875, $1,000-1,300.

Bininger's / Travelers / Guide / A.M. Bininger & Co. / No 19 Broad St. NY, medium golden amber, 6-7/8", American 1860-1875, $600-800.

Columbus / bust of Columbus coming out of a barrel / on a barrel (rooster), pale aqua, 5-3/4", American 1890-1900, $300-400.

Bininger's / Travelers / Guide / A.M. Bininger & Co / No 19 Broad St NY
Medium golden amber, 6-7/8", teardrop flask, smooth base, applied double collar mouth, American 1860-1875 ....**$600-800**

Bust of Man in Military Uniform – Falcon with Crown
Cobalt blue, pint, pontil-scarred base, sheared and tooled mouth, European 1840-1860 ....**$180-250**

Bust of Columbia – Eagle / B&W
Blue aqua, pint, open pontil, sheared and tooled lip, American 1835-1845.... **$275-375**

Bust Of Washington – Tree
Cobalt blue, calabash, open pontil, applied mouth, extremely rare, one of three known examples, American 1855-1860 ....**$15,000-20,000**

But For Joe (in banner) Woman on a Bicycle
Blue aqua, pint, smooth base, applied ringed mouth, American 1875-1885 ....**$200-250**

Columbus / (bust of Columbus coming out of a barrel) on a Barrel – (rooster)
Pale aqua, 5-3/4", half-barrel form, smooth base, tooled lip, rare, American 1890-1900 ....**$300-400**

Columbian Exposition / Bust Of Columbus / 1893 / A.E. Bros & Co – Pennsylvania / Pure Rye / Baker Whiskey
Amber, 6-3/4", pumpkinseed form, smooth base, tooled mouth, rare, American 1893-1895..**$400-600**

G. Lewis – Liquor Co. – Silver State – Victor, Colo., clear, half-pint, American 1870-1880, $700-1,000.

Exchange – Flood & Barks Props. – Main 187 – Bakersfield, clear, pumpkinseed, pint, American 1870-1885, $100-150.

Eagle / C.T. Bond (in circle) – C.T. Bond / Merchant & Trader / New Albany / Miss
Yellow with amber tone, half-pint, smooth base, applied ringed mouth, extremely rare, one of two known examples, American 1865-1875 .... **$5,000-7,000**

Eagle / Granite / Glass Co – Eagle / Stoddard N.H.
Deep amber, pint, pontil-scarred base, sheared and tooled mouth, American 1850-1860 .... **$300-400**

Eagle – New London / (anchor) Glass Works (historical flask)
Brilliant yellow olive, pint, large red iron pontil mark, applied double collared mouth, rare color and rare iron pontil, American 1856-1860, New London Glass Works, New London, Connecticut **$2,000-4,000**

Eagle – Morning Glory
Blue aqua, pint, pontil-scarred base, sheared and tooled lip, American 1830-1840 .... **$700-1,000**

Eagle (embossed) – Louisville / KY / Glass Works
Dark amber, half-pint, vertically ribbed flask, smooth base, applied top with ring, American 1860-1865 .... **$1,500-3,000**

Exchange – Flood & Barks Prop. – Tel. Main 187 – Bakersfield
Clear, pint, pumpkinseed form, smooth base, tooled top, American 1885-1895 .... **$100-160**

Frank Abadie – Wholesale Liquors – Eureka, Nev
Clear, pint, smooth base, tooled top, American 1884 -1886 .... **$100-1600**

G. Lewis – Liquor – Co. – Silver State – Victor, Colo
Clear, half-pint, smooth base, tooled top, American 1880-1895 .... **$700-1,000**

Corn For The World / ear of corn / monument / Baltimore, deep pink puce, quart, American 1865-1875, $2,500-4,000.

Geo. W. Robinson / Dog's Head / No 8 Main St / Wheeling W. VA

Blue aqua, strap-sided pint, smooth base, applied mouth, American 1870-1880 .... **$150-200**

Geo. W. Robinson / No 75 / Main St. W. VA

Blue aqua, strap-sided quart, smooth base, applied mouth, American 1870-1880 .... **$140-180**

Grotesque Face – Two Men Talking

Cobalt blue, half-pint, pontil-scarred base, sheared and tooled lip, rare, European 1850-1860 .. **$400-600**

Henry Chapman & Co. – Sole Agents – Montreal

Golden amber, 5-3/4", teardrop form, smooth base, ground lip, American 1870-1885 .... **$75-100**

In Silver We Trust / Bust Of Bryan / Bryan 1896 Sewall – United Democratic Ticket / We Shall Vote / American Eagle / 61 to 1

Medium amber, half-point, 5-1/4", smooth base, tooled lip, rare political flask made for the Presidential election of 1896, American 1896 .... **$600-800**

Isabella / Anchor / Glass Works – Factory

Blue aqua, quart, open pontil, sheared and tooled lip, American 1855-1865 .... **$275-375**

J.R. & Son – Scroll Flask

Pale Ice blue, pint, scroll in a corseted form, pontil-scarred base, sheared top, American 1830-1840, John Robinson and Son Manufacturers, Pittsburgh, Pennsylvania **$350-750**

Label Under Glass Pocket Flask – Photograph of Gentlemen – Compliments of J.P. Haddox – Winchester, VA

Clear, 5", smooth base, screw top lid with cap, American 1885-1915 .... **$1,500-1,600**

Label Under Glass Pocket Flask – Victorian Man and Woman Holding Hands

Clear, 5", smooth base, screw top lid with cap, American 1885-1915 .... **$450-550**

Label Under Glass Pocket Flask – Photograph of Victorian Woman

Clear, 5", smooth base, screw top lid with cap, American 1885-1910 .... **$1,700-1,900**

Label Under Glass Pocket Flask – Photograph of Beautiful Woman – For Fine Old Rye Whiskey

Clear, 5", smooth base, screw top lid with cap, American 1885-1910 .... **$600-800**

Label Under Glass Pocket Flask – Photograph of Naval Officer – Remember The Maine
Clear, 5-1/4", smooth base, screw top lid with cap, American 1885-1915 .... **$600-800**

Label Under Glass Pocket Flask – Photograph of Provocative Posing Woman
Clear, 5-3/4", smooth base, screw top lid with cap, American 1885-1910 .... **$1,700-1,900**

Label Under Glass Pocket Flask – Kaiser Wilhelm I. Denkmal A.D. Wittekinberg B / Perta Building
Clear, 5-3/4", smooth base, screw top lid with cap, American 1885-1920 .... **$90-110**

Label Under Glass Pocket Flask – Photograph of Provocative Posing Woman
Clear, 6", smooth base, screw top lid with cap, American 1880-1905 .... **$1,500-1,700**

Label Under Glass Pocket Flask – Photograph of Provocative Woman in Attire
Clear, 6", smooth base, screw top lid with cap, American 1885-1910 .... **$1,100-1,300**

Label Under Glass Pocket Flask – Beautiful Woman Lifting Up Her Dress
Clear, 6", smooth base, screw top lid with cap, American 1885-1920 .... **$1,300-1,400**

Label Under Glass Pocket Flask – Beautiful Victorian Woman Holding Roses
Clear, 6", smooth base, screw top lid with cap, American 1885-1915 .... **$600-800**

Label Under Glass Pocket Flask – G.W. Schmidt / Merry Christmas / (pretty woman in Victorian dress) / Happy New Year / Pittsburgh, Pa
Clear glass, 6-1/4", horizontal side ribbing, smooth base, sheared and tooled lip, original metal screw cap and neck chain, extremely rare, American 1885-1910 .... **$700-900**

Label Under Glass Pocket Flask – Theodore Roosevelt (Stars & Stripes background)
Clear, 6-1/2", smooth base, screw top lid with cap, American 1885-1920 .... **$450-550**

Layfayette – Liberty Cap Portrait Flask
Brilliant aquamarine, half-pint, pontil-scarred base, sheared mouth, extremely rare, American 1824-1825 Coventry Glass Works, Coventry, Connecticut **$5,000-10,000**

Label under glass, G.W. Schmidt / Merry Christmas / pretty woman in Victorian dress / Happy New Year / Pittsburgh, PA, clear glass, 6-1/4", American 1885-1910, $700-900.

A Merry Christmas (woman on a barrel) / And A / Happy New Year (rooster), clear glass, 7-3/4", American 1890-1900, $150-200.

Liberty / Eagle – Willington / Glass / Co / West Willington / Conn

Olive amber, half-pint, smooth base, applied double collar mouth, American 1855-1875 .... **$200-250**

M. Heims – 139 – Washington St. Indianapolis

Clear, half-pint, pumpkinseed form, lattice design, smooth base, tooled top, American 1895-1905 .... **$100-120**

Mellow Rib Pattern Flask

Yellow green, pint, 6-1/4", 20-vertical rib pattern, pontil-scarred base, sheared and tooled lip, American 1820-1830 .... **$800-1,200**

Merry Christmas – And – Happy New Year

Clear, 4", half-pint, floral design and decoration, smooth base, tooled top, American 1885-1895 .... **$100-200**

Mountain Dew (label under glass with pretty woman)

Clear, pint, smooth base, screw top (with cap), American 1910-1930 .... **$150-250**

Nailsea Flask

Clear glass with white looping, 6-3/8", polished pontil, tooled mouth, European 1850-1880 .... **$150-250**

North / American (inside map of North America) / Pan-American / South / American (inside a map of South America)

Clear, 7", smooth base, ground lip, original metal screw-on cap and screw-on shot glass cover, American 1901 .... **$350-450**

Old Rye – Wheeling / VA

Medium blue green, pint, smooth base, applied mouth, rare, American 1865-1875 .... **$600-800**

Patent – Label reads: Cognac Brandy, George L. Forbush, Pharmacist, Petersboro, New Hampshire

Yellow amber, pint, smooth base, applied double collar mouth, American 1870-1880 .... **$150-200**

Pattern Molded Flask

Clear, 7-3/8", 19-ogival pattern, pontil-scarred base, sheared and tooled wide mouth, American 1815-1825 .... **$400-700**

Pike's Peak / Prospector – Eagle

Deep blue aqua, quart, pontil-scarred base, applied mouth, American 1870-1875 .... **$140-180**

Pitkin Flask
Dark amber, 5-3/4", pint, 36 ribs swirled to the left, flattened clockface form, pontil-scarred base, sheared top, American 1800-1830 .... **$500-1,000**

Pitkin Flask
Light green aqua, 5-3/8", 30-broken rib pattern swirled to right, open pontl, sheared and tooled lip, American 1790-1810 .... **$400-600**

Pitkin Flask
Medium yellow olive green, 5-3/4", 36-broken rib pattern swirled to right, open pontil, sheared and tooled lip, American 1790-1810 .... **$600-800**

Pitkin Flask with early label (Bourbon Whiskey / Sold by Frank R. Hadley / Druggist & Chemist / New Bedford, Mass
Light olive green, 7", ribbed and swirled to left, 36-ribs, pontil-scarred base, sheared mouth, American 1783-1830, Pitkin Glass Works, Manchester, Connecticut **$1,250-2,500**

Popular – Cocktails – Rheinstron Bros. – Cincinnati USA – (two drinks embossed on reverse side)
Clear, half-pint, horseshoe shape, smooth base, screw top with pewter cap and ground and polished lip, American 1905-1915 .... **$75-120**

Return To Joe Gribble – Old Crow Saloon – Douglas, AZ.
Clear, 6", half-pint, smooth base, screw top cap with ground lip, very rare, American 1903 .... **$3,500-4,500**

Scroll Flask
Medium to deep amber, pint, red iron pontil, applied mouth, American 1845-1855 .... **$1,200-1,500**

Scroll Flask
Deep teal blue, pint, pontil-scarred base, sheared and tooled lip, American 1845-1855 .... **$4,000-5,000**

Sloop / Star
Aqua, half-pint, open pontil, sheared and tooled lip, American 1825-1835 .... **$150-200**

Soldier / Balt. MD – Ballet Dancer / Chapman
Emerald green, pint, open pontil, sheared and tooled lip, rare, American 1850-1865, Chapman's Maryland Glass Works....................................... **$1,400-1,800**

Spring Garden / Anchor / Glass Works – Cabin
Orange amber, pint, smooth base, applied double collar mouth, American 1860-1870, Spring Garden Glassworks, Baltimore, Maryland **$700-1,000**

Patrick Smith - 1313 - Sec. Ave. - NW Corner 69th St. - New York - One - Half Pint - Full Measure, 1890-1910, half-pint, $80-150.

Spirits Flask (blown)

Fiery opalescent milk glass, 4-5/8", multicolored enamel floral and bird decorations, rectangular with beveled corner panes, pontil-scarred base, sheared lip, original pewter mouth band, blown using German half-post method, German 1770-1800 ....**$400-600**

Sprits Flask (blown)

Deep cobalt blue, 5-3/8", multicolored enamel decorations of a man in colonial dress holding a glass on one side and German script writing on other side, pontil-scarred base, sheared lip, original threaded pewter mouth band, blown using German half-post method, German 1770-1800..**$500-900**

Sprits Flask (blown)

Light to medium cobalt blue, 6-7/8", tight broken rib-pattern slightly swirled to right, pontil-scarred base, tooled mouth, blown using German half-post method, European 1770-1800..**$275-375**

Spirits Flask

Sapphire blue, 6-1/4", white looping conical form tapering from a larger base to smaller neck, pontil-scarred base, applied pewter mouth with screw threads, Southern German 1760-1780 ....**$2,500-3,500**

Separation of Military Duty – Werbreu gedient hal seine Zeit Dem sei einvoller Kruggeweihl (He who diligently gave his time deserves a drink. Drink to this. In memory of the time I served in Cuxhaven 1907-10), milk glass, German 1910, $140-180.

Spirits Flask

Light purple amethyst, 7-5/8", white looping, rectangular form with wide beveled corner panels, pontil-scarred base, applied pewter mouth with screw threads, Southern German 1760-1780 .... **$1,200-1,600**

Spirits Flask

Deep cobalt blue, 7-5/8", white looping, rectangular form with wide beveled corner panels, pontil-scarred base, applied pewter mouth with screw threads, Southern German 1760-1780 .... **$1,400-1,800**

Spirits Flask

Purple amethyst, 7-1/2", white herringbone pattern, pontil-scarred base, applied pewter mouth with screw threads, Southern German 1760-1780.... **$800-1,200**

Spirits Flask

Honey amber, 6", white looping, rectangular form with wide beveled corner panels, pontil-scarred base, applied pewter mouth with screw threads, Southern German 1760-1780 .... **$1,200-1,600**

Standing Deer / Good / Game – Willow Tree

Aqua, pint, open pontil, sheared and tooled lip, American 1825-1835, Coffin & Hays Glass Works, Hammonton, New Jersey........................... **$275-375**

Standing Stag – Boar's Head, Horn, Rifle and Sword

Purple amethyst, 5-3/8", pontil-scarred base, inward rolled lip, European 1840-1870 .... **$400-600**

Stiegel-Type Spirits Flask

Clear, 4-3/4", multi-colored enamel decoration of a rabbit playing a drum on one side and German script on the other side, scarred base, tooled mouth with original pewter neck ring, blown in Geman half-post method, German 1770-1810 .... **$350-450**

Stiegiel-Type Spirits Flask

Deep purple amethyst, 5-3/4", 1-rib pattern swirled to left, pontil-scarred base, tooled lip, blown in German half-post method, German 1780-1810....... **$500-700**

Summer Tree – Winter Tree

Yellow olive, quart, pontil-scarred base, applied double collar mouth, rare, American 1850-1860 .... **$2,500-3,500**

Sunburst Flask

Medium olive green, half-pint, pontil-scarred base, tooled mouth, American 1815-1825........... **$500-700**

Sunburst flask, 1850-1850, 5-5/8", $300-400.

The Waldorf & Tavern – Reno, Nevada, clear, 10 oz., American 1910, $200-250.

Sunburst Flask

Medium yellow olive amber, half-pint, pontil-scarred base, tooled mouth, American 1815-1825 . **$500-700**

Scroll Flask

Yellow green, quart, iron pontil, sheared lip, American 1840-1850 .... **$500-700**

The Log Cabin (embossed log cabin) – 167-3rd St. Portland Ore. – Billy Winters Pro

Clear, pint, pumpkinseed form, smooth base, tooled top, American 1885-1895 .... **$325-425**

The Waldorf Cafes – Becker Bros. Inc. – San Francisco – Los Angeles – San Diego – 1915

Clear, pint, smooth base, tooled top, American 1915 .... **$100-120**

The Waldorf & Tavern – Reno, Nevada

Clear, 10 oz., smooth base, tooled top, American 1910-1915... **$200-250**

The – F.G. McCoy Co. Inc – The Wellington Saloon – Prescott, Ariz.

Clear, 6", half-pint, smooth base (Design Pat. Aug 9, 1898), tooled top, American 1902-1906..... **$700-900**

Thos. Taylor & Co – Sole Agents P. Vollmer's Old Bourbon Louisville – Virginia, Nev.

Clear, pint, coffin flask form, smooth base, tooled top, American 1867-1883 .... **$1,000-2,000**

Traveler's / Star / Companion – Ravenna / Star / Glass Co.

Blue aqua, pint, smooth base, applied ringed mouth, American 1855-1870 .... **$150-250**

Traveler's / Companion – Star

Deep amber, half-pint, iron pontil, sheared and tooled mouth, American 1850-1860 .... **$500-700**

Union / Clasped Hands / FA & CO / Cannon

Amber, pint, smooth base, applied ringed mouth, American 1860-1870, Fahnestock, Albree & Co. Glassworks, Pittsburgh, PA **$275-375**

Union Saloon – John Flack Propr. – San Bernardino

Deep purple, pint, smooth base, tooled top with glass stopper, American 1885-1905................... **$350-450**

Vertical Rib Pattern Flask with Oval Indented Panels

Aqua, pint, 8", pontil-scarred base, sheared and tooled lip, American 1835-1845, Louisville Glass Works, Louisville, Kentucky **$200-275**

Wharton's / Whisky / 1850 / Chestnut Grove, cobalt blue, 5-3/8", American 1855-1870, $350-450.

Wharton's / Whisky / 1850 / Chestnut Grove, dark amber, 5-1/4", American 1855-1870, $250-350.

W.A. Gaines & Cos. – The Capitol Old Crow Whiskey – Cheyenne Wyo.

Clear, pint, smooth base, screw top, American 1900-1920 .... **$100-200**

Washington Bar – Coleman & Granger – Tonopah, Nevada

Clear, pint, smooth base, screw top, American 1905-1806 .... **$300-500**

Westford Glass / Westford / Conn – Sheaf Of Grain

Dark amber, half-pint, smooth base, applied double collar mouth, American 1855-1865 .... **$120-160**

Wharton's Whisky – 1850 Chestnut Grove

Medium cobalt blue, 5-1/4", teardrop form, smooth base, applied lip, American 1865-1875 .... **$350-550**

Zanesville / City / Glassworks

Yellow amber, pint, smooth base, applied mouth, rare, American 1875-1885, Zanesville Glass Works, Zanesville, Ohio **$500-700**

Zanesville / City / Glassworks, yellow amber, pint, rare, American 1875-1885, $500-700.

Food and Pickle Bottles

Food bottles are one of the largest and most diverse categories in the field of collectible bottles. They were made for the commercial sale of a wide variety of food products excluding beverages, except milk. Food bottles are an ideal specialty for the beginning collector, since they are so readily available. Many collectors are attracted to food bottles for their historical value. Nineteenth and early twentieth century magazines and newspapers contained so many illustrated advertisements for food products that many collectors keep scrapbooks of ads as an aid to dating and pricing the bottles.

Before bottling, food could not be transported long distances or kept for long periods of time on account of spoilage. Bottling revolutionized the food industry and began a new chapter in American business merchandising and distribution. With the glass bottle, producers were able to save labor, use portion packaging, and sell from long distances.

Suddenly local producers faced competition from great distances, so many interesting bottles were created specifically to distinguish them from others. Green and clear peppersauce bottles, for instance, were made in the shape of Gothic cathedrals with arches and windows (green and clear); mustard jars and chili sauce bottles featured unique embossing; cooking oil bottles were tall and slim; and pickle bottles had large mouths.

The pickle bottle is one of the largest of the food bottles, with a wide mouth and a square or cylindrical shape. While the pickle bottle was often unique in shape and design, its color was almost exclusively aqua, although occasionally you'll find a multi-colored piece. Since there are many variations of designs for these Gothic looking pickle jars, it's difficult to identify exactly the contents of the bottles and the bottle manufacturer. While the oldest bottles may have used foil labels for identification, paper labels and embossing provide additional identification. When looking through ghost town dumps and digging behind older pioneer homes, you are sure to find these food and pickle bottles in large numbers, since pickles were a common and well-liked food, especially in the mining communities.

Two of the more common food bottles are the Worcestershire sauce bottles distributed by Lea & Perrins and the Heinz sauce bottles. The Worcestershire sauce in the green bottle was in high demand during the 19th century and is quite common.

Henry J. Heinz introduced his sauces in 1869 with bottled horseradish and didn't begin bottling ketchup until 1889.

Belfast / Cigars / United (inside a shield) / Cut Plug, yellow amber, 6-7/8", American 1910-1920, $120-180.

Acker's – Select Tea – Finley Acker & Co – Tea Specialist – Philadelphia USA (embossed tea leaves and elephant)
Medium green, 8", smooth base, ABM top with gold gilded stopper, American 1882-1929 .... **$600-800**

Anchor Pickle and Vinegar Works (embossed anchor)
Light green, 7-1/2", smooth base (H.N. & Co.), applied top, American 1860-1870 .... **$150-170**

Antoine – candy jar with paper label
Clear, 12", smooth base, wide mouth with original lid, American 1900-1930 .... **$100-150**

Beichs – candy store jar
Clear, 13-1/2", smooth base, wide mouth with original lid, American 1900-1930............................ **$250-350**

Borden's – The Improved – Malted Milk (display jar)
Clear, 8", smooth base, wide mouth with original lid, American 1900-1930 .... **$450-500**

Buster Brown – Mustard – Steinwender – Stoffregen – Coffee Co. – St. Louis (mustard tin)
Red tin with yellow background, 2-1/2", smooth base, American 1900-1930 .... **$200-225**

Butter Boy – You'll Like It – Sur-Nuf – Pop Corn – Always Pops (popcorn tin)
Red, yellow, and black, 4", smooth base with original lid, American 1900-1930................................ **$75-90**

Candy Bros – MF'G – Confectioners – St. Louis, Mo.
Clear, 11", smooth base, tooled top with original glass insert (Candy Bros. St. Louis C.B.), American 1890-1910 .... **$125-$150**

Cathedral Pickle Jar
Medium emerald green, 7-5/8", open pontil-scarred base, rolled lip, American 1845-1860 .... **$250-400**

Cathedral Pickle Jar
Medium emerald green, 8-1/2", iron pontil, outward rolled lip, extremely rare, American 1850-1860, Willington Glass Works, Willington, Conn **$1,000-1,500**
This is the smallest of the three sizes of the highly desirable Willington pickle jars.

Cathedral Pickle Jar
Medium blue green, 11", diamond patterns on three sides, arched shoulder panels, and a crown on top, smooth base, rolled lip, American 1860-1870 .... **$500-700**

Cathedral pepper-sauce bottle, medium blue green, 10-1/2", American 1860-1870, $200-300.

Cathedral pepper-sauce bottle, aqua, 10-1/4", American 1860-1870, $350-450.

Cathedral Pickle Jar
Blue aqua, 11", smooth base, applied ring lip, scarce variant clock face and clamshell on alternating shoulder panels, American 1855-1870.............................**$150-200**

Cathedral Pickle Jar
Blue aqua, 11-3/8", smooth base, applied mouth, leafy branches above arch, scarce, American 1860-1870 ....**$200-250**

Cathedral Pickle Jar
Medium blue green, 11-5/8", smooth base, rolled lip, American 1860-1870.. **$400-600**

Cathedral Pickle Jar
Deep blue aqua, 13-1/8", 6-sided, smooth base, rolled lip, American 1860-1870 ....**$180-250**

Cathedral Pickle Jar
Blue aqua, 13-1/4", 6-sided, smooth base, outward rolled lip, American 1855-1870 ....**$200-300**

C.L. Stickney – Peppersauce Bottle
Clear, 9", pontil-scarred base, applied top, American 1850-1860.............**$100-150**

Clover Leaf Pickle Jar
Yellow with green tone, 7-3/4", pontil-scarred base, outward rolled mouth, extremely rare, only known example in this color, American 1850-1860, Stoddard Glasshouse, Stoddard, New Hampshire **$1,500-3,000**

Coca Cola – Chewing Gum
Clear, 9", smooth base, ABM wide mouth with glass stopper, counter display jar, rare, American 1903-1905 ....**$700-1,000**

Heinz's Keystone Ketchup (produced in Heinz Glass Factory – Sharpsburg, PA), clear glass, American 1889-1913, $55-75.

Diamond display jar, label reads: Mixed Pickles from H.J. Heinz Co. / Trade Mark, H.J. Heinz Co. / Pittsburgh, U.S.A. / Purveyors to the Trade / Try our Sweet Pickles, Preserves, Celery Sauce, Ketchup, clear glass, 21", American 1915-1920, $375-475.

Coca-Cola – Pepsin Gum – Manufactured By Franklin MFG Co, Richmond VA
Clear, 10-1/2", smooth base, original glass lid, rare counter display jar, American 1905-1911 ....**$800-1,000**

C.P. Sanborn & Son / Union (inside an American shield) / Boston Pickles
Yellow olive, 5", smooth base, sheared and ground lip, American 1880-1895 ....**$150-200**

Diamond Display Jar – Label reads: Mixed Pickles from H.J.Heinz Co. / Trade Mark, H.J. Heinz Co. / Pittsburgh, U.S.A. / Purveyors to the Trade / Try our Sweet Pickles, Preserves, Celery Sauce, Ketchup
Clear glass, 21", smooth base, ground lip with original glass closure, American 1915-1920 ....**$375-475**

Dodson – Hills – St. Louis – Peppersauce Bottle
Aqua, 8", smooth base, tooled top, American 1892-1915 ....**$350-450**

Draped Shoulder Pickle Jar
Blue aqua, 11-1/4", iron pontil, rolled lip, American 1850-1865 ....**$150-220**

E.C. Flaccus Co. – Trade Mark – (embossed deer head)
Medium green, pint, smooth base, milk glass lid, American 1880-1890... **$700-1,500**

Food jar, label reads: Gordon &
Dil____th, Queen Olives, 563 & 56,
Greenwich St., New York, yellow
green, 6-1/4", American 1885-1910,
$100-150.

Goofus pickle jar, milk glass, 15",
American 1880-1900, $500-700.

Goofus jar, brilliant ruby red glass,
15-1/4", Blenko Glass Works,
Milton, WV, American 20th century,
$375-475.

EHVB / N.Y. – Pickle Jar
Pale blue green, 12", hexagonal with fancy cathedral arches around the entire mid section, pontil-scarred base, tooled outward rolled mouth, American 1840-1860 ....**$800-1,600**

Fancy Embossed Product Jar – Embossed Eagle
Light canary yellow, pint, 4-7/8", smooth base, rough sheared and ground lip, original screw-on metal band, American 1890-1910 ....**$100-150**

Food Jar – Neck and Front Label Reads: Gordon & Dil____th, Queen Olives, 563 & 56, Greenwich St., New York
Yellow green, 6-1/4", smooth base, ground lip with original clear glass lid and screw band, American 1885-1910 ....**$100-150**

Food Jar
Yellow amber with topaz tone, 8-1/4", cylindrical three-piece mold, smooth base, outward rolled mouth, American 1860-1870, Keene and Stoddard Glass, Stoddard Glasshouse, Stoddard, New Hampshire..**$750-1,500**

Four Portrait Pickle Bottle
Clear, 9-1/2", embossed faces of two women, a man, and a Roman soldier, smooth base, flared lip, American 1870-1890..**$75-100**

Goofus Pickle Jar
Milk glass, 15", embossed rose and basket decoration, smooth base, ground lip, rare, American 1880-1900 ....**$500-700**

Mustard jar, medium yellow green (citron), American 1890-1910, $100-150.

Peppersauce bottle (five embossed stars on three panels), blue aqua, 8-7/8", American 1850-1860, $200-250.

Goofus Pickle Jar
Cobalt blue, 15", floral decoration with roses, smooth base, ground mouth, extremely rare color, American 1890-1910 .... **$1,000-2,000**

Goofus Pickle Jar
Cornflower blue, 15-1/2", floral decoration with roses, smooth base, ground mouth, American 1880-1910 .... **$400-800**

Heinz Noble & Co – Pittsburgh PA
Light aqua, 8", smooth base, applied top, rare, "Z" in Heinz and "N" in Noble are backwards, American 1869-1874 .... **$175-225**

Hercules (photo of Hercules) – Winslow, Rand and Watson – Pure Coffee (coffee tin)
Light orange, 7-1/2", smooth base, original lid, American 1900-1930 .... **$400-500**

Horlick's – Malted Milk – Hot or Cold (embossed glass display jar)
Clear, 9-1/2", smooth base, wide mouth with original lid, American 1900-1930 .... **$200-275**

Huston's – Confectionary – Auburn, Maine – Candy Jar with Label
Clear, 12", smooth base, wide mouth with original lid, American 1900-1930 .... **$100-150**

Lowell & Covel – Pure Cream – Caramels – Boston. U.S.A. – Candy Jar
Clear, 10", smooth base, wide mouth with original brass lid, American 1900-1930 .... **$250-300**

P.D. Code & Co. – S.F. (Phillip D. Code)
Medium green, 11-1/2", smooth base, applied top, American 1867-1898 .... **$500-600**

Peppersauce Bottle
Green aqua, 11", 12-sided, open pontil, inward rolled lip, American 1840-1860 .... **$120-140**

Perfection – Prepared Cocoanut – Spark Place, NY (jar with label)
Aqua, 8", smooth base, threaded top with original lid, American 1900-1920 .... **$150-200**

Pickle Jar
Medium blue green, 7-1/2", square form, open pontil, rolled lip, American 1840-1860 .... **$150-200**

Pickle Jar
Medium blue green, 11-1/4", five rounded cathedral arched panels, fluted shoulders, and neck, iron pontil, applied mouth, rare, American 1850-1865 . **$500-700**

Pickle jar, medium blue green, 7-1/2", square form, American 1840-1860, $150-200.

Pickle bottle – Patented March 23, 1869 (around shoulder) – Whitney Glass Works / Glassboro N.J. (on base), blue aqua, 12-1/4", American 1870-1889, $200-300.

Pickle bottle – HY. C. Kellogg – Phila, deep green aqua, 9-1/8", American 1865-1880, $350-475.

Planters – Pennant – 5 Cents Salted – Peanuts – Sold Only in Printed Planters Red Pennant Bags (counter display jar)
Clear, 12", smooth base, wide mouth with original lid, American 1900-1920
....**$500-600**

Ribbed Utility Jar
Medium green, 8-1/4", sticky ball pontil, applied lip, American 1850-1860
....**$200-400**

Ribbed Utility Bottle
Aqua, 10", pontil-scarred base, applied top, American 1850-1860...........**$100-125**

Shriver's – Oyster – Ketchup – Baltimore
Medium green, 7-1/2", smooth base, applied top, rare, American 1865-1885
....**$800-1,100**

Shriver's – Oyster – Ketchup – Baltimore
Medium green, 9", smooth base, applied top, rare, American 1865-1885
....**$1,500-2,000**

Walla / Walla / motif of Indian chief in headress / Pepsin Gum / MFD By / Walla-Walla Gum Co. / Knoxville, Tenn, clear glass, countertop, 12-7/8", American 1890-1920, $300-450.

Smokine
Dark amber, 5", E.G. Booze type cabin, smooth base, tooled top, American 1900-1920 ....**$325-425**
Smokine was used to give meat a smoked flavor.

T.B. Smith & Co. / Philada – Pickle Jar
Aquamarine, 11-1/2", cylindrical with seven rounded vertical panels (one embossed), fluted shoulder, pontil iron mark, outward rolled collared mouth, extremely rare, American 1845-1860 ....**$1,000-2,000**

Thompson's – Double Malted Entirely Soluble – Malted Milk
Light brown, 10", porcelain canister, smooth base, original lid, American 1900-1930 ....**$200-275**

Thurber & Co – Pure Lemon Fruit Syrup – New York (label)
Clear, 10-1/4", smooth base, tooled top, American 1890-1910 ....**$40-60**

Wells, Miller & Provost – No. 217 Front St. – New York
Medium olive yellow, 8-3/8", 8-rounded panels, iron pontil, applied double collar mouth, extremely rare color, American 1845-1860 ....**$1,000-1,500**

W.M. & P / N.Y. (Wells, Miller and Provost Company) – Peppersauce Bottle
Medium blue green, 9", pontil-scarred base, wide sheared and tooled mouth, rare color, American 1840-1860 ....**$250-300**

Walla Walla – Pepsin Gum – Manufactured By Walla Walla Gum Co. – Knoxsville Tenn.
Clear, 11", smooth base, ABM mouth with glass lid, American 1890-1910 ...**$250-275**

Webster's – High Grade – Coffee (coffee tin)
Yellow can with red label, one pound, smooth base, original lid, American 1900-1930 ....**$400-450**

Fruit Jars

Unlike food bottles, fruit jars were sold empty for use in home preservation of many different types of food. They were predominant in the 1800s when pre-packaged foods weren't available and home canning was the only option. Although fruit jars carry no advertising, they aren't necessarily common or plain, since the bottle manufacturer's name is usually embossed in large letters along with the patent date. The manufacturer whose advertising campaign gave fruit jars their name was Thomas W. Dyott, who was in the market early, selling fruit jars by 1829.

For the first fifty years, the most common closure was a cork sealed with wax. In 1855, an inverted saucer-like lid was invented that could be inserted into the jar to provide an airtight seal. The Hero Glassworks invented the glass lid in 1856 and improved on it in 1858 with a zinc lid invented by John Landis Mason, who also produced fruit jars. Because the medical profession warned that zinc could be harmful, Hero Glassworks developed a glass lid for the Mason jar in 1868. Mason eventually transferred his patent rights to the Consolidated Fruit Jar Company, which let the patent expire.

In 1880, the Ball brothers began distributing Mason jars, and in 1898, the use of a semi-automatic bottle machine increased the output of the Mason jar until the automatic machine was invented in 1903.

Fruit jars come in a wide variety of sizes and colors, but the most common is aqua and clear. The rarer jars were made in various shades of blue, amber, black, milk glass, green, and purple.

Sun (inside a radiating sun) / Trade Mark – J.P. Barstow / 7 (on base) aqua, pint, American 1890-1900, $150-200.

A.B.C.

Aqua, quart, smooth base, ground lip, original glass lid embossed (Pat. April 15th 1884), metal yoke marked "Pat. April 15th 1884," American 1884-1890 ..**$375-475**

A. P. Brayton & Co. / San Francisco / Cal

Teal blue, pint, smooth base, ground lip, extremely rare, American 1860-1870 ....**$1,500-2,000**

A. Stone & Co.

Aqua, quart, smooth base, applied mouth with two internal lugs, original glass closure is embossed (A. Stone & Co. / Philada), American 1860-1875 ..**$800-1,000**

Baltimore / Glass Works

Aqua, quart, smooth base, applied wide mouth, American 1855-1860, Baltimore Glass Works, Baltimore, Maryland...... ....**$700-900**

BBGMco (monogram)

Aqua, midget pint, smooth base, rough sheared and ground lip, embossed on original glass insert (Ball Brother Glass Mfg Co. / Buffalo), zinc screw band, American 1880-1890..**$600-900**

(Beaver chewing on a log) / Beaver

Light green, midget pint, smooth base, ground lip, Canadian 1890-1900.**$200-275**

Belle – Pat. Dec. 14th 1869

Aqua, quart, smooth base with three raised feet, ground lip, original domed glass lid with metal and wire enclosure, American 1869-1875 ....**$1,500-3,000**

C.F. Spencer's / Patent / Rochester / N.Y. (lot of two), aqua, quart and half-gallon, American 1863-1870, $140-200.

Bennett's / No. 1 (over erased Adams & Co. Manufacturers Pittsburgh, PA)
Aqua, quart, smooth base, applied mouth, embossed on original glass stopper (Bennett's Patent / Feb 6th 1866), American 1866-1870..........................**$600-800**

Bloeser / Jar
Aqua, half-gallon, smooth base, ground lip, embossed lid (Pat Sept 27 1887), wire and metal clamp enclosure, American 1887-1900 ....**$350-450**

Buckeye / 4
Deep blue aqua, quart, smooth base, ground lip, glass lid embossed (Adam's Patd May 20, 1862), metal yoke, American 1862-1870.....................................**$180-275**

C. Burnham & Co / Manufacturers / Philada
Aqua, quart, smooth base, ground lip, original iron lid, American 1859-1865 ....**$500-700**

Cadiz / Jar
Aqua, half-gallon, smooth base, ground lip, embossed glass lid (Cadiz Jar Pat. 1883), American 1883-1890 ....**$750-1,000**

C.F. Spencer's / Patd 1868 / Improved Jar
Blue aqua, quart, smooth base, ground lip, original tin lid, American 1868-1875 ....**$374-475**

C.F. Spencer's / Patent / Rochester / N.Y.
Aqua, quart, smooth base, applied mouth, American 1863-1870..............**$70-100**

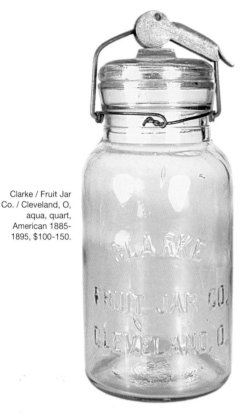

Clarke / Fruit Jar Co. / Cleveland, O, aqua, quart, American 1885-1895, $100-150.

Cohansey, aqua, half-pint, American 1872-1885, $350-450.

C.F. Spencer's / Patent / Rochester / N.Y.
Aqua, half-gallon, smooth base, applied mouth, American 1863-1870.......**$70-100**

Clarke / Fruit Jar Co. / Cleveland, O
Aqua, quart, smooth base (52), ground lip, original glass lid, impressed (Pat. M'ch 17, 1885) metal cam lever closure, American 1885-1895.........................**$100-150**

Cohansey
Aqua, pint, smooth base, ground lip, embossed glass lid (Cohansey Glass Manuf. Co. Philada. Pat. July 16, 1872), wire enclosure, American 1872-1885......**$80-120**

Commodore
Aqua, bulbous quart, smooth base, applied mouth, rare, American 1865-1870
....**$1,500-2,500**

Dexter / Improved (around circle of fruits)
Aqua, half-gallon, smooth base, ground lip, embossed glass insert (Dexter Improved / Patented Aug 8, 1865) and zinc screw band, American 1865-1875.......**$140-200**

Excelsior / Improved / 5"
Aqua, quart, smooth base, ground lip, embossed glass lid (Patd Feby 12, 56, Nov 4, 62 Dec. 6, 64 June 9, 68, Sep. 8, 68) and screw band, American 1875-1885
....**$60-90**

Dexter (encircled by fruits and vegetables), aqua, midget pint, American 1865-1880, $300-400.

F. & J. Bodine / Philada
Blue aqua, quart, smooth base, ground lip, American 1850-1865 ....**$170-250**

Franklin / R.W. King / 90 Jefferson Ave. / Detroit Mich / Fruit Jar
Aqua, quart, smooth base, ground lip, embossed glass lid (Patd Aug. 8th 1865), American 1865-1875 ....**$500-800**

Fridley & Corman's / Patent / Oct. 25th 1859 / Ladies Choice
Blue aqua, quart, smooth base, ground lip, original impress "Fridley & Corman's Patented Oct. 25th 1850," cast iron rim, American 1859-1865 ....**$800-1,400**

GEM – HGW (monogram)
Aqua, midget pint, smooth base (Pat Nov 26 76 / Pat Feb 4 73), ground lip, original embossed "HGW" monogram, dated glass insert, original zinc screw band, American 1875-1895...**$300-400**

Gilberds / (star) / Jar
Aqua, quart, smooth base, ground lip, clear glass lid embossed "Jas Gilberds / Patd / Jan 30 1883 / Jamestown, N.Y.," wire closure, American 1883-1890 ....**$250-350**

Gilberds / (star) / Jar
Aqua, half-gallon, smooth base, ground lip, original glass lid embossed "Gilberds Improved Jar Cap Jamestown, N.Y. / 3 / Pat / July 31 83," wire closure, American 1883-1890...**$375-475**

Globe
Yellow with amber tone, half-gallon, smooth base (14), ground lip, original amber glass lid embossed (Patented May 25th 1886), metal closure, American 1886-1890 ....**$170-220**

Granger
Aqua, pint, smooth base, ground lip, very rare, American 1875-1890 ......**$400-600**

Griffin's Patent Oct. 7 1862 (on lid)
Aqua, quart, smooth base, ground lip, embossed glass lid, iron cage clamp, American 1862-1870 ....**$100-150**

Hamilton Glass / Works / 1 Quart
Aqua, quart, smooth base, applied mouth, glass lid (Hamilton / Glass Works), American 1875-1885 ....**$300-400**

Hoosier Jar
Aqua, quart, smooth base, ground lip, embossed (PATD Sept 12th, 1882, Jan 3D 1883 / Hoosier Jar) on screw-on lid, American 1882-1885.....................**$400-600**

Imperial / Trade Mark (hand holding mace)
Aqua, quart, smooth base, ground lip, original clear glass lid embossed (Thomas Patent / July 12 1892), metal three-piece clamp closure, Canadian 1892-1900 ....**$600-800**

J. D. Willoughby Patented January 4 1850 (on stopper)
Aqua, quart, reddish iron pontil, applied mouth, American 1859-1865 .....**$150-200**

John M. Moore & Co. / Manufacturers / Fislerville N.J. / Patented Dec. 3rd 1861
Blue aqua, quart, smooth base, applied mouth, embossed glass lid (Patented / Dec. 3D 1861), original rounded iron yoke, American 1861-1875 ....**$300-450**

Joshua Wright / Philada
Blue aqua, 10-3/8", half-gallon, barrel form, smooth base, applied mouth, American 1855-1870..**$350-500**

Knowlton Vacuum / (star) / Fruit Jar
Aqua, pint, smooth base, smooth lip, original glass insert, "Knowlton Vacuum Full Glass Top Patented" zinc screw-on lid, American 1903-1905......................**$70-90**

Lyon & Bossard's Jar / East Stroudsburg / PA.
Aqua, pint, smooth base, ground lip, embossed (Pat. April 15th 1884) glass lid, embossed (Pat Apr 15 84) metal yoke and tightening clamp, rare, American 1884-1890 ....**$700-900**

Ludlow's Patent / June 28-1859 / August 6-1861 (on glass lid)
Aqua, quart, smooth base, ground lip, glass lid and cast iron cage clamp, American 1861-1870..**$100-150**

Made In Canada / Perfect / Seal (inside a shield) / Wide Mouth / Adjustable
Medium olive green, pint, smooth base, ABM lip, original glass lid and wire closure, word "Tight" is between the two neck bands, Canadian 1905-1925 ....**$200-300**

Mansfield
Pale green aqua, pint, smooth base (Mansfield / Knowlton May 03 / Pat / Glass W'K'S'), original embossed clear glass insert and impressed screw-on lid, American 1903-1908..**$350-450**

Mason's / Patent / Nov. 30th / 1858 – N.C.L.
Blue aqua, midget pint, smooth base (2N), sheared and ground lip, original zinc screw-on lid, scarce, American 1875-1890 ....**$300-400**

Mason's / Patent / Nov. 30th / 1858, medium amber, quart, American 1860-1895, $250-350.

Mason's / Patent / Nov. 30th / 1858
Medium amber, quart, smooth base (Pat Nov 26 67), ground lip, zinc lid, American 1860-1895 ....**$250-350**

Mason's / CJF CO (monogram) / Patent / Nov 30th / 1858
Medium yellow olive, quart, smooth base (FX605), ground lip, zinc screw lid, American 1880-1895 ....**$250-350**

Mason's CFJ CO (monogram) patent / Nov 30th / 1858
Medium golden yellow amber, quart, smooth base (79), ground lip, American 1870-1885 ....**$400-700**

Mason's / (cross) / Patent / Nov. 30th / 1858
Straw yellow, quart, smooth base (Pat Nov 26 67), ground lip, zinc screw lid, American 1880-1895 ....**$250-350**

Moore's / Patent / Dec 3D 1861
Aqua, pint, smooth base, applied mouth, original glass lid, American 1861-1870 ....**$200-250**

(Motif of star encircled by fruit)
Aqua, quart, smooth base, ground lip, American 1875-1885 ....**$350-425**

Mrs. G. E. Haller / Pat'd Feb 25 75 (on stopper)
Aqua, quart, smooth base, applied mouth, original clear glass hollow blown stopper, American 1873-1880 ....**$150-250**

NE Plus Ultra Air-Tight Fruit Jar / Made By Bodine & Bros' WMS' Town, N.J. / For Their Patent Glass Lid
Blue aqua, 1-1/2 quart size, smooth base, applied mouth, American 1858-1865 ....**$1,400-1,800**

Patent / Sept 18,
1860, blue aqua
quart, American
1860-1870,
$140-180.

Peerless
– Patented Aug
31 1863, aqua,
quart, American
1863-1870,
$200-300.

New / Paragon / 5"
Aqua, quart, smooth base, ground lip, embossed (The New Paragon Patented) glass insert and zinc screw band, American 1870-1880...................................**$180-250**

Patent / Sept 18, 1860
Blue aqua, quart, smooth base, handpressed wax seal ring, ground lip, American 1860-1870...**$140-180**

Peerless
Aqua, quart, smooth base, applied mouth, embossed glass lid (Patented Feb 13, 1863), iron yoke clamp, American 1863-1870.......................................**$200-300**

Pet
Aqua, quart, smooth base, applied mouth, embossed (Patented Aug 31 1869, T. G. Otterson) glass lid and brass wire clamp, American 1869-1875 ....**$140-180**

Petal Jar
Deep olive green, half-gallon, red iron pontil, 10-shoulder flutes, thick applied mouth, American 1850-1860 ....**$2,500-3,500**

Porcelain / Lined
Aqua, midget pint, smooth base (Pat. Nov. 26 67 / Pat Feb 4 73 / B) ground lip, zinc screw-on lid embossed (Pat'd Sept 3D, Dec. 31 1872), American 1880-1890 ....**$225-275**

Protector
Blue aqua, half-gallon, smooth base, ground lip, American 1867-1880 ....**$100-150**

Put On Rubber Before Filling / Star & Crescent (motif of moon and star) Self Sealing Jar
Aqua, pint, smooth base (Patented / Dec'r 10th 1896), ground lip, original zinc lid with milk glass insert, American 1896-1900 ....**$700-900**

Queensland / (letter "Q" inside a pineapple) / Fruit Jar
Green aqua, quart, smooth base, ground lip, Australian 1890-1900.........**$200-300**

S.B. Dewey Jr. / No. 65 / Buffalo St. / Rochester / N.Y.
Blue aqua, quart, smooth base, applied mouth, metal stopper (J.D. Willoughby, Patd Apr 4, 1859), American 1860-1870...**$1,000-1,500**

Spratt's Patent / July 18 1854 / Pat'd April 5 1864 (on lid)
Soldered in tin can, original threaded clear glass lid, American 1864-1870 ....**$250-350**

Star & Crescent / (motif of moon and star) / Pat. Mar. 11th / 1890
Aqua, quart, smooth base, ground lip, original unmarked flat glass insert and zinc screw band with wire handle, American 1890-1895 ....**$400-600**

Sun (inside a radiating sun) / Trade Mark
Aqua, pint, smooth base (J.P. Barstow / 7"), ground lip, embossed glass lid (Monier's Pat- Aprl 90, Mar 12, 95), American 1890-1900......................................**$150-200**

The / Alston – Bail Here
Clear glass, quart, smooth base (Pat'd April 1900 Dec 1901), ABM lip, original tin lid, American 1900-1905 ....**$500-700**

The / Automatic / Sealer
Aqua, half-gallon, smooth base (Clayton Bottle / Works / Clayton, N.J.), ground lip, original domed glass lid (Patd. Sept. 15, 1885), wire closure, American 1885-1895 ....**$250-450**

The / Best
Clear glass, quart, smooth base (4), ground lip, embossed glass (Patented / August 18th 1868 / The / Best) screw-on closure, American 1868-1875 ....**$800-1200**

The / CFJCO (monogram) / Queen
Aqua, midget pint, smooth base, ground lip, American 1870-1880...........**$80-140**

The / Champion / Pat. Aug. 31. 1869
Aqua, quart, smooth base, ground lip, original glass lid and metal yoke clsosure, American 1869-1875 ....**$250-300**

The Chief – K
Aqua, quart, smooth base (Pat. Nov 29 / 1870), ground lip, very rare, American 1870-1880..**$375-450**

The Daisy / Jar
Clear glass, half-gallon, smooth base, ground lip, original embossed (Pat Jan 3D 88), glass lid and metal closure, American 1888-1895 ....**$375-475**

The / Doolittle / Self Sealer
Aqua, pint, smooth base (GJCO), ABM lip, embossed glass lid (Patented / January / 1900) with wire and ear enclosure, American 1905-1910......................**$300-400**

The / Empire
Aqua, quart, smooth base (Pat. Feb. 13 1866), ground lip, original glass lid, metal clamp, and lever closure, American 1866-1875......................................**$250-350**

The / Leader, light yellow amber, half-gallon, American 1892-1895, $200-275.

The / Puritan – LSCO (monogram), aqua, quart, American 1870-1880, $150-200.

The / Leader
Light yellow amber, half-gallon, smooth base (3), ground lip, original glass lid (Patd June 28, 1892), American 1892-1895..**$200-275**

The / Leader
Golden yellow amber, half-gallon, smooth base (13), ground lip, original glass lid (Patd June 28, 1892), American 1892-1895...**$250-300**

The / Lincoln / Jar
Blue aqua, smooth base, ground lip, very rare, American 1870-1880.......**$450-600**

The Magic / (star) / Fruit Jar
Aqua, pint, smooth base (2), embossed (Clamp Pat. March 30th 1886) glass lid and metal closure, American 1886-1895...**$500-800**

The Model Jar / Patd / Aug. 1867
Aqua, quart, smooth base, ground lip, American 1867-1875 ....**$250-300**

The / Puritan – LSCO (monogram)
Aqua, quart, smooth base, ground lip, American 1870-1880 ....**$150-200**

The / Schaffer / Jar / Rochester / N.Y. – JCS (monogram)
Aqua, quart, smooth base, ground lip, American 1870-1880 ....**$250-300**

The / Scranton / Jar, aqua, quart, American 1875-1890, $800-1,200.

Trade Mark / Lighting, medium yellow green, quart, American 1875-1890, $275-375.

Trade Mark / Lightning – H.W.P., medium yellow amber, quart, American 1875-1895, $1,400-1,800.

The / Scranton / Jar
Medium yellow green, quart, smooth base (G.H.C. / 2) ground lip, aqua glass lid and spring wire with wooden roller closure, rare, American 1870-1880 ....**$800-1,500**

The / Scranton / Jar
Pale aqua, quart, smooth base, applied mouth, glass stopper (A. Kline / Patd Oct 27, 1863, Use Pin), extremely rare, American 1875-1890.................**$1,000-1,500**

The Valve Jar Co. / Philadelphia
Aqua, quart, smooth base (Pat'd Mar 10 / 1868), ground lip, American 1868-1875 ....**$400-500**

The / Val Vliet / Jar of 1881
Aqua, pint, smooth base, ground lid, original embossed glass lid (Pat May 3D, 1881), iron yoke and wire closure, rare, American 1881-1885 ....**$2,500-3,500**

Trade Mark / Lightning – HWP (monogram)
Aqua, quart, smooth base (Putnam / 2), ground lip, original glass lid with wire closure (Lightning / Patd Apr 25, 92), American 1892-1900 ....**$350-450**

Trade Mark / Lightning
Yellow olive, quart, smooth base (Putnam / 227), ground lip, dated glass lid and lightning-style closure, American 1880-1895..**$70-90**

Trade Mark / The Dandy, medium-amber, half-gallon, American 1885-1895, $250-350.

Trade Mark / Lightning
Medium yellow amber, pint, smooth base (Putnam / 109), ground lip, dated glass lid and lightning-style closure, American 1880-1895 ....**$70-90**

Trade Mark / Lightning – Salesman's Sample Fruit Jar
Aqua, 5-1/8", smooth base (Putnam / 359), ground lip, original unmarked glass lid and lightning-style closure, American 1875-1895 ....**$150-250**

Trade Mark / The Dandy
Medium amber, half-gallon, smooth base (Gilberds), ground lip, original glass lid (Pat. Oct. 13th 1885), wire closure, American 1885-1895 ....**$250-350**

Whitemore's / Patent / Rochester / NY
Aqua, quart, smooth base, ground lip, embossed (Patented Jany 14th, 68) double fin lid, original wire bail, American 1868-1875...**$200-275**

Winslow Jar
Aqua, half-gallon, smooth base, ground lip, original embossed (Patented Nov. 29th, 1870 / Patented Feb. 25th, 1873) glass lid and iron clamp, American 1870-1880
....**$80-140**

WM. L. Haller / Carlisle / PA
Aqua, quart, smooth base, sheared and tooled lip, original stopper (J.D. Willoughby Patented Jan 4 1859), American 1860-1870...**$700-900**

Ginger Beer Bottles

The origins of ginger beer can be traced back to England in the mid-1700s. But there was actually an earlier type of ginger beer produced by Mead & Metheglin in the early 1600s in colonial America. Metheglin was more of a natural carbonated, yeast-fermented beverage, often including ginger, cloves, and mace, which proved to be a popular drink in the colonies. The difference was that while ginger beer included the yeast for fermentation, it was also sweetened with honey, cane sugar, or molasses. Additional ingredients included whole Jamaica ginger root and fresh lemons. After brewing, the ginger beer was stored in stoneware bottles and corked to maintain a natural effervescence. When the carbonation process was introduced in 1899, an essence of extract was used to achieve the right taste. But the old English brewmasters observed that naturally fermented ginger beer still produced the best flavor. Until the mid-1800s, a number of ginger beers contained high alcohol content, some with as much as 11 percent.

Ginger beer was eventually introduced to the United States and Canada around 1790, with England shipping large amounts to both countries during the 1800s. England was able to continue this huge export, since its stoneware bottles were of a better quality because of a process developed in 1835 called "Improved Bristol Glaze." After brewing, the bottles were corked and wired to maintain pressure, which kept the alcohol and carbon dioxide in solution, improving preservation and extending shelf life.

The early stoneware bottle was used extensively from 1790 until 1880 to 1890 when industrialization and new manufacturing techniques introduced a new gray stoneware bottle. These new bottles were used from approximately 1885 to 1920 and were stamped with various logos and designs to attract the interest of the buyer.

In the United States, the popularity of ginger beer quickly declined after 1920, when Prohibition was signed into law and never recovered after the repeal of Prohibition in 1933. In England and Canada, the peak occurred around 1935. At one point, there were 300 ginger beer breweries in the United States, 1,000 in Canada, and 3,000 in England. While the breweries have disappeared, today's collector can still enjoy finding many varieties of bottles in green, red, blue, tan, and purple, and displaying unique slogans and logos.

While this chapter presents a good cross section of Canadian ginger beer bottles, I recommend that collectors obtain the following two books authored by Scott Wallace and Phil Culhane, a specialist in the field of Canadian glass and stoneware ginger beers: Transfer Printed Ginger Beers of Canada and Primitive Stoneware Bottles of Canada. Phil also conducts a number of auctions throughout the year and can be contacted at phil.culhane@rogers.com. His Web site address is www.cbandsc.com.

ALBERTA

Edmonton Bottling Works Co. Limited – Finest Old Fashion Brewed Scotch – Ginger Beer
Tan top, pint $350

McLaughlin's – Ginger Shandy – Made From Pure – Jamaica Ginger Root
Ivory, quart $120

Old English – Stone Ginger Beer – Phillips Bros.
Medium brown top, pint $90

BRITISH COLUMBIA

Country Club – Stone Ginger Beer – Beverage Company – Vancouver, B.C.
Tan top, pint $40

Chris Morley's – Ginger Beer – Victoria, B.C.
Tan top, pint $500

Crystal Spring Water Supply – Ginger Beer – Victoria, B.C.
Tan top, pint $275

Fairall Bros. – Victoria West
Tan top, pint $850

Kirk & Co. Ltd. – Genuine – Old English – Ginger Beer – Victoria West
Tan top, pint $90

Nelson Soda – Stone Ginger Beer – Factory
Tan top, large pint, scarce $425

Old English – Brewed English Beer – Brewed & Bottled By – Union Wholesalers – Victoria, B.C. – Contents 12 oz.
Tan top, pint $375

Regal – Mineral Water Co. – Victoria, B.C.
Tan top, pint $45

MANITOBA

Brandon Brewing Company – Brandon
Tan top, quart $210

The Golden Key – Brand – Ginger Beer – E.L. Drewery – Winnipeg
Tan top, quart $85

NEWFOUNDLAND

Gaden's Aerated Water Works – J.R. Bennett Proprietor – St. John's, N.F. – Stone Ginger Beer
Light tan, pint $1,400

ONTARIO

C. H. Norton – Berlin
Tan top, tall pint, scarce $650

Charles Wilson – Ginger Beer – Toronto
Ivory, pint $325

Clark Bros. – Toronto
Ivory, pint $70

Crescent Bottling Works – Stone Ginger Beer – Niagara Falls
Tan top, small pint $100

F.A. Meyer – Seaforth
Dark gray, large quart $80

G. Kickley (Guelph) – Brewed Ginger Beer
Tan top, pint $100

J. Tune & Son – London, Ont.
Tan top, pint $210

James Thompson – Ginger Beer – Kingston
Tan top, blue writing, pint $70

London Ginger – Beer Co. – Stone Ginger Beer
Ivory, quart $150

Ross Bros – R & B – London – Ont.
Dark metallic brown top, large pint
.... $1,050

Salisbury – Ginger Beer Of – Toronto – Stone Ginger – Old Country Home Brewed
Tan top, tall pint $50

T.H. Hutchinson – St. Thomas, Ont.
Tan top, pint $650

NEW BRUNSWICK

Dolan Bros. – Stone Ginger Beer – 1896 – 348 Brussels St. – St. John
Cobalt blue top, tall pint, internal threads, correct stopper............**$950**

Dolan Bros. – Stone Ginger Beer – 1898 – 348 Brussels St. – St. John
Cobalt blue top, tall quart, internal threads, correct stopper............**$185**

Dolan Bros. – Stone Ginger Beer – 1900 – 348 Brussels St. – St. John
Cobalt blue top, tall quart, internal threads, correct stopper............**$220**

Dolan Bros. – Stone Ginger Beer – 1913 – 348 Brussels St. – St. John
Cobalt blue top, tall quart, internal threads, correct stopper............**$125**

Harlands – Stone – Ginger Beer – 1927 – G.D. Gibbs, Sole Agent – Fredericton
Ivory, pint **$425**

Old – Homestead – International Drug Company – St. Stephen and Calais, Maine – Ginger Beer
Ivory, small quart **$230**

S. H. McKee & Sons – Stone Ginger Beer – 1894 – 121 Kings St. – Fredericton
Ivory, pint **$75**

S. H. McKee & Sons – Stone Ginger Beer – 1899 – 121 Kings St. – Fredericton
Ivory, pint **$110**

T.A. Hooley – Fairville
Dark brown top, quart...............**$425**

Terris – Ginger Beer – Saint John
Cobalt blue top, pint, original contents, original stopper **$85**

NOVA SCOTIA

Bates – English Ginger Beer – Truro, N.S.
Tan top, pint...............................**$275**

C.B. Mineral – Water Works – Thomas O'Neill – Proprietor – Bridgeport C.B.
Tan top, pint.........................**$1,100**

Felix J. Quinn – Ginger Beer Manuf'r – Halifax
Tan top, pint...............................**$55**

John Dixon – Old Time Ginger Beer – Halifax
Ivory, pint **$220**

Imperial – Mineral – Water Works – Ginger Beer – Wilson & Sullivan – Halifax
Tan top, pint...............................**$110**

J. B. Baker – Halifax
Brown glaze over gray, large quart, large donut ring on lip................**$600**

Nash & McAllister – Stone Ginger Beer – Sydney C.B.
Tan top, quart...........................**$350**

Patrick McAllister – Celebrated Brewed Ginger Beer – PMCA – Sydney
Cobalt blue top, pint...............**$1,500**

Sydney Mines Bottling Works – A.R. MacDougall, Sydney Mines N.S. – Superior Fermented – Ginger Beer
Ivory, pint **$900**

W.H. Donovan – Halifax
Ivory, pint, original stopper...........**$30**

PRINCE EDWARD ISLAND

Simmons – Charlottetown
Medium tan, pint **$70**

QUEBEC

Allan's – Ginger Beer – Montreal
Ivory, pint **$40**

C. Robillard & Cie – Ginger Beer – Montreal
Tan top, pint...............................**$80**

Elz. – Fortier & Cie – Best Ginger Beer – Quebec
Tan top, pint...............................**$30**

Gurds – Ginger Beer – The Perfect Drink – A Product of Canada

Lime green top, pint, one of only two known lime green top ginger beers ....
$1,700

Gurds – Stone Ginger Beer – The Perfect Brew

Blue green top, pint....................**$130**

J. Christian & Cie Limitee – Ginger Beer

Medium brown top, pint.............**$275**

M. Timmons & Sons – Ginger Beer

Ivory, pint **$425**

P.A. Milloy – Ginger Beer – Montreal

Ivory, pint **$160**

Seth C. Nutter – Sherbrooke – PQ.

Tan top, pint...............................**$165**

SASKATCHEWAN

Old English Brew – Crystal Spring Bottling Co. – Moose Jaw, Canada

Tan top, pint..............................**$550**

Regina Aerated – Water Company – Regina, Sask

Tan top, quart..........................**$1,600**

MANITOBA

Brandon Brewing Co. – Brandon

Tan top, quart............................**$175**

Douglas & King Limited – Kings Old Country – Stone Ginger Beer – Winnipeg

Dark brown top, pint **$45**

Empress Waters – The Empire Brewing Co.

Tan top, quart............................**$100**

Hutchinson Bottles

Charles A. Hutchinson developed the Hutchinson bottle in the late 1870s. Interestingly, the stopper, not the bottle itself, differentiated the design from others. The Hutchinson stopper, patented in 1879, was an improvement over cork stoppers, which eventually shrank and allowed air to seep into the bottle.

The new stopper consisted of a rubber disk held between two metal plates attached to a spring stem. The stem was shaped like a figure eight, with the upper loop larger than the lower to prevent the stem from falling into the bottle. The lower loop could pass through the bottle's neck and push down the disk to permit the filling or pouring of it contents. A refilled bottle was sealed by pulling the disc up to the bottle's shoulder, where it formed a tight seal. When opened, the spring made a popping sound. Thus, the Hutchinson bottle had the honor of originating the phrase "pop bottle" which is how soda came to be known as "pop."

Hutchinson stopped producing bottles in 1912, when warnings about metal poisoning were issued. As collectibles, Hutchinson bottles rank high on the scale of curiosity and value, but pricing varies quite sharply by geographical location, compared to the relatively stable prices of most other bottles.

Hutchinson bottles carry abbreviations of which the following three are the most common.

TBNTBS - This bottle not to be sold

TBMBR - This bottle must be returned

TBINS - This bottle is not sold

Albuquerque Bottling Works – Arbuquerque NM, aqua, 7-1/4", American 1880-1900, $600-700.

Brunswick Coca-Cola Bottling Co. – Brunswick, CA, clear, 7", American 1885-1900, $1,300-1,500.

A. Harsch – Albuquerque – NM
Aqua, 7", smooth base, tooled blob top, American 1885-1895 .... **$500-600**

Albuquerque – Bottling Works – Albuquerque NM
Aqua, 7-1/4", smooth base (CGW), applied blob top, (Backward "S" and "N"), American 1880-1900 .... **$600-700**

Biloxi Artesian – Bottling Works – E. Barq Prop.
Aqua, 7", smooth base, tooled blob top, American 1885-1895 .... **$95-125**

Brunswick Coca-Cola – Bottling Co. – Brunswick, CA
Clear, 7", smooth base, tooled blob top, American 1885-1900 .... **$1,300-1,500**

C.Andrae / Port Huron / Mich – C. % Co. 2
Medium cobalt blue, 6-5/8", smooth base, applied blob mouth, American 1885-1900 .... **$120-170**

Central / Bottling Works / Detroit, Mich – This Bottle Is Never Sold / C. Co. Llim No 5
Medium cobalt blue, 7", smooth base (J.J.G.), tooled blob mouth, American 1885-1900 .... **$150-220**

Birmingham – Coca-Cola
Bottling Co., clear, 7",
American 1885-1900,
$1,800-2,200.

Crystal Spring
/ Bottling Co. /
Barnet, VT., label
reads: Bottles by
Crystal Spring
Bottling Co,
Crab=Apple,
Barnet, Vt., clear
glass, 7", American
1890-1910,
$200-350.

C.W. Rider / Watertown / N.Y.
Deep teal blue, 6-3/4", smooth base, applied blob mouth, rare, American 1890-1900 color **$800-1,200**

Chr Wiegand – Las Vegas – N.M.
Medium amethyst, 7", smooth mug base, tooled blob top, American 1880-1895 ....**$500-600**

Chris Fisher – Central City, Col. – This Bottle To Be Returned to Chris Fischer
Aqua, 6", smooth base, tooled blob top, American 1885-1900...............**$300-400**

Claussen Bottling Works / Charleston / S.C.
Medium yellow with amber tone, 6-5/8", smooth base, tooled blob mouth, extremely rare, American 1885-1900 ....**$1,200-1,800**

Crystal Spring – Bottling Co. – Barnet, VT (front) – (back) Label reads: Bottled by Crystal Spring Bottling Co, Crab=Apple, Barnet, VT.
Clear, 7", smooth base, tooled blob top, American 1890-1910 ....**$200-350**

Birmingham – Coca Cola – Bottling Co.
Clear, 7", smooth base, tooled blob top, American 1885-1900 ....**$1,800-2,200**

E. A. Jennings / Hudson / N.Y.
Cobalt blue, 6-1/2", smooth base, tooled blob mouth, extremely rare, American 1880-1900...**$500-1,000**

Elko Bottling – Works – Elko Nev.
Aqua, 7-1/2", smooth base, tooled blob top, American 1899-1902 .... **$400-500**

E. Ottenville / Nashville / Tenn – MCC
Medium cobalt blue, 6-5/8", smooth base (25), tooled blob mouth, American 1885-1900 .... **$150-200**

Escambia – Pepsi Cola – Bottling Co. – Pensacola Fla.
Aqua, 7", smooth base, tooled blob top, extremely rare, American 1885-1900 .... **$700-900**

G. Layer – Raton – NM
Clear, 7", smooth mug base, tooled blob top, very rare, American 1880-1895 .... **$750-850**

G. Norris & Co. / City / Bottling Works / Detroit, Mich – C & CO LIM
Medium cobalt blue, 6-3/4", smooth base, applied blob mouth, American 1885-1900 .... **$75-125**

Gallup – Bottling Works – Gallup N.M.
Aqua, 7", smooth base, tooled blob top, American 1880-1895 .... **$450-550**

Geo. Disbro / & Co. / Chicago
Cobalt blue, 7-5/8", smooth base (D), 10-panels on side at base, applied blob mouth, American 1885-1900 .... **$150-250**

Geo. Schmuck's – Ginger Ale – Cleveland, O. – C. & Co. Lim
Yellow amber, 7-3/4", 12-sided, smooth base, tooled blob mouth, American 1885-1900 .... **$150-200**

Geo. Schmuck's – Ginger Ale – Cleveland, O.
Medium orange amber, 8", 12-sided, smooth base, tooled blob mouth, American 1885-1900 ... **$275-375**

Guyette & Company / Registered / Detroit, Mich. – This Bottle Is Never Sold / C. & Co. Lim No. 5
Medium cobalt blue, 6-7/8", smooth base (G), tooled blob mouth, American 1885-1900 .... **$125-175**

Hayes Bros / Trade Mark / NB / Registered / Chicago, ILL – MCC
Cobalt blue, 7-3/8", 10-panels on side at base, smooth base, applied blob mouth, American 1885-1900 .... **$80-150**

Hendrickson – Bros. – Diamondville – Wyo.
Aqua, 7", smooth base, tooled blob top, American 1885-1900 .... **$500-600**

Geo. Schumck's / Ginger Ale / Cleveland, O, medium amber, 8", American 1885-1900, $275-375.

Hendrickson Bros. – Diamondville Wyo., aqua, 7", American 1885-1900, $500-600.

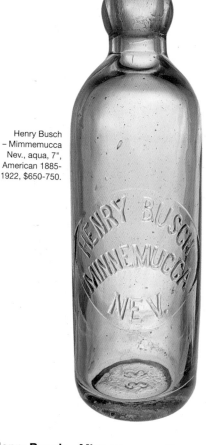

Henry Busch
– Mimmemucca
Nev., aqua, 7",
American 1885-
1922, $650-750.

Jamestown Brewing
Bottling Works N.Y.
– Jamestown, deep
aqua, 7", American
1892-1895, $75-100.

Henry Busch – Minnemucca – Nev.
Aqua, 7", smooth base, applied blob top, American 1885-1922 ....$650-750
Winnemucca is misspelled Minnemucca. There are no authentic sodas with the correct spelling.

H.L. Wigert / Burlington / Iowa – This Bottle / To Be Returned
Medium cobalt blue, 6-3/4", smooth base, applied blob mouth, rare color, American 1885-1900...$150-200

James Ray / Savannah / Geo – Ginger Ale
Deep cobalt blue, 7-3/4", smooth base, tooled blob mouth, American 1885-1900
....$300-450

Jamestown Brewing – Bottling Works N.Y. – Jamestown
Deep aqua, 7", smooth mug base, tooled blob top, American 1885-1900 .$75-100

James Dewar – Elko, Nev
Aqua, 7", smooth base, tooled blob top, American 1892-1895................$550-650

John Olbert & Co. – Durango – Colo.
Medium amethyst, 6", smooth base, tooled blob top, American 1880-1900
....$350-450

J.F. Deegan / Pottsville / PA – This Bottle / Not To / Be Sold
Deep red amber, 7", mug base, smooth base (Karl Hutter / C / New York), tooled blob mouth, rare, American 1885-1900 .... **$300-400**

J.G. Bolton / Lemont / ILLS – A. & D.H.C.
Medium cobalt blue, 6-3/4", smooth base, applied blob mouth, American 1885-1900 .... **$250-375**

J. Weilerbacher – Pittsburgh, PA. – Trade (W inside a sunburst) / Mark / Registered / C.C.C. 149
Yellow amber, 7-5/8", four front panels with a rounded back, smooth base, tooled blob mouth, American 1885-1900 .... **$150-200**

Jacob Schmidt / Pottsville, PA
Medium olive green, 6-3/4", smooth base, tooled blob mouth, very rare, American 1890-1900 ...... **$350-450**

James Dewar – Elko – Nevada
Aqua, 7", smooth base, tooled blob top, American 1892-1895 .... **$1,800-2,000**

Lascheid – Pittsburgh / PA – L (inside a wreath) / Registered / St. Clair / Carbonating / Est.
Amber, 8", four front panels and round back, smooth base (ST), tooled blob mouth, American 1885-1900 .... **$100-140**

Lohrberg Bros's / Bed Bud / ILL.
Light to medium green, 6-3/4", smooth base, tooled blob mouth, American 1885-1900 .... **$600-800**

Mayfield's – Celery Cola – J.C. Mayfield MFG Co. – Birmingham, ALA
Aqua, 7", smooth base, tooled blob top, American 1885-1895 .... **$100-200**

Mill's – Seltzer – Springs
Aqua, 6", smooth base (M), tooled blob top, American 1874-1875 .... **$100-150**

Moxie
Medium green, 7", smooth base, tooled blob top, American 1885-1900 .... **$150-250**

Norwich Bottling / Works / Norwich / N.Y.
Amber, 6-3/8", smooth base, tooled blob mouth, American 1885-1900 .... **$225-275**

Mel. Aro (around shoulder) / Eclipse Carbonating Company (inside a horseshoe) / Ecco (monogram) / St. Louis – 2 1/2 Cents Deposit / Required For Return / Of This Bottle
Deep amber, 6-1/2", smooth base (ECCO), tooled blob mouth, American 1885-1900 .... **$100-150**

J.F. Deegan / Pottsville / PA. – This Bottle / Not To / Be Sold – (on base) Karl Hutter / C / New York, deep red amber, 7", American 1885-1900, $300-400.

Moxie, medium green, 7", American 1885-1900, $150-250.

Moriarty & Carrol / Registered / Waterbury, Conn
Deep amber, 7-3/8", 10-panels on side of base, smooth base, tooled blob mouth, American 1885-1900 ....**$350-450**

National – Dope Co. – Birmingham Ala.
Aqua, 8", smooth base, tooled blob top, American 1885-1900 ....**$150-200**

Pike's Peak – M.W. Co. – Colo. City Colo.
Aqua, 7", smooth base, applied blob top, American 1880-1895 ....**$300-400**

P.J. Serwazi / Manayunk / PA
Medium olive green, 7-5/8", smooth base (S), tooled blob mouth, original loop with closure, rare, American 1890-1900 ....**$350-450**

Poudre Valley – Fort Collins Colo. – Bottling Works
Clear with amethyst, 7", smooth mug base, tooled blob top, American 1885-1900 ....**$550-650**

Registered / C. Norris & Co. / City / Bottling Works / Detroit, Mich. – C &CO. LIM
Medium cobalt blue, 6-3/4", smooth base (CN & CO), tooled blob mouth, American 1885-1900..**$140-180**

Standard / Bottling Works / Minneapolis / Minn. – 8 5 ABC
Deep amber, 6-3/4", smooth base (HR), applied blob mouth, American 1885-1900 ....**$225-275**

Standard Bottling – Silverton Colo. – Peter. Orello. Prop (on front) – Paper label on back reads: Birch Beer (large S in circle) – Colored and Flavored – Bottled By Standard Bottling Works – Silverton, Colo
Clear, 7-1/4", smooth base, tooled blob top, American 1885-1900.........**$325-425**

The Boley MFG. Co. / Bottles / & / Demijohns / 414 West 14th St. / N.Y. / Registered
Light to medium yellow-green, 6-7/8", smooth base, tooled blob mouth, American 1885-1900..**$150-250**

The City / Bottling / Works / Louisville – Seltzer Water
Cobalt blue, 6-5/8", smooth base (MK), applied blob mouth, American 1885-1900 rare color..**$800-1200**

The Pioneer Bottling Wks – Victor Colo.
Medium amethyst, 7", smooth base, tooled blob top, American 1885-1900 . **$200-250**

The Standard Bottling – Cripple Creek – Colo.
Aqua, 6", smooth base, tooled blob top, American 1880-1895 ....**$50-75**

Tonopah – Soda Works – Nev.
Aqua, 7", smooth base, tooled blob top, American 1902-1905 ....**$550-650**

Trade Mark / Jal (inside a diamond) / Registered / J.A. Lomax / 14 16 & 18 / Charles Place / Chicago – This Bottle / Must Be Returned
Deep cobalt blue, 6-3/4", smooth base (J.L.), applied blob mouth, American 1885-1900 ....**$75-100**

Union Bottling – Works – Victor Colo.
Aqua, 7", smooth base, tooled blob top, American 1885-1900 ....**$100-150**

Wagoner – Bottling Works – Wagoner, I. T. (Indian Territory Hutch)
Aqua, 7", smooth mug base, tooled blob top, American 1880-1890 ....**$50-75**
Wiseola – Bottling Co – Birmingham Ala.
Clear, 7", smooth base (star embossed on base), tooled blob top, American 1880-
1900 ....**$75-100**

Standard Bottling
– Silverton Colo., clear,
7-1/4", American
1885-1900, $325-425.

Ink Bottles

Ink bottles are unique because of their centuries-old history, which provides collectors today with a wider variety of designs and shapes than any other group of bottles. People often ask why a product as cheap to produce as ink was sold in such decorative bottles. While other bottles were disposed of or returned after use, ink bottles were usually displayed openly on desks in dens, libraries, and studies. It's safe to assume that even into the late 1880s people who bought ink bottles considered the design of the bottle as well as the quality of its contents.

Prior to the 18th century, most ink was sold in brass or copper containers. The very rich would then refill their gold and silver inkwells from these storage containers. Ink that was sold in glass and pottery bottles in England in the 1700s had no brand name identification, and, at best, would have a label identifying the ink and/or the manufacturer.

In 1792, the first patent for the commercial production of ink was issued in England, 24 years before the first American patent that was issued in 1816. Molded ink bottles began to appear in America around 1815-1816 and the blown three-mold variety came into use during the late 1840s. The most common shape of ink bottle, the umbrella, is a multi-sided conical that can be found with both pontiled and smooth bases. One of the more collectible ink bottles is the teakettle, identified by the neck, which extends upward at an angle from the base.

As the fountain pen grew in popularity between 1885 and 1890, the ink bottle gradually became less decorative and soon became just another plain bottle.

A.B. Laird's / Ink

Medium blue green, 2-1/8", 8-sided, open pontil, inward rolled lip, American 1840-1860 . **$3,500-4,500**

Albert's / Writing Fluid – Pitts. PA

Blue aqua, 2-1/4", open pontil, rolled lip, extremely rare, American 1840-1860, ... **$400-700**

B.A. Fahnestock & Co. / Ink & Ink Stand / Pittsburgh

Blue aqua, 2-3/8", open pontil, rolled lip, extremely rare, American 1840-1860 .... **$400-700**

Barrel Ink – Opdyke / Bros / Ink

Blue aqua, 2-1/2", barrel form, smooth base, tooled mouth, American 1875-1890 .... **$250-350**

Blake & Herring – N-Y

Rich emerald green, 3", 8-sided, open pontil, inward rolled lip, extremely rare, American 1840-1860 .... **$2,500-4,500**

Carters – Cloverleaf Ink

Cobalt blue, 2-3/8", 6-sided, smooth base, ABM top, American 1870-1880 .... **$100-150**

CA – RT – ER (on side at base) – Label reads: Hill and Kooken, Stationery, 11 Lyman Terrace, Waltham, Mass

Cobalt blue, 8", cathedral arch panels, smooth base (Carters), ABM lip, hard rubber dispenser, American 1920-1930... **$175-275**

Clark's / Superior / Record / Ink – Boston

Yellow amber, 6", open pontil-scarred base, flared lip, extremely rare, American 1840-1860 .... **$500-800**

Cone Ink

Medium olive green, 2-1/4", pontil-scarred base (X and 200), sheared and tooled lip, swirled glass lines, American 1840-1860 .... **$500-700**

Cone Ink

Yellow amber, 2-1/2", open pontil, inward rolled lip, American 1840-1860 .... **$600-800**

Cone Ink

Medium cobalt blue, 2-1/2" open pontil, inward rolled lip, American 1840-1860...................... **$1,500-2,500**

Cone Ink

Deep blue aqua, 2-3/8", smooth base, tooled mouth, American 1895-1910 .... **$120-180**

Cone Ink

Brilliant emerald green, 2-3/8", tubular pontil scar, outward rolled mouth, American 1840-1860 **$400-800**

Clark's / Superior / Record / Ink – Boston, yellow amber, 6", American 1840-1860, $500-800.

Stripe-pattern domed inkwell, clear glass with white and pink alternating stripe pattern swirled to right, 2-1/4", Sandwich Glass Works, Sandwich, Mass., American 1830-1850, $1,200-1,800.

Cone Ink – R.L. Higgins – Virginia City
Medium green, 2", smooth base, inward rolled mouth, American 1875-1883 ....**$800-1,000**

Cone Ink – Rogers & Cooper / St. Louis Mo (embossed)
Aqua, 3", open pontil, rolled lip, American 1840-1860...........................**$400-550**

Cone Ink
Medium cobalt blue, 3-3/4", drape pattern, panel for label, tubular pontil scar, applied double collared mouth, American 1840-1860....................................**$4,000-8,000**

Diamond / Ink Co.
Medium amber, 3-1/4", square form, smooth base (Diamond Ink Co. / Pat. Appd. For), tooled mouth, American 1885-1900...**$40-50**

Domed Ink – Bertinguiot
Yellow olive, 2-1/4", pontil-scarred base, sheared mouth, French 1840-1860 ....**$200-400**

Domed Ink – A.M. Bertinquiot
Black glass, 2-3/16", pontil-scarred base, sheared mouth, French 1840-1860 ....**$200-400**

Glass Funnel Inkwell – Simon's – Registered – Birmingham / May 30, 1845 – Clark's Patent (embossed on front)
Deep blue green, 3", polished pontil-scarred base, tooled opening, English 1845-1860 ....**$500-700**

Farleys – Ink
Yellow olive with amber tone, 3-1/2", 8-sided, open pontil, tooled flared-out lip, American 1840-1860 ....**$1,000-1,500**

Drape pattern ink, medium sapphire blue, 2-1/2", American 1840-1860, $800-1,500.

Farley's – Ink, medium olive yellow, 3-1/8", American 1840-1860, $700-900.

Harrison's / Columbian / Ink – Original Label reads: Harrison's Columbian Black Writing Fluid, South 7th Street, Philadelphia
Medium cobalt blue, 2", open pontil, inward rolled lip, American 1840-1860 ....**$700-900**

Harrison's / Columbian / Ink
Medium cobalt blue, 2", open pontil, inward rolled lip, American 1840-1860 ....**$600-800**

Harrison's / Columbian / Ink
Deep cobalt blue, 2", open pontil, inward rolled lip, American 1840-1860 **$800-1,400**

Harrison's / Columbian / Ink – Original label reads: Harrison's Columbian Black Writing Fluid, South 7th Street, Philadelphia
Medium cobalt blue, 4", open pontil, applied mouth, American 1840-1860 ....**$800-1,400**

Harrison's / Columbian / Ink
Cobalt blue, 5-3/4", open pontil, applied mouth, American 1840-1860 ....**$1,000-1,400**

Gross & Robinson's / American / Writing Fluid, deep blue aqua, 5-7/8", American 1840-1860, $500-800.

Igloo ink, medium cobalt blue, 2", American 1865-1880, $800-1,400.

Hover / Phila, sapphire blue, 5", American 1840-1860, $800-1,200.

Hohenthal / Brothers & Co / Indelible / Writing Ink / N.Y.

Yellow amber, 7", cylinder, pontil-scarred base, applied mouth with tool crimped pour spout, scarce, American 1840-1860 .... **$1,000-1,500**

Hoffman's / Ink – Label reads: Hoffman's Chemical Red Carmine Ink, Bridgeport, Connecticut

Aqua, 2-3/4", smooth base, tooled and ground lip, American 1875-1895 .... **$75-100**

Hover / Phila

Moss green, 4-1/2", cylindrical form, tubular pontil scar, tool flared mouth, American 1840-1860 .... **$300-600**

Hover / Phila

Sapphire blue, 5", cylindrical form, open pontil, tooled flared-out lip, rare, American 1840-1860 . **$800-1,200**

Igloo Ink – Label reads: Anti-Corrosive Jet Black Ink, Prepared by John Aannear, 128 Front St., Philadelphia

Aqua, 2", smooth base, sheared and ground lip, American 1865-1875 .... **$120-180**

Inkwell

Clear glass, 2", 14-vertical rib pattern, filler and four-quill opening on top, pontil-scarred base, American 1850-1870... **$200-300**

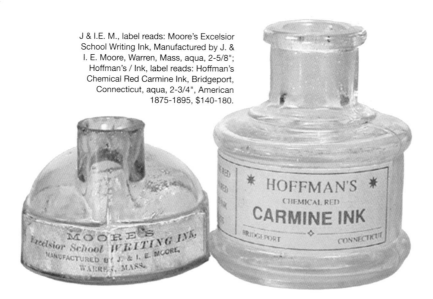

J & I.E. M., label reads: Moore's Excelsior School Writing Ink, Manufactured by J. & I. E. Moore, Warren, Mass, aqua, 2-5/8"; Hoffman's / Ink, label reads: Hoffman's Chemical Red Carmine Ink, Bridgeport, Connecticut, aqua, 2-3/4", American 1875-1895, $140-180.

J. & I.E.M. – Label Reads: Moore's Excelsior School Writing Ink, Manfactured by J. & I.E. Moore, Warren, Mass

Aqua, 2-5/8", smooth base, tooled and ground lip, American 1875-1895 **$75-100**

J. Raynald

Medium green, 2-1/2", globe form, smooth base, inward rolled mouth, American 1850-1870 .... **$250-350**

J.S. Dunham, St. Louis. M.

Brilliant aquamarine, 2-1/4", 12-sided, tubular pontil scar, inward rolled mouth, rare, unknown variant, American 1840-1860 .... **$400-800**

J.S. Mason / Philad.a

Bright blue green, 4-3/8", cylindrical, pontil-scarred base, tooled flared mouth, extremely rare, American 1840-1860 .... **$250-500**

Kosmian / Safety Ink

Brilliant blue green, 7-1/8", square with one indented embossed panel and beveled corners, smooth base, applied square collared mouth, rare, American 1860-1880 .... **$300-600**

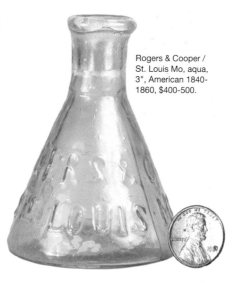

Rogers & Cooper / St. Louis Mo, aqua, 3", American 1840-1860, $400-500.

Master ink – Davids & Black – New York, light blue green, 6-3/8", American 1840-1860, $600-800.

Master ink – Collins' Ink Co. / Louisville KY, dark amber 9-7/8", American 1860-1875, $375-500.

Locomotive Ink – Trade Mark – Pat. Oct. 1874

Aqua, 2", locomotive form, smooth base, sheared and ground lip, American 1874-1880, made for Charles L. Lochman, Proprietor of Lochman's Locomotive Ink Company of Carlisle, Penn **$1,000-1,500**

Lyons Ink

Medium cobalt blue, 2-7/8", smooth base, tooled lip, American 1880-1895 .... **$300-400**

Master Ink – Carters – Label reads: Carter's – RYTO – Permanent – Blue Black – Ink

Cobalt blue, 7", smooth base, cathedral form, ABM lip, original stopper with screw top cap, American 1920-1930... **$275-325**

Master Ink – Carter – Label reads: Hill and Kocken Stationery 11 Lyman Terrace, Waltham, Mass. Tel. Waltham 3239-M

Deep cobalt blue, 8", 6-sided, cathedral form, smooth base, ABM lip, original rubber stopper with plastic screw cap, American 1920-1930 .... **$275-375**

Master Ink – Carters – Label reads: Carter's – RYTO – Permanent – Blue Black – Ink

Cobalt blue, 9", smooth base, cathedral form, ABM lip, original stopper with screw top cap, American 1920-1930... **$400-500**

Master Ink – Carters – Label reads: Carter's – RYTO – Permanent – Blue Black – Ink

Cobalt blue, 10", smooth base, cathedral form, ABM lip, original stopper with screw top cap, American 1920-1930... **$100-150**

Master Ink – Collins Ink Co / Louisville KY

Dark amber, 9-7/8", smooth base, applied mouth with hand tooled pour spout, extremely rare, American 1860-1875... **$375-500**

Master Ink – Davids & Black – New York (around shoulder)

Olive amber, 6-3/8", open pontil, applied sloping collar mouth, rare color, American 1840-1860 .. **$800-1,200**

Master Ink – Gross & Robinson's / American / Writing Fluid

Deep blue aqua, 5-7/8", iron pontil, applied mouth, rare, American 1840-1860 .... **$500-800**

Master Ink – Hover – Phila

Medium blue green, 7-1/2", open pontil, applied sloping double collar mouth with hand tooled pour spout, scarce, American 1840-1860 .... **$500-700**

Sided master ink, deep yellow olive green, half-gallon, 10", American 1845-1860, $5,000-8,000.

Saltglaze stoneware master ink – A.W. Harrison / Patent / Columbian Ink / Philadelphia, gray and brown, 10", American 1845-1860, $1,000-1,800.

Patterson's / Excelsior / Ink, deep blue aqua, 2-3/4", rare, American 1840-1860, $400-600.

Master Ink – R.L. Higgins – Virginia

Dark amber, 6", smooth base, applied mouth with pour spout, extremely rare, American 1875-1883 ....**$10,000-12,000**

Master Ink – Saltglaze Stoneware – A.W. Harrison / Patent / Columbian Ink / Philadelphia (stamped on side at shoulder)

Gray and brown, 10", handled, smooth base, mouth similar to wide applied style, American 1845-1860 ....**$1,000-1,800**

Master Ink – Stafford's / Ink

Dark puce, 7-3/4", smooth base, applied mouth, hand tooled pour spout, extremely rare color, American 1875-1885 ....**$700-800**

Multi-Sided Ink

Blue aqua, 1-3/4", 8-sided, pontil-scarred base, sheared and inward rolled lip, American 1840-1860 ....**$100-150**

NE Plus Ultra Fluid

Blue aqua, 2", cottage form, smooth base, burst sheared lip, American 1850-1860 ....**$275-325**

Patterson's / Excelsior / Ink

Deep blue aqua, 2-3/4", 8-sided, open pontil (reversed 3X), inward rolled lip, rare, American 1840-1860 ....**$400-600**

Rider on Horse (horizontal diamond) – Rider on Horse (horizontal diamond)

Dark yellow amber, 1-3/8", open pontil, tooled disk-type lip, blown in a two-piece mold, extremely rare, American 1815-1835, ...**$6,500**

S.F. Cal Ink Co

Medium amber, 2", cottage ink, smooth base, inward rolled lip, American 1850-1860 ....**$1,800-2,000**

S.O. Dunbar / Tauton / Mass., aqua, 8-5/8", American 1840-1860, $100-150.

Sheet's – Writing – Fluid – Dayton / O, blue aqua, 2-5/8", American 1840-1860, $400-700.

S. Fine / Blk. Ink
Aqua, 3-1/8", open pontil, sheared and ground lip, American 1840-1860 **$200-300**

S.O. Dunbar / Taunton / Mass
Aqua, 8-5/8", cylinder form, iron pontil, applied mouth, American 1840-1860 ....**$100-150**

Sheet's – Writing – Fluid – Dayton / O
Blue aqua, 2-5/8", 6-sided, corset-waist form, pontil-scarred base, inward rolled lip, American 1840-1860 ....**$400-700**

Teakettle Ink
Medium cobalt blue, 1-1/2", lobed melon form, smooth base, ground mouth with brass collar and cap, England 1830-1850..**$500-1,000**

Teakettle Ink (stoneware) – Compliments Of – The Letort Hotel – James F. Grandone, Prop. – Carlisle. PA
Two-tone light and dark pottery, 2-1/2", smooth base, wide smooth top, American 1880-1910...**$125-150**

Teakettle Ink
Jade clambroth, 2-1/2", smooth base, sheared and ground lip, American 1850-1870 ....**$325-425**

Teakettle Ink
Blue clambroth, 2-1/2", smooth base, sheared and ground lip, American 1850-1870 ....**$325-425**

Teakettle ink, milk glass, 2-3/8", American 1875-1885, $375-500.

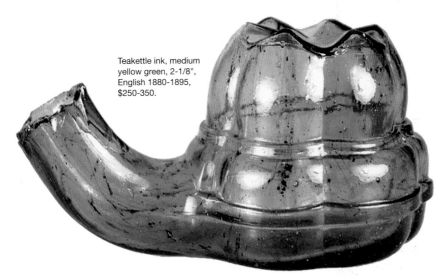

Teakettle ink, medium yellow green, 2-1/8", English 1880-1895, $250-350.

Teakettle Ink – Double Font

Clear glass, 3-1/2", embossed on upper font (D.R.G.M. No. 55922) and lower font (D.R.G.M.), smooth base, sheared lip with original metal neck ring and cap and metal separator ring, rare, double font inkwell provides two different ink colors from the same inkwell, English 1880-1895 ....**$375-475**

Teakettle Ink – Double Font

Clear glass, 4-1/2", polished pontil base, sheared and ground lip, rare, double font inkwell provides two different ink colors from the same inkwell, American 1880-1895 ....**$350-475**

Teakettle Ink – Miniature Beehive
Aqua, 1-1/8", beehive form, smooth base, sheared and ground lip, American 1880-1895 ....**$200-300**

Teakettle Ink – Beehive
Deep blue aqua, 2", beehive form, smooth base, rough sheared lip, European 1880-1895 ....**$275-375**

Teakettle Ink – Monroe's / Patent / School / Ink
Aquamarine, 2", 7-sided, two front panels embossed, smooth base, tooled and ground mouth, extremely rare, American 1860-1880...............................**$400-800**

Teakettle ink, medium apple green, 2", English 1880-1890, $275-475.

Teakettle ink, deep sapphire blue, 2", American 1875-1895, $275-450.

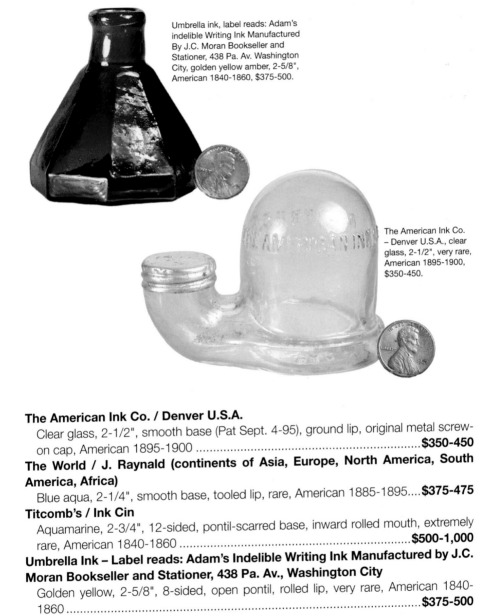

Umbrella ink, label reads: Adam's indelible Writing Ink Manufactured By J.C. Moran Bookseller and Stationer, 438 Pa. Av. Washington City, golden yellow amber, 2-5/8", American 1840-1860, $375-500.

The American Ink Co. – Denver U.S.A., clear glass, 2-1/2", very rare, American 1895-1900, $350-450.

The American Ink Co. / Denver U.S.A.
Clear glass, 2-1/2", smooth base (Pat Sept. 4-95), ground lip, original metal screw-on cap, American 1895-1900 ....**$350-450**

The World / J. Raynald (continents of Asia, Europe, North America, South America, Africa)
Blue aqua, 2-1/4", smooth base, tooled lip, rare, American 1885-1895....**$375-475**

Titcomb's / Ink Cin
Aquamarine, 2-3/4", 12-sided, pontil-scarred base, inward rolled mouth, extremely rare, American 1840-1860 ....**$500-1,000**

Umbrella Ink – Label reads: Adam's Indelible Writing Ink Manufactured by J.C. Moran Bookseller and Stationer, 438 Pa. Av., Washington City
Golden yellow, 2-5/8", 8-sided, open pontil, rolled lip, very rare, American 1840-1860 ....**$375-500**

Umbrella Ink – Boss' / Patent
Aquamarine, 2-5/8", tubular pontil scar, inward rolled mouth, American 1840-1860 ....**$400-800**

Umbrella Ink – J. Gundry / Cincinnati
Aquamarine, 3", 12-sided, tubular pontil scar, inward rolled mouth, American 1840-1860 ....**$400-600**

Umbrella ink, medium lime green, 2-5/8", American 1855-1865, $400-600.

Umbrella Ink – J.W. – Seaton – Louisville KY, medium blue green, 2-1/4", rare, American 1840-1860, $800-1,400.

Sided Ink – Zieber & Co. – Excelsior – Ink, deep blue green, 7-1/2", American 1840-1860, $4,500-6,000.

Umbrella Ink – James S. / Mason & Co.
Bright blue green, 2-1/2", octagonal form, tubular pontil scar, inward rolled lip, American 1840-1860 rare.**$400-800**

Umbrella Ink – Water's – Ink – Troy N.Y.
Light to medium blue-green, 2-3/4", 6-sided, open pontil, inward rolled lip, rare, American 1840-1860 color **$2,000-3,000**

Umbrella Ink – Wide Mouth
Medium pink amethyst, 1-7/8", 8-sided, pontil-scarred base, sheared and tool widened mouth, original cork with material wrap closure, extremely rare, American 1840-1860, found in rubble of the Glassboro N.J. building that was the office of the Whitney Glassworks **$5,000-7,000**

Umbrella Ink
Dark green, 4-1/2", smooth base, tooled lip, American 1850-1860 .... **$250-275**

Zieber & Co – Excelsior – Ink
Deep blue green, 7-1/2", 12-sided, iron pontil, applied mouth, American 1840-1860 .... **$4,500-6,000**
Zieber is one of the most sought after master inks.

FIGURAL INKS

Ink – Log Cabin
Clear glass, 2-1/2", smooth base, tooled flared mouth, American 1880-1890 .... **$350-700**

Ink – Two Story Building
Milk glass, 4-3/4", smooth base, tooled squared collared mouth, extremely rare, American 1860-1880**$500-1,000**

Teakettle Ink – Turtle
Clear glass, 1-5/8", smooth base, rough sheared lip, English 1880-1895 .... **$175-225**

Medicine Bottles

The medicine bottle group includes all pieces specifically made to hold patented medicines. Bitter and cure bottles, however, are excluded from this category because the healing powers of these mixtures were very questionable.

A patent medicine was one whose formula was registered with the U.S. Patent office, which opened in 1790. Not all medicines were patented, however, because after the passage of the Pure Food and Drug Act of 1907, the ingredients of medicines had to be listed on the bottle. As a result, most of these patent medicine companies went out of business when consumers learned that most medicines consisted of liquor diluted with water and an occasional pinch of opiates, strychnine, and arsenic. I have spent many enjoyable hours reading the labels on these bottles and wondering how anyone would survive after taking the recommended doses.

One of the oldest and most collectible medicine bottles, the embossed Turlington "Balsam of Life," was manufactured in England from 1723 to 1900. The first embossed U.S. medicine bottle dates from around 1810. When searching for these bottles, always be on the lookout for embossing and original boxes. Embossed "Shaker" or "Indian" medicine bottles are very collectible and valuable. Most embossed medicines made before 1840 are clear and aqua. The embossed greens, ambers, and blues, specifically the darker cobalt blues, are much more collectible and valuable.

H. Lakes's / Indian / Specific, deep
blue aqua, 8-1/4", American
1840-1860, $300-400.

ADR / Albany
Medium blue green, 4-3/4", oval form, smooth base, inward rolled lip, American 1840-1860 .... **$180-250**

A. Leitch & Co / Apothecaries / St. Louis
Deep blue aqua, 6", open pontil, applied mouth, extremely rare, American 1840-1860 .... **$400-600**

Alexanders / Silameau
Sapphire blue, 6-1/4", open pontil, applied mouth, American 1840-1860 .... **$1,200-1,600**

Allan's / Anti Fat – Botanic Medicine Co. – Buffalo, N.Y.
Medium cobalt blue, 7-5/8", smooth base, applied mouth, American 1875-1885 .... **$200-300**

American / Oil – Cumberland River – Kentucky
Blue aqua, 6-7/8", pontil-scarred base, wide outward rolled lip, American 1840-1860 .... **$250-300**

American – Medicinal / Oil – Burkesville / KY.
Blue aqua, 6-1/2", open pontil, applied mouth, American 1840-1860 .... **$350-450**

B. Denton's – Healing Balsam – Label reads: Denton's Vegetable Healing Balsam, Barton Denton, Madison St. Auburn, N.Y.
Aqua, 4-1/8", 8-sided, open pontil, applied sloping collar mouth, American 1840-1860 .... **$150-200**

B. Denton (embossed vine) Auburn, N.Y.
Blue aqua, 6-3/8", open pontil, applied mouth, American 1840-1860 .... **$80-120**

Barrell's – Indian – Liniment – H.C.O. Cary
Aqua, 4-3/4", open pontil, rolled lip, scarce, American 1840-1860... **$120-180**

Bartine's / Lotion
Aqua, 6-1/2", open pontil, applied mouth, American 1840-1860... **$140-180**

Beekman's – Pulmonic – Syrup – New York
Medium olive green in upper half shading to darker in the lower half, 7-1/4", 8-sided, pontil-scarred base, applied double collar mouth, very rare, American 1840-1860... **$5,000-7,000**

Bench's / Mixture Of / Cannabis Indica
Aqua Marine, 7-3/4", oval form, open pontil, applied mouth, extremely rare, American 1840-1860 **$600-800**

Blood Food / Prepared By / G. HandySide
Medium cornflower blue, 6-3/4", smooth base, applied mouth, English 1885-1900 .... **$150-200**

Blood Food / Prepared By / G. HandySide

Olive yellow, 7", smooth base, applied mouth, English 1885-1900 .... **$150-200**

Boston / Lung Institute

Clear, 2-5/8", wide-mouth jar, pontil-scarred base, outward rolled lip, American 1840-1860 ..... **$300-400**

Butler & Son – London / S.F. Urquhart – Toronto, C.W.

Blue aqua, 5-3/4", open pontil, applied mouth, extremely rare, Canadian 1840-1860 .... **$300-400**

C. Brinckerhoff – Health Restorative – Price $1.00 – New York

Medium yellow olive green, 7-3/8", pontil-scarred base, applied mouth, American 1840-1860 ..... **$1,500-2,000**

C.F. Haskell / Coloris / Capilli / Restitutuior

Blue aqua, 7-1/2", oval form, pontil-scarred base, applied mouth, American 1840-1860 .... **$250-300**

Carter's – Extract Of / Smart Weed – Erie

Aqua, 5-1/2", open pontil, applied mouth, American 1840-1860 .... **$200-300**

Carter's / Spanish / Mixture – Label reads: Carter's Spanish Mixture, Bennett & Beers, Druggists, General Agents and Proprietors, No. 3 Pearl Street, Richmond, VA

Deep olive green, 8-1/2", iron pontil, applied sloping double collar mouth, American 1840-1860 .... **$800-1,200**

Cattle Liniment – Breinig Fronefield & Co

Pale aqua, 6-1/2", pontil-scarred base, applied mouth, American 1840-1860 .... **$250-300**

Cerisiaux – Rheumatic / Antidote – Or Electric – Liniment – New York

Aqua, 5-1/4", open pontil, applied mouth, very rare, American 1840-1860 .... **$150-200**

Chloride / Calcium – St. Catharines – Canada

Blue aqua, 5-3/4", open pontil, applied mouth, Canadian 1840-1860 .... **$180-250**

Clark's / Syrup

Medium blue green, 9-3/4", smooth base, applied double collar mouth, American 1855-1865 .... **$400-600**

Clement's – Genuine Osceola / Liniment – Prepared By – J. Cochran / Lowell / Mass

Aqua, 6-7/8", open pontil, applied double collar mouth, extremely rare, American 1840-1860 .... **$500-700**

Constitutional / Beverage / W. Olmstead & Co. – New York, medium amber, 10-1/4", American 1865-1875, $275-375.

Davison & Son – Fleet Street, yellow olive green, 6", English 1770-1790, $200-350.

Dr. Cooper's Ethereal Oil for Deafness, aqua, 2-3/4", American 1840-1860, $250-300.

Cloud's Cordial – Cloud's Cordial

Straw yellow with olive tone, 10-1/2", tapered form, American 1870-1880 .... **$400-600**

Cordial Balm – Of Health – Prepared By – Dr. Braddee

Medium yellow olive, 4-1/4", open pontil rolled lip, extremely rare, currently the only known example, American 1830-1840 .... **$2,500-4,500**

Curtis & Trall / New York

Blue aqua, 9-1/4", iron pontil, applied mouth, American 1840-1860 .... **$150-200**

Davis & / Miller / Druggists / Baltimore (in a slug plate)

Medium sapphire blue, 8-1/2", iron pontil, applied mouth, American 1840-1860 .... **$700-800**

Davis' – Vegetable – Pain Killer

Aqua, 4-7/8", open pontil, applied double collar mouth, American 1840-1860 .... **$180-250**

Doctor – Geo. W. Blocksom – Druggist – Zanesville

Light sapphire blue, 8-1/4", 12-sided, iron pontil, applied squared collar mouth, extremely rare, American 1840-1860 .... **$1,000-1,500**

Doctor Oreste / Sinanide's / Medicinal / Preparation / Orestorin

Deep cobalt blue, 4-5/8", smooth base, tooled lip, American 1890-1910 .... **$200-300**

D.P. Brown – Buffalo, N.Y.

Yellow olive amber, 1-1/4", 12-sided salve jar, smooth base, rough sheared lip, American 1855-1870 .... **$400-600**

Dr. Bruce's – Indian Vegetable / Panacea – New Castle, KY

Blue aqua, 9", smooth base, applied mouth, American 1855-1865 .... **$375-475**

Dr. Cooper's – Ethereal / Oil – For / Deafness

Aqua, 2-3/4", open pontil, flared lip, rare, American 1840-1860 .... **$250-300**

Drs. D. Fahrney & Son – Preparation For / Cleansing The Blood / Boonsboro, M.D.

Medium copper topaz, 9-5/8", smooth base, applied mouth, very rare, American 1865-1875 ...... **$500-700**

Dr. D. Jaume's / Ague Mixture – Philadelphia

Aqua, 7-7/8", open pontil, applied tapered mouth, American 1840-1860 .... **$350-450**

Dr. Irish's Indian Bone Ointment, aqua, 6-1/2", American 1850-1860, $200-275.

Dr. H. James / Cannabis Indica / Craddock & Co / Proprietors / Phila / PA, aqua, 7-7/8", American 1880-1890, $250-300.

Dr. / Keeley's / Double / Chloride / Of / Gold Cure / For / Tobacco Habit / A / Tested / And / Infallible / Remedy / Discovered By / Dr. L.E. Keeley/ Dwight, Mas., K.G.C. / Leslie E. Kelley M.D., clear glass, 5-3/4", American 1890-1900, $275-375.

Dr. Duncan's – Expectorant / Remedy

Deep blue aqua, 6-3/8", open pontil, rolled lip, American 1840-1860.......**$200-250**

Dr. Edwards' – Tar Wild Cherry / & Naptha – Cough Syrup

Blue aqua, 5-1/8", open pontil, tooled top, American 1840-1860..............**$75-100**

Dr / E.J. Coxe – New Orleans – Southern / Cough Syrup

Medium green, 7-3/8", cylinder form, open pontil, applied mouth, extremely rare Southern colored pontil, American 1840-1860 ....**$3,500-4,500**

Dr. Friend's – Cough Balsam – Morristown, N.J.

Blue aqua, 6-1/8", pontil-scarred base, applied sloping collar mouth, rare, American 1840-1860..**$350-450**

Dr. Forsha's – Alternative / Balm

Green aqua, 5-1/2", open pontil, applied double collar mouth, rare color, American 1840-1860..**$400-600**

Dr. John Bull's / King Of Pain / Louisville KY

Aqua, 6-7/8", oval form, pontil-scarred base, applied sloping collar mouth, American 1840-1860..**$180-250**

Dr. H. Anders – Iodine Water (face on sun) – Hauriexhag / Fontevitale – 1855

Aqua, 8-1/8", smooth base, applied mouth, rare, American 1855-1865...**$350-450**

DRS. Ivans / & Hart / New York

Aquamarine, 7-3/8", 8-sided, open pontil, applied mouth, extremely rare, American 1840-1860..**$375-475**

Dr. Browder's / Compound Syrup / Of Indian Turnip – Label reads: Dr. Browder's Compound Syrup / Of / Indian Turnip / For The Cure Of / Consumption, Coughs, Colds, Spillage, Blood, and All Other Complications of the Chest

Aqua, 7", open pontil, applied mouth, American 1840-1860 ....**$400-650**

Dr. Henley's / Beef and Iron. Celery, medium orange amber, 11-5/8", American 1875-1885, $170-250.

Dr. Hoofland's / Balsamic Cordial, C.M. Jackson / Philadelphia, aqua, 7", American 1840-1860, $140-180.

Roback's / Scandinavien / Blood Purifier / Cincinnati, O, ice blue aqua, 7-3/4", American 1840-1860, $275-375.

Dr. Foord's – Pectoral / Syrup – New York
Aqua, 5-3/8", open pontil, applied mouth, American 1840-1860.............**$120-160**

Dr. Hamilton's – Indian / Liniment
Aqua, 5-3/8", oval form, open pontil, rolled lip, American 1840-1860.......**$275-350**

Dr. Hershey's / Worm Syrup
Aqua, 5-1/2", open pontil, inward rolled lip, rare, American 1840-1860....**$200-275**

Dr. Hoofland / Balsamic Cordial – C.M. Jackson / Philadelphia
Aqua, 7", open pontil, applied double collar mouth, American 1840-1860
....**$140-180**

Dr. Kellinger's – Magic Fluid – New York
Aqua, 3-3/4", open pontil, rolled lip, scarce, American 1840-1860..........**$120-160**

Dr. Kelling's / Pure Herb / Medicines
Aqua, 6-3/8", cylinder form, open pontil, applied mouth, American 1840-1860
....**$150-200**

Dr. Kennedy's – Medical / Discovery – Roxury, Mass
Blue aqua, 8-5/8", open pontil, applied mouth, American 1840-1860 ....**$75-100**

Dr. Meeker's Casca Rilla Tonic, The Meeker Medicine Co., Established 1854, Chicago, ILL
Olive green, 5-7/8", pontil-scarred base, applied double collar mouth, American 1855-1860..**$350-450**

Dr. H. Swayne's – Vermifuge – Philada
Aqua, 4-5/8", square form, open pontil, thin flared-out lip, American 1840-1860
....**$200-275**

Dr. S.A. Weaver's / Canker & / Salt Rheum / Syrup
Aqua, 9-1/2", oval form, iron pontil, applied mouth, American 1840-1860 .. **$150-250**

Dr. G.W. Phillips – Cough/Syrup – Cincinnati O, deep blue aqua, 7-1/2", American 1840-1860, $375-475.

Dr. Rose's – Prophylactic / Syrup – For – Consumption / Brochitis – Abscess's / & Scrofula – Philada, aqua, 6-7/8", American 1840-1860, $400-600.

E.A. Buckhout's Dutch Liniment / Prepared At / Mechanicville / Saratoga Co. NY, blue aqua, 4-3/4", American 1840-1860, $700-1,000.

Dr. S.C. Marsh / Druggist / Newark N.J.
Blue aqua, 6-1/4", open pontil, tooled lip, American 1840-1860 ....**$75-100**

Dr. S.S. Fitch – 707 B. Way, N.Y – Dr. Fitch's Tonic Wash
Deep blue aqua, 2-7/8", open pontil, flared lip, American 1840-1860.......**$100-150**

Dr. S.S. Fitch – 707 B. Way, N.Y – Dr. Fitch's Tonic Wash
Deep blue aqua, 4-1/2", open pontil, flared lip, American 1840-1860.......**$100-150**

Dr. W.J. Haas's – Expectorant – Schuylkill Haven – PA
Aqua, 5-3/8", open pontil, thin flared-out lip, extremely rare, American 1840-1860 ....**$300-400**

Dr. W.N. Handy / Easton, N.Y.
Deep olive green, 8-3/4", 12-sided, smooth base, applied mouth, extremely rare, American 1855-1860, blown at Mt. Pleasant Glass Works, New York ...**$800-1,200**

Dr. White / Cini. Ohio
Medium sapphire blue, 4", pontil base, rolled lip, very rare, American 1850-1865 ....**$200-225**

Dr. White's / Magic / Liniment
Medium sapphire blue, 4", smooth base, rolled lip, very rare, American 1850-1860 ....**$200-225**

Dr. Wistar's – Balsam Of – Wild Cherry – Philada
Aqua, 8-sided, open pontil, applied mouth, American 1840-1860 ....**$170-250**

Durno's / The / Mountain / Indian / Liniment
Blue aqua, 6", cylinder form, open pontil, inward rolled lip, very rare Indian medicine bottle, American 1840-1860 ....**$500-700**

E.A. Buckhout's / Dutch / Liniment / (standing man) – Prepared At / Mechanicville Saratoga, Co. N.Y.
Blue aqua, 4-3/4", open pontil, rolled lip, American 1840-1860.............**$700-1,000**

Flagg's Good Samaritan's Immediate Relief – Cincinnati, deep aqua, 3-7/8", American 1840-1860, $300-400.

Comstock & Brother Turkish Balm, aqua, 7-1/4", American 1840-1860, $375-550.

E.C. Allen / Concentrated / Electric Paste – OR / Arabian Pain / Extractor – Lancaster / Pa

Medium emerald green, 3-1/8", open pontil, inward rolled lip, American 1840-1860 .... **$600-800**

EDW. Wilder's / Compound Extract / Of Wild Cherry – Patented / (motif of five-story building) – EDW. Wilder & Co / Wholesale Druggists / Louisville Ky

Clear, 8-1/2", semi-cabin form, smooth base, tooled mouth, American 1885-1895 .... **$275-375**

EDW. Wilder's / Compound Extract / Of Wild Cherry – Patented / (motif of five-story building) – EDW. Wilder & Co / Wholesale Druggists / Louisville Ky

Clear, 7-1/4", semi-cabin form, smooth base, tooled mouth, American 1885-1895 .... **$275-375**

Flagg's Good – Samaritan's – Immediate – Relief – Cincinnati, O

Aqua, 3-3/4", 5-sided, open pontil, outward rolled lip, American 1840-1860 .... **$180-275**

For Colds / Coughs Croup & C / Immediate Relief / & / Speedy Cure

Amber, 4-7/8", pumpkinseed flask, smooth base, applied mouth, extremely rare form, American 1875-1885 .... **$500-700**

Follansbee's – Elixir – Of Health

Deep blue aqua, 8-3/4", iron pontil, applied mouth, extremely rare, American 1840-1860 .... **$500-700**

Forshas – Balm / Liniment

Medium green, 4-1/4", smooth base, thin flared-out lip, rare color, American 1840-1860........... **$250-350**

French's / Freckle Remover

Opaque milk glass, 5-1/8", smooth base, tooled mouth, American 1885-1895 .... **$140-180**

Gargling Oil / Lockport. N.Y.

Medium emerald green, 7-3/8", smooth base, applied sloping collar mouth, rare in this large size, American 1865-1875... **$140-180**

Genuine – Swaim's / Panacea – Philadelphia

Aqua, 7-7/8", open pontil, applied mouth, American 1840-1855... **$600-700**

Germ Bacteria Or / Fungus Destroyer / WM. Radam's / Microbe Killer / (man clubbing a skeleton) / Registered Trade Mark Dec. 13, 1887 / Cures / All / Diseases

Yellow amber, 10-1/2", smooth base, sheared and tooled lip, American 1890-1900 .... **$300-400**

G.W. Merchant / Chemist / Lockport / N.Y.

Blue green, 7", smooth base, applied tapered collar mouth, American 1860-1870 .... **$250-300**

G.W. Simonds' Vegetable Pain Curer – An Internal and External Remedy, Prepared by G.W. Simonds, Fitzwilliam, N.H., Price 25 Cents (label only)

Medium olive amber, 7-3/8", pontil-scarred base, applied sloping collar mouth, blown in a three-piece mold, American 1840-1860 .... **$375-475**

Gibb's / Bone Liniment

Medium olive green, 6-3/8", 6-sided, open pontil, applied tapered collar mouth, American 1840-1860 .... **$1,400-1,800**

Girolamo – Pagliano

Medium lime green, 4-1/4", open pontil, inward rolled lip, rare, American 1840-1860 .... **$275-375**

Gregory's Elixir of Opium – Prepared by W.L. Gregory, Pharmaceutical Chemist, 931 Main Street, Buffalo, N.Y. (label)

Yellow olive amber, 7-1/4", cylinder form, pontil-scarred base, applied double collar mouth, American 1830-1845 .... **$275-375**

Hamptons / V. Tincture / Mortimer / & Mowbray / Balto

Deep copper puce, 6-1/4", oval form, smooth base, applied square collar mouth, American 1855-1865 .... **$275-325**

Hamptons / V. Tincture / Mortimer / & Mowbray / Balto

Medium yellow topaz, 6-3/8", smooth base, applied mouth, American 1855-1865 .... **$275-325**

Holme & Kidd

Deep blue aqua, 7-5/8", iron pontil, outward rolled lip, American 1840-1860 .... **$140-180**

Honduras / Tonic / W.E. Twiss & Co / MFR

Medium golden yellow amber, 8-7/8", oval form, smooth base, tooled mouth, American 1880-1900 .... **$100-150**

Hubbell

Medium sapphire blue, 5-5/8", open pontil, applied mouth, very rare, American 1840-1860 ... **$800-1,200**

I. Covert's – Balm Of Life

Medium yellow olive green, 6", open pontil, applied mouth, American 1840-1860 .... **$800-1,200**

Jaque & Marsh's / Hive Syrup / New York, blue aqua, 4-7/8", American 1840-1860, $275-375.

Harrison's / Columbian / Tonic / Stimulant, label reads: Harrison's Columbian Tonic Stimulant, Appolos W. Harrison Manufacturer, No 10 South 7th Street, Philadelphia, clear glass 6-1/2", American 1840-1860, $600-800.

Handyside's / Blood Purifier, deep smoky olive green (black), 11", English 1875-1890, $275-375.

Hoffman's Mixture For Gonorrhea – Gleet & C. – Solomons & Co. – Savannah, Geo., aqua, 5-7/8", American 1880-1890, $80-140.

I.L. St. John's – Carminative – Balsam
Aqua, 4-5/8", pontil-scarred base, rolled lip, very rare, American 1840-1860 .... **$250-350**

Indian / Clemens (standing Indian) Tonic / Prepared By / Geo. W. House
Blue aqua, 5-1/2", open pontil, outward rolled lip, American 1840-1860 .... **$600-800**

Indian / Liniment
Blue aqua, 4-1/2", oval form, open pontil, rolled lip, American 1840-1860 .... **$140-180**

Indian – Vegetable – Balsam
Aqua, 4-1/2", open pontil, thin flared-out lip, American 1840-1860... **$140-180**

J.B. Wheatly's / Compound Syrup / Dallasburgh, KY – Label reads: Wheatley's Compound Syrup Cure of Chills & Fever, Prepared by J.B. Wheatley, Dallasburg, Ky
Blue aqua, 6", cylinder form, pontil-scarred base, applied double collar mouth, American 1840-1860 .... **$250-375**

J.B. Wilde & Co / Louisville
Blue aqua, 6-3/4", open pontil, applied mouth, American 1840-1960 .... **$100-150**

J.D. Thompsons – Rheumatic & Neuralgic / Liniment – Pitts PA
Blue aqua, 4-3/4", open pontil, rolled lip, American 1840-1860... **$375-475**

J. Folely's – Indian / Botanic – Balsam
Aqua, 6-3/4", open pontil, applied mouth, extremely rare, American 1850-1860 .... **$350-450**

John Fabers / Elixir Of / Oryza / N.Y.
Deep blue aqua, 8", rectangular wedge form, open pontil-scarred base, applied sloping double collar mouth, extremely rare in this form, American, 1840-1860 .... **$350-450**

John Gilbert & Co / Druggist / 177 North 3D. St. / Philada
Aqua, 12-1/4", 1-gallon, smooth base, applied mouth, American 1855-1865 .... **$275-325**

John Hart & Co. – John Hart
Deep amber, 7-1/8", heart form, smooth base, applied double collar mouth, American 1865-1875 **$450-550**

John / Youngson – Extract Of / American Oil
Aqua, 4", open pontil, rolled lip, American 1840-1860 .... **$90-125**

Healy & Bigelow (motif of Indian) – Indian Sagwa, aqua, 7-3/4", American 1880-1895, $140-180.

L.Q.C. Wishart's – Pine Tree / Tar Cordial / Phila. Patent (motif of pine tree / 1859, medium yellow green, 9-5/8", American 1865-1880, $200-275.

L.Q.C. Wishart's Pine Tree Cordial – Phila – Patent, medium yellow green, 9-1/2", American 1860-1870, $275-375.

Judson's – Cherry / & / Lungwort – Extract
Blue aqua, 8-1/4", open pontil, applied mouth, extremely rare, American 1840-1860 ....**$600-800**

L.P. Dodge – Rheumatic / Liniment / Newburg
Medium yellow amber, 6-1/8", open pontil, applied mouth, rare Newburg, New York colored pontil, American 1840-1860 ....**$1,800-2,700**

Lindsey's – Blood / Searcher – Pittsburgh, PA
Deep blue aqua, 8-3/4", red iron pontil, applied double collar mouth, American 1840-1860...**$1,000-1,500**

Lindsey's – Blood / Searcher – Hollidaysburg
Medium blue green, 9", smooth base, applied double collar mouth, rare in this color with Hollidaysburg embossing, American 1860-1870...............................**$350-450**

Log Cabin – Extract – Rochester, N.Y.
Amber, 7", smooth base (Pat. Sept 6th / 1887), tooled mouth, American 1887-1895 ....**$375-450**

Log Cabin – Extract – Rochester, N.Y.
Amber, 8-5/8", smooth base (Pat. Sept 6th / 1887), tooled mouth, American 1887-1895 ....**$375-450**

London – W.B. No 6
Deep green aqua, 5-1/2", pontil-scarred base, outward rolled lip, rare embossed variant, English 1830-1850...**$140-180**

Masury's / Sarsaparilla / Cathartic
Blue aqua, 9", smooth base, applied double collar mouth, American 1855-1870 ....**$275-400**

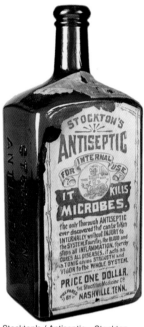

Stockton's / Antiseptic – Stockton Medicine Co. / Nashville, Tenn, label reads: Stockton's Antiseptic For Internal Use, It Kills Microbes, Price One Dollar, Prepared by the Stockton Medicine Co., Nashville, Tenn, medium amber, 10", American 1885-1895, $200-300.

Mrs. E. Kidder Dysentery Cordial – Boston, green aqua, 7-3/4", American 1840-1860, $180-275.

Mathewson's – Horse – Remedy – Price 50 CTS
Aqua, 6-3/4", pontil-scarred base, applied double collar mouth, scarce, American 1840-1860 **$275-375**

McCombie's / Compound / Restorative
Aqua, 6-7/8", open pontil, applied mouth, rare, American 1840-1860 .... **$150-200**

Morse's / Celebrate Syrup / Prov. R.I.
Deep blue green, 9-1/2", oval form, open pontil, applied mouth, American 1840-1860 ... **$2,500-3,500**

Mystic Cure – For / Rheumatism / And / Neuralgia – Mystic Cure – Label reads: Detchon's Mystic Cure for Rheumatism and Neuralgia, I.A. Detchon, M.D. Crawfordsville, Indiana, Price 75 Cents
Pale aqua, 6-1/2", smooth base, tooled lip, American 1890-1900 .... **$150-200**

Mrs. Dr. Secor / Boston, Mass
Deep cobalt blue, 9-1/2", smooth base, tooled lip, American 1885-1895 .... **$200-300**

Mrs. E. Kidder / Dysentery / Cordial / Boston
Aqua, 7-3/4", open pontil, applied sloping collar mouth, American 1840-1860 .... **$140-180**

Mrs. M. Cox's / Indian Vegetable / Decoction / Balto
Aqua, 8-3/8", cylinder form, open pontil, applied mouth, American 1850-1860 .... **$400-700**

Mrs. M. N. Gardners – Indian Balsam / Of Liverwort
Aqua, 5-1/8", cylinder form, open pontil, thin flared lip, American 1840-1860 .... **$120-160**

New York / C.F. Haskell / Coloris / Capilli / Restitutor
Aqua, 7-1/2", oval form, open pontil, applied mouth, rare, American 1840-1860 .... **$150-200**

N.Y. Medical – University – (embossed measure) – Label reads: Compound Fluid Extract of Cancer-Plant, Directions for Taking, and Prepared by the New York Medical University, Nos 6 7 8 University Place, New York City
Deep cobalt blue, 7-3/8", smooth base, tooled lip, scarce bottle made rare by the addition of the original label, American 1885-1900 .... **$300-400**

No 1 / Shaker Syrup – Canterbury, N.Y.
Blue aqua, 7-3/8", open pontil, applied mouth, American 1840-1860 .... **$200-275**

Ober & McConkey's – Specific – For – Fever & Aqua – Balt MD

Aqua, 6-5/8", 6-sided, open pontil, applied mouth, rare, American 1840-1860 .... **$500-600**

O'Rourke & Hurley / Prescription Chemists / Little Falls, N.Y.

Emerald green, 5-1/2", smooth base (C.L.C. Co.), tooled lip, American 1890-1900 .... **$80-140**

Pelletier's – Extract Of / Sarsaparilla – Hartford Conn

Blue aqua, 10-3/4", open pontil, applied double collar mouth, American 1840-1860 .... **$600-800**

Peruvian Syrup

Medium teal blue, 9-3/4", cylinder form, iron pontil, applied sloping collar mouth, rare color, American 1845-1860 .... **$1,845-1,860**

Prepared By – Dr. Easterly – St. Louis, MO

Blue aqua, 6", iron pontil, applied mouth, American 1840-1860 .... **$250-300**

Procter & Gamble / Glycerine

Clear, 7-7/8", wedge shape, smooth base, applied mouth, American 1850-1860 .... **$180-275**

Pure – Family – Nectar

Clear, 8-7/8", open pontil, applied mouth, American 1840-1860 .... **$120-160**

Radway's – Sarsaparillian / Resolvent – R.R.R. – Entd. Acord / To Act Of / Congress

Medium lime green, 7-3/8", smooth base, applied double collar mouth, American 1870-1880 **$150-250**

R.E. Sellers & Co. – Pittsburgh

Blue aqua, 6-7/8", iron pontil, applied double collar mouth, rare, American 1840-1860 .... **$120-160**

Rev. T. Hill's / Vegetable Remedy

Aqua, 5", oval form, open pontil, applied mouth, American 1840-1860 .... **$90-150**

Rev. T. Hill's / Vegetable Remedy

Aqua, 6", oval form, open pontil, applied mouth, American 1840-1860 .... **$90-150**

Roswell Van Bushkirk / Druggist / Newark N.J.

Blue aqua, 6", open pontil, applied square collar mouth, American 1840-1860 .... **$275-400**

R.R.R. / Radway's Ready Relief / One Dollar / New York – Entd Accord To – Act Of Congress

Blue aqua, 8", open pontil, applied mouth, American 1840-1860 .... **$250-350**

Paul G. Schuh Rattle Snake Oil – Cairo, Ill., clear glass, 5-1/2", American 1885-1895, $200-300.

Rees / Remedy / For / Piles, aqua, 7-1/2", American 1840-1860, $375-475.

Sims Tonic / Elixir / Pyrophosphate / Of Iron Sims Tonic Co. – Antwerp N.Y., medium amber, 7-1/4", American 1901-1905, $140-200.

Russian – Hair Rye – No. 1
Blue aqua, 3-3/8", open pontil, tool flared-out lip, American 1840-1860...**$140-160**

S & M – Label reads: Fluid Extract of Valerian, Prepared Only by Smith & Melvin, Chemist, 825 Washington Street, Boston
Pale aqua, 4-1/4", 12-sided, open pontil, tool flared-out lip, American 1840-1860 ....**$175-250**

Shakers' / Aromatic Elixir Of Malt / Pleasant Hill, / KY
Blue aqua, 8-3/4", smooth base, applied square collar mouth, American 1870-1880 ....**$150-200**

Shaker Syrup / No. 1 – Canterbury, N. H. – Label reads: Corbett's Shaker, Compound Concentrated Syrup of Sarsaparilla, Prepared at Shaker Village, Merrimack Co., N.H.
Aqua, 7-1/2", open pontil, applied mouth, American 1840-1860.............**$375-475**

Shaker Syrup – D. Miller & Co
Blue aqua, 7-1/4", open pontil, applied sloping collar mouth, American 1840-1860 ....**$400-500**

Sheperd's – Vermifuge
Aqua, 4-7/8", open pontil, rolled lip, American 1840-1860 ....**$90-125**

Smith's – Green Mountain – Renovator – East Georgia, VT
Yellow amber, 7", rectangular with wide beveled corner panels, iron pontil, applied double collar mouth, American 1840-1860 ....**$1,200-1,600**

S.M. Kier – Petroleum – Pittsburgh, PA
Blue aqua, 6-5/8", open pontil, applied collar mouth, American 1840-1860 . **$80-140**

Sweet's Blk Oil
– Rochester N.Y., deep
blue green, 5-7/8",
American 1840-1860,
$1,400-1,800.

Vaughn's
– Vegetable /
Lithontriptic /
Mixture – Buffalo,
deep blue aqua,
7-5/8", American
1855-1865,
$400-600.

Sparks / Kidney & Liver / Cure / Trade Mark / (upper torso of a man) / Perfect Health / Camden, N.J.

Medium yellow amber, 9-1/2", smooth base, tooled mouth, very rare, American 1880-1900...**$800-1,200**

Sweet's Bl'K Oil – Rochester. N.Y.

Blue green, 6", open pontil, applied sloping collar mouth, rare, American 1840-1860 ....**$1,800-2,700**

Taylor's – Indian – Ointment

Aqua, 3", 6-sided, open pontil, rolled lip, extremely rare, American 1840-1860 **$350-450**

U.S.A. / Hosp. Dept

Yellow amber olive, 9-1/4", smooth base (SDS), applied double collar, American 1863-1870...**$700-900**

U.S.A. / Hosp. Dept

Blue aqua, 9-1/4", smooth base (X), applied mouth, American 1863-1870. **$150-250**

U.S.A. / Hosp. Dept

Yellow olive green, 9-3/8", smooth base (six-pointed star), applied double collar mouth, American 1863-1870 ....**$800-1,200**

Wakelee's / Camelline

Pale ice blue, 3-1/4", smooth base, tooled lip, American 1890-1900 ....**$100-150**

Winant's / Indian / Liniment

Aqua, 4-7/8", open pontil, rolled lip, rare, American 1840-1860 ....**$350-450**

Worner's / Rattler Oil / Phoenix, ARZ

Clear, 3-1/2", smooth base, tooled lip, rare, American 1890-1900 ....**$150-200**

Milk Bottles

The first patent date for a milk bottle was issued to the "Jefferson Co. Milk Assn." in January 1875. The bottle featured a tin top with a spring clamping device. The first known standard-shaped milk bottle (pre-1930) was patented in March 1880 and was manufactured by the Warren Glass Works of Cumberland, Maryland.

In 1884, A.V. Whiteman patented a jar with a dome-type tin cap to be used with the patented Thatcher and Barnhart fastening device for a glass lid. No trace exists of a patent for the bottle itself, however. Among collectors today, the Thatcher milk bottle is one of the most prized. There are several variations on the original. Very early bottles were embossed with a picture of a Quaker farmer milking his cow while seated on a stool. "Absolutely Pure Milk" is stamped into the glass on the bottle's shoulder.

An important development in the design of the milk bottle was the patent issued to H.P. and S.L. Barnhart in September 17, 1889, for their methods of capping and sealing. They developed a bottle mouth that received and retained a wafer disc or cap. It was eventually termed the milk bottle cap and revolutionized the milk bottling industry.

Between 1900 and 1920, not many new bottles were designed or had patents issued. With the introduction of the Owens semi-automatic and automatic bottle machines, milk bottles became mass produced. Between 1921 and 1945, the greatest number of milk bottles were manufactured and used. After 1945, square milk bottles and paper cartons became common.

Recently, there has been a renewed interest in collecting milk bottles. Two types of milk bottles are especially collectible. The first is the "Baby Top" bottle, which featured an embossed baby's face on the upper part of the bottle's neck. The second is the "Cop-the-Cream," which displays a policeman's head and cap embossed into the neck. The "Baby Top" design was invented in 1936 by Mike Pecora, Sr., of Pecora's Dairy in Drums, PA. Pecora's Dairy used quart, pint, and half-pint round bottles with pryo printing. Fifteen years after the original baby face was introduced, a "twin face" Baby Top was made with two faces, back to back, on opposite sides of the bottle. The Baby Top and Cop-the-Cream, as well as Tin Tops, are very rare and valuable.

The color mentioned in the following bottle descriptions is the color of the lettering on the bottle.

Baby Tops

Associated Dairies, Los Angeles, CA
Red and blue **$125**

Bomgardner Dairy
Orange................... **$75**

Coweset Farm
Black...................... **$75**

Dickson Dairy, Dickson, PA
Red........................ **$75**

Fairyland Farms
Red........................ **$75**

Julius Anderson, Rockland, ME
Red........................ **$75**

Orchard Farm Dairy, Schenectady, NY
Orange................... **$75**

Riviera Dairy, Santa Barbara, CA
Orange and green **$100**

Reservoir Farm, Moonsocket, RI
Orange................. **$125**

Strathbar Farms, Frankfort, NY
Red and blue **$125**

Sunbury Dairy
Orange................. **$100**

Sunshine Dairy
Red........................ **$35**

Webb Brook Farm
Red........................ **$50**

Associated Dairies, Los Angeles, CA, red and green, $250.

Coweset Farm – Grade – For Particular People, black, $75.

Wait's – Belvidere, IL, red, $150.

Webb Brook Farm, red, $75.

COP THE CREAM

Bentley's Dairy, Fall River, MA
   Orange.................. **$100**

Crestall Dairy, Carlstadt, NJ
   Red...................... **$125**

Eberhart & Rhodes Dairy, Puxsutawney, Pa
   Red...................... **$125**

Glenside Dairy, Deep Water, NJ
   Brown **$100**

Harpers Dairy, Wominister, MA
   Orange.................. **$125**

Losten Dairy, Chesapeake, Md
   Red...................... **$125**

Manor Dairy, Madison, WI
   Red...................... **$150**

Old Homestead Dairy, Windsor, VT
   Red...................... **$125**

Roe Dairy
   Blue **$150**

Morningcrest – Eau Claire, WI, orange, $150.

Old Homestead – Windsor, VT, red, $125.

Roe Dairy, blue, $150.

Sweet's Dairy – Fredonia, N.Y., orange, $150.

CREAM TOPS

Bitter Root Parlor Dairy, Stevenson, MT
   Brown and red **$75**
Bordens Dairy Delivery Co.
   Red........................ **$75**
Gateway Pure Milk
   Red and blue **$200**
Graduate Milk Bottles
   Red........................ **$50**
Hanson Dairy, Watervliet, MI
   Black and tan........ **$40**

Indiana Dairy Co., Indiana, PA
   Black..................... **$45**
Locust Grove Stock Farm, Rehoboth, MA
   Red and blue **$75**
Maine Dairy, Portland, ME
   Red........................ **$45**
Miller Dairy, Connersville, IN
   Red and blue **$50**
Modern Top Dairy
   Red and tan **$75**

Mountain Meadow Dairy, Bisbee, AZ
   Brown and red **$75**
Netherland
   Red........................ **$30**
Sanitary Dairy, Fort Dodge, IA
   Red........................ **$35**
Star Dairy, New London, CT
   Red........................ **$25**
Sunshine Dairies, Utica, NY
   Red and blue **$45**

Gateway Pure Milk – Cream That Whips, blue and red, $40.

Mayflower Dairy – Vancouver, WA, red, $50.

Model Dairy – Clintonville, WI, red, $50.

Muller's – ckford, IL, ge and $75.

Round Top Farm – Dammariscota, ME, green, $50.

Shineman's Dairy – Canajoharie, N.Y., orange, $30.

QUARTER PINTS

Almida County, Oakland, CA, orange, $30.

Benty & Sons, Fairbanks, AK (semi-rare)
Red **$50**
Bill Bros., Cortland, N.Y.
Red **$20**
C.A. Dorr Dairy, Watertown, N.Y.
Orange **$20**
Casey Dairy, Cortland, N.Y.
Red **$20**
Cramers Dairy, Fairbanks, AK (semi-rare)
Red and black **$50**
Gillette & Sons Dairy
Red **$10**
H.J. Whitmore, Clayton, N.Y.
Red **$20**
J.R. McNulty, Watertown, N.Y.

Orange **$30**
Rice's Dairy, Lihue, HI (semi-rare)
Red **$50**
Rock Castle Heavy Whipping Cream, Lynchburg, VA
Green **$30**
Rutland Hills Farm, Watertown, NY
Orange **$20**
Women's Missionary Conference of the M.E. Church, Clarksburg, WV
Red **$50**

Bay City, San Leandro, CAL, red, $30.

Elkhorn Farm, Watsonville, CA, orange, $20.

Dairy Products Laboratory, blue, $50.

Wildwood Dairy, Santa Rosa, CA, black, $30.

GALLONS

Bergman's Dairy, Derry, PA
Red........................ **$50**
Carson County Creamery, Rawlins, WY
Orange................... **$50**
Indiana Dairy, Indiana, PA
Black...................... **$50**

Keystone Dairy, New Kensington, PA
Red........................ **$50**
Linger Light Dairy, New Castle, PA
Orange................... **$50**
Model Dairy, Corry, PA
Orange................... **$50**
North Hills Dairy, Pittsburgh, PA
Red........................ **$50**

Page's Milk, Pittsburgh, PA
Orange................... **$50**
P.S. McGee Dairy, Blair County, PA
Red........................ **$50**
R.W. Cramer & Sons, PA
Red........................ **$50**

Carbon Country Creamery, Rawlins Wyo., orange, $50.

Harmony Dairy, Pittsburgh, PA, red, $50.

Lewis Dairies, Grove City, PA, green, $50.

Model Dairy, Corry, PA, orange, $50.

Page's Pittsburgh Milk Co, Pittsburgh, PA, red, $50.

SQUARE QUARTS

Bechtel's Dairy, PA
    Green...................... **$10**

Brook Hill Farm, Acidophilus Milk
    Red......................... **$20**

Central Dairy, Central Bridge, N.Y.
    Red......................... **$25**

Crane Dairy Co.
    Orange................... **$10**

Guard Your Health
    Orange................... **$10**

Mauer's Dairy, PA
    Orange................... **$10**

Merry's Dairy, Ben Avon, PA
    Red and green **$30**

Meyer's Milk, 57th Anniversary
    Purple **$30**

Monence Dairy, Monence, Il
    Black..................... **$10**

Woodlawn Dairy
    Red......................... **$30**

Magic Milk, green, $10; Monence, Monence, IL, purple, $10; Crane Dairy, orange, $10; J & J Dairy, Atlantic City, NJ, red, $10; Sunflower, red, $20.

Meyer's Milk, 57th Anniversary, purple, $30.

COFFEE CREAMERS

All Star Dairies
Red........................ $20

Blanding Dairy, St. Johns, MI
Red........................ $20

Cattlemen's Café, Oklahoma City, OK
Black..................... $50

Indiana Dairy, Indiana, PA
Black..................... $40

Kenmore Lanes, Kenmore, N.Y.
Black..................... $50

Kennersley Farm, MD
Red........................ $30

Link's, Randolph, N.Y.
Red........................ $40

Marion Center Creamery, Indiana, PA
Red........................ $20

Meadow Gold Milk
Red........................ $20

New London Mohegan Dairy, CT
Brown.................... $20

Norman's Kill, Albany, N.Y.
Orange.................. $30

Potomac Farms, MD
Orange.................. $20

Rehoboth Dairy, Rehoboth, DE (semi-rare)
Red........................ $50

R.J. Murphy & Sons Dairy
Orange.................. $30

Royale Dairy, Keyser, W.V.
Red........................ $30

Indiana Dairy, Indiana, PA, black or milk glass, $40.

Johnson's Dairy – Home of Baseball, Cooperstown, NY, black, $75.

Mountain Dairy, Sunbury, PA, red, $20.

Picket's Pasteurized Products, Sheridan, IN, orange, $40.

Strickler's – It's Better – Cream, Huntingdon, PA, orange, $20.

Tin-Top Milks

Benedict Bros. – Milk & Cream – 548 Castro St.
Clear, half-pint cream **$100**

Ewells XL Dairy – Bottled Milk – Depot 21st & Folsom Streets – Trade Mark – This Bottle To Be Washed And Returned
Clear, half-pint cream **$100**

Fairmont 42 – Randall Dairy
Clear, pint, American 1885-1905........................**$100**

Jersey Creamery M.Y.S. 1413 Park St., Alameda – This Bottle Must Be Returned
Clear, pint, includes tin-top, American 1885-1905
....**$160**

Jersey Creamery M.Y.S. 1413 Park St., Alameda – This Bottle Must Be Returned
Clear, half-pint, includes tin-top, American 1885-1905 ....**$50**

Jersey Farm – 837 Howard St. – This Bottle To Be Washed and Returned
Clear, half-pint cream **$100**

Merced Dairy – Solomon Bros. – 1507 Broderick St.
Clear, pint, includes tin-top, American 1885-1905 .**$100**

Milbrae California Milk Co. – Folsom & 21st Sts. – S.F. Cal
Clear, pint, includes tin-top, American 1885-1905
....**$120**

People's Creamery Hatch and Orth 3776-24th St. – S.F.
Clear, quart, American 1885-1905 ....**$100**

Absolutely / Pure Milk (motif of man milking cow) / The Milk Protector – To Be Used Only As Designated / Milk / & Cream / Jar – Thatcher MF'F. CO. / Potsdam N.Y., clear glass quart, 1886-1895, $700-1,000.

Miscellaneous

Alta Crest Farms – Spencer Mass (embossed with cow's head)
Medium lime green, quart, smooth base, ABM top, American 1950..................................... **$1,000-1,100**

A. Rosa & Co. – Between 5th & 6th – 20 Oak Grove Ave.
Clear, pint, smooth base **$100**

Big Elm – Dairy – Company – One Quart – Liquid – Registered
Green, quart, 9-1/4", smooth base (B-34), ABM lip with cap seat, American 1920-1930........... **$180-250**

Absolutely / Pure Milk (motif of man milking cow) / The Milk Protector – To Be Used Only As Designated / Milk / & Cream / Jar, clear glass, pint, 1886-1895, $500-700.

Sorges Brand (on applied token) – Sorge's / Selected Milk / Manitowog / Dairy Co. / 1 Quart Sealed / Pat'd Sept 22 1925, clear glass, quart, 1925-1935, $200-300.

To Be Washed / And Returned / Not To Be Bought Or Sold (circular slug plate), medium amber, half-gallon, 1900-1915, $180-220.

Bordens
Ruby red, quart, U.S. Pat. No. 2,177,396 60 – Royal Ruby – Anchor Glass (around base), American 1950, manufactured by Anchor Hocking for experimental purposes for the Borden Milk Company, fewer than twelve were made **$1,800-2,000**

Dairy Delivery Co. – San Francisco – Wash and Return
Clear, pint, smooth base, American 1900-1910 .**$100**

E.F. Mayer – Phone – Glen D3887R – 289 Hollenbeck Street
Medium amber, quart, smooth base (34 & M), ABM top, American 1940-1950 .... **$80-100**

Merced Dairy – Salomon Bros. – 1507 Broderick St.
Clear, pint, smooth base, American 1940-1950 .**$100**

One Quart / Liquid / Carrigan's / Niagara / Dairy Co. / Reed
Bright green, quart, 9-3/8", smooth base, ABM lip with cap seat, American 1920-1930 .... **$375-450**

People's Dairy – 24th & Church Strs.
Clear, pint, American 1885-1905 .... **$50**

San Mateo County Dairy – Trade Mark – Phone Mission 227. 1818-1822 Howard St.
Clear, pint, American 1885-1905 .... **$100**

San Pedro & X.L. Dairy Co. – S.F. 1515 California St.
Clear, pint, smooth base, American 1990-1920 ...**$70**

Sorge's – Selected Milk / Manitowog – Dairy Co. / 1 Quart Sealed – Pat'd Sept 22 1925 – On Applied Token: Sorges Brand
Clear, quart, smooth base, ABM lip, rare, American 1925-1935 .... **$200-300**

To Be Washed – And Returned – Not To Be Bought or Sold (in circular slug plate)
Medium amber, 9-5/8", smooth base, applied double collar mouth, American 1900-1915 .... **$180-120**

Weckerle / Reg –Weckerle / 1 QT
Bright green, quart 9-1/4", smooth base (W), ABM with cap seat, American 1920-1930 .... **$275-375**

Mineral Water Bottles

Mineral water, also known as spring water, was a very popular beverage for a full century, with peak consumption between 1860 and 1900. Consequently, most collectible bottles were produced during these years. While the earliest bottles are pontilled, the majority are smooth based. The water came from various springs that were high in carbonates (alkaline), sulfurous compounds, various salts, and were often naturally carbonated. The waters were also thought to possess medical and therapeutic qualities and benefits.

Although the shapes and sizes of mineral bottles are not very creative, the lettering and design, both embossed and paper, are bold and interesting. The bottles were produced in a variety of colors and range from 7 inches to 14 inches high. Most were cork-stopped and embossed with the name of the glasshouse manufacturer. In order to withstand the the high-pressure bottling process and the gaseous pressure of the contents, the bottles were manufactured with thick, heavy glass. Their durability made them suitable to be refilled many times.

A.D. Schnackenberg & Co. / Mineral Water / Brooklyn. N. Y., medium golden amber, pint, rare, American 1870-1880, $500-700.

Albert Crook / Paradise Spring / Saratoga Co. N.Y, deep olive green, quart, extremely rare, American 1865-1875, $250-350.

Bear Lithia Water / Bear (motif of bear) Trade Mark / Near / Elkton, VA, pale aqua, half-gallon, American 1885-1895, $175-275.

A. D. Schnackenberg & Co. / Mineral Water / Brooklyn, N.Y.
Deep amber, pint, smooth base, applied mouth, very rare, American 1870-1880 ....**$500-700**

Aletic China Water / Discovered By / (coat of arms) / Prof. Lavender
Yellow olive green, half-pint, smooth base, applied mouth, American 1870-1880 ....**$180-275**

Andrew Lawrence / York, PA
Medium emerald green, 7-3/8", iron pontil, applied blob mouth, extremely rare, one of only two known examples, American 1840-1860 ....**$500-700**

A. Schroth / Sch.ll Haven – Superior / Mineral Water / Union Glass Works
Medium cobalt blue, 7-3/8", mug base, iron pontil, applied mouth, scarce, American 1840-1860..**$400-700**

Avery Lord
Medium cobalt blue, 7-1/4", smooth base, applied mouth, American 1855-1870 ....**$200-250**

Avery N. Lord – Utica N.Y.
Aqua, 7-1/4", smooth base, applied mouth, American 1855-1870...........**$200-250**

B. Bick & Co. – Mineral Water
– Cincinnati – B, cobalt blue, 7-1/2",
American 1840-1860, $350-450.

Blount Springs / Natural / Sulphur
Water – Trade / BS / Mark, deep
cobalt blue 9", American 1870-1880,
$375-550.

Buffum's Sarsaparilla & Lemon
– Mineral Water – Pittsburgh, cobalt
blue, 7-3/4", American 1840-1860,
$400-600.

A.W. Rapp's / Improved / Patent Mineral Water – Soda Water / R / New York
Emerald green, 6-7/8", iron pontil, applied mouth, American 1835-1845
....**$300-400**

B. Bick & Co – Mineral Water – Cincinnati – B
Cobalt blue, 7-1/2", 10-sided with embossed tear drop in each panel around
shoulder, iron pontil, applied blob mouth, rare, American 1840-1860 ......**$350-450**

Buffum & Co / Pittsburgh – Sarsaparilla / And / Mineral Water
Deep cobalt blue, 8", smooth base, applied mouth, American 1855-1865
....**$800-1200**

Carter & / Wilson / Manuf's / Boston – Soda & / Mineral / Water
Deep blue green, 6-7/8", iron pontil, applied sloping collar mouth, American 1840-
1860 ....**$400-600**

Carter & / Wilson / Manuf's / Boston – Soda & / Mineral / Water
Deep blue green, 6-3/4", iron pontil, applied sloping collar mouth, American 1840-
1860 ....**$400-600**

Franklin Spring / Mineral Water / Ballston Spa / Saratoga Co. N.Y., emerald green, pint, American 1865-1875, $200-275.

Colemans / Concentrated / Spring Water White Sulphur / Dallas Texas – Pat'd Aug 1 '76', medium amber, pint, American 1870-1880, $400-700.

Irondale Spring / W. VA, medium golden amber, pint, very rare, American 1865-1875, $400-600.

Champion Spouting Spring / Saratoga Mineral / Springs / (CSS monogram) / Limited / Saratoga N.Y. – Champion / Water

Blue aqua, pint, smooth base, applied mouth, American 1865-1875 ....$150-200

Clark & White / C / New York / NII

Deep olive green, pint, smooth base, applied mouth, rare, American 1860-1865 ....$180-220

Clark & White / C / New York

Deep olive green, pint, smooth base, wide mouth with rolled lip, early widemouth salt jar, extremely rare, American 1855-1865 ....$4,000-6,000

Congress & Empire Spring Co / Hotchkiss' Sons / C / W / New York / Saratoga, N.Y.

Olive green, half-pint, smooth base, applied mouth, American 1865-1875 . $500-800

Congress & Empire Spring Co / Columbian Water / Saratoga, N.Y.

Medium blue green, pint, slope shoulder, smooth base, applied mouth, American 1865-1875..$800-1,400

Covert / Morristown / N.J. – Superior / Mineral / Water

Medium cobalt blue, 6-7/8", iron pontil, applied mouth, American 1840-1860 ....$1,500-2,500

Crystal Spring Water / C.R. Brown / Saratoga Springs / N.Y.

Deep emerald green, quart, smooth base, applied mouth, rare, American 1865-1875 ....$375-475

Darling & Cobb's / Improved / Mineral Water – Boston / C

Light blue green, 6-7/8", iron pontil, applied sloping collar mouth, American 1840-1860 ....$150-275

Deep Rock Springs / Oswego, N.Y. / C. MC. N & Co., blue aqua, quart, rare, American 1870-1880, $275-450.

Gardner & Landon / Sharon / Sulphur Water, medium olive green, quart, American 1860-1875, $1,000-1,500.

Gettysburg Katalysine / Water, yellow emerald green, quart, American 1865-1875, $275-375.

Demott's / Celebrated / Soda or Mineral / Waters – Hudson County / N.J.
Cobalt blue, 7-3/8", iron pontil, applied sloping collar mouth, American 1840-1860 ....**$250-350**

Excelsior / Spring / Saratoga, N.Y.
Medium blue green, quart, smooth base, applied mouth, American 1865-1875 ....**$200-300**

Exelsior / Spring / Saratoga, N.Y.
Yellow olive green, pint, smooth base, tooled mouth, American 1865-1875..**$200-275**

Francis / Schellenberg (in a slug plate)
Blue green, 6-7/8", squat form, iron pontil, applied mouth, American 1840-1860 ....**$150-200**

Geo. Upp, Jr. / York, PA – Mineral / Water
Medium cobalt blue, 7-3/4", iron pontil, applied blob mouth, very rare, American 1840-1860..**$500-700**

Geyser Spring / Saratoga Springs / State / Of / New York – The Saratoga / Spouting Springs
Deep blue green, pint, smooth base, applied mouth, very rare color, American 1865-1875 ....**$1,800-3,000**

Geyser Spring / Saratoga Springs / New York – Avery N. Lord / 66 Broad St. / Utica, N.Y.
Blue aqua, quart, smooth base (A & HDC), applied mouth, rare, American 1865-1875 ....**$120-160**

Gettysburg – Water
Deep olive green, tall magnum quart, smooth base, applied mouth, extremely rare, American 1865-1875 ....**$2,500-3,500**

Dr. Wieber's / European / Mineral Water, medium blue green, pint, American 1865-1880, $400-600.

Hathorn Spring / Saratoga, N.Y., label reads: Saratoga Mineral Waters, Property of the State of New York, Hathorn Spring, Natural Cathartic Water. dark amber, pint, American 1865-1875, $200-275.

Hopkins / Chalybeate / Baltimore, medium yellow green, pint, American 1850-1860, $375-475.

Guilford Mineral / GMSW (monogram) / Guilford / VT. / Spring Water
Olive yellow, quart, smooth base, applied mouth, scarce color, American 1865-1875 ....**$250-350**

G.W. Weston & Co / Saratoga / N.Y.
Deep olive amber, quart, pontil-scarred base, applied mouth, American 1848-1855 ....**$275-375**

H. Borgman / Mineral Water / Manufacturer / Cumberland, MD
Blue green, 8-3/8", iron pontil, applied blob mouth, extremely rare, American 1850-1860 ....**$1,500-2,500**

Hand & Murtha / Mineral Waters – H & M
Aqua, 7-1/4", iron pontil, applied mouth, extremely rare, American 1845-1860 ....**$375-475**

Harris's / Albany / Mineral Water
Medium blue green, 7-1/4", iron pontil, applied mouth, very rare, American 1840-1860 ....**$375-450**

Highrock Congress Springs / (motif of rock) / C & W / Saratoga, N.Y.
Teal blue, pint, smooth base, applied mouth, American 1865-1875..........**$400-600**

Highrock Congress Spring / (motif of rock) / C & W / Saratoga, N.Y.
Yellow amber, pint, smooth base, applied mouth, American 1865-1875...**$200-300**

I. Sutton & Co. – Covington – KY, medium cobalt blue, 8-1/2", American 1840-1860, $800-1,200.

Frost's Magnetic Spring / Eaton Rapids Mich, medium orange amber, quart, American 1870-1875, $375-475.

Lamoille Spring, Milton VT, medium yellow amber, quart, American 1865-1875, $450-650.

I.C. / Vreeland / Newark / N.J. – Superior Water / Union Glass Works / Phila
Teal blue, 7-1/2", iron pontil, applied blob mouth, American 1840-1860...**$180-220**

J.B. Edward – Mineral Water / Columbia / PA
Deep blue, 7-5/8", iron pontil, applied mouth, American 1840-1860 ....**$200-300**

J. Dowall (in a slug plate) – Union Glass Works Phila – / Superior / Mineral Water
Deep cobalt blue, 7-1/2", mug base, iron pontil, applied blob-type mouth, American 1840-1860.....................**$600-900**

J. Lake / Schenectady , N.Y.
Deep cobalt blue, 8-1/8", iron pontil, applied mouth, American 1840-1860 ... **$500-800**

John Boardman – New York – Mineral Waters
Cobalt blue, 7-1/4", 8-sided, iron pontil, applied blob mouth, American 1840-1860
.....................**$400-600**

Knickerbocker / Mineral Water / Bottles Registered / According To Law – Boughton & Chase / Rochester
Medium cobalt blue, 7-1/2", iron pontil, applied blob-type mouth, American 1840-1860 ....**$500-800**

Lynch & Clarke / New York
Deep olive green, quart, pontil-scarred base, applied mouth, American 1825-1830
.....................**$1,200-1,600**

Massena Spring Water, golden
yellow amber, quart, American 1880-
1885, $250-375.

Oswego Deep Rock / Mineral Water
– This Bottle Must Be Returned, blue
aqua, quart, American 1870-1880,
$250-350.

Strumatic Mineral Water / N / PSM
Co., medium orange amber, pint,
American 1870-1880, $600-800.

Lynch & Clarke / New York
Yellow olive amber, pint, pontil-scarred base, applied mouth, American 1825-1835
....**$700-900**

Keys – Burlington / N.J.
Medium blue green, 7-1/8", iron pontil, applied blob mouth, American 1840-1860
....**$200-300**

Keys – Burlington (in an arch) / N.J.
Medium emerald green, 7-1/4", iron pontil, applied mouth, American 1840-1860
....**$200-300**

Massena Spring / (monogram) / Water
Medium teal blue, quart, smooth base, applied mouth, American 1865-1875
....**$275-400**

Middletown / Healing / Springs / Grays & Clark / Middletown VT
Deep emerald green, quart, smooth base, applied mouth, rare color, American
1865-1875..**$250-300**

Middletown / Healing Springs / Grays & Clark / Middletown VT
Deep yellow amber, quart, smooth base, applied mouth, American 1865-1875
....**$500-800**

Missisquoi / A / Springs – (Indian woman with papoose)
Yellow olive, quart, smooth base, applied mouth, American 1865-1875 ...**$200-300**

Richfield Springs N.Y. / Sulphur / Water, deep blue-green, pint, American 1865-1875, $250-350.

Rockbridge Alum Water, Rockbridge Co / VA, medium teal blue, half-gallon, 9-3/4", American 1865-1880, $400-700.

Round Lake / Mineral Water / Saratoga Co. / N.Y., deep red amber, quart, American 1865-1875, $375-475.

Oak Orchard / Acid Springs – H.W. Bostwick / Agt. No 574 / Broadway, New York
Dark amber, quart, smooth base (Glass From F. Hitchings Factory / Lockport, N.Y.), applied mouth, American 1865-1875 ....**$200-275**

Oak Orchard / Acid Springs – Alabama / Genesee Co. N.Y.
Medium blue-green, quart, smooth base, applied mouth, American 1865-1875..**$275-350**

Powell's – Mineral Water – Burlington – N.J.
Medium sapphire blue, 7-5/8", 8-sided, iron pontil, rare Powell bottle, American 1840-1860..**$1,800-2,700**

Powell & – Dr. Burr's Mineral Water – Burlington – N.J.
Medium cobalt blue, 7-3/4", 8-sided, iron pontil, applied mouth, American 1840-1860 ....**$1,500-2,500**

Rockbridge / VA / Alum Water
Yellow olive green, 6-7/8", squat form, pint, iron pontil, applied mouth, American 1845-1860..**$7,000-9,000**

Rockbridge / Alum / Water – Alum Springs / Virginia
Deep emerald green, 13-1/4", smooth base, applied mouth, extremely rare, American 1855-1865 ....**$10,000-20,000**

S. Keys / Burlington / N.J. – Union Glass Works / Superior / Mineral Water
Medium cobalt blue, 7-3/4", paneled mug base, iron pontil, applied mouth, American 1840-1860...**$450-650**

Saratoga Red Spring, deep blue green, quart, American 1865-1875, $200-300.

Saratoga Seltzer Spring Co. / Saratoga N.Y. – SSS, dark olive green, quart, very rare, American 1865-1875, $4,000-6,000.

Siderite Springs / SS Co. / Manchester Conn, medium emerald green, pint, extremely rare, American 1865-1875, $2,500-4,500.

Red Sulphur Springs, Monroe Co. / WV, medium amber tall, quart, American 1880-1885, $275-375.

Saratoga High Rock Spring / (motif of rock) / Saratoga, N.Y.

Emerald green, pint, smooth base, applied mouth, American 1865-1875 .... **$700-1,000**

Saratoga / (star) / Spring

Olive green, quart, smooth base, applied mouth, scarce color, American 1865-1875............. **$275-375**

Saratoga Seltzer Water

Medium green, pint, smooth base, applied mouth, American 1870-1885 .... **$200-300**

Saratoga Vichy Spouting Spring / V / Saratoga / N.Y.

Aqua, three-quarter pint, smooth base, applied mouth, rarely seen in this size, American 1765-1875 . **$350-450**

Saratoga Vichy Spouting Spring / V / Saratoga / N. Y.

Aqua, half-pint, smooth base, tooled mouth, American 1865-1875.. **$275-375**

St. Catherines / Mineral Water / G.L. Mather Agent / Astor House / New York

Medium yellow amber, 11-3/8", cylinder form, smooth base, applied sloping collar mouth, American 1865-1875 .... **$600-800**

St. Regis / Water / Massena Springs

Black olive amber, quart, smooth base, applied mouth, American 1865-1875 .... **$375-450**

Syracuse Springs / D / Excelsior /
A.J. Delantour / New York, yellow
olive, pint, American 1870-1880,
$500-800.

Vermont Spring / Saxe & Co. /
Sheldon VT, medium golden yellow
amber, quart, American 1865-1875,
$350-475.

Washington Spring, Saratoga N.Y.,
medium yellow olive, pint, American
1865-1875, $400-600.

Star Spring co / (star) / Saratoga, N.Y.
Deep amber, pint, smooth base, applied mouth, American 1865-1875 .... **$150-250**

Teller's / Mineral Water / Detroit – The Bottle / Must Be / Returned
Deep cobalt blue, 8-3/8", smooth base, applied mouth, American 1855-1865 .... **$375-450**

Vermont Spring / Saxe & Co. / Shelton, VT.
Yellow olive, quart, smooth base, applied mouth, scarce color, American 1865-1875............. **$120-150**

Vermont Spring / Saxe & Co. / Sheldon, VT.
Yellow amber, quart, smooth base, applied mouth, American 1865-1875 .... **$350-475**

Washington Spring Co (bust of Washington) / Ballston Spa / N.Y. – C
Deep blue green, pint, smooth base, applied mouth, American 1865-1875 .... **$600-800**

W. Heiss, Jr's / Mineral Water / No. 213 N. 2nd. St. / Phila – Improved / H / Patent
Medium blue green, 7", tubular pen pontil, applied mouth, American 1835-1845 .... **$350-400**

WM. P. Davis & Co – Excelsior – Mineral Water – Brooklyn
Cobalt blue, 7-3/8", 8-sided, iron pontil, applied blob mouth, American 1840-1860 .... **$400-600**

White Sulphur Water / Greenbrier,
VA, medium blue green, quart,
American 1855-1865, $375-475.

Patriotic Bottles

At the beginning of World War II, bottle manufacturers, especially milk bottle producers, began a patriotic campaign unlike any other in American history. World War II resulted in some of the most unique and collectible bottles with various slogans and images depicting tanks, soldiers, fighter planes, and "V" signs. While some milk bottles were very colorful and had detailed graphics, many displayed simple slogans such as "Buy War Savings Bonds- Keep it Up" and "Buy Bonds and Stamps" on the wings of bombers and fighter planes.

The Applied Color Label (ACL) soda pop bottle was conceived in the 1930s when Prohibition forced brewing companies to sell soda pop. They used this technology during World War II to create labels that will forever preserve unique patriotic moments and figures in American history. They include images such as American flags, the Statue of Liberty, "V" symbols, fighter planes, fighter pilots, soldiers, and stars and stripes. Bottles with images of Uncle Sam and the American flag are the most popular.

Other groups of bottles such as historical flasks, figurals, and Jim Beam bottles have depicted patriotic figures, embossed images, and paintings of important patriotic milestones in the history of America. In fact, there are 25 different types of flasks representing the American flag as a symbol of patriotism, a rallying cry for battle, and the re-establishment of the Union following the Civil War.

MILK BOTTLES

CREAM TOPS

Dairy Cooperative Assoc., Vancouver, WA
Milk – First Line – Of – Health Defense........ **$150-175**
Common Bottle
Food Fights Too – Watch What You Buy......... **$35-55**
Common Bottle
Working Together – An American Tradition (Uncle Sam standing).. **$35-45**

HALF-PINTS

All Out – For Defense – Drink Milk – Berwick Clewells Creamery (picture of bugler in the middle of United States map)
Red..$75
America – First – Last – Always (picture of American eagle)
Red..$35
Food Fights Too – Use Only What You Need – Conserve What You Buy – Balance Your Meals With Milk
Red and blue $35
For Your Health and Safety – Drink Milk – Buy Defense Bonds (picture of milk bottle in letter "V" and a soldier and flier on each side of "V") Northampton Dairy, Northampton, PA
Red..$60
Liberty – Freedom – Equality (picture of eagle with American flag) - rare
Red, white, and blue $100

WAR SLOGANS

Act For Victory (picture of eagle with wings spread) – Drink Milk
Round red quart...$45
Double Protection – For The Home – Buy War Bonds And Stamps
Round green quart..$25
Every Little Bit Helps – Win The War (in banner with stars)
Round red quart...$60

Buy Stamps To Aid Defense – Spring Grove Creamery, Willets, CA, $150.

America Is A Good Place to Live – Let's Keep It That Way, $50.

Health Helps Him – Buy War Bonds, $150.

Food Fights Too – Use it Wisely – Balance Your Meals

Round red quart..$35

He's Doing His Share – You Do Yours – Buy More War Bonds (picture of soldier fighting) – Campbells, Clovis, NM

Round red quart..$100

Keep 'Em Flying – For Victory (in letter "V" with fighter planes in the background flying around the world)

Round red quart..$75

Remember Pearl Harbor – Prepare – HiGrade Dairy, Harrington, DE, $250.

Churchill holding "V" sign – Highfield Dairy, Port Hope, Ont., $250.

For Our Defense – Milk-Defender of Health, $150.

For Victory! – Buy United States War Bonds and Stamps – Haskell's Dairy, Savannah, GA, $150.

U.S.A (Disney), $150; Columbia, $550; America at War – Our Home Front Supports Our Fighting Front, $150.

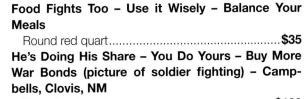

Make American Strong – Drink More Milk (picture of girl with American eagle in background)

Round red quart...$35

Milk – The First Line – Of – Health Defense

Round red quart...$35

National Defense – Starts With – Good Health – Build America's Future – Drink More Milk – Shums Jeanette, PA

Green round quart...$35

Please Return – This Bottle – When Empty – Make It Live Longer – It Does A War Job Too – Sanida Dairy, Erie, PA

Round red quart...$50

Keep Them Rolling – Buy Bonds and Stamps, $250.

Keep 'Em Flying – Buy War Bonds and Stamps, $100.
Keep 'Em Flying – V for Victory – M for Milk, $150.
Keep 'Em Flying – V for Victory – M for Milk, $100.

Buy War Bonds and Stamps – J.M. Adams & Bros., Cheasea, MA, $250.

Bottled on the Farm FOR VICTORY – Buy War Bonds – Medo-Green Dairy, $150.

Keep 'Em Flying – Drink Milk, $150.

Fortify Your Help – Drink More Milk, $250.

Illustration, Owens Illinois Salesman Sample Page.

Protect Their Future – Buy More War Bonds – Build Their Health With Milk (picture of young boy and girl)

Round red quart..$35

You Owe It To Your Country – Buy War Bonds – You Owe It To Your Health Drink Milk

Green round quart...$35

Silence Is True – Sunburst Dairy – Union City, TN

Round red quart..$50

That's The Way I Like To See It – COOPERATION

Round red quart..$35

They Guard Your Home – We Guard Your Health (picture of soldier, marine, and sailor)

Round red quart..$35

U.S.A. (picture of eagle with airplane and ship in background, surrounded by stars) – Maple Grove Dairy, Shelbyville, KY

Red, white, and blue $100

We're All Pulling For Uncle Sam – Spokane Bottle Exchange

Round red quart..$75

GALLON

You Can Keep 'Em Flying – By – Buying – U.S. War Bonds – Stamps (picture of fighter plane flying)

Red and black...$60

FIGURALS

Uncle Sam Hat

Milk glass, 2-1/2", original traditional red, white, and blue paint, smooth base, tooled rim, original tin insert and cardboard closure reads: Republican Nominees, WM. H. Taft, President and James S. Sherman, Vice President, with pictures of both candidates, American 1908, made for the 1908 Presidential campaign **$600-800**

FLASKS AND BOTTLES

Figural liberty bottle, Proclaim Liberty Throughout the Land – 1776 Centennial Exposition – 1876, clear glass, 3-1/2", American 1876, $250-250.

Albany Glassworks – Albany / NY / Bust of Washington – frigate portrait flask

Medium golden amber, pint, iron pontil, applied double collared mouth, American 1848-1850, Albany Glass Works, Albany, New York **$2,000-4,000**

Double Eagle Historical Flask – motif of American eagle

Sapphire blue, pint, pontil-scarred base, sheared top, American 1850-1855, Louisville Glass Works, Louisville, Kentucky **$500-1,000**

Eagle – motif of American eagle

Medium forest green, pint, smooth base, applied double collar mouth, American 1860-1872 **$300-600**

Phoenix Old – Trade – motif of American eagle – Mark – Bourbon

Medium amber, half-pint, smooth base, tooled top, American 1885-1895 .... **$100-200**

Pocket Flask – label under glass – 29th National Encampment – G.A. R. – 1895 – motif of eagle on an American flag – I.W. Harper's – Nelson Co. KY Whiskey

Clear glass, 6" x 3-1/2", smooth base, threaded top with original metal screw-on cap, American 1895.. **$500-700**

Eagle above wreath, half-pint, American 1860-1870, $400-600.

Pocket flask – label under glass – 33rd National – 1899 - Encampment - G.A. R. – Phila – PA – motif of American eagle and U.S. flag banner, two U.S. flags - Compliments of J.A. Brennan, US embossed on back of flask

Clear glass, 4-1/2" dia, canteen style, smooth base, threaded top with original metal screw-on cap, American 1899.. **$500-700**

80-112. Liberty eagle, Willington Glass Co., West Willington, Conn., quart, American 1855-1865, $400-700.

Clasped Hands – eagle with banner, half-pint, American 1860-1870, $275-350.

Pocket flask – label under glass – Grand Army – September – motif of American eagle on U.S. flag banner – 1894 – Encampment – Pittsburgh, PA
Clear glass, 5-1/4" x 3-1/4", smooth base, tooled top, American 1894 ....**$4,000-5,000**

Pocket Flask – label under glass – U.S. Calvary – motif of American eagle, two U.S. flags, and Dewey – Words read: E. Pluribus Unum
Clear glass, 5-3/4", smooth base, threaded top with original metal screw-on cap, American 1885-1900 ....**$400-500**

Pocket flask – label under glass – U.S. Calvary – motif of an American eagle, two U.S. flags, and a shield in red, white, and blue with stars – words read: Our Heroes
Clear glass, 5-3/4", smooth base, threaded top with original metal screw-on cap, American 1885-1900 ....**$400-500**

Stonewall Jackson – Stomach Bitters – Dr M. Perl & CO.

Deep yellow olive amber, 8-5/8", smooth base, applied sloping collar mouth, American 1865-1875 ....**$700-900**

Thomas "Stonewall" Jackson was the recognized Confederate general during the Civil War.

Washington Eagle

Aqua, pint, pontil-scarred base, sheared and tooled lip, American 1845-1855 ....**$200-300**

JIM BEAM BOTTLES

Canteen – 1980

Replica of World War II canteen..**$15-20**

D-Day – 1984

Army boot stepping on beach with the names Utah, Omaha, and Gold........**$18-22**

George Washington and Martha Washington – Bicentennial commemorative plate bottle – 1976

Biographies on back of bottles..**$15-25**

Space Shuttle – 1986

Model of space shuttle as bottle..**$50-55**

Uncle Sam Fox – 1971

Fox dressed like Uncle Sam **$18-20**

V.F.W. – Veterans of Foreign Wars – of The United States – 50th Anniversary – 1971

Department of Indian V.F.W. on back...**$5-10**

SODA BOTTLES

Enjoy Freedom Of Thirsty – Drink – Liberty – Beverages (picture of Statue of Liberty) – red and white lettering – 1962 (very rare)

Clear glass, 12 oz., Brooklyn, NY **$150-200**

Liberty – Sign Of Purity (picture of Statue of Liberty) – 1964 (very rare)

Clear glass, 10 oz., Liberty, TX **$175-200**

Victory Cola – white lettering – Stars and Stripes with Sergeant Stripes – 1947

Green glass, 12 oz., Pacoima, Ca **$150-170**

Victory Root Beer – white lettering – Stars and Stripes – 1946

Clear glass, 10 oz., Pacoima, Ca **$55-65**

Yankee Doodle – Old Fashion – Root Beer – Revolutionary Soldier Playing Fife – red, white, and blue colors – 1948

Clear glass, 10 oz., Los Angeles, CA...**$45-60**

MISCELLANEOUS

Barber Bottle – Multicolored red, white, and blue Stars and Stripes, American Shield containing the words "Sea Foam"
Milk glass, 8-7/8", smooth base (J.B.S. stands for Jim's Barber Shop, rolled lip, rare decoration, American 1885-1925..**$350-450**

Cologne Bottle – large label depicting an "American Eagle" that reads: Eau De Cologne / Superieure
Teal blue, 11", 12-sided, smooth base, tooled flared top, American 1860-1880, Boston and Sandwich Glass Works, Sandwich, Mass..........................**$500-1,000**

Patriotic Shaving Mug – The Union Forever
Red, white, and blue bands with white center band reading "The Union Forever" in gold, 3-1/4", smooth base, American 1885-1925 ....**$150-200**

Patriotic Shaving Mug – Made for Pietro – motif of American and Italian flags separated by an American Eagle
White, 3-7/8", smooth base, American 1885-1925 ....**$75-100**

Patriotic shaving mug, American 1885-1925, $70-100.

Pattern-Molded Bottles

A pattern molded bottle is one that is blown into a ribbed or pattern mold. This group includes globular and chestnut flasks. One of these, the Stiegel bottle, manufactured during the late 18th century, is considered very rare and valuable. The two types of Stiegel bottles manufactured at the Stiegel Glass Factory are the diamond daisy and hexagon designs.

Since pattern-molded bottles are among the more valuable and rare pieces, collectors need to familiarize themselves with the types, sizes, colors, and the various manufacturers of these bottles.

Pattern-molded globular bottle, 24-rib pattern swirled to left, 8", American 1815-1830, $500-800.

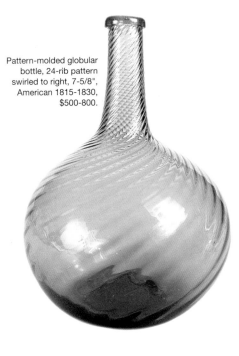

Pattern-molded globular bottle, 24-rib pattern swirled to right, 7-5/8", American 1815-1830, $500-800.

Pattern-molded globular bottle, 24-rib pattern swirled to left, 8-1/4", American 1815-1830, $600-800.

Freeblown Globular Bottle – Flattened Sides

Light olive green, 8-1/8", open pontil, applied mouth, American 1780-1810 .... **$400-600**

Freeblown Globular Bottle

Blue aqua, 9-5/8", original pressed glass stopper, open pontil, applied mouth, American 1810-1820 .... **$150-200**

Freeblown Globular Bottle

Olive green, 10-1/4", open pontil, outward lip, American 1770-1800 .... **$600-800**

Globular Bottle

Blue aqua, 5-1/2", 10-vertical rib-pattern, pontil-scarred base, sheared lip, applied ring where the shoulder meets the neck, European (possibly French) 1770-1800 .... **$275-375**

Globular Bottle

Blue aqua, 7-1/2", 24 rib-pattern swirled to right, pontil-scarred base, outward rolled lip, American 1815-1830 **$375-475**

Globular Bottle
Blue aqua, 7-3/8", 24 vertical rib-pattern, pontil-scarred base, applied mouth, American 1815-1825 ....**$275-375**

Globular Bottle
Medium green, 7-5/8", 24-rib pattern swirled to right, pontil-scarred base, outward rolled lip, American 1815-1830 ....**$500-800**

Globular Bottle
Yellow amber, 8", 24 rib-pattern swirled to left, pontil-scarred base, outward rolled lip, American 1815-1830 ....**$500-800**

Globular Bottle
Blue aqua, 8-1/4", 24 rib-pattern swirled to right, pontil-scarred base, outward rolled lip, American 1815-1830 ....**$375-475**

Globular Bottle
Amber, 8-1/2", 24 rib-pattern swirled to left, pontil-scarred base, outward rolled lip, American 1815-1830 ......**$600-800**

Globular Bottle
Dark amber, 8-3/8", 24 rib-pattern swirled to left, pontil-scarred base, outward rolled lip, American 1815-1830 ....**$600-800**

Globular Bottle
Light aqua, 9-1/4", 32 rib-pattern swirled to left, pontil-scarred base, applied sloping collar mouth, American 1815-1835 ....**$150-180**

Globular Bottle
Blue aqua, 9-3/8", 24 rib-pattern swirled to left, pontil-scarred base, outward rolled lip, American 1815-1830 ....**$500-800**

Globular Swirl Bottle
Medium amber, 7-1/2", 24 rib-pattern swirled to right, pontil-scarred base, outward rolled lip, American 1825-1835 ....**$400-600**

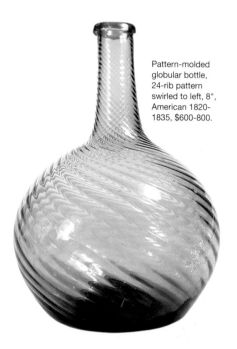

Pattern-molded globular bottle, 24-rib pattern swirled to left, 8", American 1820-1835, $600-800.

Pattern-molded globular bottle, 9-1/4", 32 rib-pattern swirled to left, American 1815-1835, $150-180.

Midwestern club bottle
7-3/4", 24 broken-rib
pattern swirled to left,
American 1815-1835,
$400-700.

Midwestern club
bottle, 8-1/2", 24
broken-rib pattern
swirled to left,
American 1815-1835,
$350-450.

Midwestern club bottle,
7-7/8", 24 broken-rib
pattern swirled to right,
American 1815-1835,
$350-450.

Midwestern club
bottle, 8-1/4", 24-rib
pattern swirled to
left, American
1815-1835,
$350-450.

Midwestern Globular Bottle

Medium amber, 7-3/4", 24 rib-pattern swirled to left, pontil-scarred base, outward rolled lip, American 1815-1835 **$400-700**

Midwestern Club Bottle

Blue aqua, 7-5/8", 24 rib-pattern swirled to right, pontil-scarred base, applied mouth, American 1815-1825 .... **$170-250**

Midwestern Club Bottle

Aqua, 7-7/8", 24 rib-pattern swirled to right, pontil-scarred base, applied mouth, American 1815-1835 .... **$350-450**

Midwestern Club Bottle

Aqua, 8-1/4", 24 broken rib-pattern swirled to left, pontil-scarred base, applied mouth, American 1815-1835 .... **$350-450**

Midwestern Globular Bottle

Golden yellow amber, 8-1/2", 24 rib-pattern swirled to left, pontil-scarred base, applied mouth, American 1815-1835 .... **$500-800**

Pattern-Molded Chestnut Flask

Blue aqua, 5", 22 rib-pattern, pontil-scarred base, sheared and tooled mouth, American 1815-1835 .... **$150-200**

Pattern-Molded Chestnut Flask

Yellow with amber and olive tone, 5-1/8", 24 rib-pattern swirled to left, pontil-scarred base, sheared and tooled lip, American 1815-1830 .... **$300-450**

Pattern-Molded Chestnut Flask

Amber, 5-1/4", 24 vertical-rib pattern, pontil-scarred base, sheared and tooled lip, American 1815-1830 .... **$200-275**

Pattern-molded chestnut flask, 5", 22-rib-pattern, American 1815-1835, $150-200.

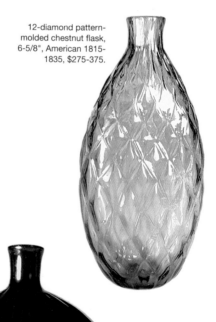

12-diamond pattern-molded chestnut flask, 6-5/8", American 1815-1835, $275-375.

Pattern-molded chestnut flask, 5-1/8", 24-rib pattern, American 1815-1830, $200-275.

Pattern-molded 10-diamond chestnut flask, 5-3/8", American 1815-1830, $1,000-1,800.

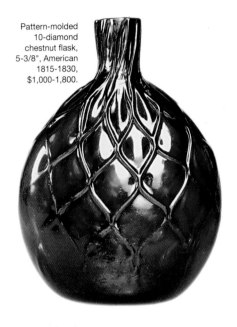

Chestnut flask, medium sapphire blue, 6-3/4", American 1820-1835, $600-800.

Pinch waist chestnut flask, clear glass, 8-1/4", European 1820-1850, $375-475.

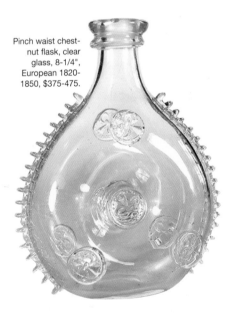

Pattern molded club bottle, 7-7/8", 28 rib-pattern swirled to left, American 1815-1825, $200-300.

Pattern-Molded Chestnut Flask
Yellow with amber tone, 5-3/8", 10-diamond pattern, pontil-scarred base, sheared lip, American 1815-1830 .... **$600-800**

Pattern-Molded Chestnut Flask
Medium yellow olive, 6-3/8", 20 vertical rib-pattern, pontil-scarred base, sheared and inward rolled lip, American 1815-1835 .... **$600-800**

Pattern-Molded Chestnut Flask
Light blue green, 6-5/8", 12-diamond pattern, pontil-scarred base, sheared lip, American 1815-1835 .... **$275-375**

Pattern-Molded Club Bottle
Deep blue aqua, 7-7/8", 28 rib-pattern swirled to left, pontil-scarred base, applied mouth, American 1815-1825 .... **$200-300**

Pattern-Molded Club Bottle
Medium blue green, 8", 24 rib-pattern swirled to left, pontil-scarred base, outward rolled lip, rare color, American 1820-1835 .... **$600-800**

Pattern-Molded Club Bottle
Medium cobalt blue, 8-1/4", 24 vertical rib-pattern swirled to left, open pontil, applied blob mouth, most sought color for a Mid-Western Club bottle, American 1815-1835 .... **$3,500-4,500**

Pattern-Molded Club Bottle
Deep blue aqua, 8-1/2", 30 rib-pattern slightly swirled to right, pontil-scarred base, applied mouth, American 1815-1835 .... **$200-300**

Pattern-Molded Club Bottle
Yellow amber with olive tone, 8-5/8", 24 rib-pattern swirled to right, open pontil, applied blob mouth, rare in this color, American 1815-1835 .... **$3,500-4,500**

Pattern-Molded Condiment Bottle
Clear, 5", 16 vertical rib-pattern with a twist to the left, pontil-scarred base, flared-out and rolled inward lip, American 1815-1835 .... **$100-200**

Pattern-Molded Decanter
Cobalt blue, 12", 16 vertical rib-pattern with tight twisting swirls in the neck, polished pontil, applied neck ring, sheared and tooled lip, European 1865-1880 .... **$150-350**

Pattern-Molded Flask
Bright yellow green, 5-3/4", 8 vertical rib-pattern, pillar molded in a flattened triangular form, pontil-scarred base, sheared mouth, American 1800-1830 **$500-1,000**

18-ogival pattern molded flask, 8", American 1815-1835, $275-375.

Pattern molded flask, medium green, 7-3/4", American 1820-1835, $500-700.

Pitkin flask, green aqua, 4-1/2", American 1815-1830, $500-700.

Rib-pattern pocket flask, 5-7/8", 18-rib pattern swirled to right, European 1800-1820, $400-700.

Pattern-Molded Flask

Light green, 6-1/8", 14 ogival pattern, pontil-scarred base, sheared and tooled lip, American 1815-1835 .... **$275-375**

Pattern-Molded Flask

Clear, 7-3/8", 19 ogival pattern, pontil-scarred base, sheared and tooled wide mouth, American 1815-1825 .... **$400-700**

Pattern-Molded Pocket Flask

Aqua, 8", 18 ogival pattern, open pontil-scarred base, sheared and tooled lip, scarce pattern, American 1815-1835 .....**$275-375**

Pattern-Molded Pocket Flask

Medium sapphire blue, 3-7/8", 20 rib-pattern swirled to right, pontil-scarred base, tool flared-out lip, American 1815-1835 .... **$700-900**

Pattern-Molded Pocket Flask

Blue aqua, 5-1/8", 15-diamond pattern, open pontil, sheared and tooled lip, American 1815-1825, possibly blown in Ohio at Mantua Glass House, which is one of the few glasshouses to use the 15-diamond pattern **$400-600**

Pattern-Molded Pocket Flask

Clear glass with light amethyst tint, 6-1/4", 30 vertical-rib pattern, pontil-scarred base, sheared and tooled lip, American 1800-1810 .... **$250-350**

Pitkin Flask

Clear, 4-5/8", 12 rib-pattern, alternating plain and horizontal lobes, pontil-scarred base, tooled mouth, European 1780-1820, possibly German **$275-400**

Pitkin Flask

Medium olive yellow, 4-7/8", 32 rib-pattern swirled to left, open pontil-scarred base, sheared and tooled mouth, American 1775-1800, Pitikin Glass Works, East Manchester, Connecticut **$700-1,000**

Pitkin Flask

Clear, 5-1/4", 34 broken-rib pattern swirled to right, pontil-scarred base, sheared and tooled lip, rare in clear glass, American 1790-1820 .... **$275-375**

Pitkin Flask

Light green aqua, 5-3/8", 30 broken rib-pattern swirled to right, open pontill, sheared and tooled lip, rare color, American 1790-1810.......**$400-600**

Pitkin Flask

Medium yellow olive green, 5-3/4", 36 broken rib-pattern swirled to right, open pontil, sheared and tooled lip, American 1790-1810 ....**$600-800**

Pitkin Flask

Blue green, 6-3/8", 32 broken-rib pattern, pontil-scarred base, sheared and tooled lip, American 1815-1825..**$500-700**

Rib-Pattern Cruet

Medium pink amethyst, 8-1/2", 20-vertical rib pattern, pontil-scarred base, tooled flared-out lip, American 1820-1840 ....**$600-800**

Rib-Pattern Flask

Yellow green, pint, 6-1/4", 20 vertical rib-pattern, pontil-scarred base, sheared and tooled lip, American 1820-1830, Keene New Hampshire Glassworks **$800-1,200**

Rib-Pattern Molded Flask

Medium olive green, 6-3/8", 30 vertical-rib pattern, open pontil, sheared and tooled lip, American 1810-1820..**$500-700**

Rib-Pattern Pocket Flask

Deep cobalt blue, 5-7/8", 18 rib-pattern swirled to right, pontil-scarred base, sheared and tooled lip, European 1880-1820, possibly German **$400-700**

Stiegel Diamond Daisy Pattern Flask

Medium amethyst, 4-3/4", diamond flute pattern, flattened bulbous form, pontil-scarred base, sheared mouth, extremely rare pattern and color, American 1763-1775, Stiegel's American Flint Glass Manufactory, Manheim PA **$3,000-6,000**

Stiegel Diamond Daisy Pattern Flask

Light amethyst, 5", large diamond pattern, flattened bulbous form, pontil-scarred base, sheared mouth, American 1763-1775, Stiegel's American Flint Glass Manufactory, Manheim PA **$2,500-5,000**

Stiegel Diamond Daisy Pattern Flask

Medium amethyst, 5-1/8", pontil-scarred base, tooled mouth, American 1770-1774, Stiegel's American Flint Glass Manufactory, Manheim, PA **$4,000-6,000**

Rib pattern flask, medium cobalt blue, 5-1/2", American 1840-1850, $1,000-1,500.

Midwestern melon-ribbed flask, medium blue green, 5-7/8", American 1820-1835, $200-300.

Perfume and Cologne Bottles

I would like to thank Penny Dolnick who provided the background and pricing information, and Randy Monsen and Rodney Baer, who provided the great photographs to the Perfume and Cologne chapter for the 6th Edition.

Penny's credentials speak for themselves as a past President of the International Perfume Bottle Association (IPBA), author of the *Penny Bank Commercial Perfume Bottle Price Guide*, 7th Edition, the *Penny Bank Miniature Perfume Bottle Price Guide*, 2nd Edition, and the *Penny Bank Solid Perfume Bottle Price Guide*, 3rd Edition. Penny, who can be contacted at alpen@gate.net, is willing to help fellow collectors identify and date bottles, although not conduct actual appraisals.

The International Perfume Bottle Association is an organization of 1,500 perfume bottle collectors in several countries. Its main objective is to foster education and comradeship for collectors through its quarterly full color magazine, its regional chapters, and its annual convention. If interested in obtaining further information on future conventions or membership, the organization's Web site is www.perfumebottles.org

In addition, every year, the IPBA convention plays host to the Monsen & Baer Perfume Bottle Auction, featuring approximately 400 perfume bottles and related items. For imformation on purchasing full-color hardbound Monsen & Baer auction catalogues, contact Randall Monsen and Rodney Baer at monsenbaer@errols.com.

Collectors look for two types of perfume bottles— decorative and commercial. Decorative bottles include any bottles sold empty and meant to be filled with your choice of scent. Commercial bottles are sold filled with scent and usually have the label of a perfume company. Since there are so many thousands of different perfume bottles, most collectors specialize in some subcategory.

Popular specialties among decorative perfume bottle collectors include many categories: ancient Roman or Egyptian bottles; cut glass bottles with or without gold or sterling silver trim or overlay; bottles by famous glassmakers such as Moser, Steuben, Webb, Lalique, Galle, Daum, Baccarat, and Saint Louis; figural porcelain bottles from the 18th and 19th centuries or from Germany between 1920 and 1930; perfume lamps (with wells to fill with scent), perfume burners, laydown and double-ended scent bottles, atomizer bottles, pressed or molded early American glass bottles, matched dresser sets of bottles, and handcut Czechoslovakian bottles from the early 20th Century.

Among collectors of commercial perfumes, there are favorite collections categorized by various characteristics, such as bottles with a certain color of glass; bottles by a particular parfumer (Guerlain, Caron, or Prince Matchabelli); bottles by famous fashion designers (Worth, Paul Poiret, Chanel, Dior, Schiaparelli or Jean Patou); bottles by a particular glassmaker or designer (Lalique, Baccarat, Viard or Depinoix); giant factice bottles (store display bottles not filled with genuine fragrance); little compacts holding solid (cream) perfume, which are often figural; tester bottles (small bottles with long glass daubers), and figural, novelty, and miniature perfumes (usually replicas of regular bottles given as free samples at perfume counters).

For the novice perfume bottle collector, it may surprise you to learn that the record price for a perfume bottle at auction was over $80,000, and those little sample bottles that were given

free at perfume counters in the '60s can now bring as much as $300 or $400! It may also surprise you that those miniature bottles are more popular with European collectors than their full-size counterparts, and bottles by American perfume companies are more desirable to European collectors than to Americans, and vice-versa. Also, most collectors of commercial perfume bottles will buy empty examples, but those still sealed with the original perfume carry a premium, and the original packaging can raise the price by as much as 300 percent. The rubber bulbs on atomizer bottles dry out over time but the lack of one or the presence of a modern replacement does not really affect the price.

Collecting perfume bottles is one of those hobbies that can begin with little or no investment. Just ask your friend who wears Shalimar to save her next empty bottle for you. But beware! Investment quality perfume bottles can be very pricey!

The rules for value are the same as for any other kind of glass—rarity, condition, age, and quality of the glass.

There are, however, some special considerations when collecting perfume bottles. You do not have an investment quality bottle (one that will appreciate in value over time) unless the bottle:

1. Has its original stopper and label (if it's commercial).

2. Is a high quality glass bottle (not a lower end eau de cologne or eau de toilette bottle) and there is no corrosion on any metal part.

With commercial perfume bottles, prior to the introduction of the plastic liners on the dowel end of the stopper in 1963, all stoppers had to be individually ground to match the neck of their specific bottle. Bottles without the liners are preferred to those that have them.

PERFUME BOTTLE VALUES

Special Note: All dates given are for the introduction of the scent (if applicable), not for the issue of the particular bottle.

DECORATIVE PERFUME BOTTLES

German ceramic crown top of Dutch boy holding flowers, 4.2", c1920....... **$150**

German ceramic crown top of seated Kewpie doll, 2.9", c1930s **$125**

Baccarat signed atomizer for Marcel Franck, 3.75", c1930s.................. **$90**

Ruby cut glass w/sterling neck and elaborate stopper, French, 3.8", c1855 .... **$575**

English ruby glass double-ended scent w/sterling mounts, signed, 4.5", 1905 .... **$350**

R. Lalique "Myosotis #3", green stain, nude stopper, signed, 9.0", c1928 .... **$4,000**

R. Lalique "Sirenes" perfume burner, blue stain, nude figures, signed, 7.0", c1920 .... **$2,750**

Webb red glass w/sterling stopper and white cameo overlay, unsigned, 4.4", c1910 .... **$950**

Limoges enameled w/lady, enameled overcap, inner stopper, 2.5", c19th C. **$700**

Volupte atomizer enameled w/Art Deco motifs, unsigned, 9.3", c1930s.... **$900**

Devilbiss black glass w/gold mica "lady leg" atomizer, label, 6.8", c1930s **$275**

Devilbiss perfume lamp enameled w/ dancing girls, metal cap and base, 7.5", c1930s....................................... **$500**

Austrian square metal filigree over glass w/glass jewels, 2.1", c1920s....... **$150**

Czech pale blue cut glass w/matching keyhole stopper, 5", c1920s........ **$175**

Birmingham engraved sterling laydown w/glass liner, hinged cover, 4.5", 1885 .... **$350**

Ingrid Czech lapis lazuli glass atomizer cut w/roses, label, 5", c1920s.... **$350**

Moser amber w/gold frieze of female warriors, signed, 6", c1920s........ **$200**

Hoffman clear w/amber lady and cherub stopper, many jewels, signed, 6.8", c1920s................................... **$1,500**

Czech clear w/pale blue nude figure dauber, blue jewels, unsigned, 5.7", c1920s................................... **$5,250**

Shuco mohair monkey figure w/perfume tube inside, 5", c1930s **$325**

American molded paperweight bottle w/bird stopper, unsigned, 5.3", c1940s **$25**

American clear bottle w/elaborate silver overlay, ball stopper, 5.1", c1930s **$155**

Kosta faceted bottle and stopper, signed V Lindstand, 3.5", c1950.............. **$65**

Galle atomizer, yellow w/maroon berry and leaf overlay, cameo signed, 7.36", c1910 .... **$2,200**

Daum, Nancy peach w/amber leaf and flower overlay, cameo signed, 6.5", c1915 .... **$1,250**

Baccarat two dolphins bottle, ball stopper, signed, 6", c1925........................ **$300**

Fenton blue opalescent coin dot atomizer for DeVilbiss, 4", c1940s **$65**

Steuben blue aurene atomizer, acorn finial, for DeVilbiss, 9.5", c1930 ... **$900**

Cambridge pink foot urn, stopper w/long dauber, label, 4.75", c1940s **$130**

L.C. Tiffany blue favrile footed urn, signed, 6', c1930s................................. **$650**

COMMERCIAL PERFUME BOTTLES

Elizabeth Arden It's You , MIB, Baccarat white figural hand in dome, 6.5", c1938 ....**$3,850**

Babs Creations Forever Yours, heart in composition hands w/dome, 3.5", c1940 ....**$138-200**

Bourjois Evening in Paris, cobalt w/fan stopper, banner label, 4.5", c1928..**$225**

Bourjois Evening in Paris, cobalt bullet-shape laydown, good label, tassel, 3.5", c1928..............................**$16-20**

Hattie Carnegie, Carnegie blue. clear head and shoulders bottle, label, 3.25", c1944 .... **$100**

Caron Nuit de Noel, MIB, black glass, gold label, faux shagreen box w/tassel, 4.36", c1922 ....**$80-99**

Chanel Chanel #5, glass giant factice, 10.5", c1921 .... **$550**

Mary Chess Souvenir d'un Soir, MIB, replica of Plaza Hotel fountain, 3.62", c1956 .... **$2,300**

Colgate Cha Ming, glass stopper, flower label, box, 3", c1917 .... **$55**

Corday Toujours Moi, MIB, clear bottle w/gold trim, glass stopper, 2.5", c1924 .... **$154**

Label under glass, "Dina Cologne," 9-3/4", American 1880-1910, $275-375.

Corday Tzigane, R Lalique tiered bottle and stopper, label, 5.5", c1940s.. **$220**

Coty Ambre Antique, R Lalique w/gray stained maidens, 6", c1913...... **$1,429**

Coty L'Origan, MIB, Baccarat, flat rectangle, sepia stained moth stopper, 3.25", c1903 .... **$265**

D'Albert Ecusson, urn w/gold label, box, 3.87", c1952 .... **$50**

Jean Desprez Votre Main. Sevres porcelain, hand w/applied flowers, 3.2", c1939 .... **$1,300**

Dior Diorissimo, MIB, clear amphora, glass stopper, 3.87", c1956 .... **$128**

Dior Diorissimo, urn w/gilt bronze flowers stopper, box, 9", c1956............ **$2,500**

D'Orsay Toujours Fidele, Baccarat, pillow shape w/bulldog stopper, box, 3.5", c1912 .... **$600**

Duchess of Paris Queenly Moments, Queen Victoria bottle on wood base, 3.5", c1938................................... **$28**

Faberge Woodhue, oversize upright logo stopper, 3.5", c1940 .... **$29**

Forvil Relief, R Lalique round bottle w/ swirl pattern, no label, 6.87", c1920 .... **$400**

Dorothy Gray Savoir Faire, bottle w/ enameled mask, gold stopper, 4", c1947 ....**$200-430**

Jacques Griffe Griffonage, square bottle, flat top glass stopper, box, 2.25", c1949 .... **$45**

Guerlain Shalimar, Baccarat signed classic winged bottle, blue stopper, 5.5", c1921 .... **$133**

Guerlain Shalimar, MIB, donut-shape cologne, pointed glass stopper, 11", c1921 .... **$36**

Houbigant Parfum Ideal, Baccarat, faceted stopper, gold label, box, 4.2", c1900 .... **$45**

Isabey Bleu de Chine, Viard, gray stain w/enameled flowers, 5.75", c1926 .... **$1,500**

Andrew Jergens, Ben Hur, rounded bottle, frosted stopper, black label, 5.25", c1904 .... **$40**

Lander Gardenia, dime store bottle w/ orange plastic tiara stopper, 4.75", c1947 .... **$10**

Lanvin Arpege, MIB, black boule w/gold logo, gold raspberry stopper, 3.5", c1927 .... **$220**

Lucien Lelong Indiscret, draped bottle, glass bow stopper, label, 4.75", c1935 .... **$80**

Prince Matchabelli Added Attraction, MIB, red crown, velvet case, 2.12, c1956 .... **$350**

Prince Matchabelli Crown Jewel, MIB, clear crown, cross stopper, chain, 2", c1945 .... **$60**

Molinard Xmas Bells, MIB, black glass figural bell, gold lettering, 4.25", c1926 .... **$750**

Solon Palmer Gardenglo, simple bottle, glass ball stopper, label, 4.75", c.1913 .... **$20**

Raphael Replique, MIB, R logo stopper, red seal, 3.25", c1944 .... **$51-60**

Nina Ricci L'Air du Temps, MIB, Lalique, double dove stopper, 4.5", c1948 **$168**

Elsa Schiaparelli Shocking, torso w/ flowers, tape measure, dome, 4", c1936 .... **$113**

Tre Jur Suivez Moi, lady figure bottle w/ long dauber, 2.5" c1925 .... **$158-306**

Vigny Golliwogg, MIB, black face stopper w/seal fur hair, 3.5", c1919 .... **$356**

Worth Dans la Nuit, R Lalique, matt blue boule, name on stopper, 5.75", c1920 .... **$705**

Ybry Femme de Paris, Baccarat, green opaque w/enameled overcap, 2.25", c1925 .... **$555**

Label under glass perfume: Solon Palmer / Perfumer / SP (monogram) New York, label reads: Palmer's – Jockey Club – Perfumes, American 1890-1910, $400-600.

Sandwich Glass cologne bottles: "Solon Palmer, Perfumer, 6-3/8" (amethyst bottle); Ricksecker, Perfumer 5-1/8" (cobalt blue bottle), American 1850-1880, $250-375.

MINIATURE PERFUME BOTTLES

Elizabeth Arden, blue grass, blown bottle w/blue horse figure inside, box, 2.2", c1934 .... **$1,257**

Bourjois Evening in Paris, cobalt mini in green bakelite shell, 2", c1928 .... **$220**

Bourjois On The Wind, peach label and cap, 1.5", c1930 .... **$12**

Hattie Carnegie A Go Go, square mini in hat box, 1.36", c1969 .... **$55**

Caron Nuit de Noel, tester, black cap and label, full, 1.75", c1922.................. **$50**

Ciro Chevalier de la Nuit, frosted figural knight, black head, 2.36", c1923. **$290**

Colgate Caprice Worn label, twisted screw cap, 2", c1893 .... **$15**

Corday Toujours Moi, shield-shape label, pink plastic cap, 1.75", c1923....... **$31**

Coty A'Suma Boule with embossed flowers, no label, 1.5", c1934........ **$60**

Jean Desprez Sheherazade, MIB, tall spire stopper, 3", c1960s **$200**

Dior Diorama, round laydown "pebble," black label, 1", c1950.................. **$125**

Dior Miss Dior, round laydown "pebble," white label, 1", c1953.................... **$33**

D'Orsay Intoxication, draped bottle, gold label, gold pouch, 1.62", c1942 .... **$30**

Evyan Great Lady, laydown heart bottle, full, 2.25", c1958........................... **$10**

Guerlain Chamade, green plastic pagoda cap, 1.25" c1969 ....**$206-211**

Guerlain L'Heure Bleu, tester, black cap w/dauber, horse label, 2.25", c1912 .... **$103**

Guerlain Mitsouko, replica mini, glass stopper, full, 1.5", c1919 .... **$25**

Richard Hudnut Le Debut Bleu, MIB, blue w/gold raspberry stopper, 1.25", c1927 .... **$250**

Richard Hudnut Le Debut Noir, MIB, black w/gold raspberry stopper, 1.25", c1927 .... **$675**

Karoff Buckarettes, set of two, cowboy and cowgirl w/wooden heads, 1.87", c1940 .... **$58**

Lanvin Arpege, tiny black boule w/logo, 1.2", c1927 .... **$665**

Le Galion Sortilege, tiny mini w/ship cap and gold label, 1.25", c1937 .... **$25**

Lucien Lelong Passionment, tiny mini w/ pearl cap, label, 1.12", c1940 .... **$18**

Germain Monteil Laughter, blown bottle, blue threaded stopper, full, 1.5", c1941 .... **$40**

Raphael Replique, MIB, Lalique, acorn in plastic case, 2", c1944............... **$172**

Revillon Detchma , MIB, urn shape, metal cap, 2.25", c1955 .... **$15**

Nina Ricci, set of 3, sunburst, leaf and heart minis in box, 1.25"-1.5", c1952 .... **$605**

Rochas Femme, round laydown "pebble," gold label, 1.5", c1945 .... **$33**

Elsa Schiaparelli Shocking, set of three torsos in Jack in Box w/flowers, 1.36", c1936 ....**$667-1,000**

Rose Valois Canotier, figural mini wearing hat in plastic case, 2.3", c1950 ....**$145-317**

Weil Cobra, MIB, ball stopper, worn box, 1.5", c1941 .... **$25**

Weil Secret of Venus (Antilope), waisted bottle, blue cap, full, 1.36", c1942. **$32**

Miscellaneous Perfume / Cologne / Scent Bottles

Cologne Bottle

Deep teal blue, 4-3/4", polygonal form, 8-sided, smooth base, rolled lip, American 1850-1870...**$250-350**

Cologne Bottle – Label reads: "Superior Cologne Water, Prepared by L.W. Glenn & Son No 20 South 4th Str. Philada"

Clear, 5-7/8", blown using the German half-post method, polished pontiled base and sides, applied lip, original ground glass stopper, American 1800-1820 .... **$150-200**

Cologne Bottle

Deep cobalt blue, 7", corset waist form, 8-sided, smooth base, tooled mouth, American 1850-1880 ....**$1,200-1,800**

Blown in three sizes, with this example the tallest. Of the three sizes, this is the most difficult to find.

Cologne Bottle – Label reads: "Our Own" Cologne Fragrant and Lasting Prepared by J.M. Holt Milford, N.H.

Deep cobalt blue, 7-1/2", 12-sided, smooth base, rolled lip, American 1850-1880 ....**$375-475**

Cologne Bottle – Label reads: "Eau de Cologne Reetifiee"

Cobalt blue, 7-3/4", 12-sided with sloped shoulders, pontil-scarred base, rolled lip, American 1860-1880 ....**$275-375**

Cologne Bottle – Front label reads: "Eau De Cologne Paris", Neck label reads: "Prepared by Chas. I. L. Atwood Apothecary, Boston"

Medium emerald green, 8-7/8", smooth base, rolled lip, rare size and labels, scarce color, American 1850-1870...**$400-600**

Sandwich cologne bottle, 12-sided, 4-1/2", American 1850-1870, $200-300.

Cologne bottle, "Jules Hauel Philadelphia," 6-5/8", American 1860-1880.

Corset waist cologne, 6-sided, 3-3/4", American 1840-1870, $400-700.

Large cologne bottle, green aqua, 9-3/8", American 1840-1860, $500-800.

Sandwich cologne bottle, 4-5/8", American 1860-1880, $400-600.

Dancing Indian cologne bottle, 4-3/4", American 1840-1860, $150-200.

Cologne Bottle
Deep fiery opalescent powder blue milk glass, 10-3/8", pontil-scarred base, rolled lip, American 1850-1870 .... **$180-150**

Cologne Bottle
Opaque lavender blue milk glass, 10-7/8", smooth base, tooled mouth, American 1850-1870 . **$140-200**

Cologne Bottle
Milk glass, 11", pontil-scarred base, tooled mouth, American 1840-1860 .... **$100-150**

Cologne Bottle
Deep blue teal, 11", 12-sided, smooth base, tooled mouth, American 1850-1870 .... **$400-700**

Cologne Bottle – Label reads: French's Bay Rum Imported by Geo. C. Goodwin & Co. 38 Hanover St. Boston
Dark amber, 11-1/2", smooth base, applied mouth, American 1870-1880 .... **$120-140**

Cologne Bottle
Medium pink amethyst, 11-3/8", 12-sided, smooth base, rolled lip, rare size, American 1850-1880 .... **$500-700**

Cologne Bottle – Etched – Label reads: Eau de Cologne
Medium amethyst, 11-7/8", copper wheel cut grape and vine decoration around center, pontil-scarred base, flared-out and rolled lip, Amereican 1840-1860 .... **$375-550**

Cologne Bottle – Label reads: Cologne Water Prepared by X. Bazin, Successor to E. Roussel, No. 114 Chestnut St. Philada.
Fiery opalescent milk glass, 12-3/8", blown, pontil-scarred base, rolled lip, American 1850-1860 **$375-475**

Fancy Cologne Bottle – Embossed: Cristiani – De Paris
Aqua, 3-1/2", open pontil, rolled lip, American 1840-1860 .... **$120-160**

Fancy Cologne Bottle – Dancing Indians
Opaque milk glass, 5", dancing Indians on two panels, pontil-scarred base, tooled lip, very rare in this color, American 1840-1860 .... **$2,500-3,500**

Fancy Cologne Bottle – Dancing Indians
Fiery opalescent milk glass, 5", dancing Indians on two panels, pontil-scarred base, tooled lip, American 1840-1860 .... **$2,500-3,500**

Fancy Cologne – Floral and Bead Pattern

Milk glass, 5-1/2", smooth base, tooled flared-out lip, American 1850-1870 .... **$300-400**

Fancy Figural Cologne Bottle – Embossed: Aux Grands – Hommes LA Patrie Reco – Nnaissanate

Clear, 5-1/2", domed building design, pontil-scarred base, flared-out lip, rare, European 1830-1860 .... **$150-250**

Fancy Figural Cologne Bottle – Embossed: Morris – Johnson – "N-York"

Clear, 6-1/4", building design, pontil-scarred base, rolled lip, American 1840-1860 .... **$250-350** Embossed "N-York" appears on early stoneware from the early 1800s.

Fancy cologne bottle, aqua, 4-1/8", American 1840-1860, $60-90.

Fancy Figural Cologne Bottle – Embossed: "J. Picard / Paris", Label reads: Cologne Water, Jules Picard Paris"

Clear, 6-7/8", smooth base, tooled lip, French 1850-1870 .... **$140-180**

Fancy Cologne Bottle – Floral label reads: De Cologne Des Princes

Sapphire blue, 9-1/2", 12-sided tapered form, smooth base, inward rolled mouth, American 1860-1880, Boston and Sandwich Glass Works, Sandwich, Mass **$600-1,200**

Fancy Cologne Bottle – Floral label with eagle reads: Eau de Cologne – Superieure

Teal blue, 11", 21-sided form, smooth base, tooled flared mouth, American 1860-1880, Boston and Sandwich Glass Works, Sandwich, Mass **$500-1,000**

Cologne bottle, clear glass, 5-5/8", American 1870-1880, $140-180.

Figural Cologne Bottle

Milk glass, 7-3/4", cylindrical tapered column form with brick pattern, smooth base, outward tooled mouth, American 1860-1880, Boston and Sandwich Glass Works, Sandwich Mass........................... **$500-1,000**

Palmer's – Ihlang Ihlang – Perfumes – Label Under Glass (Palmer signature embossed on reverse side)

Clear, 9", smooth base, ground tooled top with original round handled glass stopper, American 1875-1880 .... **$2,500-2,800** Ihlang Ihlang was a perfume obtained from the flowers of the Canada Odorarta, an East Indian tree.

Bunker Hill Monument cologne bottle, 11-3/4", American 1875-1890, $800-1,200.

Fancy cologne bottle, aqua, 3-7/8", American 1840-1860, $80-120.

Fancy cologne bottle, aqua, 4-5/8", American 1840-1860, $75-100.

Fancy cologne bottle, aqua, 4-1/2", American 1840-1860, $140-180.

Fancy cologne bottle, aqua, 6-3/8", American 1840-1860, $75-100.

Fancy cologne bottle, aqua, 6-3/8", American 1840-1860, $125-150.

Fancy cologne bottle, aqua, 4-5/8", American 1840-1860, $125-150.

Palmer's – Patchouly – Perfumes – Label Under Glass (Palmer signature embossed on reverse side)
 Clear, 8-1/2", smooth base (WM Walton Pat'd Sept. 23/62 and two reissues May 28/67 Patd Sles), ground tooled top with original round handled glass stopper, American 1875-1880 ....**$1,000-1,400**

Palmer's – Tea Rose – Perfumes – Label Under Glass (Palmer signature embossed on reverse side)
 Clear, 9", smooth base, ground tooled top with original round handled glass stopper, American 1875-1880 ....**$2,500-3,000**

Scent Bottle
 Cobalt blue, 1-1/2", plump coin form with ribs swirled to the right, pontil-scarred base, sheared mouth, American 1820-1850 ....**$400-800**

Scent Bottle
 Cobalt blue, 2-1/8", flattened ovoid form with ribbed shoulder and waist, wide raised band in center portion, smooth base, ground mouth, rare form and design, American 1800-1840..**$500-1,000**

Scent Bottle
 Cobalt blue with olive yellow overlay herringbone pattern, 2-1/2", polished pontil, sheared and ground lip, European 1840-1860 ....**$200-300**

Scent Bottle
 Amber, 3-1/2", heart and fleur-de-lis pattern, pontil-scarred base, original pewter crown cap, French 1750-1800..**$200-300**

Lion cologne, 4-3/8",
American1840-1860,
$120-160.

Scent Bottle – Cut Glass
Clear with cut overlay cobalt blue, 3-1/2", smooth base, sheared and polished lip, original cut glass stopper, American 1840-1870......................................**$250-350**

Seahorse Scent Bottle
Clear glass with white band, 2", pontil-scarred base, tooled lip, applied rigaree, American 1815-1835 ....**$85-125**

Seahorse Scent Bottle
Clear glass with white band, pontil-scarred base, tooled lip, applied rigaree, American 1815-1835..**$85-125**

Seahorse Scent Bottle
Cobalt blue, 2-3/4", pontil-scarred base, tooled mouth, applied clear glass rigaree, American 1815-1835 ....**$250-350**

Seahorse Scent Bottle – copper wheel cut letters "T.S.N." above a bird on one side and "1792" above a flower on the other side
Clear, 4-1/8", pontil-scarred base, tooled lip, applied rigaree, American 1792 ....**$275-375**

Sunset Scent Bottle
Greenish aqua, 1-3/4", clamshell form, smooth base, tooled and ground lip, American 1860-1880..**$100-125**

Sunburst Scent Bottle
Medium blue green, 1-3/4", pontil-scarred base, ground and polished lip, American 1825-1835..**$400-600**

Sunset Scent Bottle
Fiery opalescent milk glass, 2-1/2", clamshell form, smooth base, tooled and ground lip, original pewter closure, very rare, European 1860-1880......................**$100-125**

Poison Bottles

By the very nature of their contents, poison bottles form a unique category for collecting. While most people assume that poison bottles are plain, most are very decorative, making them easy to identify their toxic contents. In 1853, the American Pharmaceutical Association recommended that laws be passed requiring identification of all poison bottles. In 1872, the American Medical Association recommended that poison bottles be identified with a rough surface on one side and the word poison on the other. But as so often happened during that era, passing of these laws was very difficult and the manufacturers were left to do whatever they wanted. Because a standard wasn't established, a varied group of bottle shapes, sizes, and patterns were manufactured including skull and crossbones, or skulls, leg bones, and coffins.

The bottles were manufactured with quilted or ribbed surfaces and diamond/lattice-type patterns for identification by touch. Colorless bottles are very rare, since most poison bottles were produced in dark shades of blues and browns, another identification aid. When collecting these bottles, caution must be exercised, since it is not uncommon to find a poison bottle with its original contents. If the bottle has the original glass stopper, the value and demand for the bottle will greatly increase.

Friedgen (irregular hexagon poison)

Yellow green, 6-7/8", smooth base (C.L.G. CO. / Patent Applied For), tooled lip, extremely rare, no other example in the 12 oz. size is known to exist, American 1890-1910 .... **$4,500-5,500**

Gift / Flache (skull and crossbones)

Olive green, 6-1/4", smooth base, tooled lip, German 1890-1930 .... **$90-150**

Gift / Flasche (skull and crossbones)

Golden yellow amber, 9-3/8", 6-sided, smooth base, ABM lip, German 1920-1930 .... **$50-75**

Not To Be Taken

Cobalt blue, 5", 4-sided, smooth base, tooled top, American 1890-1910 .... **$75-100**

Not To Be Taken – Label reads: What Home Without a Clean Bed, Mexican Brand Insect Fluid Compound, (woman in bedroom using the product), Mexican Roach Food Co, Buffalo, N.Y., Under the Insecticide Act of 1910, Serial No. 269

Cobalt blue, 5-1/2", hexagonal form, smooth base (4), tooled lip, Canadian 1900-1915 .... **$140-180**

Not To Be Taken

Brilliant green, 7", ribbing and cross design around entire bottle, smooth base, tooled top, American 1900-1915 .... **$250-275**

Not To Be Taken

Dark cobalt blue, 8-1/2", 4-sided, smooth base, tooled top, American 1900-1915 .... **$150-300**

Poison

Cobalt blue, 2-1/2", star shaped, smooth base, screw top, American 1900-1930 .... **$50-60**

Poison

Medium cobalt blue, 3", coffin form, smooth base, tooled top, American 1890-1915 .... **$90-125**

Friedgen, irregular hexagon poison, 12 oz., 6-7/8", extremely rare, at present, no other examples in the 12 oz. size exist are known to exist, American 1890-1910, $4,500-5,500.

Not To Be Taken – Caution – 20 / Taylor / Liverpool (on smooth base) 8-3/8", English 1890-1915, $600-900.

Poison – cobalt blue, 4-1/4" long, American 1885-1900, $1,500-2,000.

Not To Be Taken – Poisonous, deep cobalt blue, 7-3/8", English 1890-1910, $125-150.

Poison, 3-1/4", American 1890-1910, $50-75.

Poison (skull and crossed bones) DP Co – Poison, 5", American 1890-1910, $2,500-3,500.

Poison
Medium amber, 3", 3-sided, smooth base (JTM), tooled top, American 1900-1915 .... **$35-40**

Poison
Cobalt blue, 3-1/4", triangular form, smooth base (U.D. CO.), ABM top, American 1890-1910.... **$50-70**

Poison
Cobalt blue, 3-3/4", smooth base, tooled top, American 1890-1910 .... **$100-200**

Poison
Cobalt blue, 4", quilted around entire bottle, smooth base, tooled top, original glass stopper embossed "Poison," American 1890-1910 .... **$75-100**

Poison – Use With Caution
Cobalt blue, 4", irregular hexagon, smooth base, ABM top, American 1890-1910 .... **$50-60**

Poison – Star / Skull / Crossbones – Poison
Yellow with amber tone, 4-3/4", oval form, smooth base (S&D / 231), tooled lip, American 1890-1910 .... **$700-1,000**

Poison
Medium amber, 4-7/8", smooth base (S & D), tooled mouth American 1890-1910 .... **$200-300**

Poison
Medium amber, 5", triangular form, smooth base, tooled top, American 1900-1920 .... **$650-750**

Poison (skull and crossbones) DP CO – Poison – Written on faded label: R, 3 cents a piece
Cobalt blue, 5", coffin form, smooth base, tooled mouth, rare middle size, American 1890-1910 ... **$4,000-6,000**

Poison
Green aqua, 5-5/8", rectangular form, smooth base, tooled mouth, American 1890-1910.......... **$140-180**

Poison
Cobalt blue, 5", quilted around entire bottle, smooth base, tooled top, original glass stopper embossed "Poison," American 1890-1910 .... **$75-100**

Poison
Cobalt blue, 6", quilted around entire bottle, smooth base, tooled top, original glass stopper embossed "Poison," American 1890-1910 .... **$75-100**

Poison
Violet blue, 8", quilted around entire bottle, round form, smooth base (HB CO), glass stopper, tooled top, American 1900-1915 .... **$100-130**

Poison, cobalt blue, 5-1/4" l., American 1890-1910, $150-175.

Lyons Powder – B&P/N.Y., deep red
puce, 4-1/8", American 1840-1860,
$150-250.

Poison – The Owl Drug Co. – Aqua
Ammonia Poison, deep cobalt blue,
9-5/8", American 1890-1910.

Poison
Medium amber, 8", diamond cornered design, smooth base, tooled top, American
1890-1915 .... **$300-350**

Poison
Cobalt blue, 8", triangular form, smooth base, tooled top, American 1890-1915
.... **$2,500-3,000**

Poison
Violet blue, 9-1/4", quilted around entire bottle, round form, smooth base, glass
stopper that reads "Poison" on thee sides, tooled top, American 1900-1915
.... **$175-200**

Poison
Violet blue, 12", quilted around entire bottle, round form, smooth base, glass stopper,
tooled top, American 1900-1915 .... **$550-650**

**Poison – Bowman's / Drug Stores – Poison – Label reads: Denatured Alcohol,
Poison, Bowman Drug Co., Oakland**
Cobalt blue, 7", irregular hexagon form, smooth base (G.L.G. & Co. / Patent Appl'd
For), tooled lip, American 1890-1910 .... **$1,000-1,500**

Poison – Carbolic Acid – Use With Caution
Cobalt blue, 8-3/4", smooth base, tooled top, American 1890-1915........... **$70-80**

Poison – The Owl Drug Co. (motif of owl on mortar and pestle)
Cobalt blue, 4", smooth base, ABM top, American 1900-1915 .... **$50-60**

Poison – The Owl Drug Co. (motif of owl on mortar and pestle)
Medium amber, 4-1/2", smooth base, ABM top, American 1900-1915 ... **$100-125**

Poison – The Owl Drug Co., cobalt blue, 9-5/8", American 1890-1915, $800-1,100.

Poison – F.A. Thompson & Co. – Detroit – Poison, medium amber, 3-1/4", American 1890-1910, $600-900.

Poison – The Owl Drug Co. (motif of owl on mortar and pestle) – Label reads: Solution of Formaldehyde
Cobalt blue, 7-3/4", smooth base, tooled mouth, rare with label, American 1890-1915 .... **$375-475**

Poison – The Owl Drug Co. (motif of owl on mortar and pestle)
Cobalt blue, 9-5/8", triangular form, smooth base, tooled top, American 1890-1915 .... **$800-1,100**

Poison (skull and crossbones) / H.K. Mulford Co. – Chemist – Philadelphia
Cobalt blue, 3-1/4", smooth base, tooled top, American 1900-1915...... **$175-200**

Poison (skull and crossbones) / Gift (skull and crossbones) / Veleno
Olive green, 8-1/4", smooth base, ABM lip, German 1890-1930 .... **$90-150**

Poison
Amber, 8-3/8", hexagonal form, smooth base (E.B. & CO. LO/5000), tooled lip, English 1900-1920 .... **$200-300**

Poison
Cobalt blue, 5-3/8", smooth base (U.S.P.H.S.), tooled lip with a wide mouth, American 1890-1910 .... **$150-250**

Poison
Cobalt blue, 5-5/8", smooth base (H.B. CO.), tooled lip, original stopper embossed with "Poison," scarce, American 1890-1910 .... **$140-160**

Poison – Poison,
coffin shape,
7-1/4", American
1880-1910,
$900-1,100.

Poison – Poison,
3", extremely
rare, only one
of two known
examples,
American
1890-1910,
$3,500-4,500.

Poison
Medium amber, 5", coffin form, smooth base (Norwich 16A), tooled round collared mouth, American 1890-1900 .... **$500-700**

Poison
Medium amber, 7-1/2", coffin form, smooth base (Norwich 16A), tooled round collared mouth, extremely rare, American 1890-1900 .... **$7,000-14,000**

Poison
Cobalt blue, 14-3/4", cylindrical with tall wide flutes around the circumference of the midsection, smooth base, tooled collared mouth, American 1880-1900 . **$300-600**

Poison – Poison
Medium amber, 3", coffin shape, smooth base, tooled lip, extremely rare, one of only two known examples, American 1890-1910 .... **$3,500-4,500**

Poison – Poison
Medium green, 5", irregular hexagon, smooth base, tooled top, American 1890-1915 .... **$100-150**

Poison – Poison
Light cobalt blue, 5", irregular hexagon, smooth base, tooled top, American 1890-1915 .... **$50-70**

Poison – Poison
Dark cobalt blue, 5", irregular hexagon, smooth base, tooled top, American 1890-1915 .... **$500-600**

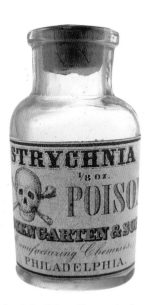

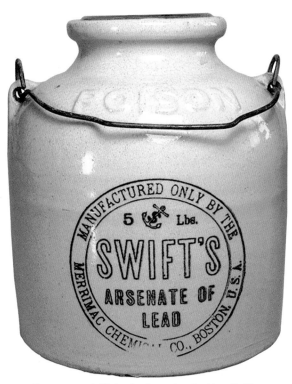

Strychnia – Poison – Rosengarten & Sons – Manufacturing Chemist – Philadelphia, clear glass, 2-1/2", American 1900-1920, $100-150.

Stoneware crock, "Poison" embossed on shoulder – Swift's Arsenate of Lead, Manufactured Only By The Merrimac Chemical Co., Boston, U.S.A., cream color, 6-3/8", American, 1890-1920.

Poison – Poison
Medium green, 5-1/2", smooth base (C.L.G. CO. / Patent Applied For), tooled mouth, rare color, American 1890-1910 ....**$250-350**

Poison – Poison (on reverse)
Cobalt blue, 7-1/4", coffin form, smooth base (Norwich 16 A), tooled top, American 1890-1910 ....**$800-1,100**

Skull and Crossbones (embossed on bottle)
Yellow amber, 2-1/2", smooth base (P.D. & CO.), tooled lip, American 1890-1910 ....**$60-80**

Strychnia / 1/8 oz. / Poison Rosengarten & Sons / Manufacturing Chemists / Philadelphia (label)
Clear, 2-1/2", smooth base, tooled lip with original cork, American 1900-1920 ....**$100-150**

Vorsicht / (skull and crossbones) / Gift! – Attention! / (skull and crossbones) Poison – Attenzione! / (skull and crossbones) / Veleno
Yellow green, 9", square form with embossing on three panels in three languages, smooth base, ABM lip, European 1915-1935...**$125-150**

Sarsaparilla Bottles

Sarsaparilla was advertised as a "cure-all" elixir, which actually makes these bottles a subset of the "cures" or "bitters" category. In the 17th century, sarsaparilla was touted as a blood purifier and later as a cure for the dreaded disease of syphilis. The drink became popular in the United States in the 1820s as a cure-all for a number of different ailments and soon was recognized as nothing more than "snake oil" sold at the medicine shows with ornate and descriptive bottle labels. One of the most popular brands among collectors is Doctor Townsend, which was advertised as "The most extraordinary medicine in the world." The bottles are usually aqua or green, with blues or dark colors considered much rarer.

Botanic Sarsaparilla, 8-1/4",
American 1875-1880,
$100-150.

C.W. Brodie / N.Z. Sarsaparilla,
9-5/8", New Zealand 1880-1890,
$180-275.

Dr. Buchans Sarsaparilla – Felton
Grimwade & Co. / Melbourne,
9-1/4", Australian 1880-1890,
$150-200.

Albright's Sarsaparilla / Prepared By / C.W. Albright Graduated In Pharmacy / Central Ave. & Kossuth St. Camden, N.J. / 100 Does 60 Cents

Aqua, 8-1/4", smooth base (W.T. & Co. / U.S.A.), tooled mouth, American 1880-1895 ....**$200-300**

B.F. Williams – Syrup Of Sarsaparilla / & / Iodid of Potass – Louisville, KY

Green aqua, 9-7/8", iron pontil, applied mouth, extremely rare, American 1850-1860… **$500-800**

Broadbent & Sons' / Sarsayeldock

Clear glass, 9-3/4", smooth base (AGM), tooled mouth, unusual composite of sarsaparilla and yellow dock, Australian 1880-1895 ....**$150-200**

Colburn's / Root, Bark, & Herb / Sarsaparilla / Pittsburgh, PA

Blue aqua, 8-7/8", smooth base, tooled mouth, American 1885-1895 .....**$140-180**

Cornell & Folsom / Wahoo & Sarsaparilla / N.Y.

Blue aqua, 9-1/2", iron pontil, applied sloping collar mouth, extremely rare, one of only two or three known examples, American 1840-1860 ....**$400-600**

Crescent / Sarsaparilla / 100 Doses 50 Cents – Crescent Drug Co – Newark, N.J.

Deep blue aqua, 9", smooth base, tooled mouth, American 1880-1895...**$180-275**

Dayton's / Sarsa / Parilla – And Coca Tonic – Blood Remedy – H.W. Veeder / Schenectady, N.Y.

Blue aqua, 8-3/4", smooth base, tooled mouth, rare, American 1885-1895 **$140-180**

Doeller's Sarsaparilla / Hamilton, Ohio

Pale blue aqua, 9-1/8", smooth base (AMF & Co.), tooled mouth, rare, American 1880-1895..**$120-160**

Dr. M.C. Parker's Sarsaparilla, 9-3/8", American 1855-1870, $350-450.

The C.D. Co's Sarsaparilla Resolvent, 8-1/2", American 1885-1895, $140-180.

Gilbert's Sarsaparilla Bitters – N.A. Gilbert & Co. – Enosburgh Falls VT, 8-sided, 8-3/4", American 1880-1890, $500-800.

Dr. Beach's Sarsaparilla Compound / M'F'D By / C.S. Welch / Wellsboro, PA
Deep blue aqua, 8-5/8", smooth base (W.T. & Co.), tooled mouth, extremely rare, American 1880-1890 ....**$150-200**

Dr. Cronk's / Sarsaparilla – NS. Wheeler
Pale blue green, 7-5/8", iron pontil, applied sloping collar mouth, extremely rare, American 1850-1860 ....**$150-200**

Dr. Dausch's / Sarsaparilla / And / Celery Comp. / Food For / Blood & Brain / Oriole / Chemical Co. / Balto, MD.
Clear glass, 6-7/8", smooth base (T.C.W. & Co.), tooled mouth, American 1890-1900 ....**$100-150**

Dr. H.K. Root – Clover Blossom / & / Sarsaparilla Comp – 7th Son
Aqua, 6-1/8", open pontil, applied sloping collar mouth, American 1840-1860 ....**$120-160**

Dr. Howe's – Shaker / Sarsaparilla – New York
Blue aqua, 9-3/4", open pontil, applied mouth, extremely rare, American 1840-1860 ....**$500-700**

Dr. James' / Stillingine & / Sarsaparilla – J.W. James & Co. – Pittsburgh, PA. U.S.A.
Aqua, 9-5/8", smooth base, tooled mouth, American 1880-1895 ....**$150-200**

Dr. / Keller / s (motif of a walking Indian) / Sarsaparilla / Sole Proprietor / New York
Blue aqua, 9-3/8", iron pontil, applied sloping collar mouth, rare, one of only four or five known examples, American 1840-1860 ....**$2,500-3,500**

Dr. J.S. Rose's Sarsaparilla –
Philadelphia, 9-1/4", American
1845-1860, $375-500.

F. Brown Boston Sarsaparilla &
Tomato Bitters, 8-5/8", American
1840-1860, $170-250.

Dr. Lameroux's – Sarsaparilla – Crane & Brigham / Wholesale Druggists / San Francisco
Medium blue green, 9-1/8", smooth base, applied square collar mouth, extremely rare, California sarsaparilla, American 1870-1880 .... **$275-375**

Dr. Martin's / Compound – Syrup Of / Snake Root – Sarsaparilla / & Burdock
Deep blue aqua, 8-3/4", smooth base, applied sloping collar mouth, American 1855-1865 ...... **$1,000-1,500**

Dr. Straus' Sarsaparilla / Philadelphia
Aqua, 9-1/4", smooth base (W.T. & Co. / U.S.A.), tooled mouth, American 1880-1895 .... **$100-150**

Dr. Townsend's – Sarsaparilla – Albany / N.Y.
Medium yellow olive, 9-1/2", pontil-scarred base, applied sloping collar mouth, American 1845-1860.... **$375-500**

Dr. Townsend's – Sarsaparilla – Albany / N.Y.
Deep yellow olive, 9-5/8", pontil-scarred base, applied sloping collar mouth, scarce New England variant with rivet circles on each panel, American 1845-1860
.... **$300-400**

Dr. Townsend's – Sarsaparilla – Albany / N.Y.
Medium yellow amber, 9-3/8", pontil-scarred base, applied sloping collar mouth, rare, true amber color, American 1845-1860 .... **$700-1,200**

Dr. Tutt's – Sarsaparilla / & Queens Delight – Augusta GA
Aqua, 7-1/2", smooth base, tooled mouth, American 1880-1895 .... **$140-180**

Dr. Wilcox's – Compound Extract – Of / Sarsaparilla
Medium blue green, 9-1/4", iron pontil, applied sloping collar mouth, variant with backwards "S" in Wilcox's, American 1845-1860 .... **$4,000-6,000**

Dr. Winslow's / Sarsaparilla Compound / And Iodine Potash / Prepared Only By / The Howard Drug & Medicine Co. / Baltimore, MD
Blue aqua, 8-7/8", smooth base, tooled mouth, American 1880-1890 .... **$140-180**

Elliott's / Arabian / Sarsa / Parilla – Elliott Medicine Co – Providence, R.I.
Blue aqua, 8-7/8", smooth base, tooled mouth, extremely rare, American 1880-1895 .... **$140-180**

George's / Sarsaparilla – Constock & BR – N.Y.
Aqua, 9-1/4", iron pontil, applied sloping collar mouth, American 1845-1860 .... **$800-1,200**

Goodwin's / Sarsaparilla

Clear glass, 9-1/2", smooth base, tooled mouth, American 1885-1895 .... **$100-150**

Gray's Sarsaparilla – Irwin M. Gray & Co. – Montrose, PA

Blue aqua, 8-1/2", smooth base, tooled mouth, American 1885-1895 .... **$150-200**

Griffiths / Sarsaparilla

Pale aqua, 9-3/4", smooth base, tooled mouth, extremely rare, American 1880-1890 .... **$100-150**

Guysott's – Compound Extract / Of Yellow Dock – & Sarsaparilla

Deep blue green, 9-1/2", smooth base, applied sloping collar mouth, rare, American 1840-1860 .... **$2,500-3,500**

Guysott's – Compound Extract / Of Yellow Dock – & Sarsaparilla

Deep blue green, 9-5/8", pontil-scarred base, applied sloping collar mouth, rare, American 1840-1860 .... **$1,800-2,700**

Masury's Sarsaparilla Compound – J&T Hawks – Rochester, N.Y., 11-1/8", American 1840-1860, $400-600.

I.C. Morrison's / Sarsaparilla – 188 Greenwich St. – New York

Dark cobalt blue, 9-1/2", iron pontil, applied mouth, American 1840-1860 .... **$4,000-6,000**

King's – Sarsaparilla / And Celery Compound (original labels)

Medium amber, 10", smooth base, tooled mouth, rare, American 1880-1895 .... **$350-450**

Levings & Co. – Sarsaparilla / And / Rose Willow

Deep blue aqua, 7-3/4", smooth base, applied double collar mouth, American 1865-1880 .... **$375-450**

Lippmans – Compounds / Extract – Sarsaparilla / With Iod Potass – Savannah GA.

Aqua, 8-1/2", smooth base, tooled mouth, rare Southern sarsaparilla with "arrowhead" indented side panels, American 1880-1895 .... **$200-300**

Munger's Sarsaparilla / Three Rivers, Mich

Clear glass, 9", smooth base, tooled mouth, extremely rare, from small Michigan town, American 1885-1895 .... **$200-300**

Neat's / Sarsa / Parilla – Neat Richardson Drug Co. – Louisville, KY

Clear glass, 8-5/8", smooth base, tooled mouth, American 1890-1900 .... **$100-150**

Charles Joly – Philadelphia – Jamaica Sarsaparilla, 9-5/8", American 1875-1890, $100-150.

Putman & Walker's Ruby Sarsaparilla, 9-3/4", American 1880-1895, $100-200.

Buffum's Sarsaparilla & Lemon Mineral Water – Pittsburgh, 10-sided, 7-1/8", American 1840-1860, $400-700.

Turner's Sarsaparilla – Buffalo N.Y., 12-1/8", American 1855-1865, $800-1,200.

Old Homestead / Sarsaparilla – McGarrick & Lewis / Wholesale Druggists / Norfolk, VA

Aqua, 7-3/8", smooth base, tooled mouth, American 1880-1895... **$150-200**

Pelletier's – Extract Of / Sarsaparilla –Hartford Con.

Aqua, 10-5/8", open pontil, applied double collar mouth, American 1840-1860 .... **$400-600**

Queens / Sarsa / Parilla – Standard Medicine Co. – Howell Mich.

Blue aqua, 8-7/8", smooth base, tooled mouth, American 1880-1895 .... **$200-300**

Seward's – Fluid Extract / Sarsaparilla – Buffalo. N.Y.

Aqua, 7-3/4", smooth base, applied double collar mouth, extremely rare, American 1840-1860 **$400-600**

Thos. A. Hurley's – Compound Syrup / Of Sarsaparilla – Louisville KY.

Medium amber, 9-7/8", smooth base (S.G.W. Lou. KY.), tooled mouth, American 1880-1890... **$150-200**

Totten's / Ssarsaparilla / 672 NTH 10th Street / Philada, PA

Aqua, 7-5/8", smooth base, tooled mouth, extremely rare, American 1885-1895 .... **$200-300**

Whipple's / Sarsaprilla / Portland, ME

Aqua, 9-1/8", smooth base, tooled mouth, American 1880-1895... **$100-150**

Whitney's / Sarsaparilla / Put Up By / Miller & Whitney / Healdsburg, Cal

Blue aqua, 9-1/2", smooth base (W.T. & Co.), tooled mouth, American 1880-1890 .... **$150-200**

Wilsons – Tonic & / Sarsaparillian – Elixir – J.W. Brayley / Proprietor

Blue aqua, 8-1/2", smooth base, tooled mouth, American (or possibly Canadian) 1888-1895 **$150-200**

Woodman's – Sarsaparilla

Blue aqua, 6-1/8", open pontil, applied sloping collar mouth, American 1840-1860 .... **$200-300**

Worlds – Columbian / Sarsaparilla – Worcester, Mass. – World's Columbian / Sarsaparilla Co.

Aqua, 8-5/8", smooth base, tooled mouth, American 1885-1895... **$100-150**

Wynkoop's / Katharismic Honduras / Sarsaparilla – New York

Deep cobalt blue, 10-1/4", open pontil, applied sloping collar mouth, rare, only a few sarsaparillas exist in cobalt blue, American 1840-1860 .... **$,3500-4,500**

Snuff Bottles

Snuff was a powdered form of tobacco mixed with salt, various scents, and flavors such as cinnamon and nutmeg. Inhaling snuff was much more fashionable than smoking or chewing tobacco. It was yet another substance touted as a cure-all for ailments like sinus problems, headaches, and numerous other problems.

Most snuff bottles from the eighteenth and early nineteenth centuries were embossed and dark brown or black, with straight sides. They were either square or rectangular in shape, with beveled edges and narrow bodies with wide mouths. In the latter part of the 19th century, the bottles were colorless or aqua and rectangular or cylindrical, with occasional embossing and labels.

Leonard Appleby / Rail Road / Mills Snuff, 4-5/8", American 1840-1860, $600-900.

E. Roome / Troy / New York, 4-1/4", American 1835-1860, $400-600.

Snuff bottle, medium olive green, 6-1/8", European 1850-1870, $250-350.

Leonard Appleby / Rail Road / Mills Snuff
Golden amber with red tone, 4-3/8", rectangular with beveled corners, tubular pontil scar, tooled flared-out lip, very rare, embossed, American 1840-1860 **$1,500-3,000**

Leonard Appleby / Rail Road / Mills Snuff
Yellow amber with olive tone, 4-5/8", open pontil, sheared and tooled flared-out lip, very rare, embossed, American 1840-1860...**$600-900**

Otto Landberg & Co. – Beroemoe Snuif – Celebrated Snuff – Capetown (on reverse)
Cobalt blue, 5-1/4", smooth base, tooled top, England 1800-1830............**$50-100**

Snuff Bottle
Medium plum amethyst, 4-1/4", rectangular with wide beveled corners, pontil-scarred base, tooled flared mouth, American 1820-1850 ....**$500-1,000**

Snuff Bottle
Deep orange amber, 3-1/2", square form, open pontil, tooled flared-out lip, American 1790-1820..**$140-180**

Snuff Bottle
Dark chocolate amber, 4-1/4", square form, large open pontil, tooled flared-out lip, American 1790-1820 ....**$150-200**

Snuff Blown Bottle – Label reads: Best Virgin – Scotch Snuff – Manufactured by Sweetser Brothers, Boston, Mass
Medium olive emerald green, 4-1/4", open pontil-scarred base (F), tooled flared-out lip, American 1825-1835..**$350-450**

Snuff Bottle
Forest green, 4-1/4", square made in a dip mold, pontil-scarred base, sheared mouth, American 1800-1830 ....**$300-600**

Snuff bottle,
dark yellow
amber, square
form, 4-3/8",
American
1800-1825,
$200-300.

Freeblown snuff jar,
6-3/8", American
1780-1810,
$200-300.

Snuff Bottle
Medium olive yellow, 4-3/8", open pontil, sheared and tooled lip, American 1900-1820 ....**$275-350**

Snuff Bottle
Yellow amber, 4-3/8", pontil-scarred base, sheared and tooled lip, American 1815-1830 ....**$150-200**

Snuff Bottle
Olive yellow, 4-3/8", pontil-scarred base, sheared and tooled lip, American 1815-1830 ....**$150-200**

Snuff Bottle
Medium yellow olive, 4-5/8", open pontil, sheared and tooled lip, English 1870-1810 ....**$120-160**

Snuff Bottle – Freeblown – Label reads: Spirits of Camphor
Forest green, 4-3/4", rectangular form, pontil-scarred base, tooled flared mouth, American 1740-1840 ....**$200-400**

Snuff Bottle – Freeblown
Yellow olive, 4-3/4", rectangular form, pontil-scarred base, tooled flared mouth, American 1740-1840 ....**$200-400**

Snuff Bottle
Yellow olive, 4-7/8", rectangular form, open pontil, sheared and tooled lip, blown in a dip mold, European 1780-1810..**$275-375**

Snuff Bottle
Medium olive green, 5", square with beveled corner panels, open pontil, tooled flared-out lip, American 1790-1820 ....**$400-600**

Large snuff jar, yellow olive green, 9-7/8", European 1850-1870, $250-400.

Black glass snuff jar, 4-3/8", American 1815-1830, $140-180.

Black glass snuff jar, 6-3/4", blown in dip mold, English 1780-1810, $200-300.

Snuff Bottle
Yellow amber, 5", rectangular with wide beveled corner panels, pontil-scarred base, tooled flared-out lip, American 1790-1820 ....**$150-200**

Snuff Bottle
Medium olive green, 5-1/2", square form, open pontil, sheared and tooled lip, American 1790-1810 ....**$350-450**

Snuff Bottle
Olive amber, 5-3/4", square with rounded corner panels, pontil-scarred base, tooled and flared-out lip, American 1790-1820 ....**$400-700**

Snuff Bottle
Emerald green, 6-1/8", square form, open pontil, sheared and tooled lip, blown in a dip mold, very rare in this color, American 1790-1810 ....**$400-600**

Snuff Bottle – Freeblown
Medium blue green, 6-3/8", cylinder form, open pontil, outward rolled lip with cork closure, American 1780-1810 ....**$200-300**

Snuff Bottle
Deep olive amber, 6-1/2", rectangular form with wide beveled corner panels, pontil-scarred base, sheared mouth with wide applied lip, blown in a dip mold, English 1780-1810..**$275-375**

Snuff Bottle – Black Glass
Olive green, 6-3/4", pontil-scarred base, outward rolled lip, blown in a dip mold, English 1780-1810..**$200-300**

Snuff Bottle
Dark olive green, 7-1/2", rectangular with wide corner panels, smooth base, tooled large wide mouth, German 1860-1880..**$180-275**

Soda Bottles

After years of selling, buying, and trading, I have come to believe that soda bottles support one of the largest collector groups in the United States. Even collectors who don't normally search for soda bottles always seem to have a few on their table (or under the table) for sale.

Soda is basically artificially flavored or unflavored carbonated water. In 1772, an Englishman named Joseph Priestley succeeded in defining the process of carbonation. Small quantities of unflavored soda were sold by Professor Benjamin Silliman in 1806. By 1810, New York druggists were selling homemade seltzer as cure-all for stomach problems, with flavors being added to the solution in the mid-1830s. By 1881, flavoring was a standard additive in these seltzers.

Because of pressure caused by carbonation, bottle manufacturers had to use a much stronger type of bottle, which eventually led to the heavy-walled blob-type soda bottle. Some of these more common closures were the Hutchinson-type wire toppers, lightning stoppers, and Codd stoppers.

Soda bottles generally aren't unique in design, since the manufacturers had to produce them as cheaply as possible to keep up with demand. The only way to distinguish among bottles is by the lettering, logos, embossing, or labels (not very common).

Burr & Water's Bottlers – Buffalo N.Y.
– This Bottle Not To Be Returned,
7-1/8", American 1840-1860,
$600-800.

Brownell & Wheaton / New Bedford
– This Bottle Never Sold, 7-3/8",
American 1855-1865, $180-275.

Carbutt & Hamilton Manufacturers
– Cincinnati, ten-pin shape, 7-7/8",
American 1855-1870, $375-450.

A. Allen / Lumberton / N.J. – Milford Glass Works
Blue green, 6-3/4", squat form, iron pontil, applied mouth, American 1840-1860
....**$400-600**

A. R. Cox / Norristown
Deep blue green, 7-1/4", iron pontil, applied mouth, American 1840-1860. **$150-200**

A. W. Cudworth / & Co / San Francisco / Cal (in a slug plate)
Emerald green, 7-1/2", iron pontil, applied blob mouth, American 1850-1860
....**$250-375**

A. Wood / Pittsg / PA
Medium blue green, 7-3/8", tubular open pontil, applied sloping collar mouth, very
rare, American 1840-1860 ....**$1,400-1,800**

Blanchard & Defreest / Troy, N.Y. – Superior / B & D / Soda Water
Sapphire blue, 7-3/4", iron pontil, applied blob mouth, American 1840-1860**$375-550**

Block & / Brandon / FRL – Levenworth / City / K.T.
Blue aqua, 7-1/2", pontil-scarred base, applied top mouth, rare, Kansas Territory,
American 1858-1860 ....**$2,000-3,000**

Boughton & Chase
Medium cobalt blue, 7", graphite pontil base, 10-sided, applied top, American 1865-
1875 ....**$2,500-3,000**

Brownell / & Wheaton / New Bedford – This Bottle / Never Sold
Deep sapphire blue, 7-3/8", smooth base, applied blob type mouth, American 1855-
1865 ....**$180-275**

Carpenter & Co Knickerbocker Soda
Water – Saratoga – Springs, 7-1/2",
American 1840-1860, $400-700.

California Natural Seltzer Water /
H&G, 7-1/2", rare color, American
1875-1880, $3,000-4,000.

Crystal Palace Premium Soda Water
/ W. Eagle / New York / Union Glass
Works, 7-3/8", American 1845-1860,
$800-1,200.

Carbutt & Hamilton / Manufacturers / Cincinnati
  Blue aqua, 7-7/8", smooth base, applied mouth, American 1855-1870 ...**$375-450**
Carpenter – & Cobb – Knickerbocker – Soda Water – Saratoga – Springs
  Blue green, 7-1/2", 10-sided, iron pontil, applied blob mouth, rare, American 1840-
  1860 ....**$400-700**
Cassin's English Aerated Waters
  Emerald green, 10", rounded smooth bottom, applied top, Western soda, American
  1875-1885 ....**$325-425**
C.B. Hale & Co – Camden / N.J. (in an oval)
  Medium emerald green, 7", iron pontil, applied sloping double collar mouth, very
  rare, one of only three or four known to exist, American 1840-1860 ....**$500-700**
**C.C. Haley / & Co / Celebrated / California / POP Beer – Patented / Oct. 29th
1872 / This Bottle / Is Never Sold**
  Deep amber, 11-1/8", smooth base, applied mouth, scarce, American 1872-1875
  ....**$250-350**
C. Garforth / Wheeling – G
  Blue aqua, 7-1/2", iron pontil, applied reverse sloping collar mouth, American 1840-
  1860 ....**$350-450**
Chas. Grove / Cola. PA (in a slug plate) – Brown / Stout
  Blue aqua, 6-1/2", squat form, iron pontil, applied mouth, rare, American 1840-
  1860 ....**$300-400**

Crystal Soda Water Co. / Patented Nov. 12, 1872 / U.S.PT., 7-1/2", American 1875-1885, $200-300.

F. Gleason – Rochester, N.Y., ten-pin shape, 8-3/8", American 1855-1865, $400-600.

Cha's Grove / Columbia, PA (in a slug plate)
Medium blue green, 6-7/8", iron pontil, applied mouth, rare, American 1840-1860 .... **$300-400**

C. M. Walter / M. Holly / N.J. (in a slug plate)
Deep green aqua, 7", squat form, smooth base, applied mouth, American 1855 -1865 .... **$400-600**

Cream / Ale – A. Templeton / Louisville (around mug base)
Deep red amber, quart, smooth base (L & W), applied sloping double collar mouth, American 1870-1880 .... **$250-300**

C. Whittemore / New York
Light blue green, 7-1/2", iron pontil, applied "top hat" mouth, American 1840-1860 .... **$100-150**

Davenport & Cos. / Mineral & Soda / Water – D.G. & K / Patent
Deep blue green, 6-7/8", pontil-scarred base, applied mouth, American 1830-1840 .... **$400-600**

D. Harkins / Richmond / PA (in a slug plate)
Deep blue green, 7-1/4", iron pontil, applied mouth, extremely rare, found in the Port Richmond, Pennsylvania area, where many early glass houses were located in Kensington and Union, American 1840-1860 .... **$400-600**

D.L. Ormsby
Cobalt blue, 7-1/8", iron pontil, applied blob mouth, American 1840-1860 .... **$375-450**

E. Bigelow / & Co / Springfield / Mass – Soda / Water
Deep emerald green, 7-1/8", iron pontil, applied mouth, scarce color, American 1840-1860. **$140-180**

Elias Barth / Burlington / N.J.
Blue green, 7", smooth base (B), applied blob mouth, American 1855-1865 .... **$150-250**

F. Gleason / Rochester. N.Y.
Medium blue green, 7", iron pontil, applied inverted cone sloping collar mouth, American 1840-1860 .... **$400-600**

F. Gleason / Rochester / N.Y.
Medium sapphire blue, 7-1/2", backward "N" in Gleason and "NY", iron pontil, applied blob type mouth, American 1840-1860 .... **$250-350**

G. – S.
Emerald green, 7-1/4", 8-sided, pontil-scarred base, applied blob mouth, very rare, American 1840-1860 .... **$275-375**

**G.A. Cook & Bro / Philipsburg / N.J. (in a slug plate)
– Dyottville Glass Works / Philada**
Medium blue green, 6-1/2", iron pontil, applied sloping double collar mouth, extremely rare, one of only three known examples, American 1840-1860 ..... **$500-800**

Geo. Eagle
Deep blue green, 7", rib body pattern, iron pontil, applied mouth, American 1840-1860 ...... **$800-1,200**

Golden Gate
Dark green, 7", smooth base, applied top, San Francisco soda, American 1865-1875........ **$250-350**

H. Ferneding / Dayton. O. (on shoulder)
Deep olive amber, quart, pontil-scarred base, applied sloping double collar mouth, three-piece mold, American 1851-1852 .... **$180-275**

H. Nash & Co / Root Beer / Cincinnati
Deep cobalt blue, 8-1/2", 12-sided, iron pontil, applied blob mouth, American 1840-1860 .... **$500-700**

H. Sproatt
Medium cobalt blue, 10", 15-sided , smooth base, applied top American, 1865-1875........ **$1,500-1,700**

H. & V.B. / Newton / N.J.
Emerald green, 7", smooth base, applied mouth, American 1860-1870 .... **$180-275**

Hausmann & Co. / Belvidere, N.J.
Medium blue green, 7-1/4", smooth base, applied mouth, extremely rare, American 1855-1865 **$275-375**

Henke & Maack
Emerald green, 9", smooth base, round bottom, applied mouth, extremely rare Washington D.C. soda bottle, American 1855-1865 .... **$1,800-2,500**

Hogan & Thompson / San Francisco / Cal. (in a slug plate) – Union Glass Works / Philada
Deep cobalt blue, 7-1/2", pontil-scarred base, applied blob top, rare, American 1853-1856 .... **$400-600**

Howell & Smith / Buffalo
Medium sapphire blue, 7-3/8", iron pontil, applied "top hat" type mouth, American 1840-1860 ...... **$140-180**

IRA Harvey – H
Emerald green, 6-3/4", squat form, iron pontil, applied mouth, American 1840-1860 .... **$150-200**

J.B. Edwards / Columbia / PA (in a slug plate) – Brown / Stout
Emerald green, 6-1/4", squat form, iron pontil, applied mouth, very rare, American 1840-1860 ...... **$375-475**

Henke & Maack, 9", extremely rare, American 1855-1865, $1,800-2,500.

J. & A. Dearborn & Co. / New York – Soda Water, 7-1/8", American 1840-1860, $275-375.

J. Lake – Schenectady, N.Y., 7-7/8",
American 1840-1860, $700-900.

Polk & Co. / Barnums / Build-
ing – Cor Fayette & St. Pauls St. /
Baltimore, MD, ten-pin shape, 8",
American 1850-1860, $500-800.

J. Foy / Burlington / N.J. (in a slug plate) – Brown Stout
Medium blue-green, 7-1/8", squat form, iron pontil, applied mouth, very rare, one of only two known examples, American 1840-1860 .... **$1,000-1,500**

J. & H. Casper / Lancaster / PA – Cold Cream / Soda
Aqua, 6", smooth base, applied mouth, American 1870-1880 .... **$100-150**

J. Lake / Schenectady, N.Y.
Sapphire blue, 7-7/8", iron pontil, applied mouth, rare color, American 1840-1860 .... **$700-900**

J. Lukens / Wheeling
Brilliant cobalt blue, 7-3/8", iron pontil, applied sloping collar mouth, American 1840-1860 ...... **$1,200-1,600**

J. Marbacher / Easton / PA – Improved / M / Patent
Medium green, 7-3/8", iron pontil, applied mouth, American 1840-1860 .... **$220-275**

John R. Owens / Parkesburg
Emerald green, 7", squat form, iron pontil, applied mouth, scarce, American 1840-1860 .... **$275-375**

L.L. Belland / Newark / N.J. (in a slug plate)
Deep green aqua, 6-3/4", iron pontil, applied mouth, American 1840-1860 .... **$120-160**

L. Schmitt / Columbia (in a slug plate)
Medium sapphire blue, 7", iron pontil, applied mouth, very rare, Pennsylvania soda, American 1840-1860 .... **$300-400**

L. Snider / Wheeling
Deep emerald green, 7-1/2", iron pontil, applied blob type mouth, very rare, American 1840-1860 .... **$800-1,400**

J. Wismann / Dayton / Ohio
Deep blue aqua, 7-5/8", 12-sided, red iron pontil, applied blob mouth, American 1840-1860 . **$350-450**

(Star) / Morton / 1851 / Newark, N.J. (in a slug plate)
Light blue green, 6-3/4", squat form, iron pontil, applied mouth, American 1840-1860 .... **$375-475**

Nash & Co / Root Beer / Cincinnati
Deep cobalt blue, 8-3/8", 12-sided, iron pontil, applied blob mouth, American 1840-1860 .... **$800-1,200**

O.G.M. / Gaines / Columbia / PA (in a slug plate) – Brown Stout
Blue green, 6-3/8", squat form, iron pontil, applied mouth, American 1840-1860 .... **$350-450**

Pomroy & Hall, 7-1/4", rare, American 1840-1860, $500-800.

Robinson, Wilson & Legallee – 102 Sudbury St. / Boston, 6-5/8", American 1840-1860, $140-160.

S & C Elkton / M.D. (in a slug plate), 6-7/8", very rare, American 1840-1860, $300-400.

P. Kellett / Newark / N.J.
Medium blue, 7-3/8", iron pontil, applied blob type mouth, American 1840-1860
....**$150-200**

Polk & Co / Barnums / Building – Cor Fayette / & St. Pauls St / Baltimore, MD
Medium cobalt blue, 8", smooth base, applied tapered collar mouth, extremely rare, American 1850-1860 ....**$500-800**

Polk & Co. / Barnums / Building / Balto
Medium cobalt blue, 8-3/4", smooth base, rounded bottom, applied mouth, rare, American 1850-1860 ....**$1,000-1,500**

Pomroy & Hall
Medium emerald green, 7-1/4", mug base, iron pontil, applied blob mouth, original neck ring is stamped "Allenders Patent July 24, 18_ Mauf'd by S.A. Bailey, New London, Ct," rare, American 1840-1860..**$500-800**

Robinson, Wilson & Legallee / 102 / Sudbury St. / Boston
Medium emerald green, 6-5/8", iron pontil, applied sloping double collar mouth, American 1840-1860 ....**$140-160**

San Francisco / Glass Works
Deep blue aqua, 7-1/8", smooth base, applied mouth, American 1870-1876
....**$150-200**

S & C / Elkton / M.D. (in a slug plate)
Deep blue green, 6-7/8", iron pontil, applied sloping collar, rare, Maryland soda, American 1840-1860 ....**$300-400**

S. Smith – Auburn N.Y. – 1857, 7-3/4", American 1840-1860, $400-600.

Southwick & G.O. Tupper – New York – ADNA – H, 7-1/2", American 1840-1860, $400-700.

S.S. Smith – Auburn N.Y., 8-1/4", American 1855-1865, $600-800.

Steinke & Kornahrens Soda Water – Return This Bottle – Charleston S.C., 8-1/4", American 1840-1860, $500-600.

Shaw & Co / Cape May (in a slug plate)
Medium blue green, 7-1/8", smooth base, applied mouth, American 1855-1865 .... **$100-170**

Southwick – & – Tupper – New York
Medium blue green, 7-5/8", 10-sided, iron pontil, applied blob mouth, American 1840-1860 . **$275-400**

Smedley & Brandt (in a slug plate)
Emerald green, 7-1/4", iron pontil, applied mouth, rare, American 1840-1860 .... **$300-400**

S.W. Bell / 1861 / New Brunswick – B
Light blue green, 7-1/4", smooth base, applied blob, mouth, American 1860-1870 .... **$100-170**

Taylor's – Best
Deep cobalt blue, 8-1/4", 6-sided, cucumber form, iron pontil, applied mouth, extremely rare, only one of two examples known, American 1848........ **$600-800**
This soda bottle was produced to coincide with Whig Parties nomination of Zachary Taylor for President at the Philadelphia Convention in June 1848.

T.H. Paul Glassboro – N.J., 7-1/2",
American 1840-1860, $400-600.

U & I.D. Clinton – Woodbridge /
Conn. Premium Soda Water, 7-3/8",
American 1840-1860, $140-180.

Union Lava Works / Conshohocken
/ Patented 1852, 7-1/8", American
1852-1860, $400-600.

T.H. Paul / Glassboro / N.J.
Medium blue green, 7-1/2", squat form, iron pontil, applied double collar mouth, extremely rare, American 1840-1860 ....**$400-600**

Tiffany & Allen / Washington Market / Cor / Fair & Washington / St. / Patterson / N.J. Spruce Beer – Please / Return Bottle / Soon As / Empty
Cobalt blue, 7-5/8" pint, cylinder form, smooth base, applied mouth, American 1865-1875...**$700-1,000**

T.M. Richardson / Burlington / N. J.
Medium blue-green, 7-1/4", squat form, iron pontil, applied mouth, American 1840-1860 ....**$250-350**

Toram's / Brown Stout – 65 / South St. / Phila
Medium green, 7-1/4", iron pontil, applied mouth, American 1840-1860..**$100-150**

T & R Morton / 1851 / Newark, N.J. – M
Light blue green, 7-5/8", iron pontil, applied mouth, American 1840-1860**$140-180**

Tweddle's / Soda Water / New York – Patent
Emerald green, 6-5/8", pontil-scarred base, applied mouth, American 1830-1840 ....**$375-475**

U & I.D. Clinton / Woodbridge / Conn. – Premium / Soda Water
Medium blue green, 7-3/8", iron pontil, applied blob mouth, American 1840-1860 ....**$140-180**

Warning Webster & Co. – 192 West St. N.Y. – Soda Water, 7-1/2", American 1840-1860, $250-350.

W. Dean / Newark / N.J. 6-3/4", American 1840-1860, $120-170.

W. M. & DT Cox / Port Jervis N.J., 7-1/8", American 1840-1860, $400-600.

Union Lava Works / Conshohocken / Patented 1852 (blank slug plate on reverse side of bottle)
Deep cobalt blue, 7-1/8", iron pontil, applied blob mouth, very rare, American 1852-1860 ....**$400-800**

Valentine / & Vreeland / Newark / N.J. – Supr. Soda Water / Union Glass Works / Phila
Cobalt blue, 7-1/2", iron pontil, applied blob mouth, American 1840-1860. **$200-300**

W. Eagle / Canal St. NY – Philadelphia / Porter / 1860
Blue green, 7", smooth base, applied mouth, rare, American 1855-1865.**$180-220**

W. Ryer – R / Union Glass Works / Philada
Deep cobalt blue, 7-1/8", iron pontil, applied blob mouth, American 1840-1860 ....**$400-600**

Willis & Ripley / Portsmouth – W & R
Sapphire blue, 7-3/8", iron pontil, applied mouth, American 1840-1860...**$375-400**

W.M. & DT Cox / Port Jervis / N. Y.
Medium blue green, 7-1/8", iron pontil, applied sloping collar mouth, rare, American 1840-1860..**$400-600**

WM. H. Weaver / Belvidere (in a slug plate) – Mineral / Water
Medium emerald green, 7", iron pontil, applied blob top, American 1840-1860 ....**$800-1,000**

WM. H. Weaver / Hackettstown (in slug plate) – This Bottle Is Never / Sold
Blue green, 7", squat form, iron pontil, applied mouth, American 1840-1860. **$400-600**

Soda Fountain Syrup Dispensers

When was the last time anyone remembers hanging out at the local corner drugstore, or sitting down at the soda fountain counter and ordering an ice cream soda or a rootbeer float, where the syrup was squirted into the glass from a decorative ceramic dispenser? Sounds good, doesn't it? Unless you entered that drugstore 75, or maybe even 100 years ago, you didn't have the fun of enjoying that experience.

U.S. pharmacists first began selling all types of fountain drinks for a number of various physical ailments from the common cold to lung diseases during the 1850s. In fact, the majority of these early drink mixes consisted of various drugs such as codeine, alcohol, and cocaine mixed with water. The pharmacists soon realized that by mixing different fruit extracts, along with sugar and carbonated water, they could produce a drink that everyone would buy.

Following the early successes of Coca-Cola and Pepsi with their flavored drinks in the late 1880s and 1890s, other new soft-drink companies began to produce additional soda flavors and sold their syrup bases to drugstores. As the competition heated up and soda syrup began to be mass-produced, it didn't take long for the pharmacists to figure out that having a soda fountain in their drugstore might make more money than selling drugs.

As a gimmick to sell the syrups, the companies gave the dispensers away as free advertising to drugstore owners who continued to purchase large amounts of soda syrup. This wasn't difficult, since the use of soda fountains became extremely popular during the 1920s with the help of Prohibition. The active use of a small number of drugstore soda fountains, with their unique and ornate dispensers, continued into the 1950s. But, with the arrival of modern technology and the onslaught of fast food chains, drugstore soda fountains became a thing of the past. It should be noted that while all the dispensers are decorative and valuable, the ceramic dispenser demands the highest prices at auctions.

Always Drink – Fowler's – Cherry (picture of red drink cup with 5 cents in middle of green leaf) – Smash – Our Nation's Beverage

Tan, red and green label, 14", pump at top of dispenser, American 1900-1930 ....**$2,000-2,200**

Always Drink – Fowler's Cherry (picture of cherries in middle of green leaf) Our Nation's Beverage

Tan, red and green label, 16", pump at top of dispenser, American 1900-1930 ....**$2,000-2,500**

Always Drink – Fowler's Cherry (picture of cherries in middle of green leaf) Our Nation's Beverage

Dark tan, orange and green label, 16", pump at top of dispenser, American 1900-1930.....................**$2,000-2,500**

Armours – Vigoral (decoration of red carnations)

White, 19", porcelain, copper reservoir, spigot at base of dispenser, five matching cups, lid, American 1910-1935 ....**$600-700**

Buckeye – Label reads: Cleveland Fruit Juice Co. – Root Beer (Buckeye Root Beer embossed)

Light brown glaze, 14", pump at top of dispenser, American 1900-1925 ....**$2,000-3,000**

Buckeye – Root – Beer (painted on front) – Label reads: Cleveland Fruit Juice Co.

Tan, 15", pump at top of dispenser, American 1900-1925 .....**$2,000-3,000**

Buckeye – Root Beer

Dark brown in tree stump shape, 14", pump at top of dispenser,American 1910-1930..........................**$500-600**

Buckeye – Root Beer

Black in heart type shape, 14", pump at top of dispenser, American 1910-1930 ....**$1,000-1,200**

Cherri Bon

Red with green base with cherry leaves, cherry shape, 14", original pump at top of dispenser, American 1900-1925 **$23,750**

Christo – Ginger Ale – Christo Manufacturing Co. – Richmond, VA

White, 16", barrel form, pump at top of dispenser, American 1900-1920..**$4,250**

Drink – California – Iron Port – 5 cents (picture of man holding world on shoulders) 5 cents – You'll Like It

White with red color on the label, pump at top of dispenser, American 1900-1910 ....**$10,000-11,000**

Drink – Clayton's – Smack – Trade Mark Reg. U.S. Pat. OFE – Artificial Flavor and Color – Ice Cold

White with blue label, 16", ceramic, pump at top of dispenser, American 1890-1920...........................**$17,250**

Drink – Crawford's – Cherry-Fizz – It's Jake-A-Loo

White, 16", pump at top of dispenser, American 1910-1930 ....**$8,750**

Drink – Dr. Swett's – Root Beer – On The Market Seventy Five Years

White with yellow, 14", pump at top of dispenser, American 1900-1920..**$5,600**

Drink – Dixie-Flip – The Wonder Drink (encircled with wreath of grapes)

White, 16", ceramic, horseshoe-style pump at top of dispenser, American 1900-1915............................**$34,750**

Drink – Dr. Pepper – The Year Round – An Ideal Beverage – 5 cents

White, 17", ceramic, spigot center of dispenser, American 1900-1920 ....**$25,250**

Drink – Fan-Faz – "Drink of the Fans" – A Pennant Winner

White, ceramic, 16", baseball shape original pump at top of dispenser marked "Fan-Taz," American 1900-1920 ....**$25,700**

Drink – Grapefruitola – 5 cents

Light yellow, green leaves around dispenser top, white base, 15", ceramic, plunger cap insert at top of dispenser, American 1913...................... **$31,750**

Drink – Grape – Julep

Purple with white base, 16", pump at top of dispenser, American 1905-1925 ....**$1,800-2,000**

Drink – Hires – It Is Pure

Tan, 14", hourglass shape, pump at top of dispenser, American 1905-1925 ....**$300-400**

Drink Hires Rootbeer – Drink Hires 5 cents – Hires Rootbeer – Is Luscious and Pure (picture of Hires "ugly" boy in blue dress and pink bib)

Brown trim and light cream, ceramic, spigot center of dispenser, Germany 1880-1930, Villeroy and Boch, Mettlach, Germany................. **$61,000**

Drink – Howel's – Original – Orange – Julep – 5 cents

Red with white base, 16", pump at top of dispenser, American 1905-1930 ....**$5,500-6,000**

Drink – Orange – Julep

Orange with white base, 16", pump at top of dispenser, American 1905-1925 ....**$1,800-2,000**

Drink – Rosary – Root Beer – Try It

White, 16", barrel shape, pump at top of dispenser, American 1910-1930 ....**$3,400**

Dr. Swett's – Root Beer

White, 16", barrel shape, pump at top of dispenser, American 1910-1930 ....**$6,500**

Drink – Stein's – Famous – Root Beer

White, 16", original style pump at top of dispenser, American 1910-1930 ....**$7,000**

Getz Blend – Root Beer

White, 16", pump at top of dispenser, American 1900-1930 .... **$3,900**

Green's – Muscadine – Punch

Light brown, 16", barrel shape, pump at top of dispenser, extremely rare, American 1900-1910 .....**$3,000-4,000**

Indian Rock – Ginger Ale

White, 16", original pump with Indian Rock Ginger Ale on ball, American 1905-1930.............................**$11,000**

Jersey – Crème – Perfect – Trade Mark (monogram with JC in middle)

White, 15-1/2", original pump at top of dispenser, American 1905-1930 ....**$900-1,000**

Jim Dandy – Root Beer – Delicious and Refreshing

White, 15", ceramic, pump at top of dispenser, American 1900-1930 **$40,750**

Liberty – Root Beer – Big Stein – 5 cents

Dark brown, 14", barrel shape, pump at middle of dispenser, American 1900-1920 ....**$1,000-2,000**

Magnus – Concordia Punch

Cream color porcelain over metal, 14", pump at top of dispenser, American 1910-1930.............................. **$1,000**

Mission Orangeade – Ice Cold

Orange art deco design depicting slices of oranges, 15-1/2", spigot on back side of dispenser, American 1930 **$1,000-1,100**

Mission Rickey – Lime – Ice Cold

Lime green Art Deco design depicting slices of limes, 15-1/2", spigot on back side of dispenser, American 1930 ....**$900-1,000**

Murray's – Old Fashion – Root Beer

Tan and dark brown, 12", barrel sitting on tree stump, dispenser in the middle of barrel, American 1910-1935.... **$550**

Pepsi – Cola, Dispenser lid reads: "Strengthening – Refreshing – Satis-fying – Invigorating"

Blue and green with forest background, ceramic, 19", original spigot marked "Avon Co." in center, American 1902, Avon Works, Wheeling, WV.... **$31,750**

Philadelphia Soda Fountain Co – Patented # 1128 (very ornate engraving on entire dispenser)

Silver plated, 26" h. x 19" w., two fancy dispensers, one on each side, American 1880 ....$2,000-2,500

Richardson's – Liberty – Root Beer

Tan and dark brown, 13", barrel sitting on tree stump, dispenser in the middle of barrel, American 1910-1935.... $700

Schuster's – Root Beer

Light and dark brown, 15", barrel shape, pump is not correct and incomplete, American 1901-1925 .... $500

So. Cas. Co. – Orange Ale – Artificially Colored – Mixed Citric Acid

Orange, 16", ceramic, original pump at top of dispenser, American 1900-1925 .... $25,750

Texberry

White with metal bands, 16", barrel shape, pump at top of dispenser, American 1910-1925 .... $900

Ward's – Lemon – Crush

Yellow with green base, 13", lemon shape, original pump at top of dispenser, American 1900-1930 .....$2,800-3,000

Ward's – Lime – Crush – Color Added

Lemon, 14", lime shape, pump at top of dispenser, American 1900-1930 ....$5,000-6,000

Ward's – Orange – Crush – Color Added

Orange, 15", orange shape, pump at top of dispenser, American 1900-1930 ....$900-1,000

Zipp's – 5 cents – Cherri-o

White, 15", barrel shape, pump at top of dispenser, American 1905-1925 .... $3,800

Zipps's – Root Bee r

White, 15", barrel shape, pump at top of dispenser, American 1905-1925 .... $2,100

Target Balls

Target balls, round bottles the size of a baseball, were filled with confetti, ribbon, and other items. Used for target practice from the 1850s to early 1900s, they gained considerable popularity during the 1860s and 1870s in exhibitions and Wild West shows with Buffalo Bill Cody and Annie Oakley. During one summer, the Bohemian Glass Works manufactured target balls at the rate of 1,250,000 over a six-month period. Others such as Bogardus and Ira Paine had their target balls manufactured by various glassmakers throughout the country, as well as Europe, especially England.

Some of the most popular colors were amber, various shades of light blue, purple (amethyst), and green. Around 1900, clay pigeons began to be used in place of target balls. Because they were made to be broken, they are, unfortunately ,extremely difficult to find, and have become very rare, collectible, and valuable.

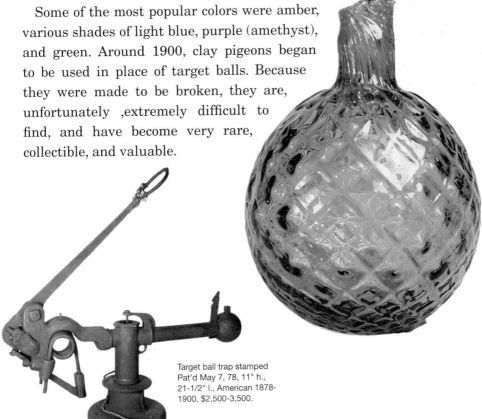

Target ball trap stamped Pat'd May 7, 78, 11" h., 21-1/2" l., American 1878-1900, $2,500-3,500.

Bogaradus' Glass Ball Pat'd Apr. 10, 1877, 2-5/8" dia., English 1877-1900, $700-900.

C. Bogardus / Patd / Apr 10th / 1877 / Glass Ball (on base), 2-5/8" dia., extremely rare, English 1877-1900, $5,000-7,000.

Bogardus Glass Ball – Pat'd Aprl 10 1877

Brilliant emerald green, amethyst striation in lower half of ball and overall diamond pattern above and below the center band, 2-3/4" dia., rough sheared mouth, embossed "8" inside one of the diamonds above the "A" in Aprl, American 1877-1900..... **$1,000-1,500**

Bogardus Glass Ball – Pad'd Aprl 10 1877

Yellow amber with light olive tone, 2-3/4" dia., overall diamond pattern above and below center band, rough sheared mouth, American 1877-1900.**$500-700**

Bogardus Glass Ball – Pat'd Apr. 10 1877

Medium sapphire blue, 2-5/8" dia., diamond pattern above and below center band, smooth base, rough sheared lip, English 1877-1900.................**$700-900**

C. Bogardus / Patd / Apr 10th / 1877 / Glass Ball (on base)

Yellow amber with olive tone, 2-5/8" dia., overall diamond pattern, rough sheared lip, rarest and most sought after of the Bogardus grouping, American 1877-1900 ....**$5,000-7,000**

E. Jones Gunmaker – Lancaster Blackburn

Cobalt blue, 2-1/2" dia., lattice embossed ball with cross on base, rough sheared lip, English 1880-1900 ....**$500-800**

For Hockey's Patent Trap

Pale olive yellow, 2-3/8" dia., rough sheared lip, English 1880-1900 ....**$1,000-1,500**

Glasshutten Dr. A. Frank – Charlottenburg

Yellow olive, 2-3/4" dia., overall diamond pattern, rough sheared lip, German 1880-1900 ....**$350-450**

Ira Paine's Filled – Ball Pat. Oct 23 1877

Yellow amber, 2-1/2" dia., smooth base, rough sheared mouth, blown in three-piece mold, American 1877-1900 ....**$300-400**

Ira Paine's Filled – Ball Pat. Oct 23, 1877

Light yellow with olive tone, 2-5/8" dia., smooth base, rough sheared lip, blown in a three-part mold, American 1877-1900 ....**$350-450**

Target balls, 2-5/8" dia., blown in three-piece molds, 1880-1900, $220-260.

Mauritz – Widfors

Yellow with amber tone, 2-5/8" dia., blown in two-piece mold, rough sheared lip, extremely rare, possibly only one of two known examples, Swedish 1880-1900 ....**$600-800**

N.B. Glass works Perth – N.B. Glass Works Perth

Green aqua, 2-5/8" dia., diamond pattern above and below center band, smooth base, rough sheared lip, English 1880-1900..........................**$150-200**

N.B. Glass Works Perth – N.B. Glass Works Perth

Deep cobalt blue, 2-5/8" dia., upside down "P" and backward "S", diamond pattern above and below center band, rough sheared mouth, English 1880-1900 ....**$150-200**

Range Ball (five pointed stars on both sides)

Medium cobalt blue, 2-1/8" dia., rough sheared long neck, English 1880-1910 ....**$120-160**

Range Ball (embossed star on either side)

Medium sapphire blue, 2-1/8" dia., rough sheared mouth, long neck, English 1880-1900..............**$150-200**

Mauritz – Widfors, 2-5/8" dia., Swedish 1880-1900, $600-800.

Range ball with five pointed star on both sides, 2-1/8"dia., English 1880-1910, $120-160.

Target ball "II" (on shoulder), 2-5/8" dia., American 1880-1900, $100-150.

Target ball, 2-5/8" dia., English 1880-1900, $200-300.

Range Ball
Deep purple amethyst, 2-1/2" dia., smooth base, rough sheared lip, blown in a two-piece mold, American 1880-1900 ....**$140-180**

Target Ball
Olive yellow, 2-5/8" dia., smooth base, rough sheared lip, blown in three-piece mold, scarce, American 1880-1900 ....**$150-200**

Target Ball "II" (on shoulder)
Light sapphire blue, 2-5/8" dia., smooth base (G2 embossed), sheared mouth, blown in three-piece mold, scarce, American 1880-1900 ....**$100-150**

Target Ball – Stars Ball
Yellow amber center shading to a deep color amber in the upper and lower areas, 2-5/8" dia., sheared lip, blown in a three-part mold, a number of rows of four pointed stars covering the entire ball, rare, American 1880-1900 ......**$3,500-5,000**

Target Ball – Stars and Bars
Yellow with amber and olive tones, 2-5/8" dia., rough sheared lip, intricate pattern of a series of horizontal lines along both mold seams with closely patterned dots on both sides and base, American 1880-1900 ....**$2,500-3,700**

Target Ball (man pointing a shotgun in two opposite side circles)
Light to medium emerald green, 2-5/8" dia., smooth base, rough sheared lip, English 1880-1900..............**$400-800**

Target Ball
Cobalt blue, 2-5/8" dia., smooth base, rough sheared lip, French 1880-1900 ....**$40-60**

Target Ball
Medium sapphire blue, 2-5/8" dia., square pattern above and below blank center band, rough sheared mouth, English 1880-1900..............**$200-300**

Target Ball
Medium golden yellow amber, 2-5/8" dia., embossed with line across center of bases, rough sheared mouth, blown in three-piece mold, American 1880-1900 ....**$120-160**

Target Ball
Bright yellow green, 2-5/8" dia., overall diamond pattern, long neck, rough sheared, Czechoslovakian 1885-1900 ....**$200-300**

Target ball, 2-5/8" dia., Czechoslovakian 1885-1890, $200-300.

Target ball, 2-5/8" dia., American 1877-1900, $500-700.

Target ball, 2-5/8" dia., American 1880-1900, $120-160.

Target ball, 2-5/8" dia., American 1880-1900, $100-150.

Target Ball
Dark amber, 2-1/2" dia., 7 horizontal rings around the entire ball, smooth base, rough sheared lip, American 1880-1900..........................**$600-800**

Target Ball – "K" embossed on the side
Amber, 2-1/2" dia., smooth base, rough sheared lip, American 1880-1900 ....**$300-600**

Target Ball
Medium cobalt blue, 2-1/2" dia., smooth base (G.8), three raised dots on shoulder, rough sheared lip, blown in three-part mold, rare, American 1880-1900..........................**$350-450**

Target Ball
Medium amber, 2-1/2" dia., smooth base, rough sheared mouth, blown in three-piece mold, large diamond on base, American 1880-1900 ....**$120-150**

Target Ball
Deep Prussian blue, 2-1/2" dia., rough sheared lip, overall diamond pattern, European 1880-1900..........**$180-275**

Target ball, 2-3/4" dia., German 1880-1900, $250-300.

W.W. Greener St – Marys Works – Birmm & 68 Haymarket London, 2-5/8"dia., English 1880-1900, $400-600.

Target Ball – Patd Sept 25th 1877 (around shoulder)

Deep sapphire blue, 2-1/2" dia., overall sand grain finish, rough sheared lip, blown in three-piece mold, extremely rare, American 1877-1900, manufactured by Corning Glass Company **$4,000-6,000**
The sand grain texture was applied so the shot would not slide off when hitting the ball, giving a better chance of breakage. Only a few of these types exist.

Target Ball

Cobalt blue, 2-1/2" dia., large square pattern above and below an unembossed center band, smooth base, rough sheared lip, French 1880-1900 ....**$150-250**

Target Ball – Wide Mouth

Clear glass with medium turquoise blue, 2-3/4" dia., overall mottled pattern and sand grain finish, sheared and ground 1" mouth, English 1890-1910 ....**$1,000-1,500**

Van Cutsem – A St Quentin

Cobalt blue, 2-1/2" dia., diamond pattern above and below the embossed center band, smooth base, rough sheared lip, French 1880-1900...............**$130-170**

W.W. Greener – St. Marys Works – Birmm & 68 Haymarket London

Medium amethyst, 2-5/8" dia., diamond pattern above and below center band, smooth base, rough sheared lip, English 1880-1900..........................**$400-600**

W.W. Greener – St. Marys Works – Birmm & 68 Haymarket London

Smoky olive green, 2-5/8" dia., diamond pattern above and below center band, smooth base, rough sheared lip, rare color, English 1880-1900**$1,200-1,600**

W.W. Greener – St. Marys Works – Birmm & 68 Haymarket London

Cobalt blue, 2-5/8" dia., diamond pattern above and below center band, smooth base, rough sheared lip, English 1880-1900..........................**$180-275**

Warner Bottles

The Warner bottle was named for H.H. Warner, who sold a number of remedies developed by a Doctor Craig. Warner developed his bottle for those and other cures and began producing great volumes and varieties (over twenty) in 1879 in Rochester, New York. In addition, Warner bottles were marketed and sold overseas in major cities such as London, Melbourne, Frankfurt, and Prague.

Warner Bottles, which can be categorized in the following varieties, can frequently be found with their original labels and boxes, giving additional value to these already expensive and rare pieces.

- Warner's Safe Kidney & Liver Remedy
- Warner's Safe Diabetes Remedy
- Warner's Safe Cure
- Warner's Safe Bitters
- Warner's Safe Rheumatic Cure
- Warner's Safe Cure (around shoulders – rare)
- Log Cabin Cough & Consumption Remedy
- Log Cabin Hop & Buchu Remedy
- Log Cabin Sarsaparilla
- Log Cabin Scalpine (hair tonic)
- Log Cabin Scalpine
- Long Cabin Extract, Rochester, N.Y.
- Log Cabin Rose Cream (extremely rare)

Warner's Log Cabin Extract – Rochester N.Y., 8-5/8",
American 1887-1895, $375-450.

Warner's Log Cabin Sarsaparilla – Rochester N.Y., 9-1/8",
American 1887-1895, $250-350.

Warner's / (Trade Mark on motif of safe) / Safe / Compound

Medium amber, 6", smooth base, tooled lip, rare with different embossing, English 1885-1895..............**$250-350**

16 Fl. Oz / Warner's / Safe / Kidney & Liver / Remedy / (Trade Mark on motif of safe) / Rochester, N.Y.

Yellow green, 6-1/2", smooth base, tooled blob mouth, very rare in this color, American 1885-1895.**$275-450**

Tippecanoe – H.H. Warner & Co. – Label reads: Tippecanoe – Trade Mark – The Best – For – Dyspepeia – Stomach Disorder

Medium amber, 9", log shape, smooth base, applied mouth with mushroom style top, American 1880-1900 ....**$325-425**

Warner's / Safe / Nervine / (motif of safe) Trade Mark / Rochester N.Y. / U.S.A. / London – England / Toronto – Canada

Orange amber, 7-1/2", smooth base, applied double collar mouth, rare, Canadian 1885-1895 ....**$400-600**

Warner's / Safe / Tonic Bitters / (motif of safe) Trade Mark / Rochester. N.Y.

Yellow amber, 7-1/2", smooth base, tooled mouth, American 1880-1895 ....**$500-700**

Warner's / Safe / Tonic / (Trade Mark on motif of safe) / Rochester, N.Y. (in a slug plate)

Amber, 7-1/2", smooth base (A. & D.H.C.), applied mouth, American 1885-1895.........................**$400-600**

Warner's Safe Cure (around shoulder), 9-3/4", American 1880-1890, $275-450.

Warner's Safe Cure – Trade Mark – Melbourne Aus – London Eng – Toronto Can – Rochester N.Y. U.S.A., 9-1/2", New Zealand, 1885-1895, $375-450.

Warner's / Safe / Cure / (Trade Mark on motif of safe) / Melbourne

Red amber, 7-1/4", smooth base, applied mouth, Australia 1885-1895 ..**$150-200**

Warner's / Safe / Cure / (motif of safe) Trade Mark / Rochester / N.Y. U.S.A. – London – England – Toronto – Canada

Orange amber, 9-1/2", smooth base, applied double collar mouth, rare, Three Cities, Canadian or American 1880-1895 ....**$350-500**

Warner's / Safe / Cure / (motif of safe) Trade Mark / Melbourne Aus / London Eng / Toronto Can / Rochester. N.Y. U.S.A.

Medium yellow topaz, 9-1/2", smooth base, applied blob type mouth, New Zealand 1885-1895 ....**$375-450**

Warner's / Safe / Kidney & Liver / Core / (Trade Mark on motif of safe) / Rochester, N.Y.

Medium amber, 9-1/2", smooth base, applied double collar mouth, rare

variant with cure misspelled, American 1885-1895 ....**$150-200**

Warner's / Safe / Nervine / (motif of safe) Trade Mark / Melbourne Aus / London Eng / Toronto Can / Rochester N.Y. U.S.A.

Yellow with orange tone, 9-1/4", smooth base, applied blob type mouth, scarce in this color, New Zealand 1885-1900 ....**$140-180**

Warner's / Safe / Cure / (Trade Mark on motif of safe) / Melbourne Aus. / London Eng / Toronto Can / Rochester N.Y. U.S.A.

Deep yellow amber with olive tone, 9-1/4", smooth base, tooled blob-type mouth, rare in this color, New Zealand 1885-1895 ....**$150-200**

Warner's / Safe / Nervine / (motif of safe) / London

Medium yellow topaz, 9-1/4", smooth base, applied blob mouth, English 1880-1895 ....**$180-275**

Warner's Safe Bitters – Rochester, N.Y., orange amber, 9-1/2", American 1880-1895, $600-800.

Warner's Safe Diabetes Cure – Trade Mark – London, 9-3/4", English 1885-1895, $500-700.

Warner's Safe Cure – Trade Mark – London, 10-3/4", English 1880-1895, $600-800.

Warner's / Safe Cure / (on motif of safe) / Pressburg

Yellow olive green, 9-1/2", smooth base, applied blob mouth, rare, Czechoslovakia 1890-1895 **$800-1,400** Warner's had an agent in Pressburg for only two years.

Warner's / Safe / Bitters / (motif of safe) Trade Mark / Rochester. N.Y. (in a slug plate)

Medium orange amber, 9-5/8", smooth base (A. & D.H.C.), applied double collar mouth, American 1880-1890 .... **$600-800**

Warner's / Safe / Diabetes / Cure / (Trade Mark on motif of safe) / Melbourne

Red amber, 9-3/4", smooth base, applied blob mouth, rare variant lacking the AUS after MELBOURNE, Australian 1885-1895................................. **$250-350**

Warner's Safe Cure – Trade Mark – London, 7-3/8" and 9-3/8", English 1890-1900, $150-250.

Warner's – Trade Mark – Safe Compound, 5-3/8", English 1880-1895, $700-900.

Warner's / Safe / Cure / (motif of safe) / London
Olive green, 9-7/8", smooth base, applied top, English 1885-1900.. **$150-250**

Warner's / Safe / Cure / (motif of safe) / London
Orange amber, quart, 10-3/4", smooth base, applied blob mouth, English 1885-1895 .... **$700-900**

Warner's / Safe / Cure / (Trade Mark on motif of safe) / London
Medium olive green, 11", smooth base, applied blob mouth, largest of the Warner bottle series, English 1885-1895.. **$1,200-1,800**

Warner's / Safe / Cure / (Trade Mark on motif of safe) / London
Yellow topaz, 11-1/4", smooth base, applied blob mouth, largest of the Warner bottle series, English 1885-1895.. **$700-900**

Warner's Safe Cure – London, orange amber, 9-1/2", English 1885-1895, $700-900.

Whiskey Bottles

Whiskeys, sometimes referred to as spirits, come in an array of sizes, designs, shapes, and colors. The whiskey bottle dates back to the 19th century and provides the avid collector with numerous examples of rare and valuable pieces.

In 1860, E.G. Booz manufactured a whiskey bottle in the design of a cabin embossed with year 1840 and the words "Old Cabin Whiskey." According to one theory, the word booze was derived from his name to describe hard liquor. The Booz bottle is also given the credit of being the first to emboss the name on whiskey bottles.

After the repeal of Prohibition in 1933, the only inscription that could be found on any liquor bottles was "Federal Law Forbids Sale or Re-use of This Bottle" which was continued through 1964.

Always Pure / Old (elk's head) Elk / Whiskey (decanter)

Lime green, 8-3/4", ear-of-corn form, smooth base, molded handle American 1885-1910 .....**$140-180**

A.M. Bininger & Co. / 19 Broad St. / N.Y.

Yellow amber,12-1/4", cannon barrel form, smooth base, rough ground mouth, American 1860-1880 ....**$500-1,000**

B.F. & Co. / N.Y. – Seal Whiskey Jug

Golden amber, 9", pattern-molded conical form, 26 vertical rib-pattern, applied handle with seal applied to the rigaree of the handle, applied double collar mouth with pour spout, rare, American 1840-1860 ....**$500-1,000**

Bininger's / Knickerbocker / A.M. Bininger & Co. / No. 19 Broad St. N.Y.

Medium yellow amber, 6-1/2", open pontil, applied sloping collar mouth, handle second hardest to obtain of the four handled Bininger bottles, American 1855-1875 ....**$500-700**

Buchanans / Absolutely Pure / Malt / Whiskey

Medium orange amber, 8-7/8", cannon shape, smooth base, tooled mouth, American 1875-1885 ....**$350-450**

Callahan's / Old Cabin / Whiskey

Yellow amber, 9", rectangular tall log cabin form with cathedral arched windows and doors, smooth base, applied sloping collared mouth, American 1865-1880 ....**$8,000-16,000**
This very bottle was used for the 33 cent American Glass postage stamp developed by Richard Sheaf. Bottle is on display at the Corning Museum of Glass, Corning, New York.

Chestnut Grove / (crown) / Whiskey / C.W. – label reads: Diploma Awarded by the Pennsylvania State Agricultural Society, to Chas. Wharton, Jr. for Chestnut Grove Whiskey at the Exhibition of 1859, Chas Wharton, Jr Wholesale Agent, No 116 Walnut St., Philada

Yellow amber, 9-1/8", open pontil, applied ringed mouth, handle, American 1859-1870 .....**$375-475**

Cognac / W & Co. – On Applied Seal

Medium amber, 6", globular form, pontil-scarred base, applied ring mouth, handle, American 1860-1875 ....**$700-900**

Applied handled whiskey, label reads: Fine Old Bourbon Whiskey, The Travellers, Sol. Age 8-1/4", American 1860-1875, $250-350.

Buchanans Absolutely Pure Malt Whiskey, 8-7/8", American, 1875-1885, $350-450.

Crane & Brigham / San Francisco (inside a leaf)
Medium yellow amber, 10-1/4", smooth base, applied ringed mouth, American 1880-1890..........................**$500-800**

Dr. Girard's / Ginger Brandy / London
Medium amber, 10", pontil-scarred base, applied double collar top, applied handle, American 1855-1875.............**$650-750**

E.G. Booz's / Old Cabin / Whiskey – 1840 – 120 Walnut St. / Philadelphia – E.G. Booz's / Old Cabin / Whiskey
Medium amber, 7-5/8", cabin form, smooth base, applied mouth, rare, few peaked corner bottles exist, American 1860-1875, Whitney Glassworks, Glassboro, N.J..............**$4,500-5,550**

E.G. Booz's / Old Cabin / Whiskey – 1840 – 120 Walnut St. / Philadelphia – E.G. Booz's / Old Cabin / Whiskey
Dark amber, 7-7/8", cabin form, smooth base, applied sloping collar mouth, rare, few peaked corner bottles exist, American 1860-1875, Whitney Glassworks, Glassboro, N.J. **$4,500-5,500**

E.I.J. – Seal Whiskey Bottle
Yellow olive, quart, applied shoulder seal, large iron pontil mark, applied sloping collared mouth with ring, extremely rare, only known example, American 1845-1860 ....**$1,000-2,000**

Fine Old Bourbon Whiskey, The Travellers, Sol. Age (label)
Deep strawberry puce, 8-1/4", open pontil, applied mouth, applied handle, American 1860-1875 ....**$250-350**

Forest / Lawn / J.V.H.
Yellow olive green, 7-1/2", bulbous form, pontil-scarred base, applied mouth, American 1865-1875............**$600-800**

Golden Eagle / (motif of embossed eagle) / Distilleries Co. / San Francisco Cal.
Dark amber, 11", smooth base, tooled top, American 1902-1910 ...**$300-600**

Golden Treasure
Blue aqua, 4-3/4", barrel form, smooth base, applied square collar mouth, American 1855-1865 ....**$140-200**

I.R.T. & Co. / Philad
Medium amber, 7", pontil-scarred base, applied double collar top, applied handle, American 1855-1875.............**$500-600**

Embossed Star / IXL Valley Whiskey / E & B Bevan / Pittston Pa / Embossed Star
Dark amber, 8", pontil-scarred base, applied double collar top, American 1855-1875....................**$2,500-2,800**

Flora Temple / Standing Horse / Harness Trot 2.19 – Label on reverse reads: Established 1839 / S.T. Suits / Kentucky / Salt River Bourbon / Whiskey / Distilleries / Jefferson, Co. Ky.
Deep strawberry puce, 8-1/2", smooth base, applied ring mouth and handle, American 1859-1869, Whitney Glass Works, Glassboro, N.J. **$600-800**

Fort Trumbull Glass Co.
Yellow amber, quart, three-piece mold, smooth base, applied sloping collared mouth with ring, extremely rare Fort Trumbull Glass Works, New London, Connecticut, American 1865-1868 ....**$750-1,500**

Greeley's / Bourbon Whiskey / Bitters
Deep plum purple, 9-3/8", barrel form, smooth base, applied square collared mouth, American 1860-1880 ....**$1,000-2,000**

Greeting / Theodore Netter / 1232 Market St / Philadelphia
Medium cobalt blue, 6", barrel form, smooth base, tooled mouth, American 1885-1895.........................**$200-300**

G.W. Huntington – On Applied Seal
Medium teal, 11-3/4", large iron pontil, applied mouth, extremely rare, American 1845-1865 ....**$600-800**

H.A Graef's Son / N.Y. / Canteen, 6-3/4", American 1875-1885, $700-900.

H.A. Graef's Son – N.Y. – Canteen, olive green, 6-3/4", American 1875-1885, $700-900.

Heidelberg / Branntwein – A.M. Bininger & Co.

Olive green, 9-5/8", smooth base, applied sloping collar mouth, rare, American 1865-1875 ....**$700-900**

HF & B / NY (embossed lettering in embossed shield)

Yellow with a green tone, 9", melon form, smooth base, applied sloping collared mouth with ring, rare, American 1860-1870......................**$500-1,000**

HF & B / NY (embossed lettering in embossed shield)

Apricot puce, 9-1/8", melon form, smooth base, applied sloping collared mouth with ring, rare, American 1860-1870 ....**$500-1,000**

Hopatkong / Whiskey / J.C. Hess & Co. Phila

Deep cobalt blue, 10-1/4", 12-fluted panels in lower half, smooth base, applied ring mouth, extremely rare, American 1865-1875 ....**$2,500-3,500**

I. Nelson's / Old Bourbon / Maysville, KY

Yellow amber, 7-3/8", barrel form, smooth base, applied mouth, rare, American 1860-1870 ....**$2,500-3,500**

Jacob A. Wolford – Chicago (around shoulder) / Wolford / Z – Whiskey

Yellow amber, 8-5/8", smooth base (A & D.H. Chambers Pittsburgh, PA / Pat Aug 6th 72), applied mouth with internal screw threads, original threaded stopper is embossed "Pat. Aug. 6th 72, American 1875-1880 ....**$500-800**

J.F.T. & Co. / Philad

Amber, 7-1/8", jug, molded vertical rib pattern, open pontil, applied double collar mouth, handle, American 1860-1875 ....**$500-900**

JH Cutter / Old / Bourbon / A.P. Hotling & Co. / Sole Agents – "A No 1" on reverse

Medium amber, 12", smooth base, applied top, American 1877-1880 ....**$125-150**

Golden Treasure, 4-3/4", American 1855-1865, $140-200.

J.T. Gayen / Altona

Red amber, 13-5/8", cannon form, smooth base, applied blob mouth, American 1865-1875 ....**$1,500-2,000**

J. Moore / (antlers) / Old Bourbon / Trade Mark

Dark amber, 11-1/4", smooth base, applied top, American 1875-1888 ....**$300-600**

Jockey Club / Whiskey / GW Chesley & Co. / SF

Golden amber, 11-7/8", smooth base, applied top, extremely rare, American 1873-1878....................**$5,000-8,000**

John Coyne / Cor Fayette & Seneca STS / Utica, N.Y.

Medium yellow green, strap-side pint, smooth base, applied double collar mouth, American 1875-1885 ....**$150-200**

Label Under Glass – Rum Punch – Label: picture of lady with orange and green background

Clear glass, 12", smooth base, applied top, American 1875-1895 ....**$1,800-2,000**

Label Under Glass – Cherry – Label: picture of lady with orange and green background

Clear glass, 12", smooth base, applied top, American 1875-1895 ....**$1,500-1,700**

Label Under Glass – Gin – Label: picture of lady with peach and gold background

Clear glass, 12", smooth base, applied top, American 1875-1895 ....**$2,000-2,200**

Label Under Glass – Kummel – Label: picture of lady with orange and green background

Clear glass, 11", fluted shape, smooth base, applied top, American 1875-1895 ....**$1,300-1,500**

Label Under Glass – Encased Whiskey Bottle – Multicolored label with a pretty woman – Label reads: Benj. F. Stratton, Pottstown, PA

Wicker basket, 11-3/4", tooled mouth, metal and cork stopper on chain, extremely rare, American 1880-1895 ....**$500-700**

Label Under Glass – Label reads: Our Private Stock / (motif of whiskey barrels) / Bourbon / McLeod Hatje Proprietors / San Francisco

Clear glass, 12", smooth base, applied top, American 1875-1895 ....**$1,800-2,000**

Lancaster / Glass Works / Lancaster N.Y. (embossed on base)

Yellow amber, 9-1/4 ", barrel form, smooth base, applied square collared mouth, American 1860-1870 ....**$500-1,000**

Lancaster / Glass Works / Lancaster N.Y. (embossed on base)

Brilliant yellow amber with topaz tone, 9-1/2", smooth base, applied double collared mouth, American 1860-1870 .... **$500-1,000**

Lilienthal & Co. / (motif of embossed monogram and crown) / San Francisco

Light yellow with green tone, 11-1/2", smooth base, applied top, American 1885-1895 .... **$500-1,200**

M. Gruenberg & Co. / Old Judge KY / San Francisco (light embossing)

Medium amber, 11-3/8", four-piece mold, smooth base, applied top, American 1879-1881 .... **$700-1,500**

M. Gruenberg & Co. / Old Judge KY / San Francisco (strong embossing)

Dark amber, 11-3/8", four-piece mold, smooth base, applied top, American 1879-1881 .... **$700-1,500**

M. Schwartzkoff / Liquors / 301 / Penn Ave. / Scranton, PA

Brilliant yellow olive, 9-3/4", strap sided quart, smooth base, applied double collar mouth, American 1880-1890 .... **$350-450**

May & Fairall / Grocers / Baltimore

Yellow amber, 11-3/8", smooth base, applied mouth, American 1870-1880 .... **$375-475**

McKennas / Nelson County / Extra / Kentucky Bourbon / Whiskey / W & K Sole Agents

Medium amber, 12", smooth base, applied top, American 1874-1878 .... **$1,500-1,700**

Milton J. Hardy / Old / Bourbon / Trade Mark (eagle) / Wellington A. Hardy / Manufacturer / Louisville / K.Y.

Yellow amber with faint olive tone, 11-3/4", smooth base, applied mouth, American 1878-1880 .... **$5,000-8,000**

Neal's Ambrosia / Philada / Whiskey – On Applied Seal

Cobalt blue, 9-1/4", smooth base, applied collar mouth, American 1865-1875 .... **$3,500-4,500**

Old / Fashion / Hand / Made / Sour / Mash / Belle / Of / Anderson

Milk glass, 6-7/8", smooth base, tooled lip, American 1885-1900 .... **$75-100**

Old / Fashion / Hand / Made / Sour / Mash / Belle / Of / Anderson

Milk glass, 8-1/8", smooth base, tooled lip, American 1885-1900 .... **$75-100**

May & Fairall Grocers / Baltimore 11-3/8", American 1870-1880, $375-475.

Neal's Ambrosia / Philada Whiskey (on applied seal), 9-1/4", American 1865-1875, $3,500-4,500.

Old Monogahela / B / Rye Whiskey (on applied seal), 9-3/8", American 1870-1875, $250-350.

P.F. Goddard & Co / 233 Dock St. / Phila 11-1/4", American 1870-1880, $600-800.

Old Monogahela / B (sheath of grain) / Rye Whiskey – On Applied Seal

Deep olive amber, 9-3/8", smooth base, applied sloping double collar mouth, American 1870-1875 .... **$250-350**

Old Monogahela / C (sheath of grain) H / Rye Whiskey – On Applied Seal

Dark amber, 9-1/2", smooth base, applied sloping double collar mouth, American 1870-1875 **$250-350**

Old Wheat / 1835 / Whiskey

Golden amber, 12-1/4", iron pontil, tooled mouth with ring, American 1845-1860 .... **$500-1,000**

P.F. Goddard & Co / 223 / Dock / St. / Phila – On Applied Seal

Lime green, 11-1/4", smooth base (Whitney Glass Works), "Patent" on shoulder, applied collar mouth, American 1870-1880 .... **$600-800**

P & V – Seal Whiskey Bottle

Aquamarine, 11-1/4", smooth base, three-piece mold, applied sloping collared mouth with ring, extremely rare, only known example, American 1860-1870 .... **$1,000-2,000**

Pure Cognac – On Applied Seal

Medium amber, 9", cone form, pontil-scarred base, applied double collar mouth, handle, American 1865-1875 .... **$700-900**

Redington & Co / R & Co (monogram) / San Francisco

Medium yellow amber, 10-1/4", smooth base, applied ring mouth, scarce, American 1880-1890 .. **$500-700**

Reed's / Old Lexington Club

Medium amber, 11-3/4", smooth base, applied top, very rare, American 1887-1895, Whitney Glass Works, Glassboro, New Jersey **$2,000-3,000**

Renault & Co. / Cognac / 1805 / W.H.Y. – Seal Whiskey Bottle

Yellow olive, 11", smooth base (Dyottville Glass Works Phila) applied sloping collared mouth with ring, three-piece mold, American 1860-1870, Dyottville Glass Works, Philadelphia, Pennsylvania........ **$1,500-3,000**

Russ's / Aromatic – Schnapps – New York

Olive green, 9-7/8", smooth base, applied sloping double collar mouth, American 1865-1875 .... **$140-180**

R.B. Cutter /
Louisville, KY,
8-1/2", American
1855-1870,
$550-750.

Russ's Aromatic Schnapps /
New-York,
9-7/8",
American
1865-1875,
$140-180.

Schreiber Bros. Co. / (motif of two deer with SB emblem) The Largest Jewish Liquor House Of The West / Chicago, ILL

Clear, 9-1/4", smooth base, ABM lip with wooden handle, American 1900-1920 .... **$200-300**

SOP / S.M. & Co – On Applied Seal

Medium orange amber, 7-1/2", cone form, pontil-scarred base, applied ring mouth, handle, American 1860-1875 .... **$500-700**

T. Goddard & Co / 233 Dock / St. / Philada – Seal Whiskey Bottle

Bright yellow green, 11", embossed seal applied upside down, smooth base, applied sloping collared mouth with ring, extremely rare, seal is upside down, American 1860-1870 .... **$750-1,500**

Tabec / De / A. Delpit / Nouvelle / Orleans – On Applied Seal

Deep olive amber, smooth base, applied collar mouth, blown in three-piece mold, American 1860-1870 .... **$350-450**

The Duffy Malt / (monogram) / Whiskey Co. – Sample Bottle

Medium amber, 4", smooth base, tooled top, American 1885-1900 .... **$75-100**

Star Whiskey / New York / W.B. Crowell Jr., 8-1/2", American 1860-1875, $500-800.

Tabec De A. Delpit / Nouvelle / Orleans (on applied seal), blown in three-piece mold, American 1860-1870, $350-450.

The Old Mill / Whitlock & Co., 8-1/4", American 1860-1875, $600-800.

Turner Brothers – New York, yellow amber, 10", American 1855-1860, $400-600.

The / Old Mill / Whitlock & Co. – On Applied Seal
Yellow amber, 8-1/4", cone form, pontil-scarred base, applied double collar mouth, large seal with neck chain and handle, American 1860-1875 ....**$600-800**

Trade Mark / Gold Dust / (motif of embossed horse) Kentucky Bourbon / N. Van Bergen & Co. / Sole Proprietors
Blue aqua, 11-3/4 ", smooth base, applied drippy top, American 1877-1883 ....**$700-1,400**

Trade Mark / Gold Dust / (motif of embossed horse) Kentucky Bourbon / N. Van Bergen & Co. / Sole Proprietors
Medium amethyst, 11-7/8", smooth base, tooled top, extremely rare variant, one of only five known examples, American 1880-1882...................................**$500-1,000**

Turner Brothers / New York
Orange amber, 9-3/4", barrel form, smooth base, applied square collared mouth, American 1860-1880 ....**$500-1,000**

Van Beil & Co. / Phila / 1861 – On Applied Seal
Yellow olive, 12-1/8", smooth base (Whitney Glass Works Glassboro, NJ), applied mouth with internal screw threads, embossed on correct screw-in stopper (Pat. Jan 1861), three-piece mold, American 1865-1875 ....**$400-700**

Van Biel & Co. / Phila / 1861 (on applied seal), 12-1/8", American 1865-1875, $400-700.

82-580. W.B. Bordman Old Bourbon, 9-1/4", American 1860-1870, $200-275.

Wharton's Whisky – 1850 – Chestnut Grove, aqua, 5-5/8", American 1855-1870, $200-300.

Weeks & Potter – Boston (on shoulder)
Medium golden amber, 11-1/2", smooth base, applied sloping double collar mouth with internal threads, original glass screw stopper embossed "PAT," blown in three-piece mold, American 1875-1885 . **$120-160**

W.F. & B / N.Y.
Dark amethyst, 11", 6-sided, smooth base, applied mouth, rare, American 1865-1875 .... **$700-900**

W.B. Bordman/ Old Bourbon
Yellow amber, 9-1/4", case gin form, smooth base, applied double collar mouth, very rare, American 1860-1870... **$200-275**

Wharton's / Whiskey / 1850 / Chestnut Grove
Orange amber, Jug, smooth base (Whitney Glass Works / Glassboro, N.J.), applied handle, sheared and tooled lip with pour spout, American 1860-1875..... **$350-475**

Whitlock & Co. / New York – BM & EA
Medium grass green, 9-3/8", smooth base, applied mouth, rare, American 1865-1875 .... **$700-900**

Whitlock & Co. / New York – BM & EA, 9-3/8", American 1865-1875.

BACK BAR BOTTLES AND DECANTERS

Back bar decanters (set of two) Rye and Scotch, 1880-1900, 8-1/2", $100-150 (for set).

Bar Bottle – Pattern Molded
Medium teal green, 10", 16 vertical rib-pattern, open pontil, applied top, American 1780-1840..**$800-1,000**

Bar Bottle
Fiery opalescent cranberry, 11", red with white swirl pattern, smooth base, tooled mouth, American 1885-1910 ....**$375-475**

Bar Bottle
Cobalt blue, 11-3/8", cylinder, smooth base, applied ringed mouth, raised oval panel on front, blown in three-piece mold, American 1870-1880 ....**$375-450**

Crystal Spring (white lettering)
Clear, 11-1/4", swirled glass, smooth base, applied top, American 1885-1900 ....**$250-400**

Decanter – Buffalo Club (picture of buffalo in brown enamel)
Clear, 9-1/4", corset waist form, cut shoulder and panel, polished pontil, tooled lip, original glass stopper, American 1890-1910..**$700-800**

Guckenheimer / Rye Whiskey / Nothing Better (white lettering)
Clear, 11-1/4", swirled glass, smooth base, applied top, American 1885-1900 ....**$250-400**

Label Under Glass – Portrait of beautiful Victorian woman wth red, gold, blue, black, and white background
Clear, 10", smooth base (W.N. Walton Pat. Sept. 23/62), tooled flared top, American 1860-1880..**$400-800**

Thos Jacobs & Co (on seal), 1850-1860, 11-3/4", $150-250 (large iron pontil).

Union Clasped Hands - Eagle, 1860-1865, 8-7/8", $350-450.

Label Under Glass – John H. Hamm / (motif of lady) / Rye Whiskey

Clear, 10", smooth base, tooled lip with original ground glass closure, American 1880-1900......**$1,100-1,300**

Label Under Glass – Fine Old / Port

Clear, 11", smooth base, tooled lip with original ground glass closure, American 1880-1900......**$300-400**

Label Under Glass – Brandy (motif of lady)

Clear, 11", smooth base, tooled lip with original ground glass closure, American 1880-1900......**$1,600-1,800**

Large Rye (in gold lettering)

Clear, 11", 12 panel base and cut-glass fluted shoulders, smooth base, applied top, American 1885-1900 ......**$200-300**

Magnet (motif of red and white magnet) Whiskey

Clear, 9", smooth base, tooled lip with original ground glass closure, American 1880-1900 ......**$500-700**

Pride Of Kentucky / (motif of "L" (Livingston) in diamond) / Sour Mash

Clear, 8", smooth base, tooled lip, applied handle, American 1895-1910 ......**$300-600**

Puritan Rye (white lettering)

Clear, 11", swirled glass, smooth base, applied lip, American 1895-1900... **$250-400**

Rye

Deep cobalt blue, 11", smooth base, silver closure, American 1895-1900 . **$250-300**

Pottery and Stoneware Whiskey Jugs

Back bar decanter, Scotch, 1880-1910, 11", $250-350; Cartan, McCarthy & Co (monogram) San Francisco, 1880-1894, 11-7/8", $75-100.

Blackbird Distillery (picture of blackbird on a branch) Guild Auld / Scotch Whiskey (pottery whiskey jug)
Cream with brown glaze on neck and handle, 7-3/4", rare, American 1890-1915 ....**$600-800**

Chas. D. Moul / Wines / & Liquors / York, Pa
Cream color body with dark brown top, 4", smooth base, small open double handles, American 1885-1910 **$150-250**

Compliments / I.W. Harper / Nelson Co. / Kentucky
Brown and light brown pottery, 3", smooth base, American 1890-1915..**$50-60**

English Pub Jug – Henry White & Co's / Old Jamaica / Rum (inside a heart with an African Caribbean man on each side) London / Trade Mark
Cream color body with burnt orange glaze on neck, 6-3/8", smooth base (Frank Beardmore & Co), handled, American 1880-1920 ....**$275-375**

Helmet / Rye / Max Fruhauf & Co. / Cincinnati, O
Dark and light brown, 3", smooth base, American 1890-1915 ....**$100-125**

Mark Twain / Hotel / Hannibal, Mo
Dark brown glaze, 2-3/4", smooth base (Hall / made in U.S.A.), handled, American 1905-1935, Hull Pottery, Crooksville, Ohio **$80-120**

Meredith's / Diamond Club / (motif of diamond) / Pure Rye / Whiskey / Expressly For Medicinal Use / East Liverpool Ohio
White, 4-1/2", smooth base (KT & K China – Knowles, Taylor & Knowles Company), handled jug, American, 1870-1900...**$50-100**
The word "China" on base refers to type of whiteware.

Meredith's / Diamond Club / (motif of diamond) / Pure Rye / Whiskey / Expressly For Medicinal Use / East Liverpool Ohio
White, 7", smooth base (KT & K China – Knowles, Taylor & Knowles Company), handled jug, American 1870-1900 ....**$50-100**
The word "China" on base refers to type of whiteware.

S. Harrison / Lincoln (stoneware whiskey flask)
Gray, 6-1/2", smooth base, raised slab seal, English 1840-1860...**$140-180**

Spring Lake / Hand Made / Sour Mash / Bourbon
White, 7-3/4", smooth base (KT & K China – Knowles, Taylor & Knowles Company), handled jug, American 1870-1900..**$50-100**

Wicklow Distillery (owl on branch) / Old Irish Whiskey / Guaranteed 1/4 Gallon (pottery whiskey jug)
Cream with brown glaze neck, 7-3/4", handled, Irish 1890-1915..**$100-150**

New Bottles (Post-1900)

The bottles in this section have been listed by individual categories and/or type since the contents hold little interest for the collector. New bottles covered in this section are valued for their decorative, appealing, and unique designs.

The objective of most new-bottle collectors is to collect a complete set of items designed and produced by a favorite manufacturer. With reproductions, like the bottles Coca-Cola has released, or with new items, such as those made by Avon, the right time to purchase is when the first issue comes out on the retail market, or prior to retail release if possible. As with the old bottles, the following listings provide a representative cross section of new bottles in various price ranges and categories rather than listing only the rarest or most collectible pieces.

The pricing shown reflects the value of particular item listed. Newer bottles are usually manufactured in limited quantities without any reissues. Since retail prices are affected by factors such as source, type of bottle, desirability, condition, and the possibility the bottle was produced exclusively as a collectors' item, the pricing can fluctuate radically at any given time.

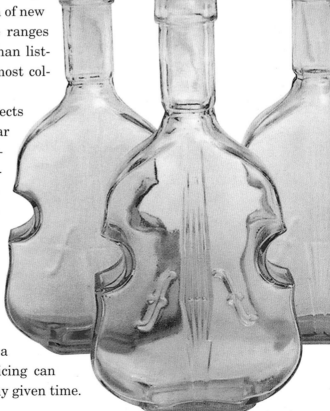

Avon Bottles

The cosmetic empire known today as Avon began as the California Perfume Company. It was the creation of D.H. McConnell, a door-to-door book salesman who gave away perfume samples to stop the doors from being slammed in his face. Eventually, McConnell gave up selling books and concentrated on selling perfumes instead. Although based in New York, the name "Avon" was used in 1929 along with the name California Perfume Company or C.P.C. After 1939, the name Avon was used exclusively. Bottles embossed with C.P.C. are very rare and collectible due to the small quantities issued and the even smaller number that have been well preserved.

Today, Avon offers collectors a wide range of products in bottles shaped like cars, people, chess pieces, trains, animals, sporting items (footballs, baseballs, etc.) and numerous other objects. The scarcest and most sought after pieces are the Pre-World War II figurals, since very few were well preserved.

To those who collect Avon items, anything Avon-related is considered collectible. That includes boxes, brochures, magazine ads, or anything else labeled with the Avon name. Since many people who sell Avon items are unaware of their value, collectors can find great prices at swap meets, flea markets, and garage sales.

While this book offers a good representation of Avon collectibles, I recommend that serious collectors obtain Bud Hastin's book *Avon Products & California Perfume Co. (CPC) Collector's Encyclopedia*, 18th Edition, which offers pricing and pictures of thousands of Avon & California Perfume Co. (CPC) products from 1886 to present.

A Man's World, Globe On Stand, 1969 .... **$7-10**

A Winner, Boxing Gloves, 1960 **$20-25**

Abraham Lincoln, Wild Country After Shave, 1970-1972 .... **$3-5**

After Shave On Tap, Wild Country **$3-5**

Aladdin's Lamp, 1971 .... **$7-10**

Alaskan Moose, 1974 .... **$5-8**

Alpine Flask, 1966-1967 .... **$35-45**

American Belle, Sonnet Cologne, 1976-1978 .... **$5-7**

American Buffalo, 1975 .... **$6-8**

American Eagle Pipe, 1974-1975 **$6-8**

American Eagle, Windjammer After Shave, 1971-1972 .... **$3-4**

American Ideal Perfume, California Perfume Comp., 1911 .... **$125-140**

American Schooner, Oland After Shave, 1972-1973 .... **$4-5**

Andy Capp Figural (England), 1970 .... **$95-105**

Angler, Windjammer After Shave, 1970 .... **$5-7**

Apple Blossom Toilet Water, 1941-1942 .... **$50-60**

Apothecary, Lemon Velvet Moist Lotion,1973-1976 .... **$4-6**

Apothecary, Spicy After Shave, 1973-1974 .... **$4-5**

Aristocat Kittens Soap (Walt Disney) **$5-7**

Armoire Decanter, Charisma Bath Oil, 1973-1974 .... **$4-5**

Armoire Decanter, Elusive Bath Oil, 1972-1975 .... **$4-5**

Auto Lantern, 1973 .... **$6-8**

Auto, Big Mack Truck, Windjammer After Shave, 1973-1975 .... **$5-6**

Auto, Cord, 1937 Model, Wild **Country** After Shave, 1974-1978 .... **$7-8**

Auto, Country Vendor, Wild Country After Shave, 1973 .... **$7-8**

Auto, Duesenberg, Silver, Wild Country After Shave, 1970-1972 .... **$8-9**

Powder Sachet, 1912-1915, large size bottle with brass cap, $75-100.

Auto, Dune Buggy, Sports Rally Bracing Lotion, 1971-1973 .... **$4-5**

Auto, Electric Charger, Avon Leather Cologne, 1970-1972 .... **$6-7**

Auto, Hayes Apperson, 1902 Model, Avon Blend 7 After Shave, 1973-1974 .... **$5-7**

Auto, Maxwell 23, Deep Woods After Shave, 1972-1974 .... **$5-6**

Auto, MG, 1936, Wild Country After Shave, 1974-1975 .... **$4-5**

Auto, Model A, Wild Country After Shave, 1972-1974 .... **$4-5**

Auto, Red Depot Wagon, Oland After Shave, 1972-1973 .... **$6-7**

Auto, Rolls Royce, Deep Woods After Shave, 1972-1975 .... **$6-8**

Auto, Stanley Steamer, Windjammer After Shave, 1971-1972 .... **$6-7**

Auto, Station Wagon, Tai Winds After Shave, 1971-1973 .... **$7-8**

Auto, Sterling 6, Spicy After Shave, 1968-1970 .... **$6-7**

Auto, Sterling Six Ii, Wild Country After Shave, 1973-1974 .... **$4-5**

Station Wagon, 1971-1973, 6 oz. green glass car with tan plastic top, $14.

Gaylord Gator, 1967-1969, 10" l., green and yellow rubber soap dish with yellow soap, $3 Gator only, $10 entire set.

Auto, Stutz Bearcat, 1914 Model, Avon Blend 7 After Shave, 1974-1977 **$5-6**

Auto, Touring T, Tribute After Shave, 1969-1970.................................. **$6-7**

Auto, Volkswagen, Red, Oland After Shave, 1972 .... **$5-6**

Avon Calling, Phone, Wild Country After Shave, 1969-1970 .... **$15-20**

Avon Dueling Pistol Ii, Black Glass, 1972 .... **$10-15**

Avonshire Blue Cologne, 1971-1974 .... **$4-5**

Baby Grand Piano, Perfume Glace, 1971-1972.............................. **$8-10**

Baby Hippo, 1977-1980 .... **$4-5**

Ballad Perfume, 3 Drams, 3/8 Ounce, 1939 .... **$100-125**

Bath Urn, Lemon Velvet Bath Oil, 1971-1973................................. **$4-5**

Beauty Bound Black Purse, 1964 .... **$45-55**

Bell Jar Cologne, 1973 .... **$5-10**

Benjamin Franklin, Wild Country After Shave, 1974-1976...................... **$4-5**

Big Game Rhino, Tai Winds After Shave, 1972-1973...................... **$7-8**

Big Whistle, 1972 .... **$4-5**

Bird House Power Bubble Bath, 1969 .... **$7-8**

Bird Of Paradise Cologne Decanter, 1972-1974.............................. **$4-5**

Blacksmith's Anvil, Deep Woods After Shave, 1972-1973...................... **$4-5**

Bloodhound Pipe, Deep Woods After Shave, 1976 .... **$5-6**

Blue Blazer After Shave Lotion, 1964 .... **$25-30**

Blue Blazer Deluxe, 1965 .... **$55-65**

Blue Moo Soap On A Rope, 1972**$5-6**

Blunderbuss Pistol, 1976 .... **$7-10**

Bon Bon Black, Field & Flowers Cologne, 1973............................ **$5-6**

Bon Bon White, Occur Cologne, 1972-1973 .... **$5-6**

Bon Bon White, Topaze Cologne, 1972-1973.................................. **$5-6**

Boot Gold Top, Avon Leather After Shave, 1966-1971...................... **$3-4**

Boot Western, 1973 .... **$4-5**

Boots And Saddle, 1968.......... **$20-22**

Brocade Deluxe, 1967 .... **$30-35**

Buffalo Nickel, Liquid Hair Lotion, 1971-1972.................................. **$4-5**

Bulldog Pipe, Oland After Shave, 1972-1973.................................. **$4-5**

Bunny Puff And Talc, 1969-1972. **$3-4**

Bureau Organizer, 1966-1967 . **$35-55**

Butter Candlestick, Sonnet Cologne, 1974 .... **$7-8**

Butterfly Fantasy Egg, First Issue, 1974 .... **$20-30**

Butterfly, Unforgettable Cologne, 1972-1973.................................. **$4-5**

Butterfly, Unforgettable Cologne, 1974-1976.................................. **$1-2**

Sachet, 1908, glass bottle with metal cap, two-piece gold label, $100-135.

Cable Car After Shave, 1974-1975
.... **$8-10**
Camper, Deep Woods After Shave,
1972-1974................................. **$6-7**
Canada Goose, Deep Woods Cologne,
1973-1974................................. **$4-5**
Candlestick Cologne, Elusive, 1970-
1971 .... **$5-6**
Car, Army Jeep, 1974-1975 .... **$4-5**
Casey's Lantern, Island Lime After
Shave, 1966-1967.................. **$30-40**
Catch A Fish, Field Flowers Cologne,
1976-1978................................. **$6-7**
Centennial Express 1876, Locomotive
1978 .... **$11-12**
Chevy '55, 1974-1975................... **$6-8**
Christmas Ornament, Green or Red,
1970-1971................................. **$1-2**
Christmas Ornament, Orange, Bubble
Bath, 1970-1971 .... **$2-3**
Christmas Tree Bubble Bath, 1968
.... **$5-7**
Classic Lion, Deep Woods After
Shave, 1973-1975..................... **$4-5**
Club Bottle, 1906 Avon Lady, 1977
.... **$25-30**

Club Bottle, 1st Annual, 1972 **$150-200**
Club Bottle, 2nd Annual, 1973 . **$45-60**
Club Bottle, 5th Annual, 1976 .. **$25-30**
Club Bottle, Bud Hastin, 1974.. **$70-95**
Club Bottle, Cpc Factory, 1974 **$30-40**
Collector's Pipe, Windjammer After
Shave, 1973-1974..................... **$3-4**
Colt Revolver 1851, 1975-1976 **$10-12**
Corncob Pipe After Shave, 1974-
1975 .... **$4-6**
Corvette Stingray '65, 1975........ **$5-7**
Covered Wagon, Wild Country After
Shave, 1970-1971..................... **$4-5**
Daylight Shaving Time, 1968-1970 **$5-7**
Defender Cannon, 1966 .... **$20-24**
Dollar's 'N' Scents, 1966-1967 **$20-24**
Dutch Girl Figurine, Somewhere,
1973-1974............................... **$8-10**
Duck After Shave, 1971.............. **$4-6**
Dueling Pistol 1760, 1973-1974 **$9-12**
Dueling Pistol Ii, 1975................ **$9-12**
Eight-ball Decanter, Spicy After
Shave, 1973 .... **$3-4**
Electric Guitar, Wild Country After
Shave, 1974-1975..................... **$4-5**
Enchanted Frog Cream Sachet,
Sonnet, 1973-1976 .... **$3-4**
Fashion Boot, Moonwind Cologne,
1972-1976................................. **$5-7**

American Ideal - powder sachet, 1912-1915, brass cap, $75-100.

First Class Male, 1970-1971, 4-1/2" h., 4 oz., blue glass with red cap, $10.

Thomas Jefferson handgun, 1978-1979, 10" l., 2-1/2 oz., dark amber glass with gold and silver plastic cap, $11.

Fashion Boot, Sonnet Cologne, 1972-1976 .... **$5-7**

Fielder's Choice, 1971-1972 .... **$4-6**

Fire Alarm Box, 1975-1976 .... **$4-6**

First Class Male, Wild Country After Shave, 1970-1971 .... **$3-4**

First Down, Soap On A Rope, 1970-1971 .... **$7-8**

First Down, Wild Country After Shave **$3-4**

First Volunteer, Tai Winds Cologne, 1971-1972 .... **$6-7**

Fox Hunt, 1966 .... **$25-30**

French Telephone, Moonwind Foaming Bath Oil, 1971 .... **$20-24**

Garnet Bud Vase, To A Wild Rose Colgone, 1973-1976 .... **$3-5**

Gavel, Island Lime After Shave, 1967-1968 .... **$4-5**

George Washington, Spicy After Shave, 1970-1972 .... **$2-3**

George Washington, Tribute After Shave, 1970-1972 .... **$2-3**

Gold Cadillac, 1969-1973 .... **$7-10**

Gone Fishing, 1973-1974 .... **$5-7**

Grade Avon Hostess Soap, 1971-1972 .... **$6-8**

Hearth Lamp, Roses, Roses, 1973-1976 .... **$6-8**

Hobnail Decanter, Moonwind Bath Oil, 1972-1974 .... **$5-6**

Hunter's Stein, 1972 .... **$10-14**

Indian Chieftan, Protein Hair Lotion, 1972-1975 .... **$2-3**

Indian Head Penny, Bravo After Shave, 1970-1972 .... **$4-5**

Inkwell, Windjammer After Shave, 1969-1970 .... **$6-7**

Iron Horse Shaving Mug, Avon Blend 7 After Shave, 1974-1976 .... **$3-4**

Jack-in-the-box, Baby Cream, 1974 .... **$4-6**

Jaguar Car, 1973-1976 .... **$6-8**

Jolly Santa, 1978 .... **$6-7**

Joyous Bell, 1978 .... **$5-6**

King Pin, 1969-1970 .... **$4-6**

Kodiak Bear, 1977 .... **$5-10**

Koffee Klatch, Honeysuckle Foam Bath Oil, 1971-1974 .... **$5-6**

Liberty Bell, Tribute After Shave, 1971-1972 .... **$4-6**

Liberty Dollar, After Shave, 1970-1972 .... **$4-6**

Lincoln Bottle, 1971-1972 .... **$3-5**

Lip Pop Colas, Cherry, 1973-1974 **$1-2**

Lip Pop Colas, Cola, 1973-1974 .. **$1-2**

Lip Pop Colas, Strawberry, 1973-1974 .... **$1-2**

Longhorn Steer, 1975-1976 .... **$7-9**

Looking Glass, Regence Cologne, 1970-1972 .... **$7-8**

Mallard Duck, 1967-1968 .... **$8-10**

Mickey Mouse, Bubble Bath, 1969 .... **$10-12**

Talcum Powder, 1912-1915, 3.5 oz. metal can, different types of caps on each can, $300-360.

Seahorse, 1970-1972, clear glass, 6 oz., gold cap, $10.

Mighty Mitt Soap On A Rope, 1969-1972 .... **$7-8**

Ming Cat, Bird Of Paradise Cologne, 1971 .... **$5-7**

Mini Bike, Sure Winner Bracing Lotion, 1972-1973 .... **$3-5**

Nile Blue Bath Urn, Skin So Soft, 1972-1974 .... **$3-4**

Nile Blue Bath Urn, Skin So Soft, 1972-1974 .... **$4-6**

No Parking, 1975-1976 .... **$5-7**

Old Faithful, Wild Country After Shave, 1972-1973 .... **$4-6**

One Good Turn, Screwdriver, 1976. **$5-6**

Opening Play, Dull Golden, Spicy After Shave, 1968-1969 .... **$8-10**

Opening Play, Shiny Golden, Spicy After Shave, 1968-1969 .... **$14-17**

Owl Fancy, Roses, Roses, 1974-1976 .... **$3-4**

Owl Soap Dish And Soaps, 1970-1971 .... **$8-10**

Packard Roadster, 1970-1972 ..... **$4-7**

Pass Play Decanter, 1973-1975 .. **$6-8**

Peanuts Gang Soaps, 1970-1972 **$8-9**

Pepperbox Pistol, 1976 .... **$5-10**

Perfect Drive Decanter, 1975-1976 **$7-9**

Pheasant, 1972-1974 .... **$7-9**

Piano Decanter, Tai Winds After Shave, 1972 .... **$3-4**

Pipe, Full, Decanter, Brown, Spicy After Shave, 1971-1972 .... **$3-4**

Pony Express, Avon Leather After Shave, 1971-1972 .... **$3-4**

Pony Post "Tall", 1966-1967 .... **$7-9**

Pot Belly Stove, 1970-1971 .... **$5-7**

President Lincoln, Tai Winds After Shave, 1973 .... **$6-8**

President Washington, Deep Woods After Shave, 1974-1976 .... **$4-5**

Quail, 1973-1974 .... **$7-9**

Rainbow Trout, Deep Woods After Shave, 1973-1974 .... **$3-4**

Road Runner, Motorcycle **$4-5**

Rook, Spicy After Shave, 1973-1974 .... **$4-5**

Royal Coach, Bird Of Paradise Bath Oil, 1972-1973 .... **$4-6**

Scent With Love, Elusive Perfume, 1971-1972 .... **$9-10**

Scent With Love, Field Flowers Perfume, 1971-1972 .... $9-10

Scent With Love, Moonwind Perfume, 1971-1972 .... **$9-10**

Side-Wheeler, Tribute After Shave, 1970-1971 .... **$4-5**

Side-Wheeler, Wild Country After Shave, 1971-1972 .... **$3-4**

Small World Perfume Glace, Small World, 1971-1972 .... **$3-4**

Snoopy Soap Dish Refills, 1968-1976 .... **$3-4**

Snoopys Bubble Tub, 1971-1972 **$3-4**

Spark Plug Decanter, 1975-1976 **$2-5**
Spirit Of St Louis, Excalibur After
    Shave, 1970-1972 .... **$3-5**
Stage Coach, Wild Country After
    Shave, 1970-1977 .... **$5-6**
Tee Off, Electric Pre-Shave, 1973-1975
    .... **$2-3**
Ten Point Buck, Wild Country After
    Shave, 1969-1974 .... **$5-7**
Twenty-Dollar Gold Piece,
    Windjammer After Shave, 1971-1972
    .... **$4-6**
Uncle Sam Pipe, Deep Woods After
    Shave, 1975-1976 .... **$4-5**
Viking Horn, 1966 .... **$12-16**
Western Boot, Wild Country After
    Shave, 1973-1975 .... **$2-3**
Western Saddle, 1971-1972 .... **$7-9**
Wild Turkey, 1974-1976 .... **$6-8**
World's Greatest Dad Decanter, 1971
    .... **$4-6**

Aromatic Bay Rum, 1927-1929, 4 oz. metal cork embossed stopper, $100-125.

Ballantine Bottles

Ballantine bottles, brightly colored and ceramic, contain imported Scotch whiskey and usually read "Blended Scotch Whiskey, 14 Years Old." Most of these bottles are based on sporting or outdoor themes, such as ducks and fishermen, whose heads are incorporated into the cap on the bottle. The more collectible items, however, are the older bottles (1930), which are non-figural and very decorative.

Charioteer	$8-10	Mallard Duck	$15-20
Discus Thrower	$8-10	Mercury	$7-10
Duck	$8-10	Old Crow Chessman	$9-10
Fisherman	$20-25	Scottish Knight	$10-12
Gladiator	$8-10	Seated Fisherman	$10-12
Golf Bag	$20-25	Silver Knight	$12-15
Knight	$15-20	Zebra	$15-20

Ballantine's Liqueur Blended Scotch Whiskey, Product of Scotland, 1950-1955, $50-75.

Barsottini Bottles

The Barsottini bottle, manufactured in Italy, does not use any American or non-geographic themes for the U.S. marketplace. These bottles are ceramic and are manufactured in gray and white to represent the brick work of buildings, and usually represent European subjects such as the Eiffel Tower or the Florentine Steeple.

Alpine Pipe, 10"........................ $10-12

Antique Automobile, Ceramic, Coupe $7-10

Antique Automobile, Open Car $7-10

Clock, With Cherub............... $30-40

Clowns, Ceramic, 12" Each $10-12

Eiffel Tower, Gray And White, 15" $10-12

Florentine Cannon, L, 15" $14-20

Florentine Steeple, Gray And White $10-12

Monastery Cask, Ceramic, 12" $15-20

Paris Arc De Triomphe, 7-1/2" $10-12

Pisa's Leaning Tower, Gray And White $10-12

Roman Coliseum, Ceramic $10-12

Trivoli Clock, Ceramic, 15" $12-15

Jim Beam Bottles

The James B. Beam distilling company was founded in 1778 by Jacob Beam in Kentucky and now bears the name of Col. James B. Beam, Jacob Beam's grandson. Beam whiskey was very popular in the South during the 19th and 20th century but was not produced on a large scale. Because of low production, the early Beam bottles are very rare, collectible, and valuable.

In 1953, the Beam company packaged bourbon in a special Christmas/New Year ceramic decanter—a rarity for any distiller. Because the decanters sold well, Beam decided to redevelop its packaging, leading to production of a number of decanter series in the 1950s. The first was the Ceramics Series in 1953. In 1955 the Executive Series was issued to commemorate the 160th anniversary of the corporation. In 1955, Beam introduced the Regal China Series, issued to honor significant people, places, and events with a focus on America and contemporary situations. In 1956, political figures were introduced with the elephant and the donkey, as well as special productions for customer specialties made on commission. In 1957, the Trophy Series honored various achievements within the liquor industry. The State Series was introduced 1958 to commemorate the admission of Alaska and Hawaii into the Union. The practice has continued with Beam still producing decanters to commemorate all 50 states.

In total, over 500 types of Beam bottles have been issued since 1953. For further information, contact: International Association of Jim Beam Bottle and Specialties Clubs, PO Box 486, Kewanee, IL 61443, (309) 853-3370, www.beam-wade.org.

AC Spark Plug 1977
Replica of a spark plug in white, green, and gold....................................**$22-26**

AHEPA 50th Anniversary 1972
Regal China bottle designed in honor of AHEPA'S (American Hellenic Education Progressive Association) 50th Anniversary **$4-6**

Aida 1978
Figurine of character from the opera Aida **$140-160**

Akron Rubber Capital 1973
Regal China bottle honoring Akron, Ohio...**$15-20**

Alaska 1958
Regal China, 9-1/2", star-shaped bottle **$55-60**

Alaska 1964-1965
Re-issue of the 1958 bottle **$40-50**

Alaska Purchase 1966
Regal China, 10", blue and gold bottle **$4-6**

American Samoa 1973
Regal China, with the seal of Samoa **$5-7**

American Veterans **$4-7**

Antique Clock **$35-45**

Antioch 1967
Regal China, 10", commemorates Regal's Diamond Jubilee **$5-7**

Antique Coffee Grinder 1979
Replica of a box coffee mill used in mid-19th century.....................**$10-12**

Antique Globe 1980
Represents the Martin Behaim globe of 1492 ....**$7-11**

Antique Telephone (1897) 1978
Replica of an 1897 desk phone, second in a series.........................**$50-60**

Antique Trader 1968
Regal China, 10-1/2", represents Antique Trader newspaper................**$4-6**

Appaloosa 1974
Regal China, 10", represents favorite horse of the Old West **$12-15**

Arizona 1968
Regal China, 12", represents the state of Arizona....................................**$4-6**

Armadillo **$8-12**

Armanetti Award Winner 1969
Honors Aramnetti, Inc. of Chicago as "Liquor Retailer of the Year"..........**$6-8**

Armanetti Shopper 1971
Reflects the slogan "It's fun to Shop Armanetti - Self Service Liquor Store", 11-3/4" **$6-8**

Armanetti Vase 1968
Yellow toned decanter embossed with flowers **$5-7**

Bacchus 1970
Issued by Armanetti Liquor Stores of Chicago, Illinois,11-3/4" **$6-9**

Barney's Slot Machine 1978
Replica of the world's largest slot machine.......................................**$14-16**

Barry Berish 1985
Executive series **$110-140**

Barry Berish 1986
Executive series, bowl..........**$110-140**

Bartender's Guild 1973
Commemorative honoring the International Bartenders Assn **$4-7**

Baseball 1969
Issued to commemorate the 100th anniversary of Baseball.............**$18-20**

Bean Pot 1980
Shaped like a New England bean pot; club bottle for the New England Beam Bottle and Specialties Club **$12-15**

Beaver Valley Club 1977
A club bottle to honor the Beaver Valley Jim Beam Club of Rochester **$8-12**

Bell Scotch 1970
Regal China, 10-1/2", in honor of Arthur Bell & Sons.......................**$4-7**

Beverage Association, NLBA **$4-7**

The Big Apple 1979
Apple-shaped bottle with "The Big Apple" over the top **$8-12**

Bing's 31st Clam Bake Bottle 1972
Commemorates 31st Bing Crosby National Pro-Am Golf Tournament in January 1972 ....**$25-30**

Bing Crosby National Pro-Am 1970
....**$4-7**

Bing Crosby National Pro-Am 1971
....**$4-7**

Bing Crosby National Pro-Am 1972
.... **$15-25**

Bing Crosby National Pro-Am 1973
....**$18-23**

Bing Crosby National Pro-Am 1974
....**$15-25**

Bing Crosby National Pro-Am 1975
....**$45-65**

Bing Crosby 36th 1976 ....**$15-25**

Bing Crosby National Pro-Am 1977
....**$12-18**

Bing Crosby National Pro-Am 1978
....**$12-18**

Black Katz 1968
Regal China, 14-1/2" **$7-12**

Blue Cherub Executive 1960
Regal China, 12-1/2" **$70-90**

Blue Daisy 1967
Also know as Zimmerman Blue Daisy
....**$10-12**

Blue Gill, Fish **$12-16**

Blue Goose Order **$4-7**

Blue Jay 1969 ....**$4-7**

Blue Goose 1979
Replica of blue goose, authenticated by Dr. Lester Fisher, Dir. of Lincoln Park Zoological Gardens in Chicago **$7-9**

Blue Hen Club **$12-15**

Blue Slot Machine 1967...........**$10-12**

Bobby Unser Olsonite Eagle 1975
Replica of the racing car used by Bobby Unser...........................**$40-50**

Bob DeVaney...............................**$8-12**

Bob Hope Desert Classic 1973
First genuine Regal China bottle created in honor of the Bob Hope Desert Classic **$8-9**

Bob Hope Desert Classic 1974..**$8-12**

Bohemian Girl 1974
Issued for the Bohemian Cafe in Omaha, Nebraska to honor the Czech and Slovak immigrants in the United States, 14-1/4" **$10-15**

Bonded Gold **$4-7**

Bonded Mystic 1979
Urn-shaped bottle, burgundy-colored
....**$4-7**

Bonded Silver...............................**$4-7**

Boris Godinov, with Base 1978
Second in Opera series **$350-450**

Bourbon Barrel **$18-24**

Bowling Proprietors **$4-7**

Boys Town Of Italy 1973
Created in honor of the Boys Town of Italy **$7-10**

Bowl 1986
Executive series **$20-30**

Broadmoor Hotel 1968
To celebrate the 50th anniversary of this famous hotel in Colorado Springs, Colorado "1918-The Broadmoor-1968"
....**$4-7**

Buffalo Bill 1971
Regal China, 10-1/2", commemorates Buffalo Bill **$4-7**

Bull Dog 1979
Honors the 204th anniversary of the United States Marine Corps **$15-18**

Cable Car 1968
Regal China, 4-1/2".....................**$4-6**

Caboose 1980 ....**$50-60**

California Mission 1970
This bottle was issued for the Jim Beam Bottle Club of Southern California in honor of the 20th anniversary of the California Missions, 14" **$10-15**

California Retail Liquor Dealers Association 1973
Designed to commemorate the 20th anniversary of the California Retail Liquor Dealers Association **$6-9**

Cal-neva 1969
Regal China, 9-1/2"......................**$5-7**

Camellia City Club 1979
Replica of the cupola of the State
Capitol building in Sacramento.**$18-23**

Cameo Blue 1965
Also known as the Shepherd Bottle.**$4-6**

Cannon 1970
Bottle issued to commemorate the
175th anniversary of the Jim Beam Co.
Some of these bottles have a small
chain shown on the cannon and some
do not. Those without the chain are
harder to find and more valuable, 8"
Chain **$2-4**
No Chain...................................**$9-13**

Canteen 1979
Replica of the canteen used by the
Armed Forces **$8-12**

Captain And Mate 1980...........**$10-12**

Cardinal (Kentucky Cardinal) 1968
....**$40-50**

Carmen 1978
Third in the Opera series **$140-180**

Carolier Bull 1984
Executive series **$18-23**

Catfish **$16-24**

Cathedral Radio 1979
Replica of one of the earlier dome-
shaped radios **$12-15**

Cats 1967
Trio of Cats; Siamese, Burmese, and
Tabby...**$6-9**

Cedars Of Lebanon 1971
Bottle issued in honor of the Jerry
Lewis Muscular Dystrophy Telethon in
1971 ....**$5-7**

Charisma 1970
Executive series **$4-7**

Charlie McCarthy 1976
Replica of Edgar Bergen's puppet from
the 1930s...............................**$20-30**

Cherry Hills Country Club 1973
Commemorating 50th anniversary of
Cherry Hills Country Club **$4-7**

Cheyenne, Wyoming 1977 ....**$4-6**

Chicago Cubs, Sports Series
....**$30-40**

Chicago Show Bottle 1977
Commemorates 6th Annual Chicago
Jim Beam Bottle Show.............**$10-14**

Christmas Tree.....................**$150-200**

Churchill Downs – Pink Roses 1969
Regal China, 10-1/4"...................**$5-7**

Churchill Downs – Red Roses 1969
Regal China, 10-1/4"..................**$9-12**

Circus Wagon 1979
Replica of a circus wagon from the late
19th century............................**$24-26**

Civil War North 1961
Regal China, 10-1/4"...............**$10-15**

Civil War South 1961
Regal China, 10-1/4"...............**$25-35**

Clear Crystal Bourbon 1967
Clear glass, 11-1/2" **$5-7**

Clear Crystal Scotch 1966 ....**$9-12**

Clear Crystal Vodka 1967............**$5-8**

Cleopatra Rust 1962
Glass, 13-1/4" **$3-5**

Cleopatra Yellow 1962
Glass, 13-1/4", rarer than Cleopatra
Rust..**$8-12**

Clint Eastwood 1973
Commemorating Clint Eastwood Invi-
tational Celebrity Tennis Tournament in
Pebble Beach **$14-17**

Cocktail Shaker 1953
Glass, Fancy Diz. Bottle, 9-1/4" ...**$2-5**

Coffee Grinder **$8-12**

Coffee Warmers 1954
Four types are known: red, black,
gold, and white **$7-12**

Coffee Warmers 1956
Two types with metal necks and
handles **$2-5**

Coho Salmon 1976
Offical seal of the National Fresh Water
Fishing Hall of Fame is on the back
....**$10-13**

Colin Mead **$180-210**

Cobalt 1981
Executive Series........................**$18-23**
Collector's Edition 1966
Set of six glass famous paintings: The Blue Boy, On the Terrace, Mardi Gras, Austide Bruant, The Artist Before His Easel, and Laughing Cavalier (each) **$2-5**
Collectors Edition Volume II 1967
A set of six flask-type bottles with famous pictures: George Gisze, Soldier and Girl, Night Watch, The Jester, Nurse and Child,and Man on Horse (each)..**$2-5**
Collectors Edition Volume III 1968
A set of eight bottles with famous paintings: On the Trail, Indian Maiden, Buffalo, Whistler's Mother, American Gothic, The Kentuckian, The Scout, and Hauling in the Gill Net (each)..**$2-5**
Collectors Edition Volume IV 1969
A set of eight bottles with famous paintings: Balcony, The Judge, Fruit Basket, Boy with Cherries, Emile Zola, The Guitarist Zouave, and Sunflowers (each) **$2-5**
Collectors Edition Volume V 1970
A set of six bottles with famous paintings: Au Cafe, Old Peasant, Boaring Party, Gare Saint Lazare, The Jewish Bride, and Titus at Writing Desk (each) **$2-5**
Collectors Edition Volume VI 1971
A set of three bottles with famous art pieces: Charles I, The Merry Lute Player, and Boy Holding Flute (each) **$2-5**
Collectors Edition Volume VII 1972
A set of three bottles with famous paintings: The Bag Piper, Prince Baltasor, and Maidservant Pouring Milk (each) **$2-5**
Collectors Edition Volume VIII 1973
A set of three bottles with famous portraits: Ludwig Van Beethoven, Wolfgang Mozart, and Frederic Francis Chopin (each)..............................**$2-5**

Collectors Edition Volume IX 1974
A set of three bottles with famous paintings: Cardinal, Ring-Neck Pheasant, and the Woodcock (each) **$3-6**
Collectors Edition Volume X 1975
A set of three bottles with famous pictures: Sailfish, Rainbow Trout, and Largemouth Bass (each) **$3-6**
Collectors Edition Volume XI 1976
A set of three bottles with famous paintings: Chipmunk, Bighorn Sheep, and Pronghorn Antelope (each)....**$3-6**
Collectors Edition Volume XII 1977
A set of four bottles with a different reproduction of James Lockhart on the front (each)...................................**$3-6**
Collectors Edition Volume XIV 1978
A set of four bottles with James Lockhart paintings: Raccoon, Mule Deer, Red Fox, and Cottontail Rabbit (each)....**$3-6**
Collectors Edition Volume XV 1979
A set of three flasks with Frederic Remington's paintings: The Cowboy 1902, The Indian Trapper 1902, and Lieutenant S.C.Robertson 1890 (each) **$2-5**
Collectors Edition Volume XVI 1980
A set of three flasks depicting duck scenes: The Mallard, The Redhead, and the Canvasback (each)..........**$3-6**
Collectors Edition Volume XVII 1981
A set of three flasks bottles with Jim Lockhart paintings: Great Elk, Pintail Duck, and the Horned Owl (each) **$3-6**
Colorado 1959
Regal China, 10-3/4"...............**$20-25**
Colorado Centennial 1976
Replica of Pike's Peak **$8-12**
Colorado Springs..........................**$4-7**
Computer, Democrat 1984.......**$12-18**
Computer, Republican 1984 ....**$12-18**
Convention Bottle 1971
Commemorate the first national convention of the National Association of Jim Beam Bottle and Specialty Clubs hosted by the Rocky Mountain Club, Denver, CO **$5-7**

Convention Number 2 – 1972

Honors the second annual convention of the National Association of Jim Beam Bottle and Specialty Clubs in Anaheim, CA **$20-30**

Convention Number 3 – Detroit 1973

Commemorates the third annual convention of Beam Bottle Collectors in Detroit, MI **$10-12**

Convention Number 4 – Pennsylvania 1974

Commemorates the annual convention of the Jim Beam Bottle Club in Lancaster, PA **$80-100**

Convention Number 5 – Sacramento 1975

Commemorates the annual convention of the Camellia City Jim Beam Bottle Club in Sacramento, CA **$5-7**

Convention Number 6 – Hartford 1976

Commemorates the annual convention of the Jim Beam Bottle Club in Hartford, CT **$5-7**

Convention Number 7 – Louisville 1978

Commemorates the annual convention of the Jim Beam Bottle Club in Louisville, KY **$5-7**

Convention Number 8 – Chicago 1978

Commemorates the annual convention of the Jim Beam Bottle Club in Chicago, IL **$8-12**

Convention Number 9 – Houston 1979

Commemorates the annual convention of the Jim Beam Bottle Club in Houston, TX **$20-30**

Cowboy, beige **$35-45**

Cowboy, in color **$35-45**

Convention Number 10 – Norfolk 1980

Commemorates the annual convention of the Jim Beam Bottle Club at the Norfolk Naval Base, VA **$18-22**

Waterman, pewter **$35-45**

Waterman, yellow **$35-45**

Convention Number 11 – Las Vegas 1981

Commemorates the annual convention of the Jim Beam Bottle Club in Las Vegas, NV **$20-22**

Showgirl, blonde **$45-55**

Showgirl, brunette **$45-55**

Convention Number 12 – New Orleans 1982

Commemorates the annual convention of the Jim Beam Bottle Club in New Orleans, LA **$30-35**

Buccaneer, gold **$35-45**

Buccaneer, in color **$35-45**

Convention Number 13 – St. Louis 1983 (Stein)

Commemorates the annual convention of the Jim Beam Bottle Club in St. Louis, MO **$55-70**

Gibson girl, blue **$65-80**

Gibson girl, yellow **$65-80**

Convention Number 14 – Florida, King Neptune 1984

Commemorates the annual convention of the Jim Beam Bottle Club in Florida **$15-20**

Mermaid, blonde **$35-45**

Mermaid, brunette **$35-45**

Convention Number 15 – Las Vegas 1985

Commemorates the annual convention of the Jim Beam Bottle Club in Las Vegas, NV **$40-50**

Convention Number 16 – Pilgrim Woman, Boston 1986

Commemorates the annual convention of the Jim Beam Bottle Club in Boston, MA **$35-45**

Minuteman, color **$85-105**

Minuteman, pewter **$85-105**

Convention Number 17 – Louisville 1987

Commemorates the annual convention of the Jim Beam Bottle Club in Louisville, KY **$55-75**

Santa Claus 1983, $60; Santa Claus paperweight 1983, $30; Gibson Girl (blond) 1983, $60; Gibson Girl (brunette) 1983, $60; Thirteenth Convention Stein 1983, $60.

Kentucky Colonel, blue **$85-105**
Kentucky Colonel, gray **$85-105**
Convention Number 18 – Bucky
 Beaver 1988 ....**$30-40**
 Portland rose, red **$30-40**
 Portland rose, yellow **$30-40**
Convention Number 19 – Kansas City
 1989
 Commemorates the annual convention of the Jim Beam Bottle Club in Kansas City, MO................................... **$40-50**
Cowboy 1979
 Awarded to collectors who attended the 1979 convention for the International Association of Beam Clubs **$35-50**
CPO Open **$4-7**
Crappie 1979
 Commemorates the National Fresh Water Fishing Hall of Fame.......**$10-14**
Dark Eyes Brown Jug 1978..........**$4-6**
D-Day...**$12-18**
Delaware Blue Hen Bottle 1972
 Commemorates the state of Delaware **$4-7**
Delco Freedom Battery 1978
 Replica of a Delco battery **$18-22**
Delft Blue 1963.............................**$3-5**
Delft Rose 1963............................**$4-6**

Del Webb Mint 1970
 Metal stopper...........................**$10-12**
 China stopper **$50-60**
Devil Dog **$15-25**
Dial Telephone 1980
 Fourth in a series of Beam telephone designs **$40-50**
Dodge City 1972
 Issued to honor the centennial of Dodge City....................................**$5-6**
Doe 1963
 Regal China, 13-1/2"...............**$10-12**
Doe – Reissued 1967 ....**$10-12**
Dog 1959
 Regal China, 15-1/4"...............**$20-25**
Don Giovanni 1980
 The fifth in the Opera series..**$140-180**
Donkey And Elephant Ashtrays 1956
 Regal China, 12" (pair).............**$12-16**
Donkey And Elephant Boxers 1964
 (pair) **$14-18**
Donkey And Elephant Clowns 1968
 Regal China, 12" (pair).................**$4-7**
Donkey And Elephant Football
 Election Bottles 1972
 Regal China, 9-1/2" (pair) **$6-9**
Donkey New York City 1976
 Commemorates the National Democratic Convention in New York City **$10-12**

Ducks Unlimited (American Widgeon pair) 1989, $65; Football, 1989, $50; American Brands 1989, $300; Nutcracker 1989, $50; Nutcracker 1989, $100.

Duck 1957
 Regal China, 14-1/4".............**$15-20**
Ducks And Geese 1955.................**$5-8**
Ducks Unlimited Mallard 1974 $40-50
Ducks Unlimited Wood Duck 1975
 ....**$45-50**
Ducks Unlimited 40th Mallard Hen
 1977 ....**$40-50**
Ducks Unlimited Canvasback Drake
 1979 ....**$30-40**
Ducks Unlimited Blue-Winged Teal
 1980
 The sixth in a series, 9-1/2" **$40-45**
Ducks Unlimited Green-Winged Teal
 1981 ....**$35-45**
Ducks Unlimited Wood Ducks 1982
 ....**$35-45**
Ducks Unlimited American Widgeon
 Pair 1983 ....**$35-45**
Ducks Unlimited Mallard 1984 $55-75
Ducks Unlimited Pintail Pr 1985 $30-40
Ducks Unlimited Redhead 1986
 ....**$15-25**
Ducks Unlimited Blue Bill 1987..**$40-60**
Ducks Unlimited Black Duck 1989
 ....**$50-60**
Eagle 1966
 Regal China, 12-1/2".............**$10-13**

Eldorado 1978.............................**$7-9**
Election, Democrat 1988.........**$30-40**
Election, Republican 1988 ....**$30-40**
Elephant And Donkey Supermen
 1980 (Set Of Two) **$10-14**
Elephant Kansas City 1976
 Commemorates the National Demo-
 cratic Convention in New York City**$8-10**
Elks **$4-7**
Elks National Foundation...........**$8-12**
Emerald Crystal Bourbon 1968
 Green glass, 11-1/2" **$3-5**
Emmett Kelly 1973
 Likeness of Emmett Kelly as sad-faced
 Willie the Clown........................**$18-22**
Emmett Kelly, Native Son **$50-60**
Ernie's Flower Cart 1976
 In honor of Ernie's Wines and Liquors
 of Northern California **$24-28**
Evergreen, Club Bottle **$7-10**
Expo 1974
 Issued in honor of the World's Fair held
 at Spokane, WA..........................**$5-7**
Falstaff 1979
 Second in Australian Opera series, Lim-
 ited edition of 1,000 bottles.....**$150-160**
Fantasia Bottle 1971....................**$5-6**
Fathers Day Card.....................**$15-25**

Female Cardinal 1973................$8-12
Fiesta Bowl, Glass......................$8-12
Fiesta Bowl 1973
The second bottle created to commemorate the Fiesta Bowl..........$9-11
Figaro 1977
Character Figaro from the opera Barber of Seville $140-170
Fighting Bull.............................$12-18
Fiji Islands $4-6
First National Bank Of Chicago 1964
Commemorates the 100th anniversary of the Firt National Bank of Chicago. Approximatley 130 were issued with 117 being given as momemtos to the bank directors with none for public distribution. This is the most valuable Beam Bottle known. Also, beware of reproductions................$1,900-2,400
Fish 1957
Regal China, 14" $15-18
Fish Hall Of Fame $25-35
Five Seasons 1980
Club bottle for the Five Seasons Club of Cedar Rapids honors the state of Iowa $10-12
Fleet Reserve Association 1974
Issued by the Fleet Reserve Association to honor the Career Sea Service on their 50th anniversary $5-7
Florida Shell 1968
Regal China, 9 ....$4-6
Floro De Oro 1976....................$10-12
Flower Basket 1962
Regal China, 12-1/4"...............$30-35
Football Hall Of Fame 1972
Reproduction of the new Professional Football Hall of Fame building...$14-18
Foremost – Black And Gold 1956
First Beam bottle issued for a liquor retailer, Foremost Liquor Store of Chicago $225-250
Foremost – Speckled Beauty 1956
The most valuable of the Foremost bottles.................................$500-600

Fox 1967, Blue Coat $65-80
Fox 1971, Gold Coat................$35-50
Fox, Green Coat.......................$12-18
Fox, White Coat $20-30
Fox, On A Dolphin....................$12-15
Fox, Uncle Sam...........................$5-6
Fox, Kansas City, Blue, Miniature
....$20-30
Fox, Red Distillery..........$1,100-1,300
Franklin Mint $4-7
French Cradle Telephone 1979
Third in the Telephone Pioneers of America series $20-22
Galah Bird 1979....................$14-16
Gem City, Club Bottle..............$35-45
George Washington Commemorative Plate 1976
Commemorates the U.S. Bicentennial, 9-1/2" $12-15
German Bottle – Weisbaden 1973
....$4-6
German Stein $20-30
Germany 1970
Issued to honor the American Armed Forces in Germany $4-6
Glen Cambell 51st 1976
Honors the 51st Los Angeles Open at the Riviera Country Club in February 1976 ....$7-10
Golden Chalice 1961 ....$40-50
Golden Jubilee 1977
Executive Series......................$48-12
Golden Nugget 1969
Regal China, 12-1/2"...............$35-45
Golden Rose 1978 ....$15-20
Grand Canyon 1969
Honors the Grand Canyon National Park 50th Anniversary $7-9
Grant Locomotive 1979...........$55-65
Gray Cherub 1958
Regal China, 12" $240-260
Great Chicago Fire Bottle 1971
Commemorates the great Chicago fire of 1871 and to salute Mercy Hospital, which helped the fire victims.....$18-22

Great Dane 1976 ....$7-9

Green China Jug 1965
  Regal Glass, 12-1/2" $4-6

Hank Williams, Jr $40-50

Hannah Dustin 1973
  Regal China, 14-1/2" $10-12

Hansel And Gretel Bottle 1971 $44-50

Harley Davidson 85th Anniversary
  Decanter $175-200

Harley Davidson 85th Anniversary
  Stein $180-220

Harolds Club – Man-in-a-Barrel 1957
  First in a series made for Harolds Club
  in Reno, Nevada $380-410

Harolds Club – Silver Opal 1957
  Commemorates the 25th anniversary
  of Harolds Club $20-22

Harolds Club – Man-in-a-Barrel 1958
  ....$140-160

Harolds Club – Nevada (Gray) 1963
  Created for the "Nevada Centennial
  - 1864-1964 as a state bottle. This is a
  rare and valuable bottle $90-110

Harolds Club – Nevada (Silver) 1964
  ....$90-110

Harolds Club – Pinwheel 1965 .$40-45

Harolds Club – Blue Slot Machine
  1967 ....$10-14

Harolds Club – VIP Executive 1967
  Limited quantity issued............$50-60

Harolds Club – VIP Executive 1968
  ....$55-65

Harolds Club – Gray Slot Machine
  1968 ....$4-6

Harolds Club – VIP Executive 1969
  This bottle was used as a Christmas
  giftv to the casino's executives
  ....$260-285

Harolds Club – Covered Wagon
  1969-1970................................$4-6

Harolds Club 1970 ....$40-60

Harolds Club 1971 ....$40-60

Harolds Club 1972 ....$18-25

Harolds Club 1973 ....$18-24

Harolds Club 1974 ....$12-16

Harolds Club 1975 ....$12-18

Harolds Club Vip 1976.............$18-22

Harolds Club 1977 ....$20-30

Harolds Club 1978 ....$20-30

Harolds Club 1979 ....$20-30

Harolds Club 1980 ....$25-35

Harolds Club 1982 ....$110-145

Harp Seal.................................$12-18

Harrahs Club Nevada – Gray 1963
  This is the same bottle used for the
  Nevada Centennial and Harolds Club
  ....$500-550

Harry Hoffman $4-7

Harveys Resort Hotel At Lake Tahoe
  ....$6-10

Hatfield 1973
  The character of Hatfield from the stor
  of the Hatfield and McCoy feud
  ....$15-20

Hawaii 1959
  Tribute to the 50th state $35-40

Hawaii – Reissued 1967 ....$40-45

Hawaii 1971.................................$6-8

Hawaii Aloha 1971 ....$6-10

Hawaiian Open Bottle 1972
  Honors the 1972 Hawaiian Open Golf
  Tournament.................................$6-8

Hawaiian Open 1973
  Second bottle created in honor of the
  United Hawaiian Open Golf Classic
  ....$7-9

Hawaiian Open 1974
  Commemorates the 1974 Hawaiian
  Open Golf Classic $5-8

Hawaiian Open Outrigger 1975 .$9-11

Hawaiian Paradise 1978
  Commemorates the 200th anniversary
  of the landing of Captain Cook.$15-17

Hemisfair 1968
  Commemorates the "Hemisfair 68-San
  Antonio".....................................$8-10

Herre Brothers $22-35

Hobo, Australia $10-14

Hoffman 1969.............................$4-7

Holiday - Carolers....................$40-50

Holiday - Nutcracker $40-50

Home Builders 1978
Commemorates the 1979 convention of the Home Builders $25-30

Hone Heke............................$200-250

Honga Hika 1980
First in a series of Maori warrior bottles. Honga Hika was a war-chief of the Ngapuke tribe $220-240

Horse (Appaloosa)......................$8-12

Horse (Black) $18-22

Horse (Black) Reissued 1967...$10-12

Horse (Brown) $18-22

Horse (Brown) Reissued 1967 .$10-12

Horse (Mare And Foal) $35-45

Horse (Oh Kentucky) $70-85

Horse (Pewter $12-17

Horse (White) $18-20

Horse (White) Reissued 1967...$12-17

Horseshoe Club 1969 ....$4-6

Hula Bowl 1975 ....$8-10

Hyatt House – Chicago $7-10

Hyatt House – New Orleans.......$8-11

Idaho 1963................................$30-40

Illinois 1968
Honors Illinois Sesquicentennial 1818-1968 ....$4-6

Indianapolis Sesquicentennial $4-6

Indianapolis 500.........................$9-12

Indian Chief 1979 ....$9-12

International Chili Society 1976 $9-12

Italian Marble Urn 1985
Executive series $12-17

Ivory Ashtray 1955 ....$8-10

Jackalope 1971
Honors the Wyoming Jackalope...$5-8

Jaguar...$18-23

Jewel T Man – 50th Anniversary
....$35-45

John Henry 1972
Commemorates the legendary Steel Drivin' Man..............................$18-22

Joliet Legion Band 1978
Commemorates the 26th national championships.......................$15-20

Kaiser International Open Bottle 1971
Commemorates the 5th Annual Kaiser International Open Golf Tournament$5-6

Kangaroo 1977.........................$10-14

Kansas 1960
Commemorates the "Kansas 1861-1961 Centennial" $35-45

Kentucky Black Head – Brown Head 1967
Black Head $12-18
Brown Head...............................$20-28
White Head $18-23

Kentucky Derby 95th, Pink, Red Roses 1969 ....$4-7

Kentucky Derby 96th, Double Rose 1970 ....$15-25

Kentucky Derby 97th 1971..........$4-7

Kentucky Derby 98th 1972..........$4-6

Kentucky Derby 100th 1974......$7-10

Key West 1972
Honors the 150th anniversary of Key West, Florida..............................$5-7

King Kamehameha 1972
Commemorates the 100th anniversary of King Kamehameha Day..........$8-11

King Kong 1976
Commemorates Paramount's movie release in December 1976 ....$8-10

Kiwi 1974 ....$5-8

Koala Bear 1973........................$12-14

Laramie 1968
Commemorates the "Centennial Jubilee Laramie Wyo. 1868-1968"......$4-6

Largemouth Bass Trophy Bottle 1973
Honors the National Fresh Water Fishing Hall of Fame $10-14

Las Vegas 1969
Bottle used for Customer Specials, Casino series $4-6

Light Bulb 1979
Honors Thomas Edison............$14-16

Lombard 1969
Commemorates "Village of Lombard, Illinois-1869 Centennial 1969" $4-6

London Bridge $4-7
Louisville Downs Racing Derby 1978
....$4-6
Louisiana Superdome $8-11
LVNH Owl $20-30
Madame Butterfly 1977
Figurine of Madame Butterfly, music
box plays "One Fine Day" from the
opera $340-370
The Magpies 1977
Honors an Australian football team
....$18-20
Maine 1970 ....$4-6
Majestic 1966 ....$20-24
Male Cardinal $18-24
Marbled Fantasy 1965 ....$38-42
Marina City 1962
Commemorates modern apartment
complex in Chicago $10-15
Marine Corps $25-35
Mark Antony 1962 ....$18-20
Martha Washington 1976 ....$5-6
McCoy 1973
Character of McCoy from the story of
the Hatfield and McCoy feud $14-17
McShane – Mother-of-Pearl 1979
Executive series $85-105
McShane – Titans 1980 ....$85-105
McShane – Cobalt 1981
Executive series $115-135
McShane – Green Pitcher 1982
Executive series $80-105
McShane – Green Bell 1983
Executive series $80-110
Mephistopheles 1979
Figurine depicts Mephistopheles from
the opera Faust, Music box plays
Soldier's Chorus $160-190
Michigan Bottle 1972 ....$7-9
Milwaukee Stein $30-40
Minnesota Viking 1973 ....$9-12
Mint 400 1970 ....$80-105
Mint 400 1970 ....$5-6
Mint 400 1971 ....$5-6

Mint 400 1972
Commemorates the 5th annual Del
Webb Mint 400 ....$5-7
Mint 400 1973
Commemorates the 6th annual Del
Webb Mint 400 ....$6-8
Mint 400 1974 ....$4-7
Mint 400 7th Annual 1976 ....$9-12
Mississippi Fire Engine 1978 ..$120-130
Model A Ford 1903 (1978) $38-42
Model A Ford 1928 (1980) $65-75
Montana 1963
Tribute to "Montana, 1864 Golden
Years Centennial 1964" $50-60
Monterey Bay Club 1977
Honors the Monterey Bay Beam Bottle
and Specialty Club $9-12
Mortimer Snerd 1976 ....$24-28
Mother-of-Pearl 1979 ....$10-12
Mount St. Helens 1980
Depicts the eruption of Mount St.
Helens $20-22
Mr. Goodwrench 1978 ....$24-28
Musicians On A Wine Cask 1964 $4-6
Muskie 1971
Honors the National Fresh Water Fish-
ing Hall of Fame $14-18
National Tobacco Festival 1973
Commemorates the 25th anniversary
of the National Tobacco Festival ...$7-8
Nebraska 1967 ....$7-9
Nebraska Football 1972
Commemorates the University of
Nebraska's national championship
football team of 1970-1971 ....$5-8
Nevada 1963 ....$34-38
New Hampshire 1967 ....$4-8
New Hampshire Eagle Bottle 1971
....$18-23
New Jersey 1963 ....$40-5o
New Jersey Yellow 1963 ....$40-50
New Mexico Bicentennial 1976 .$8-12
New Mexico Statehood 1972
Commemorates New Mexico's 60
years of statehood $7-9

New York World's Fair 1964 ....$5-6

North Dakota – 1965 ....$45-55

Northern Pike 1977

The sixth in a series designed for the National Fresh Water Fishing Hall of Fame $14-18

Nutcracker Toy Soldier 1978 .$90-120

Ohio 1966 ....$5-6

Ohio State Fair 1973

In honor of the 120th Ohio State Fair $5-6

Olympian 1960 ....$2-4

One Hundred First Airborne Division 1977

Honors the division known as the Screaming Eagles $8-10

Opaline Crystal 1969 ....$4-6

Oregon 1959

Honors the centennial of the state $20-25

Oregon Liquor Commission $25-35

Osco Drugs $12-17

Panda 1980...............................$20-22

Paul Bunyan $4-7

Pearl Harbor Memorial 1972

Honoring the Pearl Harbor Survivors Association $14-18

Pearl Harbor Survivors Association 1976 ....$5-7

Pennsylvania 1967 ....$4-6

Pennsylvania Dutch, Club Bottle

....$8-12

Permian Basin Oil Show 1972

Commemorates the Permian Basin Oil Show in Odessa, Texas $4-6

Petroleum Man $4-7

Pheasant 1960 ....$14-18

Pheasant 1961 Re-issued; Also '63, '66, '67, '68 ....$8-11

Phi Sigma Kappa (Centennial Series) 1973

Commemorates the 100th anniversary of this fraternity $3-4

Phoenician 1973 ....$6-9

Pied Piper Of Hamlin 1974 ....$3-6

Ponderosa 1969

A replica of the Cartwrights of the Bonanza TV show $4-6

Ponderosa Ranch Tourist 1972

Commemorates the one millionth tourist to the Ponderosa Ranch $14-16

Pony Express 1968 ....$9-12

Poodle – Gray And White 1970 ....$5-6

Portland Rose Festival 1972

Commemorates the 64th Portland, Oregon Rose Festival $5-8

Portola Trek 1969

Bottle was issued to celebrate the 200th anniversary of San Diego....$3-6

Poulan Chain Saw 1979 ....$24-28

Powell Expedition 1969

Depicts John Wesley Powell's survey of the Colorado River $3-5

Preakness 1970

Issued to honor the 100th anniversary of the running of the Preakness....$5-6

Preakness Pimlico 1975...............$4-7

Presidential 1968

Executive series $4-7

Prestige 1967

Executive series $4-7

Pretty Perch 1980

8th in a series, this fish is used as the official seal of the National Fresh Water Fishing Hall of Fame.................$13-16

Prima-Donna 1969........................$4-6

Professional Golf Association $4-7

Queensland 1978 ....$20-22

Rabbit $4-7

Rainbow Trout 1975

Produced for the National Fresh Water Fishing Hall of Fame.................$12-15

Ralph Centennial 1973

Commemorates the 100th anniversary of the Ralph Grocery Co...........$10-14

Ralph's Market.........................$8-12

Ram 1958................................$40-55

Ramada Inn 1976 ....$10-12

Red Mile Racetrack...................$8-12

Redwood 1967 ....$6-8

Reflections 1975
Executive series $8-12
Regency 1972...............................$7-9
Reidsville 1973
Issued to honor the centennial of
Reidsville, North Carolina..............$5-6
Renee The Fox 1974
Represents the companion for the
International Association of Jim Beam
Bottle and Specialities Club's mascot
....$7-9
Rennie The Runner 1974...........$9-12
Rennie The Surfer 1975..............$9-12
Reno 1968
Commemorates "100 Years - Reno **$4-6**
Republic Of Texas 1980...........$12-20
Republican Convention 1972.............
$500-700
Republican Football 1972 ....$350-450
Richard Hadlee $110-135
Richards – New Mexico 1967
Created for Richards Distributing Co.
of Alburquerque, New Mexico $8-10
Robin 1969 ....$5-6
Rocky Marciano 1973..............$14-16
Rocky Mountain, Club Bottle ..$10-15
Royal Crystal 1959.........................$3-6
Royal Di Monte 1957 ....$45-55
Royal Emperor 1958 ....$3-6
Royal Gold Diamond 1964 ......$30-35
Royal Gold Round 1956...........$80-90
Royal Opal 1957 ....$5-7
Royal Porcelain 1955...........$380-420
Royal Rose 1963 ....$30-35
Ruby Crystal 1967.........................$6-9
Ruidoso Downs 1968
Pointed ears............................$24-26
Flat ears $4-6
Sahara Invitational Bottle 1971
Introduced in honor of the Del Webb
1971 Sahara Invitational Pro-Am Golf
Tournament..................................$6-8
San Bear – Donkey 1973
Political series $1,500-2,000
Samoa..$4-7

San Diego 1968
Issued by the Beam Co. for the 200th
anniversary of its founding in 1769.. **$4-6**
San Diego – Elephant 1972 ......$15-25
Santa Fe 1960 ....$120-140
SCCA, Etched $15-25
SCCA, Smoothed.......................$12-18
Screech Owl 1979......................$18-22
Seafair Trophy Race 1972
Commemorates the Seattle Seafair
Trophy Race.................................$5-6
Seattle World's Fair 1962 ....$10-12
Seoul – Korea 1988...................$60-75
Sheraton Inn.................................$4-6
Short Dancing Scot 1963 ....$50-65
Short-timer 1975......................$15-20
Shriners 1975 ....$10-12
Shriners – Indiana.......................$4-7
Shriners Pyramid 1975
Issued by the El Kahir Temple of Cedar
Rapids, Iowa $10-12
Shriners Rajah 1977 ....$24-28
Shriners Temple 1972...............$20-25
Shriners Western Association.$15-25
Sierra Eagle...............................$15-22
Sigma Nu Fraternity 1977 ....$9-12
Sigma Nu Fraternity – Kentucky $8-12
Sigma Nu Fraternity – Michigan $18-23
Smiths North Shore Club 1972
Commemorating Smith's North Shore
Club, at Crystal Bay, Lake Tahoe **$10-12**
Smoked Crystal 1964 ....$6-9
Snow Goose 1979......................$8-10
Snowman $125-175
South Carolina 1970
In honor of celebrating its Tri-centen-
nial 1670-1970............................$4-6
**South Dakota – Mouth Rushmore
1969** $4-6
South Florida – Fox On Dolphin 1980
Bottled sponsored by the South
Florida Beam Bottle and Specialties
Club $14-16
Sovereign 1969
Executive series $4-7

St. Louis Glass Convention bottles, 1983: bourbon, vodka, scotch, gin, brandy, tequila, Canadian whiskey, $5 each.

Treasure Chest 1979..................$8-12

Trout Unlimited 1977
To honor the Trout Unlimited Conservation Organization $14-18

Truth Or Consequences Fiesta 1974
Issued in honor of Ralph Edwards radio and televison show..........$14-18

Turquoise China Jug 1966 ....$4-6

Twin Bridges Bottle 1971
Commemorates the largest twin bridge between Delaware and New Jersey $40-42

Twin Cherubs 1974
Executive series $8-12

Twin Doves 1987
Executive series $18-23

US Open 1972
Honors the US Open Golf Tourney at Pebble Beach, CA.....................$9-12

Vendome Drummers Wagon 1975
Honored the Vendomes of Beverly Hills, CA..................................$60-70

VFW Bottle 1971
Commemorates the 50th anniversary of the Department of Indana VFW **$5-6**

Viking 1973................................$9-12

Volkswagen Commemorative Bottle – Two Colors 1977
Commemorates the Volkswagen Beetle $40-50

Vons Market $28-35

Walleye Pike 1977
Designed for the National Fresh Water Fishing Hall of Fame.................$12-15

Walleye Pike 1987 ....$17-23

Washington 1975
A state series bottle to commemorate the Evergreen State.....................$5-6

Washington – The Evergreen State 1974
The club bottle for the Evergreen State Beam Bottle and Specialties Club
.... $10-12

Washington State Bicentennial 1976
....$10-12

Waterman 1980 ....$100-130

Western Shrine Association 1980
Commemorates the Shriners convention in Phoenix, Arizona...........$20-22

West Virginia 1963 ....$130-140

White Fox 1969
Issued for the 2nd anniversary of the Jim Beam Bottle and Specialties Club in Berkley, CA..........................$25-35

Wisconsin Muskie Bottle 1971 $15-17

Woodpecker 1969 ....$6-8

Wyoming 1965...........................$40-50

Yellow Katz 1967
Commemorates the 50th anniversay of the Katz Department Stores $15-17

Julian McShane bottle 1983, $60; Noel Executive 1983, $50; Stein 1983 $19; Zimmerman Liquors 50th Anniversary 1983, $25; 1904 "100 Digit" Dial Telephone 1983, $46.

Yellow Rose 1978
Executive series $7-10
Yellowstone Park Centennial......$4-7
Yosemite 1967..............................$4-6
Yuma Rifle Club $18-23
Zimmerman – Art Institute..........$5-8
Zimmerman Bell 1976
Designed for Zimmerman Liquor Store
of Chicago $6-7
Zimmerman Bell 1976 ....$6-7
Zimmerman – Blue Beauty 1969$9-12
Zimmerman – Blue Daisy............$4-6

Zimmerman Cherubs 1968 ....$4-6
Zimmerman – Chicago.................$4-6
Zimmerman – Eldorado..............$4-7
Zimmerman – Glass 1969 ....$7-9
Zimmerman Oatmeal Jug $40-50
Zimmerman – The Peddler Bottle
1971 ....$4-6
Zimmerman Two-Handled Jug 1965
....$45-60
Zimmerman Vase, Brown............$6-9
Zimmerman Vase, Green $6-9
Zimmerman – 50th Anniversary $35-45

AUTOMOBILE AND
TRANSPORTATION SERIES

CHEVROLET

1957 Convertible, Black, New..$85-95
1957 Convertible, Red, New $75-85
1957, Black..............................$70-80
1957, Dark Blue, PA $70-80
1957, Red................................$80-90
1957, Sierra Gold $140-160
1957, Turquoise.......................$50-70
1957, Yellow Hot Rod $65-75
Camaro 1969, Blue $55-65
Camaro 1969, Burgundy $120-140
Camaro 1969, Green............$100-120
Camaro 1969, Orange $55-65
Camaro 1969, Pace Car $60-70
Camaro 1969, Silver $120-140
Camaro 1969, Yellow, PA $55-65

Corvette 1986, Pace Car, Yellow,
New $60-85
Corvette 1984, Black $70-80
Corvette 1984, Bronze.........$100-200
Corvette 1984, Gold............$100-120
Corvette 1984, Red...................$55-65
Corvette 1984, White...............$55-65
Corvette 1978, Black $140-170
Corvette 1978, Pace Car $135-160
Corvette 1978, Red..................$50-60
Corvette 1978, White..............$40-50
Corvette 1978, Yellow..............$40-50
Corvette 1963, Black, PA $75-85
Corvette 1963, Blue, NY $90-100
Corvette 1963, Red..................$60-70

Corvette (black) 1989, $95; Corvette (bronze) 1989, $110; Corvette (gold) 1989 $110; Nineteenth Convention bottle 1989, $40.

Corvette 1963, Silver $50-60
Corvette 1955, Black, New ..$110-140
Corvette 1955, Copper, New..$90-100
Corvette 1955, Red, New $110-140
Corvette 1954, Blue, New $90-100
Corvette 1953, White, New ..$100-120

DUESENBERG

Convertible, Cream $130-140
Convertible, Dark Blue $120-130
Convertible, Light Blue..........$80-100
Convertible Coupe, Gray......$160-180

FORD

International Delivery Wagon, Black
....$80-90
International Delivery Wagon, Green
....$80-90
Fire Chief 1928 ....$120-130
Fire Chief 1934 ....$60-70
Fire Pumper Truck 1935 ....$45-60
Model A, Angelos Liquor......$180-200
Model A, Parkwood Supply .$140-170
Model A 1903, Black................$35-45
Model A 1903, Red...................$35-45
Model A 1928 ....$60-80
Model A Fire Truck 1930 .....$130-170
Model T 1913, Black $30-40
Model T 1913, Green $30-40
Mustang 1964, Black...........$100-125
Mustang 1964, Red..................$35-45
Mustang 1964, White...............$25-35
Paddy Wagon 1930 ....$100-120
Phaeton 1929 ....$40-50

Ford Fire Engine (1930 Model A) 1983, $205.

Pickup Truck 1935 ....$20-30
Police Car 1929, Blue $75-85
Police Car 1929, Yellow........$350-450
Police Patrol Car 1934.............$60-70
Police Tow Truck 1935.............$20-30
Roadster 1934, Cream, PA, New
....$80-90
Thunderbird 1956, Black.........$60-70
Thunderbird 1956, Blue, PA $70-80
Thunderbird 1956, Gray............$50-60
Thunderbird 1956, Green $60-70
Thunderbird 1956, Yellow........$50-60
Woodie Wagon 1929................$50-60

MERCEDES

1974, Blue.................................$30-40
1974, Gold $60-80
1974, Green $30-40
1974, Mocha.............................$30-40
1974, Red..................................$30-40
1974, Sand Beige, PA $30-40
1974, Silver, Australia $140-160
1974, White...............................$35-45

Ford Woodie (1929) 1983, $90; Police Patrol Wagon (1931) 1983, $155.

Casey Jones with Tender 1989, $50; Casey Jones Caboose 1989, $30.

TRAINS

Baggage Car	$40-60
Box Car, Brown	$50-60
Box Car, Yellow	$40-50
Bumper	$5-8
Caboose, Gray	$45-55
Caboose, Red	$50-60
Casey Jones With Tender	$65-80
Casey Jones Caboose	$40-55
Casey Jones Accessory Set	$50-60
Coal Tender, No Bottle	$20-30
Combination Car	$55-65
Dining Car	$75-90
Flat Car	$20-30
General Locomotive	$60-70
Grant Locomotive	$50-65
Log Car	$40-55
Lumber Car	$12-18
Observation Car	$15-23
Passenger Car	$45-53
Tank Car	$15-20
Track	$4-6
Turner Locomotive	$80-100
Watertower	$20-30
Wood Tender	$40-45
Wood Tender, No Bottle	$20-25

OTHER

Ambulance	$18-22
Army Jeep	$18-20
Bass Boat	$12-18
Cable Car	$25-35
Circus Wagon	$20-30
Ernie's Flower Cart	$20-30
Golf Cart	$20-30
HC Covered Wagon 1929	$10-20
Jewel Tea	$70-80
Mack Fire Truck 1917	$120-135
Mississippi Pumper Firetruck 1867	$115-140
Oldsmobile 1903	$25-35
Olsonite Eagle Racer	$40-35
Police Patrol Car 1934, Yellow	$110-140
Space Shuttle	$20-30
Stutz 1914, Gray	$40-50
Stutz 1914, Yellow	$40-50
Thomas Flyer 1909, Blue	$60-70
Thomas Flyer 1909, Ivory	$60-70
Vendome Wagon	$40-50
Volkswagen, Blue	$40-50
Volkswagen, Red	$40-50

San Francisco Cable Car, 1983, $60; Duesenberg Convertible Coupe, 1983, $250-275.

Bischoff
Bottles

Bischoffs, which was founded in Trieste, Italy, in 1777, issued decorative figurals in the 18th century long before any other company. The early bottles are rare because of the limited production and the attrition of the bottles over the years. Modern Bischoffs were imported into the United States beginning in 1949. Collectors haven't shown intense interest in modern imports, and since sales have not been made often enough for accurate values to be established, prices are not included in this book. Three other types of Bischoffs will be covered: Kord Bohemian Decanters, Venetian Glass Figurals, and Ceramic Decanters and Figurals.

KORD BOHEMIAN DECANTERS

These decanters were handblown and handpainted glass bottles created in Czechoslovakia by the Kord Company with a tradition of Bohemian cut, engraved, etched, and flashed glass. Stoppers and labels with the bottles are considered very rare and valuable today. The cut glass and ruby-etched decanters were imported to the U.S. in the early 1950s, with the ruby-etched being considered rare only if complete with the stopper. In addition, most of these decanters have a matching set of glasses to provide an even greater increase in value if the entire set is intact.

Amber Flowers 1952
Two-toned glass decanter, 15-1/2",
dark amber stopper **$30-40**

Amber Leaves 1952
Multi-toned bottle with long neck,
13-1/2" **$30-40**

Anisette 1948-1951
Clear glass bottle with ground glass
stopper, 11" **$20-30**

Bohemian Ruby-Etched 1949-1951
Round decanter, tapered neck, etched
stopper, 15-1/2" **$30-40**

Coronet Crystal 1952
Round tall bottle, multi-toned with a
broad band of flowers, leaves, and
scrolls circle, 14" **$30-40**

Cut Glass Decanter (Blackberry) 1951
Geometric design, handcut overall,
ground stopper, 10-1/2" **$32-42**

Czech Hunter 1958
Round thick clear glass, heavy round
glass base, 8-1/2" **$18-26**

Czech Hunter's Lady 1958
"Mae West" shaped decanter of
cracked clear glass, 10" **$18-26**

Dancing - Country Scene 1950
Clear glass handblown decanter with
peasant boy and girl doing a country
dance beside a tree, 12-1/4"....**$25-35**

Dancing - Peasant Scene 1950
Pale and amber glass decanter, peas-
ants in costume dancing to music of
bagpipes, 12" **$25-35**

Double Dolphin 1949-1969
Fish-shaped twin bottles joined at the
abdomen, handblown clear glass.
.... **$20-30**

Flying Geese Pitcher 1952
Green glass handle and stopper, glass
base, 9-1/2" **$15-25**

Flying Geese Pitcher 1957
Clear crystal handled pitcher, gold
stopper, 9-1/2" **$15-25**

Horse Head 1947-1969
Pale amber-colored bottle in the shape
of a horse's head, round pouring spout
on top, 8"................................. **$15-25**

Jungle Parrot - Amber Glass 1952
Handetched jungle scenes with a yellow amber color, 15-1/2" **$25-35**

Jungle Parrot - Ruby Glass 1952
Handetched jungle scenes with a ruby
colored body, 15-1/2" **$20-30**

Old Coach Bottle 1948
Pale amber color, round glass stopper,
10"... **$25-35**

Old Sleigh Bottle 1949
Glass decanter, handpainted, signed,
10"... **$22-32**

Wild Geese - Amber Glass 1952
Tall round decanter with tapering
etched neck, flashed with a yellow
amber color, 15-1/2" **$25-35**

Wild Geese - Ruby Glass 1952
Tall round decanter with tapering
etched neck, flashed with ruby red
color,15-1/2" **$25-35**

VENETIAN GLASS FIGURALS

These figurals are produced in limited editions by the Serguso Glass Company in Morano, Italy and are unique in design and color with Birds, Fish, Cats, and Dogs.

Black Cat 1969
Glass black cat with curled tail, 12" l
....**$18-25**

Dog - Alabaster 1966
Seated alabaster glass dog, 13"
....**$33-45**

Dog - Dachschund 1966
Alabaster long dog with brown tones,
19" l..**$40-50**

Duck 1964
Alabaster glass tinted pink and green,
long neck, upraised wings, 11", l
....**$42-52**

Fish - Multicolor 1964
Round fat fish, alabaster glass, green,
rose, yellow...............................**$18-25**

Fish - Ruby 1969
Long, flat, ruby glass fish, 12" l.**$25-35**

CERAMIC DECANTERS AND FIGURALS

These are some of the most interesting, attractive, and valuable of the Bischoff collection and are made of ceramic, stoneware, and pottery. Decanters complete with handles, spouts, and stoppers demand the highest value.

African Head 1962 .... $15-18	Christmas Tree 1957................ $50-55
Alpine Pitcher 1969.................. $25-30	Dachshund Figural $35-45
Amber Flower 1952.................. $30-35	Deer Figural 1969.................... $20-25
Amber Leaf 1952...................... $30-35	Duck Figural............................. $35-45
Amphora, Two Handles 1950 ..$20-25	Egyptian Dancing Figural 1961 $12-17
Ashtray, Green-Striped 1958 .. $10-15	Egyptian Pitcher - Two Musicians
Bell House 1960 .... $30-40	1969 .... $15-24
Bell Tower 1960........................ $15-30	Egyptian Pitcher - Three Musicians
Boy (Chinese) Figural 1962 ..... $30-40	1959 .... $20-28
Boy (Spanish) Figural 1961 ..... $25-35	Girl In Chinese Costume 1962 $30-40
Candlestick, Antique 1958...... $20-25	Girl In Spanish Costume 1961 $30-40
Candlestick, Clown 1963 .... $8-10	Greek Vase Decanter 1969 ..... $13-19
Canteen, Floral 1969 .... $15-20	Mask - Gray Face 1963 .... $16-26
Canteen, Fruit 1969 .... $18-20	Porcelain Cameo 1962........... $15-20
Cat, Black 1969....................... $20-25	Oil And Vinegar Cruets - Black And
Clown With Black Hair 1963 ... $30-40	White 1959 .... $18-25
Clown With Red Hair 1963 ...... $15-25	Vase - Black And Gold 1959 ... $19-22
Chariot Urn 1966 (2 Sections). $20-25	Watchtower 1960.................... $12-16

Borghini Bottles

Borghini bottles are ceramics of modernistic style with historical themes manufactured in Pisa, Italy. They vary greatly in price depending on distribution points. The lowest values are in areas closest to the point of distribution or near heavy retail sales. Recent bottles are stamped "Borghini Collection Made In Italy."

Cats
Black with red ties, 6"..............**$11-15**

Cats
Black with red ties, 12".............**$10-15**

Female Head
Ceramic, 9-1/2" **$11-15**

Penguin
Black and white, 6" **$8-11**

Penguin 1969
Black and white, 12" **$12-16**

Fruit bowl, 1970, $15-20; Penguin, 1969, $10-12; Cardinal, 1969, $10-12; Black Cat, 1969, $10-15.

Ezra Brooks Bottles

The Ezra Brooks Distilling Company began to issue figurals in 1964, ten years after the Jim Beam company, and quickly became a strong competitive rival due to their effective distribution, promotion strategy, unique design, and choice of subjects.

While many of the Brooks bottles depict the same themes as Jim Beam (Sports and Transportation series), they also produced bottles based on original subjects. One of these is the Maine lobster that looks good enough to put on anyone's dinner table. The most popular series depict antiques such as an Edison phonograph and a Spanish cannon. Yearly, new editions highlight American historical events and anniversaries. One of my favorites is the bucket-shaped bottle Bucket of Blood (1970) named for the Virginia City, Nevada saloon.

While these bottles are still filled with Kentucky bourbon, most purchases for these figural bottles are by collectors who want the bottle rather than the contents.

Alabama Bicentennial 1976 .....**$12-14**

American Legion 1971
Distinguished embossed star emblem
from WWI................................**$30-40**

American Legion 1972
Salutes Illinois American Legion 54th
National Convention **$50-60**

American Legion 1973
Salutes Hawaii, which hosted the
American Legion's 54th National Con-
vention **$20-25**

American Legion – Miami 1974 . **$15-20**

American Legion – Denver 1977
....**$15-20**

American Legion – Chicago 1982
....**$20-25**

American Legion – Seattle 1983
....**$30-35**

Amvets – Polish Legion 1973.. **$14-18**

Amvets – Dolphin 1974.............**$10-15**

Antique Cannon 1969 ....**$10-12**

Antique Phonograph 1970 ......**$20-25**

Arizona 1969
Man with burro in search of Lost
Dutchman Mine.......................**$20-25**

Auburn 1932 Classic Car 1978 .. **$30-35**

Bucky Badger No. 1 Boxer 1973
....**$30-35**

Bucky Badger No. 2 Football 1974
....**$30-35**

Bucky Badger No. 3 Hockey 1974
....**$30-35**

Baltimore Oriole Wildlife 1979 .**$20-30**

Bare Knuckle Fighter 1971 ......**$35-40**

Baseball Hall Of Fame 1973.....**$20-22**

Baseball Player 1974 ....**$20-25**

Bear 1968 ....**$10-12**

Beaver 1972...............................**$10-15**

Bengal Tiger Wildlife 1979 ....**$20-30**

Betsy Ross 1975 ....**$15-20**

Bicycle, Penny-Farthington 1973
....**$10-15**

Big Bertha
Nugget Casino's very own elephant,
with a raised trunk...................**$10-13**

Big Daddy Lounge 1969
Salute to South Florida's state liquor
chain and Big Daddy Lounges .**$10-12**

Bighorn Ram 1972 ....**$18-20**

Bird Dog 1971 ....**$12-14**

Bordertown 1970
Salutes Borderline Club on border of
California and Nevada **$10-15**

Bowler 1973 ....**$15-20**

Bowling Tenpins 1973................**$9-12**

Brahma Bull 1972......................**$10-12**

Bronco Buster 1973..................**$15-20**

Bucket Of Blood 1970
Salutes the famous Virginia City, Nevada saloon. Bucket-shaped bottle
....**$15-20**

Bucking Bronco, Rough Rider 1973
....**$10-12**

Bucky Badger, Football...........**$20-25**

Bucky Badger, Hockey 1975....**$18-24**

Bucky Badger, No. 1 Boxer 1973
....**$9-12**

Buffalo Hunter 1971..................**$10-12**

Bulldog 1972
Mighty canine mascot and football
symbol **$10-14**

Bull Moose 1973 ....**$12-15**

Busy Beaver **$4-7**

Cabin Still **$20-35**

Cable Car 1968 ....**$5-6**

California Quail 1970 ....**$8-10**

Canadian Honker 1975...............**$9-12**

Canadian Loon Wildlife 1979 ...**$25-35**

Cardinal 1972 ....**$20-25**

Casey At Bat 1973 ....**$75-80**

Ceremonial Dancer 1970.........**$20-25**

Cb Convoy Radio 1976...............**$5-9**

Charolais Beef 1973 ....**$10-14**

Cheyenne Shoot-Out 1970
Honoring the Wild West and its Cheyenne Frontier Days **$10-12**

Chicago Fire 1974.....................**$20-30**

Chicago Water Tower 1969........**$8-12**

Christmas Decanter 1966 ....**$5-8**

Christmas Tree 1979.................**$13-17**

Churchill 1970

Commemorating Churchill's "Iron Curtain" speech at Westminster College $5-9

Cigar Store Indian 1968...........$10-12

Classic Firearms 1969

Embossed gun set consisting of Derringer, Colt 45, Peacemaker, over and under flintlock, and pepper box$15-19

Clowns, Imperial Shrine 1978..$30-35

Clown Bust No. I Smiley 1979..$30-35

Clown Bust No. 2 Cowboy 1979 $30-35

Clown Bust No. 3 Pagliacci 1979 ....$30-35

Clown Bust No. 4 Keystone Cop $30-35

Clown Bust No. 5 Cuddles.......$30-35

Clown Bust No. 6 Tramp $30-35

Clown With Accordion 1971 ....$30-35

Clown With Balloon 1973........$30-35

Club Bottle, Birthday Cake $9-12

Club Bottle, Distillery $9-12

Club Bottle 1973

The third commemorative Ezra Brooks Collectors Club in the shape of America...$14-18

Clydesdale Horse 1973 ....$8-12

Colonial Drummer 1974 ....$10-15

Colt Peacemaker Flask 1969.....$5-10

Conquistadors – 1971

Tribute to the great drum and bugle corps $10-15

Conquistadors Drum And Bugle 1972 ....$12-15

Corvette Indy Pace Car 1978...$45-55

Corvette 1957 Classic 1976.$110-140

Court Jester $10-15

Dakota Cowboy 1975 ....$30-35

Dakota Cowgirl 1976................$30-35

Dakota Grain Elevator 1978.....$20-30

Dakota Shotgun Express 1977 $18-22

Dead Wagon 1970

Made to carry gunfight loser to Boot Hill..$5-7

Delta Belle 1969 ....$6-7

Democrat Convention 1976.....$10-16

Derringer Flask 1969 ....$5-10

Dirt Bike, Riverboat 1869........$10-16

Distillery 1970

Reproduction of the Ezra Brooks Distillery in Kentucky $10-12

Duesenberg..............................$24-33

Elephant 1973 ....$7-9

Elk

Salutes those organizations who practiced benevolence and charity ..$20-28

English Setter – Bird Dog 1971$14-17

Equestrienne 1974....................$15-17

Esquire, Ceremonial Dancer....$10-16

Farmer – Iowa 1977 ....$30-35

Farthington Bike 1972 ....$6-8

Fire Engine 1971 ....$14-18

Fireman 1975............................$30-35

Fisherman 1974 ....$15-18

Flintlock 1969 (Two Versions: Japanese And Heritage)

Japanese $10-15

Heritage $10-15

Florida "Gators" 1973

Tribute to the University of Florida Gators football team $9-11

Foe Eagle 1978.........................$15-20

Foe Flying Eagle 1979 ....$20-25

Foe Eagle 1980.........................$35-40

Foe Eagle 1981.........................$35-40

Football Player 1974.................$20-25

Ford Mustang Pace Car 1979..$25-35

Ford Thunderbird – 1956 1976.$70-80

Foremost Astronaut 1970

Tribute to major liquor supermart, Foremost Liquor Store $5-7

Fresno Decanter........................$5-12

Fresno Grape With Gold...........$48-60

Fresno Grape 1970 ....$6-11

Gamecock 1970.........................$9-13

Go Big Red No. 1, No. 2, And No. 3 – Football-Shaped Bottle

No. 1 with football 1972 ....$20-28

No. 2 with hat 1971 ....$18-22

No. 3 with rooster 1972 ....$10-14

Golden Antique Cannon 1969
Symbol of Spanish power **$10-12**
Golden Eagle 1971...................**$18-22**
Golden Grizzly Bear 1970........**$10-12**
Golden Horseshoe 1970
Salute to Reno's Horseshoe Club **$15-20**
Golden Rooster No. 1
Replica of solid gold rooster on display
at Nugget Casino in Reno, Nevada
....**$35-50**
Gold Prospector 1969 ....**$10-12**
Gold Seal 1972..........................**$12-14**
Gold Turkey...............................**$35-45**
Golfer 1973................................**$25-30**
Go Tiger Go 1973......................**$10-14**
Grandfather Clock 1970...........**$10-12**
Grandfather Clock 1970...........**$12-20**
Greater Greensboro Open 1972
....**$25-30**
**Greater Greensboro Open Golfer
1973**...**$25-30**
Greater Greensboro Open Map 1974
....**$40-45**
Greater Greensboro Open Cup 1975
....**$25-30**
Greater Greensboro Open Cup 1976
....**$25-30**
**Greater Greensboro Open Club And
Ball 1977**..................................**$25-30**
**Great Stone Face – Old Man Of The
Mountain 1970**.......................**$10-14**
Great White Shark 1977 ....**$8-14**
Hambletonian 1971...................**$13-16**
Happy Goose 1975 ....**$12-15**
Harolds Club Red Dice 1968....**$20-25**
Hereford 1971 ....**$12-15**
Hereford 1972 ....**$12-15**
Historical Flask Eagle 1970 ....**$5-10**
Historical Flask Flagship 1970...**$5-10**
Historical Flask Liberty 1970 .....**$5-10**
Historical Flask Old Ironsides 1970
....**$5-10**
Hollywood Cops 1972 ....**$12-18**
Hopi Indian 1970
Kachina Doll............................**$15-20**

Hopi Kachina 1973...................**$50-75**
Horseshoe Casino Gold............**$8-10**
Idaho – Ski The Potato 1973
Salutes the State of Idaho **$8-10**
Indianapolis 500.......................**$30-35**
Indy Pace Car 1978...................**$50-60**
Indian Ceremonial 1970 ....**$13-18**
Indian Hunter 1970 ....**$12-15**
Iowa Farmer 1977.....................**$55-65**
Iowa Grain Elevator 1978........**$25-34**
Iron Horse Locomotive **$8-14**
Jack O'Diamonds 1969 ....**$4-6**
Jay Hawk 1969............................**$6-8**
Jester 1971...................................**$6-8**
Jug, Old Time 1.75 Liter **$9-13**
Kachina Doll No. 1 1971 ....**$80-100**
Kachina Doll No. 2 1973...........**$75-85**
Kachina Doll No. 3 1974...........**$80-90**
Kachina Doll No. 4 1975...........**$40-45**
Kachina Doll No. 5 1976...........**$50-55**
Kachina Doll No. 6 1977...........**$50-55**
Kachina Doll No. 7 1978...........**$55-60**
Kachina Doll No. 8 1979...........**$85-90**
Kachina Doll No. 9 1980...........**$30-35**
Kansas Jayhawk 1969.................**$4-7**
Katz Cats 1969
Siamese cats are symbolic of Katz
Drug Co. of Kansas City, Kansas**$8-12**
Katz Cats Philharmonic 1970
**Commemorating its 27th annual Star
Night**..**$6-10**
Keystone Cop 1980 ....**$32-40**
Keystone Cops 1971 ....**$70-75**
Killer Whale 1972......................**$15-20**
King Of Clubs 1969.....................**$4-6**
King Salmon 1971......................**$18-24**
Liberty Bell 1970 ....**$5-6**
Lincoln Continental Mark I 1941 $20-25
Lion On The Rock 1971 ....**$5-7**
Liquor Square 1972 ....**$5-7**
Little Giant 1971
Replica of the first horse-drawn steam
engine to arrive at the Chicago fire in
1871 ....**$11-16**
Maine Lighthouse 1971 ....**$18-24**

Maine Lobster 1970.................$15-18
Mako Shark 1962 & 1979.........$15-20
Man-o-War 1969......................$10-16
M & M Brown Jug 1975b..........$15-20
Map, USA Club Bottle 1972.........$7-9
Masonic Fez 1976....................$12-15
Max, The Hat, Zimmerman 1976 $25-30
Military Tank 1971....................$15-22
Minnesota Hockey Player 1975
....$18-22
Minuteman 1975......................$15-20
Missouri Mule, Brown 1972.........$7-9
Moose 1973.............................$20-28
Motorcycle..............................$10-14
Mountaineer 1971
One of the most valuable Ezra Brooks
figural bottles..........................$40-55
Mr. Foremost 1969......................$7-10
Mr. Maine Potato 1973...............$6-10
Mr. Merchant 1970....................$10-12
Mule..$8-12
Mustang Indy Pace Car 1979...$20-30
Nebraska – Go Big Red............$12-15
New Hampshire State House 1970
....$9-13
North Carolina Bicentennial 1975
....$8-12
Nugget Classic
Replica of golf pin presented to golf
tournament participants.............$7-12
Oil Gusher.................................$6-8
Old Captial 1971......................$30-40
Old Ez No. 1 Barn Owl 1977.....$25-35
Old Ez No. 2 Eagle Own 1978..$40-55
Old Ez No. 3 Show Owl 1979...$20-35
Old Man Of The Mountain 1970
....$10-14
Old Water Tower 1969
Famous landmark, survived the Chi-
cago fire of 1871......................$12-16
Oliver Hardy Bust......................$40-45
Ontario 500 1970.....................$18-22
Overland Express 1969...........$17-20
Over-Under Flintlock Flask 1969.$6-9
Panda – Giant 1972.................$12-17

Penguin 1972.............................$8-10
Penny Farthington High-Wheeler
1973...$9-12
Pepperbox Flask 1969..............$5-10
Phoenix Bird 1971....................$20-26
Phoenix Jaycees 1973.............$10-14
Phonograph.............................$15-20
Piano 1970...............................$12-13
Pirate 1971..............................$15-20
Polish Legion American Vets 1978
....$18-26
Portland Head Lighthouse 1971
Honors the lighthouse that has guided
ships safely into Maine Harbor since
1791.......................................$18-24
Pot-Bellied Stove 1968................$5-6
Queen Of Hearts 1969
Playing card symbol with royal flush in
hearts on front of the bottle........$5-10
Raccoon Wildlife 1978.............$30-40
Ram 1973.................................$13-18
Razorback Hog 1969................$12-18
Razorback Hog 1979................$20-30
Red Fox 1979...........................$30-40
Reno Arch 1968
Honoring the Biggest Little City in the
World, Reno, Nevada...............$10-12
Sailfish 1971...............................$7-11
Salmon, Washington King 1971. $20-26
San Francisco Cable Car 1968....$4-8
Sea Captain 1971....................$15-20
Sealion – Gold 1972.................$11-14
Senators Of The US 1972
Honors the Senators of the United
States of America....................$10-15
Setter 1974..............................$10-15
Shrine – Fez 1976....................$10-15
Shrine – Clown 1978................$25-30
Shrine King Tut Guard 1979.....$20-25
Shrine – Golden Pharaoh.........$35-40
1804 Silver Dollar 1970.............$8-10
Silver Saddle 1973...................$22-25
Silver Spur Boot 1971
Cowboy-boot-shaped bottle with silver
spur buckled on "Silver Spur-Carson

City Nevada" embossed on side of
boot..$15-20
Simba 1971................................$9-12
Ski Boot 1972............................$5-7
Slot Machine 1971
A replica of the original nickel Liberty
Bell slot machine invented by Charles
Fey in 1895............................$20-25
Snowmobiles 1972......................$8-11
**South Dakota Air National Guard
1976**.......................................$20-25
Spirit Of '76 1974.........................$5-7
**Spirit Of St. Louis 1977, 50th
Anniversary**..............................$6-11
Sprint Car Racer.......................$30-40
Stagecoach 1969......................$10-12
Stan Laurel Bust 1976............$40-45
Stock Market Ticker 1970
A replica of a tickertape machine$8-11
Stonewall Jackson 1974..........$30-35
Strongman 1974.......................$20-25
Sturgeon 1975...........................$20-28
John L. Sullivan 1970..............$15-20
Syracuse – New York 1973......$11-16
Tank Patton 1972
Reproduction of a U.S. Army tank
....$16-20
Tecumseh 1969
Figurehead of the U.S.S. Delaware,
this decanter is an embossed repli-
cas of the statue at the United States
Naval Academy..........................$8-15
Telephone 1971
Replica of the old-time upright handset
telephone................................$16-19
Tennis Player 1972...................$20-25
Tennis Player 1973...................$20-25
Terrapin, Maryland 1974..........$14-16
Texas Longhorn 1971...............$18-22
Ticker Tape 1970.......................$8-12
Tiger On Stadium 1973
Commemorates college teams who
have chosen the tiger as their mascot
....$12-17
Tom Turkey...............................$18-24

Tonopah 1972............................$15-20
Totem Pole 1972.......................$20-25
Totem Pole 1973.......................$20-25
Tractor 1971
A model of the 1917 Fordson made by
Henry Ford...............................$9-11
Trail-Bike Rider 1972................$10-12
Trojan Horse 1974....................$15-18
Trojans – USC Football 1973....$10-14
Trout And Fly 1970.....................$7-11
Truckin' & Vannin' 1977.............$7-12
Vermont Skier 1972...................$10-12
**VFW – Veterans Of Foreign Wars
1973**...$10-15
**VFW – Veterans Of Foreign Wars
1974**..$10-12
VFW –veterans Of Foreign Wars 1982
....$25-30
**VFW – Veterans Of Foreign Wars
1983**...$25-30
Virginia – Red Cardinal 1973....$10-15
Walgreen Drugs 1974...............$16-24
Weirton Steel 1973...................$15-18
Western Rodeos 1973..............$17-23
West Virginia – Mountaineer 1971
....$65-75
West Virginia – Mountain Lady 1972
....$20-25
Whale 1972...............................$14-20
Wheat Shocker 1971
The mascot of the Kansas football
team in a fighting pose.................$5-7
Whiskey Flasks 1970
Reproduction of collectible American
patriotic whiskey flask of the 1800s: Old
Ironsides, Miss Liberty, American Eagle,
Civil War Commemorative.........$12-14
Whitetail Deer 1974..................$18-24
White Turkey 1971....................$20-25
Wichita...$4-8
Wichita Centennial 1970.............$4-6
Winston Churchill 1969.............$7-10
Zimmerman's Hat 1968
A salute to "Zimmerman's-World's
Largest Liquor Store"....................$5-6

J.W. Dant
Bottles

J.W. Dant Distilling Co. produces bottles similar to the Brooks and Beam bottles and have strong collector appeal. These bottles usually depict American themes such as patriotic events and folklore in addition to various types of animals.

Because Dant has such a liking for American history and its traditions, most of these bottles are decorated with historical scenes in full color. Some bottles carry an embossed American eagle and shield with stars. One other unique item about these bottles is that they are limited editions and the molds are not reused.

Alamo 1969	$5-10
American Legion 1969	$5-10
Atlantic City 1969	$5-10
Bobwhite 1969	$6-8
Boeing 747	$5-10
Boston Tea Party, Eagle To Left	$5-7
Boston Tea Party, Eagle To Right	$9-12
Bourbon	$3-5
Paul Bunyan 1969	$5-7
California Quail 1969	$7-9
Chukar Partridge	$7-9
Clear Tip Pinch	$10-12
Constitution And Guerriere	$5-7
Duel Between Burr And Hamilton	$8-10
Eagle	$10-12
Fort Sill Centennial 1969	$10-12
Patrick Henry 1969	$5-8
Indianapolis 500 1969	$10-12
Mountain Quail 1969	$10-12
Mt. Rushmore 1969	$10-12
Prairie Chicken	$10-12
Reverse Eagle	$10-12
Ring-necked Pheasant	$10-12
Ruffed Grouse 1969	$10-12
San Diego Harbor 1969	$5-8
Speedway 500	$6-9
Stove – Pot Belly 1966	$10-12
Washington Crossing Delaware	$8-10
Woodcock 1969	$10-12
Wrong-Way Charlie	$15-20

Garnier Bottles

Garnet Et Cie, a French firm founded in 1858, has long been given credit as the pioneer of the modern "collectible" bottle for liquor, and introduced the Garnier figural bottles in 1899. During the Prohibition and World War II, there was a temporary halt in production, which quickly resumed in the 1950s.

The bottles manufactured before World War II are the rarest and most valuable but are not listed in this book due to the difficulty in establishing accurate prices. Among these are the Cat (1930), Clown (1910), Country Jug (1937), Greyhound (1930), Penguin (1930), and the Marquise (1931).

Cardinal; Robin; Goldfinch; Mockingbird; Road Runner, all 1971, $10-15 (all).

Aladdin's Lamp 1963 ....$40-50
Alfa Romeo 1913 1970.............$20-30
Alfa Romeo 1929 1969.............$20-30
Alfa Romeo Racer 1969 ....$20-30
Antique Coach 1970 ....$25-30
Apollo 1969
Apollo Spaceship, 13-1/2" $17-22
Aztec Vase 1965......................$15-20
Baby Foot – Soccer Shoe 1963
   Black with white trim 3-3/4" x 8-1/2"
   ....$10-20
   1962 soccer shoe, large...........$10-15
Baby Trio 1963 ....$7-10
Baccus Figural 1967 ....$20-25
Bahamas
   Black policeman, white jacket and hat,
   black pants, red stripe, gold details
   ....$15-24
Baltimore Oriole 1970...............$10-16
Bandit Figural 1958...................$10-14
Bedroom Candlestick 1967 .....$20-25
Bellows 1969............................$14-21
Bird Ashtray 1958 ....$3-4
Bluebird 1970 ....$12-18
Bouquet 1966 ....$15-25
Bull (And Matador) Animal Figural
   1963 ....$17-23

Burmese Man Vase 1965.........$15-25
Canada $11-14
Candlestick 1955 ....$25-35
Candlestick Glass 1965...........$15-25
Cannon 1964 ....$50-60
Cardinal State Bird – Illinois 1969
   ....$15-20
Cat – Black 1962 ....$15-25
Cat – Gray 1962........................$15-25
Chalet 1955 ....$40-50
Chimney 1956 ....$55-65
Chinese Dog 1965....................$15-25
Chinese Statuette – Man 1970.$15-25
Chinese Statuette – Woman 1970
   ....$15-25
Christmas Tree 1956................$60-70
Citroen 1970.............................$20-30
Classic Ashtray 1958................$20-30
Clock 1958................................$20-30
Clown's Head 1931 ....$65-75
Clown Holding Tuba 1955 ....$15-25
Coffee Mill 1966 ....$20-30
Coffee Pot 1962 ....$30-35
Columbine Figural 1968
   Female partner........................$20-30
   Harlequin $30-40
Diamond Bottle 1969.............. $10-15

Frog (France) 1936, $65-75;
Elephant (France) 1961, $20-30.

Drunkard – Drunk On Lamp Post
....**$15-20**
Duckling Figural 1956...............**$18-26**
Duo 1954
Two clear glass bottles stacked, two
pouring spouts.........................**$12-18**
Egg Figural 1956 ....**$70-80**
Eiffel Tower 1951
13-1/2" **$15-25**
12-1/2" **$14-20**
Elephant Figural 1961..............**$20-30**
Empire Vase 1962 ....**$10-18**
Fiat 500 1913 1970
Yellow body...........................**$20-30**
Fiat Neuvo 1913 1970
Blue body **$20-30**
Flask Garnier 1958....................**$9-12**
Flying Horse Pegasus 1958 .....**$50-60**
Football Player 1970................**$13-17**
Ford 1913 1969.........................**$20-30**
Fountain 1964...........................**$25-35**
Giraffe 1961 ....**$20-35**
Goldfinch 1970 ....**$15-20**
Goose 1955 ....**$14-24**
Grenadier 1949.........................**$55-65**
Guitar And Mandolin **$20-25**
Harlequin Standing 1968..........**$13-19**
Harlequin With Mandolin 1958 $30-40

Hockey Player 1970.................**$15-20**
Horse Pistol 1964.....................**$15-25**
Hula Hoop 1959 ....**$25-30**
Hunting Vase 1964....................**$25-35**
Hussar 1949
French cavalry soldier of 1800s **$25-35**
India **$10-15**
Indian 1958 ....**$15-20**
Indy 500, No. 1 1970 .... **$40-45**
Indy 500, No. 2 1970 ....**$40-45**
Jockey 1961 ....**$25-35**
Lancer 1949...............................**$15-22**
Locomotive 1969 ....**$15-25**
Log – Round 1958.....................**$20-30**
London – Bobby........................**$12-18**
Loon 1970..................................**$10-18**
Maharajah 1958 ....**$70-80**
Mallard Duck.............................**$15-20**
Meadowlark 1969 ....**$15-20**
M.G. 1933 1969.........................**$25-30**
Mockingbird 1970 ....**$15-20**
Montmartre Jug 1960 ....**$12-18**
Monuments 1966
A cluster of Parisian monuments
....**$15-25**
Napoleon On Horseback 1969 $20-30
Nature Girl 1959 ....**$10-15**
New York Policeman **$9-13**

Nice Pitcher; Centaur Pitcher; Biarritz Pitcher; Pegasus Pitcher; Deauville Pitcher, all 1971, $20-25 each.

Oriole 1969 ....$15-20	Saint Tropez Jug 1961b............$20-30
Packard 1930 1970 ....$20-30	Scarecrow 1960 ....$25-35
Painting 1961 ....$25-35	Sheriff 1958 ....$15-25
Paris, French Policeman..........$10-15	Snail 1950 ....$58-68
Paris Taxis 1960 ....$20-30	Soccer Shoe 1962.....................$30-40
Partridge 1961...........................$15-20	Soldier With Drum And Rifle....$15-20
Pheasant 1969 ....$20-25	S.S. France – Large 1962 ......$80-130
Pigeon – Clear Glass 1958 ......$10-15	S.S. France – Small 1962.........$50-60
Pony 1961..................................$25-35	S.S. Queen Mary 1970 ....$25-35
Poodle 1954...............................$12-15	Stanley Steamer 1907 1970 .....$20-30
Quail 1969..................................$15-10	Teapot 1961 ....$15-25
Rainbow Trout...........................$20-25	Teapot 1935...............................$20-30
Renault 1911 1969 ....$20-30	Train 1971 ....$10-15
Road Runner 1969.....................$10-15	Trout 1967...................................$17-22
Robin 1970 ....$10-15	Valley Quail 1969.........................$8-12
Rocket 1958 ....$10-15	Violin 1966 ....$30-36
Rolls Royce 1908 1970 ....$20-30	Watch – Antique 1966...............$20-30
Rooster 1952.............................$15-20	Water Pitcher 1965 ....$12-18
	Woman With Jug.......................$20-25

Hoffman Bottles

Hoffman bottles are considered limited editions since each issue is produced in a restricted quantity. When this number is reached, the molds are destroyed, which quickly makes the designs rare and valuable.

While these bottles often portray European figures in various occupations, they have also depicted American subjects, such as the 1976 Centennial Bottle and the 1976 Hippie Bottle.

OCCUPATION SERIES

Mr. Bartender With Music Box
"He's a Jolly Good Fellow"........**$25-30**

Mr. Charmer With Music Box
"Glow Little Glow Worm"..........**$10-15**

Mr. Dancer With Music Box
"The Irish Washerwoman" **$18-22**

Mr. Doctor With Music Box
"As Long as He Needs Me"......**$20-25**

Mr. Fiddler With Music Box
"Hearts and Flowers" **$20-22**

Mr. Guitarist With Music Box
"Johnny Guitar".........................**$20-22**

Mr. Harpist With Music Box
"Do-Re-Mi" **$10-15**

Mr. Lucky With Music Box
"When Irish Eyes Are Smiling" ..**$15-20**

Mrs. Lucky With Music Box
"The Kerry Dancer" **$12-15**

Mr. Policeman With Music Box
"Don't Blame Me" **$30-35**

Mr. Sandman With Music Box
"Mr. Sandman"..........................**$10-20**

Mr. Saxophonist With Music Box
"Tiger Rag" **$15-20**

Mr. Shoe Cobbler
"Danny Boy"............................**$15-20**

Bears and Cubs, 1977, $10-20; Duck Decoy, 1976, $15-20; Leprechaun "Mr." Carpenter, 1979, $20-25.

BICENTENNIAL SERIES 4/5 QT. SIZE

Betsy Ross With Music Box
"Star Spangled Banner" $30-40
Generation Gap
Depicts "100 Years of Progress", 2 oz.
size $30-38
Majestic Eagle With Music Box
"America the Beautiful"............$60-80

C.M. RUSSELL SERIES 4/5 QT. SIZE

Buffalo Man 1976 ....$45-50
Cowboy 1978 ....$30-35
Flathead Squaw 1976 ....$45-50
Half-Breed Trader 1978 ....$40-45
I Rode Him 1978 ....$35-40
Indian Buffalo Hunter 1978 ......$40-45
Last Of Five Thousand 1975 ....$25-30
Northern Cree 1978 ....$35-40
Prospector 1976 ....$30-35
Red River Breed 1976...............$23-30
The Scout 1978 ....$30-40
The Stage Coach Driver 1976..$40-45
The Stage Robber 1978............$45-50
Trapper 1976 ....$40-45

PISTOL SERIES WITH STAND

Civil War Colt 1975 ....$25-35
Dodge City Frontier 1975 ....$25-35
45 Automatic 1975 ....$25-35
German Luger 1975 ....$20-30
Kentucky Flintlock 1975...........$30-35
The Lawman 1978.....................$35-40
The Outlaw 1978 ....$35-40

PISTOL FRAMED SERIES

Civil War Colt 1978 ....$30-35
Derringer – Gold 1978 ....$25-30
Derringer – Silver 1978............$25-30
Dodge City Frontier 1978 ....$30-35
45 Automatic 1978...................$30-35
German Luger 1978 ....$30-35
Kentucky Flintlock 1978...........$15-20
Lawman 1978 ....$15-20
Outlaw 1978 ....$15-20

CHEERLEADER SERIES

Dallas 1979...............................$30-35
Houston 1980 ....$25-30
Rams 1980................................$25-30
St. Louis 1980...........................$25-30
Washington 1980 ....$25-30

CHILDREN OF THE WORLD SERIES

France With Music Box 1979 ...$30-35
Jamaica With Music Box 1979 $30-35
Mexico With Music Box 1979 ..$30-35
Panama With Music Box 1979.$30-35
Spain With Music Box 1979 .....$30-35
Yugoslavia With Music Box 1979
....$30-35

Japanese Bottles

While bottle making in Japan is an ancient art, the collectible bottles now produced are mainly for export. Even though these bottles are available in higher numbers in the American marketplace, prices have remained reasonable.

Daughter 1970.........................$15-20
Faithful Retainer 1970 ....$25-35
"Kiku" Geisha, Blue 13-1/4", 1970
....$20-30
Maiden 1970........................... $20-25
Noh Mask 1961 ....$50-60
Okame Mask 1961 ....$50-60
Playboy 1970 ....$20-25
Princess 1970..........................$50-55
Sake God, Colorful Robe, Porcelain
    10", 1969..............................$20-30
Sake God, White, Bone China 10",
    1969 ....$15-20
"Yuri" Geisha, Pink, Red Sash
    13-1/4", 1969........................$35-45

HOUSE OF KOSHU

Angel, With Book 7 Oz. $5-10
Child, Sitting On A Barrel 17 Oz.. $5-10
Beethoven Bust 7 Oz.................$5-10
Centurian Bust 7 Oz. $5-10
Children 7 Oz. $7-10
Declaration Of Independence $4-6
Geisha, Blue 1969 ....$40-45
Geisha, Cherry Blossom 1969 $30-35
Geisha, Lily 1969.....................$25-35
Geisha, Violet 1969 ....$30-40
Geisha, Wisteria 1969.............$30-40
Geisha, Lavender With Fan 1969
....$45-50
Geisha, Reclining 1969...........$60-70
Geisha, Sitting 1969................$45-50
Lantern – Doro 1961 ....$55-65
Lionman, Red 1967..................$25-35
Lionman, White 1969 ....$35-40

House of Koshu, "Boy," 1969, $20-25.

Pagoda, Green 1969 ....$25-30
Pagoda, White 1961.................$20-25
Pagoda, Gold 1970 ....$15-20
Sailor With A Pipe 1969............$6-10

KAMOTSURU BOTTLES

Daokoru, God Of Wealth 1965 $15-20
Ebisu, God Of Fishermen 1965 $15-20
Fukurokujin – God Of Wisdom 1965
....$15-20
Goddess Of Art 1965 ....$15-20
Golden House 1969 ....$15-20
Hotei, God Of Wealth 1965......$15-20
Jurojin – God Of Longevity 1965 $15-20
Sedan Chair 1966.....................$15-20
Treasure Tower 1966 ....$20-25

Kentucky Gentlemen Bottles

These bottles are similar in design to the Beam and Brooks bottles but are released less frequently. As a rule, these bottles depict costumes of various periods of American history, most notably around the Civil War.

Confederate Infantry Soldier (1969)
In gray uniform with sword, 13-1/2"
....**$20-25**

Frontiersman (1969)
Coonskin cap, fringed buckskin, power horn, long rifle, 14" **$20-25**

Pink Lady (1969)
Long bustle skirt, feathered hat, pink parasol, 13-1/4".....................**$20-30**

Kentucky Gentlemen (1969)
Figural bottle, frock coat, top hat and cane; "Old Colonel", gray ceramic, 14"
....**$20-25**

Revolutionary War Officer
In dress uniform and boots, holding sword, 14" **$20-25**

Union Army Sergeant
In dress uniform with sword, 14"**$20-25**

Lionstone Bottles

Lionstone bottles, manufactured by Lionstone Distillery, incorporate a great deal of detail and realism in their designs. For example, the "Shoot-Out at O.K. Corral" bottle set consists of three bottles with nine figures and two horses.

The Lionstone bottles are issued in series form such as the Sport, Circus, and Bicentennial series. The most popular among collectors is the Western series. Since the prices of these bottles have continued to be firm in the market, collectors should always be on the lookout for old uncirculated stock.

Bar Scene No. 1 1970 ....$125-140	Chinese Laundryman 1969 ......$15-20
Bartender 1969 ....$35-40	Annie Christmas 1969 ....$20-25
Belly Robber 1969....................$15-20	Annie Oakley 1969 ....$25-35
Blacksmith 1973 ....$25-30	Circuit Judge 1969...................$15-20
Molly Brown 1973 ....$30-35	Corvette, 1.75 Liters................$60-75
Buffalo Hunter 1973..................$25-35	Country Doctor 1969 ....$12-18
Calamity Jane 1973 ....$35-40	Cowboy 1969 ....$15-20
Camp Cook 1969 ....$25-30	Frontiersman 1969...................$14-16
Camp Follower 1969.................$25-30	Gambels Quail 1969.................$15-20
Canadian Goose 1980 ....$75-100	Gentleman Gambler 1969 ....$25-35
Casual Indian 1969 ....$8-12	God Of Love 1969 ....$17-22
Cavalry Scout 1969....................$8-12	God Of War 1978......................$35-40
Cherry Valley Club - Gold 1971 .. $25-35	Goddess Of War 1978..............$35-40
Cherry Valley Club - Silver 1971 . $35-45	Gold Panner 1969 ....$15-20

Old Time Steam Engine, 1976, $20-25; Insignia of "I.A.F.F.", 1976, $20-25; Old Time Fire Engine, 1976, $20-30.

Top Row: Proud Indian, 1969, $10-15; Cowboy, 1969, $15-20; Gambler, 1969, $25-35.
Bottom Row: Casual Indian, 1969, $8-12; Cavalry Scout, 1969, $8-12; Sheriff, 1969, $10-12.

Highway Robber 1969 ....$15-20	Riverboat Captain 1969..........$10-15
Jesse James 1969 ....$18-23	Roadrunner 1969 ....$28-36
Johnny Lightining #1 – Gold 1972 ....$50-65	Saturday Night Bath 1976 ....$60-70
	Sheepherder 1969...................$50-60
Judge Roy Bean 1973 ....$20-30	Sheriff 1969 ....$10-12
Lonely Luke 1974.....................$35-45	Sod Buster 1969 ....$13-16
Lucky Buck 1974 ....$35-40	Squawman 1969 ....$20-30
Mallard Duck 1972...................$35-45	Stagecoach Driver 1969........$45-60
Miniatures – Western (Six) $85-110	STP Turbocar - Red 1972.......$25-35
Mint Bar With Frame 1970 ..$700-900	STP Turbocar With Gold And Platinum (Pair) 1972 ....$150-185
Mint Bar With Nude And Frame $1,000-1,250	Telegrapher 1969 ....$15-20
Mountain Man 1969................$15-20	Tinker 1974..............................$25-35
Pintail Duck 1969....................$40-55	Tribal Chief 1973 ....$25-35
Proud Indian 1969...................$10-15	Al Unser No. 1 ....$15-20
Railroad Engineer 1969..........$15-18	Wells Fargo Man 1969.............$8-12
Renegade Trader 1969...........$15-18	Woodhawk 1969 ....$35-40

BICENTENNIAL SERIES

Firefighers No. 1 1972 ....$110-120
Firefighter No. 3 1975 ....$55-65
Mail Carrier 1975 ....$25-30
Molly Pitcher 1975 ....$25-30
Paul Revere 1975 ....$25-30
Betsy Ross 1975 ....$25-30
Sons Of Freedom 1975.............$35-40
George Washington 1975........$20-25
Winter At Valley Forge 1975.....$30-35

BICENTENNIAL WESTERNS

Barber 1976.............................$30-40
Indian Weaver 1976 ....$30-35
Photographer 1976...................$35-40
Rainmaker 1976 ....$22-28
Trapper 1976 ....$30-35

BIRD SERIES 1972-1974

Bluebird – Eastern $18-24
Bluebird – Wisconsin...............$20-30
Bluejay....................................$20-25
Peregrine Falcon $15-18
Meadowlark $15-20
Mourning Doves $50-70
Swallow $15-18

CIRCUS SERIES (MINIATURES) 1973

The Baker $10-15
Burmese Lady $10-15
Fat Lady..................................$10-15
Fire-Eater $10-15
Giant With Midget....................$10-15
Giraffe-Necked Lady $10-14
Snake Charmer........................$10-15
Strong Man..............................$10-15
Sword Swallower......................$10-15
Tattooed Lady $10-15

DOG SERIES (MINIATURES) 1975-1977

Boxer $10-15
Cocker Spaniel $9-12
Collie......................................$10-15
Pointer $10-15
Poodle....................................$10-15

EUROPEAN WORKER SERIES 1974

The Cobbler $20-35
The Horseshoer $20-35
The Potter...............................$20-35
The Silversmith $25-35
The Watchmaker $20-35
The Woodworker $20-35

Capistrano Swallow, 1974, $15-20 (middle).

ORIENTAL WORKER SERIES 1974

Basket Weaver	$25-35
Egg Merchant	$25-35
Gardner	$25-35
Sculptor	$25-35
Tea Vendor	$25-35
Timekeeper	$25-35

SPORTS SERIES 1974-1980

Baseball	$22-30
Basketball	$22-30
Boxing	$22-30
Football	$22-30
Hockey	$22-30

TROPICAL BIRD SERIES (MINIATURES) 1974

Blue-crowned Chlorophonia	$12-16
Emerald Toucanet	$12-16
Northern Royal Flycatcher	$12-16
Painted Bunting	$12-16
Scarlet Macaw	$12-16
Yellow-Headed Amazon	$12-16

MISCELLANEOUS LIONSTONE BOTTLES 1971-1974

Buccaneer	$25-35
Cowgirl	$45-55
Dancehall Girl	$50-55
Falcon	$15-25
Firefighter No. 2	$80-100
Firefighter No. 3	$25-35
Firefighter No. 5, 60th Anniversary	$22-27
Firefighter No. 6, Fire Hydrant	$40-45
Firefighter No. 6, In Gold Or Silver	$250-350
Firefighter No. 7, Helmet	$60-90
Firefighter No. 8, Fire Alarm Box	$45-60
Firefighter No. 8, In Gold Or Silver	$90-120
Firefighter No. 9, Extinguisher	$55-60
Firefighter No. 10, Trumpet	$55-60
Firefighter No. 10, Gold	$200-260
Firefighter No. 10, Silver	$125-175
Indian Mother And Papoose	$50-65
The Perfesser	$40-45
Roses On Parade	$60-80
Screech Owls	$50-65
Unser-Olsonite Eagle	$35-45

MISCELLANEOUS MINIATURES 1978

Bartender	$12-15
Cliff Swallow Miniature	$9-12
Dancehall Girl Miniature	$15-22
Firefighter Emblem	$24-31
Firefighter Engine No. 8	$24-31
Firefighter Engine No. 10	$24-31
Horseshoe Miniature	$14-20
Kentucky Derby Race Horse, Cannonade	$35-45
Lucky Buck	$10-12
Rainmaker	$10-15
Sahara Invitational No. 1	$35-45
Sahara Invitational No. 2	$35-45
Sheepherder	$12-15
Shootout At OK Corral, Set Of Three	$250-300
Woodpecker	$10-15

Luxardo Bottles

The Girolamo Luxardo bottle is made in Torreglia, Italy, and was first imported into the United States in 1930. The Luxardo bottle usually contained wine or liquors, as Luxardo also produces wine.

Luxardo bottles are well designed and meticulously colored, adding to the desirability of this line. Most are figural and consist of historical subjects and classical themes. The most popular bottle, the Cellini, was introduced in the early 1950s and is still used. The names and dates of many of the earlier bottles are not known, due to owners removing the tags. Bottles in mint conditions with the original label, whether with or without contents, are very rare, collectible, and valuable. One of the rarer and more valuable of these bottles is the Zara, which was made prior to World War II.

African Head $20-25
Alabaster Fish Figural (1960-1968)
....$30-40
Alabaster Goose Figural (1960-1968)
   Green and white, wings............$25-35
Ampulla Flask (1958-1959) $20-30
Apothecary Jar (1960)
   Handpainted multicolor, green and black.......................................$20-30
Assyrian Ashtray Decanter (1961)
   Gray, tan, and black $15-25

Autumn Leaves Decanter (1952)
   Handpainted, two handles **$35-45**
Autumn Wine Pitcher (1958)
   Handpainted country scene, handled pitcher......................................**$30-40**
Babylon Decanter (1960)
   Dark green and gold.................**$16-23**
Bizantina (1959)
   Gold embossed design, wide body
....**$28-38**

Baroque gold ruby pitcher, 1958, $15-20; Baroque green and gold amphora, 1958, $20-30; white topaz Majolica pitcher, 1958, $20-30.

Blue And Gold Amphora (1968)
Blue and gold with pastoral scene in
white oval................................**$20-30**

Blue Fimmmetta Or Vermillian (1957)
Decanter....................................**$20-27**

Brocca Pitcher (1958)
White background pitcher with handle,
multicolor flowers, green leaves
....**$28-37**

Buddha Goddess Figural (1961)
Goddess head in green-gray stone
....**$14-19**
Miniature....................................**$11-16**

Burma Ashtray Specialty (1960)
Embossed white dancing figure, dark
green background....................**$20-25**

Burma Pitcher Specialty (1960)
Green and gold, white embossed
dancing figure.........................**$14-19**

Calypso Girl Figural (1962)
Black West Indian girl, flower head-
dress in bright color.................**$20-25**

Candlestick Alabaster (1961)...$30-35

Cannon (1969)
Brass wheels............................**$20-25**

Cellini Vase (1958-1968)
Glass and silver decanter, fancy..**$14-19**

Cellini Vase (1957)
Glass and silver handled decanter with
serpent handle.........................**$14-19**

Ceramic Barrel (1968)
Barrel shaped with painted flowers
....**$14-19**

Cherry Basket Figural (1960)
White basket, red cherries.......**$14-19**

Classical Fragment Specialty (1961)
Roman female figure and vase .**$25-33**

Cocktail Shaker (1957)
Glass and silver decanter, silver
painted top...............................**$14-19**

Coffee Carafe Specialty (1962)
Old-time coffee pot, white with blue
flowers......................................**$14-19**

Curva Vaso Vase (1961)
Green, white, ruby red.............**$22-29**

Deruta Amphora (1956)
Colorful floral design on white...**$11-16**

Deruta Cameo Amphora (1959)
Colorful floral scrolls and cameo head
on eggshell white.....................**$25-35**

Deruta Pitcher (1953)
Multicolor flowers on base perugia
....**$11-16**

Diana Decanter (1956)
White figure of Diana with deer on
black...**$11-16**

**Dogal Silver And Green Decanter
(1952-1956)**
Handpainted gondola..............**$14-19**

Dogal Silver Ruby (1952-1956)
Handpainted gondola..............**$14-18**

Dogal Siver Ruby Decanter (1956)
Handpainted Venetian scene and flow-
ers..**$17-22**

**Dogal Silver Smoke Decanter (1952-
1955)**
Handpainted gondola..............**$14-19**

**Dogal Silver Smoke Decanter (1953-
1954)**
Handpainted gondola..............**$11-16**

Dogal Silver Smoke Decanter (1956)
Handpainted silver clouds and gon-
dola..**$11-16**

Dogal Silver Smoke Decanter (1956)
Handpainted gondola, buildings, flow-
ers..**$14-18**

Dolphin Figural (1959)
Yellow, green, blue..................**$42-57**

"Doughnut" Bottle (1960)........**$15-20**

Dragon Amphora (1953)
Two-handled white decanter with
colorful dragon and flowers......**$10-15**

Dragon Amphora (1958)
One handle, white pitcher, color
dragon......................................**$14-18**

Duck-Green Glass Figural (1960)
Green and amber duck, clear glass
base...**$35-45**

Eagle (1970)..............................**$45-55**

Egyptian Specialty (1960)
Two-handled amphora, Egyptian design on tan and gold **$14-19**

Etruscan Decanter (1959)
Single-handled black Greek design on tan background.....................**$14-19**

Euganean Bronze (1952-1955) .**$14-19**

Euganean Coppered (1952-1955)
....**$13-18**

Faenza Decanter (1952-1956)
Colorful country scene on white single-handled decanter **$21-28**

Fighting Cocks (1962)
Combination decanter and ashtray
....**$14-19**

Fish - Green And Gold Glass Figural (1960)
Green, silver, and gold, clear glass base....................................**$30-40**

Fish - Ruby Murano Glass Figural (1961)
Ruby-red tone of glass.............**$30-40**

Florentine Majolica (1956)
Round-handled decanter, painted pitcher....................................**$20-30**

Fruit (1960)...............................**$10-15**

Gambia (1961)
Black princess, kneeling holding tray
....**$8-12**

Golden Fakir, Seated Snake Charmer With Flute And Snakes
1961 gold **$26-37**
1960 black and gray **$26-37**

Gondola (1959)
Highly glazed abstract gondola and gondolier in black.....................**$21-27**

Gondola (1960).........................**$24-30**

Gondola (1968).........................**$25-30**

Grapes, Pear Figural **$25-40**

Mayan (1960)
Mayan temple god head mask .**$15-25**

Mosaic Ashtray (1959) Combination Decanter Ashtray
Black, yellow, green 11-1/2".....**$15-25**
Black, green; miniature 6" **$10-14**

Nubian (1959)
Kneeling black figure **$15-20**

Opal Majolica (1957)
Two gold handles, translucent top
....**$14-19**

Penguin Murano Glass Figural (1968)
Black and white penguin **$25-30**

Apple, 1960-1961, $25-30; Pear, 1960-61, $25-30; Queen Chess Piece, $75-85; Orange, 1960-1961, $25-30; Banana, 1960-1961, $25-30.

Pheasant Murano Glass Figural (1960)
Red and clear glass on a crystal base
....$35-45

Pheasant Red And Gold Figural (1960)
Red and gold glass bird $40-60

Primavera Amphora (1958)
Two-handled vase shape..........$14-19

Puppy Cucciolo Glass Figural (1961)
Amber and green glass $26-37

Puppy Murano Glass Figural (1960)
Amber glass.............................$26-37

Silver Blue Decanter (1952-1955)
Handpainted silver flowers and leaves
....$22-28

Silver Brown Decanter (1952-1955)
Handpainted silver flowers and leaves
....$26-37

Sir Lancelot (1962)
Figure of English knight in full armor
....$14-19

Springbox Amphora (1952)
Leaping African deer $14-19

Squirrel Glass Figural (1968)
Amethyst-colored squirrel on crystal
base..$40-50

Sudan (1960)
African motif in browns, blue, yellow
and gray..................................$14-19

Torre Rosa (1962)
Rose tinted tower of fruit $16-24

Torre Tinta (1962)
Multicolor tower of fruit.............$18-22

Tower Of Flowers (1968) $15-20

Tower Of Fruit (1968)
Various fruit in natural colors.....$16-24

**Tower Of Fruit Majolicas Torre
Bianca (1962)**
White and gray tower of fruit $16-24

Venus (1969) $15-20

McCormic Bottles

McCormic bottles are similar in design to the Beam and Brooks bottles but are released in limited numbers. The McCormic Distilling Company was purchased by Midwest Grain Products in 1950, and the company discontinued making the decanters in 1987.

The bottles, which contain McCormic Irish Whiskey, are manufactured in four series: Cars, Famous Americans, Frontiersmen Decanters, and Gunfighters. The Famous Americans series has been the most produced and portrays celebrities from colonial times to the 20th century.

BARREL SERIES

Barrel, With Stand And Shot Glasses
1958 ....$25-30
Barrel, With Stand And Plain Hoops
1968 ....$15-20
Barrel, With Stand And Gold Hoops
1968 ....$20-25

BICENTENNIAL SERIES

Benjamin Franklin 1975............$25-30
Betsy Ross 1975 ....$35-40
George Washington 1975........$40-45
John Hancock 1975..................$25-30
John Paul Jones 1975 ....$25-30
Patrick Henry 1975 ....$20-25
Paul Revere 1975.....................$40-50
Thomas Jefferson 1975............$25-30
Bincentennial Set 1976 (All Of The
    Above Figurals).................$250-300
Spirit Of '76 1976 ....$90-100

George Washington, 1976, $20-30; Betsy Ross, 1976, $20-25; Ben Franklin, 1976, $15-20.

Right: John Hancock, 1976, $15-20; Paul Revere, 1976, $20-25.

Below: Patrick Henry, 1976, $15-20; John Paul Jones, 1976, $15-20; Thomas Jefferson, 1976, $15-20.

Bird Series

Blue Jay 1971	$20-25
Canadian Goose, Miniature	$18-25
Gambel's Quail 1982	$45-55
Ring Neck Pheasant 1982	$45-55
Wood Duck 1980	$30-35

Car Series

Packard 1937	$25-35
The Pony Express	$20-25
The Sand Buggy Commemorative Decanter	$35-50

Confederate Series

JEB Stuart (1976)	$55-65
Jefferson Davis (1976)	$55-65
Robert E. Lee (1976)	$50-60
Stonewall Jackson (1976)	$60-65

Entertainer Series

Hank Williams Sr. 1980	$150-175
Hank Williams Jr. 1980	$90-100
J.R. Ewing (1980)	$55-60
Jimmy Durante (1981)	$65-70
Louis Armstrong (1983)	$80-85
Marilyn Monroe (1984)	$600-650
Tom T. Hall 1980	$80-90

Elvis Presley Series

Elvis #1 '77 1978	$85-90
Elvis #1 '77 Mini 1979	$85-90
Elvis #2 '55 1979	$55-65
Elvis #2 '55 Mini 1980	$20-30
Elvis #3 '68 1980	$80-85
Elvis #3 '68 Mini 1980	$50-55
Elvis Bust 1978	$65-70

Elvis Designer I 1981
Music box plays "Are You Lonesome Tonight?"......................$150-160
Elvis Designer II
Music box plays "It's Now or Never"
....$170-180
Elvis Gold 1979 ....$165-175
Elvis Karate $385-390
Elvis Sergeant......................$355-365
Elvis Silver 1980 ....$175-180

FAMOUS AMERICAN PORTRAIT SERIES

Abe Lincoln With Law Book In Hand
....$35-45
Alexander Graham Bell With Apron
....$10-15
Captain John Smith.................$12-20
Charles Lindbergh....................$24-28
Eleanor Roosevelt $12-20
George Washington Carver $28-40
Henry Ford...............................$20-25
Lewis Meriwether $16-20
Pocahontas $30-42
Robert E. Perry $25-35
Thomas Edison $35-45
Ulysses S. Grant With Coffee Pot And Cup $15-25
William Clark $15-20

FOOTBALL MASCOTS

Alabama Bamas........................$26-34
Arizona Sun Devils $39-48
Arizona Wildcats......................$21-27
Arkansas Hogs 1972 ....$42-48
Auburn War Eagles.................$16-24
Baylor Bears 1972....................$24-30
California Bears $20-25
Drake Bulldogs, Blue Helmet And Jersey 1974...........................$15-20
Georgia Bulldogs, Black Helmet And Red Jersey...........................$12-19
Georgia Tech Yellowjackets $15-25
Houston Cougars 1972 ....$20-30
Indiana Hoosiers 1974.............$15-25

Iowa Cyclones 1974 ....$45-55
Iowa Hawkeyes 1974...............$60-70
Iowa Purple Panthers...............$32-42
Louisiana State Tigers 1974 ....$15-20
Michigan State Spartans $15-20
Michigan Wolverines 1974 ......$15-25
Minnesota Gophers 1974..........$8-12
Mississippi Rebels 1974............$8-12
Mississippi State Bulldogs, Red Helmet And Jersey 1974......$12-18
Nebraska Cornhuskers 1974...$12-18
Nebraska Football Player $35-45
Nebraska, Johnny Rogers, No. 1 ....$230-260
New Mexico Lobo....................$32-40
Oklahoma Sooners Wagon 1974.$20-28
Oklahoma Southern Cowboy 1974 ....$14-18
Oregon Beavers 1974..............$10-18
Oregon Ducks 1974 ....$12-18
Purdue Boilermaker 1974 ....$15-25
Rice Owls 1972 ....$20-30
SMU Mustangs 1972 ....$17-24
TCU Horned Frogs 1972 ....$25-30
Tennessee Volunteers 1974 ......$8-12
Texas A&M Aggies 1972..........$22-30
Texas Tech Raiders 1972.........$20-26
Texas Horns 1972 ....$23-33
Washington Cougars 1974......$20-25
Washington Huskies 1974.......$15-25
Wisconsin Badgers 1974.........$15-25

FRONTIERSMEN COMMEMORATIVE DECANTERS 1972

Daniel Boone...........................$15-22
Davy Crockett $17-25
Jim Bowie................................$12-15
Kit Carson $14-18

GENERAL

A&P Wagon $50-55
Airplane, Spirit Of St. Louis 1969
....$60-80

American Bald Eagle 1982......$30-40
American Legion Cincinnati 1986
....$25-35
Buffalo Bill 1979 ....$70-80
Cable Car $25-30
Car, Packard 1980.....................$30-40
Chair, Queen Anne.....................$20-30
Ciao Baby 1978 ....$20-25
Clock, Cuckoo 1971 ....$25-35
De Witt Clinton Engine 1970....$40-50
French Telephone 1969 ....$20-28
Globe, Angelica 1971.................$25-32
Henry Ford 1977.........................$20-24
Hutchinson Kansas Centennial 1972
....$15-25
Jester 1972................................$20-28
Jimmy Durante 1981
  With music box, plays "Inka Dinka Do"
....$31-40
Joplin Miner 1972 ....$15-25
J.R. Ewing 1980
  With music box, plays theme song
  from "Dallas" $22-27
J.R. Ewing, Gold Colored.........$50-55
Julia Bulette 1974 ....$140-160
Lamp, Hurricane $13-18
Largemouth Bass 1982 ....$20-28
Lobsterman 1979.......................$20-30
Louis Armstrong $60-70
Mark Twain 1977.......................$18-22
Mark Twain, Mini.......................$13-18
McCormick Centennial 1956 .$80-120
Mikado 1980...............................$60-80
Missouri Sesquicentennial China
  1970 ....$5-7
Missouri Sesquicentennial Glass
  1971 ....$3-7
Ozark Ike 1979 ....$22-27
Paul Bunyan 1979 ....$25-30
Pioneer Theatre 1972 ....$8-12
Pony Express 1972 ....$20-25
Renault Racer 1969 ....$40-50
San Houston 1977 ....$22-28
Stephen F. Austin 1977.............$14-18
Telephone Operator...................$45-55

Thelma Lu 1982.........................$25-35
U.S. Marshal 1979.....................$25-35
Will Rogers 1977 ....$18-22
Yacht Americana 1971 ....$30-38

GUNFIGHTER SERIES

Bat Materson $20-30
Billy The Kid $25-30
Black Bart..................................$26-35
Calamity Jane $25-30
Doc Holiday...............................$25-35
Jesse James $20-30
Wild Bill Hickok........................$21-30
Wyatt Earp................................$21-30

JUG SERIES

Bourbon Jug $62-70
Gin Jug $6-10
Old Holiday Bourbon 1956........$6-18
Platte Valley 1953......................$3-6
Platte Valley, 1/2 Pt...................$3-4
Vodka Jug..................................$6-10

KING ARTHUR SERIES

King Arthur On Throne.............$30-40
Merlin The Wizard With His Wise Old
  Magical Robe 1979.................$25-35
Queen Guinevere, The Gem Of Royal
  Court $12-18
Sir Lancelot Of The Lake In Armor, A
  Knight Of The Roundtable....$12-18

THE LITERARY SERIES

Huck Finn 1980 ....$20-25
Tom Sawyer 1980.....................$22-26

MINIATURES

Charles Lindbergh Miniature 1978
....$10-14
Confederates Miniature Set (Four)
  1978 ....$40-50
Henry Ford Miniature 1978 ......$10-14
Mark Twain Miniature 1978......$12-18
Miniature Gunfighters (Eight) 1977
....$110-140
Miniature Noble 1978 ....$14-20

Miniature Spirit Of '76 1977 .....$15-25
Patriot Miniature Set (Eight) 1976
....$250-350
Pony Express Miniature 1980 ..$15-18
Will Rogers Miniature 1978 ......$12-16

PIRATE SERIES

Pirate No. 1 1972 ....$10-12
Pirate No. 2 1972 ....$10-12
Pirate No. 3 1972 ....$8-12
Pirate No. 4 1972 ....$8-12
Pirate No. 5 1972 ....$8-12
Pirate No. 6 1972 ....$8-12
Pirate No. 7 1972 ....$8-12
Pirate No. 8 1972 ....$8-12
Pirate No. 9 1972 ....$8-12
Pirate No.10 1972 ....$20-28
Pirate No.11 1972 ....$20-28
Pirate No.12 1972 ....$20-28

RURAL AMERICANA SERIES

Woman Feeding Chickens 1980 $25-35
Woman Washing Clothes 1980 ..$30-40

SHRINE SERIES

Circus $20-35
Dune Buggy 1976 ....$25-35
Imperial Council $20-25
Jester (Mirth King) 1972 ....$30-40
The Noble 1976 ....$25-32

SPORTS SERIES

Air Race Propeller 1971 ....$15-20
Air Race Pylon 1970 ....$10-15
Johnny Rodgers No. 1 1972 .$160-195
Johnny Rodgers No. 2 1973 .....$70-85
KC Chiefs 1969 ....$18-25
KC Royals 1971 ....$10-15
Mohammud Ali 1980 ....$20-30
Nebraska Football Player 1972 $33-45
Skibob 1971 ....$10-11

TRAIN SERIES

Jupiter Engine 1969 ....$20-25
Mail Car 1970 ....$25-28
Passenger Car 1970 ....$35-45
Wood Tender 1969 ....$14-18

Miniature Bottles

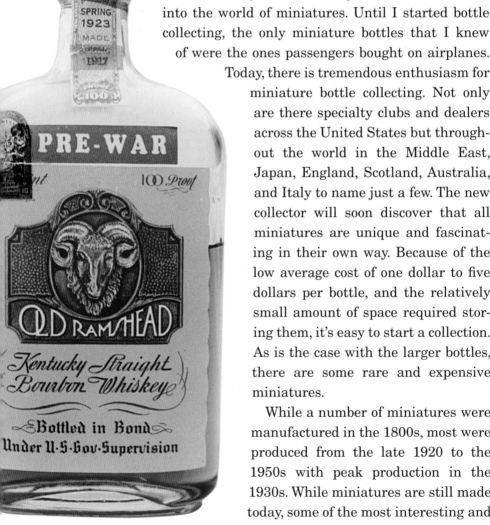

When a discussion on bottle collecting begins, it's clear that most collectors focus their attention on the physically large bottles such as beer, whiskey, or maybe bitters. But there is a distinct group of collectors who eschew big finds and set their sights on the small. Their quest for that special find leads them into the world of miniatures. Until I started bottle collecting, the only miniature bottles that I knew of were the ones passengers bought on airplanes.

Today, there is tremendous enthusiasm for miniature bottle collecting. Not only are there specialty clubs and dealers across the United States but throughout the world in the Middle East, Japan, England, Scotland, Australia, and Italy to name just a few. The new collector will soon discover that all miniatures are unique and fascinating in their own way. Because of the low average cost of one dollar to five dollars per bottle, and the relatively small amount of space required storing them, it's easy to start a collection. As is the case with the larger bottles, there are some rare and expensive miniatures.

While a number of miniatures were manufactured in the 1800s, most were produced from the late 1920 to the 1950s with peak production in the 1930s. While miniatures are still made today, some of the most interesting and sought after are those produced before 1950. The state of Nevada legalized the sale of miniatures in 1935, Florida in 1935, and Louisiana in 1934.

If you are looking for a nineteenth century miniature, you might seek out miniature beer bottles. They are a good example of a bottle that was produced for more than one use. Most of the major breweries produced them as advertisements, novelties, and promotional items. In fact, most of the bottles did not contain beer. A number of these bottles came with perforated caps so that they could be used as salt and pepper shakers. The Pabst Blue Ribbon Beer Company was the first brewery to manufacture a beer bottle miniature commemorating the Milwaukee Convention of Spanish American War Veterans. Pabst's last miniature was manufactured around 1942. Most of the miniature beers you'll find today date from before World War II. In 1899 there were as many as 1,507 breweries, all of which produced miniatures.

Beyond the whiskey, beer, and soda pop bottles identified in this chapter, don't overlook earlier chapters, such as Barsottini, Garnier, Lionstone, and Luxardo, which also list miniatures.

Collecting miniature liquor bottles has become a special interest for other than bottle collectors. A number of the state liquor stamps from the early 1930s and 1940s have specific series numbers that sought by stamp collectors. As a reference for pricing, I have consulted Robert E. Kay's *Miniature Beer Bottles & Go-Withs* price guide and reference manual with corresponding pricing codes (CA-1, California, MN-1, Minnesota, etc).

BEER BOTTLES

PRE-PROHIBITION – CIRCA 1890-1933

Grand Rapids – Brewing Co. Silver Foam – Grand Rapids, Mich. (MI-2)
Embossed and paper label, 5-1/8", Grand Rapids, MI, 1900 ....**$100-150**

Indianapolis Brewing Co. (IN-2)
Paper label, embossed, 4-1/2", Indianapolis, IN, 1890.....................**$30-50**

Pabst Brewing Co – Milwaukee (WI-4)
Paper label, 5-1/2", Milwaukee, WI 1900 ....**$100-150**

POST PROHIBTION – CIRCA 1933-PRESENT

A-1 Pilsner Beer, Arizona Brewing Co. (AZ-3) 1958
Foiled paper label, 4", Phoenix, AZ
....**$5-10**

Acme Beer, Acme Breweries (CA-6) 1940
Decal paper label, 3", San Francisco, CA **$10-20**

Acme Beer, Acme Breweries (CA-10) 1950
Paper label, 4-1/4", San Francisco, CA
....**$5-10**

Budweiser Lager Beer – Anheuser-Busch, Inc. (MO-17) 1950
Paper label, 4-1/4", St. Louis, MO
....**$10-20**

Camden Pilsner Beer – Camden County Beverage Co. (NJ-1) 1940
Decal paper label, 3", Camden, NJ
....**$75-100**

Canadian Brand Cream Ale – George F. Stein Brewery, Inc. (NY-17) 1950
Decal paper label, 4", Buffalo, NY
....**$10-20**

Carling Black Label Beer – Brewing Corp. of America (OH-16) 1950
Paper label, 4-1/4", Cleveland, OH
....**$5-10**

Citizens Beer, Joliet Citizens Brewing Co. (IL-32) 1940
Decal paper label, 3", Joilet, IL
....**$100-150**

Congress Beer – Haberle Congress Brewing Co., Inc. (NY-40) 1940
Decal paper label, 4-1/4", Syracuse, NY **$100-150**

Country Club Pilsener Beer – M.K. Goetz Brewing Co. (MO-6) 1940
Decal paper label, 4-1/4", St. Joseph, MO **$5-10**

Crystal Rock Beer – Cleveland & Sandusky Brewing Co. (OH-23) 1935
Decal paper label, 4-1/4", Sandusky, OH..**$50-75**

Doerschuck Beer – North American Brewing Co. (NY-28) 1940
Decal paper label, 3", Brooklyn, NY
....**$75-100**

Drewrys Beer, Drewrys Ltd. U.S.A. Inc. (IN-6) 1955
Paper label, 4-1/4", South Bend, IN
....**$30-50**

Drewrys Beer, Drewrys Ltd. U.S.A. Inc. (IL-31) 1952
Decal paper label, 4-1/4", Chicago, IL
....**$20-30**

Goebel 22 Beer – Goebel Brewing Co (MI-9) 1952
Foiled paper label, 4-1/4", Detroit, MI
....**$5-10**

Gold Bond Beer – Cleveland Sandusky Brewing Co. (OH-22) 1935
Decal paper label, 4-1/4", Cleveland, OH..**$10-20**

Gluek's Pilsener Pale Beer – Gluck Brewiing Co. (MN-10) 1945
Decal paper label, 4", Minneapolis, MN **$10-20**

Falstaff Beer, Falstaff Brewing Company (CA-16) 1953
Foiled paper label, 3", San Jose, CA **$5-10**

Falstaff Pale Beer – Falstaff Brewing Corp. (MO-23) 1936
Decal paper label, 4-1/4", St. Louis, MO **$10-20**

Fleck's Beer – Ernst Fleckenstein Brewing Co. (MN-2) 1936
Decal paper label, 4-1/4", Faribault, MN..**$10-20**

Hamm's Preferred Stock Beer – Theodore Hamm Brewing Co. (MN-17) 1950
Paper label, 4-1/4", St. Paul, MN **$10-20**

Meister Brau – Peter Hand Brewery Co.(IL-16) 1952
Foiled paper label, 4", Chicago, IL **$5-10**

Prager Beer – Atlas Brewing Co. (IL-25) 1950
Paper label, 4-1/4", Chicago, IL .**$5-10**

Primo Lager Beer – Hawaii Brewing Corp (HA-1) 1940
Decal paper label, 3", Honolulu, HI **$100-150**

Ruppert Knickerbocker Beer – Jacob Ruppert (NY-31) 1955
Foiled paper label, 4", Brooklyn, NY **$10-20**

Schmidt's Beer – Jacob Schmidt Brewing Co. (MN -23) 1955
Foiled paper label, 4-1/4", St. Paul, MN..**$5-10**

Schaefer Beer – The F. & M. Schaefer Brewing Co. (NY-26) 1950
Foiled paper label, 4-1/4", Brooklyn, NY **$5-10**

Schmidt's – The Schmidt Brewing Co. (MI-6) 1950
Paper label, 4-1/4", Detroit, MI...**$5-10**

Stein's Ale – George F. Stein Brewery, Inc. (NY-10) 1940
Decal paper label, 3", Buffalo, NY **$10-20**

Stein's Canandaigua Light Ale – Geo. F. Stein Brewery, Inc. (NY-4) 1950
Paper label, 4", Buffalo, NY **$10-20**

Tip Top Bohemian Brand Beer – The Sunrise Brewing Co. (OH-25) 1939
Decal paper label, 3", Cleveland, OH **$10-20**

Trophy Beer, Birk Bros. Brewing Co.(IL-23) 1950
Paper label, 4", Chicago, IL........**$5-10**

FOREIGN BEER BOTTLES

Milwaukee Brew Cerveza – German Pacific Brewery (Pan -1) 1940
Decal paper label, 3", Panama .**$75-100**

Castle Ale – Rhodesian Breweries Ltd. (RHOD-1) 1960
Paper Label, 4-1/4", Rhodesia .**$10-20**

Castle Golden Pilsener – South African Breweries Ltd. (RHOD-6) 1960
Paper label, 4-1/2", South Africa **$10-20**

Chivo Clausen – Columbia (COLM-1) 1957
Paper label, 4-1/4", Columbia, South America **$10-20**

Superior (Mex – 5) 1958
Enamel label, 4-1/4", Mexico....**$10-20**

WHISKEY FLASKS (CIRCA 1928-1936)

Antique Straight Whiskey (1934) $100

Barclay's Gold Label (1936) $125

Bourbon De Luxe (1932)............... $90

Brigadier (1930)............................. $80

Calvert's "Reserve" (1935) $100

Cedar Arms (1930)...................... $125

Cobbs Creek (1936) $75

Daniel Webster (1933) $100

Four Seasons Brand (1936).......... $75

Golden Oak (1935) $125

Green Mill (1936) $75

Kentucky Boy (1934).................... $100

Kentucky Tavern (1936)................. $75

Major Paul's (1934) $75

Mattingly & Moore (1934)............ $100

Old "73" -93 Proof – Straight
Whiskey (1934)......................... $200

Old 3-G Brand – Straight Bourbon
Whiskey................................... $100

Old Underproof – Kentucky Straight
Bourbon Whiskey $80

Rosemont – Kentucky Straight
Bourbon Whiskey) $125

Royal Oak (1936 .... $80

Atherton, 1932, $25-35.

Black Gold, 1933,
$25-35.

Bond & Lillard,
1933, $25-35.

Three Musketeers, 1933, $25-35; Crown's Old Camel Brand, 1933, $35-45; Nite Club Special, 1933, $25-35.

Deep Springs – Tennessee Whisky, 1935; Old McCall's, 1940; Ben Franklin, 1933, $20-30.

Gallant Knight, 1933, $35-45.

Mount Vernon, 1933, $35-45.

Pre-War, Old Ram's Head, 1923, $50-75.

Old Barbee, 1930, $45-50.

Old Rip Van Winkle, Many Years In The Woods, 1933, $40-50.

SCOTCH WHISKEY

Auld Nicholas	$90-175
Beverages Finest Liqueur	$130-175
Black Horse	$130-175
Black Rod – Grand North Country	$90-175
Campbells	$45-90
Campbelltown	$175-255
Cardow	$250-350
Clangrant	$90-175
Daire's	$130-175
Dalmore – 12 Years Old	$90-175
Gayscot	$175-255
Glencory	$250-350
Glen Grant	$45-90
Golden Drop	$250-350
Henekeys – H.R.H. – Henekeys Ltd	$45-90
Iliska	$90-175
Johnny Lauder's	$130-175
Kingburn	$130-175
Linkwood – 5 Years Old	$90-175
MacLagan's	$175-255
Offiler's	$175-255
Old Argyll	$175-255
Rothsay	$90-175
Royal No. 1	$90-175
Strathglass House	$175-255

Whiskey Nipper, Happy Voyage, 1930s, $45-55.

HAPPY VOYAGE

Whiskey Nipper, Make Him Happy – Give Him A Little Scotch, 1930s, $40-50.

MAKE HIM HAPPY GIVE HIM A LITTLE SCOTCH

SODA POP BOTTLES
(3" TO 5", CIRCA 1930s-1950s)

APPLIED COLOR PAINTED LABEL (ACL)

Canada Dry Water	$10	O-So Beverages	$10
Double Cola	$10	Pepsi-Cola	$40
Hires (RB)	$18	Pioneer Valley	$15
Nesbitt's	$10	Royal Crown Cola	$15

Old Blue Ribbon Bottles

These bottles, containing Old Blue Ribbon liquor, are figural bottles made from 1969 to 1974. They are noted for their realistic depiction of historical themes and railroad cars from the 19th century. In addition, Blue Ribbon is the only manufacturer to produce a hockey series, with each bottle commemorating a different team.

Air Race Decanter $18-26
Blue Bird..............................$14-19
Caboose Mkt...........................$20-30
Eastern Kentucky University ...$15-21
Jupiter '60 Mail Car $13-17
Jupiter '60 Passenger Car $16-23
Jupiter '60 Wood Tender $13-17
Jupiter '60 Locomotive $15-22
KC Royals.............................$19-26
Pierce Arrow $13-15
Santa Maria Columbus Ship....$15-20
Titanic Ocean Liner $100-125

TRANSPORTATION SERIES
Balloon..................................$9-12
5th Ave Bus $14-21
Prairie Schooner.....................$10-11
River Queen $10-15
River Queen, Gold $20-25

HOCKEY SERIES
Boston Bruins $14-18
Chicago Black Hawks..............$14-18
Detroit Red Wings $14-18
Minnesota North Stars............$14-18
New York Rangers...................$14-18
St. Louis Blues $14-18

Old Commonwealth Bottles

The Old Commonwealth brand, produced by J.P. Van Winkle and Son, is one of the newer companies (1974) to produce whiskey in collectible decanters. The ceramic decanters themselves are manufactured in Asia, while the whiskey is produced and bottled at Hoffman Distilling Co. in Lawrenceburg, Kentucky.

Today, most of the decanters are produced in regular and miniature sizes, with the titles of most pieces appearing on the front plaques.

Alabama Crismson Tide 1981
University of Alabama symbol...**$15-20**

Bulldogs 1982
The mascot of the Georgia Bulldogs
....**$40-45**

Chief Illini No. 1 1979
The mascot for the University of Illinois
....**$75-85**

Chief Illini No. 2 1981
The mascot for the University of Illinois
....**$60-65**

Chief Illini No. 3 1979
The mascot for the University of Illinois
....**$65-75**

Coal Miner No. 1 1975
Standard size **$80-100**
Mini 1980................................**$20-30**

Coal Miner No. 2 1976
Standard size **$40-45**
Mini 1982................................**$20-25**

Coal Miner No. 3 1977
Standard size **$80-85**
Mini 1981................................**$25-30**

Coal Miner – Lunch Time No. 4 1980
Standard size **$40-45**
Mini..**$20-25**

Cottontail 1981........................**$25-35**

Elusive Leprechaun 1980 ....**$24-30**

Fisherman, "A Keeper" 1980 ...**$20-30**

Golden Retriever 1979.............**$30-40**

Kentucky Thoroughbreds 1976 . **$30-40**

Kentucky Wildcat.....................**$35-40**

LSU Tiger 1979.........................**$45-50**

Lumberjack **$15-25**

Missouri Tiger **$35-45**

Old Rip Van Winkle No. 1 1974 $40-50

Old Rip Van Winkle No. 2 1975 $35-45

Old Rip Van Winkle No. 3 1977 $30-40

Pointing Setter Decanter 1965 $16-23

Quail On The Wing Decanter 1968
....**$7-12**

Rebel Yell Rider 1970...............**$23-32**

Rip Van Winkle Figurine 1970 ..**$32-40**

Songs Of Ireland 1972.............**$15-20**

Sons Of Erin 1969 ....**$6-9**

South Carolina Tricentennial 1970
....**$12-19**

Tennessee Walking Horse 1977. **$24-35**

USC Trojan 1980
Standard size **$45-55**
Mini..**$10-15**

Weller Masterpiece 1963..........**$26-35**

Western Boot Decanter 1982
Standard size **$30-35**
Mini..**$20-25**

Western Logger 1980 ....**$25-34**

Wings Across The Continent 1972
....**$16-23**

Yankee Doodle........................**$25-32**

MODERN FIREFIGHTERS SERIES

Modern Hero No. 1 1982
Standard size $65-70
Mini...$25-30
The Nozzleman No. 2 1982
Standard size $70-75
Mini...$25-30
On Call No. 3 1982
Standard size $70-75
Mini...$20-25
Fallen Comrade No. 4 1982
Standard size $75-80
Mini...$25-30
Fireman #1 1976..................$110-115
Cumberland Valley
Fireman #2 1978......................$75-80
Volunteer
Fireman #3 1980......................$80-85
Valiant Volunteer
Fireman #4 1981......................$80-85
Heroic Volunteer
Fireman #5 1982......................$75-80
Lifesaver
Fireman # 6 1982......................$75-80
Breaking Through

WATERFOWLER SERIES

Waterfowler No. 1 1978...........$55-60
Here They Come No. 2 1980...$45-50
Good Boy No. 3 1981...............$45-50

Old Fitzgerald Bottles

Old Fitzgerald bottles are manufactured by the Fitzgerald Distilling Co. to package its brands of whiskey and bourbon. These bottles are often called Old Cabin Still Bottles, based on one of the brand names under which they were distributed and sold.

The bottles are issued in both decanter and figural designs in various types and colors portraying various Irish and American subjects. The bottles are produced in very limited numbers.

American Sons 1976................$15-20
America's Cup Commemorative 1970
....$20-25
Birmingham 1972.....................$45-50
Blarney Castle 1970.................$10-15
Browsing Deer Decanter 1967 $15-22
California Bicentennial 1970....$15-22
Cabin Still, Hillbilly 1854..........$75-80
Cabin Still, Hillbilly 1954..........$15-20
Candelite Decanter 1955...........$9-12
Classic 1972.............................$5-10
Colonial Decanter 1969...............$4-7
Crown Decanter..........................$5-9
Diamond 1961..........................$10-15
Eagle 1973.................................$5-10
Fleur De Lis 1962......................$5-10
Gold Coast Decanter 1954.......$10-15
"Golden Bough" Decanter 1971..$4-9
Gold Web Decanter 1953.........$10-16
Hillbilly Pt. 1969.......................$13-18
Hillbilly Bottle 1954 Pt.............$13-18
Hillbilly Bottle 1954 Qt.............$13-18
Hillbilly Bottle 1954 Gal. (Very Rare)
....$60-85

Hospitality 1958.........................$5-10
Irish Charm 1977.....................$20-25
Irish Luck 1972........................$25-30
Irish Patriots 1971...................$15-20
Jewel Decanter 1951-1952.......$9-15
Leaping Trout Decanter 1969..$11-16
Leprechaun Bottle 1968..........$25-32
LSU Alumni Decanter 1970.....$25-32
Man O' War Decanter 1969.....$10-15
Memphis Commemorative 1969
....$15-20
Nebraska 1971.........................$27-32
Nebraska 1972.........................$25-30
Ohio State Centennial 1970.....$20-25
Old Cabin Still Decanter 1958..$16-23
Old Ironsides 1970.....................$5-10
Pilgrim Landing Commemorative
1970.....................................$14-24
Rip Van Winkle – Blue 1971.....$30-40
Sons Of Erin 1969...................$15-20
Tree Of Life 1964.......................$5-10
Triangle – Snowflake 1975.........$5-10

Ski-Country Bottles

Ski-Country bottles are produced by The Foss Company in Golden, Colorado. They are issue in limited editions and offer a variety of subjects such as Indians, owls, game birds, Christmas themes, and customer specialties. Since Foss didn't start manufacturing decanters until 1973, a number of limited editions have high quality detailing. These bottles are rated high on the list of most collectors.

ANIMALS

African Safari Lions 1981
Standard size $65-70
Mini $35-40

Badger Family 1981
Standard size $60-65
Mini $30-35

Bobcat Family 1981
Standard size $75-80
Mini $35-40

Coyote Family 1978
Standard size $60-65
Mini $35-40

Fox Family 1979
Standard size $70-75
Mini $45-50

Jaguar Family 1983
Standard size $180-200
Mini $55-60

Kangaroo
Standard size $40-45
Mini $35-40

Koala $45-50

Raccoon
Standard size $60-65
Mini $45-50

Skunk Family
Standard size $65-70
Mini $35-40

Snow Leopard
Standard size $60-65
Mini $35-40

BIRDS

Blackbird
Standard size $60-65
Mini $30-35

Black Swan
Standard size $75-80
Mini $55-60

Blue Jay
Standard size $95-100
Mini $70-75

Cardinal
Standard size $85-90
Mini $60-65

Condor
Standard size $60-65
Mini $40-45

Gamecocks
Standard size $175-200
Mini $50-55

Gila Woodpecker
Standard size $80-85
Mini $40-45

Peace Dove
Standard size $70-75
Mini $40-45

Peacock
Standard size $115-120
Mini $75-80

Penguin Family
Standard size $70-75
Mini $45-40

Sage Grouse, 1974, $40-50; Red Shouldered Hawk, 1973, $60-70; Peacock, 1972, $80-100.

Wood Duck
Standard size $175-200
Mini....................................$125-150

CHRISTMAS
Bob Cratchit
Standard size $60-65
Mini......................................$40-45
Mrs. Cratchit
Standard size $80-85
Mini......................................$40-45
Scrooge
Standard size $65-70
Mini......................................$20-25

CIRCUS
Clown
Standard size $44-52
Mini......................................$27-33
Elephant On Drum
Standard size $35-45
Mini......................................$35-45
Jenny Lind, Blue Dress
Standard size $55-75
Mini......................................$48-60
Lion On Drum
Standard size $31-36
Mini......................................$23-28

P.T. Barnum, 1976, $30-40; Circus Lion, 1975, $30-35; Circus Clown, 1974, $45-55.

Palomino Horse
Standard size $40-48
Mini $30-40
P.T. Barnum
Standard size $32-40
Mini $20-25
Ringmaster
Standard size $20-25
Mini $15-18
Tiger On Ball
Standard size $35-44
Mini $31-37
Tom Thumb
Standard size $20-25
Mini $16-21

CUSTOMER SPECIALTIES

Ahrens-Fox Engine $140-180
Bonnie And Clyde (Pair)
Standard size $60-70
Mini $55-62
Caveman
Standard size $16-23
Mini $18-22
Mill River Country Club $38-47
Olympic Skier, Gold $85-110
Olympic Skier, Red
Standard size $22-30
Mini $30-35
Olympic Skier, Blue
Standard size $25-32
Mini $35-40
Political Donkey And Elephant $50-60

DOMESTIC ANIMALS

Basset Hound
Standard size $45-55
Mini $26-32
Holstein Cow $45-60

EAGLES, FALCONS, AND HAWKS

Birth Of Freedom
Standard size $85-95
Mini $65-75

Eagle On The Water
Standard size $90-110
Mini $38-45
Easter Seals Eagle
Standard size $48-60
Mini $22-29
Falcon Gallon $350-425
Gyrfalcon
Standard size $54-60
Mini $27-34
Happy Eagle
Standard size $85-105
Mini $80-95
Mountain Eagle
Standard size $130-150
Mini $100-120
Osprey Hawk
Standard size $140-160
Mini $100-120
Peregrine Falcon
Standard size $75-85
Mini $18-25
Prairie Falcon
Standard size $65-80
Mini $35-48
Red Shoulder Hawk
Standard size $60-70
Mini $34-40
Redtail Hawk
Standard size $75-95
Mini $33-40
White Falcon
Standard size $68-75
Mini $30-40

FISH

Muskellunge
Standard size $30-37
Mini $17-21
Rainbow Trout
Standard size $40-50
Mini $24-30
Salmon
Standard size $30-35
Mini $18-22
Trout $27-32

Landlocked Salmon, 1976, $40-50; Trout, 1975, $30-35; Muskie, 1977, $30-40.

GAME BIRDS

Banded Mallard............................$50-60
Chukar Partridge
  Standard size.............................$33-40
  Mini...$16-21
King Eider Duck........................$50-60
Mallard 1973..............................$50-60
Pheasant, Mini $52-62
Pheasant, Golden
  Standard size.............................$40-45
  Mini...$24-30
Pheasant In The Corn
  Standard size.............................$50-60
  Mini...$30-39
Pheasants Fighting
  Standard size.............................$70-80
  Mini...$35-45
Pheasants Fighting, 1/2 Gal
  ....$145-165
Pintail..$76-85
Prairie Chicken $55-65
Ruffed Grouse
  Standard size.............................$40-50
  Mini...$22-28
Turkey
  Standard size.............................$80-100
  Mini...$100-120
Desert Sheep
  Standard size.............................$75-90
  Mini...$25-30

Mountain Sheep
  Standard size.............................$50-60
  Mini...$24-30
Stone Sheep
  Standard size.............................$50-65
  Mini...$27-34

HORNED AND ANTLERED ANIMALS

Antelope $45-60
Big-Horn Ram
  Standard size.............................$65-75
  Mini...$25-31
Mountain Goat
  Standard size.............................$30-45
  Mini...$38-48
Mountain Goat, Gal $525-600
White Tail Deer
  Standard size.............................$30-95
  Mini...$34-40

INDIANS

Ceremonial Antelope Dancer
  Standard size.............................$52-62
  Mini...$36-45
Ceremonial Buffalo Dancer
  Standard size.............................$150-185
  Mini...$32-38
Ceremonial Deer Dancer
  Standard size.............................$85-100
  Mini...$40-48

Ceremonial Eagle Dancer
Standard size $185-205
Mini...$24-34
Ceremonial Falcon Dancer
Standard size $85-100
Mini...$34-45
Ceremonial Wolf Dancer
Standard size $50-60
Mini...$32-40
Chief No.1
Standard size $105-125
Mini...$14-20
Chief No.2
Standard size $105-125
Mini...$14-20
Cigar Store Indian....................$32-40

DANCERS OF THE SOUTHWEST

Dancers Of The Southwest, Set
Standard size $250-300
Mini.....................................$140-175
Arizona Ceremonial Eagle Dancer 1978
Standard Size $100-125
Mini...$20-30
Acoma 1975
Standard Size $40-50
Mini...$15-20
Drummer 1975
Standard Size $35-45
Mini...$15-20
Eagle Dancer 1975
Standard Size $35-45
Mini...$15-20
Hoop Dancer 1975
Standard Size $35-40
Mini...$15-20

Shield Dancer 1975
Standard Size $40-50
Mini...$15-20
Sun Dancer 1975
Standard Size $40-50
Mini...$15-20

OWLS

Barn Owl
Standard size $48-55
Mini...$20-24
Great Gray Owl
Standard size $48-55
Mini...$20-25
Horned Owl
Standard size $60-70
Mini...$70-80
Horned Owl, Gal $700-800
Saw Whet Owl
Standard size $40-45
Mini...$20-25
Screech Owl Family
Standard size $80-90
Mini...$68-75
Spectacled Owl
Standard size $70-85
Mini...$58-68

RODEO

Barrel Racer
Standard size $58-68
Mini...$20-26
Bull Rider
Standard size $42-49
Mini...$22-28
Wyoming Bronco
Standard size $48-66
Mini...$25-35

Soda Bottles
Applied Color Label

Anyone who has ever had a cold soda on a hot summer day from a bottle with a painted label probably didn't realize that the bottle would become rare and collectible. Today, collecting Applied Color Label (ACL) Soda Bottles has become one of the fastest growing and most affordable areas of bottle collecting. This rapid growth has resulted in the Painted Soda Bottle Collectors Association, which is the national collectors group dedicated to the promotion and preservation of ACL Soda Bottles.

So, what is an Applied Color Label soda bottle? The best description is this excerpt from an article written by Dr. J.H. Toulouse, a noted expert on bottle collecting and glass manufacturing in the late 1930s:

"One of the developments of the last few years has been that of permanent fused on labels on glass bottles. The glass in a glass furnace is homogenous in character, all of one color and composition. When the bottles are ready for decoration, the color design is printed on them in the process that superficially resembles many printing or engraving processes. The color is applied in the form of a paste-like material, through a screen of silk, in which the design has been formed. The bottles which contains the impression of that design must then be dried and then fired by conducting it thorough a lehr, which is long, tunnel-like enclosure through which the bottles pass at a carefully controlled rate of speed and in which definite zones of temperature are maintained. The maximum temperature chosen is such that the glass body will not melt, but the softer glass involved in the color will melt and rigidly fuse on the glass beneath it."

The first commercially sold soda, Imperial Inca Cola—whose name was inspired by the Native American Indian—promoted medical benefits. Coca-Cola was developed in 1886 by Dr. John Styth

Pemberton of Atlanta, Georgia and became the first truly successful cola drink. Carbonated water was added in 1887, and by 1894 bottled Coca-Cola was in full production. The iconic shape of the Coke bottle, the hobbleskirt design, was created in 1915 by Alex Samuelson. Numerous inventors attempted to ride on the coattails of Coke's success. The most successful of these inventors was Caleb Bradham, who started Brad's drink in 1890 and in 1896 changed its name to Pep-Kola. In 1898, it was changed to Pipi-Cola and by 1906 to Pepsi-Cola.

The ACL soda bottle was conceived in the 1930s when Prohibition forced numerous brewing companies to experiment with soda. What started out as a temporary venture saved many brewing companies from bankruptcy, and some companies never looked back. From the mid-1930s to the early 1960s, with the peak production in the 1940s and 1950s, many small, local bottlers throughout the United States created bottle labels that will forever preserve unique moments in American history. The labels featured Western scenes, cowboys, Native Americans, aircraft from biplanes to jets, clowns, famous figures, birds, bears, boats, Donald Duck, and even Las Vegas (Vegas Vic).

Since Native Americans and cowboys were popular American figures, these bottles are among the most popular and collectible. In fact, the Big Chief ACL sodas are the most popular bottles, even more than the embossed types. The small bottlers actually produced most of the better-looking labels. in contrast to the largely uniform bottles by major bottlers such as Coca-Cola and Pepsi-Cola. Because these bottles were produced in smaller quantities, they are rarer and, hence, more valuable. While rarity will affect value, a bottle with a larger label is even more desirable for collectors. The most sought-after bottles are those with a two-color label, each color adding more value to the bottle.

Unless noted otherwise, all ACL soda bottles listed have a smooth base and a crown top:

Chronology of the glass package for Coca-Cola, 1894 to 1975, from the archives of the Coca-Cola Company, Atlanta, Georgia

Left to Right, top row:

A. 1894, Hutchinson-Style Bottle. Joseph A. Biedenharn, the first Coca-Cola bottler, began using this bottle in Vicksburg, Mississippi, in 1894.

B. 1899-1902, Hutchinson-Style Bottle. This bottle style was used by Coca-Cola bottlers after November 1899 and before 1903.

C. and D. 1900-1916, Straight-Side Bottle. These bottles had the trademark Coca-Cola embossed in glass. They were designed for crown closures and were distributed with the diamond-shaped label from 1900 through 1916. Both flint and amber bottles were used by Coca-Cola bottlers during this period.

E. Nov. 16, 1915, Hobbleskirt Design: This was the first glass package for Coca-Cola using the classic contour design. It was introduced to the market in 1916.

Left to Right, bottom row:

F. and G. December 25, 1923 (known as the Christmas bottle), and August 3, 1937 (Patent No. D-105529). These two successive designs with patent revisions were used between 1923 (patent date December 25, 1923) and 1951 when the 1937 patent (D-105529) expired. In 1960, the contour design for the bottle was registered as a trademark.

H. 1957. Applied Color Label (ACL). The ACL Coca-Cola trademark was incorporated on all sizes of classic contour bottles.

I. 1961. One-Way Bottle (OWB). The one-way, or no-return glass bottle was later modified for the twist top.

J. 1975. One-Way Bottle (Plastic). This experimental 10 oz. package was made in the classic contour design with twist-top cap. It was tested 1970-1975.

APPLIED COLOR LABEL BOTTLES

A Treat, Allentown, PA
White, 12 oz., 1952.......................**$35**

Aircraft Beverages, Stratford, CT
White and red, 24 oz., 1958..........**$43**

Arrowhead Famous Beverages, Los Angeles, CA
White, 10 oz., 1953......................**$15**

Bauneg Beg Beverages, Springvale, ME
Green and white, 7-1/2 oz., 1944 . **$15**

Belfast Sparkling Beverages, San Francisco, CA
White, 10 oz., 1957......................**$10**

Big Boy Beverages, Cleveland, OH
Red and white, 7 oz., 1947 ....**$15**

Big Chief Soda Water, Natchitoches, LA
Red and white, 8 oz., 1951 ....**$20**

Big Chief Beverages, Modesto, CA
Green bottle with red label, 10 oz., 1956 ....**$300-400**

Blue Jay Beverages, Junction City, KN
Blue and white, 9 oz., 1956...........**$45**

Capitol Club Beverages, Norristown, PA
White, 7 oz., 1954.........................**$15**

Champ of Thirst Quenchers, Philadelphia, PA
Brown, white and yellow, 8 oz., 1960
....**$25**

Chase Flavors, Jackson / Memphis, TN
Brown and white, 10 oz., 1952 .....**$15**

Cherry River Beverages, Richmond, WV
Red and white, 10 oz., 1958 ....**$20**

Chief Muskogee Fine Beverages, Muskogee, OK
Red, black and white, 8-1/2 oz., 1950-52 ....**$30**

Clipper Old Fashioned Root Beer, New Castle, ME
Amber glass with black and white label, 10 oz., 1953 ....**$35**

Daniel Boone Mix, Spencer, NC
Black and white, 7 oz., 1946.........**$12**

Drink–O Delicious, Knoxville, TN
Green and white, 10 oz., 1955-56. **$40**

Simba $10; Sperky $5; Smile $27; Smile $23; Smarty $12; Son-E-Boy $11; Setzler's $5; Stevens $17.

TIP $5; Top's $10; Tecumseh $19; Tom Tucker $41; Ted's Root Beer $20; Tiny Tim $16; Tiny Tim $10; TNT $22.

Duke Beverages, Alton, IL
Red and white, 12 oz., 1954 .... **$75**

Dumpy Wumpy Beverages, Dunbar, WV
Purple and white, 6 oz., 1948 ..... **$150**

Excel, Breese, IL
Red and white, 10 oz., 1961 .... **$7**

Fawn Beverage Co., Elmira, NY
White, 12 oz., 1951 .... **$36**

Fontinalis Berverages, Grayling, MI
Red and white, 8 oz., 1946 .... **$125**

Fox Beverages, Fremont, OH
Red and white, 10 oz., 1963-68 ...... **$5**

Frontier Beverages, North Platte, NE
Brown and white, 8 oz., 1948 ..... **$250**

Gholson Bros. Beverages, Albuquerque, NM
White, 7 oz., 1953-58 .... **$10**

Go – For Brand, Austin, MN
Orange and white, 7 oz., 1948 ...... **$15**

Golden Dome Ginger Ale, Montpelier, VT
Yellow and white, 28 oz., 1948 ...... **$15**

Grantman Beverages, Antigo, WI
Red and white, 7 oz., 1965 .... **$10**

LIX $33; Lane's $5; Lucky Club $25; Lincoln $75; Lemmy $25; Lift $11; Little Joe $11; Long Tom $8.

Ma's $6; Mayville $8; Mid-Valley $13; Mix-Up $7; Mission $6; Oscar's $8.

Hamakua, Paauilo, HI
White, 12 oz., 1941.......................**$15**

Harris Springs Ginger Ale, Waterloo, SC
Green glass with white label, 12 oz., 1938-48..**$70**

Harrison's – Heart –O-Orange, Globe, AZ
Orange and white, 10 oz., 1941 ....**$16**

Heep Good Beverages – Wenatchee Bottling Works, Wenatchee, WA
Green, 7 oz., 1937 ....**$80**

Hy-Plane Beverages, Connersville, IN
Yellow, white, and red, 7 oz., 1945 **$35**

Indian Mound Springs Quality Beverages – Ace of Them All, Bridgeville, PA
Red and white, 7 oz., 1966 ....**$18**

Iwana Beverages, Dover, OH
Black and white, 8 oz., 1944-50 ...**$25**

Jacks – Up, Gillespie, IL
Green glass with white label, 7 oz., 1954 ....**$45**

Jay Cola Sparkling Beverages, Oklahoma City, OK
Red, black, and yellow, 10 oz., 1947 ....**$320**

Jet Up Space-Age Beverages, Grove City, PA
Red and black, 7 oz., 1960 ....**$15**

Johnny Bull Root Beer, Wheeling, WV
Green glass with red and white label, 7-1/2 oz., squat shape 1952-56 . **$170**

K.C. Beverages – Kit Carson Love, Muskogee, OK
Red and white, 10 oz., 1957 ....**$35**

K's Fruit Beverages, Los Angeles, CA
Blue and white, 7 oz., 1944...........**$20**

Kelly's Cream-Top Root Beer, Mishawaka, IN
Red and white, 10 oz., 1953 ....**$45**

King Orange Soda, W. Barrington, RI / Buff, NY
Red, blue, and white, 12 oz., 1941 **$15**

Lammi Beverages, Iron Mountain, MI
Red and white, 7 oz., 1959-1960.. **$20**

Land – O – Lakes Beverages, Paris, MI
White, 7 oz., 1948........................**$10**

Lazy-B Beverages, Fremont, OH
Red and white, 8 oz., 1957 ....**$15**

Lincoln, Chicago, IL
Blue and red, 12 oz., Abe Lincoln with cabin in background, 1957............**$75**

Little Joe, Perry, IA
Green glass with red and white label,
7 oz., 1947 .... **$20**

Mac Fuddy Beverages, Flint, MI
Green, red, and white, 10 oz., 1963 .**$25**

Magic City Beverages, Birmingham, AL
Red and white, 7 oz., 1947 .... **$150**

Maple Spring Beverages, E. Wareham, MA
Red, green, and white, 7 oz., 1962-67
.... **$15**

Mingo Beverages, Williamson, WV
Black and orange, 9 oz., 1922 and
1950 .... **$75**

Mixer Man Beverages, Elkins, WV
White and green, 16 oz., 1955 ...... **$65**

Nemasket Springs Beverages, Middleboro, MA
Red and white, 8 oz., 1948 .... **$70**

New Yorker Beverages, Detroit, MI
White, 7 oz., 1947 .... **$25**

Nezinscot Beverages, Turner, ME
Red, white, and black, 6 oz., 1941 **$10**

Nu-Life Grape – For Better Life, New Orleans, LA
Black and white, 7 oz., 1947 .... **$75**

Old Jamaica Beverages, Waldoboro, ME
Red, 7 oz., 1964 .... **$20**

Old Nassua – Pale Dry – Ginger Ale, Mineola, NY
Green and white, 7 oz., 1947 .... **$20**

Old Smoky Beverages, Greenville, TN
Red and white, 10 oz., 1952-58.... **$35**

Out West Beverages, Colorado Springs, CO
White, 10 oz., 1959-1956 .... **$150**

PA-Poose Root Beer, Coshocton, OH
Red and yellow, 12 oz., 1941-43... **$50**

Pacific (Surfer and Surfer Girl), Honolulu, HI
Green and white, 6-1/2 oz., 1950-53
.... **$50**

Pelican Beverages, Alexandria, LA
Red and white, 10 oz., 1964-70.... **$30**

Peter Pan – Delicious – Refreshing, Buffalo, NY
Red and white, 7 oz., 1948 .... **$30**

Polar Pak Beverages, San Diego, CA
Green and white, 7 oz., 1944-46... **$25**

Quality Flower's Beverages, Charlotte, NC
Blue and white, 10 oz., 1969.......... **$7**

Ralph's Beverages, Zanesville, OH
Red and yellow, 10 oz., 1961 .... **$30**

Red Arrow Beverages – Taste Better, Detroit, MI
Red and white, 7 oz., 1946-47 ..... **$15**

Red Lodge Beverage Company, Red Lodge, MT
Red and white, 7 oz., 1950 .... **$44**

Rocket Beverages, Greeley, CO
White, 10 oz., 1965...................... **$50**

Royal Palm, Ft. Myers, FL
Red and white, 8 oz., 1955-58 ..... **$10**

Sioux Beverages, Sioux Falls, SD
Red and white, 7 oz., 9148-52 ..... **$80**

Sno-Maid, Reading, PA
Green and white, 7 oz., 1966 .... **$25**

Snow White Beverages, Saxton, PA
Green and white, 12 oz., 1961 ..... **$10**

T & T Beverages, Gipsy, PA
White, 7 oz., 1957........................ **$30**

Tasty Maid, Madera, CA
White, 10 oz., 1968...................... **$20**

Uncle Tom's Root Beer, San Bernardino, CA
Red, white, and yellow, 10 oz., 1955
.... **$520**

Variety Club Junior Beverages, Columbus, OH
Red and white, 7-1/2 oz., 1943..... **$60**

Vino – Pride of Florida – Punch, Wildwood, FL
Red and white, 7 oz., 1960 .... **$25**

Walker's Root Beer, Melrose, MA
White, 12 oz., 1949...................... **$35**

Devil Shake $80; Dew $8; Diamond $15; Diet-Way $6; Dodger $6; Double Cola $20; Double Cola $7; Double Cola $5.

Western Beverages, Albuquerque, NM
White, 8 oz., 1947........................**$50**
Zeeh's Beverages, Kingston, NY
Red and white, 12 oz., 1949.........**$35**
Zills's Best Soda, Rapid City, SD

Yellow, 7 oz., 1948.......................**$20**
7-UP – Star Beverage Co. (lady in bathing suit around bubbles)
Amber, 7 oz.., crown top, American 1920-1930...........................**$100-150**

EMBOSSED
ALL BOTTLES HAVE A SMOOTH BASE
UNLESS NOTED OTHERWISE

COCA-COLA

Coca-Cola – Los Angeles (embossed around lower part of bottle)
Aqua, 7", crown top, American 1910-1925.....................................**$100-150**
Coca-Cola – Los Angeles
Amber, 7", crown top, American 1910-1920..................................**$150-200**
Coca-Cola – Richfield, Utah
Clear, 9", crown top, American 1910-1925.....................................**$100-150**

Coca-Cola Co. – Seattle
Aqua, 8", crown top, American 1910-1925.......................................**$75-100**
Coca-Cola – Ten Fl. Oz. – Bottling Works – Rochester NY – 10 Fl. Oz.
Amber, 8", crown top, American 1910-1925.....................................**$300-400**
Coca-Cola – Trade Mark Registered – Boise Idaho
Aqua, 7", crown top, American 1910-1925.....................................**$100-200**

Coca-Cola – Trade Mark Registered – Crown – Bottling Works – Contents 6 Fl. Oz – Cheyenne Wyo
Clear, 7-3/4", crown top, American 1910-1930.............................**$750-950**

Coca-Cola – Trade Mark Registered – Dr. J.C. Bogue – Sherman, Texas
Clear, 8", crown top, American 1915-1930 ....**$100-150**

Coca-Cola – Trade Mark Registered – Pueblo Coca-Cola – Pueblo Colo. – Bottling Works
Clear, 7", crown top, American 1910-1925 ....**$100-150**

Coca-Cola Bottling Co – Las Cruces – Deming – New Mexico
Clear, 8", ABM top, 6-panel arches, American 1900-1915 ....**$100-120**

Coca-Cola Bottling Works – Los Angeles (embossed around the base)
Clear, 8-1/2", CCBW on base, tooled crown top, American 1905-1915
....**$100-160**

Coca-Cola – Denver
Clear, 8-3/4", crown top, American 1905-1916...........................**$150-200**

Coca-Cola – San Francisco Cal.
Clear, 8", tooled top, American 1905-1925 ....**$200-250**

Colorado – Coca-Cola (in script) – Springs
Clear, 9", crown top, American 1910-1925 ....**$150-230**

Indian Rock – Ginger Ale – Coca-Cola – Bottling Co. – Washington N.C.
Light green aqua, 7-3/4", ten-pin shape, crown top, American 1910-1930 ....**$300-500**

Property of Salt Lake Coca-Cola – Bottling Co. – Coca-Cola (in script) – Salt Lake City – Registered
Clear, 8", tooled top, American 1905-1925 ....**$100-150**

Property of – Salt Lake – Coca-Cola (in script) – Bottling Co. – Salt Lake City Utah
Blue aqua, 10", tooled top, American 1905-1920.........................**$325-425**

The Best By A Dam Site – Boulder – Products – Las Vegas Nev (Las Vegas Coke)
Clear, 7-1/2", ABM top, American 1905-1920...........................**$150-200**

The – Coca-Cola – Trade Mark Registered – Bottling Co. – Denver, Colo
Clear, 7", crown top, American 1905-1920 ....**$75-100**

The Salt Lake Coca-Cola Bottling Co. – Red Seal Brand
Aqua, 7-1/2", ABM top, American 1905- 1915...........................**$50-100**

PEPSI-COLA

Indian Rock – Ginger Ale – Richmond – Pepsi-Cola Co. – Richmond VA – 7 Fluid Ounces
Clear, 7-3/4", ten-pin shape, crown top, American 1910-1930 ....**$300-500**

Pepsi-Cola (prototype bottle)
Clear, 7", crown top, American 1906-1910 ....**$900-1,000**

Registered – Pepsi Cola (In script on four of the eight panels)
Clear, 8", ABM top, base reads: Ideal Bottling Works – L.A. Calif., American 1906-1920.........................**$200-400**

Violin and Banjo Bottles

While roaming the aisles of bottle and antique shows, I have often seen a violin- or banjo-shaped bottle on a table, admired its shape and color, then set it back down and moved on to whiskey and medicine bottles. I didn't fully appreciate these uniquely shaped bottles until I attended the June 1999 National Bottle Museum Antique Bottle Show in Saratoga, NY, to participate in a book signing. Before the show, a silent auction was held that included a spectacular display of violin and banjo bottles. At that time, I had the pleasure of meeting several knowledgeable collectors and members of the Violin Bottle Collectors Association and received a short lesson about the characteristics and history of violin bottles. With the help of many dedicated members of the Violin Bottle Collectors Association, we've written a chapter that will assist both the veteran and the novice collector with understanding the fun and collecting of violin and banjo bottles.

While gathering the information for this chapter, it became clear that most bottle and antique collectors and dealers (including this collector) had very little knowledge about violin and banjo bottles and their beginnings. Are they considered antiques? How old are violin bottles? Why and where were they manufactured?

First, most were manufactured in the 20th century, with heavy production beginning in the 1930s. Interestingly, violin and banjo bottles are completely original designs and not copied from any earlier bottle forms such as historic flasks or bitters. This makes these bottles antique in that they are the first of their design and style.

As with other specialty groups, violin and banjo bottles have specific categories, and specific classes and codes within each category. For the serious collector, I recommend *The Classification of Violin Shaped Bottles*, 2nd Edition 1999, and 3rd Edition 2004, by Robert A. Linden and *Violin Bottles, Banjos, Guitars, and Other Novelty Glass*," 1st Edition 1995, by Don and Doris Christensen. Information on the association can be obtained by writing to the Violin Bottle Collector's Association, 1210 Hiller Road, McKinleyville, CA 95519 or by contacting Frank Bartlett, Membership Chairman, at e-mail fbviobot@hotmail.com.

Selection of Bard's Town violin bottles, $50-75 each
Top: Bard's Town, 1939, 5"; Bard's Town, 1940, 4-7/8"; Bard's Town, 1938, 4-7/8"; Bard's Town Bond, 1940, 4-7/8"; Bourbon Springs, 1938, 4-7/8".
Bottom: Bourbon Springs, 1939, 4-7/8"; Old Anthem Brand, 1938, 4-7/8"; Old Bard Brand, 1938, 4-7/8"; Old Fiddle, 1950, 4-3/4"; Old Fiddle, 1950, 4-3/4".

VIOLIN BOTTLES

Category 1: American Styles
LV: Large Violin-Shaped Bottle

FIGURE 1

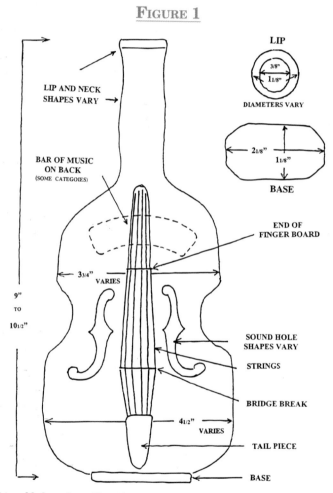

LIP

3/8"

1 1/8"

DIAMETERS VARY

LIP AND NECK SHAPES VARY →

2 1/8"

1 1/8"

BASE

BAR OF MUSIC ON BACK
(SOME CATEGOIES)

END OF FINGER BOARD

3 3/4" VARIES

9"
TO
10 1/2"

SOUND HOLE SHAPES VARY

STRINGS

BRIDGE BREAK

4 1/2" VARIES

TAIL PIECE

BASE

- Eight molds have been identified:
  - Molds 1, 4, and 6: Produced at Clevenger Brothers Glass Works
  - Molds 2, 3, and 7: Produced at Dell Glass Company
  - Mold 5: Maker unidentified
  - Mold 8: Produced in Japan
- Bottles had no contents and were made only for decorative purposes.
- Production began in the 1930s; first identified in the marketplace in the 1940s.
- Height range of 9" to 10-1/4"; body width 4-1/4" to 4-3/8"; 1-1/2" thick near base.
- Colors: amber, amberina, amethyst, blue, cobalt, green, yellowish, and vaseline.

FIGURE 2

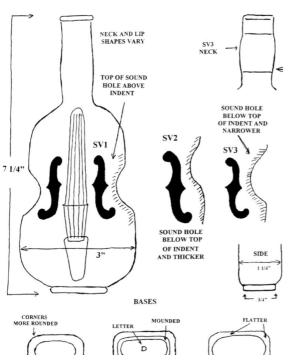

SV: Small Violin-Shaped Bottle

- Three molds have been identified:
  - Mold 1: Produced at Clevenger Brothers Glass Works and Old Jersey Glass Co (a Dell Glass Company)
  - Mold 2: Produced at Dell Glass Company
  - Mold 3: Produced at Clevenger Brothers Glass Works
- Less common than large violin bottles.
- Bottles had no contents and were made only for decorative purposes.
- First identified in the marketplace in the 1940s.
- Height range of 7-1/4"; body width 3"; 1-1/4" thick near base.
- Colors: cobalt, clear, blue, green, amber, and amethyst.

EV: Violin-Shaped Bottle with Tuning Pegs or "Ears" on the neck. (Figure 3)

- Four molds have been identified. Four neck shapes represent four mold patterns and numerals 1-7 are cavity numbers (Figure 4).
  - EVA1 up to EVA7: Each has an "A" neck shape.
  - EVB1 up to EVB7: Each has a "B" neck shape.
  - EVC1 up to EVC7: Each has a "C" neck shape.
  - EVD1 up to EVD7: Each has a "D" neck shape.
- Produced at Maryland Glass Company.
- ABM product (mold line goes up through neck, ears, and lip).
- Bottles had contents such as cosmetic lotion.
- Labeled as flasks, figurals, vases, and cosmetic bottles.
- Production began in the mid-1930s and lasted through the mid-1950s.
- Height 8"; body width 4".
- Colors: blue, amber, and clear.

Violin bottle (EV) with tuning pegs, or "ears," cobalt blue, $10-20.

Violin bottles (EV) with tuning pegs, or "ears," cobalt blue, amber, $10-20 each.

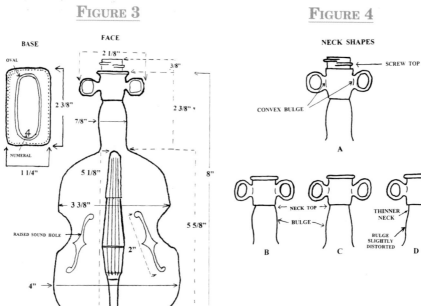

FIGURE 3

BASE

FACE

OVAL

2 3/8"

NUMERAL

1 1/4"

2 1/8"

3/8"

2 3/8"

7/8"

5 1/8"

8"

3 3/8"

RAISED SOUND HOLE

2"

5 5/8"

4"

FIGURE 4

NECK SHAPES

SCREW TOP

CONVEX BULGE

A

NECK TOP

BULGE

THINNER NECK

BULGE SLIGHTLY DISTORTED

B   C   D

FIGURE 5

Dec. 7, 1937.   H. D. HENSHEL   Des. 107,353

BOTTLE

Filed Oct. 19, 1937

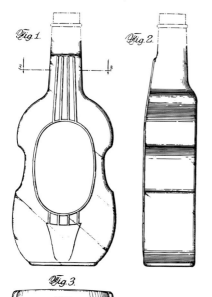

FIGURE 6

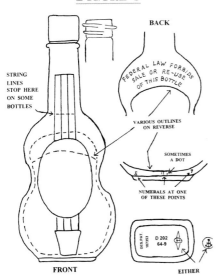

BV: Bardstown Violin-Shaped Whiskey Bottle (Figures 5 and 6)

During the late 1930s, bourbon whiskey was distilled in Bardstown, Kentucky, and distributed throughout the Eastern United States and Canada. Bardstown used several sizes of violin-shaped bottles with attractive labels that became a common identifier until production ceased in 1940. Interestingly, the violin bottle molds spanned 16 years, but the molds were only used for four years. Due to the limited production, Bardstown bottles with full labels are very difficult to find.

- Two molds have been identified (Produced at Owens-Illinois and Anchor-Hocking)
- Mold 1 – Cork Top
  - BVC1: 11", quart
  - BVC2: 11", 4/5 quart
  - BVC3: 10-1/8", pint
  - BVC4: 9-5/8", pint
  - BVC5: 8-1/8", 1/2 pint
- Mold 2 - Screw Top
  - BVS1: 14", half gallon
  - BVS2: 9-1/2" to 10", pint
  - BVS3: 7-3/4" to 8-1/8", half pint
  - BVS4: 4-3/4" to 4-7/8", nip
- Only American violin figural designed and patented specifically with alcoholic content.
- Production began in the 1930s and lasted until 1940 when production ceased.
- Color: amber.

Category 2: European Styles

DV: Definitive violin-shaped bottles.

FV: Violin-shaped bottle embossed "Bottles Made in France" on base.

CV: Violin-shaped bottle etched "Czecho" and "Slovakia" on base.

Category 3: Special Styles

OV: Other violin-shaped bottles, including miniatures.

Category 4: Banjo-Shaped Bottles (Figure 7)

LB: Large Banjo-Shaped Bottles

- Six molds have been identified.
  - LB1: Does not have a base (mold line goes all around the body) and has no embossing
  - LB2: Plain oval base and no embossing. Possible prototype for future models.
  - LB3: Only type produced to contain alcohol. LB3 bottles have the following embossed legend "Federal Law Forbids Sale or Reuse of this Bottle," which was required from 1933 (repeal of prohibition) to 1966.
  - LB4: Minor changes with a "new" face and a clean reverse side.
  - LB5: Same as LB4 with a pontil mark but with the famous base embossing removed.
  - LB6: No pontil marks, since snap case tools were used. Finer and more delicate string and sound hole embossing.
- All large banjos have the same discus body shape, approximate height, width, and neck measurements. (Height 9-1/2"; diameter 5-1/4"; thickness 1-5/8" ; oval base 1-1/2" long by 3/4" wide)
- Production began in 1942 and continued until 1975.
- Produced at Clevenger Brothers Glass Works, Dell Glass Company, and the Maryland Glass Company.
- Colors: amber, green, blue, and amethyst.

FIGURE 7

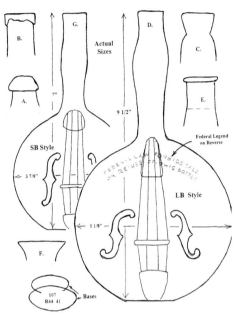

FIGURE 7

SB: Small Banjo-Shaped Bottles

- Two molds have been identified:
  - SB1: Smaller version of LB; height 7"; discus diameter 3-7/8"; lady's neck 3-1/8"; oval base 1-1/8" by 3/4".
  - SB2: Squared sides; height 7-7/8"; discus diameter 4-1/2"; straight neck 3-1/2"; oval base 2" by 1-1/8" with 1" kickup in center of bottle (scarce).
- Produced at Clevenger Brothers Glass Works, Dell Glass Company, and the Maryland Glass Company.
- Colors: amber, green, blue, amethyst

OB: Other Banjo-Shaped Bottles

- Three molds have been identified:
  - OB1: cork stopped whiskey measuring 10-3/4" tall; 5-5/8" wide; and 2-1/2" thick. Embossed on back is "Medley Distilling Company, Owensboro, Kentucky 4/5 Quart." Color: clear
  - OB2: Produced in Italy for 8" to 12" liquor bottles. Base embossing with "Patent Nello Gori." Color: clear
  - OB3: Possible miniature, 4-1/2" tall, cobalt salt and pepper shakers in the image of a banjo. Produced by Maryland Glass Company in the 1930s.

Violin Bottle Pricing

LV1a1 (United Church Bandstand)
Amethyst.......**$150-250**
LV1a2 (Auburn Die Company)
Amethyst.......**$250-350**
LV1a3 (VBCA, 1997)
Cobalt.............**$50-100**
LV1a4 (VBCA, 1999)
Amethyst.........**$50-150**
LV1 (Clevenger)
Blue **$20-30**
Green................**$20-30**
Amethyst...........**$30-45**
Jersey green **$30-45**
Amber...............**$40-50**
Cobalt.............**$50-100**
Amberina **$400-550**
LV2 (Dell)
Blue **$15-25**
Green................**$15-25**
Amethyst...........**$30-45**
LV3 (Dell)
Blue **$15-25**
Green................**$15-25**
Amethyst...........**$30-45**
LV4 (Clevenger)
Green................**$50-60**
Amethyst...........**$50-60**
Amber...............**$50-60**
Cobalt.............**$80-100**
LV5 (Dell Glass)
Royal blue **$50-70**
Clear **$50-70**
Deep green **$90-110**
Golden amber
....................**$100-120**
Yellow **$100-120**
Florescing green
....................**$250-350**

Large violin bottle (LV1a3), cobalt blue, $50-100.

Large violin bottle (LV1), amber, $40-50.

Large violin bottle (LV3), amethyst, $30-45.

Large violin bottle (LV5), yellow, $100-120.

Large violin bottle (LV6), blue, $20-30, green, $20-30, amber, $40-50.

Large violin bottle (LV7), light amethyst, $30-45.

Large violin bottle (LV8), light blue, $60-80.

LV6 (Clevenger)

Blue **$20-30**
Green **$20-30**
Jersey green **$25-40**
Amethyst........... **$30-45**
Amber **$40-50**
Clear **$40-50**
Cobalt **$50-100**
Vaseline......... **$250-350**

LV7 (Dell glass)

Light blue **$25-35**
Light green **$25-35**
Light amethyst .. **$30-45**
Milk glass .... **$400+**

LV8 (Japan)

Light blue **$60-80**
Dark blue **$60-80**
Dark green **$60-80**
Dark amethyst... **$60-80**

SV1 (Clevenger)

Blue **$25-35**
Green **$25-35**
Amethyst........... **$35-45**
Jersey green **$35-45**
Amber **$45-60**

Small violin bottles (SV1), green ($25-35), clear ($45-60), cobalt blue ($45-60), blue ($25-35), amber ($45-60).

Clear **$45-60**
Cobalt **$45-60**

SV2 (Dell)
Blue **$15-25**
Green **$15-25**
Amethyst.......... **$20-30**

SV3 (Clevenger)
Blue **$25-35**
Green **$25-35**
Amethyst.......... **$35-45**
Amber.............. **$45-60**
Cobalt **$45-60**

SV3app (Pairpoint Glass)
Ruby red .... **$60+**

EVs (Maryland Glass Company)
Light cobalt **$10-20**
Dark cobalt **$10-20**
Amber.............. **$10-20**
Clear **$10-20**

DV1 (Unknown)
Blue **$30-50**
Green............... **$30-50**

Small violin bottle (SV2), amethyst, $20-30.

Definitive violin bottle (DV1), blue, $30-50.

Definitive violin bottles (DV 2 and 3), ruby red, $60-100 (each).

Clear	**$30-50**
Amber	**$40-60**
Red	**$80-100**

DV2 (Unknown)
Clear	**$15-25**
Blue	**$20-30**
Green	**$20-30**
Amber	**$25-40**
Red	**$60-100**

DV3 (Unknown)
Clear	**$15-25**
Blue	**$20-30**
Green	**$20-30**
Amber	**$25-40**
Red	**$60-100**

FV1-3 (French)
Clear	**$15-30**
Blue tint	**$40-60**
Green tint	**$40-60**
Light peach	**$50-75**

OV2 (Wheaton)
Clear	**$5-10**
Blue	**$5-10**
Green	**$5-10**

OV12 (George West)
Amber	**$150-250**
Cobalt	**$500+**

OV14 (Stumpy)
Light blue	**$40-60**
Green	**$50-80**
Amethyst	**$50-80**

OV16 (Decanter)
Light blue	**$150-300**
Green	**$150-300**
Amethyst	**$150-300**
Clear	**$150-300**

French violin bottle (FV1-3), blue tint $40-60, green tint $40-60, light peach, $50-75.

Special style violin bottle, amber, $150-250.

Banjo Bottle Pricing

LB1: 9"- No base or embossing, mottled glass, small applied tooled lip. Unknown origin.
Green............**$75-$125**

LB2: 9-1/2" - Oval base, no embossing. Unknown origin.
Blue ....**$40-$70**
Amethyst.........**$40-$70**
Green...........**$60-$100**

LB3: 9-1/2" - 107 R44 41 embossed on base. **"FEDERAL LAW FORBIDS SALE OR REUSE OF THIS BOTTLE"** embossed on reverse. Maryland Glass pre-1966.
Blue ....**$60-$100**

LB4: 9-1/2" - 107 R44 41 embossed on base, strings, and soundholes. Dell Glass 1940s.
Blue ....**$25-$40**
Amethyst.........**$25-$40**
Green..............**$25-$40**

LB5: 9-1/2" - No embossing on base, strings, and soundholes. Dell Glass 1940s.
Blue ....**$25-$40**
Amethyst.........**$25-$40**
Green..............**$25-$40**

Large banjo (LB1-9"), green, $75-125.

Large banjo (LB4 and 5, 9-1/2"), blue, amethyst, green, $25-40.

Large banjo (LB6b), amber
$100-150.

LB6: 9-1/2" - No embossing on base, strings, and soundholes. Clevenger 1940s.
Type E Neck
Blue .... $25-$50
Amethyst......... $25-$50
Green.............. $25-$50
Cobalt .... $75-$100
Flared Lip
Blue .... $75-$100
Amethyst......... $50-$75
Green.............. $50-$75
Amber .... $150-$200

LB6: 9-1 2" – Embossed Slug plate Commemoratives. No embossing on base, strings and sound holes. Clevenger 1970s.

LB6a: Depiction of East Bridgewater Church.
Amber .... $150-$250

LB6b: Just the words "American Handmade, Clevenger Brothers Glass Works, Clayton, NJ."
Amber......... $100-$150

LB6c: Depiction of two glassblowers and the words "Clevenger Brothers Glass Works, American Made Mouth Blown."
Blue .... $75-$100
Amethyst....... $75-$100
Green............ $75-$100
Amber .... $75-$100

LB6d: Bicentennial "Celebrating 200 Years of Freedom 1776-1976."
Green............ $50-$100

LB6: 9-1/2" – Embossed slug plate commemoratives. No embossing on base, strings, and sound holes. Pairpoint Glass 2001.

LB6e: VBCA 2000 Commemorative.
Cobalt .... $45-$65
LB6f: VBCA blank slug plate.
Cobalt .... $45-$65
LB6g: Chelmsford Historical Society/ Ezekial Byam Commemorative.
Teal .... $30-$50
SB1: 7" - Embossed strings and sound holes. Old Jersey Glass/Dell 1940s.
Blue .... $25-$50
Amethyst......... $25-$50
Green............ $75-$100
SB2: 7-7/8" with 4-1/2" diameter disk body, embossed strings, no sound holes. Origin unknown.
Blue .... $35-$60
Amethyst......... $35-$60
Green............ $75-$100

Small banjo (SB1-7"), blue $25-50; amethyst $25-50; green $75-100.

Reference

The information in the "Reference" section has been compiled and updated to help collectors enhance their knowledge and enjoyment of the hobby. For example, a collector at a show often has nothing but a trademark on the bottom of the bottle, but isn't aware of how important it is in the identification process. As you'll read in the "Trademark" chapter, this is an excellent way, and sometimes the only way, to identify the bottle's manufacturer, date of production, and contents of the bottle. In addition, the following glossary, bibliography, and lists of clubs, museums, and auction houses provide invaluable supplementary information.

Trademarks

Trademarks are helpful for determining the history, age, and value of bottles. In addition, researching trademarks will give the bottle collector a deeper knowledge of the many glass manufacturers that produced bottles and the companies that provided the contents.

What is a trademark? By definition, a trademark is a word, name, letter, number, symbol, design, phrase, or a combination of all of these items that identifies and distinguishes a product from its competitors. For bottles, that mark usually appears on the bottom of the bottle and possibly on the label if a label still exists. Trademark laws only protect the symbol that represents the product, not the product itself.

Trademarks have been around for a long time. The first use of an identification mark on glassware was during the 1st century by glassmaker Ennion of Sidon and two of his students, Jason and Aristeas. They were the first glassmakers to identify their products by placing letters in the sides of their molds. In the 1840s, English glass manufacturers continued this practice using a similar technique.

Identifying marks have been found on antique Chinese porcelain, on pottery from ancient Greece and Rome, and on items from India dating back to 1300 B.C. In addition, stonecutter's marks have been found on many Egyptian structures dating back to 4000 B.C. In medieval times, craft and merchant owners relied on trademarks to distinguish their products from makers of inferior goods in order to gain buyers' loyalty. Trademarks were applied to almost everything, including paper, bread, leather goods, weapons, silver, and gold.

In the late 1600s, bottle manufacturers began to mark their products with a glass seal that was applied to the bottle while still hot. A die with the manufacturer's initials, date, or design, was permanently molded on the bottles. This was both efficient and effective because cutting wasn't required, and the mark could be easily seen by the buyer.

Since the concept of trademarks spread beyond Europe, they were quickly adopted in North America as the number of immigrants grew. For many early trademark owners, protection for the trademark owner was almost nonexistent. While the U.S. constitution provided rights of ownership in copyrights and patents, there wasn't any trademark protection until Congress enacted the first federal trademark law in 1870. Significant revisions and changes were made to the 1870 trademark law in 1881, 1905, 1920, and 1946. Research indicates that registration of trademarks began in 1860 on glassware, with a major increase in the 1890s by all types of glass manufacturers.

Determining Bottle Makers and Dates

If you're able to determine the owner of a trademark, as well as when it might have been used, you will likely be able to determine the date of a piece. If the mark wasn't used long, it is much easier to pinpoint the bottle's age. If, however, the mark was used over an extended period of time, you will have to rely on additional references. Unfortunately, most numbers appearing with trademarks are not part of the trademark and, therefore, will not provide any useful information.

Approximately 1,200 trademarks have been created for bottles and fruit jars. Of these, 900 are older marks (1830s-1940) and 300 are more modern marks (1940s to 1970). Very few manufacturers used identical marks, which is amazing, considering how many companies have produced bottles.

Note: Words and letters in bold are the company's description with the trademarks as they appeared on the bottle. Each trademark is followed by the complete name and location of the company and the approximate period in which the trademark was used.

UNITED STATES TRADEMARKS

A

A: Adams & Co., Pittsburgh, PA, 1861-1891

A: John Agnew & Son, Pittsburgh, PA, 1854-1866

A: Arkansas Glass Container Corp., Jonesboro, AR, 1958-Present (if machine made)

A (in a circle): American Glass Works, Richmond, VA, and Paden City, WV, 1908-1935

A & B together (AB): Adolphus Busch Glass Manufacturing Co, Belleville, IL, and St. Louis, MO, 1904-1907

ABC: Atlantic Bottle Co., New York City, NY, and Brackenridge, PA, 1918-1930

ABCo.: American Bottle Co., Chicago, IL, 1905-1916; Toledo, OH, 1916-1929

ABCO (in script): Ahrens Bottling Company, Oakland, CA, 1903-1908

A B G M Co.: Adolphus Busch Glass Manufacturing Co, Belleville, IL, 1886-1907; St. Louis, MO, 1886-1928

A & Co.: John Agnew and Co., Pittsburgh, PA, 1854-1892

A C M E: Acme Glass Co., Olean, NY, 1920-1930

A & D H C: A. & D.H. Chambers, Pittsburgh, PA, Union Flasks, 1843-1886

AGCo: Arsenal Glass Co. (or Works), Pittsburgh, PA, 1865-1868

AGEE and Agee (in script): Hazel Atlas Glass Co., Wheeling, WV, 1919-1925

AGNEW & CO.: Agnew & Co., Pittsburgh, PA, 1876-1886

AGWL, PITTS PA: American Glass Works, Pittsburgh, PA, 1865-1880; American Glass Works Limited, 1880-1905

AGW: American Glass Works, Richmond, VA, and Paden City, WV, 1908-1935

Ahrens Bottling (AB Co. in middle) Oakland Cal.: 1903-1908, listed in business directories as Diedrich Ahrens

Alabama Brewing (W over B in middle) San Francisco: 1899-1906

Albany Brewing (Trade AB Mark in middle): 1858-1918 (business ended with prohibition)

AMF & Co.: Adelbert M. Foster & Co., Chicago, IL; Millgrove, Upland, and Marion, IN, 1895-1911

Anchor figure (with H in center): Anchor Hocking Glass Corp., Lancaster, OH, 1955

A. R. S.: A. R. Samuels Glass Co., Philadelphia, PA, 1855-1872

A S F W W Va.: A. S. Frank Glass Co., Wellsburg, WV, 1859

ATLAS: Atlas Glass Co., Washington, PA, and later Hazel Atlas Glass Co., 1896-1965

B

B: Buck Glass Co., Baltimore, MD, 1909-1961

B (in circle): Brockway Machine Bottle Co., Brockway, PA, 1907-1933

Ball and Ball (in script): Ball Bros. Glass Manufacturing Co., Muncie, IN, and later Ball Corp., 1887-1973

Baker Bros. Balto. MD.: Baker Brothers, Baltimore, MD, 1853-1905

BAKEWELL: Benjamin P. Bakewell Jr. Glass Co., 1876-1880

Baltimore Glass Works: 1860-1870

BANNER: Fisher-Bruce Co., Philadelphia, PA, 1910-1930

Beer Steam Bottling Company (WG & Son in diamond and W Goeppert & Son in middle) San Francisco: 1882-1886

BB Co: Berney-Bond Glass Co., Bradford, Clarion, Hazelhurst, and Smethport, PA, 1900

BB48: Berney-Bond Glass Co., Bradford, Clarion, Hazelhurst, and Smethport, PA, 1920-1930

BBCo: Bell Bottle Co, Fairmount, IN, 1910-1914

Bennett's: Gillinder & Bennett (Franklin Flint Glass Co) Philadelphia, PA, 1863-1867

Bernardin (in script): W.J. Latchford Glass Co., Los Angeles, CA, 1932-1938

The Best: Gillender & Sons, Philadelphia, PA, 1867-1870

B F B Co.: Bell Fruit Bottle Co., Fairmount, IN, 1910

B. G. Co.: Belleville Glass Co., IL, 1882

Bishop's: Bishop & Co., San Diego and Los Angeles, CA, 1890-1920

BK: Benedict Kimber, Bridgeport and Brownsville, PA, 1825-1840

BLUE RIBBON: Standard Glass Co., Marion, IN, 1908

Boca (BOB in a circle in middle) Beer: 1875-1891

BOLDT: Charles Boldt Glass Manufacturing Co., Cincinnati, OH, and Huntington, WV, 1900-1929

Boyds (in script): Illinois Glass Co., Alton, IL, 1900-1930

BP & B: Bakewell, Page & Bakewell, Pittsburgh, PA, 1824-1836

Brelle (in script) Jar: Brelle Fruit Jar Manufacturing Co., San Jose, CA, 1912-1916

Brilliante: Jefferis Glass Co., Fairton, NJ, and Rochester, PA, 1900-1905

C

C (in a circle): Chattanooga Bottle & Glass Co. and later Chattanooga Glass Co., 1927 – Present

C (in a square): Crystal Glass Co., Los Angeles, CA, 1921-1929

C (in a star): Star City Glass Co., Star City, WV, 1949-Present

C (in upside-down triangle): Canada Dry Ginger Ale Co., New York City, NY, 1930-1950

Canton Domestic Fruit Jar: Canton Glass Co., Canton, OH, 1890-1904

C & Co. or C Co: Cunninghams & Co., Pittsburgh, PA, 1880-1907

C. Beck, Santa Cruz: (Big Trees Brewery), 1894-1917

CCCo: Carl Conrad & Co., St. Louis, MO, (Beer), 1860-1883

C.V.Co. No. 1 & No 2: Milwaukee, WI, 1880-1881

C C Co.: Carl Conrad & Co., St. Louis, MO, 1876-1883

C C G Co.: Cream City Glass Co., Milwaukee, WI, 1888-1894

C.F.C.A.: California Fruit Canners Association, Sacramento, CA, 1899-1916

CFJCo: Consolidated Fruit Jar Co., New Brunswick, NJ, 1867-1882

C G I: California Glass Insulator Co., Long Beach, CA, 1912-1919

C G M Co: Campbell Glass Manufacturing Co., West Berkeley, CA, 1885

C G W: Campbell Glass Works, West Berkeley, CA, 1884-1885

C & H: Coffin & Hay, Hammonton, NJ, 1836-1838, or Winslow, NJ, 1838-1842

C & I: Cunningham & Ihmsen, Pittsburgh, PA, 1865-1879

C V No 2 – MILW: Chase Valley Glass Co. No 2, Milwaukee, WI, 1880-1881

C L G Co.: Carr-Lowrey Glass Co., Baltimore, MD, 1889-1920

CLARKE: Clarke Fruit Jar Co., Cleveland, OH, 1886-1889

CLIMAX: Fisher-Bruce Co, Philadelphia, PA, 1910-1930

CLOVER LEAF (In arch with picture of a clover leaf): 1890 (marked on ink and mucilage bottles)

Clyde, N. Y.: Clyde Glass Works, Clyde, NY, 1870-1882

The Clyde (in script): Clyde Glass Works, Clyde, NY, 1895

C. Milw: Chase Valley Glass Co., Milwaukee, WI, 1880-1881

Cohansey: Cohansey Glass Manufacturing Co., Philadelphia, PA, 1870-1900

CO-SHOE: Coshocton Glass Corp., Coshocton, OH, 1923-1928

C R: Curling, Robertson & Co., Pittsburgh, PA, 1834-1857, or Curling, Ringwalt & Co., Pittsburgh, PA, 1857-1863

CRYSTO: McPike Drug Co., Kansas City, MO, 1904

D

D 446: Consolidated Fruit Jar Co., New Brunswick, NJ, 1871-1882

DB: Du Bois Brewing Co., Pittsburgh, PA, 1918

Dexter: Franklin Flint Glass Works, Philadelphia, PA, 1861-1880

Diamond: (Plain) Diamond Glass Co., 1924-Present

The Dictator: William McCully & Co., Pittsburgh, PA, 1855-1869

Dictator: William McCully & Co., Pittsburgh, PA, 1869-1885

D & O: Cumberland Glass Mfg. Co., Bridgeton, NJ, 1890-1900

D O C: D.O. Cunningham Glass Co., Pittsburgh, PA, 1883-1937

DOME: Standard Glass Co., Wellsburg, WV, 1891-1893

D S G Co.: De Steiger Glass Co., LaSalle, IL, 1879-1896

Duffield: Dr. Samuel Duffield, Detroit, MI, 1862-1866, and Duffield, Parke & Co., Detroit, MI, 1866-1875

Dyottsville: Dyottsville Glass Works, Philadelphia, PA, 1833-1923

E

E4: Essex Glass Co., Mt. Vernon, OH, 1906-1920

Economy (in script) TRADE MARK: Kerr Glass Manufacturing Co., Portland, OR, 1903-1912

Electric Trade Mark (in script): Gayner Glass Works, Salem, NJ, 1910

Electric Trade Mark: Gayner Glass Works, Salem, NJ, 1900-1910

Erd & Co., E R Durkee: E.R. Durkee & Co., New York, NY, Post-1874

The EMPIRE: Empire Glass Co., Cleveland, NY, 1852-1877

E R Durkee & Co: E.R. Durkee & Co., New York, NY, 1850-1860

Eureka 17: Eurkee Jar Co., Dunbar, WV, 1864

Eureka (in script): Eurkee Jar Co., Dunbar, WV, 1900-1910

Everett and EHE: Edward H. Everett Glass Co. (Star Glass Works), Newark, OH, 1893-1904

Everlasting (in script) JAR: Illinois Pacific Glass Co., San Francisco, CA, 1904

E W & Co: E. Wormser & Co., Pittsburgh, PA, 1857-1875

F

F (inside a jar outline or keystone): C.L. Flaccus Glass Co., Pittsburgh, PA, 1900-1928

F WM. Frank & Sons: WM. Frank & Co., Pittsburgh, PA, 1846-1966, WM. Frank & Sons, Pittsburgh, PA, 1866-1876

F & A: Fahnstock & Albree, Pittsburgh, PA, 1860-1862

FERG Co: F.E. Reed Glass Co., Rochester, NY, 1898-1947

FF & Co: Fahnstock, Fortune & Co., Pittsburgh, PA, 1866-1873

F G: Florida Glass Manufacturing Co., Jacksonville, FL, 1926-1947

FL or FL & Co.: Frederick Lorenz & Co., Pittsburgh, PA, 1819-1841

FLINT–GREEN: Whitney Glass Works, Glassborough, NJ, 1888

FOLGER, JAF&Co., Pioneer, Golden Gate: J. A. Folger & Co., San Francisco, CA, 1850-Present

G

G in circle (bold lines): Gulfport Glass Co., Gulfport, MS, 1955-1970

G E M: Hero Glass Works, Philadelphia, PA, 1884-1909

G & H: Gray & Hemingray, Cincinnati, OH, 1848-1851; Covington, KY, 1851-1864

G & S: Gillinder & Sons, Philadelphia, PA, 1867-1871 and 1912-1930

Geo. Braun Bottler (C over B in arrowhead in middle) 2219 Pine St. S.F.: 1893-1906

Gillinder: Gillinder Bros., Philadelphia, PA, 1871-1930

Gilberds: Gilberds Butter Tub Co., Jamestown, NY, 1883-1890

GLENSHAW (G in a box underneath name): Glenshaw Glass Co., Glenshaw, PA, 1904

GLOBE: Hemingray Glass Co., Covington, KY (the symbol "Parquet-Lac" was used beginning in 1895)–1886

Greenfield: Greenfield Fruit Jar & Bottle Co., Greenfield, IN, 1888-1912

G W K & Co.: George W. Kearns & Co., Zanesville, OH, 1848-1911

H

H and H (in heart): Hart Glass Manufacturing Co., Dunkirk, IN, 1918-1938

H (with varying numerals): Holt Glass Works, West Berkeley, CA, 1893-1906

H (in a diamond): A.H. Heisey Glass Co., Oakwood Ave., Newark, OH, 1893-1958

H (in a triangle): J. T. & A. Hamilton Co., Pittsburgh, PA, 1900

Hamilton: Hamilton Glass Works, Hamilton, Ontario, Canada, 1865-1872

Hansen & Kahler (H & K in middle) Oakland Cal.: 1897-1908

Hazel: Hazel Glass Co., Wellsburg, WV, 1886-1902

H.B.Co: Hagerty Bros. & Co., Brooklyn, NY, 1880-1900

Helme: Geo. W. Helme Co., Jersey City, NJ, 1870-1895

Hemingray: Hemingray Brothers & Co. and later Hemingray Glass Co., Covington, KY, 1864-1933

Henry Braun (beer bottler in middle) Oakland Cal.: 1887-1896

H. J. Heinz: H.J. Heinz Co., Pittsburgh, PA, 1860-1869

Heinz & Noble: H.J. Heinz Co., Pittsburgh, PA, 1869-1872

F. J. Heinz: H.J. Heinz Co., Pittsburgh, PA, 1876-1888

H. J. Heinz Co.: H.J. Heinz Co., Pittsburgh, PA, 1888-Present

HELME: Geo. W. Helme Co., NJ, 1870-1890

HERO: Hero Glass Works, Philadelphia, PA, 1856-1884 and Hero Fruit Jar Co., Philadelphia, PA, 1884-1909

H F J Co (in wings of Maltese cross): Hero Glass Works, 1884-1900

HP (close together in circle): Keene Glass Works, Keene, NH, 1817-1822

HS (in a circle): Twitchell & Schoolcraft, Keene, NH, 1815-1816

I

IDEAL: Hod c. Dunfee, Charleston, WV, 1910

I G Co.: Ihmsen Glass Co., Pittsburgh, PA, 1855-1896

I. G. Co: Ihmsen Glass Co., 1895

I. G. Co.: Monogram, Ill. Glass Co. on fruit jar, 1914

IPGCO: Ill. Pacific Glass Company, San Francisco, CA, 1902-1926

IPGCO (in diamond): Ill. Pacific Glass Company, San Francisco, CA, 1902-1926

IG: Illinois Glass, F inside a jar outline, C. L. Flaccus 1/2 glass 1/2 co., Pittsburgh, PA, 1900-1928

Ill. Glass Co.: 1916-1929

I G: Illinois Glass Co., Alton, IL, before 1890

I G Co. (in a diamond): Illinois Glass Co., Alton, IL, 1900-1916

Improved G E M: Hero Glass Works, Philadelphia, PA, 1868

I P G: Illinois Pacific Glass Co. San Francisco, CA, 1902-1932

I X L: I X L Glass Bottle Co., Inglewood, CA, 1921-1923

J

J (in keystone): Knox Glass Bottle Co. of Miss., Jackson, MS, 1932-1953

J (in square): Jeannette Glass Co., Jeannette, PA, 1901-1922

JAF & Co., Pioneer and Folger: J.A. Folger & Co., San Francisco, CA, 1850-Present

J D S: John Duncan & Sons, New York, NY, 1880-1900

J. P. F.: Pitkin Glass Works, Manchester, CT, 1783-1830

J R: Stourbridge Flint Glass Works, Pittsburgh, PA, 1823-1828

JBS monogram: Joseph Schlitz Brewing Co., Milwaukee, WI, 1900

JT: Mantua Glass Works, later Mantua Glass Co., Mantua, OH, 1824

JT & Co: Brownsville Glass Works, Brownsville, PA, 1824-1828

J. SHEPARD: J. Shepart & Co., Zanesville, OH, 1823-1838

K

K (in keystone): Knox Glass Bottle Co., Knox, PA, 1924-1968

Kensington Glass Works: Kensington Glass Works, Philadelphia, PA, 1822-1932

Kerr (in script): Kerr Glass Manufacturing Co. and later Alexander H. Kerr Glass Co., Portland, OR; Sand Spring, OK; Chicago, IL; Los Angeles, CA, 1912-Present

K H & G: Kearns, Herdman & Gorsuch, Zanesville, OH, 1876-1884

K & M: Knox & McKee, Wheeling, WV, 1824-1829

K & O: Kivlan & Onthank, Boston, MA, 1919-1925

KO – HI: Koehler & Hinrichs, St. Paul, MN, 1911

K Y G W and KYGW Co: Kentucky Glass Works Co., Louisville, KY, 1849-1855

L

L (in keystone): Lincoln Glass Bottle Co., Lincoln, IL, 1942-1952

L: W.J. Latchford Glass Co., Los Angeles, CA, 1925-1938

Lamb: Lamb Glass Co., Mt. Vernon, OH, 1855-1964

LB (B inside L): Long Beach Glass Co., Long Beach, CA, 1920-1933

L. G. (with periods): Liberty Glass Co., 1924-1946

L-G (with hyphen): Liberty Glass Co., 1946-1954

L G (with no punctuation): Liberty Glass Co., since 1954

L & W: Lorenz & Wightman, PA, 1862-1871

LGW: Laurens Glass Works, Laurens, SC, 1911-1970

L G Co: Louisville Glass Works, Louisville, KY, 1880

Lightning: Henry W. Putnam, Bennington, VT, 1875-1890

LP (in keystone): Pennsylvania Bottle Co., Wilcox, PA, 1940-1952

L K Y G W: Louisville Kentucky Glass Works, Louisville, KY, 1873-1890

M

"Mascot, "Mason" and M F G Co.: Mason Fruit Jar Co., Philadelphia, PA, 1885-1890

Mastadon: Thomas A. Evans Mastadon Works, and later Wm. McCully & Co. Pittsburgh, PA, 1855-1887

MB Co: Muncie Glass Co., Muncie, IN, 1895-1910

M B & G Co: Massillon Bottle & Glass Co., Massillon, OH, 1900-1904

M B W: Millville Bottle Works, Millville, NJ, 1903-1930

M. Casey, Gilroy Brewery Cal.: Chicago Bottle Works, San Francisco, CA, 1896-1906

McL (in circle): McLaughlin Glass Co., Vernon, CA, 1920-1936, Gardena, CA, 1951-1956

MEDALLION: M.S. Burr & Co., Boston, MA (mfgr. of nursing bottles), 1874

M (in keystone): Metro Glass Bottle Co., Jersey City, NJ, 1935-1949

MG: Straight letters 1930-1940; slanted letters, Maywood Glass, Maywood, CA, 1940-1958

M.G. CO.: Modes Glass Co., Cicero, IN, 1895-1904

M. G. W.: Middletown Glass Co., NY, 1889

Moore Bros.: Moore Bros., Clayton, NJ, 1864-1880

MOUNT VERNON: Cook & Bernheimer Co., New York, NY, 1890

N

N (in keystone): Newborn Glass Co., Royersford, PA, 1920-1925

N: H. Northwood Glass Co., Wheeling, WV, 1902-1925

N (bold N in bold square): Obear-Nester Glass Co., St. Louis, Missouri and East St. Louis, IL, 1895

N 17: American Bottle Co., Toledo, OH, Div. of Owens Bottle Co., 1917-1929

N B B G Co: North Baltimore Bottle Glass Co., North Baltimore, OH, 1885-1930

N. Cervelli (N over C in middle) 615 Francisco ST. S.F.: 1898-1906

N G Co: Northern Glass Co., Milwaukee, WI, 1894-1896

N - W: Nivison-Weiskopf Glass Co., Reading, OH, 1900-1931

O

O (in a square): Owen Bottle Co., 1911-1929

O B C: Ohio Bottle Co., Newark, OH, 1904-1905

O-D-1-O & Diamond & I: Owens Ill. Pacific Coast Co., CA, 1932-1943. Mark of Owens-Ill. Glass Co. merger in 1930

O G W: Olean Glass Co. (Works), Olean, NY, 1887-1915

O (in keystone): Oil City Glass Co., Oil City, PA, 1920-1925

OSOTITE (in elongated diamond): Warren Fruit Jar Co., Fairfield, IA, 1910

O-U-K I D: Robert A Vancleave, Philadelphia, PA, 1909

P

P (in keystone): Wightman Bottle & Glass Co., Parker Landing, PA, 1930-1951

PCGW: Pacific Coast Glass Works, San Francisco, CA, 1902-1924

PEERLESS: Peerless Glass Co., Long Island City, NY, 1920-1935 (was Bottler's & Manufacturer's Supply Co., 1900-1920)

P G W: Pacific Glass Works, San Francisco, CA, 1862-1876

Picture of young child in circle: M.S. Burr & Co., Boston, MA (mfgr. of nursing bottles), 1874

Premium: Premium Glass Co., Coffeyville, KS, 1908-1914

P in square or pine in box: Pine Glass Corp., Okmulgee, OK, 1927-1929

P S: Puget Sound Glass Co., Anacortes, WA, 1924-1929

Putnam Glass Works (in a circle): Putnam Flint Glass Works, Putnam, OH, 1852-1871

P & W: Perry & Wood and later Perry & Wheeler, Keene, NH, 1822-1830

Q

Queen (in script) Trade Mark (all in a shield): Smalley, Kivian & Onthank, Boston, MA, 1906-1919

R

Rau's: Fairmount Glass Works, Fairmount, IN, 1898-1908

R & C Co: Roth & Co., San Francisco, CA, 1879-1888

Red (with a key through it): Safe Glass Co., Upland, IN, 1892-1898

R G Co.: Renton Glass Co., Renton, WA, 1911

Root: Root Glass Co., Terre Haute, IN, 1901-1932

S

S (in a side of a start): Southern Glass Co., L.A., 1920-1929

S (in a triangle): Schloss Crockery Co., San Francisco, CA, 1910

S (in keystone): Seaboard Glass Bottle Co. Pittsburgh, PA, 1943-1947

SB & GCo: Streator Bottle & Glass Co., Streator, IL, 1881-1905

SF & PGW: San Francisco & Pacific Glass Works, San Francisco, CA, 1876-1900

S & C: Stebbins & Chamberlain or Coventry Glass Works, Coventry, CT, 1825-1830

S F G W: San Francisco Glass Works, San Francisco, CA, 1869-1876

SIGNET (blown in bottom): Chicago Heights Bottle Co., Chicago, Heights, IL, 1913

Squibb: E.R. Squibb, M.D., Brooklyn, NY, 1858-1895

Standard (in script, Mason): Standard Coop. Glass Co., and later Standard Glass Co., Marion, IN, 1894-1932

Star Glass Co: Star Glass Co., New Albany, IN, 1867-1900

Swayzee: Swayzee Glass Co. Swayzee, IN, 1894-1906

T

T (in keystone): Knox Glass Bottle Co. of Miss., Palestine, TX, 1941-1953

T C W: T.C. Wheaton Co., Millville, NJ, 1888-Present

THE BEST (in an arch): Gotham Co., New York, NY, 1891

TIP TOP: Charles Boldt Glass Co., Cincinnati, OH, 1904

T W & Co.: Thomas Wightman & Co., Pittsburgh, PA, 1871-1895

T S: Coventry Glass Works, Coventry, CT, 1820-1824

U

U: Upland Flint Bottle Co., Upland, Inc., 1890-1909

U in Keystone: Pennsylvania Bottle Co., Sheffield, PA, 1929-1951

U S: United States Glass Co., Pittsburgh, PA, 1891-1938, Tiffin, OH, 1938-1964

W

WARRANTED (in arch) FLASK: Albert G. Smalley, Boston, MA, 1892

W & CO: Thomas Wightman & Co., Pittsburgh, PA, 1880-1889

W C G Co: West Coast Glass Co., Los Angeles, CA, 1908-1930

WF & S MILW: William Franzen & Son, Milwaukee, WI, 1900-1929

W G W: Woodbury Glass Works, Woodbury, NJ, 1882-1900

WYETH: Drug manufacturer, 1880-1910

W. T. & Co. (in rectangle): Whitall-Tatum & Co., Millville, NJ, 1875-1885

W.T. & Co. - E (in small rectangle within big rectangle): Whitall Tatum, Millville, NJ, 1885-1895

W.T. & Co. – C – U.S.A. (in small rectangle within big rectangle): Whitall Tatum, Millville, NJ, 1891-1984

W.T. & Co. – U.S.A. (in small rectangle within big rectangle): Whitall Tatum, Millville, NJ, 1890-1901

W T R Co.: W.T. Rawleigh Manufacturing Co., Freeport, IL, 1925-1936

FOREIGN TRADEMARKS

A (in a circle): Alembic Glass Industries, Bangalore, India

Big A (in center of it GM): Australian Glass Mfg. Co. Kilkenny, So. Australia

A.B.C.: Albion Bottle Co. Ltd., Oldbury, Nr. Birmingham, England

A.G.W.: Alloa Glass Limited, Alloa, Scotland

A G B Co.: Albion Glass Bottle Co., England; trademark is found under Lea & Perrins, 1880-1900

B & C Co. L: Bagley & Co. Ltd., Est. 1832, England (still operating)

AVH: A. Van Hoboken & Co., Rotterdam, the Netherlands, 1800-1898

Beaver: Beaver Flint Glass Co., Toronto, Ontario, Canada, 1897-1920

Bottle (in frame): Veb Glasvoerk Drebkau Drebkau, N. L., Germany

Crown with three dots: Crown Glass, Waterloo, N.S., Wales

Crown (with figure of a crown): Excelsior Glass Co., St. Johns, Quebec and later Diamond glass Co., Montreal, Quebec, Canada, 1879-1913

CS & Co.: Cannington, Shaw & Co., St. Helens, England, 1872-1916

CSTS (in center of hot air balloon): C. Stolzles Sohne Actiengeselischaft fur Glasfabrikation, Vienna, Austria, Hungary, 1905

D (in center of a diamond): Dominion Glass Co., Montreal, Quebec, Canada

D.B. (in a book frame): Dale Brown & Co., Ltd., Mesborough, Yorks, England

Fish: Veb Glasvoerk Stralau, Berlin, Germany

Excelsior: Excelsior Glass Co., St. John, Quebec, Canada, 1878-1883

HH: Werk Hermannshutte, Czechoslovakia

Hamilton: Hamilton Glass Works, Hamilton, Ontario, Canada, 1865-1872

Hat: Brougba, Bulgaria

Hunyadi Janos: Andreas Saxlehner, Buda-Pesth, Austria-Hungary, 1863-1900

IYGE (all in a circle): The Irish Glass Bottle, Ltd. Dublin, Ireland

KH: Kastrupog Holmeqaads, Copenhagen, Denmark

L (on a bell): Lanbert S.A., Belgium

LIP: Lea & Perrins, London, England, 1880-1900

LS (in a circle): Lax & Shaw, Ltd., Leeds, York, England

M (in a circle): Cristales Mexicanos, Monterey, Mexico

N (in a diamond): Tippon Glass Co., Ltd. Tokyo, Japan

NAGC: North American Glass Co., Montreal, Quebec, Canada, 1883-1890

NP: Imperial Trust for the Encouragement of Scientific and Industrial Research, London, England, 1907

NS (in middle of bottle shape): Edward Kavalier of Neu Sazawa, Austria-Hungary, 1910

P & J A: P. & J. Arnold, LTD., London, England, 1890-1914

PRANA: Aerators Limited, London, England, 1905

PG: Verreries De Puy De Dome, S.A. Paris

R: Louit Freres & Co., France, 1870-1890

S (in a circle): Vetreria Savonese. A. Voglienzone, S.A. Milano, Italy

S.A.V.A. (all in a circle): Asmara, Ethiopia

S & M: Sykes & Macvey, Castleford, England, 1860-1888

T (in a circle): Tokyo Seibin., Ltd. Tokyo, Japan

vFo: Vidreria Ind. Figuerras Oliveiras, Brazil

VT: Ve.Tri S.p.a., Vetrerie Trivemta, Vicenza, Italy

VX: Usine de Vauxrot, France

WECK (in a frame): Weck Glaswerk G. mb.H, ofigen, Bonn, Germany

Y (in a circle): Etaria Lipasmaton, Athens, Greece

Bottle Clubs

(Listed alphabetically by State, Country, and Club Name)

Bottle clubs are one of the best sources for beginners and offer a great opportunity to meet veteran bottle collectors, learn from them, gather information, and have a good time. The bottle clubs listed here reflect the latest information available at the time of publication and are subject to change. The list represents an excellent cross-section across the United States, Europe, and Asia-Pacific. Any active bottle club or organization that requires a change of information or wishes to be included in the next edition of *Antique Trader® Bottles: Identification & Price Guide*, should send the required information to Michael F. Polak, P.O. Box 30328, Long Beach, CA 90853 or e-mail at bottleking@earthlink.net.

UNITED STATES

ALABAMA

Alabama Bottle Collectors Society
2768 Hanover Circle
Birmingham, AL 35205
(205) 933-7902

Azalea City Beamers Bottle & Spec.
  Club
8001 Pawnee Circle
Mobile, AL 36695

Dixie Jewels Insulator Club
P.O. Box 2674
Huntsville, AL 35804
(256) 880-1460

Mobile Bottle Collectors Club
8844 Lee Circle
Irvington, AL 36544
(205) 957-6725

Montgomery Bottle & Insulator Club
2021 Merrily Drive
Montgomery, AL 36111
(205) 288-7937

North Alabama Bottle & Glass Club
P.O. Box 109
Decatur, AL 35602-0109

Tuscaloosa Antique Bottle Club
1617 11th St.
Tuscaloosa, AL 35401

Vulcan Beamers Bottle & Spec. Club
5817 Avenue Q
Birmingham, AL 35228
(205) 831-5151

West Alabama Bottle Club
16760 Northfork Farm Road
Northport, AL 35476
(914) 325-3844

ALASKA

Alaska Bottle Club
8510 E. 10th
Anchorage, AK 99504

ARIZONA

Avon Collectors Club
P.O. Box 1406
Mesa, AZ 86201

Grand Canyon State Insulator Club
8331 W. Foothill Drive
Peoria, AZ 85383
(623) 566-0121

Phoenix Antiques, Bottles &
  Collectibles Club
4702 W. Lavey Road
Glendale, AZ 85306
(480) 962-9182

Pick & Shovel A.B.C. of Arizona, Inc
P.O. Box 7020
Phoenix, AZ 85011

Southern AZ Historical Collector's
  Association, Ltd.
6211 Piedra Seca
Tuscon, AZ 85718

Tri-City Jim Beam Bottle Club
2701 E. Utopia Road, Sp.#91
Phoenix, AZ 85024
(602) 867-1375
jbeam4@juno.com

Valley of the Sun Bottle & Specialty Club
212 E. Minton
Tempe, AZ 85281

White Mountain Antique Bottle
   Collectors Association
P.O. Box 503
Eager, AZ 85925

Wildcat Country Beam Bottle & Spec.
   Club
2601 S. Blackmoon Drive
Tucson, AZ 85730
(602) 298-5943

ARKANSAS

Fort Smith Area Bottle Collectors Assn.
2201 S. 73rd St.
Ft. Smith, AR 72903

Hempsted County Bottle Club
710 S. Hervey
Hope, AR 71801

Indian Country A.B. & Relic Soc
3818 Hilltop Drive
Jonesboro, AR 72401

Little Rock Antique Bottle Collectors
   Club
16201 Highway 300
Roland, AR 72135

Madison County Bottle Collectors Club
Rt. 2, Box 304
Huntsville, AR 72740

Razorback Jim Beam Bottle & Spec. Club
5412 Amber Circle
Benton, AR 72015
(501) 945-5028

CALIFORNIA

American Cut Glass Assoc.
P.O. Box 482
Ramona, CA 92065-0482

Amethyst Bottle Club
3245 Military Ave.
Los Angeles, CA 90034

Antique Bottle Collectors of Orange
   County
223 E. Pomona
Santa Ana, CA 92707

Antique Poison Bottle Collectors
   Association
3739 Amador Court
Chino, CA 91710

Argonaut Jim Beam Bottle Club
8253 Citadel Way
Sacramento, CA 95826
(916) 383-0206

Avon Bottles & Collectible Club
Central California Divison
P.O. Box 232
Amador City, CA 95601

Avon Bottle & Specialties Collectors
Southern California Division
9233 Mills Ave.
Montclair, CA 91763

Avon California Perfume Collectors
8104 Shirley Ave.
Reseda, CA 91335

Avon Collectors
San Diego Division
8135 Whelen Drive
San Diego, CA 92119

Bakersfield Bottle & Insulator
Collectors
1023 Baldwin Road
Bakersfield, CA 93304

Bay Area Vagabonds Jim Beam Club
224 Castleton Way
San Bruno, CA 94066
(415) 355-4356

Beaming Rebel Foxes Jim Beam Club
1114 Coronado Terrace
Los Angeles, CA 90026

Bidwell Bottle Club
Box 546
Chico, CA 95926

Bishop Belles & Beaux Bottle Club
P.O. Box 1475
Bishop, CA 93514

Blossom Valley Jim Beam Bottle &
Spec. Club
431 Grey Ghost Ave.
San Jose, CA 95111
(408) 227-2759

Bodfish Beamers Jim Beam Bottle Club
P.O. Box 907
Bodfish, CA 93205
(760) 379-8218

California Milk Bottle Collectors
2592 Mayfair Court
Hanford, CA 93230

California Miniature Bottle Club
1911 Willow St.
Alameda, CA 94501

California Ski Country Bottle Club
212 South El Molino St.
Alhambra, CA 91801

Camellia City Jim Beam Bottle Club
53705 Engle Road
Carmichael, CA 95608
(916) 488-1038

Cherry Valley Beam Bottle & Specialty
Club
6851 Hood Drive
Westminster, CA 92683

Fiesta City Beamers
329 Mountain Drive
Santa Barbara, CA 93103

First Double Springs Collectors Club
13311 Illinois St.
Westminster, CA 92683

Five Cities Beamers
756 Mesa View Drive, Sp. 57
Arroyo Grande, CA 93420

Fostoria Glass Collectors, Inc.
P.O. Box 1625
Orange, CA 92668

Fresno Antique Bottle & Collectors
Club
4318 Kenmore Drive South
Fresno, CA 92703

Glass Belles of San Gabriel
518 W. Neuby Ave.
San Gabriel, CA 91776

Glasshopper Figural Bottle Association
P.O. Box 6642
Torrance, CA 90504

Golden Gate Beam Club
35113 Clover St.
Union City, CA 94587
(415) 487-4479

Golden Gate Historical Bottle Society
752 Murdell Lane
Livermore, CA 94550
(925) 373-6758

Golden State Insulator Club
P.O. Box 2194
Rocklin, CA 95677
(916) 415-1555

Hoffman's Mr. Lucky Bottle Club
2104 Rhoda St.
Simi Valley, CA 93065

International Perfume Bottle
    Association
3519 Wycliffe Drive
Modesto, CA 95355

Jim Beam Bottle Club
139 Arlington
Berkley, CA 94707

Jim Beam Bottle Club of So. Calif
1114 Coronado Terrace
Los Angeles, CA 90066

Lilliputian Bottle Club
5626 Corning Ave.
Los Angeles, CA 90056
(213) 294-3231

Livermore Avon Club
6385 Claremont Ave.
Richmond, CA 94805

Los Angeles Historical Bottle Club
515 El Centro St.
South Pasadena, CA 91030

Miniature Bottle Club of Southern
    California
836 Carob
Brea, CA 92621

Mission Bells (Beams)
1114 Coronada Terrace
Los Angeles, CA 90026

Mission Trail Historical Bottle Club
1075 Hart St.
Seaside, CA 93955

Modesto Beamers
3216 Cato Court
Modesto, CA 95354

Modesto Old Bottle Club (MOBC)
P.O. Box 1791
Modesto, CA 95354

Monterey Bay Beam Bottle & Specialty
    Club
P.O. Box 258
Freedom, CA 95019

Mt. Diablo Bottle Club
4166 Sandra Circle
Pittsburg, CA 94565

Napa-Solano Bottle Club
1409 Delwood
Vallejo, CA 94590

National Insulator Assoc.
28390 Saffron Ave.
Highland, CA 92346
(909) 862-4312

Northern California Carnival Glass
    Club
1205 Clifton Drive
Modesto, CA 95355

Northwestern Bottle Collectors
    Association
P.O. Box 1121
Santa Rosa, CA 95402

Ocean Breeze Beamers
4841 Tacayme Drive
Oceanside, CA 92054
(714) 757-9081

Orange County Jim Beam Bottle &
   Specialties Club
546 W. Ash Ave.
Fullerton, CA 92632
(714) 875-8241

Original Sippin Cousins
   Ezra Brooks Specialties Club
12206 Malone St.
Los Angeles, CA 90066

Pepsi-Cola Collectors Club
P.O. Box 817
Claremont, CA 91711

Painted Soda Bottle Collectors Assn
9418 Hilmer Drive
LaMesa, CA 91942
(619) 461-4354

Relic Accumulators
P.O. Box 3513
Eureka, CA 95501

Santa Barbara Beam Bottle Club
5307 University Drive
Santa Barbara, CA 93111

San Bernardino County Historical
   Bottle and Collectible Club
P.O. Box 6759
San Bernardino, CA 92412
(619) 244-5863

San Diego Antique Bottle Club
11602 Via Casilina
El Cajon, CA 92019

San Joaquin Valley Jim Beam
   Bottle & Specialties Club
4085 N. Wilson Ave.
Fresno, CA 93704

San Jose Antique Bottle Collector Club
1037 Hazelwood Ave.
Campbell, CA 95008
(408) 259-7564

San Luis Obispo Bottle Society
124-21 St.
Paso Robles, CA 93446
(805) 238-1848

Sequoia Antique Bottle Society
1900 4th Ave.
Kingsburg, CA 93631

Sequoia Antique Bottle
   and Collectors Society
P.O. Box 3695
Visalia, CA 93278
(559) 732-3734

Sierra Gold Ski Country Bottle Club
5081 Rio Vista Ave.
San Jose, CA 95129

Ski-Country Bottle Club
   of Southern California
3148 N. Walnut Grove
Rosemead, CA 91770

Solar Country Beamers
940 Kelly Drive
Barstow, CA 92311
(714) 256-1485

Southern Wyoming Avon Bottle Club
301 Canyon Highlands Drive
Oroville, CA 95965

Sunnyvale Antique Bottle Collectors Assn
613 Torrington
Sunnyvale, CA 94087

Superior California Bottle Club
3220 Stratford Ave.
Redding, CA 96001
The California Miniature Club
1911 Willow St.
Alameda, CA 94501

The Stretch Glass Society
P.O. Box 3305
Quartz Hill, CA 93586

Tinseltown Beam Club
4117 E. Gage Ave.
Bell, CA 90201
(213) 699-8787

Violin Bottle Collector's Assoc.
Karen Larkin, Newsletter Editor
1210 Hiller Road
McKinleyville, CA 95519

Wildwind Jim Beam Bottle & Spec. Club
905 Eaton Way
Sunnyvale, CA 94087
(408) 739-1558

'49er Historical Bottle Assn
1111 24th St. #103
Sacramento, CA 95816

COLORADO

American Breweriana Association, Inc
P.O. Box 11157
Pueblo, CO 81001

Antique Bottle Collectors of Colorado
3776 Easter Circle South
Centennial, CO 80122
(303) 290-9016

Avon Collectors of Colorado
1530 Sawyer Way
Colorado Springs, CO 80909

Avon Collectors
Rocky Mountain Division
7961 East Hampden Circle
Denver, CO 80237

Colorado Antique Bottle Club
9545 Oak Tree Court
Colorado Springs, CO 80925
(719) 390-5621

Mile-Hi Jim Beam Bottle & Spec. Club
13196 W. Green Mountain Drive
Lakewood, CO 80228
(303) 986-6828

National Ski Country Bottle Club
1224 Washington Ave.
Golden, CO 80401
(303) 279-3373

Northern Colorado Antique Bottle Club
227 W. Beaver Ave.
Ft. Morgan, CO 80701

Northern Colorado Beam Bottle &
   Spec. Club
280 Sequoia Circle
Windsor, CO 80550

Ole Foxie Jim Beam Club
Attn: Shirley Engel, President
7530 Wilson Court
Westminster, CO 80030
(303) 429-1823

Pikes Peak Antique Bottle & Collectors
   Club
308 Maplewood Drive
Colorado Springs, CO 80907-4326

Triple Ridge Insulator Club
7176 Newport St.
Commerce City, CO 80022
(303) 478-5603

Western Slope Bottle Club
P.O. Box 354
Palisade, CO 81526
(303) 464-7727

CONNECTICUT

The National Assn. of Milk Bottle
  Collectors
18 Pond Place
Cos Cob, CT 06807
(203) 869-8411

The Somers Antique Bottle Club
Box 373
Somers, CT 06071

Southern Connecticut Antique Bottle
  Collectors Assn
11 Paquonnock Road
Trumbull, CT 06033

DELAWARE

Blue Hen Jim Beam Bottle & Spec.
  Club
303 Potomac Drive
Wilmington, DE 19803
(302) 652-6378

Delmarva Antique Bottle Club
28947 Lewes Georgetown Highway
Lewes, DE 19958
(302) 945-7072

Tri-State Bottle Collectors and Diggers
  Club
20 Boston Place
New Castle, DE 19720
(302) 353-6429

FLORIDA

Antique Bottle Collectors of Florida,
  Inc.
2512 Davie Blvd.
Ft. Lauderdale, FL 33312

Antique Bottle Collectors of North
  Florida
3867 Winter Berry Road
Jacksonville, FL 32210

Avon Collectors Club
P.O. Box 11004
Ft. Lauderdale, FL 33339

Central Florida Insulator Collectors Club
3557 Nicklaus Drive
Titusville, FL 32780
(321) 480-1800

Central Florida Jim Beam Bottle Club
2131 Kewannee Trail
Casselberry, FL 32707

Crossarms Collectors Club
1756 N.W. 58th Ave.
Lauderhill, FL 33313

Emerald Coast Bottle Collectors
P.O. Box 863
DeFuniak Springs, FL 32435
(850) 892-5474

Everglades Antique Bottle Club
6981 S.W. 19th St.
Pompano, FL 33068

Everglades Antique Bottle & Collectors
  Club
400 S. 57 Terrace
Hollywood, FL 33023
(305) 962-3434

International Perfume Bottle Assoc.
3314 Shamrock Road
Tampa, FL 33629
(813) 837-5845

Mid-State Antique Bottle Collectors
3400 East Grant St.
Orlando, FL 32806

M.T. Bottle Collectors Assn., Inc.
1030 Blue Horizon Drive
Deltona, FL 32725
(904) 734-3651

Ridge Area Antique Bottle Collectors
1219 Carlton
Lake Wales, FL 33853

Sanford Antique Bottle Collectors
2656 Grandview Ave.
Sanford, FL 33853
(305) 322-7181

South Florida Jim Beam Bottle & Spec.
   Club
14302 South West 76th St.
Miami, FL 33183

Suncoast Antique Bottle Club
12451 94th Ave N.
Seminole, FL 33772
(727) 393-8189

Treasure Coast Bottle Collectors
6301 Lilyan Parkway
Ft. Pierce, FL 34591

GEORGIA
The Desoto Trail Bottle Collectors
   Club
406 Randolph St.
Cuthbert, GA 31740

The Dixie Jewels Insulator Club
6220 Carriage Court
Cummings, GA 30130
(707) 781-5021

Flint Antique Bottle & Coin Club
C/O Cordele-Crisp Co.
Recreation Dept.
204 2nd St. North
Cordele, GA 31015

Georgia Bottle Club
2996 Pangborn Road
Decatur, GA 30033

Macon Antique Bottle Club
P.O. Box 5395
Macon, GA 31208

Peanut State Jim Beam Bottle & Spec.
   Club
767 Timberland St.
Smyra, GA 30080
(404) 432-8482

Southeastern Antique Bottle Club
143 Scatterfoot Drive
Peachtree City, GA 30269

HAWAII
Hauoli Beam Bottle Collectors Club of
   Hawaii
45-027 Ka-Hanahou Place
Kaneohe, HI 96744

Hawaii Historic Bottle Collectors
   Club
2056 Puu Place, Apt. F
Wahiawa, HI 96785

Hilo Bottle Club
287 Kanoelani St.
Hilo, HI 96720

IDAHO

Buhl Antique Bottle Club
500 12th
N. Buhl, ID 83316

Eagle Rock Beam & Spec. Club
3665 Upland Ave.
Idaho Falls, ID 83401
(208) 522-7819

Em Tee Bottle Club
P.O. Box 62
Jerome, ID 83338

Idaho Beam & Spec. Club
2312 Burrell Ave.
Lewiston, ID 83501
(208) 743-5997

ILLINOIS

Alton Area Bottle Club
2448 Alby St.
Alton, IL
(618) 462-4285

Antique Bottle Club of Northern
Illinois
270 Stanley Ave.
Waukegan, IL 60085
(815) 338-2567

Avon Calling Collectors Club
128 Arizona Ave.
Joliet, IL 60433

Avon Hobby Collectors Club
5 Petunia Circle
Matteson, IL 60443

Blackhawk Jim Beam Bottle & Spec.
Club
3229 Hayes Road
Rochelle, IL 61068

Central & Midwestern States Beam &
Spec. Club
44 S. Westmore
Lombard, IL 60148

Chicago Ezra Brooks Bottle & Spec.
Club
3635 W. 82nd St.
Chicago, IL 60652

Dreamers Beamers
5721 Vial Parkway
LaGrange, IL 60525
(847) 824-1097

1st Chicago Antique Bottle Club
P.O. Box 224
Dolton, IL 60419
(708) 841-4068

Greater Chicago Insulator Club
515 Main St., Unit 403
West Chicago, IL 60185
(630) 231-4171

Heart of Illinois Antique Bottle Club
2010 Bloomington Road
East Peoria, IL 61611

International Assn. of Jim Beam Bottle
and Specialties Clubs
P.O. Box 486
Kewanee IL 661443
(309) 853-3370
www.beam-wade.org

Land of Lincoln Bottle Club
2515 Illinois Circle
Decatur, IL 62526

Lewis & Clark Jim Beam Bottle &
Spec. Club
P.O. Box 451
Wood River, IL 62095

Metro East Bottle & Jar Assn
309 Bellevue Drive
Delleville, IL 62223

Pekin Bottle Collectors Assn.
409 E. Forrest Hill Ave.
Peoria, IL 61603

Rock River Valley Jim Beam Bottle &
   Spec. Club
1107 Ave. A
Rock Falls, IL 61071
(815) 625-7075

The Greater Chicago Insulator Club
34273 Homestead Road
Gurnee, IL 60031
(708) 855-9136

Tri-County Jim Beam Bottle Club
3702 W. Lancer Road
Peoria, IL 61615
(309) 691-8784

INDIANA

Avon Collectors, Ding Dong Chapter
3061 S. State Road 3
Hartford City, IN 47348

City of Bridges Jim Beam Bottle &
   Spec. Club
1017 N. 6th St.
Logansport, IN 46947
(219) 722-3197

Crossroads of America Jim Beam
   Bottle Club
114 S. Green St.
Brownsburg, IN 46112
(317) 852-5168

Hoosier Jim Beam Bottle & Spec. Club
P.O. Box 24234
Indianapolis, IN 46224

Jelly Jammers
6086 West Boggstown Road
Boggstown, IN 46110

Lafayette Antique Bottle Club
3664 Redondo Drive
Lafayette, IN 47905

Mid-West Antique Fruit Jar & Bottle
   Club
P.O. Box 38
Flat Rock, IN 47234
(812) 587-5560

National Greentown Glass Association
P.O. Box 107
Greentown, IN 46936-0107

The Ohio Valley Antique Bottle and Jar
   Club
214 John St.
Aurora, IN 47001

Wabash Valley Antique Bottle &
   Pottery Club
10655 Atherton Road
Rosedale, IN 47874
(812) 466-1559

We Found 'Em Bottle & Insulator Club
P.O. Box 578
Bunker Hill, IN 46914

IOWA

Avon of Waterloo Collectors Club
2211 Washington
Cedar Falls, IA 50613

Avon Collectors, Hawkeye Des Moines
   Chapter
702 E. Jefferson St.
Knoxville, IA 50138

Early American Pattern Glass Society
P.O. Box 266
Colesburg, IA 52035

Five Seasons Beam & Spec. Club of
Iowa
609 32nd St., NE
Cedar Rapids, IA 52402
(319) 365-6089

Gold Dome Jim Beam Bottle & Spec.
Club
2616 Hull
Des Moines, IA 50317
(515) 262-8728

Hawkeye Jim Beam Bottle Club
658 Kern St.
Waterloo, IA 60703
(319) 233-9168

Iowa Antique Bottlers
2815 Druid Hill Drive
Des Moines, IA 50315
(515) 282-6901

Iowa Great Lakes Jim Beam Bottle &
Spec. Club
Green Acres Mobile Park, Lot 88
Estherville, IA 51334
(712) 362-2759

Larkin Bottle Club
107 W. Grimes
Red Oak, IA 51566

Quad Cities Jim Beam Bottle & Spec.
Club
2425 W. 46th St.
Davenport, IA 52806

Shot Tower Beam Club
284 N. Booth St.
Dubuque, IA 52001
(319) 583-6343

KANSAS

Air Capital City Jim Beam Bottle &
Spec. Club
3256 Euclid
Wichita, KS 67217
(316) 942-3162

Cherokee Strip Ezra Brooks Bottle &
Spec. Club
P.O. Box 631
Arkansas City, KS 67005

Kansas City Bottle Collectors
1050 West Blue Ridge Blvd.
Kansas City, MO 64145

National Depression Glass Assoc.
P.O. 8264
Wichita, KS 67208

Southeast Kansas Bottle & Relic Club
1015 South Allen
Chanute, KS 66720
(620) 431-2662

Walnut Valley Jim Beam Bottle & Spec.
Club
P.O. Box 631
Arkansas City, KS 67005
(316) 442-0509

KENTUCKY

Derby City Jim Beam Bottle Club
583 Crittendon St.
Gratz, KY 40359

Gold City Jim Beam Bottle Club
286 Metts Court, Apt. 4
Elizabethtown, KY 42701
(502) 737-9297

Kentucky Bluegrass Ezra Brooks
Bottle Club
6202 Tabor Drive
Louisville, KY 40218

Kentucky Cardinal Beam Bottle Club
428 Templin
Bardstown, KY 41104

LOUISIANA

Bayou Bottle Bugs
216 Dahlia
New Iberia, LA 70560

"Cajun Country Cousins" Ezra Brooks
    Bottle & Spec. Club
1000 Chevis St.
Abbeville, LA 70510

Crescent City Jim Beam Bottle & Spec.
    Club
733 Wright Ave.
Gretna, LA 70053
(504) 367-2182

Historical Bottle Assn. of Baton Rouge
1843 Tudor Drive
Baton Rouge, LA 70815

New Orleans Antique Bottle Club
2605 Winifed St.
Metairie, LA 70003

MAINE

New England Antique Bottle Club
89 New York Ave.
South Portland, ME 04106
(603) 778-9692

Pine Tree State Beamers
15 Woodside Ave.
Saco, ME 04072
(207) 284-8756

MARYLAND

Baltimore Antique Bottle Club
P.O. Box 36061
Baltimore, MD 21268
(410) 531-9459

Chesapeake Bay Insulator Club
12604 Eldrid Court
Silver Springs, MD 20904
(301) 680-8910

International Chinese Snuff Bottle
    Society
2601 North Charles St.
Baltimore, MD 21218

Paperweight Collectors Assoc.
P.O. Box 1263
Beltsville, MD 20704-1263

Potomac Bottle Collector's
8008 Eastern Drive, Apt. 101
Silver Spring, MD 20910
(301) 588-2174

Potomac Highlands Antique Bottle &
    Glass Collector's Club
709 St. Mary's Ave.
Cumberland, MD 21502
(301) 777-1107

MASSACHUSETTS

Berkshire Antique Bottle Assn.
Box 971
Lenox, MA 01240

Candy Container Collectors of
    American
P.O. Box 426
Reading, MA 01864-0426

Insulator Collectors on the Net
103 Canterbury Court
Carlisle, MA 01741
(978) 369-0208

Little Rhody Bottle Club
784 King St.
Raynham, MA 02767
(508) 880-4929

Merrimack Valley Antique Bottle Club
17 Locust Road
Chelmsford, MA 01824
(978) 256-2738

Scituate Bottle Club
54 Cedarwood Road
Scituate, MA 02066

Violin Bottle Collectors Association of
America
24 Sylvan St.
Danvers, MA 01923

Yankee Pole Cat Insulator Club
C/O Jill Meier
103 Canterbury Court
Carlisle, MA 01741-1860
(978) 369-0208

MICHIGAN

Avon Collectors Mustang '64 Chapter
8470 Dogwood Lane
Warren, MI 48093

Central Michigan Krazy Korkers Bottle
Club
Mid-Michigan Community College
Clare Ave.
Harrison, MI 48625

Dickinson County Bottle Club
717 Henford Ave.
Iron Mountain, MI 49801

Flint Antique Bottle Collectors Assn.
450 Leta Ave.
Flint, MI 48507

Flint Antique Bottle & Collectors Club
11353 W. Cook Road
Gaines, MI 48436
(517) 271-9193

Flint Eagles Ezra Brooks Club
1117 W. Remington Ave.
Flint, MI 48507

Grand Rapids Antique Bottle Club
1368 Kinney N.W.
Walker, MI 49504

Grand Valley Bottle Club
31 Dickinson S.W.
Grand Rapids, MI 49507

Great Lakes Miniature Bottle Club
P.O. Box 230460
Fairhaven, MI 48023

Huron Valley Bottle Club
12475 Saline-Milan Road
Milan, MI 48160

Huron Valley Bottle & Insulator Club
2475 West Walton Blvd.
Waterford, MI 48329
(248) 673-1650

Jelly Jammers
4300 W. Bacon Road
Hillsdale, MI 49242

Kalamazoo Antique Bottle Club
607 Crocket Ave.
Portage, MI 49024
(616) 329-0853

Lionstone Collectors Bottle & Spec.
Club of Michigan
3089 Grand Blanc Road
Swartz Creek, MI 48473

Manistee Coin & Bottle Club
207 E. Piney Road
Manistee, MI 49660

Metropolitan Detroit Antique Bottle
   Club
2725 Creek Bend Road
Troy, MI 48098

Michigan Bottle Collectors Assn.
144 W. Clark St.
Jackson, MI 49203

Michigan's Vehicle City Beam Bottles
   & Spec. Club
G5348 W. Court St.
Flint, MI 48504
(810) 732-2936

Mid-Michee Pine Beam Club
609 Webb Drive
Bay City, MI 48706

Red Run Jim Beam Bottle & Spec.
   Club
172 Jones St.
Mt. Clemens, MI 48043
(313) 465-4883

West Michigan Antique Bottle Club
10895 Settlewood
Lowell, MI 49331

World Wide Avon Bottle Collectors
   Club
22708 Wick Road
Taylor, MI 48180

Ye Old Corkers
C/O Janet Gallup
Box 7
Gaastra, MI 49927

MINNESOTA

Lake Superior Antique Bottle Club
P.O. Box 67
Knife River, MN 55609

Minnesota 1st Antique Bottle Club
5001 Queen Ave.
N. Minneapolis, MN 55430
(512) 521-9874

North-Star Historical Bottle Assn. Inc.
3308-32 Ave. S.
Minneapolis, MN 55406
(612) 721-4165

North Western Insulator Club
5424 Dufferin Drive
Savage, MN 55378
(952) 447-2422

Paul Bunyan Jim Beam Club
8773 Centerline Road N.W.
Solway, MN 56678
(218) 467-3355

Red Wing Collectors Society Inc. (Red
   Wing & American Pottery)
P.O. Box 50
Red Wing, MN 550660-0050

Society of Inkwell Collectors
5136 Thomas Ave. S.
Minneapolis, MN 55410

Truman, Minnesota Jim Beam Bottle
   & Spec. Club
Truman, MN 56088
(507) 776-3487

Viking Jim Beam Bottle & Spec. Club
8224 Oxborough Ave. S.
Bloomington, MN 55437
(612) 831-2303

MISSISSIPPI

Gum Tree Beam Bottle Club
104 Ford Circle
Tupelo, MS 38801

Magnolia Beam Bottle & Spec. Club
1079 Maria Drive
Jackson, MS 39204-5518
(601) 372-4464

Mississippi Antique Bottle Club
P.O. Box 601
Carthage, MS 39501
(601) 267-7128

MISSOURI

Arnold, Missouri Jim Beam Bottle &
Spec. Club
1861 Jean Drive
Arnold, MO 63010
(314) 296-0813

Avon Times Collectors
P.O. Box 9868
Kansas City, MO 64134

Avon Collectors Mid America Chapter
6100 Walnut
Kansas City, MO 64113

Barnhart, Missouri Jim Beam Bottle &
Spec. Club
2150 Cathlin Court
Barnhart, MO 63012

Beer Can Collectors of America
747 Merus Court
Fenton, MO 63026-2092
(636) 343-6486

Chesterfield Jim Beam Bottle & Spec.
Club
2066 Honey Ridge
Chesterfield, MO 63017

"Down in the Valley" Jim Beam Bottle
Club
528 St. Louis Ave.
Valley Park, MO 63088

The Federation of Historical Bottle
Clubs
10118 Schuessler
St. Louis, MO 63128
(314) 843-7573

First Avon Collectors Club of St. Louis
10714 Wheeling Court
St. Louis, MO 63136

Florissant Valley Jim Beam Bottles &
Spec. Club
25 Cortez
Florissant, MO 63031

Kansas City Antique Bottle Collectors
Assn.
1131 E. 77 St.
Kansas City, MO 64131

Maryland Heights Jim Beam Bottle &
Spec. Club
2365 Wesford
Maryland Heights, MO 63043

Midwest Miniature Bottle Collectors
12455 Parkwood Lane
Blackjack, MO 63033

Missouri Arch Jim Beam Bottle &
Spec. Club
2900 N. Lindbergh
St. Ann, MO 63074
(314) 739-0803

Missouri Valley Insulator Club
10143 Coburg Lands Drive
St. Louis, MO 63137

Mound City Jim Beam Decanter
Collectors
42 Webster Acres
Webster Groves, MO 63119

North-East County Jim Beam Bottle &
Spec. Club
10150 Baron Drive
St. Louis, MO 63136

Rock Hill Jim Beam Bottle & Spec.
Club
9731 Graystone Terrace
St. Louis, MO 63119
(314) 962-8125

Sho Me Jim Beam Bottle & Spec. Club
Rt. 7, Box 314-D
Springfield, MO 65802
(417) 831-8093

St. Louis Antique Bottle Collectors
Assn.
71 Outlook Drive
Hillsboro, MO 63050

St. Louis Jim Beam Bottle & Spec.
Club
2900 Lindbergh
St. Ann, MO 63074
(314) 291-3256

Troy, Missouri Jim Beam Bottle &
Spec. Club
121 E. Pershing
Troy, MO 63379

Vaseline Glass Collectors
P.O. Box 125
Russellville, MO 65074

Vera Young, Avon Times
P.O. Box 9868
Kansas City, MO 64134
(816) 537-8223

West County Jim Beam Bottle & Spec.
Club
11707 Momarte Lane
St. Louis, MO 63141

MONTANA

Montana Bottle Collector's Assoc.
2575 Winchester Drive
East Helena, MT 59635
(406) 227-5301

NEBRASKA

Cornhusker Jim Beam Bottle & Spec.
Club
5204 S. 81st St.
Ralston, NE 68127
(402) 331-4646

Nebraska Antique Bottle & Collectible
Club
407 N. 13th St.
Ashland, NE 68003
(407) 944-2168

Nebraska Big Red Bottle & Spec. Club
N Street Drive-in, 200S
18th St.
Lincoln, NE 68508

NEVADA

Las Vegas Antique Bottle &
Collectibles Club
3901 E. Stewart #19
Las Vegas, NV 89110
(702) 452-1263

Las Vegas Bottle Club
2632 E. Harman
Las Vegas, NV 89121
(702) 731-5004

Lincoln County Antique Bottle Club
P.O. Box 191
Calente, NV 89008
(702) 726-3655

Reno/Sparks Antique Bottle Club
P.O. Box 1061
Verdi, NV 89439
(775) 345-0171

Virginia & Truckee Jim Beam
    Bottle & Spec. Club
P.O. Box 1596
Carson City, NV 89701

NEW HAMPSHIRE

New England Antique Bottle Club
4 Francour Drive
Somersworth, NH 03878

Yankee Bottle Club
382 Court St.
Keene, NH 03431-2534

NEW JERSEY

Antique Bottle Collectors Club of
    Burlington County
18 Willow Road
Bordentown, NJ 08505

Artifact Hunters Assn. Inc
C/O 29 Lake Road
Wayne, NJ 07470

Central Jersey Bottle
    & Collectible Club
92 North Main St.
New Egypt, NJ 98553

Glass Research Society of New Jersey
Wheaton Village
Millville, NJ 08332

Jersey Jackpot Jim Beam
    Bottle & Spec. Club
197 Farley Ave.
Fanwood, NJ 07023
(201) 322-7287

Jersey Shore Bottle Club
P.O. Box 995
Toms River, NJ 08754
(732) 244-5171

New Jersey Antique Bottle Club Assn.
24 Charles St.
South River, NJ 08882
(732) 238-3238

South Jersey Antique Bottle
    & Glass Club, Inc.
25 High St.
Glassboro, NJ 08028

Trenton Jim Beam Bottle Club, Inc.
17 Easy St.
Freehold, NJ 07728

West Essex Bottle Club
76 Beaufort Ave.
Livingston, NJ 07039

NEW MEXICO

Enchantment Insulator Club
5516 Kachina NW
Albuquerque, NM 87120
(505) 899-8755

Billy the Kid Jim Beam
    Decanter & Specialties Club
P.O. Box 353
Alto, NM 88312

New Mexico Historical Bottle Society
1463C State Road 344
Sandia Park, NM 87047
(505) 281-5223

Roadrunner Bottle Club of New Mexico
2341 Gay Road S.W.
Albuquerque, NM 87105

New York

Ball Metal Container Group
One Adams Road
Saratoga Springs, NY 12866

Capital District Insulator Club
41 Crestwood Drive
Schenectady, NY 12306

Capital Region Antique Bottle &
   Insulator Club
50 Pershing Drive
Scotia, NY 12302
(518) 528-1774

Chautauqua County Bottle Collectors
   Club
Morse Motel
Main St.
Sherman, NY 14781

Eastern Monroe County Bottle Club
C/O Bethlehem Lutheran Church
1767 Plank Road
Webster, NY 14580

Empire State Bottle Collectors Assn.
4 Vinette Road
Central Square, NY 13036

Finger Lakes Bottle Collectors Assn.
P.O. Box 3894
Ithaca, NY 14852

Genesee Valley Bottle Collector's Assoc.
5330 Henty Road
Avon, NY 14414
(585) 373-6758

Greater Buffalo Bottle Club
66 Chassin Ave.
Amherst, NY 14226
(716) 834-2249

Hudson River Jim Beam Bottle & Spec.
   Club
48 College Road
Monsey, NY 10952

Hudson Valley Bottle Club
201 Filors Lane
Stony Point, NY 10980

Lions Club of Ballston Spa
37 Grove St.
Ballston Spa, NY 12020

Long Island Antique Bottle Assn.
10 Holmes Court
Sayville, NY 11782

Mohawk Valley Antique Bottle Club
1108 Rutger St.
Utica, NY 13501
(315) 768-7091

National Bottle Museum
76 Milton Ave.
Ballston Spa, NY 12020
(518) 885-7589

National Insulator Association
41 Crestwood Drive
Schenectady, NY 12306

Society of Inkwell Collectors
Jane Betrus, Executive Director
10 Meadow Drive
Spencerport, NY 14459
(716) 352-4114

The Corning Museum of Glass
One Museum Way
Corning, NY 14830-2253

Tryon Bottle Badgers
P.O. Box 146
Tribes Hill, NY 12177

Western New York Bottle Club Assn.
Attn: Tom Karapantso
62 Adams St.
Jamestown, NY 14701
(716) 487-9645

West Valley Bottleique Club
P.O. Box 204
Killbuck, NY 14748
(716) 945-5769

NORTH CAROLINA

Catawba Valley Jim Beam Bottle &
　Spec. Club
265 5th Ave.
N.E. Hickory, NC 28601
(704) 322-5268

Kinston Collectors Club, Inc.
1905 Greenbriar Road
Kinston, NC 28501-2129
(919) 523-3049

Tar Heel Jim Beam Bottle & Spec. Club
6615 Wake Forest Road
Fayetteville, NC 20301
(919) 488-4849

The Johnnyhouse Inspector's Bottle
　Club
1972 East US 74 Highway
Hamlet, NC 28345

Raleigh Bottle Club
P.O. Box 18083
Raleigh, NC 27619
(919) 789-4545

Southeast Bottle Club
P.O. Box 13736
Durham, NC 27709
(919) 789-4545

The Robeson Antique Bottle Club
1830 Riverside Blvd.
Lumberton, NC 28358

Western North Carolina Antique Bottle
　Club
P.O. Box 1391
Candler, NC 28715

Wilmington Bottle & Artifact Club
183 Arlington Drive
Wilmington, NC 28401
(919) 763-3701

Yadkin Valley Bottle Club
General Delivery
Gold Hill, NC 28071

OHIO

Buckeye Bottle Club
229 Oakwood St.
Elyria, OH 44035

Central Ohio Bottle Club
931 Minerva Ave.
Columbus, OH 43229

Collectors of Findlay Glass
P.O. Box 256
Findlay, OH 45939-0256

Diamond Pin Winners Avon Club
5281 Fredonia Ave.
Dayton, OH 45431

The Federation of Historical Bottle
　Clubs
C/O Gary Beatty, Treasurer
9326 Court Road 3C
Galion, OH 44833

Findlay Antique Bottle Club
P.O. Box 1329
Findlay, OH 45840
(419) 442-3183

Gem City Beam Bottle Club
1463 E. Stroop Road
Dayton, OH 45429

Glass Collectors Club of Toledo
6122 Cross Trails Road
Sylvania, OH 43560-1714

Greater Cleveland Jim Beam Club
5398 W. 147th St.
Brook Park, OH 44142
(216) 267-7665

Heart of Ohio Bottle Club
P.O. Box 353
New Washington, OH 44854
(419) 492-2829

Maple Leaf Beamers
8200 Yorkshire Road
Mentor, OH 44060
(216) 255-9118

Midwest Miniature Bottle Club
5537 Cleander Drive
Cincinnati, OH 45238

National Fenton Glass Society
P.O. Box 4008
Marietta, OH 45750

National Trail Insulator Club
8784 Grubbs Rex Road
Arcanum, OH 45304
(937) 884-7379

Northern Ohio Jim Beam Bottle Club
43152 Hastings Road
Oberlin, OH 44074
(216) 775-2177

North Eastern Ohio Bottle Club
P.O. Box 57
Madison, OH 44057
(614) 282-8918

Ohio Bottle Club
P.O. Box 585
Barberton, OH 44203

Pioneer Beamers
44610 Parsons Road
Oberlin, OH 44074

Rubber Capitol Jim Beam Club
151 Stephens Road
Akron, OH 44312
(614) 263-7110

Southwestern Ohio Antique Bottle &
 Jar Club
273 Hilltop Drive
Dayton, OH 45415
(513) 836-3353

St. Bernard Swigin Beamers
4327 Greenlee Ave.
Cincinnati, OH 45217
(513) 793-3318

Superior Bottle Club
22000 Shaker Blvd.
Shaker Heights, OH 44122

Western Reserve Insulator Club
P.O. Box 33661
North Royalton, OH 44133
(440) 237-2242

West Virginia Bottle Club
39304 Bradbury Road
Middleport, OH 45760

OKLAHOMA

Bar-Dew Antique Bottle Club
817 E. 7th St.
Dewey, OK 74029

Frontier Jim Beam Bottle & Spec. Club
P.O. Box 52
Meadowbrook Trailer Village, Lot 101
Ponca City, OK 74601
(405) 765-2174

Midwest Miniature Bottle Collector
3108 Meadowood Drive
Midwest City, OK 73110-1407

Oklahoma Territory Bottle & Relic
Club
1300 S. Blue Haven Drive
Mustang, OK 73064
(405) 376-1045

Prairie Signals Insulator Club
11825 Lancashire Circle
Oklahoma City, OK 73162
(405) 721-6578

Sooner Jim Beam Bottle & Spec. Club
570 Oak Park Circle
Choctaw, OK 73020

Tri-State Historical Bottle Club
817 E. 7th St.
Dewey, OK 74029

Tulsa Antique and Bottle Club
P.O. Box 4278
Tulsa, OK 74159
(918) 835-0278

OREGON

Central Oregon Bottle & Relic Club
671 N.E. Seward
Bend, OR 97701

Gold Diggers Antique Bottle Club
1958 S. Stage Road
Medford, OR 97501

Jefferson State Antique Bottle
Collectors
P.O. Box 1565
Jacksonville, OR 97530
(541) 899-8411

Jefferson State Insulator Club
5508 Pioneer Road
Medford, OR 97501
(541) 608-1043

Lewis & Clark Historical Bottle &
Collectors Soc.
8018 S.E. Hawthorne Blvd.
Portland, OR 97501

Oregon Beaver Beam Club
2514 N. E. Douglas
Roseburg, OR 97470

Oregon Bottle Collectors Assn.
1762 Sunset Ave.
West Linn, OR 97068
(503) 657-1726

Pacific Northwest Fenton Assoc.
P.O. Box 881
Tillamook, OR 97141
(503) 842-4815

Pioneer Fruit Collectors Assn.
P.O. Box 175
Grand Ronde, OR 97347

Promotional Glass Collectors
Association
528 Oakley
Central Point, OR 97502

Siskiyou Antique Bottle Collectors
Assn.
2668 Montana Drive
Medford, OR 97504

PENNSYLVANIA

American Collectors of Infant Feeders
1819 Ebony Drive
York, PA 17402-4706

Beaver Valley Jim Beam Club
1335 Indiana Ave.
Monaca, PA 15061

Coal Crackers Bottle Club
Rod Walck
168 Sunrise Terrace Lane
Lehighton, PA 18235
(610) 377-1484

Delaware Valley Bottle Club
12 Belmar Road
Halboro, PA 19040

Del Val Miniature Bottle Club
57-104 Delaire Landing Road
Philadelphia, PA 19114

East Coast Ezra Brooks Bottle Club
2815 Fiddler Green
Lancaster, PA 17601

Endless Mountain Antique Bottle Club
P.O. Box 75
Granville Summit, PA 16926

H.C. Fry Glass Society
P.O. Box 41
Beaver, PA 15009

Indiana Bottle Club
240 Oak St.
Indiana, PA 15701

International Perfume Bottle
   Association
295 E. Swedesford Road
PMB 185
Wayne, PA 19087

Jefferson County Antique Bottle Club
6 Valley View Drive
Washington, PA 15301

Kiski Mini Beam and Spec. Club
C/O John D. Ferchak Jr.
816 Cranberry Drive
Monroeville, PA 15146
(412) 372-0387

Laurel Valley Bottle Club
P.O. Box 201
Hostetter, PA 15638
(412) 238-9046

Middletown Area Bottle Collectors
   Assn.
P.O. Box 1
Middletown, PA 17057
(717) 939-0288

Pagoda City Beamers
735 Florida Ave.
Riverview Park
Reading, PA 19605
(215) 929-8924

Penn Beamers' 14th
15 Gregory Place
Richboro, PA 18954

Pennsylvania Bottle Collectors Assoc.
251 Eastland Ave.
York, PA 17402
(717) 854-4965

Pennsylvania Dutch Jim Beam Bottle
   Club
812 Pointview Ave.
Ephrata, PA 17522

Philadelphia Bottle Club
8203 Elberon Ave.
Philadelphia, PA 19111

Pittsburgh Antique Bottle Club
694 Fayette City Road
Fayette City, PA 15438
(412) 233-8109

Pittsburgh Bottle Club
1528 Railroad St.
Sewickley, PA 15143

Seaview Jim Beam Bottle & Spec. Club
362 Lakepoint Drive
Harrisburg, PA 17111
(717) 561-2517

Susquehanna Valley Jim Beam Bottle
   & Spec. Club
64 E. Park St.
Elizabethtown, PA 17022
(717) 367-4256

Valley Forge Jim Beam Bottle Club
1219 Ridgeview Drive
Phoenixville, PA 19460

Washington County Antique Bottle
   Club & Insulator Club
366 N. Main St.
Houston, PA 15342
(724) 743-3334

RHODE ISLAND
Little Rhody Bottle Club
P.O. Box 15142
Riverside, RI 02915-0142
www.littlerhodybottleclub.org

SOUTH CAROLINA
Anderson Collectors Club
2318 Highway 29, N.
Anderson, SC 29621

Berkeley Antique Bottle & Collectibles

Club
P.O. Drawer 429
Moncks Corner, SC 29461
(843) 761-0316

Horse Creek Antique Bottle Club
P.O. Box 1176
Langley, SC 29834
(803) 593-2271

Palmetto State Beamers
908 Alton Circle
Florence, SC 29501
(803) 669-6515

South Carolina Bottle Club
1091 Daralynn Drive
Lexington, SC 29073
(803) 957-4807

TENNESSEE
East Tennessee Antique Bottle &
   Collectibles Society
314 Patty Road
Knoxville, TN 37924

Memphis Bottle Collectors Club
3706 Deerfield Cove
Bartlett, TN 38135

Middle Tennessee Bottle Collectors Club
1221 Nichol Lane
Nashville, TN 37205

Music City Beam Bottle Club
12175 Sparta Pike
Watertown, TN 37184

Painted Soda Bottle Collectors
   Association (PSBCA)
1966 King Springs Road
Johnson City, TN 37601

State of Franklin Antique Bottle &
  Collectibles Association
728 Fairway Drive
Elizabethton, TN 37643

Tennessee Valley Traders and
  Collectors Club
821 Hiwassee St.
Newport, TN 37821
(865) 835-0278

TEXAS

Cowtown Jim Beam Bottle Club
2608 Roseland
Ft. Worth, TX 76103
(817) 536-4335

El Paso Insulator Club
Martha Stevens, Chairman
4556 Bobolink
El Paso, TX 79922

Foursome (Jim Beam)
1208 Azalea Drive
Longview, TX 75601

Gulf Coast Bottle and Jar Club
907 W. Temple
Houston, TX 77009

Lone Star Insulator Club
5415 Lexington Circle
Lumberton, TX 77657
(409) 755-3993

Houston Glass Club
5338 Creekbend Drive
Houston, TX 77096

Republic of Texas Jim Beam Bottle &
  Spec. Club
2000 Serrano
Bedford, TX 76021
(817) 283-7863

Sidewinders Jim Beam Club
3205 Windy Hill
Denton, TX 76208

UTAH

Golden Spike Jim Beam Club
1114 N. 390 W.
Sunset, UT 84015
(801) 773-2605

Utah Antique Bottle & Collectible Club
1123 E. 2100 S.
Salt Lake City, UT 84106
(801) 467-8636

VIRGINIA

Antique Poison Bottle Collectors Assoc.
312 Summer Lane
Huddleston, VA 24104
(540) 297-4498

Apple Valley Bottle Collectors Club
P.O. Box 2201
Winchester, VA 22604
(540) 877-1093

Buffalo Beam Bottle Club
P.O. Box 434
Buffalo Junction, VA 24529
(804) 374-2041

Historical Bottle Diggers of Virginia
172 McKinley Drive
Broadway, VA 22815

International Perfume Bottle Assoc.
Box 529
Vienna, VA 22183

Merrimac Beam Bottle & Spec. Club
433 Tory Road
Virginia Beach, VA 23462
(804) 497-0969

Potomac Bottle Collectors
8411 Porter Lane
Alexandria, VA 22308

Richmond Area Bottle Collectors Assn.
4718 Kyloe Lane
Moseley, VA 23120
(804) 231-1088

Shenandoah Valley Beam Bottle &
    Spec. Club
11 Bradford Drive
Front Royal, VA 22630
(703) 743-6316

The Richmond Area Bottle Collectors
    Association
4718 Kyloe Lane
Moseley, VA 23120

WASHINGTON

Apple Capital Beam Bottle & Spec.
    Club
300 Rock Island Road
E. Wenatchee, WA 98801
(509) 884-6895

Blue Mountain Jim Beam Club
3802 Old Milton Highway
Walla Walla, WA 99362
(509) 525-3278

Evergreen State Beam Club
14328 60th Ave.
West Edmund, WA 98026
(425) 745-1824

Inland Empire Bottle & Collectors Club
7703 E. Trent Ave.
Spokane, WA 99206

Mt. Rainer Ezra Brooks Bottle Club
P.O. Box 1201
Lynwood, WA 98178

Mt. Tahoma Jim Beam Club
14609 18th Ave. S.W.
Seattle, WA 98166
(206) 243-5069

Northwest Treasure Hunter's Club
E. 107 Astor Drive
Spokane, WA 99208

Pacific Northwest Avon Bottle Club
25425 68th S.
Kent, WA 98031

Skagit Bottle & Glass Collectors
1314 Virginia
Mt. Vernon, WA 98273

Violin Bottle Collectors Association of
    America
21815 106th St. East
Buckley, WA 98321

Washington Bottle Collector's Assoc.
905 24th Ave. S.
Seattle, WA 98144
(206) 329-8412

Washington County Antique Bottle
    Club
905 24th St.
Seattle, WA 92144

WEST VIRGINIA

Fenton Art Glass Collectors
P.O. Box 384
Williamstown, WV 26187
Wild Wonderful W. Virginia Jim Beam

Bottle & Spec. Club
3922 Hanlin Way
Weirton, WV 26062
(304) 748-2675

WISCONSIN

Badger Jim Beam Club of Madison
P.O. Box 5612
Madison, WI 53705

Belle City Jim Beam Bottle Club
8008 104th Ave.
Kenosha, WI 53140
(414) 694-3341

Cream Separator Collectors Association
W20772 State Road 95
Arcadia, WI 54612

Heart of the North Beam Bottle and
    Bottle Club
1323 Eagle St.
Rhinelander, WI 54501
(715) 362-6045

Milwaukee Antique Bottle &
    Advertising Club, Inc.
4090 Lake Drive
West Bend, WI 53095

Milwaukee Jim Beam Bottle and Spec.
    Club, Ltd.
16548 Richmond Drive
Menomonee Falls, WI 53051

Packerland Beam Bottle & Spec. Club
1366 Avondale Drive
Green Bay, WI 54303
(414) 494-4631

Sportsman's Jim Beam Bottle Club
6821 Sunset Strip
Wisconsin Rapids, WI 54494
(715) 325-5285

Watkins Collectors Club
W24024 St. Road 54/93
Galesville, WI 54630

WYOMING

Cheyenne Antique Bottle Club
4417 E. 8th St.
Cheyenne, WY 82001

International Perfume Bottle Assoc.
Box 529
Vienna, VA 22183

FOREIGN

AUSTRALIA

Blue Jay Beamers
3 Rednall Stree
Tree Tea Gully
South Australia 5091

Jim Beam Collectables Club of New
  South Wales
19 Goodacre Ave.
Winton Hills 2153 NSW Australia

Miniature Bottle Collectors of
  Australia
P.O. Box 59, Ashburton
Victoria 3147, Australia

CANADA

Bytown Bottle Seekers' Club
564 Courtenay Ave.
Ottawa
Ontario, Canada K2A 3B3

Four Seasons Bottle Collectors Club
5 Greystone Walk Drive, Apt. 1902
Scarborough
Ontario, Canada M1K 515

Ottawa Valley Insulator Collectors
RR #4
Almonte
Ontario, Canada KOA 1AO
(613) 256-7638

Sleeping Giant Bottle Club
P.O. Box 1351
Thunder Bay
Ontario, Canada P7C 5W2

Violin Bottle Collectors Association
33 East 35th St.
Hamilton
Ontario, Canada L8V 3R7

Western Canadian Insulator Collectors
(403) 823-3045

CHINA

Hong Kong Miniature Liquor Club
  LTD
180 Nathan Road
Bowa House
Tsim Sha Tsui, Kowloon
Hong Kong
(852) 721-3200

ENGLAND

The Mini Bottle Club
47 Burradon Road, Burradon
Cramlington, Northumberland, NE
  237NF
England

GERMANY

Miniatur Flaschensammler
  Duetschlands E.V
Keltenstrasse 1a, 5477
Nickenich, Germany

IRELAND

Northern Ireland Antique Bottle Club
David Scott
52 Ormiston Crescent
Belfast, Ireland B74 3JQ

ITALY

Club Delle Mignonnettes
Via Asiago 16, 60124
Ancona, AN, Italy

JAPAN

Osaka Miniature Bottle Club
11-2 Hakucho 1-Chome, Habikinoshi
Osaka 583, Japan

Miniature Bottle Club of Kobe
3-5-41, Morigocho, Nada-ku
Kobe, 657 Japan

NEW ZEALAND

Port Nicholson Miniature Bottle Club
86 Rawhiti Road
Pukerua Bay
Wellington, New Zealand

Southern Cross Jim Beam Bottle and
Specialties Club
61 Port Hills Road
Heathcote Valley
Christchurch 8002, New Zealand

SCOTLAND

Cumbria Antique Bottle Club
Steve Davison, 01-228-26634

Moray Bottle Club
Ian Gosling, 01-343-830-512

Northumberland & Durham Bottle
Club
D. Robertson, 01-91-236-4304

Auction Companies

ABIC Absentee Auctions
139 Pleasant Ave.
Dundas
Ontario, Canada L9H 3T9
Phone: (519) 443-4162 or (905) 628-3433
E-mail: info@auctionsbyabc.com
Web site: http://www.auctionsbyabc.com

American Bottle Auctions
2523 J St., Suite #203
Sacramento, CA 95816
Phone: (800) 806-7722
Fax: (916) 443-3199
E-mail: info@americanbottle.com
Web site: http://www.americanbottle.com

Armans of Newport
207 High Point Ave.
Portsmouth, RI 02871

Robert Arner Auctioneer
153 Pinehill Road
New Ringgold, PA 17960
Phone: (570) 386-4586
e-mail: Lentigo&ptd.net
Web site: Arnerauctioneers.com

Australian & Collectables Auctions
David Wescott
P.O. Box 245
Deniliquin NSW 2710, Australia
Phone: 011-61-35881-2200
Fax: 011-61-35881-4740
E-mail: dwescott@wescottdavid.com
Web site: www.westcottdavid.com

B B Auctions/Bottles & Bygones
30 Brabant Road
Cheadle Hulme, Cheadle
Cheshire, England SK8 7AU
Phone: 011-44-7931-812156
E-mail: bygonz@yahoo.com
Web site: www.bygonz.co.uk

BBR Auctions
5 Ironworks Row, Wath Road, Elsecar
Barnsley, S. Yorkshire, S74 8HJ
England
Phone: 011-44-1226-745156
Fax: 011-44-1226-361561

BottleAuction.Com
P.O. Box 2146
Vista, CA 92085
Phone: (760) 415-6549
E-mail: randy@bottleauction.com

Cerebro Tobacco Ephemera Auctions
P.O. Box 327
East Prospect, PA 17317
Phone: (800) 695-2235
E-mail: cerebrolab@aol.com
Web site: http://www.cerebro.com

CB & SC Auctions
Rhonda Bennett
179D Woodridge Crest
Nepean
Ontario, Canada K2B 712
Phone: (613) 828-8266

Collectors Sales & Services
P.O. Box 4037
Middletown, RI 02842
Phone: (401) 849-5012
E-mail: collectors@antiquechina.com
Web site: http://www.antiqueglass. com

Down-Jersey Auction
15 Southwest Lakeside Drive
Medford, NJ 08055
Phone: (609) 953-1755
Fax: (609) 953-5351
E-mail: dja@skyhigh.com
Web site: http://www.down-jersey.com

Gallery at Knotty Pine Auction Service
Route 10, P.O. Box 96 W.
Swanzey, NH 03469
Phone: (603) 352-2313
Fax (603) 352-5019
E-mail: kpa@inc-net.com
Web site: www.knottypineantiques.com

Galleria Auctions & Bottles and More
  magazine
P.O. Box #6
Lehighton, PA 18235
Phone: (610) 377-1484
E-mail: rodwalck@ptd.net
Web site: www.bottlemagazine.com and
  www.galleriaauctions.com

Garth's Auctions
2690 Stratford Road, Box 369
Delaware, OH 43015
Phone: (740) 362-4771
Fax: (740) 363-0164
E-mail: info@garths.com
Web site: http://www.garths.com

Glass Works Auctions
Box 187
East Greenville, PA 18041
Phone: (215) 679-5849
Fax: (215) 679-3068
E-mail: glswrk@enter.net
Web site: http://www.glswrk-auction.com

Glass International
134 Meeshaway Trail
Medford, NJ 08055
Phone: (609) 714-2595
E-mail: glassinternational@comcast.net
Web site: www.glassinternational.com.

Gore Enterprises
William D. Emberley
P.O. Box 158
Huntington, VT 05462
Phone: (802) 453-3311

Harmer Rooke Galleries
32 East 57th St.
New York, NY 10022
Phone: (212) 751-1900

Norman C. Heckler & Co.
79 Bradford Corner Road
Woodstock Valley, CT 06282
Phone: (860) 974-1634
Fax: (860) 974-2003
E-mail: info@hecklerauction.com
www.hecklerauction.com

James E. Hill Auctions
P.O. Box 366
Randolph, VT 05060
Phone: (802) 728-5465
E-mail: jehantqs@sover.net

KIWI Auctions Ltd.
19A Annalong Road
Howick
Auckland 1705, New Zealand
Phone: +64 29 206 2000
E-mail: kiwi.auctions@xtra.co.nz
Web site: www.kiwiauctions.co.nz

McMurray Antiques & Auctions
P.O. Box 393
Kirkwood, NY 13795
Phone/Fax: (607) 775-2321

Wm. Morford
Rural Route #2
Cazenovia, NY 13035
Phone: (315) 662-7625
Fax: (315) 662-3570
E-mail: morf2bid@aol.com
Web site: http://morfauction.com

Morphy Auctions
P.O. Box 8
2000 N. Reading Road
Denver, PA 17517
Phone: (717) 335-3435

New England Absentee Auctions
16 Sixth St.
Stamford, CT 06905
Phone: (203) 975-9055
Fax: (203) 323-6407
E-mail: NEAAuction@aol.com

Nostalgia Publications, Inc.
P.O. Box 4175
River Edge, NJ 07661
Phone: (201) 488-4536
Fax: (201) 883-0938
E-mail: nostpub@webtv.net

NSA Auctions/R. Newton-Smith
  Antiques
88 Cedar St.
Cambridge
Ontario, Canada N1S IV8
E-mail: info@nsaauctions.com
Web site: http://www.nsaauctions.com

Open-Wire Insulator Services
28390 Ave.
Highland, CA 92346
Phone: (909) 862-9279
E-mail: insulators@open-wire.com
Web site: http://www.open-wire.com

Don Osborne Auctions
33 Eagleville Road
Orange, MA 01354
Phone: (978) 544-3696
Fax: (978) 544-8271

Howard B. Parzow
Drug Store & Apothecary Auctioneer
P.O. Box 3464
Gaithersburg, MD 20885-3464
Phone: (301) 977-6741

Pettigrew Antique & Collector Auctions
1645 Tejon St.
Colorado Springs, CO 80906
Phone: (719) 633-7963
Fax: (719) 633-5035

Phillips International Auctioneers &
  Valuers
406 E. 79th St.
New York, NY 10021
Phone: (212) 570-4830
Fax: (212) 570-2207
Web site: www.phillips-auctions.com

Pop Shoppe Auctions
10556 Combie Road #10652
Auburn, CA 95602
Phone: (530) 268-6333
E-mail: PopShoppe@aol.com

Carl Pratt Bottle Auctions
P.O. Box 2072
Sandwich, MA 02563
Phone: (508) 888-8794

Shot Glass Exchange
Box 219
Western Springs, IL 60558
Phone/Fax: (708) 246-1559

Skinner Inc.
The Heritage on the Garden
63 Park Plaza
Boston, MA 02116
Phone: (617) 350-5400
Fax: (617) 350-5429
E-mail: info@skinnerinc.com
Web site: http://www.skinnerinc.com

Mike Smith's Patent Medicine Auction
Veterinary Collectibles Roundtable
7431 Covington Highway
Lithonia, GA 30058
Phone: (770) 482-5100
Fax: (770) 484-1304
E-mail: Petvetmike@aol.com

Glassman Auctioneers
16943 East Y Ave.
Fulton, MI 49052
Phone: (888) 996-8243
E-mail: e-mail@glassmanauction.com
Web site: glassmanauction.com

Sotheby's Online Auctions
Web site: www.sothebys.com

Steve Ritter Auctioneering
34314 W. 120th St.
Excelsior Springs, MO 64024
Phone: (816) 833-2855

Stuckey Auction Co.
315 West Broad St.
Richmond, VA 23225
Phone: (804) 780-0850

T.B.R. Bottle Consignments
P.O. Box 1253
Bunnell, FL 32110
Phone: (904) 437-2807

Victorian Images
Box 284
Marlton, NJ 08053
Phone: (856) 354-2154
Fax: (856) 354-9699
E-mail: rmascieri@aol.com
Web site: www.TradeCards.com

Bruce & Vicki Waasdorp
Antique Pottery/Stoneware Auctions
P.O. Box 434
Clarence, NY 14031
Phone: (716) 759-2361
Fax: (716) 759-2379
E-mail: waasdorp@antiques-stoneware.
com
Web site: http://www.antiques-
stoneware.com

Museums and Research Resources

Canadian Museum of Civilization
100 Laurier St.
Hull
Quebec, Canada J8X 4H2
Phone: (819) 776-7000 or (800) 555-5621
Web site: www.civilization.com

Central Nevada Museum
Logan Field Road
P.O. Box 326
Tonopah, NV 89049
Phone: (775) 482-9676

Coca-Cola Company Archives
P.O. Drawer 1734
Atlanta, GA 30301
Phone: (800) 438-2653
Web site: cocacola.com.

Corning Museum of Glass
One Museum Way
Corning, NY 14830-2253
Phone: (607) 974-8271 or (800) 732-6845
Web site: www.cmog.com

Dr. Pepper Museum
300 S. 5th St.
Waco, TX 76701
Phone: (254) 757-2433

The Glass Museum
309 S. Franklin
Dunkirk, IN 47336-1209
Phone/Fax: (765) 768-6872

Hawaii Bottle Museum
27 Kalopa Mauka Road
P.O. Box 1635
Honokaa, HI 96727-1635

Henry Ford Museum & Greenfield
    Village
20900 Oakwood Blvd.
Dearborn, MI 48121
Phone: (313) 271-1620

Heritage Glass Museum
25 High St. East
Glassboro, NJ 08028
Phone: (856) 881-7468

Historical Glass Museum
1157 Orange St.
Redlands, CA 92374-3218
Phone: (909) 798-0868
Web site: www.historicalglassmuseum.com

Mark Twain's Museum and Books
111 S. C St.
P.O. Box 449
Virginia City, NV 89440-0449

The McGill Historical Drug Company
#11 Fourth St. (Highway 93)
McGill, NV 89318
Phone: (775) 235-7082

Museum of American Glass
  at Wheaton Village
1501 Glasstown Road
Millville, NJ 08332-1568
Phone: (856) 825-6800 or (800) 998-
  4552
Web site: www.wheatonvillage.org.

Museum of Connecticut Glass
27 Plank Lane
Glastonbury, CT 06033-2523
Phone: (860) 633-2944
Web site: www.glassmuseum.org

National Bottle Museum
76 Milton Ave.
Ballston Spa, NY 12020
Phone: (515) 885-7589
Web site: www.crisny.org/not-for-profit/
  nbm.

National Heisey Glass Museum
169 W. Church St.
Newark, OH 43055
Phone: (740) 345-2932

Nevada State Museum
600 N. Carson St.
Carson City, NV 89701
Phone: (775) 687-4810

Pepsi-Cola Company Archives
One Pepsi Way
Somers, NY 10589
Phone: (914) 767-6000
Web site: www.pepsi.com

Philadelphia Museum of Art
26th Street and the Benjamin Franklin
  Parkway
Philadelphia, PA 19130
Phone: (215) 763-8100
Web site: www.philamuseum.com

Sandwich Glass Museum
P.O. Box 103
129 Main St.
Sandwich, MA 02563
Phone: (508) 888-0251
Fax: (508) 888-4941
e-mail: sgm@sandwichglassmuseum.org.

Schmidt Museum of Coca-Cola
109 Buffalo Creek Drive
Elizabethtown, KY 42701
Phone: (270) 234-1100
Web site: www.schmidtmuseum.com

Glossary

ABM (Automatic Bottle Machine):
This innovation by Michael Owens
in 1903 allowed an entire bottle to be
made by machine in one step. ABM
bottles are identified by the seam
going to the top of the mouth. By
1913 all bottles were manufactured
by ABMs.

ACL (Applied Color Label): A
method of labeling or decorating a
bottle by applying borosilicate glass
and mineral pigments with a low
melting point to the bottle through a
metal screen and baking it in a furnace. The molten glass and pigment
form the painted label.

Agate Glass: A glass made from mix
incorporating blasting furnace slag.
Featuring striations of milk glass in
off-white tints, the glass has been
found in shades of chocolate brown,
caramel brown, natural agate, and
tanned leather. It was made from the
1850 to the 1900s.

Amethyst-Colored Glass: A clear
glass that when exposed to the sun
or bright light for a long period of
time turns various shades of purple.
Only glass that contains manganese
turns purple.

Amber-Colored Glass: Nickel was
added in the glass production to obtain this common bottle color. It was
believed that the dark color would
prevent the sun from ruining the
contents of the bottle.

Annealing: The gradual cooling of hot
glass in a cooling chamber or annealing oven.

Applied Lip / Top: On pre-1880s
bottles, the neck was applied after
removal from the blowpipe. The neck
may be just a ring of glass trailed
around the neck.

Aqua-Colored Glass: The natural
color of glass. The shades depend on
the amount of iron oxide contained in
the glass production. Produced until
the 1930s.

Bail: A wire clamp consisting of a wire
that runs over the top of the lid or
lip, and a "locking" wire that presses
down on the bail and the lid, resulting in an airtight closure.

Barber Bottle: In the 1880s, these colorful bottles decorated the shelves of
barbershops and were usually filled
with bay rum.

Batch: A mixture of the ingredients
necessary in manufacturing glass.

Battledore: A wooden paddle used to flatten the bottom or sides of a bottle.

Bitters: Herbal "medicines" containing a great quantity of alcohol, usually corn whiskey.

Black Glass: A glass produced between 1700 and 1875 that is actually a dark olive-green or olive-amber color caused by the carbon in the glass production.

Blob Seal: A way of identifying an unembossed bottle by applying a molten coin-shaped blob of glass to the shoulder of the bottle, into which a seal with the logo or name of the distiller, date, or product name was impressed.

Blob Top: A lip on a soda or mineral water bottle made by applying a thick blob of glass to the top of the bottle. A wire held the stopper, which was seated below the blob and anchored the wire when the stopper was closed, to prevent carbonation from escaping.

Blown in Mold, Applied Lip (Bimal): A bottle formed when a gather of glass was blown into a mold to take the shape of the mold. The lip on these bottles were added later and the bases often have open-pontil scars. Side seams stop before the lip.

Blowpipe: A hollow iron tube wider and thicker at the gathering end than at the blowing end. The blowpipe was used by the blower to pick up the molten glass, which was then blown in the mold or free blown outside the mold. Pipes can vary from 2-1/2 to 6 feet long.

Blow-Over: A bubble-like extension of glass above a jar or bottle lip blown so the blowpipe could be broken free from the jar after blowing. The blow-over was then chipped off and the lip ground.

Bocca: An opening on the side of the furnace where the pot was placed. The glass batch was placed in the pot where the gather was taken.

Borosilicate: A type of glass originally formulated for making scientific glassware.

Bruise: Identical to a "fish eye," except that some bruises may be more transparent. A faint bruise is clearer, while a bigger bruise resembles the white eye of a fish.

Bubbles / Blisters: Air or gas pockets that became trapped in the glass during the manufacturing process. The term "seed" is also used to describe these shapes.

Calabash: A type of flask with a rounded bottom. These bottles are known as "Jenny Lind" flasks and were common in the 19th century.

Camphor Glass: A white cloudy glass that looks somewhat like refined gum camphor. This glass was made in blown, blown-mold, and pressed forms.

Carboys: Cylindrical bottles with short necks.

Casewear: Wear marks to the high points of embossing, sides, or base of a bottle due to contact with other bottles in cases while being transported.

Clapper: A glassmaker's tool used in shaping and forming the footing of an object.

Closed Mold: Bottle mold in which the base, body, shoulder, neck, and lip of the bottle all form at one time.

Cobalt Colored Glass: This color was used with patented medicines and poisons to distinguish them from regular bottles. Excessive amounts resulted in "cobalt blue" color.

Codd: A bottle enclosure that was patented in 1873 by Hiram Codd of England. A small ball is blown inside of the bottle. When the ball is pushed up by carbonation, it forms a seal.

Cork Press: Hand tool designed to squeeze a cork into the required shape for use as a bottle closure.

Crown Cap: A tin cap crimped tightly over the rolled lip of a bottle. The inside of the cap was filled with a cork disk, which created an airtight seal.

Cullet: Clean, broken glass added to the batch to bring about rapid fusion to produce new glass.

Date Line: The mold seam or mold line on a bottle. This line can be used to help determine the approximate date a bottle was manufactured.

De-Colorizer: A compound added to natural aquamarine bottle glass to make the glass clear.

Dimple: A small molded depression or hole in a bottle neck where a lever wire or a toggle enclosure is hooked.

Dip Mold: A one-piece mold open at the top.

Embossing: Raised letters or symbols formed in a mold. They typically identify the maker, contents, and trademark.

Fire Polishing: The reheating of glass to eliminate unwanted blemishes.

Flared Lip: A bottle whose lip has been pushed out, or flared, to increase the strength of the opening. These bottles were usually made before 1900.

Flash: A very faint crack that is difficult to see. The bottle must be turned in a certain position to see the crack.

Flashing: A method of coloring glass by dipping a bottle into a batch of colored glass.

Flint Glass: Glass composed of a silicate of potash and lead. Commonly referred to as lead crystal in present terminology.

Free-Blown Glass: Glass produced with a blowpipe rather than a mold.

Frosted Glass: Frosting occurs when a bottle's surface is sandblasted.

Gaffer: A term for the master blower in early glasshouses.

Gather: The gob of molten glass gathered on the end of the blowpipe, which the glassmaker then expanded by blowing until it formed a bottle or other glass object.

Glass Pontil: The earliest type of pontil, in which a sharp glass ring remained after the bottle was broken off the pontil rod.

Glory Hole: The small furnace used for the frequent reheating necessary during the making of a bottle. The glory hole was also used in fire polishing.

Green Glass: Refers to a composition of glass and not a color. The green color was caused by iron impurities in the sand, which could not be controlled by the glassmakers.

Ground Pontil: A smooth circular area of glass created after a rough pontil scar has been ground off.

Hobbleskirt: The iconic paneled shape with curved waist used to make the classic Coca-Cola bottle.

Hobnail: Pattern of pressed glass characterized by an all-over pattern of bumps that look like hobnail heads.

Hutchinson Stopper: A spring-type internal closure used to seal soda bottles, patented by Charles Hutchinson in 1879.

Imperfections: Flaws such as bubbles, or tears, bent shapes and necks, imperfect seams, and errors in spelling and embossing.

ISP (Inserted Slug Plate): Special or unique company names, or names of people, were sometimes embossed on ale, whiskey, and wine bottles, using a plate inserted into the mold.

Iron Pontil: The solid iron rod heated and affixed to a bottle's base created a scar as a black circular depression often turning red upon oxidation. This is also referred to as a bare iron pontil or improved pontil.

Iridescence: A stain found on an old bottle that has been dug from the ground. The stain has an opaline or rainbow color due to the minerals in the ground fusing with the glass. Therefore, this stain is very difficult to clean and usually remains in the glass.

Jack: A steel or wooden tong-like tool the gaffer used to manipulate hot glass.

Keyed Mold: A variation of a two-piece hinge mold, in which the bottom mold seam is not straight but arches up at the middle of the bottle base.

Kick-Up: The deep indentation added to the bottom of a bottle. The indentation is formed by pressing a piece of wood or metal into the base of the mold while the glass is still hot. The kickup is common on wine bottles and calabash flasks.

Laid-On-Ring: A bead of glass that has been trailed around the neck opening to reinforce the opening.

Lady's Leg: A bottle with a long curving neck.

Lehr: An annealing oven or furnace in which a new blown bottle was gradually cooled to increase its strength and reduce cooling breakage.

Lightning Closure: A closure with an intertwined wire bail configuration to hold the lid on fruit jars. This closure was also common with soda bottles.

Lipper: A wood tool used to widen lips and form rims and spouts of pitchers, carafes, and wide-mouthed jars.

Manganese: A mineral used as a decolorizer between 1850 and 1910. Manganese causes glass to turn purple when exposed to ultraviolet rays from the sun.

Melting Pot: A clay pot used to melt silicate in the process of making glass.

Metal: Molten glass.

Milk Glass: White glass formed by adding tin to the molten glass. Milk glass was primarily used for making cosmetic bottles.

Moil: Residual glass remaining on the tip of a blowpipe after detaching the blowpipe from the blown bottle.

Mold, Full-Height Three-Piece: A mold in which the entire bottle was formed in one piece. The two seams on the bottle run from the base to below the lip on both sides.

Mold, Three-Piece Dip: A mold that formed a bottle in three pieces that were later joined together. In this mold, the bottom part of the bottle mold is one piece and the top, from the shoulder up, has two separate pieces. Mold seams appear circling the bottle at the shoulder and on each side of the neck.

Opalescence: Opalescence is found on "frosty" or iridescent bottles that have been buried in the earth in mud or silt. The minerals in these substances have interacted with the glass to create these effects.

Open Mold: A mold in which only the base and body of the bottle is formed in the mold, with the neck and lip being added later.

Open Pontil: The blowpipe, rather than a separate rod, was affixed to the base, leaving a raised or depressed circular scar called a moil.

Owens Automatic Bottle Machine: The first automatic glass-blowing machine was patented in 1904 by Michael Owens of the Libby Glass Company, Toledo, Ohio,

Painted Label: Abbreviation for Applied Color Label (ACL), which is baked on the outside of the bottle and was used commonly used on soda pop and milk bottles.

Panelled: A bottle that isn't circular or oval and that is made with four to twelve panels.

Paste Mold: A mold made of two or more pieces of iron and coated with a paste to prevent scratches on the glass, thereby eliminating the seams as the glass was turned in the mold.

Pattern Molded: Glass that was formed into a pattern before being completed.

Plate Glass: Pure glass comprised of lime and soda silicate.

Pontil, Puntee, or Punty Rod: The iron rod attached to the base of a bottle by a gob of glass to hold the bottle during the finishing.

Pontil Mark: A glass scar on the bottom of a bottle formed when the bottle was broken off the pontil rod. To remove a bottle from a blowpipe, an iron pontil rod with a small amount of molten glass was attached to the bottom of the bottle. A sharp tap removed the bottle from the pontil rod, leaving the scar.

Potstones: Flaws resembling white stones created by impurities in the glass batch.

Pressed Glass: Glass that has been pressed into a mold to take the shape of the mold or the pattern within the mold.

Pucellas: Called "the tool" by glassmakers, this implement is essential in shaping both the body and opening in blown bottles.

Pumpkinseed: A small round flat flask, often found in the Western United States. Generally made of clear glass, the shape resembles the seed of the grown pumpkin. Pumpkinseeds are also known as "mickies," "saddle flasks," and "two-bit ponies."

Punt: A term used in the wine bottle trade to describe a kick-up or push-up at the bottom of the bottle.

Ribbed: A bottle with vertical or horizontal lines embossed into the bottle.

Rolled Lip or Finish: A smooth lip formed when the blowpipe was removed from the bottle. The hot glass at the removal point was rolled or folded into the neck to form and smooth out the top of the finish and to strengthen the neck.

Round Bottom: A soda bottle made of heavy glass and shaped like a torpedo. The rounded bottom ensured that the bottle would be placed on its side, keeping the liquid in contact with the cork and preventing the cork from drying and popping out of the bottle.

Satin Glass: A smooth glass manufactured by exposing the surface of the glass to hydrofluoric acid vapors.

Scant Size: Term for a bottle (normally liquor) referred to as a "pint" or "quart" but that actually held less capacity.

Seal: A circular or oval slug of glass applied to the shoulder of a bottle with an imprint of the manufacturer's name, initials, or mark.

Seam: A mark on a bottle where the two halves meet caused by glass assuming the shape of the mold.

Servitor: An assistant to the master glassblower (gaffer).

Sheared Lip: A plain lip formed by clipping the hot glass of the bottle neck from the bottle using a pair of scissors like shears. No top was applied, but sometimes a slight flange was created.

Sick Glass: Glass bearing superficial decay or deterioration with a grayish tinge caused by erratic firing.

Slug Plate: A metal plate approximately 2 inches by four inches with a firm's name on it that was inserted into a mold. The slug plate was removable, allowing a glasshouse to use the same mold for many companies by simply switching slug plates.

Smooth Base: A bottle made without a pontil.

Snap Case: Also called a snap tool, the snap case had arms that extended from a central stem to hold a bottle firmly on its sides during finishing of the neck and lip. The snap case replaced the pontil rod, and thus eliminated the pontil scars or marks. It sometimes left grip marks on the side of the bottle, however.

Squat: A bottle designed to hold beer, porter, and soda.

Tooled Top: A bottle with a top that is formed in the bottle mold. Bottles of this type were manufactured after 1885.

Torpedo: A beer or soda bottle with a rounded base meant to lie on its side to keep the cork wet and prevent air from leaking in or the cork from popping out.

Turn-Mold Bottles: Bottles turned in a mold using special solvents. The continuous turning with the solvent erased all seams and mold marks and added a distinct luster to the bottle.

Utility Bottles: Multipurpose bottles that could be used to hold a variety of products.

WCF: Wire Cork Fastener.

Wetting Off: Touching the neck of a hot bottle with water to break it off the blowpipe.

Whittle Marks: Small blemishes on the outside of bottles made in carved wooden molds. These blemishes also occurred when hot glass was poured into cold molds early in the morning, which created "goose pimples" on the surface of the glass. As the molds warmed, the glass became smoother.

Wiped Top: A bottle in which the mold lines end before the top due to the neck being wiped smooth after the top was tooled onto the bottle. This method was used before 1915.

Xanthine Glass: Yellow glass achieved by adding silver to the glass batch.

Bibliography

BOOKS

Agee, Bill. *Collecting All Cures*. East Greenville, PA: Antique Bottle & Glass Collector, 1973.

Albers, Marilyn B. *Glass Insulators From Outside North America*, 2nd revision. Houston, TX: Self Published, 1993.

Apuzzo, Robert. *Bottles of Old New York, A Pictorial Guide to Early New York City Bottles, 1680-1925*. New York: R&L Publishing, 1997.

Ayers, James. *Pepsi-Cola Bottles Collectors Guide*. Mount Airy, NC: R.J. Menter Enterprises, 1998.

———.*Pepsi: Cola Bottles & More*. Mount Airy, NC: R.J. Menter Enterprises, 2001.

Arnold, Ken. *Australian Preserving & Storage Jars Pre 1920*. Chicago: McCann Publishing, 1996.

Babb, Bill. *Augusta on Glass*, 2007. Bill Babb, 2352 Devere St., Augusta, GA 30904.

Badders, Veldon. *The Collector's Guide to Inkwells: Identification & Values*. Paducah KY: Collector Books, Schroeder Publishing Co., 2001.

Barnett, Carl and Ken Nease. *Georgia Crown Top Bottle Book*, 2003. Georgia Soda Bottle Book, 1211 St. Andrews Drive, Douglas, GA 31533.

Barnett, R.E. *Western Whiskey Bottles*, 4th edition. Bend, OR: Maverick Publishing, 1997.

Barrett II, William J. *Zanesville and the Glass Industry, A Lasting Romance*, 1997. Self Published, Zanesville, OH.

Beck, Doreen. *The Book of Bottle Collecting*. Gig Harbor, WA: Hamlin Publishing Group, Ltd., 1973.

Berguist, Steve. *Antique Bottles of Rhode Island*, 1998. Self Published, Cranston, RI.

Binder, Frank and Sara Jean. A Guide to American Nursing Bottles, 2001, revised edition to 1992 edition. Self Published, 1819 Ebony Drive, York, PA 17402.

Blake, Charles E. *Cobalt Medicine Bottles*, 2001. Glendale, AZ. Self Published, (602) 938-7277.

Blakeman, Alan. *A Collectors Guide to Inks*. Elsecar, England: BBR Publishing, 1996.

———. *A Collectors Guide: Miller's Bottles & Pot Lids*. Octopus Publishing Group Ltd., 2002.

Bossche, Willy Van den. *Antique Glass Bottles, A Comprehensive Illustrated Guide*, 2001. Self Published, Antique Collectors Club, Wappingers Falls, NY.

Bound, Smyth. *19th Century Food in Glass*. Sandpoint ID: Midwest Publishers, 1994.

Bowman, Glinda. *Miniature Perfume Bottles*. Atglen, PA: Schiffer Publishing, Inc., 2000.

Bredehoft, Tom and Neila. *Fifty Years of Collectible Glass 1920-1970, Identification and Price Guide*, Volume I. Dubuque, IA: Antique Trader Books, 1998.

Breton, Anne. *Collectible Miniature Perfume Bottles*. Flammarion Publications, 2001.

Burnet, Robert G. *Canadian Railway Telegraph History*. Ontario, Canada, 1996: Self Published.

Champlin, Nat. *Nat Champlin's Antique Bottle Cartoons*. Bristol, RI: Self Published, 1998.

Chapman, Tom. *Bottles of Eastern California*, 2003. Hungry Coyote Publishing, Tom Chapman, 390 Ranch Rd., Bishop, CA 93514, (760) 872-2427.

Christensen, Don and Doris. *Violin Bottles: Guitars & Other Novelty Glass*. Privately Published, 1995, 21815 106th St. E. Buckley, WA 98321.

Cleveland, Hugh. *Bottle Pricing Guide*, 3rd edition. Paducah, KY: Collector Books, 1996.

Creswick, Alice M. *Redbook Number 6: The Collectors Guide to Old Fruit Jars*, 1992. Privately Published, 8525 Kewowa SW. Grand Rapids, MI 49504.

Culhane, Phil and Scott Wallace. *Transfer Printed Ginger Beers of Canada*, 2002. E-mail: phil.culhane@rogers.com.

———. *Primitive Stoneware Bottles of Canada*, 2002. E-mail: phil.culhane@rogers.com.

DeGrafft, John. *American Sarsaparilla Bottles*. East Greenville, PA: Antique Bottle & Glass Collector, 1980.

———. *Supplement to American Sarsaparilla Bottles*, 2004. Self-Published, John DeGrafft, 8941 E. Minnesota Ave., Sun Lakes, AZ 85248.

Diamond, Freda. *Story of Glass*. New York: Harcourt, Brace and Co., 1953.

Dodsworth, Roger. *Glass and Glassmaking*. London, England: Shire Publications, 1996.

Dumbrell, Roger. *Understanding Antique Wine Bottles*. Ithaca, NY: Antique Collectors Club, 1983.

Duncan, Ray H. *Dr. Pepper Collectible Bottles, Identification & Values*, 2004. Black Creek Publishing, 1606 CR 761, Devine TX 78016.

Eatwell, John M. and David K. Clint III. *Pike's Peak Gold*, 2002. Self Published, 2345 So. Federal Blvd, Suite 100, Denver, CO 80219.

Edmondson, Bill. *The Milk Bottle Book of Michigan*. Privately Published, 1995, 317 Harvest Ln., Lansing, MI 48917.

Edmundson, Barbara. *Historical Shot Glasses*. Chico, CA: Self Published, 1995.

Eilelberner, George and Serge Agadjanian. *The Complete American Glass Candy Containers Handbook*. Adele Bowden, 1986.

Elliott, Rex R. and Stephen C. Gould. *Hawaiian Bottles of Long Ago*. Honolulu, HI: Hawaiian Service Inc., 1988.

Ferraro, Pat and Bob. *A Bottle Collector's Book*. Sparks, NV: Western Printing & Publishing Co., 1970.

Ferguson, Joel. *A Collectors Guide to New Orleans Soda Bottles*. Slidell, LA: Self Published, 1999.

Field, Anne E. *On the Trail of Stoddard Glass*. Dublin, NH: William L. Bauhan, 1975.

Fike, Richard E. *The Bottle Book*, The Blackburn Press, Caldwell, NJ (973) 228-7077, 2006.

Fletcher, W. Johnnie. *Kansas Bottle Book*. Mustang, OK: Self Published, 1994.

———. *Oklahoma Bottle Book*. Mustang, OK: Self Published, 1994.

Gardner, Paul Vickers. *Glass. New York: Smithsonian Illustrated Library of Antiques*, Crown Publishers, 1975.

Gerth, Ellen C. *Bottles from the Deep, Patent Medicines, Bitters, and Other Bottles from the Wreck of the Steamship "Republic."* Shipwreck Heritage Press, August 2006.

Graci, David. *American Stoneware Bottles, A History and Study*. South Hadley, MA: Self Published, 1995.

———. *Soda and Beer Bottle Closures, 1850-1910*, 2003. P.O. Box 726, South Hadley, MA 01075.

Ham, Bill. *Bitters Bottles*, 1999, supplement 2004. Self Published, P.O. Box 427, Downieville, CA 95936.

———. *The Shaving Mug Market*. Downieville, CA: Self Published, 1997.

Hastin, Bud. *AVON Products & California Perfume Co. Collector's Encyclopedia*, 16th edition. Kansas City, MO: Bud Hastin Publications, 2001.

———. *AVON Products & California Perfume Co. Collector's Encyclopedia*, 17th edition. Kansas City, MO: Bud Hastin Publications, 2003.

Haunton, Tom. *Tippecanoe and E.G. Booz Too!*, 2003. Tom Haunton, 48 Hancock Ave, Medford, MA 02155.

Heetderks, Dewey R, M.D. *Merchants of Medicine, Nostram Peddlers-Yesterday & Today*, 2003. Dewey Heetderks, 4907 N. Quail Crest Drive, Grand Rapids, MI 49546.

Higgins, Molly. *Jim Beam Figural Bottles*. Atglen, PA: Schiffer Publishing, 2000.

Holiner, Richard. *Collecting Barber Bottles*. Paducah, KY: Collector Books, 1986.

Hudson, Paul. *Seventeenth Century Glass Wine Bottles and Seals Excavated at Jamestown*, Journal of Glass Studies. Vol. III, Corning, NY: The Corning Museum of Glass, 1961.

Holabird, Fred and Jack Haddock. *The Nevada Bottle Book*. Reno, NV: R.F. Smith, 1981.

Hopper, Philip. *Anchor Hocking Commemorative Bottles and other Collectibles*. Atglen, PA: Schiffer Publishing, 2000.

Hudgeons III, Thomas E. *Official Price Guide to Bottles Old & New*. Orlando, FL: House of Collectibles, 1983.

Hunter, Frederick William. *Stiegel Glass*. New York: Dover Publications, 1950.

Hunting, Jean and Franklin. *The Collector's World of Inkwells*. Atglen, PA: Schiffer Publishing, 2000.

Husfloen, Kyle. *American Pressed Glass & Bottles Price Guide*, 1st edition. Dubuque, IA: Antique Trader Books, 1999.

———. *American Pressed Glass & Bottles Price Guide*, 2nd edition. Dubuque, IA: Antique Trader Books, 2001.

Innes, Lowell. *Pittsburg Glass 1797-1891*. Boston, MA: Houghton Mifflin Company, 1976.

Jackson, Barbara and Sonny. *American Pot Lids*. East Greenville, PA: Antique Bottle & Glass Collector, 1992.

Jarves, Deming. *Reminiscences of Glass Making*. New York: Hurd and Houghton, 1865.

Kendrick, Grace. T*he Antique Bottle Collector*. Ann Arbor, MI: Edwards Brothers Inc., 1971.

Ketchum, William C. Jr. *A Treasury of American Bottles*. Los Angeles: Rutledge Publishing, 1975.

Klesse, Brigitt and Hans Mayr. *European Glass from 1500-1800, The Ernesto Wolf Collection*. Germany: Kremayr and Scheriau, 1987.

Knittle, Rhea Mansfield. *Early American Glass*. NY: Garden City Publishing Company, 1948.

Kovel, Terry and Ralph. *The Kovels' Bottle Price List*, 11th edition, 1999. New York: Crown Publishers, Inc., 1996.

Kovill, William E. Jr. I*nk Bottles and Ink Wells*. Taunton, MA: William L. Sullwold, 1971.

Kosler, Rainer. Flasche, *Bottle Und Bouteille*. Ismaning, Germany: WKD-Druck Gmbh Publishing Company, 1998.

Lastovica, Ethleen. *An Illustrated Guide to Ginger Beer Bottles for South African Collectors*. Cape Town, South Africa, 2000, ISBN 0-620-25981-7.

Lee, Ruth Webb. *Antique Fakes and Reproductions*. Privately Published, Northborough, MA, 1971.

Lefkowith, Christie Mayer. *Masterpieces of the Perfume Industry*. Editions Stylissimo Publications, 2000.

Leybourne, Doug. *Red Book #8, Fruit Jar Price Guide*. Privately Published, North Muskegon, MI, 1998.

———. *Red Book #9, Fruit Jar Price Guide*. Privately Published, North Muskegon, MI, 2001.

———. *Red Book #10, Fruit Jar Price Guide*. Privately Published, North Muskegon, MI, 2008.

Linden, Robert A. *The Classification of Violin Shaped Bottles*, 2nd edition. Privately Published, 1999.

———. *Collecting Violin & Banjo Bottles, A Practical Guide*, 3rd edition. Privately Published, 2004.

Maust, Don. *Bottle and Glass Handbook*. Union Town, PA: E.G. Warman Publishing Co., 1956.

Markota, Peck and Audie. *Western Blob Top Soda and Mineral Water Bottles*, 1st edition. Sacramento, CA: Self Published, 1998.

———. *California Hutchinson Type Soda Bottles*, 2nd edition. Sacramento, CA, Self Published, 2000.

Markowski, Carol. *Tomart's Price Guide To Character & Promotional Glasses*. Dayton, OH: Tomart Publishing, 1993.

Martin, Byron and Vicky. *Here's To Beers, Blob Top Beer Bottles 1880-1910*, 1973, supplement 2003. Byron Martin, P.O. Box 838, Angels Camp, CA 95222.

McCann, Jerry. *2007 Fruit Jar Annual*. Chicago: J. McCann Publisher, 2007,5003 W. Berwyn Ave, Chicago, IL 60630-1501.

———, Jerry. 2008 Fruit Jar Annual. Chicago: J. McCann Publisher, 2008,5003 W. Berwyn Ave, Chicago, IL 60630-1501.

McDougald, John and Carol. *1995 Price Guide for Insulators*. St. Charles, IL: Self Published, 1995.

McKearin, Helen and George S. *American Glass*. New York: Crown Publishers, 1956.

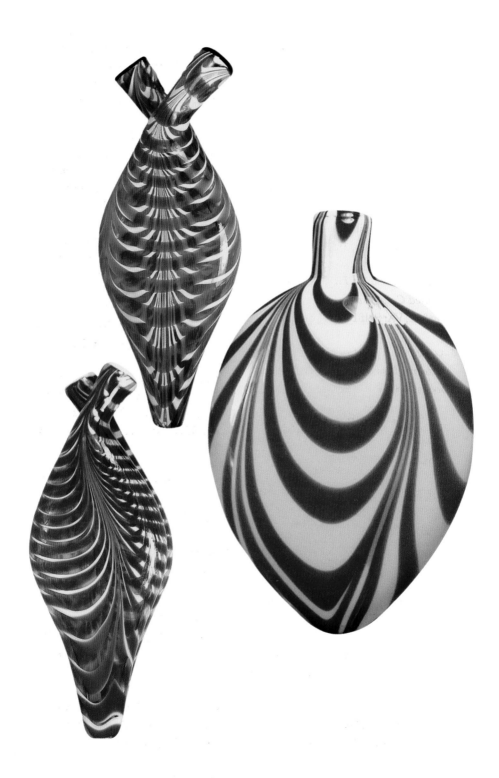

———. *Two Hundred Years of American Blown Glass*. New York: Crown Publishers, 1950.

———. *American Bottles and Flasks and Their Ancestry*. New York: Crown Publishers, 1978.

Megura, Jim. *Official Price Guide to Bottles*, 12th edition. New York: House of Collectibles, The Ballantine Publishing Group, 1998.

Meinz, David. *So Da Licious, Collecting Applied Color Label Soda Bottles*. Norfolk, VA: Self Published, 1994.

Metz, Alice Hulett. *Early American Pattern Glass*. Paducah, KY: Collector Books, 2000.

———. *Much More Early American Pattern Glass*. Paducah, KY: Collector Books, 2000.

Miller, Mike. *Arizona Bottle Book. 2000*. Self Published, 9214 W. Gary Rd., Peoria, AZ.

Milroy, Wallace. *The Malt Whiskey Almanac*. Glasgow G38AZ Scotland: Neil Wilson Publishing Ltd., 1989.

Monsen & Baer. *The Beauty of Perfume, Perfume Bottle Auction VI*. Vienna, VA: Monsen & Baer Publishing, 1998.

———. *The Legacies of Perfume, Perfume Bottle Auction VII*. Vienna, VA: Monsen & Baer Publishing, 1998.

Montague, H.F. *Montague's Modern Bottle Identification and Price Guide*, 2nd edition. Overland Park, KS: H.F. Montague Enterprises, Inc., 1980.

Morgan, Roy and Gordon Litherland. *Sealed Bottles: Their History and Evolution (1630-1930)*. Burton-on-Trent, England: Midland Antique Bottle Publishing, 1976.

Munsey, Cecil. *The Illustrated Guide to Collecting Bottles*. New York: Hawthorn Books, Inc., 1970.

———. *The Illustrated Guide to The Collectibles of Coca-Cola*. New York: Hawthorn Books, Inc., 1972.

Murschell, Dale L. *American Applied Glass Seal Bottles*. Self Published, Dale Murschell, HC 65 Box 2610, Arnold Stickley Rd., Springfield, WV, 1996.

Namiat, Robert. *Barber Bottles with Prices*. Radnor, PA: Wallace Homestead Book Company, 1977.

Newman, Harold. *An Illustrated Dictionary of Glass*. London: Thames and Hudson Publishing, 1977.

Nielsen, Frederick. *Great American Pontiled Medicines*. Cherry Hill, NJ: The Cortech Corporation, 1978.

North, Jacquelyne. *Perfume, Cologne, and Scent Bottles*, Revised 3rd Edition Price Guide, Atglen, PA: Schiffer Publishing, Inc., 1999.

Northend, Mary Harrod. *American Glass*. New York: Tudor Publishing Company, 1940.

Odell, John. *Digger Odell's Official Antique Bottle & Glass Price Guides*, I - 11. Lebanon, OH: Odell Publishing, 1995.

———. *Indian Bottles & Brands*. Lebanon, OH: Odell Publishing, 1998.

———. *Pontil Medicine Encyclopedia*, Lebanon, OH: Odell Publishing, 2003.

Ojea, Ed and Jack Stecher. *Warner's Reference Book*, 1999. Self Published, 1192 San Sebastian Ct., Grover Bend, CA 93433.

Ostrander, Diane. *A Guide to American Nursing Bottles*. York, PA: ACIF Publications, 1992.

Padgett, Fred. *Dreams of Glass, The Story of William McLaughlin and His Glass Company*. Livermore, CA. Self Published, 1997.

Pepper Adeline, *The Glass Gaffers of New Jersey*. New York: Charles Scribners Sons, 1971.

Peterson, Arthur G. *400 Trademarks on Glass*. L-W Book Sales, P.O. Box 69, Gas City, IN 46933, 2002.

Petretti, Alan. *Petretti's Coca-Cola Collectibles Price Guide*, 11th edition. Iola, WI: Krause Publications, 2001.

———. *Petretti's Soda Pop Collectibles Price Guide*, 1st edition. Dubuque, IA: Antique Trader Books, 2001.

———. *Petretti's Soda Pop Collectibles Price Guide*, 3rd edition. Dubuque, IA: Antique Trader Books, 2003.

———. *Warman's Coca-Cola Collectibles, Identification and Price Guide*. Iola, WI: Krause Publications, 2006.

Pickvet, Mark. *The Encyclopedia of Glass*. Atglen, PA: Schiffer Publishing, 2001.

Polak, Michael. *Antique Trader-Bottles: Identification and Price Guide*, 4th edition. Iola, WI: Krause Publications, 2002.

———. *Antique Trader Bottles: Identification and Price Guide*, 5th edition. Iola, WI: Krause Publication, 2005.

———. *Antique Trader-Bottles: Identification and Price Guide*, 6th edition. Iola, WI: Krause Publication, 2009.

———. *Warman's Bottles Field Guide, Value and Identification*, 1st edition. Iola, WI: Krause Publications, 2005.

———. *Warman's Bottles Field Guide, Value and Identification*, 2nd edition. Iola, WI: Krause Publications, 2007.

———. *Official Price Guide to American Patriotic Memorabilia*, 1st edition. New York: House of Collectibles, 2002.

Putnam, H.E. *Bottle Identification*. New York: H.E. Putnam Publisher, 1965.

Rensselaer, Van Stephen. *Early American Bottles and Flasks*. Stratford, CT: J. Edmund Edwards Publisher, 1969.

Richardson, Charles G. and Lillian C. *The Pill Rollers, Apothecary Antiques and Drug Store Collectibles*, 3rd edition, 2003. Charles G. Richardson, 1176 S. Dogwood Drive, Harrisonburg, VA 22801-1535.

Ring, Carlyn. *For Bitters Only*. Concord, MA: The Nimrod Press, Inc., 1980.

Ring, Carlyn and W.C. Ham. *Bitters Bottles*. Downieville, CA, Self Published (530) 289-0809, 2000.

Roller, Dick. *Fruit Jar Patents*, Volume III, 1900-1942. Chicago: McCann Publisher, 1996.

———. *Indiana Glass Factories Notes*. Chicago: McCann Publisher, 1994.

Russell, Mike. *Collector's Guide to Civil War Period Bottle and Jars*, 3rd edition. Herndon, VA: Self Published, 2000.

Schwartz, Marvin D. "American Glass" Antiques, Volume 1, 1974, Blown and Molded, Princeton, NJ: Pyne Press.

Seeliger, Michael. *H.H. Warner His Company & His Bottles*. East Greenville, PA: Antique Bottle & Glass Collector, 1974.

Sloan, Gene. *Perfume and Scent Bottle Collecting*. Radnor, PA: Wallace Homestead Book Company, 1986.

Snyder, Bob. *Bottles in Miniature*. Amarillo, TX: Snyder Publications, 1969.

———. *Bottles in Miniature II*. Amarillo, TX: Snyder Publications, 1970.

———. *Bottles in Miniature III*. Amarillo, TX: Snyder Publications, 1972.

Soetens, Johan. *Packaged in Glass: European Bottles, Their History and Production*. Amsterdam: Batavlan Lion International, October 2001.

Spaid M. David and Harry A. Ford. *101 Rare Whiskey Flasks (Miniature)*. Palos Verdes, CA: Brisco Publications, 1989.

Spiegel, Walter Von. *Glas*. Battenberg Verlag, Munchen, 1979.

Spillman, Jane Shadel. *Glass Bottles, Lamps and Other Objects*. New York: Alfred A. Knopf, 1983.

Southard, Tom and Mike Burggraaf. *The Antique Bottles of Iowa*. Des Moines, IA: Self Published, 1998.

Sweeney, Rick. *Collecting Applied Color Label Soda Bottles*, 2nd edition. La Mesa, CA: Painted Soda Bottles Collectors Assoc., 1995.

———. *Collecting Applied Color Label Soda Bottles*, 3rd edition. La Mesa, CA: Painted Soda Bottles Collectors Assoc., 2002.

Taber, George, M. "To Cork or Not to Cork." Scribner: New York, N.Y. 2007.

Thompson, J.H. *Bitters Bottles*. Watkins Glen, NY: Century House, 1947.

Toulouse, Julian Harrison. *Bottle Makers and Their Marks*. Camden, NJ: Thomas Nelson Incorporated, 1971.

Townsend, Brian. *Scotch Missed (The Lost Distilleries of Scotland)*. Glasgow G38AZ Scotland: Neil Wilson Publishing Ltd., 1994.

Tyson, Scott. *Glass Houses of the 1800s*. East Greenville, PA: Antique Bottle & Glass Collector, 1971.

Tucker, Donald. *Collectors Guide to the Saratoga Type Mineral Water Bottles*. East Greenville, PA: Antique Bottle & Glass Collector, 1986.

Tutton, John. *Udderly Delightful*. Stephens City, VA: Commercial Press, Inc., 1996.

————. *Udderly Splendid*. Stephens City, VA: Commercial Press, Inc., 2003.

Umberger, Joe and Arthur. *Collectible Character Bottles*. Tyler, TX: Corker Book Company, 1969.

Van, P. Dale. *American Breweries II*. North Wales, PA: Eastern Coast Breweriana Association, 1995.

Van Rensselaer, Stephen. "Early American Bottles and Flasks." Peterborough, NH: Transcript Printing Company, 1926.

Vesilind, Priit J. *Lost Gold of the Republic, The Remarkable Quest for the Greatest Shipwreck Treasure of the Civil War Era*, Shipwreck Heritage Press, 2005.

Watkins, Laura Woodside. *American Glass and Glassmaking*. New York: Chanticleer Press, 1950.

Watson, Richard. *Bitters Bottles*. New York: Thomas Nelson & Sons, 1965.

————. *Supplement to Bitters Bottles*. New York: Thomas Nelson & Sons, 1968.

Wichmann, Jeff. *Antique Western Bitters Bottles*, 1st edition. Sacramento, CA: Pacific Glass Books Publishing, 1999.

Wilson, Betty and William. *Spirit Bottles of the Old West*. Wolfe City: Henington Publishing Company, 1968.

Wilson, Kenneth M. *New England Glass and Glass Making*. New York: Thomas Y. Crowell Company, 1972.

Wood, Zang. *New Mexico Bottle Book*. Flora Vista, NM. Self published, 1998.

Yates, Don. *Ginger Beer & Root Beer Heritage, 1790-1930*, 2004. Don Yates, 8300 River Corners Road, Homerville, OH 44235, (330) 625-1025.

Young, Susan H. "A Preview of Seventh-Century Glass From The Kourin Basilica, Cyprus", Journal of Glass Studies, Vol. 35, Corning Museum of Glass, 1993.

Yount, John T. *Bottle Collector's Handbook & Pricing Guide*. Action Printery, 10 No. Main, San Angelo, TX 76901, 1967.

Zumwalt, Betty. *Ketchup, Pickles, Sauces*. Sandpoint, ID: Mark West Publishers, 1980.

SANBORN FIRE INSURANCE MAPS – RESOURCES

EDR Sanborn Maps
Environmental Data Resources, Inc.
3530 Post Road
Southport, CT 06890
Phone: (800) 352-0050
Web Site: http://www.edrnet.com/index.
   php

Pro-Quest (Previously Chadwyk-Healy,
   Inc.)
789 E. Eisenhower Parkway
Ann Arbor, MI 48106-1346
Phone: (800) 752-0515 or (734) 761-
   4700
E-mail: info@proquest.com
Web site: www.proquest.com

San Jose Public Library – San Jose,
   California
Web site: www.sjlibrary.org
 www.sjlibrary.org

Stanford University – Stanford,
   California
Web site: www.sul.stanford.edu
E-mail: seleniteman@comcast.net

University of California at Berkley
   – Berkley, California
Web site: www.lib.berkeley.edu
   www.lib.berkeley.edu/EART/sanborn.
   html

Vlad Shkurkin, Publisher
6025 Rose Arbor
San Pablo, CA 94806-4147
Phone: (510) 232-7742
Fax: (510) 236-7050
E-mail: shkurkin@ix.netcom.com

Vista
505 Huntmar Park Drive, Suite 200
Herndon, VA 20170
Phone: (800) 989-0402 or (703) 834-
   0600
Fax: (703) 834-0606

PERIODICALS

Ale Street News
P.O. Box 1125
Maywood, NJ 07607
E-mail: JamsOD@aol.com
Web site: www.AleStreetNews.com

American Digger Magazine–For
Diggers and Collectors of America's
Heritage
P.O. Box 126
Acworth, GA 30101

Antique Bottle & Glass Collector
Jim Hagenbuch
102 Jefferson St.
P.O. Box 187
East Greenville, PA 18041
Antique Bottle Collector UK Limited
Llanerch, Carno, Caersws
Powys SY17 5JY Wales

Australian Antique Bottles and
Collectibles
AABS, Box 235
Golden Square, 3555 Australia

BAM (Bottles and More) Magazine
P.O. Box #6
Lehighton, PA 18235

Bottles & Bygones
30 Brabant Road
Cheadle Hulme, Cheadlek
Cheshire, SKA 7AU England
Bottles & Extra Magazine
1966 King Springs Road
Johnson City, TN 37601

British Bottle Review (BBR)
Elsecar Heritage Centre
Barnsley
S. York S74 8HJ, England

Canadian Bottle & Stoneware Collector
Magazine
102 Abbeyhill Drive
Kanata
Ontario, Canada K2L 1H2
Web site: www.cbandsc.com

Crown Jewels of the Wire
P.O. Box 1003
St. Charles, IL 60174-1003

Root Beer Float
P.O. Box 571
Lake Geneva, WI 53147
The Australian Bottle & Collectables
Review
84 Black Flat Road
Whittlesea, Victoria, 3757, Australia
E-mail: travisdunn@bigpond.com.au
Web site:www.abcreview.com.

The Miniature Bottle Collector
Brisco Publications
P.O. Box 2161
Palos Verdes Peninsula, CA 92074

The Soda Spectrum
A Publication by Soda Pop Dreams
P.O. Box 23037
Krug Postal Outlet
Kitchener
Ontario, Canada N2B 3V1

Treasure Hunter's Gazette (Collector's
Newsletter)
George Streeter, Publisher & Editor
14 Vernon St.
Keene, NH 03431

Index

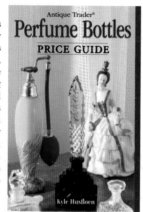

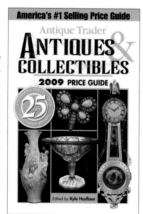